Yearbook of Islamic and Middle Eastern Law

Volume 5

1998–1999

Yearbook of Islamic and Middle Eastern Law

Volume 5
1998–1999

General Editor

Eugene Cotran, LLD
Circuit Judge, Visiting Professor of Law, SOAS
Chairman, CIMEL

Published for
the Centre of Islamic and Middle Eastern Law
at the School of Oriental and African Studies
University of London

CIMEL

SOAS

KLUWER LAW INTERNATIONAL
LONDON – THE HAGUE – BOSTON

Published by
Kluwer Law International Ltd
Sterling House
66 Wilton Road
London SW1V 1DE
United Kingdom

Kluwer Law International incorporates the
publishing programmes of
Graham & Trotman Ltd,
Kluwer Law & Taxation Publishers
and Martinus Nijhoff Publishers

Sold and distributed
in the USA and Canada by
Kluwer Law International
675 Massachusetts Avenue
Cambridge MA 02139
USA

In all other countries sold and distributed by
Kluwer Law International
P.O. Box 322
3300 AH Dordrecht
The Netherlands

ISSN 1384-2835
ISBN 90-411-1320-7
© Eugene Cotran 2000
First published in 2000

British Library Cataloguing in Publication Data is available

This publication is to be cited as *Yearbook of Islamic and Middle Eastern Law*, Volume 5 (1998–1999)

Typeset by On Screen, West Hanney, Oxfordshire
Printed and bound in Great Britain by MPG Books Ltd, Bodmin, Cornwall

Contents

Part V – Book Reviews, Notes and News 555

Biographical Notes

Husain M. Al-Baharna gained a doctorate in international law from the University of Cambridge, and is a Barrister-at-Law of Lincoln's Inn and a member of the Bahrain Bar Society. He is a member of both the UN International Law Commission and the International Council for Commercial Arbitration (ICCA). He is the former Minister for Legal Affairs in the State of Bahrain, and is now an attorney and legal consultant in Bahrain. He is also a registered arbitrator.

Fares Al-Hejailan (LLB) took his degree at the School of Oriental and African Studies in 1999 and was admitted to the Bar in Saudi Arabia in the same year.

Sabah Al-Mukhtar (LLB, LLM) is a legal consultant in Iraqi, Arab and Islamic law. He is a founding member and partner of the Arab Lawyers Network, and a member of the Iraqi Bar Association, the Arab Lawyers' Federation and the International Bar Association. He is also a Member of the Chartered Institute of Arbitrators, and the Arab Arbitration Association and is a registered arbitrator with the ICC. He is a fellow both of the British Institute of Management and the Institute of Petroleum. He is also a member of the Bar Human Rights Committee of England and Wales, the Royal Institute of International Affairs (Chatham House), the Muslim Council of Britain (National Legal Committee) and the National Civil Rights Movement (National Steering Committee). He is President of the Arab Lawyers Association (UK) and a member of the editorial board of *Arab Law Quarterly*.

Najeeb Al-Nauimi (LLB, PhD) is a Qatari lawyer with degrees in law gained in Egypt and the United Kingdom. He was formerly Minister of Justice for the State of Qatar and was a Professor of Public Law at Qatar University. He was the Agent and Counsel of the Government of Qatar to the International Court of Justice in the case *Qatar v. Bahrain*, Qatar's representative to the International Court of Justice on Request for advisory opinion on the legality of the threat or use of nuclear weapons, Vice-Chairman of the Working Group of Experts focusing on "liability and compensation for environmental damage from the Iraqi military activities against Kuwait" organized by the United Nations Environment Programme, National President of the World Jurist Association, former President of the Asian African Consultative Committee and Chairman of the Committee of Arab Legal Experts of the Arab League on the

Law of the Sea. He has been head of Qatari delegations to various international seminars and conferences. He is a writer, author and co-editor of books, and a member of various lawyers' associations, the Cairo Regional Centre for International Commercial Arbitration and the World Commission for the Oceans. Dr Al-Nauimi has also acted as sole arbitrator in various business disputes involving major companies. He is also the Chairman of the International Trading and Investment Company involved in various investment and commercial activities.

Anis Al-Qasem (LLM, PhD), a Barrister-at-Law of Lincoln's Inn, was formerly Legal Adviser to the Government of Libya and Chairman of the Libyan Petroleum Commission during the monarchy. He is presently a practising lawyer and consultant in London in the laws of the Middle East, a licensed legal consultant in Dubai, a former visiting examiner and Associate Fellow of the Institute of Advanced Legal Studies, University of London, and Chairman of the Legal Committee of the Palestine National Council.

Lu'ayy Minwer Al-Rimawi holds a Master's degree in law from Cambridge University and a Master of Science in international relations from the London School of Economics. He is a doctoral researcher in the regulation of Arab securities markets, and a part-time lecturer in public international law at the LSE. He has had contributions on a wide range of legal and socio-political issues published in the *European Business Law Review*, the *Journal of Financial Crime*, *Journal of Financial Regulation and Compliance*, *The Company Lawyer*, *Millennium: Journal of Business Studies*, *CCH: Financial Services Law Reporter*, the *International Herald Tribune*, the *Guardian*, the *Guardian Manchester Weekly*, the *Independent*, the *Independent on Sunday*, the *Yorkshire Post*, the *Jordan Times*, the *Jerusalem Post*, *Al-Quds Al-Arabi*, *Al-Hayat*, *Al-Sharq Al-Awsat*, *El Rai* and *Ed Dostour*. He is currently the principal Middle Eastern correspondent to the *European Financial Services Law Journal*.

Abdullahi An-Na'im is a Charles Howard Chandler Professor of Law, School of Law, Emory University. He holds an LLB (Khartoum, 1970), LLB (Cambridge, 1973) and a PhD in Law (Edinburgh, 1976). Dr An Na'im was Associate Professor of Law at the University of Khartoum until 1985, and has been visiting professor at UCLA (USA), University of Saskatchewan (Canada) and Uppsala (Sweden). He has also served as Executive Director of Human Rights Watch/Africa (1993–5) before becoming Professor of Law at Emory University, Atlanta, GA, USA in 1995. His research interests are in the fields of Islamic law and human rights, human rights in cross-cultural perspectives and comparative constitutionalism.

M. A. Ansari-Pour was a judge in the Iranian judiciary before coming to England to study for the LLM and a doctorate. He is the Chairman of the Iranian Law Institute and he has written widely (including both articles and books) in English and Persian.

Nayla Comair-Obeid is Doctor of Laws of the Panthéon-Assas University, Paris II, Attorney at the Beirut Bar, and Professor of the Lebanese Faculty of Law. Her speciality is international commercial law, in which connection she has made comparative studies in the field of law of arbitration, particularly arbitration in Arab countries. This research has led her to make a detailed comparative study of the civil and commercial codes of the states of the Middle East. She is the author of important works in the field, notably *Les Contrats en droit musulman des affaires* (Economica, Paris, 1995); *The Law of Business Contracts in the Arab Middle East* (Kluwer, 1996), and *Arbitration in Lebanese Law: A Comparative Study* (Delta 1999).

Eugene Cotran (LLD) has been a circuit judge in England since 1992. He is a Visiting Professor of Law at the School of Oriental and African Studies, University of London, and the Chairman of the Centre of Islamic and Middle Eastern Law within the School. He was formerly a practising Barrister-at-Law in England and the Commonwealth, a Law Commissioner and High Court judge in Kenya and an international arbitrator. He is also a Board Member of the Palestinian Independent Commission for Citizens Rights. He has numerous publications on the laws of Africa, the Commonwealth, the Middle East and international and immigration law.

John Donohue has been at St Joseph University, Beirut, since 1970 and is now Director of the Center for the Study of the Modern Arab World. He specializes in classical Arab history.

Mustafa El-Alem (LLB, LLM) is a Libyan practising lawyer and legal adviser and a member of the Libyan Bar Association. He is a member of the Board of Directors of the Arab Association for International Arbitration and the Libyan member of the Alliance of Arab Lawyers and a full Member of the Euro–Arab Arbitration Board in London. He is a Lecturer at the Faculty of Law, University of Garyounis Benghazi, and Vice-Chairman of the Arbitration Board of Benghazi Chamber of Commerce.

Nicholas Edmondes is a Solicitor of the Supreme Court of England and Wales and has worked for Trowers & Hamlins in London and Oman since 1984, specializing in project development and project finance, capital markets, corporate and international law.

Nadia El-Cheikh is Assistant Professor in the Department of History and Archaeology at the American University of Beirut. She completed her doctorate in 1992 at Harvard University. Her most recent research includes "Surat al-Rum: a Study of the Exegetical Literature", *Journal of the American Oriental Society*, 118:3 (1998) amd "Muhammad and Heraclitus: A Study in Legitimacy", to appear in *Studia Islamica*.

Jacques el-Hakim (LLD) is *agrégé* from the French Faculties of Law and has graduated in law in Syria, Lebanon and the USA. He is a member of the Damascus Bar and is currently a Professor and Head of the Commercial Law Department, Faculty of Law of Damascus University and an Attorney-at-Law. He has produced several publications on Syrian and other laws and on economics and acts as a legal adviser to banks, insurance companies, oil and airline companies.

Nicholas Foster was educated at Trinity Hall, Cambridge, and the University of Aix-Marseille. After qualifying as a solicitor he practised company, commercial and banking law with Clifford Chance and Nabarro Nathanson. He now lectures in Middle Eastern and commercial law at the School of Oriental and African Studies, University of London.

Afif Gaigi gained a degree in private law from the University of Tunis and went on to receive postgraduate diplomas in general private law and criminal science from the University of Paris. He is an attorney at the Tunis Court of Cassation, a member of the Tunis Bar and a university lecturer.

Hamzeh Haddad is the Minister of Justice of Jordan. He was educated at Cairo University, from which he graduated as a Doctor of Laws, and the University of Bristol, where he gained a doctorate. He is the author of numerous books and articles and a speaker at many regional and international conferences. He is a member of the Jordan Bar Association and of the Arbitration Board of the Arab–Swiss Chamber of Commerce, and was a practising attorney and arbitrator.

Vernon Handley (BA) is an attorney with the Law Firm of Salah Al-Hejailan ("LFSH"). Since 1994 Mr Handley has been based in the Middle East and, before joining LFSH, worked for Clifford Chance, a leading London-based law firm, first on secondment to Clifford Chance's associate office in Bahrain and, latterly, on secondment to Clifford Chance's Dubai office. Vernon Handley is a British subject. He holds a BA from Durham University.

Sibel Inceoglu (LLM, PhD) is Associate Professor of Constitutional Law, Faculty of Law, Marmara University. She has studied at Istanbul and Marmara universitites, and has been a visiting scholar in the Faculty of Law, University of California, Los Angeles.

Yamina Kebir is a practising attorney authorized to appear before the Supreme Court of Algeria. She is a member of the Algerian Bar. She graduated in law and English literature and holds a postgraduate degree in business law from the University of Paris II. She specializes particularly in international commercial contracts and transactions, business litigation, investments and corporations and in intellectual property. She has published several articles on Algerian law in English.

The Law Firm **Kosheri, Rashed & Riad** was established in 1974 by Professor Dr Ahmed El-Kosheri and Professor Dr Samia Rashed. The firm has a strong commercial and litigation practice which includes international law, corporate law, commercial agencies, licensing contracts, commercial and maritime matters, joint ventures, privatization, insurance, foreign investments, local and international business contracts, BOT projects, banking, mining and petroleum concessions, real estate, telecommunications, tax, construction, labour law, intellectual property, business litigation, international and domestic arbitrations. The firm is composed of seventeen lawyers, including two partners who are members of the New York Bar (Tarek Riad and Hala Riad), in addition to the support staff.

Martin Lau is a Barrister and lecturer in law at the School of Oriental and African Studies, University of London, where he teaches South Asian law. He studied at the

University of Heidelberg, Germany, and at the University of London. He has published extensively on South Asian law and frequently acts as an expert in proceedings for the International Chamber of Commerce and English courts.

John Wuol Makec is a Justice of the Supreme Court of the Sudan. He has an LLB, University of Khartoum (1964–1969) and an LLM, University of London (SOAS) (1978–1980). He was formerly Minister of Cooperative and Rural Development of the High Executive Council Juda, Southern Sudan and Speaker of Bahr el Ghazal Regional Assembly. He has published extensively on the Customary Laws of the Sudan, in particular of the Dinka people.

Fadi B. Nader is Partner and Legal Counsel of The International Investor KCSC, an Islamic Investment Bank based in Kuwait which is currently managing US$3.6 billion of local and international investment products, and is widely considered as one of the leading players in Islamic finance. He qualified in 1985; was an associate 1986–1988 with Samir Saleh and Associates, London; a company secretary 1988–1992 UB (Suisse) SA, Geneva; in private banking 1992–1993 with Crédit Commercial de France, London; and a Partner since 1987 in Moghaizel Law Offices, Beirut. He is a member of the Beirut Bar Association and the International Bar Association. He was educated at College des Frères Mont La Salle, Lebanon; St Joseph University, Beirut (LLB, June 1985); Queen Mary College, London (LLM, September 1986).

Adel Omar Sherif is a Counsellor for the Supreme Constitutional Court of Egypt. He earned his LLB, Advanced Studies Diploma in Public Law, Advanced Studies Diploma in Adminsitrative Law and PhD in Commercial Law from Cairo and Ain Shams universities. He served on the Council of the State, between 1980 and 1992. He first worked at the Supreme Constitutional Court in 1992 and was assigned Acting Head of the Commissioners' Body in 1993. Judge Sherif was a visiting Fellow at the Human Rights Law Centre of the College of Law, University of Chicago, II, in 1992, the Human Rights Law Centre of the University of Essex from 1993–94, the Federal Judicial Center in Washington DC in 1996 and a Visiting Professor at the Faculty of Law, McGill University from 1998–99. He has served as a legal adviser in several government agencies, including the Prime Minister's office, the Real-Estate Bank of Egypt and the Cairo Regional Centre for International Commercial Arbitration. Judge Sherif often attends international conferences and seminars as a representative for Egpyt. He is the Rapporteur of a series of international human rights conferences known collectively as "The Cairo Conference". He is the author of *Constitutional Adjudication in Egypt* (Cairo, Dar El-Shaab, 1988), *Judicial Independence: Requirements and Rewards* (Washington, DC, the Federal Judicial Center, 1996) and many published articles on Islamic and Egyptian law. He is also the co-editor of the following texts from the Kluwer Law International: *Human Rights and Democracy: The Role of the Supreme Constitutional Court of Egypt* (with Professor Kevin Boyle of Essex University, 1996), and *The Role of the Judiciary in the Protection of Human Rights* (with Judge Eugene Cotran, 1997) and *Democracy, the Rule of Law and Islam* (with Judge Eugene Cotran, 1999).

Richard Price was until May 1999 the Gulf Resident Partner of Clifford Chance based in Dubai. Since 1982 he has spent much of his career in the UAE and Saudi Arabian offices of Clifford Chance specializing particularly in international maritime and trade law. He is now a consultant to Clifford Chance on Middle Eastern matters. He is the author of *The Maritime Laws of the Arabian Gulf Cooperation Council States* (Graham & Trotman) and numerous articles on all aspects of Gulf shipping and commercial law appearing in various legal and business journals. he is also the co-author of *UAE Court of Cassation Judgments 1989-1997* (Kluwer, 1998).

Tarek Riad (SJD) has a doctorate in law from Harvard University and is a partner in the Law Firm Kosheri, Rashed & Riad. He is a special legal adviser to the Speaker of the Egyptian People's Assembly.

Nageeb Shamiri (LLD) is a member of the Supreme Judicial Council of Yemen and of the Constitutional Division of the Supreme Court of Yemen. He was formerly the Chief Justice of South Yemen. He is the Chairman of the Judicial Inspection Commission, the Secretary of the Law Reform Unit at the Ministry of Legal and Parliamentary Affairs and contributed to the drafting of the Republic's main unified laws. He is a member of the National Committee regarding the Arbitration with Eritrea, and of the Joint Commission with Saudi Arabia regarding Maritime Boundaries.

Mona Siddiqui is a Lecturer in Arabic and Islamic Studies in the Department of Theology and Religious Studies at Glsgow University. She is also Director of the Centre for the Study of Islam at the university. Her major research interests are classical Islam, Islamic law and modern Arabic literature. She is also a regular presenter on Radio 4's, *Thought for the Day*, and BBC Scotland's *Thought for the Day* and comments frequently on radio on Muslim interests in Britain.

Michèle Zirari-Devif is a Professor at the Faculty of Juridical, Economic and Social Sciences, University Mohammed V, Rabat, Morocco.

Preface

This volume of the *Yearbook* which covers the year 1998 to 1999 celebrates the fifth year of publication and takes us into the millennium when we hope to continue from strength to strength.

Part I opens with a formidable article by my colleague and friend Judge Adel Omar Sherif which deals historically with the Egyptian judicial system and in particular with the judicial function and its development. It is followed by Professor Abdullahi An-Na'im's article based on his 1998 Coulson Memorial Lecture at the School of Oriental and African Studies where he asks and answers the question "*Shari'a* and Positive Legislation: is an Islamic State Possible or Viable?" There follow four articles on commercial and business law by Nicholas Foster, on "Guarantees in the UAE"; Lu'ayy Minwer al-Rimawi on the "Kuwaiti, Jordanian and Omani Securities Markets"; Tarek Riad on "Doing Business in Egypt"; and John Donohue with "A Note on the Theory and Practice of Islamic Banking".

The next three articles all deal with personal law: Nadia El-Cheikh traces the abortive attempt to introduce a civil marriage law in the Lebanon, Yamina Kebir discusses the status of children and their protection in Algeria, and Mona Siddiqui the concept of *wilaya* in Hanafi law.

Part II surveys as in each year the developments in the laws of every country normally covered in the *Yearbook*, and we have now filled in the gaps for Kuwait, Iran and Algeria missed in volume 4.

The documents section of Part III includes an update on resolutions on Iraq, the Wye River Memorandum and the Sharm el-Sheikh Agreement moving the Israeli–Palestinian peace process a step forward; and finally the all-important Casablanca Declaration of the Arab Human Rights Movement, the Sana'a Declaration of the Emerging Democracies Forum and the Beirut Declaration reflecting the recommendations of the First Arab Conference on the Independence of the Judiciary and the Legal Profession.

In Part IV we have reproduced Chapters I and X of the arbitral award in the first stage of the proceedings between Eritrea and the Yemen regarding the Red Sea Islands. The unanimous award was done at London on 9 October 1998 (see the postscript to the Yemen survey in the *Yearbook*, vol. 4 (1997–1998), page 416. This is followed by a full transcript of the judgment of the Court of Appeal in England in *Osman v. Elasha* on the subject of the abduction of two Sudanese children, with a case comment by Judge David Pearl on "Cross-border Abduction of Children".

Part V has a variety of book reviews and an obituary of Tan Sri Datuk Professor Ahmad Mohamed Ibrahim, doyen of Islamic law in Singapore and Malaysia.

My deep thanks again go to all who assisted me in producing this fifth volume of the *Yearbook*, in particular to the contributors and to Hilary Scannell and Rachel Amphlett of Kluwer Law International.

Finally, the production of this fifth volume would not have been possible without the continued financial support of Sheikh Salah al-Hejailan to the Centre for Islamic and Middle Eastern Law.

Eugene Cotran
December 1999

Part I

Articles

An Overview of the Egyptian Judicial System, and its History

Adel Omar Sherif *

1 INTRODUCTION

The aim of this article is to explore ideas about the judicial function at the global level and also its development in Egypt, a country where many legal traditions have historically operated to produce the legal system that exists today. In order to fully appreciate the current judicial structure in Egypt, this article, therefore, will be dedicated to discussion of two topics. First, in section 2, the history of the judicial function in general and its developments, with special emphasis on the Egyptian application; and second, in section 3, the current organizational structure of the Egyptian judicial system. This section demonstrates the history of the judicial function in modern Egyptian history.

From a political perspective, the modern era began in Egypt in 1805 when Mohammed Ali took power and adopted some of the Western rules of government systems instead of Islamic *shari'a* rules that had been prevalent in the country since the Islamic spread in Egypt in the seventh century. In order to demonstrate the dramatic change that occurred regarding the judicial function, I will start by examining the position of this function under Islamic *shari'a* rules prior to the era of Mohammed Ali. I will then describe its position under the rule of Mohammed Ali's family. Finally, I will illustrate the current developments which have taken place since the Egyptian revolution of July 1952.[1]

---

* Commissioner Counsellor, The Supreme Constitutional Court of Egypt; Visiting Professor, Faculty of Law, McGill University (1998–99). The author would like to acknowledge Professor William Tetley of the Faculty of Law, McGill University, for his critical and enormously helpful comments on the final draft of this article.

[1] Some parts of this article are drawn from the author's previously published work on "The origins and developments of the Egyptian judicial system" in Kevin Boyle and Adel Omar Sherif (eds.), *Human Rights and Democracy: The Role of the Supreme Constitutional Court of Egypt*, London, Kluwer Law International, 1996, Chapter 2.

2 THE HISTORY OF THE JUDICIAL FUNCTION: ITS ROOTS AND ITS DEVELOPMENTS

2.1 The meaning of judicial function

In an abstract sense, the expression "judicial function" implies two concepts. The first is based on a formal criterion defined by the formalities and procedures related to this function; the second determines function in light of substance rather than form, i.e. on the basis of the elements of which judicial function is composed.[2] Consequently, what is meant by the expression may vary. In light of the formal criteria, judicial function refers to those bodies that are formally established by the state in order to resolve litigation and to try crimes within certain legal procedures. Within the material criteria, judicial function is recognized as a power to dispose of cases in a judicial manner. This power *per se* is the characteristic that distinguishes judicial activities from other forms of public authority activities. Nevertheless, the current common tendency in defining judicial function has been in accordance with both the formal and material elements to be regarded as a power and function as well. The state organizes judicial function to dispose of litigation and crimes peacefully through qualified judges and within specific legal methods, formalities and procedures. Accordingly, the general usage of the expression most properly refers to many different topics relating to the judicial rules, procedures and the means of disposing cases.

This modern concept of the judicial function, now widespread throughout the world's democratic systems, did not emerge, in its early stages, in the same form in which it is seen today. In fact, the history of judicial function as an essential method for settling conflicts between people is ancient rather than modern. It is as old as the human race, and exists in some form at each rung of human society, irrespective of the structure of the society or its boundaries. There have been, as will be observed from reviewing the following examples on the applications of the judicial function throughout history in various legal systems, many successive political and historical events which have led to the development of this function and its crystallization into what it is today, namely, one of the key activities of the state and a cornerstone of all democratic systems of government.

2.2 Comparative systems

2.2.1 The family system and the tribes

Historically, the earliest attempts at exercising the judicial function started with the "old family system" wherein the head of the family, usually the father, would act as a judge among his family members to resolve their disputes. When the fam-

---

[2] The distinction between formal and substantive criteria in defining legal acts has been one of the main characteristics of the civil law system. In France, and also in Egypt, it is very common for distinctions within legal acts to be based on either formal or substantive views.

ilies began to merge and live in tribes, this power was transferred to, and applied by, the tribal council which consisted of its eldest men.[3]

2.2.2 The early organized state

At the early stages of establishing a state, and due to the prevalent totalitarian approach of the government system, all powers, including the judicial function, were entrusted to the rulers who, within their unlimited powers, would try criminal offences and resolve other litigation of whatever nature.[4] Perhaps the best example of this is found in Ancient Egypt, where the pharaohs were viewed as gods and consequently held absolute power in their hands – a system that was maintained over thousands of years. The notion of judicial independence did not exist[5] as it was only one facet of the all-encompassing powers available to and exercised by the pharaohs.[6] Similarly, in Ancient Rome the concentration of power also resided with the rulers.[7] In examining the successive historical periods of Roman law we find that:

(a)   During the monarchy (735–509 BC), there were some popular bodies within the system of government in the state, e.g. the senate and the people's assemblies, but these bodies did not effectively participate in the governing process as their role was overshadowed by the increasing dominance of the emperor through his exercise of a wide range of absolute powers.

(b)   Starting with the republic period (509–27 BC), some of the power was passed over to two consuls and later to various other magistracies (such as the censors in 433 BC, the praetor and the minor officials in 367 BC) who assumed a share of the responsibility, and exercised some judicial activities through delegations from the consuls.

(c)   During the principate period (27 BC–284 AD) the emperor maintained the republic in theory, but for all practical purposes, he had absolute powers and the institutions of the republic became mere tools in his hands, and their influence rapidly declined.

(d)   With the beginning of the dominate period, the last of the development periods of the Roman Empire in 284 AD, which witnessed the decline of the

---

[3]   During the early stages of history, including the Roman law period, family was not based upon marriage, but upon power. Those who formed the family were all subject to the rights or power of the same family head. See Andrew Stephenson, *A History of Roman Law*, Boston, Little, Brown, 1912, p. 26.

[4]   The emperor, or ruler, under Roman law possessed in full that power over the community which belonged to the father in his household. He sat in judgment over all private and criminal processes. Some of his functions, including the judicial function, were delegated to subordinates, but in the last analysis these functions were controlled by him. Stephenson, *Roman Law*, p. 26.

[5]   Mahmmoud Salam Zanaty, *Mogaz Tarekh El Qannon El Masry* [A Brief on the History of Egyptian Law] (Cairo, 1986), p. 75.

[6]   However, it has been historically proven that the pharaoh occasionally delegated his judicial power to either civil or religious judges. Mahmmoud El-Sakka, *Tarekh El Qannon El Masry* [The History of Egyptian Law] Cairo, Dar El Nahda El Arabia, p. 60.

[7]   For more details on the successive historical periods of Roman law, see Stephenson, *Roman Law*.

Empire, the emperor became an absolute monarch, and was viewed as a master and god with real absolute powers over all public functions and affairs.

In effect, these historical developments confirm that, at first, the rulers would exercise the judicial function by themselves or with the assistance of their agents and other assistants. This meant that the exercise of such power was largely related to the ruler and was affected by his personal whims in controlling the administration of justice and imposing his own judgments, and exercising the jurisdiction of dispensation and absolution. Nevertheless, in a voluntary manner, or at other times as a result of public pressure, the rulers gradually relinquished much of their power by delegation to others, either public officers or ordinary individuals. However, they kept their control by many means, including selecting judges, hearing appeals against certain judgments and determining the legal rules to which the individual's conduct should conform.

2.2.3 *The medieval ages*

Many legal systems emerged following the collapse of the Roman Empire, with each having different respective judicial applications. From among these systems and applications, the following examples are provided.

2.2.3.1 The feudal law period
In the development of the feudal system, the feudal lord (or count) had the right to hold his own court. From the holding of his court he would obtain financial benefits, whilst at the same time it gave him effective power over the locality.[8] The experience that best exemplifies the form of justice administration proceedings in the feudal law period, however, is that of the people's direct participation in the administration of justice within the count's courts in France. Before the crumbling of the government in the civil wars, the invasions during the ninth and tenth centuries and the diminishing of the popular element in the administration of justice, the count's area of authority was divided into groups numbering hundreds of persons. From each group the count would summon all free men to his court, known as the *mallus*, where the assembly would elect law-finders who would give their verdicts under the presidency of the count. Initially, the presence of these free men was essential; however, the burden of attendance was later eased, and was required only three times a year to review major cases. As for minor cases, they would simply be dealt with by the elected persons known as *sabini* who thereafter were usually seven for each hundred, elected for life, and usually sitting under the presidency of the count's deputy. This is, in fact, considered to be the origin of the distinction between the high and low degrees of justice.

---

[8] Penny Darbyshire, *Eddey on The English Legal System*, 5th edn., London, Sweet & Maxwell, 1992, p. 184.

2.2.3.2 The canon law period

Canon law was primarily concerned with the administration of the church and its rules. By the year 1140, because of the prevalence of this law, the judiciary was clearly coloured by ecclesiastical traits, as canon law was primarily concerned with the administration of the church and its rules. By then, all Christendom was divided into dioceses. The bishop of each diocese was ordinarily the judge who had universal jurisdiction in both civil and criminal issues within his diocese, unless there was a specific referral to some other court. He played a positive role in investigating each case and in evaluating the evidence. The proceedings were written, and appeal was permitted in both interlocutory matters and final rulings. The appeals against the bishop's decisions were handled by both the metropolitan and the pope in Rome. In addition, the papacy reserved for itself some of the more serious causes such as claims against bishops, and dispensations and absolutions of certain types. However, the pope did not hear cases in person, in every case. He was assisted by auditors who became full delegates between the twelfth and fourteenth centuries. At first they would hear cases individually. However, each of them was required to consult his colleagues, and this led to the establishment of panels of judges as of 1331.

2.2.3.3 The old common law of England

Prior to the Norman conquest of 1066 there was no central judicial system in England, nor was there any common law.[9] England was administratively divided into shires within which smaller units of hundreds were formed. Within the units of hundreds, there existed the tithing system wherein every free man was enrolled in a group of ten. Judicial activity was generally entrusted by the Wessex kings to the shire courts, presided over by the alderman and the local bishop of each shire. The court met twice annually, and under the same two men existed the borough courts which would convene three times annually. There also existed the hundred courts which met every four weeks. These courts dealt with both ecclesiastical and lay issues. In general, the administration of justice was largely a domain of the king, the shire president and the sheriff. The procedures were simple as there was no distinction between private and criminal law. The trial by ordeal and the oath both played an important role in establishing the evidence. Appeals to the king were permitted but restricted to those cases in which redress could not be obtained.

In 1066 the Norman conquest gave effect to the feudal concept that all land was held for the king, and consequently the administration of justice became largely affected by this feudal tendency, producing many developments, including: the diminishing of the importance of the shire courts by entrusting all litigation concerning the great lords' tenants to the newly-established honour court; the reliance on the trial by battle in both civil and criminal jurisdiction; the increasing use of sworn juries and the sending out of royal justice in eyre; the bishops' relinquishing their joint presidency of the shire courts; and the transference of some courts, such as the hundred courts, into the private hands of the feudalists.

---

[9] Calob Berry Patterson, *The Administration of Justice in Great Britain*, Austin, University of Texas, p. 1. Also, see Edward Jenks, *The Book of English Law*, Boston and New York, Houghton Mifflin, 1929, pp. 12 and 28.

2.2.4 The judicial experience in Islam

Under Islamic *shari'a* rules, the judicial function is viewed not only as one of the state's functions but also as a power to be exercised by the ruler to resolve disputes with justice between individuals, in accordance with God's commands. As clearly seen from this definition, the judicial function is one of the ruler's many duties. This shows that the separation of powers doctrine in its contemporary application was not followed in the early Islamic state. In fact, at the early stages of Islam, the doctrine of separation of powers was not recognized; thus, all of the state's powers were entrusted to the Prophet Mohammed, who was effectively the first judge in Islam. The Prophet would either adjudicate disputes himself or by delegating judicial power to his Companions to dispose of certain cases. When the State began to grow, through successive Islamic spreads, this power was entrusted to the Islamic ruler or governor (*el-wali*) for each of the newly gained lands, by a delegation from the Prophet Mohammed and later by his successors, the caliphs. After the Prophet's death, this power was exercised by the caliphs who, in turn, delegated it to the governors of the newly gained countries and sometimes to specialized judges other than the governor. It was not uncommon for the caliph to direct the governors and judges to follow certain standards in their actions and behaviour in order to administer justice in compliance with Islamic rules.[10]

As the state expanded an even more, significant distinction took place – the separation of the judicial function of the *wali* from his other functions, and vesting it in specialized judges by assignment from the caliph, or the *wali* in certain cases. Nevertheless, the assignments of these judges did not prevent the caliph or the *wali* from acting as judges whenever it was appropriate.

These general developments also occurred in Egypt during the Islamic spread wherein the judicial power at the outset of the spread over was exercised by the *wali* and later by specialized judges by virtue of assignments either from the *wali* or the caliph.[11]

2.2.5 Judicial function and separation of powers

By looking at the above examples, one can easily observe that the judicial function, from the earliest forms of the organized state until the middle ages, was centralized in the hands of the rulers to the extent that there was no clear distinction between judicial function and the other functions of the state. Furthermore, one must take note that in addition to the ruler's powers, there were times, throughout different ages, in which the religious powers of Judaism, Christianity and Islam had a great impact on governmental systems and the judicial function of each. It used to be a

---

[10] For more details, see Omar Sherif, *Nozom Elhokm Wa El Edara Fe El Islam* [The Systems of Government and Administration in Islam], Cairo, Islamic Studies Institute, 1989.

[11] Abd El Hameed Metwaly, *Mabadee Nezam Elhokm Fe El Islam* [Principles of Government Systems in Islam], Cairo, Dar El Mareef, 1966, p. 633.

function of the state to defend religious beliefs in ecclesiastical matters, thus serving, for the most part, the interests of the leaders of the clergy.

Nevertheless, the exercise of judicial power – whether by the rulers, the religious institutions or the people's representatives – did not reflect the real role played by those who carried out their judicial burdens in the justice administration process, as the achievement of justice was always subject to and governed by various political and ecclesiastical considerations, and consequently there were no clear defining lines to distinguish the judicial function. In actuality, such a role is only clearly defined when the judicial function has its own identity and independence, which did not practically exist until the doctrine of the separation of powers became one of the principal tenets of the present-day democratic systems of governments.

The belief that the state has various functions is not a modern one; rather, it has a long history extending back for centuries. It is deeply rooted in the early philosophical works of Plato, Aristotle and Polybius, and could be found in some works of medieval philosophers, such as Marsilius de Padua. Moreover, it was adopted by Locke in 1690. However, this idea has been commonly attributed to the French political philosopher Montesquieu, as he adopted it and thoroughly explained it in 1748 in his famous book, *The Spirit of Laws*. He properly conceived the idea of the three functions of government as exercised by the three different organs, each juxtaposed against the others, and saw the necessity of separating the judiciary from the executive and legislative branches of government. The separation of powers he aimed to achieve is not a complete one. In fact, he envisioned the three organs acting in concert and considered the necessity of some overlapping in competence among them, in order to fulfil the exigencies of the checks and balances theory. Although he did not conceive a new idea – it was an existing one which he simply put in a more metaphysical form – he did succeed in convincing the world, as noted by Holdworth, that he had discovered a new constitutional principle which was universally valid.

In fact, it has become commonly accepted that the prevalence of the separation of powers doctrine helped manifest the judicial role and explore the extent to which justice is secured and maintained in society. The conveyance of the judicial function to competent courts would certainly aid the process of justice administration through judicial specialization, impartiality and independence.

What is also noteworthy in this regard is the fact that the prevalence of this doctrine has led to a vital change in the nature and position of the judicial function within the total system of government. Today, in accordance with this doctrine, the judicial function is viewed not only as one of the basic functions of the modern state, but also as a popular power emerging from the people themselves.[12] Such a view justifies the enrolment of the people, either directly or through their representatives, in the justice administration process by taking part, together with the other concerned powers in the state, in effecting this process.

---

[12] The Constitution of Egypt, for instance, provides in Art. 3 that the people are the source of the state's powers.

2.3 The Egyptian experience

2.3.1 The organized judiciary in Egypt

The existence of an organized judicial function has always been a firmly established feature in most successive systems of government in Egypt since the early Pharaonic period.[13] Nevertheless, this feature does not necessarily mean that such a function has always been efficient, impartial and independent, as it is historically proven that there were some eras during which the judicial function was used as a tool by the rulers to realize personal gains, regardless of public justice considerations. Rather, this feature simply demonstrates the fact that Egyptians became accustomed to having their disputes resolved by judicial bodies established by the state and empowered to apply the legal rules the state has adopted, regardless of the extent to which these bodies can guarantee justice. The Egyptian experience in this regard may be summarized as follows.

2.3.2 Judicial function after the Islamic spread in Egypt

Following the Islamic spread in Egypt in the seventh century and until the beginning of the rule of the Mohammed Ali family in the early nineteenth century, the organization of the judicial function had been governed in accordance with Islamic *shari'a* rules. During this period, the judicial procedures, as well as the substantive laws, were all derived from, and basically founded on, Islamic *shari'a* law.[14]

The judicial system in Islam is based on the single-judge court. The judgments of the court are final and generally not subject to review, with the exception of certain cases, as I will demonstrate later, wherein the judgment might be struck down either by the judge who rendered it or another competent judge.[15]

2.3.3 The general organization of the judicial function

2.3.3.1 The selection and removal of judges

Judges were required to possess a set of qualifications as candidates. The adherence to such qualifications in the exercise of the selection of judges was precisely followed in Egypt during the Islamic spread. These qualifications may be summarized as follows.[16] The candidate had to:

(a)   possess a certain degree of maturity, wisdom and intelligence, as the lack of maturity would undoubtedly deprive him of the ability to arrange his own affairs, and obviously the wisdom to judge other people's affairs;

---

[13] Fathy El Marsafawy, *Tarekh El Qannon El Masry* [The History of Egyptian Law], Cairo, Dar El Fekr El Araby, p. 161.
[14] Ibrahim Awad, *Al Qadda Fe El Islam* [The Judiciary in Islam: Its History and Organization], Cairo, Islamic Research Institute Publications, 1975, p. 101.
[15] Adel Omar Sherif, *El Qadda El Dostory Fe Mesr* [Constitutional Adjudication in Egypt] Cairo, Dar El Shaab, 1988, p. 52.
[16] Omar Sherif, *Nozom Elhokm Wa El Edara Fe El Islam*, p. 124.

(b)   be male, as this is a requirement set by the majority of Muslim jurists. How-
       ever, there are some schools of thought in Islam which permit the assign-
       ment of women as judges;
(c)   be a free man and not a slave of any person;
(d)   be a Muslim, as the prevailing rule states that a non-Muslim person has no
       power over any Muslim. Nevertheless, non-Muslims can be assigned as judges
       in the opinion of some Islamic schools of thought; and some schools permit
       their assignment as judges among the non-Muslims (of their religion), while
       others accept their assignment as judges of Muslims and non-Muslims alike.
(e)   be honest, fair and just;
(f)   be very knowledgeable of the basic rules of Islamic *shari'a*, and able to apply
       them in the different litigation brought before him;
(g)   have proper vision, hearing and pronunciation, in order to perform his du-
       ties perfectly.

The caliph or the *el-wali* of the gained lands selected judges at his discretion from
among the qualified candidates. In addition to this power of selecting and assigning the judges, the ruler also has the power to remove the appointed judge
from his office if he does not maintain the good behaviour required of judges or
commits a grave mistake which would render him ineligible to handle cases judicially.[17]

2.3.3.2 Judicial procedures
In accordance with Islamic *shari'a* rules, judicial jurisdiction was vested in the *shari'a*
courts. Each of these courts consisted of a single judge. As I mentioned earlier, multi-
judge courts do not exist in Islamic *shari'a* law. Judges were empowered with general jurisdiction, within their territories, to handle all sorts of disputes brought before
them, including civil, criminal and family matters. Their judgments were final and,
as a general rule, not subject to review. Nevertheless, under Islamic *shari'a* law, there
have always been, and still are, some exceptions to this general rule where the judgment might be struck down, either by the judge who rendered it or any other competent judge. These exceptions may be summarized as follows.[18] If the judgment:

(a)   was rendered in the absence of the concerned party (in this situation, the
       party must be given the opportunity to appear and present their arguments);
(b)   was rendered in a case over which the judge did not have jurisdiction, such as
       a matter involving a member of his family or a friend;
(c)   was rendered by a person without a proper judicial appointment; or
(d)   contradicted a clear-cut provision in the Qur'an, Sunna or Islamic jurispru-
       dence.

With the exception of these cases, all judicial rulings were final and not subject to
review. In addition, Islamic law provided a unified legal code, which helped to avoid
problems associated with conflicting laws.

---

[17] Awad, *Al Qadda Fe El Islam*, p. 184.
[18] Omar Sherif, *El Qadda El Dostory Fe Mesr*, p. 52.

Under Islamic law, the judicial function was performed in a very simple manner. The concerned litigants would appear before the competent judge and present their arguments. The judge would evaluate each party's evidence and render his decision. In exercising the judicial function, the judge was guided by the Qur'an (the Holy Book of Islam), the Sunna (the Prophet's traditions) and *ijma'* (the consensus of opinion reached by the early Muslim jurists), respectively. After exhausting these sources, he could then apply his own reasoning.[19]

2.3.4 The judicial function during the rule of the Mohammed Ali family

With the beginning of the reign of the Mohammed Ali family in 1805, Egypt's judicial system underwent a significant transformation. The regime discarded many Islamic rules of judicial procedure and replaced them with new procedures derived from the legal systems of Western Europe. The regime also expanded the scope of the judicial function during this period, which increased the need for new judges. The regime fulfilled this need by reducing the requirements for appointment to a judicial post. In particular, the requirement that candidates for the judiciary be proficient in Islamic law was steadily eased. Eventually, holding a law degree became the main qualification for a judicial appointment. These appointments were left entirely to the discretionary power of the ruler.

The hallmark of this period was the deterioration of the Islamic identity of Egypt's legal system. Mohammed Ali and his successors were foreigners (Turkish) and thus felt greater empathy and loyalty to European culture than to Egyptian culture. Mohammed Ali tried to reform the system of government as a whole, including the judiciary, without losing control over these public bodies. Consequently, he was always keen on having the final word in all significant matters. He started by establishing some specialized councils to hear certain types of disputes over judicial, commercial, administrative and military matters.[20] In reality, these councils were staffed not only by judges, but also by public officials and army officers. In addition, their decisions were not final; they had to be approved either by the ruler (*el-wali*) or some other higher council in order to become enforceable. By establishing these councils and vesting in them broad judicial jurisdiction, the judicial power became largely controlled by the *wali*. Most of the jurisdiction of the *shari'a* courts was transferred to the newly created councils; the *shari'a* courts retained very limited jurisdiction, relating only to family status issues.[21] This limited jurisdiction became even more restricted in 1856, when an act was passed establishing new councils to handle family status issues for every non-Muslim group within the state. Fourteen of these councils were established and worked alongside the *shari'a* courts, which maintained jurisdiction whenever the litigants were both Muslims or when the litigants were of different religions. Moreover, the Councils and representatives of foreign countries that had special privileges in Egypt had the power

---

[19] Omar Sherif, *Nozom Elhokm Wa El Edara Fe El Islam*, p. 130.
[20] Aziz Khanky, "El Mohamaa" [The Legal Profession], in *The Golden Book of the National Courts*, 2nd edn., Cairo, 1990, p. 386.
[21] Fathy Wally, *Qannon El Qadda El Madany* [The Civil Judiciary Law], Cairo, Dar El Nahda El Arabia, 1980, p. 220.

to decide disputes in which their natives were involved, even when Egyptian nationals were parties to the case.

From 1875 to 1883, Mohammed Ali's successors took additional steps to reform the judicial system. Due to pressures from those countries that enjoyed special privileges in Egypt, and in accordance with their agreement with the Egyptian government, a new type of court, known as "the mixed courts", was established in 1875. These courts handled any case in which foreigners were parties, or at least had a stake in the outcome. In addition, other new courts, known as "national courts", were established in 1883 to handle litigation between citizens that did not fall under the jurisdiction of the mixed courts.[22] Each of these two categories of courts, the mixed and national, applied different sets of civil, commercial, criminal and procedural codes. These codes did not adhere to the Islamic *shari'a* law, the original law of the country. In fact, they were all derived from foreign sources, primarily French law, which explains the continuing influence of French law on Egyptian legal culture.

After this wave of reforms at the end of the nineteenth century, the Egyptian judicial system consisted of the following codes and institutions:

(a) mixed codes applied by the mixed courts;
(b) national codes applied by the national courts;
(c) Islamic *shari'a* law applied by the *shari'a* courts;
(d) religious rules applied by the different religious councils, based on the litigants' religions.[23]

Undoubtedly, this plethora of different laws and competent courts led to many conflicts of jurisdiction and created great confusion. For these reasons, subsequent governments sought to reform the system with the aim of ensuring that all litigants were treated equally, regardless of their nationality or religion. As a result of these efforts the mixed courts were abolished in 1949, pursuant to an international treaty (Montreux Convention) between Egypt and those countries which enjoyed certain privileges in Egypt. In accordance with this treaty, signed in 1937, all privileges granted to foreigners, including the mixed courts system, were abolished, and the jurisdiction of these courts was transferred to the national courts.[24] Furthermore, both *shari'a* courts and religious councils were abolished in 1955, and their jurisdiction were also transferred to the national courts.[25] However, this streamlining of the court system did not affect the rules applied to family-status cases. These cases are still governed substantively in accordance with the religious rules observed by the concerned parties.[26]

These reforms left the national courts, which are known in the Egyptian judicial system as the ordinary courts or ordinary judiciary, as the competent organ within the Egyptian judiciary with general jurisdiction over judicial litigation of

---

[22] Mohammed Hamed Fahmy, *El Morafaat El Madania Wa El Togaria* [Civil and Commercial Procedures], Cairo, Maktabet El Nasr, 1938, pp. 44, 224.
[23] Omar Sherif, *El Qadda El Dostory Fe Mesr*, p. 67.
[24] *Ibid.*, p. 68.
[25] Wally, *Qannon El Qadda El Madany*, p. 222.
[26] Omar Sherif, *El Qadda El Dostory Fe Mesr*, p. 68.

nationals and aliens alike, in accordance with unified rules embodied in Egyptian laws.

In addition, the State Council (*Le Conseil d' Etat*) was established in 1946 to handle certain kinds of administrative disputes. Later, it became the public law judge with general jurisdiction over all kinds of administrative disputes.

Accordingly, by the mid-1950s the general shape of the judicial function was founded on a two-fold structure that embodied the ordinary courts on the one hand, and the State Council on the other. As the Egyptian Revolution of 1952 developed, more changes in the organization of the judicial function took place.

2.4 The Egyptian judicial system today

2.4.1 The judicial function since the 1952 Revolution

2.4.1.1 The multiplicity of judicial bodies

As a result of the 1952 revolution, the Republic was proclaimed and the rule of the Mohammed Ali family was terminated in 1953. In addition, the British occupation of the country came to an end in 1954. Since then, many constitutional developments have occurred in order to establish a new system of government and to reform some of the existing public institutions. The judicial function has been significantly affected by these developments.

These constitutional developments included the establishment of several new organs that exercise a share of judicial authority, alongside the courts of the ordinary judiciary and the state council. There has always been a common understanding among Egyptian jurists, founded on constitutional and legislative texts, that the courts of the ordinary judiciary and state council have general jurisdiction within certain limits, to be determined in accordance with the will of the legislature and the nature of the litigation. However, this fact does not prevent the legislature from establishing new judicial bodies and empowering them with specified jurisdiction to judge certain types of cases, in accordance with the public interest considerations. Based on this understanding, a number of judicial bodies have been established and vested with judicial jurisdiction to be exercised exclusively by them without any outside interference. Among these bodies are the Supreme Court of Egypt (the Supreme Constitutional Court), the Military Judiciary, the Special Courts, the Administrative Committees which are vested with judicial jurisdiction, the State Lawsuits Body, the Public Prosecution Body, the Administrative Prosecution Body and the Socialist Public Prosecution Body.

As this system of multiple judicial bodies demonstrates, the concept of judicial organs in Egypt has a very broad meaning. Judicial authority is not confined to those who have the power to decide cases such as courts of law; rather, other bodies that participate in applying judicial procedures are also considered judicial organs. Consequently, some of the existing judicial bodies in Egypt do not judge cases or render judgments. However, they are deemed judicial organs because of their participation in judicial procedures before courts, and because of their role in the process of administering justice in the society.

As the main objective of this part is to provide a comprehensive understanding of the development of the Egyptian judicial system, with the ultimate goal of providing the reader with a simple and clear picture of the structure of this system and its mechanisms, it would be helpful now to identify the numerous existing judicial bodies and their jurisdiction in the following sections.

2.5 Courts of law: the judicial bodies with the power to decide cases

The main characteristics of the judicial power in Egypt are its independence, specialization and distribution among so many judicial bodies. The 1971 Constitution provides, in Article 165, that: "[t]he judicial power is independent, and is exercised by courts of different kinds and levels . . . its judgments are to be rendered according to the law". It also provides, in Article 167, that: "[t]he law shall determine the judicial bodies and their jurisdiction; regulate the way of their formation; and prescribe the conditions and procedures for appointing their members and transferring them." Along the same lines, the Constitution delegated to the legislature the power to regulate and specify the jurisdiction of some judicial bodies. It provides, in Article 171, that: "[t]he law shall regulate the hierarchy of the State Security Courts, and prescribe their jurisdiction, as well as the conditions to be fulfilled by those who exercise the judicial power through these courts". In addition, it provides, in Article 172, that: " [t]he State Council is an independent judicial body competent to decide administrative disputes and disciplinary cases, with other competence to be determined by law". Furthermore, it provides, in Article 183, that: "[t]he law shall regulate the Military Judiciary, and prescribe its jurisdiction within the principles contained in the constitution".

In considering the listed provisions, the group of judicial bodies that have the power to decide cases according to the law and judicial procedures, and therefore are considered courts of law, include the Supreme Constitutional Court, the ordinary courts, the State Council, the military courts, the special courts and the administrative committees vested with judicial jurisdiction.

Each group of courts falling under any of these bodies is deemed a specialized judicial body. The courts within each single group are organized in a hierarchy under the ultimate supervision of the highest court in the concerned group; the Court of Cassation prevailing over the ordinary courts; the High Administrative Court prevailing over the administrative courts of the State Council. The powers of these high courts are determined within the limits of the jurisdiction of the concerned judicial body, and thus these limits are binding upon the inferior courts while not restricting the courts of other judicial bodies. In fact, this approach may lead to legal conflicts among the different judicial bodies. When this happens, the mandate to resolve such conflicts lies with the Supreme Constitutional Court, in its capacity as the supreme court of the country.

Therefore, apart from what is called exceptional courts, whose formation is considered inconsistent with the conception of the "natural judge",[27] all other courts in Egypt are specialized ones and their jurisdiction is defined with respect to the sub-

---

[27] According to Art. 68 of the 1971 Constitution, the term "natural judge" means the competent judge over the subject matter of the dispute. The said article states, "The right to litigation is inalienable for all, and every citizen has the right to be referred to his or her natural judge".

ject matter of the dispute. Hence, one can say, under the Egyptian judicial system, specialized courts are recognized and embrace the civil courts, family issues courts, administrative courts, military courts, and so on.

In practice, the term "ordinary courts" refers to the civil, criminal, commercial and family issues courts affiliated with the ordinary judicial body headed by the court of cassation. This body, which the vast majority of judges belong to, is administratively ruled by what is called the High Council of the Judiciary whose mandate is confined to the ordinary courts' body together with the public prosecution body, and does not extend to any other judicial body. This council is different from the Supreme Council of judicial bodies. The latter exercises some general administrative competence over the different judicial bodies. It is presided over by the President of the Republic, and its membership includes the Minister of Justice and heads of different judicial bodies, with the Chief Justice of the Supreme Constitutional Court first in seniority among them.

As to the term "administrative courts", it refers to those courts affiliated with the administrative judicial body (the State Council) headed by the high administrative court. This body is also administratively ruled by a special council parallel to the high council of the ordinary courts' body. Similarly, all other judicial bodies have their own higher councils to handle their internal affairs.

In general, the judiciary is a career usually initiated upon graduation from law school. Members of different judicial bodies are ranked among themselves based on their seniority. The highest rank, succeeding to the president and the deputies of the concerned judicial body, is called Counsellor. Thus every counsellor is a judge, but not every judge is a counsellor.

Now, let us discuss further the courts of law, meaning those judicial bodies with the power to decide cases.

2.5.1 The Supreme Constitutional Court

The Supreme Constitutional Court sits at the apex of the Egyptian judicial system. It is the court that has exclusive power to exercise judicial review in constitutional issues. Through the exercise of this power, the Court unifies the interpretation of the constitution which necessitates balancing the need for consistency with the requirements for progressive development.

When the present-day constitution was proclaimed in 1971, it devoted Chapter Five of Part Five to the Supreme Constitutional Court. It was the first time this court was mentioned in any Egyptian constitution. In fact, it was the first time in the evolution of Egyptian constitutional history that a real of concern was given to the aforementioned court. Chapter Five consists of five articles which are as follows:

Article 174
The Supreme Constitutional Court shall be an independent judicial body, having its own juristic personality in the Arab Republic of Egypt, and having its seat in Cairo.

Article 175
The Supreme Constitutional Court alone shall undertake the judicial control in respect of the constitutionality of laws and regulations, and shall undertake the interpretation of the legislative texts, all of which in accordance and in the manner prescribed by law.

The law shall determine the other competence of the Court, and regulate the procedures to be followed before it.

Article 176
The law shall organize the way of formation of the Supreme Constitutional Court, and prescribe the conditions required of its members, their rights and immunities.

Article 177
The status of members of the Supreme Constitutional Court shall be irrevocable. The Court shall call to account its members, in the manner prescribed by law.

Article 178
The judgments issued by the Supreme Constitutional Court in constitutional cases, and its decisions concerning the interpretation of legislative texts, shall be published in the Official Gazette. The law shall organize the effects subsequent to a decision concerning the unconstitutionality of a legislative text.

2.5.1.1 The historical background and the establishment of the Court

The Supreme Court was established pursuant to Decree Law No. 81 of the year 1969. That Court was replaced by the current Supreme Constitutional Court by virtue of Law No. 48 of the year 1979 concerning the establishment of the Supreme Constitutional Court, and like its predecessor, it has been assigned the exclusive power of judicial review.

As Dr Awad Mohammed El-Morr, former Chief Justice of the Supreme Constitutional Court of Egypt, wrote in his article about human rights in the constitutional systems of Islamic countries:

The creation of a Supreme Court vested with the power of judicial review, to pass upon the validity of legislation in order to ascertain their compliance or irreconcilable variance with the provisions of the Constitution, is largely considered as the introduction of an arbiter between the government and individuals, as well as a trustworthy custodian of all rights embodied in that constitution including fundamental human rights and freedoms in respect of which the Court aims at: (a) easing social strains resulting from state sponsored abuses of human rights which have dramatically increased, and the traditional patterns of social solidarity which have significantly decreased, along with the use of technological advances which provided sophisticated devices for the intrusion of the privacy of one's life; (b) adopting liberal conceptions of interpretation capable of sustaining the unity of the nation, enhancing its development and of meeting the new pressing needs, especially when the Court has the last word, and its decisions are regarded as binding and final; (c) subjecting alleged encroachments on fundamental human rights to stringent judicial scrutiny due to their vital importance, their impact on the individual's person, and the role they play in the Court's efforts to reconstruct the balance envisaged by the framers of the constitution in order to advance the new required norms and conceptions being inevitable safeguards for the prospects of a more adaptable and stable society; (d) and transforming abstract constitutional commands into concrete restrictions which would make real the conceived or anticipated protection of human rights, particularly in the field of economic rights which had been long ignored or avoided.[28]

---

[28] Dr Awad Mohammed El-Morr, "Human Rights and the Constitutional Systems of Islamic Countries", *Cairo University Law Review*, Cairo, 1988, p. 7.

Before the establishment of these two courts, the constitutionality of legislative enactments underwent the following developments:

(a) Through the first half of the twentieth century, all courts in principle viewed judicial review of constitutionality as being in contradiction with the separation of powers principle.

(b) With the establishment of the State Council in the year 1946, assigned with the task of deciding administrative controversies, that Council assumed – as from the year 1948 – the power of judicial review. The Council argued that where a legislative provision violates the Constitution, which is the supreme law and the ultimate source of all powers, the latter shall prevail in the case to which they both apply. Civil courts followed the practice of refraining from applying the invalid provision to the case under their consideration. However, during that era neither civil courts nor administrative courts claimed the power to invalidate the unconstitutional provision, but only abstained from applying it to the particular case. In addition, courts were not committed to adopt in other cases the opinion they had held in a previous case.

(c) Decree Law No. 81 of the year 1969 established the Supreme Court. The core of its jurisdiction was the power of judicial review, which entails the invalidation of statutes inconsistent with the constitution. Upon the completion of the formation of the Supreme Constitutional Court, the former Supreme Court ceased to exist and the new Court retained the power of judicial review. The newly established Court has been mandated to exercise this power by the express provisions of the Constitution. And as a result of its creation, all other courts have been excluded from sharing this power with the Supreme Constitutional Court. Hence the power of judicial review is now centralized in the current Court.

2.5.1.2 Formation of the Court

All members of the Court and its Commissioners' Body are appointed by presidential decrees, after being nominated by the Court's general assembly, with the exception of the Chief Justice, whose nomination is left to the discretion of the President. Basically, they are all highly ranked judges selected from other judicial bodies. However, the provisions of the Court's law permit assigning experienced law professors and lawyers as members of the Court and in the Commissioner's Body.

The structure of the Court consists of the Court as such on the one hand and the Commissioners' Body on the other, whose mandate embraces the preliminary examination of cases submitted to the court or its Commissioners' Body. The law does not specify the maximum number of members of the court nor of its Commissioners' Body. However, normally up to eleven justices sit on the bench and engage in discussions of the Court and about the same number of commissioners work with the Court. In all events, a quorum of seven justices is required, but in rendering the decision, votes of all justices are counted.

Before deciding a case, the Commissioners' Body thoroughly examines the facts relevant to the case submitted to the Court, as well as the legal points attached thereto, and finally prepares an advisory legal opinion, which shall either be adopted or disapproved, entirely or partially, by the Court in its final judgment.

2.5.1.3 Competence of the Court
Other than the power of judicial review, the Court exercises other jurisdiction. The following fall within the exclusive jurisdiction of the Court:

(a)   the power of judicial review, which is the core of its competence;
(b)   the adjudication of disputes that may arise in connection with the execution of two contradictory final judgments passed on the same subject matter by two different judicial bodies;
(c)   ascertaining the intent of the legislature whenever a request is submitted to the court for the interpretation of laws and of regulations having the force of law under the constitution. The request for that purpose is presented by the Minister of Justice upon the demand of the Prime Minister or the Speaker of the People's Assembly or the Supreme Council for Judicial Bodies.

2.5.1.4 Scope of the power of judicial review
This power extends to parliamentary acts as well as regulations of the executive branch. Judicial self-restraint as practised by the Supreme Court of the United States has been adopted by the court, including the principle according to which the Court shall not decide constitutional issues unless shown to be strictly necessary for the disposition of the case on the merits. Moreover, this power is confined to allegations of contradiction between a specific legislative provision and the constitution. It does not extend to matters left by the constitution to the discretionary power of the legislature or discussion of the motives behind legislation.

2.5.1.5 Constitutional violations
Violations of the constitution are of either a procedural or substantive nature. The former refers to non-compliance by the legislature with the formalities prescribed by the constitution, either with respect to the manner of proposing legislation or its adoption or promulgation. Substantive violations involve infringements upon constitutional limitations on the contents of legislation enacted by the People's Assembly.

2.5.1.6 Channels for bringing constitutional issues to the Court
A case can only be brought to the Court as prescribed by the Court's Law No. 48 of the year 1979. There are three channels bringing constitutional issues to the Court. These channels are:

(a)   either party to the case before the Court of merits may challenge the validity of a statute applicable thereto. Where the allegations of unconstitutionality are found by the court of merits as prima facie plausible, it shall prescribe for that party a time-limit within which to bring his case before the Supreme Constitutional Court;
(b)   where the court of merits, in the course of deciding a case, prima facie considers an applicable statute invalid, it shall *ex officio* refer the constitutional issue to the Supreme Constitutional Court; or
(c)   where the Supreme Constitutional Court itself perceives that a legislative provision linked to a case under its consideration is prima facie unconstitu-

tional, it may then refer the preliminary examination of the constitutional issue to the Commissioners' Body.

2.5.1.7 Judgments of the Court

Judgments of the Court in all cases within its jurisdiction are not reviewable. In addition, while its judgments with respect to conflict of jurisdiction and contradictory judgments bind only the parties to the case before the Court of merits, its decisions on constitutional controversies and legislative interpretation bind all individuals and public authorities. Sentences rendered by the Court in constitutional cases shall have retroactive effect in the sense that the provision held void by the Court shall be considered as if it had never been enacted. However, in matters other than criminal proceedings, the retroactive effect of the Court's decisions in constitutional cases shall not affect the *res judicata* of other judgments passed by other courts. With respect to criminal provisions, their invalidation removes the *res judicata* effect of convictions rendered in pursuance of the invalidated provision.

2.5.2 *The ordinary courts (the ordinary judicial body)*

In their capacity as the judiciary of general jurisdiction, the ordinary courts handle the bulk of judicial activity in Egypt. They mainly hear all civil, commercial, criminal and family-status cases, unless the jurisdiction is transferred to another judicial body according to the law.

The structure of the ordinary courts is three-tiered.[29] The first tier includes two types of courts, summary and primary tribunals. At the second tier are the courts of appeal; whereas the Court of Cassation (*Cour de Cassation*) occupies the third tier as the highest court within this judicial body.

Each of these courts is usually divided into a number of specialized departments to take on certain types of cases, such as civil and criminal cases. Other than the Summary tribunals, which are single-judge courts, the rest of the courts are multi-judge courts. The judicial quorum applied is three judges in both Primary and Appeal courts, and five judges in the Court of Cassation.

All working judges in these different tiers of courts are eligible to try criminal cases as well as to hear civil, commercial, and family-status litigation. Their appointment to a certain tier, court or department is purely an internal matter that is left absolutely to the discretion of their supreme council, which is presided over by the President of the Court of Cassation. The supreme council's members include senior judges representing all tiers of the ordinary courts and the Attorney General. This council is responsible for supervising the ordinary courts' activities and regulating the affairs of their judges and the public prosecutors.

2.5.2.1 The primary and summary tribunals

The distinction between primary and summary tribunals is based on the degree and scope of their jurisdiction. In fact, the summary tribunals are a branch of the pri-

---

[29] "The Court of Cassation", in *An Outline of the Judicial System*, Cairo, 1972.

mary tribunals with the authority to hear matters of minor importance within certain territorial limits. There is one primary tribunal in each governorate in Egypt, with the exception of Cairo which has two to cover the large territorial jurisdiction in the northern and southern parts of this capital city of 17 million inhabitants.

As for the summary tribunals, they are located within each primary tribunal's circuit of jurisdiction; consequently, their numbers vary from one governorate to another based on the circumstances of the judicial work in the concerned primary tribunals. Basically, the distribution of jurisdiction among the primary and summary tribunals is determined by the codes of civil and criminal procedure, as well as other legislative texts. The criteria applied in this respect provide that certain simple crimes and litigation are to be judged by the summary tribunals, whereas the rest of the caseload is to be dealt with, in most cases, by the primary tribunals.

Decisions on misdemeanours and minor litigation rendered by summary tribunals can be appealed by the concerned parties before the competent primary tribunal sitting as a court of appeal. However, decisions rendered in petty litigation are final and may not be appealed, as prescribed by law.

The primary tribunal sits as an appellate court to hear appeals, on the facts and the law, brought against the summary tribunals' decisions. It also acts as a first-degree court to try and hear cases and controversies within their jurisdiction, as stipulated by law. Generally, the courts' decisions as courts of appeals are final and enforceable, while their decisions as first-degree courts are subject to appeal, on both facts and law, before the courts of appeal.

2.5.2.2 The courts of appeal

The jurisdiction of the courts of appeal is determined on a geographical basis. In this respect, the governorates of Egypt are categorized and divided into territorial groups, and each group is covered by one court of appeal. Nevertheless, there are some courts of appeal with jurisdiction over only one governorate, as is the case of Cairo and Giza, due to their importance and large population.

Through its different departments, the court of appeal handles both criminal and civil cases. Appeals require a complete rehearing. The court reviews the appealed decisions of the primary courts on the facts and the law. It also tries criminal cases, since the primary tribunal's jurisdiction is limited to misdemeanours.

With the exception of capital punishment cases, which must be affirmed by the Court of Cassation before execution, all judgments of the courts of appeal are final, enforceable and executed immediately. However, these judgments are subject to revocation by the Court of Cassation that also has the power to stay the execution of the challenged judgment until it renders its final judgment.

2.5.2.3 The Court of Cassation

The Court of Cassation is the highest court among the ordinary courts, with its seat in Cairo. The mandate of this court is mainly to review the final judgments of the courts of appeal upon submission of a motion for cassation from any of the interested parties, including the Attorney General, on the basis of allegations of misapplication or misinterpretation of law, irregularity in the language of the judgment, or procedural errors.

Only within these limits can the motions for cassation be admitted, since the Court of Cassation, as a court of law, reviews findings of law – not fact. Hence, objections founded on facts are inadmissible. However, due to their importance, the Court examines both facts and law in some cases that involve capital punishment, besides cases submitted to it for revocation for a second time (for final disposition). When the Court finds that the challenged judgment is defective, it returns the case again to the court that rendered that judgment. This court, which must be composed of judges other than those who participated in the revoked judgment, will rehear the case *de novo*.

The judgments rendered by this Court are highly respected and followed by the lower courts even though the system of judicial precedents is not applied in Egypt. This is based on a logical understanding that there is a good likelihood that this Court's interpretation of the law in a particular case will most likely be followed in future cases; and hence, it would be safer for the lower courts if they act within this interpretation.

2.5.3 *The State Council (the administrative judicial body)*

As a result of the great influence of French legal culture on Egyptian jurisprudence, it has always been recognized in Egypt that the legal rules governing the administrative activities of the government, as an authority empowered by the people, are different from those regulating the private affairs of individuals. This is due to the fact that while the ultimate goal of the government when acting as a public power is to achieve and promote the common interests of the society, the main concern of private individuals' is primarily to achieve personal goals. Consequently, governmental administrative activities have to be viewed, treated and examined differently.

Unlike the usual practice in most systems that follow the Anglo American tradition, where both governmental and private activities are subject to the same legal rules and courts, governmental administrative activities in Egypt, as in France, are regulated according to special legal rules and subject to special judicial review exercised by specialized courts. This is what is known as the dualistic legal system wherein, on the one hand, the State Council examines the administrative activities of the state considering a set of special legal rules to which such activities should conform; while, on the other hand, the individual's activities are subject to the general jurisdiction of the ordinary courts, and must comply with the general ordinary rules of law applied in the country.

The State Council was established in Egypt in the year 1946, and since that time it has been legislatively reorganized in 1949, 1955, 1959 and 1972. Since its inception, the Council has played a very significant role in the Egyptian judicial system by reviewing the administrative activities of the government and protecting individuals' rights and freedoms. Moreover, the Council's mandate has not been confined to its power of exercising judicial review in administrative cases; rather, it has always had the competence to review draft laws and regulations, and to offer legal advice to the different bodies of the government. What is noteworthy is that although the various functions of the Council have always existed, they certainly were not as comprehensive and general as they are today. In fact, the scope of power which was given to the Council upon its establishment was somewhat limited and restricted. However, its very effective participation in the legal system of Egypt has led to a gradual increase in its powers. At first, the judicial mandate of the Council was confined to certain types of administrative litigation specified precisely by the law – such as elections of local administrative councils, administrative contracts and disputes involving government employees and their relatives (over issues such as appointments, promotions, disciplinary decisions, retirement, salaries, pensions and compensation). As this mandate developed over time, the Council became the public law judge with comprehensive jurisdiction over a wide range of administrative litigation. It has become the judicial body that has general jurisdiction in administrative issues, and serves as the counterpart to the ordinary courts that have general jurisdiction to dispose of non-administrative cases. However, as is the case with ordinary courts, this general jurisdiction does not prevent the legislature from assigning part of this jurisdiction to another judicial body due to public interest considerations.

In fact, the core judicial jurisdiction of the Council is its power of judicial review in administrative issues. The concept of judicial review in Egypt has two components: review of constitutionality and review of legality. Constitutional review aims at securing the conformity of legislation with the Constitution. Legality review seeks to ensure the compliance of governmental activities with the applicable laws and public regulations. Hence, the power of judicial review is divided between the Supreme Constitutional Court for constitutional issues on the one hand, and the State Council for administrative issues on the other. Both the court and the Council have exclusive power in regard to their jurisdiction. Nevertheless, the ordinary courts sometimes extend their jurisdiction to cover certain administrative actions of the government wherein such actions are deemed in manifest violation of the law to the extent that they cannot be recognized as a real implementation of the applied laws. However, neither the State Council nor the ordinary courts can exercise judicial review involving constitutional issues, as this jurisdiction is exclusively reserved for the Supreme Constitutional Court.

According to Law No. 47 of 1972, which is the current law regulating the State Council, the Council is divided into three judicial sections: the judiciary section, the opinion section and the legislative section. It is worth mentioning that members of the State Council, who are all judges, are eligible to sit on any of these three sections.

2.5.3.1 The judicial section
The judicial section of the State Council consists of three levels of courts besides the State Commissioners' Body. At the first level sit the administrative tribunals, followed by the administrative adjudication courts, and then the high administrative court at the third and highest level. The State Commissioners' Body acts within all three levels of courts.

Beside these courts, there are other specialized courts with the competency to decide disciplinary issues involving employees of governmental agencies, known as the disciplinary courts. At the initial stage, these courts consist of two levels, according to the accused employee's rank; and, in all cases, their decisions are subject to appellate review by the disciplinary circle of the High Administrative Court.

In general, the distribution of the State Council's jurisdiction among these courts is governed by specific rules embodied in the Council's law. According to these rules, disputes that are to be heard are apportioned among the disciplinary courts, the administrative tribunals and the administrative adjudication courts as courts of first degree, and the administrative adjudication courts and the high administrative court as courts of appeals. However, while the appellate jurisdiction of the Administrative Adjudication Courts covers both the facts and the law, the appellate jurisdiction of the High Administrative Court is mainly confined to points of law, and cannot be extended to the facts unless otherwise prescribed by a clear legislative provision.

The High Administrative Court has its seat in Cairo, whereas the disciplinary courts, administrative tribunals and administrative adjudication courts are distributed among the different governorates of Egypt, with each court having territorial jurisdiction over more than one governorate. Cairo is an exception, as its courts are totally devoted to the affairs of that city alone.

All the State Council's courts are multi-judge courts, with a quorum of five judges at the High Administrative Court and three judges at all other courts. There is, however, a special circle of eleven senior judges within the High Administrative Court. The mandate of this circle is concerned with unifying judicial rules and principles in case of conflict or contradiction between decisions of different units of the State Council. In addition, the High Administrative Court is divided into a number of circles, each of which is concerned with certain types of disputes. Some of the administrative judiciary courts have a similar system of specialization.

The judicial and internal affairs of the State Council are left to the absolute discretion of its Supreme Council, which is composed of the President of the State Council and the six most senior vice-presidents of the Council. The Supreme Council, which is known as the Private Council for the Administrative Affairs, is concerned with the judicial activity of the Council as a whole, as well as requests submitted by the judges.

The State Commissioners' Body is a part of the judicial section. The State Commissioners are judges. Their duties involve preparing a preliminary examination of the cases submitted to the Council's courts and drafting an advisory legal opinion report on each case, in order to assist the concerned court in reaching a final judgment.

2.5.3.2 The opinion section
The mandate of the opinion section of the State Council is to provide governmental bodies with legal advice. In addition, it must review any draft contract to which the government is a party whose value exceeds a certain amount of money (i.e. LE5,000).

This section is composed of three levels. At the first level, there are a number of departments, known as the opinion departments, each of which specializes in a particular ministry and its subordinate agencies. Each of these departments is composed of a president of the department and a sufficient number of members. On the second level, there are three committees known as the Presidents of the Departments Committees. Each of these committees is presided over by a vice-president of the State Council, and includes a number of department presidents to discuss the important issues referred to the committee by any of these departments, and to review draft governmental contracts that exceed a certain amount of money (i.e. LE50,000). Finally, at the third level sits the General Assembly of Opinion and Legislation Sections. The Assembly encompasses all the Presidents of the opinion departments, the presidents of the committees, and the President and members of the legislative section. It is presided over by the first vice-president of the State Council. The Assembly gives its legal opinion on international, constitutional and legislative issues upon request from any of the committees, the President of the State Council, any government minister, the Prime Minister, the Speaker of the Parliament or the President of the Republic. Any request submitted by any other entity is considered inadmissible.

In general, it is not mandatory to seek the section's opinions, nor are the opinions binding. This means that governmental agencies are free to seek the legal advice of the section whenever they like, and they are not obligated to follow its opinions. However, it has been proven, in practice, that these agencies are increasingly turning to the section for advice, and they rarely disregard its opinions.

In addition to this rule there are some cases where it becomes imperative to obtain the opinion of the section, and other cases in which the opinion must be enforced.

The first type of case concerns the review of drafts of governmental contracts that exceed a certain amount of money (i.e. LE5,000). Such drafts must be reviewed by the section (either by the competent department or committee, according to the monetary value of the contract) before signing. The law requires this compulsory revision and does not state clearly whether or not the final remarks of the review must be adopted by the concerned agency. However, in practice, such remarks are frequently adopted in response to the spirit of the law, and in order to avoid any future legal liabilities.

The second type of case is related to governmental disputes. In the Egyptian legal system, legal disputes between governmental agencies are not heard by the courts. The idea behind this is that such disputes are seen as family disputes, and thus must be resolved outside the judicial process circle. The State Council, ever since its establishment, has been the competent authority to resolve these types of disputes. Currently, this competence is exercised by the General Assembly of the Opinion and Legislation Sections. According to the State Council law, the Assembly has the exclusive power to resolve these disputes, and its decisions in this regard are enforceable and compulsory.

2.5.3.3 The legislative section

The legislative section reviews the legality and constitutionality of all draft laws and public regulations before their issuance. This review is compulsory, as stipulated by the law. However, it has been firmly established in Egyptian jurisprudence that if legislation is passed without prior review by the section, this would not deprive the legislation of its legal effect. However, it would increase the political responsibility of the government.

In practice, this section is presided over by a vice-president of the State Council, and includes some counsellors and assistant counsellors, to be assigned by the Private Council according to the exigencies of the section's activity.

2.5.4 The Military Judiciary

The military judiciary was established in Egypt pursuant to Law No. 25 of the year 1966. The 1971 Constitution assured the existence of such a judiciary within the Egyptian judicial system by providing, in Article 183, that "The law shall regulate the military judiciary, and prescribe its jurisdiction within the principles contained in the constitution."

The mandate of the military judiciary, as a specialized judiciary, is confined to crimes committed by or against military officers. The military court, and the special procedures and substantive rules applied by them, are all determined by law.

2.5.5 *The special courts and the administrative committees vested with judicial jurisdiction*

As a system based on the principle of specialization, the Egyptian judicial system recognizes many different courts and judicial committees other than the ordinary judicial bodies. Some of these courts are established during extraordinary circumstances. Examples of this are the Revolutionary Courts that followed the political changes in the years 1952 and 1971, and the Emergency State Security Courts that were established according to the Emergency Law to try some crimes during extraordinary times. Other categories of these courts are permanently established to try crimes and handle litigation pursuant to their specialization. They mainly include the state security courts that try some crimes relating to the public domain, the ethics courts that try cases of illicit enrichment and the Political Parties Court that hears disputes relating to the establishment of such parties.

In addition to these specialized courts, there are a huge number of administrative committees, almost in every ministry. Each committee consists of public officials and judges who hear certain administrative litigation relating to the agency wherein the committee is founded. The decisions of such committees are not final. They can be appealed to the State Council. Furthermore, there are many disciplinary councils with the competence to try disciplinary violations committed by employees of certain agencies. Likewise, the decisions of these councils are appealable before the State Council, and reviewable by the High Administrative Court.

3 THE JUDICIAL BODIES PARTICIPATING IN THE JUDICIAL PROCESS WITHOUT RENDERING JUDGMENTS

The judicial bodies participating in the judicial process without rendering judgments are four organs. Three out of these four handle prosecution in different types of cases. These are the Public Prosecution Body, the Administrative Prosecution Body and the Socialist Public Prosecution Body. The main mandate of the remaining body, the State Lawsuits Body, is to defend the government and its affiliated units in lawsuits before courts of law.

3.1 The Public Prosecution Body

The Public Prosecution body is presided over by the Attorney General, and consists of a large number of prosecutors of different ranks covering all parts of the country.

The mandate of this body includes carrying out criminal investigations and seeking indictments before criminal courts. Also, the Public Prosecutor must be represented before the competent courts, other than criminal courts, as required by law.

In addition, the body follows up the enforcement of the sentences handed down by the criminal courts.

According to the law and in practice, both the ordinary courts and the Prosecution Body are integral parts within the structure of the judicial system. Their members are independent, have the same rights and immunities, and perform the same duties. Thus, it is not uncommon in practice that they exchange their posts whenever the supreme council of the judiciary deems necessary, according to the judicial business requirements.

3.2 The Administrative Prosecution Body

The mandate of the Administrative Prosecution Body is mainly to conduct administrative investigations related to crimes committed by government employees and those who work in private institutions that are wholly or partially owned by the government, and which have a great impact on the public function of the concerned institution. This body has no criminal jurisdiction. Hence, if the prohibited act committed by the employee includes a crime, then the investigation of the criminal aspect should be conducted by the Public Prosecution Body, as the task of the Administrative Prosecution Body is limited to disciplinary, and not criminal, issues. Sometimes, criminal and disciplinary investigations can be conducted by the two bodies at the same time as each aspect of the prohibited act has distinct repercussions on the public's interests.

The Administrative Prosecution Body is headed by a president and includes a large number of Prosecutors distributed among the different governorates of Egypt. They are all treated on the same footing as public prosecutors with regards to their rights, immunities and duties.

3.3 The Socialist Public Prosecution Body

This body was first established under Article 179 of the 1971 Constitution. This Article provides that "[t]he Socialist Public Prosecutor shall be responsible for taking the measures which secure the people's rights, the safety of the society and its political regime, the preservation of socialist achievements and commitment to socialist behaviour. The law shall prescribe his other competence. He shall be subject to the control of the People's Assembly according to what is prescribed by law".

The Socialist Public Prosecutor Body exercises all of the competence mentioned in the Constitution. In practice, it pays particular attention to crimes of illicit enrichment. It investigates these crimes and then initiates indictment proceedings in the Ethics Court.

The body is headed by the Socialist Public Prosecutor, who is appointed by a Presidential decree after the consent of the Parliament (the People's Assembly). In practice, the Socialist Public Prosecutor is always chosen from among retired senior members of the different judicial bodies. Members of the body are not permanent appointees. They are members of other judicial bodies who serve on the Socialist Prosecutor's Body for a fixed term (generally one year), which is renewable.

3.4 The State Lawsuits Body

The State Lawsuits Body is the government attorney. Its mandate is to represent governmental agencies in lawsuits brought before all courts, nationally and internationally. The body is divided into specialized central departments in Cairo that are responsible for following up on certain areas of the body's work such as taxation, licenses and administrative disputes. The body also has a large number of non-central departments distributed among the different governorates of Egypt, which perform the body's duties throughout the entire country.

The body is presided over by a President and includes many members of different ranks. According to the law, all the members enjoy the same rights and assume the same responsibilities as their peers in the other judicial bodies.

4 CONCLUSION

This article is a brief overview of the Egyptian judicial system. Although far from comprehensive, its main object is to familiarize the outsider with the system, not only throughout its historical evolution, but also as it exists today. The article has examined the judicial system of Egypt during the Islamic spread and throughout the prevalence of the Islamic *shari'a* period. Thereafter, it points out that the rule of the Mohammed Ali family (1805–1953)[30] had brought fundamental changes to the system. An explanation is particularly given of how the rule of this family generally moved away from the existing Islamic model, and replaced it with modern European models. Finally, the article examined recent developments in the judicial system which have continued to the present day.

The focus of this article has been limited to judicial bodies and therefore has not included the Bar (and the legal profession), which was established in Egypt following the arrival of Mohammed Ali in 1805. It should be mentioned, however, that the Bar has always played a significant role in the evolution of Egyptian society and protecting human rights.[31]

---

[30] The rule of the Mohammed Ali family ceased to exist in 1953, upon proclaiming the republic system in the country, which was one of the most significant changes that followed the outbreak of the Egyptian revolution in 1952.

[31] The topic of the Egyptian Bar – its history, functioning and independence – was addressed in the author's previously published work on *The Origins and Developments of the Egyptian Judicial System*, Chapter 2. It should be mentioned however, that the Bar has faced several internal problems in the recent years, either between the Bar and the government or among members of the Bar themselves. Because of these problems the Bar was placed under court supervision in 1996. Furthermore, the increasing role of the syndicates and public associations, including the Bar, in both political and public life in Egypt has led the government to pass several pieces of legislation during the 1990s to reorganize the conditions of membership in these syndicates and consequently limit their political role in the society. The new promulgated legislation in this matter is viewed by human rights advocates as dramatically reducing the autonomy of syndicate elections, and allowing the government to control the elected councils.

Shari'a and Positive Legislation: is an Islamic State Possible or Viable?

1 INTRODUCTION

I wish to open this lecture with a clear and categorical answer to the question posed in the title, subject to clarification and substantiation later. In my view, *shari'a* cannot be enforced as positive legislation and remain the source of a religiously sanctioned normative system.[1] That is to say, *shari'a* ceases to be what it is purported or assumed to be by the very act of enacting it as positive law. Consequently, any claim to establish an Islamic state to enforce *shari'a* as the positive law is a contradiction in terms. An Islamic state is conceptually impossible because, as a political institution, a state cannot be characterized as either Islamic or non-Islamic, and its attempt to enforce *shari'a* as positive law repudiates the Islamic basis of this normative system. Moreover, in view of the nature and role of the state in the modern global context, an Islamic state would not be practically viable. I will also argue not only that these views are valid from an Islamic, rather than a so-called secular, perspective, but that this distinction itself is misconceived and unhelpful.

But let me first begin by expressing my gratitude to the organizers of this Memorial Lecture for inviting me to join the distinguished group of legal scholars who spoke before me in honour of one of the leading scholars of *shari'a* of our time. As a Sudanese Muslim, I grew up learning about *shari'a* throughout the stages of school, and as a subject of systematic study at the Faculty of Law, University of Khartoum,

---

* Charles Howard Chandler Professor of Law, Emory University, Atlanta, GA, USA. This article was originally presented as a paper at the 1998 Professor Noel Coulson Memorial Lecture, School of Oriental and African Studies, University of London, 7 December 1998.
[1] By the term *shari'a*, I mean the religious normative system of Islam. I prefer to use this term rather than Islamic law precisely because my argument here is that *shari'a* cannot be enacted into law and remain a religiously sanctioned normative system.

© Kluwer Law International 2000

Sudan, some thirty years ago. When I first came to the United Kingdom for post-graduate studies in 1971, I began to encounter the work of Professor Noel Coulson. My initial impression, as I recall now, was amazement that an English scholar could master *shari'a* and Islamic history as he did, from their original sources and in their finest details. Since that time, I have come to appreciate Professor Coulson's work in broader perspective. I admire his rare combination of outstanding legal scholarship, an integrated command of related fields, profound insights and sober empathy with Islamic societies in their present civilizational predicament. This last element in his life's work is particularly important for me because technical scholarly skill, however superb and masterly it may be, is stale and uninspiring without understanding and compassion for human beings and their communities, and genuine appreciation of the contributions of their culture to human civilization at large. Although I never met Professor Coulson in person, I would like to think of myself as one of his students. Since a person can best honour his or her teachers by continuing their work, I will attempt here to address some of the profound legal issues facing Islamic societies in the present context, as indicated throughout Professor Coulson's work, and highlighted in *Conflicts and Tensions in Islamic Jurisprudence*.[2]

As a Muslim lawyer, especially at a time when my own people in Sudan are suffering horrendous oppression and abuse in the name of purported enforcement of *shari'a*, I will attempt a personally engaged, yet hopefully scholarly, discussion of what I see as the fundamental question underlying these issues. In particular, I wish to examine the possibility and viability of integrating *shari'a* into the legal systems of Islamic societies today. Instead of resorting to rhetorical proclamations, as many Muslims tend to do, about Islam and *shari'a* as abstract ideals that should somehow be observed by Muslims everywhere, I prefer to confront the question of whether the enforcement of *shari'a* should be attempted, or what role should it have in the legal system of Islamic countries. In other words, is it possible or desirable to enforce *shari'a* as positive legislation in the present context? If not, how can Muslims around the world define and express their Islamic identity in everyday life?

As I have already stated at the beginning, an Islamic state which can enforce *shari'a* through positive legislation is neither conceptually possible nor practically viable. In my view, Muslims do have a right to self-determination, including the right to define and express their Islamic identity as they deem fit. But that cannot be on the basis of the enactment and enforcement of *shari'a* as such, because whatever norms are enforced as positive law is the political will of that state, and can never be *shari'a* as commonly understood by Muslims to mean the expression of divine will. Consequently, I hold, the pretence of enforcing *shari'a* through positive legislation (as claimed by the present governments of Iran, Afghanistan, Pakistan, Saudi Arabia and Sudan, or advocated by Muslim political activists in many other countries) is dangerous naivety, if not cynical manipulation of the sentiments of Muslims.

Moreover, contrary to the claims of its proponents, a so-called Islamic state that would enforce *shari'a* as positive legislation is the *negation* of the possibility of an Islamic way of life, not its realization. In other words, these efforts are not only doomed to failure at horrendous human and material costs, but are in fact counter-productive. If one is to speak at all of a religious mandate regarding the relation-

---

[2] Chicago and London, University of Chicago Press, 1969.

ship between Islam and the state, one should categorically oppose the illusion of an Islamic state and dangers of enforcing *shari'a*. In my view, Muslims everywhere must openly reject the alleged possibility of enforcement of *shari'a* as the law of any state in order to be able to freely express their religious identity, and begin to reflect the high ideals of their faith in the daily working of their state and its institutions, including the administration of justice.

Before elaborating on and substantiating these views, I wish to emphasize two points about the approach I am presenting in this lecture. First, although the formulation of the issues in these terms is inspired by recent and current political developments or trends in Islamic countries and communities, I propose to address them *irrespective* of the particular political context of any Islamic society today. In other words, I am primarily concerned here with the broader and more fundamental theoretical question of the relevance of *shari'a* to the lives of Muslims today, rather than with commentary or reflection on current political trends in Islamic societies. By seeking to frame the issues in these terms I want to avoid futile debates about whether one "experiment" or another, like that of Iran or Sudan today, is better able to enforce *shari'a* in a so-called "true" or "legitimate" manner. The question I am raising is whether any state, of whatever ideological orientation or practical capabilities, can ever enforce *shari'a*. While I appreciate that this issue is profoundly political, and can see that serious political implications follow from my analysis, that is not my focus in this lecture.

Second, I believe that my position is as Islamic as any human proposition can be. In other words, I believe that the views I am advancing here are valid, indeed imperative I would suggest, from an Islamic point of view, rather than as a concession to political expediency or the product of a so-called secular perspective. Moreover, as I hope it will become clear from the following discussion of the unavoidable role of human agency in the development of *shari'a* as a normative system based on Islamic religious texts, a sharp dichotomy between the secular and religious in this context is seriously misconceived and unhelpful.

In making this argument from an Islamic point of view, I remain convinced that succeeding generations of Muslims have always sought to discover *hukm* Allah (what God had decreed or willed for them to do or be), as they believe that to be divine guidance for all aspects of their daily life. As Professor Coulson described it, "Islamic jurisprudence is a speculative essay to comprehend the precise terms of Allah's law".[3] One can also assume that generations of Muslims through the ages generally earnestly strove to live up to the ideals set by the Prophet and early generations of Muslims as a matter of personal conviction. I am not concerned here with an assessment or evaluation of whether, and to what extent, any generation or group of Muslims have failed or succeeded in either discovering God's decree or will regarding any matter, or whether and how they have managed to live up to that ideal from a sociological or anthropological point of view. The question I am addressing here is whether it is possible for any state, however constituted and rationalized, to enforce *shari'a* through positive legislation.

I believe that it is impossible for any state to enforce *shari'a* as such, as opposed to voluntary compliance by Muslims, because of the essential nature of *shari'a* it-

---

[3] *Conflicts and Tension*, p. 41.

self, in relation to the nature and role of the state in the modern context. The argument I wish to make in the next section consists of two parts. First, *shari'a*, as commonly understood by Muslims to mean the divinely ordained way of life, cannot retain that quality once it is enacted as positive legislation. Second, the state cannot function in the modern context except through positive legislation and formal adoption of general policies. In other words, the state cannot enforce any principle of *shari'a* except through enacting it as legislation which would immediately negate its quality as *shari'a*. In the third section of this lecture, I will argue that Islamic societies are certainly entitled to exercise their right to self-determination in terms of an Islamic identity, including the enforcement of some Islamic norms through constitutionally sanctioned political, legislative and judicial processes, but not as immutable or divinely ordained *shari'a*.

2 THE IMPOSSIBILITY OF ENFORCEMENT OF *SHARI'A* THROUGH POSITIVE LEGISLATION

To be clear on the task here, what is at issue is whether *shari'a* can in fact be enforced as such by the state, as distinguished from voluntary compliance with its dictates by Muslims out of personal religious conviction or choice. An example of the significance of this distinction is the difference between the formal legal prohibition of paying or taking interest for loans (as in a modern banking system) because that would constitute *riba*, or outlawing modern insurance contracts as too speculative or contingent (*gharar*), on the one hand, and personal abstention from engaging in these practices because one believes them to be *haram* (a religious sin), on the other hand. Another way of explaining this point is to emphasize the difference between enforcing legal principles and rules in accordance with the constitutional standards and legislative process of the country, regardless of their original source, as distinguished from enforcing them because that is *required* by *shari'a* as the will of God. Accordingly, past or current claims or demands to enforce *shari'a* through positive legislation by the state are based on a historical fallacy because that is inconsistent with the nature of *shari'a* itself, and impossible for the state as constituted today in any country in the world. In other words, it is neither possible to conceive of this possibility in theoretical terms, nor is it true that such a model existed in the past so that it can be re-enacted today.

It is probably an article of faith for Muslims to believe that the Prophet's state in Medina (622–632 AD) did in fact implement *shari'a* in the life of the community. While I believe this to be true in that particular historical context, the implementation of *shari'a* in that instance was neither done through positive legislation, nor was it replicated by any other state after the Prophet's death. Aside from the extraordinary fact of the actual existence of the Prophet who continued to receive and explain revelation throughout that time, and his personal charisma and moral leadership, that state was constituted of close-knit tribal communities of highly motivated new converts who lived within an extremely limited space. In other words, the Medinan state was based more on the moral authority of social conformity than the coercive power of the state in other human societies. The key point to emphasize for our purposes is that the model of the Prophet's state in Medina cannot be applied in the present context of any Islamic society. However one wishes to characterize that historical experience, the Prophet's state was a unique phenomenon that ended with his death. The forms of political and social organization by which all Muslims live today, and the types of economic activities on which they all depend for their survival, make even the much more recent history of Muslim imperial states in the Middle East and India too "alien" to be revived or resurrected in the present postcolonial world of global economic and political interdependence and integration. Accordingly, claims to establish an Islamic state to enforce *shari'a* today are dangerously naive, if not cynical and manipulative.

As clearly explained by Professor Coulson in *A History of Islamic Law*,[4] and I have highlighted this elsewhere,[5] what came to be known among Muslims as *shari'a* was in fact the product of a very slow, gradual and spontaneous process of interpretation of the Qur'an, and collection, verification and interpretation of Sunnah during the first three centuries of Islam (the seventh to the ninth centuries AD). This process took place among scholars and jurists who developed their own methodology for the classification of sources, derivation of specific rules from general principles, and so forth. That technical aspect of their work came to be known as *ilm usul al-fiqh* (the science of the foundations or principles of human understanding of divine sources). As one would expect, there was much disagreement and disputation among those early scholars about the meaning and significance of different aspects of the sources with which they were working. Moreover, although those founding scholars are generally accepted to have been acting independently from the political authorities of the time, their work could not have been in isolation from the prevailing conditions of their communities, in local as well as broader regional contexts. Those factors must have also contributed to disagreements among the jurists, and sometimes to differences in the views expressed by the same jurist from one time to another, as is reported of the changes in Al-Shafi'i's views when he moved from Iraq to Egypt. Even after those disagreements eventually evolved into separate schools of thought, *madhahib*, differences of opinion persisted among scholars of the same schools, as well as between different schools.

The significant question to ask here is how can *shari'a* be divinely predetermined, if it can only be discovered through human understanding of the Qur'an and Sunnah? Ebrahim Moosa, the South African Muslim scholar, recently raised this question as follows:

When jurists claim that their extrapolation of the rules [of *shari'a*] from the sources constitute Allah's law (*hukm Allah*) one immediately realises that the law in Islam involves a transcendental dimension. One of the more intriguing questions encountered in the study of *shari'a* concerns the legal ruling or rule (*hukm*). How is it possible for the jurist (*faqih*) to conclude at the end of a very empirical evaluation and research of facts and texts that his conclusions constitute a transcendental and divine authority?[6]

The obvious answer, in my view, is that it is simply impossible for the conclusion of the jurist to ever constitute transcendental and divine authority, and should never be accepted as such. Jurists or scholars, however highly respected they may be, and

---

[4] Edinburgh, University of Edinburgh Press, 1964.
[5] See Abdullahi Ahmed An-Na'im, *Toward an Islamic Reformation: Civil Liberties, Human Rights and International Law,* Syracuse, NY, USA, Syracuse University Press, 1990, Chapter 2.
[6] "Allegory of the rule (*hukm*): law as simulacrum in Islam?" *History of Religion*, 1998, pp. 1–24, at p. 12.

even if their views came to be universally accepted by Muslims everywhere (which of course never happened for any of them), can only present their own personal views of what "*hukm* Allah" is on a given matter.

A distinction is commonly drawn in Islamic discourse between *shari'a* and *fiqh*. As recently explained by Bernard Weiss, "*shari'a* law is the product of legislation (*shari'a*), of which God is the ultimate subject (*shari'*). *Fiqh* law consists of legal understanding, of which the human being is the subject (*faqih*)."[7] This distinction can be useful in a technical sense of indicating that some principles or rules, as compared to others, are more based on speculative thinking than textual support from the Qur'an and/or Sunnah. But this does not mean that those which are taken to be *shari'a*, rather than *fiqh*, are the direct product of revelation because the Qur'an and Sunnah cannot be understood or have any influence on human behaviour except through the effort of fallible human beings. Weiss makes this point as follows:

Although the law is of divine provenance, the actual construction of the law is a human activity, and its results represent the law of God *as humanly understood*. Since the law does not descend from heaven ready-made, it is the human understanding of the law – the human *fiqh* (literally meaning understanding) – that must be normative for society.[8]

Because the founding jurists and scholars of *shari'a* were highly aware of all these factors, and sensitive to the risks of imposing what might be an erroneous view, they exercised profound acceptance of diversity of opinion, while seeking to enhance consensus among themselves and their communities. This was done through the notion that whatever is accepted as valid by consensus (*ijma'*) among all jurists (or the wider Muslim community according to some jurists) is deemed to be permanently binding on subsequent generations of Muslims.[9] Once again, however, the many practical difficulties of applying this notion were clear from the beginning. For those who wanted to confine the binding force of *ijma'* to consensus among a select group of jurists, the problem was how to agree on the criteria for identifying those jurists, and how their opinions are to be identified and verified. If one is to say that the authority of *ijma'* is to come from the consensus of the Muslim community at large, the question still remains how to determine and verify that this has happened on any matter. Whether the consensus is supposed to be of a group of scholars or of the community at large, why should the view of one generation bind subsequent generations? Whatever solutions one may find for such conceptual and practical difficulties, that will always be itself the product of human judgement. In other words, *shari'a* norms cannot possibly be drawn from the Qur'an and Sunnah except through human understanding, which necessarily means both the inevitability of differences of opinion and the possibility of error, whether among scholars or the community in general.

In this light, the question becomes how and by whom can such differences of opinion be properly and legitimately settled in practice in order to determine what is the positive law to be applied in specific cases. The basic dilemma here can be explained as follows. On the one hand, there is the paramount importance of a min-

---

[7] Bernard Weiss, *The Spirit of Islamic Law*, Athens, GA, USA, University of Georgia Press, 1998. p. 120.
[8] *Ibid.*, p. 116. Emphasis in original.
[9] *Ibid.*, pp. 120–122.

imum degree of certainty in the determination and enforcement of positive law for any society. The nature and role of positive law in the modern state also require the interaction of a multitude of actors and complex factors which cannot possibly be contained by an Islamic religious rationale. This is more true of Islamic societies today than ever before, because of their growing interdependence with non-Muslim societies throughout the world, as briefly discussed below. On the other hand, a religious rationale is key for the binding force of *shari'a* norms for Muslims. Precisely because *shari'a* is supposed to be binding on Muslims out of religious conviction, a believer cannot be religiously bound except by what he or she personally believes to be a valid interpretation of relevant texts of the Qur'an and Sunnah. Yet, given the diversity of opinions among Muslim jurists, whatever the state elects to enforce as positive law is bound to be deemed an invalid interpretation of Islamic sources by some of the Muslim citizens of that state.

This dilemma was clearly explained by Professor Coulson as follows. Because of the religious nature of *shari'a*, the strong traditional view has always been that "each individual Muslim was absolutely free to follow the school [of jurisprudence] of his choice and that any Muslim tribunal was bound to apply the law of the school to which the individual litigant belonged".[10] Accordingly, an individual also had the right to change his or her school of law on a particular issue. This state of affairs continued until the introduction of *Al-Majallah* by the Ottoman Empire in the late nineteenth century, and more widely through the enactment of family law codes in most Islamic countries over the last few decades. As Professor Coulson put it:

The principle underlying the codes [of Islamic family law] is that the political authority has the power, in the interest of uniformity, to choose one rule from among equally authoritative variants and to order the courts of his jurisdiction to apply that rule to the exclusion of all others; and the choice of this rule or that has been made simply on grounds of social desirability, the codes embodying those variants which were deemed most suited to the present standards and circumstances of the community.[11]

Moreover, I would emphasize, the imperatives of certainty and uniformity in national legislation are now stronger than they used to be even three decades ago when Professor Coulson made those remarks. This is not only due to the growing complexity of the role of the state at the domestic or national level, but also because of the global interdependence of all peoples and their states. Regardless of the relative weakness or strength of some states in relation to others, the realities of national and global political, economic, security and other relations remain firmly embedded in the existence of sovereign states that have exclusive jurisdiction over their citizens and territories. For Islamic societies, this point has recently been painfully and traumatically emphasized by the eight years of the Iran–Iraq war of the 1980s, and the composition of the international alliance of Muslim and non-Muslim countries which forced Iraq out of Kuwait in 1991. The governments of Islamic countries on both sides of the latter conflict were acting (and continue to act) as nation states, and not as part of a uniform or united global Islamic community, or on behalf of the totality of Muslims at large (traditionally referred to as the *Umma*).

---

[10] *Conflicts and Tensions in Islamic Jurisprudence*, p. 34.
[11] *Ibid.*, pp. 35–36.

The point I am making here is not that the nature of the state is identical for all societies, because the processes of state formation and consolidation vary from one country to another. Rather, the point is that there are certain common characteristics that all states need to have in order to be part of the present international system because membership is conditional upon recognition by other members. For the states of Islamic societies to be and remain accepted as members of the international community, they must comply with a recognizable set of minimum features of statehood in the present sense of the term. In particular, the ability to determine and enforce the law in everyday life is central to the existence of any state, whatever its philosophical or ideological orientation may be. Moreover, as explained in the next section, the nature of the state and its present global context preclude the possibility of the application of *shari'a* as historically understood by its founding jurists, and as still commonly accepted among Muslims.

In conclusion of this section, I wish to emphasize that whether in its traditional formulation, as known to Muslims today, or through some new or modernist elaboration and articulation, *shari'a* will always remain a historically conditioned human understanding of the Qur'an and Sunnah of the Prophet. While sharing the belief of all Muslims that these sources are divine, it is clear to me that their interpretation and expression as *shari'a* norms will always remain a human endeavour, open to challenge and reformulation though alternative human efforts. In other words, the divine sources of *shari'a* cannot influence human life and experience except through human agency in the understanding and implementation of those sources in the specific historical context of Islamic societies.

This does not mean, of course, that Islamic societies are not entitled to realize their right to self-determination in terms of an Islamic identity or that they are incapable of achieving that objective. On the contrary, I believe that they do indeed have that right and can realize it in practice. For that to happen, however, I am suggesting that Islamic societies must categorically renounce any commitment to a romantic ideal of an Islamic state that never was, and expressly abandon expectations of the enforcement of *shari'a* as such by the state. I will now turn to a general exploration of the conditions and context of the right to self-determination for Islamic societies today.

3 SELF-DETERMINATION FOR ISLAMIC SOCIETIES TODAY

Much of the current public discourse in many Islamic societies is dominated by support for or opposition to the notion of an "Islamic state" which is supposed to implement *shari'a* in a comprehensive and systematic manner. Proponents of this idea are commonly known as "Islamists" and its opponents described as "secularists", each addressing their own constituency with little interaction between the two groups in their different orientations – traditionalist or fundamentalist on the Islamist side, and liberals or nationalists, on the other side. In this section, I wish to challenge this alleged Islamist/secularist dichotomy and the assumptions on which it is based. Then I will attempt to outline the parameters within which Islamic societies should seek to exercise their right to self-determination in the present context. In other words, I will first attempt to show what the right to self-determination *cannot* mean for Islamic societies, and then offer some suggestions for what it can mean today.

To begin with some terminological clarification; while the term "Islamic state" may serve as shorthand for referring to states where Muslims constitute a clear majority of the population, the adjective "Islamic" logically applies to a people, rather than to a state as a political institution. Some scholars tend to use the term "Islamic state" to refer to those countries which have officially proclaimed Islam to be the state religion, or where *shari'a* is a formal source of legislation. However, I find this characterization misleading because such features do not accurately reflect an "Islamic" quality of the state itself as a political institution. Unless one is willing to accept every claim by a state to be "Islamic", the question becomes one of who has the authority to determine the quality of being Islamic, and according to which criteria. For example, the religious and political establishment of Saudi Arabia is unlikely to accept the claim of the present government of Iran that it is an "Islamic republic", or even accept the notion of an Islamic republic. From the Iranian point of view, the Saudi monarchy is by definition un-Islamic, and cannot possibly be legitimized by its purported commitment to the enforcement of *shari'a*.

Moreover, I suggest, an Islamic state as a political institution is conceptually impossible, historically inaccurate, and practically not viable today. In support of this proposition, I recall here my earlier argument that an Islamic state is conceptually impossible because for a political authority to claim to implement the totality of the precepts of *shari'a* in the everyday life of a society is a contradiction in terms: enforcement through the will of the state is the negation of the religious rationale of the binding force of *shari'a* in the first place. Since enforcement by the state today requires formal enactment as the law of the land or adoption of clear policies specifying certain action by organs of the state, the legislature and government of the day (whatever their form may be) will have to choose among equally authoritative but different interpretations of the Qur'an and Sunnah. In other words, any principles or rules of *shari'a* simply cease to be part of a religious normative system by the very effort to enact and enforce them by the organs of the state because the state can only enforce its own political will, not that of God. The practical impossibility of enforcing *shari'a* as positive law is also emphasized by the fact that Muslims in general acknowledge that there has never been an Islamic state in this sense since the Medinan state of the Prophet. As briefly explained above, however, there is no basis for comparison between that early city state and subsequent Muslim imperial states of the past, let alone present day complex states with their diverse populations and global context.

The lack of historical precedent is more significant, I would add, in view of the total transformation of the local and global context in which the state has to operate today. As briefly explained below, a state constituted according to the theory of *shari'a* is simply unworkable in the present national and international context. Difficulties facing this model include the profound ambivalence of the founding jurists of *shari'a* to political authority. They neither sought to control nor knew how to make those who hold it accountable to the *shari'a* itself. Economic activities would be crippled by the formal enforcement of prohibition of a fixed rate of interest on loans (*riba*), and of insurance as based on speculative contracts (*gharar*). The enforcement of corporal punishments for certain specified offences (*hudud*) faces serious unresolved procedural and evidentiary objections, let alone human rights concerns about cruel, inhuman or degrading treatment or punishment. Another type of problem is that the denial of basic citizenship rights for women and non-Muslims will face serious challenge by these groups internally, and by the international community at large.

All the above objections to the enforcement of *shari'a* through positive law and the notion of an Islamic state do not, of course, preclude Muslims from personally conforming with every aspect of *shari'a*. The fact that *riba* and *gharar* contracts are not illegal in a given country does not mean that Muslims have to engage in these practices. Any person can simply abstain from any form of commercial transaction or personal behaviour in accordance with his or her own religious or moral convictions. As emphasized above, the arguments I am making here are against enforcement by the state, and not to combat private conformity with the dictates of one's beliefs. Indeed, people may seek to reinforce the religious or moral values through the activities of non-governmental organizations and other forms of agency of civil society. It is true that legal prohibition will reinforce the authority of religious norms, as in the Arabic maxim: "inna Allaha yazi'u bil-Sultan ma la yazi'u bil-Qur'an" (which may be translated as: "God may enforce through political authority what God does not achieve through moral authority"). To my knowledge, this maxim is attributed to Ali ibn Abi Talib (the fourth Caliph of Medina and first Imam for all the Shi'ah), but even if it was said by the Prophet himself or expressed in the Qur'an, it must be interpreted by human beings in context, like any other text. For instance, this formulation does not say which norms or policies are to be enforced in one way or the other, and how. Human judgement about such questions will necessarily have to be made in terms of a balance of the benefits and costs of legal enforcement of any norm, in contrast to other ways of promoting social policy. In the present limited space, I will focus on the general framework within which any Islamic text, including the Qur'an and Sunnah, can influence public policy.

The underlying assumption of claims to enforce *shari'a* through positive legislation is that Islamic societies and communities have the right and responsibility to organize their public and private lives in accordance with the dictates of Islam. In modern terms, one can say that this is a matter of political and cultural self-determination. But self-determination is not an absolute right, because the manner in which one group or entity exercises the right will have consequences or implication for the rights of others. As Asbjorn Eide put it,[12] it is really the right to co-determination, to be exercised in collaboration with others, rather than an exclusive right of the self, whatever that may mean. In particular, all the states of Islamic societies are bound by customary international law and humanitarian law, like any other state in the world, as well as by all the international treaties they have ratified, such as the Charter of the United Nations which is binding on all of them as members of that organization. All these sources set clear and categorical limits on what the states of Islamic societies may or may not do, both within their own borders as well as in their dealings with other states and their citizens. As a practical matter, moreover, other states do act on these principles in their economic, political, security and other dealings with the states of Islamic societies. Whether it is the organization and operation of the state in general, the treatment of vulnerable per-

---

[12] During discussion at a seminar commemorating the 50th anniversary of the Declaration of Human Rights, Royal Netherlands Academy of Science, Amsterdam, The Netherlands, 10–11 December 1998.

sons and groups who are their own citizens, or the treatment of citizens of other countries, the states of Islamic societies are not free to behave as they please.

As I have elaborated elsewhere,[13] many traditional formulations of *shari'a* are fundamentally inconsistent with universally accepted principles of domestic constitutionalism as well as certain foundational principles of international law. It would therefore follow that even if *shari'a* can be enforced by the state, those problematic principles are morally untenable and practically impossible to maintain. It is not therefore surprising that there is no state in the world today, including self-proclaimed so-called Islamic states like Iran, Saudi Arabia and Sudan, that is practically capable of actually living by all the dictates of *shari'a*, as commonly understood by Muslims everywhere. Instead of insisting on these futile and profoundly hypocritical pretensions, I hereby reiterate my earlier call on Muslims everywhere to openly and categorically reject such approaches, and face the realities of their daily life in the present context of global interdependence and mutual influence. Islamic societies must also create and safeguard the political and social space for uninhibited and creative reflection on the Qur'an, Sunnah and the wealth of experience of their own history. Only then will Islamic societies begin to explore ways of making the positive contributions they can make to human civilization out of the spiritual and moral resources of Islam as a major world religion.

To emphasize a point I made in the introduction, attempts to establish a so-called Islamic state to enforce of *shari'a* through positive legislation is a negation of the possibility of an Islamic way of life because selecting certain interpretations of the Qur'an and Sunnah for such enforcement will necessarily mean denying some Muslims citizens the right to personally conform with what they accept as valid interpretation of the Qur'an and Sunnah. Moreover, such enforcement will also stifle possibilities of free and open debate about alternative interpretations. This point can also be expressed in terms of self-determination in that the enforcement of *shari'a* as the law of the land will lead to suppressing political dissent as apostasy, and possibly treason. That is why I am calling for categorical rejection of such attempts from an Islamic point of view.

But it is equally important to also categorically reject any attempt to impose a so-called "secular state", as we have seen in the case of Turkey, Iran under the Shah, and the Ba'thist regimes of Syria and Iraq. Such authoritarian efforts are not only doomed to failure, as they invariably have to be maintained by force, but are also objectionable as a matter of principle because the suppression of the political expression of an Islamic identity constitutes a total repudiation of the right of Muslims to self-determination. Despotic authoritarianism must be rejected, whether it is in the name of enforcement of *shari'a* or in opposition to that claim. While fully appreciating the dangers of efforts to establish a so-called Islamic state, as discussed above, I am equally convinced that its rejection can only be achieved through encouraging, rather than suppressing, public debate about these issues. The model I am calling for here is one of a constitutional, democratic state that fully protects and promotes human rights for all citizens, Muslims and non-Muslims alike, purported Islamists as well as self-proclaimed secularists.

---

[13] See generally, An-Na'im, *Toward an Islamic Reformation*.

Some Muslims may seek to dismiss what I am expressing here as "secular", in the sense of attempting to separate between Islam and the state or politics, and relegate Islam to the private domain. In my view, it is grossly misleading to speak of complete separation or total union of any religion and the state. Any state, as well as its constituent organs and institutions, are conceived and operated by people whose religious or philosophical beliefs will necessarily be reflected in their thinking and behaviour. In other words, I am not only saying that Islam does not require unity between religion and the state, but also that the issue itself is misconceived. The authority of religion and power of the state are two sides of the same coin, rather than being separate or opposing paradigms. Since every state will seek to legitimize its authority in terms of the prevailing religious and moral beliefs of its citizens, the states of Islamic societies will attempt to do that in terms of an Islamic frame of reference. There is no point in arguing against this fundamental political principle. What I have attempted to argue for in this lecture is the meaning and implications of an Islamic frame of reference in the modern context, not its negation or rejection as dated or irrelevant. The crucial question, in my view, is not whether Islam and the state are united or can be separated. Rather, it is the nature and implications of that relationship which must be defined and specified by each Islamic society for itself. There is no single so-called Islamic model for this relationship, but there can be distinctive models for each society in accordance with its own struggle to understand and live by the spiritual and moral precepts of Islam, as understood and applied in the present global context.

4 CONCLUDING REMARKS

In the introduction to this lecture, I have indicated that my focus here is on the fundamental jurisprudential and ideological confusion that underlies disastrous schemes to establish an Islamic state in order to enforce *shari'a* through positive legislation. But that does not mean, of course, that I am not concerned with current political trends in Islamic countries today. On the contrary, my objective is to influence those trends through critical reflection and well substantiated arguments. As a Muslim lawyer, especially from Sudan, I can hardly ignore the tragic costs of futile efforts to enforce *shari'a* through positive legislation in any Islamic society. I hope that I have succeeded in at least raising serious doubts about the possibility and desirability of such misguided, if not cynical, adventures.

I am painfully aware that most of the views I have expressed in this lecture are not only controversial, but also psychologically and intellectually difficult for the vast majority of Muslims to accept today. But this hardly means that my position is necessarily wrong from an Islamic point of view, or that it is unlikely to be accepted by the majority of Muslims in due course. On the other hand, however, my position is not necessarily right or likely to be widely accepted simply because it is now resisted by so many. But I hope that my analysis will at least attract serious consideration and reflection, and that it will stand or fall on its own merits, not because it is not accepted by the majority of Muslims today. For my part, I will keep trying to improve and clarify the argument presented here precisely because there is no alternative to their voluntary acceptance by the majority of Muslims today.

In conclusion, let me openly state what is probably already clear to you from some of my opening remarks, namely, that I am an active advocate of the views presented above, rather than a detached scholar engaged in purely academic analysis. For me the issues are too important and the stakes are too high to simply engage in abstract reflection on the relationship between *shari'a* and positive legislation in Islamic societies today.

To Muslims in the audience, let me close by reiterating what my ultimate teacher and mentor, *Ustadh* Mahmoud Mohamed Taha, used to say to Sudanese intellectuals who used to tell him that his ideas sounded convincing, but when would people accept and act on them? In response, *Ustadh* Mahmoud used to say: "You *are* the people; when will you accept these ideas and act accordingly?"

Guarantees in the UAE: a Comparative Analysis in the Light of English Law, French Law and the *Shari'a*

Nicholas Foster*

1 INTRODUCTION

A previous article[1] examined the law of the United Arab Emirates[2] relating to security over movables in the commercial field. This article complements that earlier piece by examining the UAE law of guarantees. It takes a similar approach, looking at guarantees in comparative perspective in the light of English law,[3] French law and the *shari'a*. This article is intended to stand alone, and some repetition is inevitable, but therefore it has been kept to a minimum. In particular, the reader is referred to the first article for an account of the background to the commercial and security law of the UAE.

This work has several aims: to provide an account of the guarantee law of a Middle East jurisdiction; to contribute to the corpus of writing on the law of the UAE; and to provide a comparative study of the law of guarantees across several legal systems.[4]

---

* School of Oriental and African Studies, London University. Ian Edge, Sabah Mahmoud of Gulf Legal Services and Peter O'Brien of Clifford Chance, Dubai were kind enough to comment on a draft. Ruchdi Maalouf provided very helpful assistance in research. The usual disclaimer applies.

[1] Nicholas Foster, "Commercial security over movables in the UAE: a comparative analysis in the light of English law, French law and the *shari'a*", in *Yearbook of Islamic and Middle Eastern Law*, vol. 4 (1997–1998), p. 3.

[2] "The UAE". For introductions to the UAE and its legal system, see Richard Price, "United Arab Emirates", in *Yearbook of Islamic and Middle Eastern Law*, vol. 1 (1994), pp. 307 *et seq.*; Butti Sultan Butti Al-Muhairi, "The development of the UAE legal system and unification with the judicial system", *Arab Law Quarterly*, 1996, p. 116; and Sabah M. Ali Mahmoud, *UAE Company Law and Practice*, 3rd edn., Gulf Legal Services, 1997, pp. 1–5.

[3] Despite the existence of the Welsh Assembly, the words "England" and "English" are still used herein, for the sake of convenience, to refer to the jurisdiction of England and Wales.

[4] This is a novel endeavour in all these areas, but in the case of the general study of the comparative law of guarantees, only because unfortunate circumstances have intervened to

One of the aims of the first article was to use the topic of movable security as an example of legal transplants in order to test the rival hypotheses extant in this area. This theme is not pursued herein to any great extent, since the UAE law in question is largely derived from the *shari'a*, which cannot properly be said to be "received" into a Muslim country such as the UAE. Questions do arise, though, relating to the choice of the *shari'a* over Western rules, such as their efficacy for the modern commercial world, and the way in which they fit in with a contemporary Middle East legal system.

2 TERMINOLOGY AND SCOPE

The word "guarantee" has many meanings, both inside particular jurisdictions and across jurisdictions.[5]

In the widest sense, it can be used to mean "security" generally.[6] This is not the sense in which it is used here – in this article it denotes a mechanism of personal security, i.e. an obligation of a person, C (the guarantor) to satisfy the obligation of B (the principal debtor) to A (the creditor) under A's contract with B (the principal contract) if B fails fully to satisfy that obligation. Such a mechanism is prima facie only enforceable by action by A against the person of C (hence "personal" security). Such obligations are contrasted with rights granted in relation to a thing (*res* in Latin, hence "real" security).[7]

A hybrid category exists, in English practice called "third party security", in French writing *cautionnement réel* (real guarantee). This is the provision by a third party of real security as a protection of the principal contract, without a guarantee. The difference in terminology is illuminating: English law has, somewhat surprisingly, always considered third party security as security only, and has not extended to it protective rules concerning guarantees, such as the lapse of the guarantee on the amendment of the principal contract. French law acknowledges the hybrid nature of the mechanism.[8] These mechanisms are not dealt with here.

---

cont.

    prevent the completion and publication of the section on guarantees in the *International Encyclopaedia of Comparative Law* (Mohr, 1971–). For a review of the law of numerous countries, see Winnibald E. Moojen and Matthieu Van Sint Truiden (eds.), *Bank Security and Other Credit Enhancement Methods: a Practical Guide on Security Devices Available to Banks in Thirty Countries Throughout the World*, Kluwer Law International, 1995.

5 The word "surety" is a synonym in English both for "guarantee" and "guarantor" (the ambiguity creates few problems in practice). As far as French and English are concerned, it is a "false friend", since *sûreté* means "security", and, for that reason, it will not be used herein, except where it occurs in quotations. The history of the terminology demonstrates the common tendency to fail to distinguish adequately between the different types of security. The word "pledge" in medieval usage denoted a guarantor: see Frederick Pollock and Frederic Maitland, *The History of English Law Before the Time of Edward I*, 2nd edn., Cambridge University Press, 1923, p. 185, n. 2.

6 Although the terminology is not fixed, there is a trend in recent French writing to use the word *garantie* in this way: see Dominique Legeais, *Sûretés et garanties de crédit*, Librairie Générale de Droit et de Jurisprudence, 1996: §1 (but note the existence in French of the calqued expression *garanties autonomes* to denote demand guarantee type mechanisms).

7 There is of course nothing to prevent security over an asset (real security) being taken in order to provide an assurance of payment by a guarantor, and this is very commonly done.

8 See Philippe Simler and Philippe Delebecque, *Droit civil. Les sûretés, la publicité foncière*, 2nd edn., Dalloz, 1995, §17 and, for example, Art. 2171 of the Civil Code, which provides that the

The word "guarantee" can also be used to denote, in some systems of law such as the *shari'a*, a mechanism akin to the English bail. This is applicable in civil rather than criminal matters, and is used to enforce the presence of a defendant before the court.[9]

Numerous types of guarantee, in the sense of "personal security", exist in modern legal systems, such as the civil law *aval* mechanism and its near equivalent in English law, the quasi-endorsement of a bill of exchange,[10] absolute undertakings such as standby letters of credit, performance bonds and bank guarantees, and so on.[11] This discussion, however, centres on what one might call the "traditional guarantee": a promise by the guarantor to pay the creditor if the principal debtor fails to pay a simple debt, where usually the creditor is a bank or other type of financial institution. By necessity, it also examines mechanisms which fulfil the same function in the same type of transaction, such as the indemnity in English law and the *hawala* in the *shari'a*. It does not deal with the special rules applicable to consumer transactions. (Unless otherwise stated or apparent from the context, the word "guarantee" refers only to the "traditional guarantee", not to such other mechanisms.)

3 ENGLISH, FRENCH AND *SHARI'A* APPROACHES TO GUARANTEES

3.1 Comparing guarantee regimes

Although the law of guarantees and the law of real security are classified as parts of the law of "security" in general, and although the two interact and are very often inseparable in practice, they form distinct areas of law, each with very much its own history, rules and "feel".

The concept of a guarantee is essentially very simple. The guarantor promises to pay the creditor if the principal debtor fails to do so. Yet the English law guarantee is not alone in being "encrusted with law".[12] The principal reasons for this

---

cont.

benefit of discussion (the right of the guarantor to demand that the creditor sue the principal creditor before taking action against the guarantor) is not applicable to real security, and Art. 1415, relating to the effects on spouse A's property of a guarantee given by spouse B, which has been held to apply to a real guarantee – Civ. 1re, 11 April 1995: Bull. civ. 1, No. 165; D. 1995. Somm. 327, obs. Grimaldi; D. 1996. Somm. 204, obs. S. Piedelièvre; JCP 1995. I. 3869, No. 9, obs. Simler; Defrénois 1995. 1484, obs. Champenois.

[9] Old French law had a similar idea: see Art. 2017 of the Civil Code, which still mentions the *contrainte par corps*, abolished by the Law of 22 July 1867. A similar institution existed in Germanic customary law (the *borh* or frankpledge system of Anglo-Saxon law) which was essentially an institutionalized form of hostage-taking. See James O'Donovan and John Phillips, *The Modern Contract of Guarantee*, 3rd edn., LBC Information Services, 1996, pp. 4–7 and below (section 6.1 "Comparative analysis").

[10] R. Goode, *Commercial Law*, 2nd edn., Harmondsworth, Penguin, 1995, pp. 551–555.

[11] In default of a universally accepted term, and following the example of Professor Goode, the increasingly common expression "demand guarantees", sanctioned by the ICC in its *Uniform Rules on Demand Guarantees*, is used herein.

[12] Philip R. Wood, *Comparative Law of Security and Guarantees*, Sweet & Maxwell, 1995, p. 313.

are (a) the existence of two contracts, rather than just one, and therefore at least three parties, rather than two (the "triangular"[13] nature of the relationship); and (b) the usually gratuitous nature of the guarantee, which is often given by non-commercial persons, who may also be imprudent in commercial matters, dependent on the principal debtor, or both.

3.1.1 The triangular nature of the relationship

In any guarantee transaction, there are at least three parties and two contracts. Various questions arise out of this situation, such as:

(a)   What is the relationship between the contracts? In particular, what happens if the principal contract is invalid? What happens if the principal contract is varied in some way?
(b)   What is the legal relationship between the guarantor and the principal debtor (for example, does the guarantor have a right to be indemnified)?
(c)   What is the legal relationship between the guarantor and the creditor?
(d)   If the creditor holds real security over the assets of the principal debtor, does the guarantor receive the benefit of the security (subrogation)? If so, in what circumstances?
(e)   If there is more than one guarantor, what rules are there relating to their liability *vis-à-vis* the creditor and between themselves?
(f)   Can the principal creditor demand payment from the guarantor without demanding payment first from the principal debtor?

3.1.2 Gratuitous nature of the transaction/protection of the dependent and the imprudent

Guarantees are usually gratuitous. This poses two related, but distinct, types of problem, one relevant to individual (non-corporate) parties, the other to corporate guarantors.

Guarantees by individuals are usually granted because of some emotional or family tie between the guarantor and the principal debtor. It follows that guarantors tend to be more vulnerable and less knowledgeable than a person habitually involved in business and are often dependent upon the principal debtor. Should these vulnerable parties be protected? If so, how?

The problem of corporate guarantors is rather different. A corporation is usually set up with the aim of making profit for the shareholders, and all transactions must have the potential for "corporate benefit". Since each corporation is, at least in principle, considered as an isolated unit, even from other members of the same group, the guaranteeing of the obligations of other corporations, even those within the same group, can cause problems. What rules exist relating to this problem?

These characteristics make traditional guarantees different in nature from other commercial mechanisms. Although they are almost without exception used for com-

---

[13] A term borrowed from Simler and Delebecque, *Droit civil. Les sûretés*, §22.

mercial purposes, many of the rules concerning them are not what one would expect of commercial law rules, particularly where individual guarantors are concerned. It is no accident, for example, that both the French and UAE legislators placed guarantees in their respective civil codes. This also partially explains the existence of other types of guarantee referred to below, such as demand guarantees, to which quite different, much more draconian and "commercial" rules apply, the underlying assumption being that demand guarantee type instruments will be entered into only by solely commercial parties, who know, or should know, what they are doing, and are therefore not granted the same degree of protection as the grantors of traditional guarantees.[14]

From a comparative point of view, differences in the treatment of guarantees in different legal systems arise out of different attitudes to these issues and different techniques for solving the problems.

The English, French, *shari'a* and UAE regimes will be discussed in turn. In each discussion, given the fairly close equivalence of the mechanisms, the English word "guarantee" will be used as the translation of the basic guarantee mechanism in each jurisdiction.

3.2 The English approach to the law of guarantees[15]

3.2.1 *General characteristics*

The English law of guarantees derives from a combination of the law of contract and case law, especially the rules of equity, which devised, among other things, the rules pursuant to which time or indulgence discharge the guarantee and the rules of contribution among co-guarantors.[16] The basic principle is that it is a contract, but of a specialized kind, with its own rules. It has received scant attention from the legislature. Standard form wording is well established and effectively creates a regime of rules distinct from the "official" law.[17]

---

[14] Another reason is that traditional guarantees work well where the guaranteed obligation is a simple debt, but sometimes it can be difficult to ascertain whether the underlying obligation exists, for example where the obligation guaranteed arises upon breach by the principal debtor of its obligations under a construction contract, and there is a dispute over whether there has been a breach. In such cases, they are much less effective. Demand guarantees constitute an absolute obligation to pay and do not suffer from this problem.

[15] Some detailed works are, *inter alia*, O'Donovan and Phillips, *The Modern Contract of Guarantee* (written from an Australian point of view); David G. M. Marks and Gabriel Moss, *Rowlatt on the Law of Principal and Surety*, 5th edn., Sweet & Maxwell, 1997; Geraldine Andrews and Richard Millett, *Law of Guarantees*, 2nd edn., Sweet & Maxwell, 1995. Sealy and Hooley, *Text and Materials in Commercial Law*, Chapter 25 ("Guarantees"). Goode, *Commercial Law*, Chapter 30 ("Guarantees") is a case book approach. For the sake of brevity, references herein will be mainly to Goode, *Commercial Law*.

[16] The rules were fairly well established by the seventeenth century: see W. S. Holdsworth, *A History of English Law*, vol. V, Methuen, 1924, p. 321.

[17] See Ali Malek, "A critical review of standard clauses", in *Guarantees: the Problem Areas*, Legal Studies and Services Limited, papers of a conference held on 7 December 1990; and the example of a standard form in Sealy and Hooley, *Text and Materials in Commercial Law*, pp. 971–976.

English guarantee law is an ancient branch of the law, and rather resembles a musty corner of an old attic, in which one discovers obscure wording based on rather quaint old rules, formulated to deal with the problems of another age. As such, it contains numerous traps for the unwary – an English law guarantee should be amended only by an expert![18]

3.2.2 Basic forms

Traditionally, much stress is laid on the distinction between a guarantee and an indemnity. A guarantee is an undertaking which is secondary, or accessory, to the principal contract, and therefore stands or falls with it: Lord Selborne said: "a man [cannot] guarantee anybody else's debt unless there is a debt of some other person to be guaranteed".[19] It follows that if the principal contract is invalid in any way, then the guarantee is also invalid. An indemnity, on the other hand, is independent from the principal contract, so if the principal contract is defective, the indemnity is unaffected.[20] However, standard form documents, colloquially called "guarantees", typically contain both a guarantee and an indemnity, and, so long as such a document is indeed drafted so that the contract does constitute an indemnity (for this area of the law is difficult and full of pitfalls), the distinction can be rendered theoretical rather than real.[21]

Various other mechanisms exist which fulfil similar functions to that of the traditional guarantee, such as demand guarantees and the acceptance of a bill of exchange.[22]

A major difference, however, between English law on the one hand, and all the other three systems studied on the other, is the way in which the systems view assignment of debt[23] (the obligation to pay) and novation of the principal contract,

---

[18] A good example of this is the difference between a guarantee of the entire principal debt, with a limitation on the liability of the guarantor to a specified amount, and a guarantee of part only of the debt. A very small difference in wording can, in certain circumstances, make an enormous difference in the amount recovered by the beneficiary, as a guarantor of part only is subrogated to any real security the beneficiary may have immediately upon payment of that part, whereas a guarantor of the whole with limitation of liability is not subrogated upon payment. See Goode, *Commercial Law*, pp. 836–837.

[19] *Lakeman v. Mountstephen* [1874] LR 7 HL 17, 24–25, quoted in Sealy and Hooley, *Text and Materials in Commercial Law*, Butterworths, 1994, p. 858.

[20] An often quoted passage describing the difference is to be found in *Birkmyr v. Darnell* [1704] 1 Salk 27 at 28 (cited in Sealy and Hooley, *Text and Materials in Commercial Law*, p. 859): "If two come in a shop, and one buys, and the other, to gain him credit, promises the seller, *if he does not pay you, I will*; this is a collateral undertaking, and void without writing, by the Statute of Frauds: but if he says, *Let him have the goods, I will be your paymaster*, or *I will see you paid*, this is an undertaking as for himself, and he shall be intended to be the very buyer, and the other to act as his servant".

[21] See for example *Yeoman Credit v. Latter* [1961] 1 WLR 828, CA, cited in Sealy and Hooley, *Text and Materials in Commercial Law*, p. 856 and references cited at p. 860. The word "indemnity" can itself cause problems, in that the word is also used to denote the right of a guarantor to be reimbursed by the principal debtor.

[22] See Goode, *Commercial Law*, pp. 1030–1044.

[23] The English word "debt" is ambiguous, in that it can refer either to the right to receive payment or the obligation to pay. The latter two expressions are used here in preference to the word "debt" when discussing assignments.

and in the use of assignment of the obligation to pay as a mechanism equivalent
to a guarantee. The English position is that an assignment of an obligation is not
possible, so an assignment of the obligation to pay cannot happen, except by novation. The other systems consider that an assignment of the obligation to pay is
possible (although in both French and UAE law the consent of the creditor is required, making the "assignment", in effect, a kind of novation). Such an assignment is used to create the same effect as a guarantee, by the original debtor transferring the obligation to pay to the assignee, while remaining liable jointly with the
assignee. English law novation is not used in this way, even though there is in
theory no reason why it should not be, and is restricted to the situation where an
obligation is taken over by another party.[24]

3.2.3 Civil and commercial law

There is no formal distinction between civil and commercial law, so there is no
distinction between "civil" or "commercial" guarantees. The practical result, however, of the way in which the rules on undue influence and unconscionability are applied results in there being a marked difference between the treatment of "civil" (non-
commercial) and "commercial" guarantors. It would, for example, be a brave
barrister who argued undue influence on behalf of a commercial guarantor.[25]

3.2.4 Validity and proof

The basic contract rules apply, including, in principle, the rules as to consideration. In fact, these rules are stretched, both by the way in which the offer and acceptance pertaining to the guarantee are analysed and by the practice of the courts.
As regards offer and acceptance, in a normal situation where the creditor is not bound
to lend to the principal debtor, the guarantor is viewed as making an offer to the
creditor, and the creditor as accepting the offer when the loan is made, the making
of the loan being the consideration for the contract. As regards the courts, they
look askance at arguments based on consideration, which are regarded as technical
and of little worth.[26] In any event, any potential problems of consideration can
easily be avoided by having the document executed as a deed.

A guarantee need not be in writing, but it is not enforceable unless it is evidenced
by writing, signed by the "partie to be charged therewith" (the guarantor) or some
person authorized by the guarantor.[27] That writing does not have to specify the con-

---

[24] For a fuller discussion, see below (sections 3.3.2 "Basic forms", 3.4.2 "Basic forms" and 6.1
"Comparative analysis").

[25] The possibility is, of course, always there, but the facts of the case would, it is submitted, have
to be exceptional even for it to be argued.

[26] Oral advice given to the author by a commercial QC.

[27] S. 4 Statute of Frauds 1677.

sideration.[28] Guarantees are not registrable, although some have suggested that they should be.

As there is no formal distinction between civil and commercial law, there is no difference in the means of proof between guarantees entered into by business people and companies and individuals.

3.2.5 The gratuitous nature of the guarantee

The gratuitous nature of the guarantee has always posed problems. These have been dealt with in two different ways, depending on whether the guarantor was an individual or a company. As regards individuals, the matter was approached by looking at the capacity of the guarantor and various protective rules, such as those concerning the lapse of the guarantee. As regards corporations, the concept of *ultra vires* has been employed, in conjunction with the idea that a company exists for the benefit of its shareholders, together with the equitable doctrines of fiduciary duty and notice.

The basic principle used to be that a transaction which was outside the company's objects was void.[29] This rule has been largely abolished by Companies Act 1989 in respect of companies governed by the Companies Acts.[30] However, the Companies Act 1989 did not give carte blanche to directors, who are still obliged to observe limitations on their powers, nor did it validate transactions entered into in contravention of these limitations (such transactions are voidable), or abolish the equitable rule of tracing in regard to such transactions.[31]

The gratuitous nature of the transaction may also lay it open to attack as a transaction at an undervalue if the guarantor becomes insolvent.[32]

3.2.6 The extent of the guarantee

As in other security mechanisms, English law does not impose any limitation on the debt guaranteed (so long, of course, as the principal contract is not invalid for public policy reasons, including illegality affecting the guarantee). Future debts may be guaranteed, as may all of the obligations of the principal debtor. Guaranteed obligations, although usually referred to as "debts", are not limited to simple obligations to pay money, although this is by far the commonest type of obligation guaranteed, especially since other types of obligations pose practical problems for traditional guarantees.

---

[28] S. 3 Mercantile Law Amendment Act 1856.
[29] See, for example, *Ashbury Railway Carriage and Iron Company Limited v. Riche* [1875] LR 7 HL 653, *Rolled Steel Products v. British Steel Corporation* [1986] Ch 246, [1982] 3 All ER 52, CA.
[30] See Paul L. Davies and Dan Prentice, *Gower's Principles of Modern Company Law*, 6th edn., Sweet & Maxwell, 1997. The old rules still apply to corporations other than such companies.
[31] See ss. 35(3), 35A and 322A Companies Act 1989 and Nigel Furey and David Parkes, *The Companies Act 1989: A Practitioner's Guide*, Jordan's, 1990, pp. 55–62.
[32] S. 238 Insolvency Act 1986.

3.2.7 Protection of the dependent and the imprudent

Unlike other areas of commercial law, in the law of guarantees English judges tried to protect the dependent and the imprudent, presumably on the basis that guarantors were non-commercial actors, deriving no benefit from the transaction. This was done in three ways: by the rule of interpretation *contra proferentem*, which provides that a guarantee is to be strictly construed as against the creditor;[33] by devising strict rules providing for the lapse of the guarantee if the principal contract was altered in any way; and by the Court of Chancery applying to the guarantee situation rules of general application such as those relating to undue influence and unconscionability of bargains. In terms of the way in which English law effectively, if not formally, distinguishes between civil and commercial transactions and actors, these rules have, until now at any rate, been used mainly in the context of non-commercial guarantors (undue influence and unconscionability have been used exclusively in this context), thus effectively creating two regimes. Demand guarantees, to which the protective rules do not apply, have as a matter of practice only been granted by commercial actors.

As regards the rules concerning the lapse of the guarantee, the slightest variation of the principal obligation (with a few exceptions) releases the guarantor. However, these rules only demonstrate the shortcomings of judge-made law in attempts to provide protection to contracting parties. The protective rules were subservient to the overriding principle of freedom of contract, so that guarantors could contract out of their application. They are therefore ineffective in the vast majority of cases, since nearly all guarantees contain clauses negating the effect of the protective rules. The only practical result of the rules is, in the vast majority of cases, an addition in length and obscurity to standard form guarantees, and the provision of traps for any unwary person foolhardy enough to amend the standard guarantee form incorrectly. The same applies to the *contra proferentem* rule, which can be easily circumvented by competent drafting. Effectively an area of law with its own rules has been created by the standard forms, with results quite different from those given by the general law. It is only in the exceptional case of a guarantee which is not in standard form that the legal rules really come into their own.

The rules relating to undue influence and unconscionability, on the other hand, have proved far more effective weapons, since they do not depend on contract, but conduct, and have enjoyed a renaissance in recent years, with an explosion of cases. Very simply, if the principal debtor exerts undue influence on the guarantor to enter into the guarantee, then the guarantor has a right to set aside the transaction as against the principal debtor, and also as against the creditor if the creditor knew, or ought to have known, of the relevant facts.[34]

---

[33] See *Blest v. Brown* [1862] 4 De GF and J 367 at 376, cited in Sealy and Hooley, *Text and Materials in Commercial Law*, p. 864, where Lord Campbell said: "You bind [the guarantor] to the letter of his engagement. Beyond the proper interpretation of that engagement you have no hold upon him. *He receives no benefit and no consideration*." (emphasis added)

[34] The leading modern cases are *Barclays Bank plc v. O'Brien* [1994] 1 AC 180, [1993] 4 All ER 417, HL and *CIBC Mortgages plc v. Pitt* [1994] 1 AC 200, [1993] 4 All ER 433, HL (heard together). See also *Royal Bank of Scotland v. Etridge (No. 2)* [1998] 4 All ER 705, CA. There is voluminous academic comment: a recent article is Paula Giliker, "*Barclays Bank v. O'Brien* revisited: what a difference five years can make" (1999) 62 *Modern Law Review*, 609. The Unfair Contract Terms Act 1977 applies to guarantees. The Unfair Terms in Consumer Contracts

3.2.8 The relationship between the contracts

As noted above, in theory there is a fundamental theoretical difference between a guarantee, which is dependent upon the validity of the principal contract, and an indemnity, which is not. A simple guarantee is co-extensive with the principal contract, and, if the principal contract is invalid, the guarantee is also invalid. In practice the use of a carefully drafted document containing both mechanisms reduces the practical importance of this principle. However, an indemnity does not go as far as a demand guarantee, which is completely independent from the underlying obligation, as in an indemnity the indemnifier undertakes to indemnify the creditor against loss. There are numerous situations where the indemnifier could claim that the creditor has suffered no loss.

3.2.9 The relationship between the guarantor and the principal debtor: the right to indemnity

The guarantor has an automatic right to an indemnity from the principal debtor. However, this right is usually limited in standard form guarantees, so that the guarantor is barred from competing with the creditor in the insolvency of the principal debtor.[35]

3.2.10 The relationship between the guarantor and the creditor: the right of subrogation

The guarantor also has an automatic right (which is not contractual, but granted by law) to take the place of the creditor as regards any real security which the creditor may hold, but only upon full payment of sums due under the guarantee.[36]

3.2.11 Co-guarantors

Co-guarantors have an automatic (non-contractual) right to recover sums paid beyond their proportionate share of the obligations due under the principal contract.[37]

---

cont.

Regulations 1994 (SI 1994/3159) only applies to consumer transactions, but the Unfair Contract Terms Act is not so restricted. For a concise discussion of this legislation, see for example Robert Upex, *Davies on Contract*, 8th edn., Sweet & Maxwell, 1999, pp. 90–95.

[35] The right to indemnity only arises where the guarantor has entered into the liability at the request of the principal debtor or was compelled to do so, not otherwise: see Goode, *Commercial Law*, p. 835.

[36] Where the guarantor has guaranteed the whole debt, but with a limitation of liability, payment of the full amount due does not count as payment in full for the purposes of subrogation.

[37] Goode, *Commercial Law*, pp. 840–841.

3.2.12 Enforcement

The creditor is not obliged to sue the principal debtor before making demand under the guarantee, or even to make a demand upon the principal debtor (unless there is a provision in the guarantee to this effect).[38]

3.3 The French approach to the law of guarantees[39]

3.3.1 General characteristics

Guarantee law was a significant part of Roman law. It was ancient and complex, with various types of guarantee having evolved over the centuries, and a considerable amount of legislation, including provisions which removed capacity from women to grant guarantees. The French law derives largely from Roman law, but has a much simplified regime as regards the basic mechanisms.[40]

The basics of modern French law are contained in the Civil Code.[41] The framers of the Civil Code, in accordance with the practice of the time, saw the guarantee as an essentially civil transaction, being entered into by family members and friends, rather than as a part of the world of commerce. Case law plays a very significant role in the interpretation (and, occasionally, the effective amendment) of the Civil Code provisions.

A guarantee is a contract, and the general rules of contract apply to it, but so do special rules, provided in the Civil Code. The legislator has intervened rather more than in England. Contracting out of most of the rules is possible, so that standard

---

[38] Goode, *Commercial Law*, p. 839, citing *Moschi v. Lep Air Services Limited* [1973] AC 331, [1972] 2 All ER 393, HL, per Lord Diplock at 348; *Hitchcock v. Humfrey* (1843) 5 Man & G 559; and *Re Brown's Estate* [1893] 2 Ch 300.

[39] Of the various books on the subject Simler and Delebecque, *Droit civil. Les sûretés* will, for the sake of concision, be the main work to which reference is made herein. Others include Dominique Legeais, *Sûretés et garanties du crédit*, Librairie Générale de Droit et de Jurisprudence, 1996; and Laurent Aynès, *Les sûretés. La publicité foncière*, 8th edn., Cujas, 1996. Two concise but scholarly works, very useful for an overview, are Laurent Aynès, *Le cautionnement*, 2nd edn., Dalloz, 1997; and Dominique Legeais, *Le cautionnement*, Economica, 1995 (this work is particularly strong on the practical aspects of how the law is actually used, and contains a precedent at pp. 93–97 and a practical guide for advisers of both guarantor and creditor at pp. 99–103).

[40] On Roman law, see for example R. O. Donnellan, Chapter I ("Historical: the Roman law") of R. Caney, *The Law of Suretyship in South Africa*, 2nd edn., Cape Town, Juta, 1970; P. Van Warmelo, *An Introduction to the Principles of Roman Civil Law*, Juta, 1976, §§426–433, §§513–514, §520, §521; W. W. Buckland and Arnold D. McNair, *Roman Law and Common Law: a Comparison in Outline*, 2nd edn., Cambridge University Press, revised by F. H. Lawson, 1965, pp. 324–328, which provides a succinct treatment and comparison with English law; and H. F. Jolowicz, *Historical Introduction to the Study of Roman Law*, Cambridge University Press, 1939, pp. 314–317. The possible origins of the differences between French law and Roman law are discussed below.

[41] Third Book, Title 14, Arts. 2011–2043. All further references in this section to articles without more are references to the French Civil Code.

form exceptions create in effect, as in England, a different legal situation in practice from that which seems to apply just from a reading of the texts. French guarantee law is not encrusted with such a patina of ancient rules as English law, but is a quite separate branch of law from that of real security.

3.3.2 Basic forms

The basic guarantee mechanism is the *cautionnement*, which is defined by Article 2011: "He who makes himself a guarantor of an obligation submits himself to the creditor to satisfy this obligation, if the debtor does not satisfy it himself."[42]

The latter part of this definition has been used to arrive at the same result as in English law, that the guarantee is a secondary, or accessory obligation, which is dependent upon the principal obligation.[43] The provisions protective of the guarantor[44] have resulted, using a rather similar line of thinking to that of English law, in the widespread use of the *cautionnement solidaire*, which one might translate as "joint-debt guarantee". This mechanism relies on the guarantor being a joint debtor with the principal debtor.[45] It is not an indemnity (which exists, but is very rarely used).[46] It is not even, in reality, a joint debt, for it is considered to be simply a variation of the traditional guarantee,[47] but it enjoys certain advantages, such as the absence of the benefits of discussion and division.[48]

It is also worth mentioning that guarantees are divided into three categories, depending on the source of the reason for the guarantee being given: contractual, legal (which one might translate as statutory) and judicial. In each case the guarantee is a contract, but legal guarantees are entered into as a result of a statutory obligation, judicial guarantees as a result of an order of the court.[49]

Intriguingly from the point of view of a common lawyer, the assignment of an obligation to pay is allowed in French law, as it is in the *shari'a* and the UAE, and this can be used as a substitute for a traditional guarantee in all the three systems.[50]

---

[42] "Celui qui se rend caution d'une obligation, se soumet envers le créancier à satisfaire à cette obligation, si le débiteur n'y satisfait pas lui-même ". "Obligor" and "obligee" would be more precise, if less elegant, translations of *débiteur* and *créancier*, since these words are not limited, as in English, to debt obligations.

[43] This is confirmed by other provisions of the Civil Code, such as Arts. 2012, 2013 and 2036.

[44] See below (section 3.3.6 "Protection of the dependent and imprudent").

[45] The Civil Code impliedly authorizes the joint-debt guarantee: see Art. 2021.

[46] The *constitut*, which dates back to Roman times (*constitutum debiti alieni*). See Simler and Delebecque, *Droit civil. Les sûretés*, §10.

[47] Simler and Delebecque, *Droit civil. Les sûretés*, §40, §135 and Cass. req. 19 févr. 1908, S. 1911, 1, 529, note Wahl: ("la clause de solidarité ne change pas la nature du cautionnement, mais modifie seulement certains de ses effets").

[48] The benefits of discussion and division are described below (section 3.3.6 "Protection of the dependent and the imprudent"). Note also the existence of two specific sub-categories: the *certification de caution* and the *sous-cautionnement*. Confusingly, the former is a specifically recognized sub-guarantee, or guarantee of a guarantee liability; the latter is a specific guarantee by the principal debtor granted to the guarantor. See Simler and Delebecque, *Droit civil. Les sûretés*, §46–48.

[49] *Ibid.*, §37.

[50] *Ibid.*, §254–257 for a full discussion of *délégation* as guarantee.

In French law such an assignment is called *délégation* and is uncannily like the *shari'a* mechanism of *hawala*.[51] As noted above, *délégation* resembles an English novation in that the consent of all three parties is required and indeed, in the Civil Code, Article 1275, the only provision concerning *délégation*, is contained in the novation section. However, one cannot simply equate the two, since French law also has the concept of *novation*, which is distinguished from *délégation*.[52] *Novation*, like a typical English law novation, renews the principal debt, with the principal debtor being replaced by a third party. *Délégation* is considered to be a kind of assignment, and is of two sorts, commonly, and rather misleadingly, called "perfect" and "imperfect".[53] A perfect *délégation* has the same effect as an assignment. It leads to the release of the original debtor and is effectively a novation. An imperfect *délégation* (the much commoner form) results in the original debtor remaining liable jointly with the new debtor, and it is this form which is commonly used as a substitute for a guarantee. The *délégation*, since it creates a joint debt, has the same advantages as the joint-debt guarantee.[54]

Demand guarantees, although only introduced into France in the 1970s as a result of international contracts, play just as important a role as do their counterparts in English law; indeed, they have gone a step beyond the English situation, in that they are increasingly being used where guarantee commitment is sought from individuals as a substitute for traditional guarantees. The French courts have sanctioned their use in such situations, relying on the principle of freedom of contract contained in Article 1134,[55] although with circumspection, using the provisions as to validity and defects of consent in order to protect lay guarantors where possible.[56]

---

[51] On which see below (section 6.1 "Comparative analysis"). For a general discussion of the transfer of rights and obligations, see François Terré, Philippe Simler and Yves Lequette, *Droit civil. Les obligations*, 6th edn., Dalloz, 1996, §1173–1176 (assignment of obligations), §1177–1206 (assignment of the right to receive payment), §1207–1211, §1207–1215 (assignment of the obligation to pay); §1339–1357 (*délégation*). For a detailed treatment of *délégation*, see M. Billiau, *La délégation de créance*, Thèse Paris I, Librairie Générale de Droit et de Jurisprudence, 1989, préface Ghestin.

[52] Art. 1275 itself makes this distinction by providing: "The assignment by which a debtor gives to the creditor another debtor who undertakes to be bound towards the creditor, does not effect a novation, unless the creditor has expressly declared that he meant to discharge his debtor who made the assignment" ["La délégation par laquelle un débiteur donne au créancier un autre débiteur qui s'oblige envers le créancier, n'opère point de novation, si le créancier n'a expressément déclaré qu'il entendait décharger son débiteur qui a fait la délégation".]

[53] Simler and Delebecque call them respectively "simple" and "novatory" for this reason: Simler and Delebecque, *Droit civil. Les sûretés*, §254.

[54] Simler and Delebecque, *Droit civil. Les sûretés*, §256.

[55] "Les conventions légalement formées tiennent lieu de loi à ceux qui les ont faites ". ["Agreements legally formed take the place of law for those who made them".]

[56] Simler and Delebecque, *Droit civil. Les sûretés*, §211 and case law cited therein. Other guarantee-type mechanisms exist, notably the direct action (*action directe*), which allows certain creditors to proceed directly against a third party in certain cases specified by law and the *promesse de porte-fort*, which allows a third party to undertake that one party to a contract, unable to execute the contract, for example by reason of incapacity, will execute that contract, as well as numerous other mechanisms: see Simler and Delebecque, *Droit civil. Les sûretés*, §11 for a full list.

3.3.3 *Civil and commercial law*[57]

The distinction between civil and commercial law has very significant consequences in this area. Among other things, a commercial guarantee is presumed to be a joint-debt guarantee, therefore one in which the guarantor does not enjoy the benefit of discussion, nor that of division.[58] Other important consequences include the facts that the court of competent jurisdiction is the commercial court, that the limitation period (*prescription*) is ten years (rather than thirty)[59] and that an arbitration clause (*clause compromissoire*) is allowed.

Strictly speaking, there is no separate mechanism of "commercial guarantee" as, for example, there is a separate mechanism of pledge of commercial undertaking, but only a guarantee which is of a commercial nature. The complications of the distinction are augmented by the fact that certain commercial rules, such as the rule on more flexible means of proof, are only applicable as between merchants, regardless of the categorization of the transaction itself. In addition, a merchant can enter into a guarantee which is not a commercial transaction, for example where the guarantee does not fall within the commercial activity of that merchant. This gives three possibilities: "two degrees of commerciality"[60] (a commercial transaction entered into by merchants and a commercial act not entered into by merchants) as well as a non-commercial transaction entered into by merchants, in which case the transaction is mixed and some civil, some commercial rules apply.[61]

Despite the strong linkage between the principal contract and the guarantee, the categorization of the principal contract is irrelevant for the purposes of categorization of the guarantee (an inconvenient consequence of this is that the creditor may well be required to sue in two different fora, the ordinary court and the commercial court). The basic rule is that a guarantee is a civil transaction, even if the principal contract is commercial or the guarantor is a merchant, and regardless of whether the guarantor has received payment for the grant of the guarantee. The main test is whether the guarantor has a personal proprietary interest (*intérêt patrimonial personnel*), so, for example, a merchant's guarantee given to further his business interests is a commercial transaction. However, the matter is far from clear in principle and has given rise to much litigation and case law.

The categorization is clear in certain important cases, such as that of a spouse (where the transaction is civil),[62] a financial institution and a *société* which is commercial by virtue of its form (where the transaction is commercial).

---

[57] Simler and Delebecque, *Droit civil. Les sûretés*, §§41–45.

[58] *Ibid.*, §41.

[59] *Prescription* is used to designate both prescription in the English sense and a limitation period: see Arts. 1234, 2219 and 2262.

[60] Simler and Delebecque, *Droit civil. Les sûretés*, §41.

[61] This complexity is a good example of the problems caused by a rigid distinction between civil and commercial matters. For mixed transactions, see Simler and Delebecque, *Droit civil. Les sûretés*, §45.

[62] CA Amiens 13 June 1961, D. 1962, Som. 57. Simler and Delebecque, *Droit civil. Les sûretés*, §43.

3.3.4 *Validity and proof*

General contractual rules apply; consideration is not, of course, an issue as such, since it does not exist in French law, but there is just as much a problem in theory with the concept of *cause*. Like the question of consideration in the English guarantee, however, this is largely an academic debate.[63]

The situation as to formal validity and proof is quite complex.

As regards validity, a guarantee is a consensual contract and, formally, an oral contract is valid, but Article 2015 stresses that a guarantee must be express and that it cannot be presumed. This article should be read in conjunction with Article 1162, which provides a general contractual rule of *contra proferentem*.[64]

As regards proof, civil guarantees are subject to Article 1341 in the unlikely event of their value not exceeding FF5,000 (evidence in writing) and, more pertinently, to Article 1326[65] (a unilateral undertaking must be set out in a document containing the signature of the promisor and a statement of the relevant amount in figures and letters). By virtue of Article 109 of the Commercial Code, these requirements do not apply to commercial guarantees.

The courts have complicated the situation by using the proof requirements as requirements of validity. This is discussed in more detail below.[66] As in England, guarantees are not registrable.

3.3.5 *The gratuitous nature of the guarantee*

The gratuitous nature of the guarantee does not cause a particular problem in the case of individual guarantors, the only requirement being that they have the capacity to contract. The situation for corporate guarantors is reasonably similar to that obtaining in England, but with some significant variations.[67] The basic rule is that the guarantee must be *intra vires* the corporation. The rule is very strict, in that a corporation cannot remedy the situation by simply including a main objects clause allowing it to grant guarantees generally, the grant of which as an object is reserved by law to financial institutions.[68] The grant of the guarantee must fall within the object of the corporation by there being a "community of interest" between the guarantor and the principal debtor.[69]

This rule is relaxed for *sociétés à responsabilité limitée* (SARLs) and *sociétés anonymes* (SAs) by the Commercial Companies Law, which provides that any restrictions may not be relied upon by the corporation as against third parties, unless such third

---

[63] Simler and Delebecque, *Droit civil. Les sûretés*, §§65–71.

[64] "Dans le doute, la convention s'interprète contre celui qui a stipulé et en faveur de celui qui a contracté l'obligation" ["In the case of doubt, an agreement is interpreted against him who stipulated and in favour of him who undertook the obligation".]

[65] As inserted by Law No. 80-525 of 12 July 1980. The sum of FF5,000 is fixed by decree, the relevant decree is at present Decree No. 80-533 of 15 July 1980. This provision is discussed in more detail below (section 3.3.6 "Protection of the dependent and the imprudent").

[66] See section 3.3.6 "Protection of the dependent and the imprudent".

[67] Simler and Delebecque, *Droit civil. Les sûretés*, §60 for individuals and §§62–64 for corporations.

[68] Law of 24 January 1983, Art. 3, alinéa 1.

[69] Prior approval by the shareholders is an effective method of ensuring the validity of the guarantee.

parties had actual or constructive notice of that restriction.[70] In the case of SAs, however, the guarantee must be authorized in advance by the relevant body (either the *conseil d'administration* or the *conseil de surveillance*). This rule is very strictly applied. The general exception for third parties acting in good faith does not apply, so the creditor must be absolutely sure that the authority is in good order. No subsequent ratification is allowed. The sanction is the nullity of the guarantee.[71]

A guarantee which is entered into in order to harm the interests of third party creditors may be struck down as a fraud on the creditors. There is no specific statutory provision.[72]

3.3.6 *Protection of the dependent and the imprudent*[73]

We have seen that there is some degree of protection in the civil guarantee rules on validity and proof. The general rules on the matrimonial regime provide further protection for spouses, in that Article 1415, as inserted by Law No. 85-1372 of 23 December 1985, requires the express consent of one spouse for a guarantee given by the other to be enforceable against the first spouse's property.[74]

In view of the primacy given to freedom of contract and the existence of standard forms contracting out of protective rules, the theoretical protection given by the civil nature of the guarantee is not particularly effective.

So far, then, there seems little effective protection. The absence of a doctrine of undue influence and the disappearance of the special protection granted to women in Roman law add to this impression.[75] The protection function is fulfilled, however, by other means, which are quite similar to English law. The first technique is a distinction drawn by case law between lay and commercial guarantors. This is not the traditional civil/commercial distinction, which has not proved very effective, but is flexible and, like its English counterpart, works by applying the protective rules differently to lay and commercial guarantors.[76] The means of protection just referred to are readily available to the lay, but not to the commercial, guarantor.

---

[70] Law No. 66-537 of 24 July 1966. Art. 49 applies to SARLs, Arts. 98 and 113 to SAs. Certain types of guarantee are banned, such as guarantees by the corporation of the liabilities of the management.

[71] Art. 113 Commercial Companies Law. See Jean-François Barbiéri, "Cautionnement et sociétés. Dix ans de jurisprudence", Juris-classeur périodique, *La semaine juridique, Cahiers de droit de l'entreprise*, Supplément 2, 1992, p. 16 at p. 23.

[72] But see Art. 1167, which enshrines the "Paulian action": "They [the creditors] may also, in their own name, attack acts fraudulently made by their debtor against their rights". ["Ils (les créanciers) peuvent aussi, en leur nom personnel, attaquer les actes faits par leur débiteur en fraude de leurs droits".] See Terré, Simler and Lequette, *Droit civil. Les obligations*, §1057–1089. On fraudulent collusion (*collusion frauduleuse*) see Barbiéri, "Cautionnement et sociétés", p. 22.

[73] Simler and Delebecque, *Droit civil. Les sûretés*, §24 contains a detailed discussion.

[74] *Ibid.*, §61.

[75] L. Caney, *The Law of Suretyship*, Chapter XIV ("Women Sureties"). Caney gives the justification for this as: "It was easy for women to become involved, for their feelings to be played upon, not only by unscrupulous persons, but also by well-meaning genuine persons, over-optimistic about their own affairs, and so a woman's natural inclination to help another in need had to be curtailed and she be protected by the law" (pp. 163–164).

[76] Legeais, *Le cautionnement*, pp. 15–16.

The main means available are: the use of ordinary contractual defects of consent; the manuscript acknowledgement requirements of Article 1326, combined with the Article 2015 requirement that the will of the guarantor to be bound must be express and cannot go beyond the limits of what has been agreed; and tortious lender liability. In addition, the general contractual requirement of good faith contained in Article 1134 has recently begun to be used quite extensively by the courts in the area of guarantees.

Classically, there are three defects of consent: *erreur* (mistake), *dol* (no exact equivalent – somewhere between fraud and misrepresentation) and *violence* (duress). Mistake is often alleged, but is not a common cause of nullity,[77] and the possibility of using the doctrine of *violence* to create something like the English undue influence has not been exploited. Lay guarantors are much more likely to use *dol* and this tactic is the most successful.[78] *Dol* is defined by Article 1116 as follows: "*Dol* is a cause of nullity of the agreement when manoeuvres practised by one of the parties are such that it is evident that, without these manoeuvres, the other party would not have contracted."[79]

On a literal interpretation, this provision would not be particularly helpful, as it only concerns the parties to the guarantee contract, i.e. the creditor and the guarantor, whereas in most instances the *dol* will have been practised by the principal debtor. However, the article has been widely interpreted by the courts in order to circumvent this aspect, so that a simple failure to inform by a creditor amounts to *dol* (*dol par réticence*), effectively imposing an obligation on the creditor to provide the guarantor with full information about the principal debtor. Where the creditor is a bank, this is quite an onerous obligation. There are parallels here with the English doctrine of undue influence: both use the idea of the knowledge of the creditor and both have been interpreted to the limit in order to provide protection for lay guarantors, to such a degree indeed that they have practically become fictions.[80]

The combination of Articles 1326 and 2015 has been used by the courts in order to protect guarantors. As seen above, a statement of the amount guaranteed must be set out "in manuscript" (*écrite de sa main*) (this has been construed to mean writing of any kind, including typing). In the 1980s the Court of Cassation interpreted the provisions as a requirement of validity, rather than proof. The Court has since modified its stance, holding that the articles only constitute requirements of proof. However, the latter interpretation remains very relevant, since the Court has also stated that the requirements exist in order to protect the guarantor. These requirements therefore give guarantors a potential escape route. In particular, they provide lay guarantors with a means of avoiding liability under all-money guarantees by holding invalid any but the most comprehensive statements of awareness of the implications of entering

---

[77] See the slightly differing views of Simler and Delebecque, *Droit civil. Les sûretés*, §54–57 and Legeais, *Le cautionnement*, pp. 21–22.
[78] Simler and Delebecque, *Droit civil. Les sûretés*, §58 and Legeais, *Le cautionnement*, pp. 22–23.
[79] "Le dol est une cause de nullité de la convention lorsque les manœuvres pratiquées par l'une des parties sont telles, qu'il est évident que sans ces manœuvres, l'autre partie n'aurait pas contracté."
[80] There may also be an argument that the creditor has acted in bad faith.

into the guarantee (leading banks to prefer limited amount guarantees).[81] Article 1326 does not apply to commercial guarantees given by a merchant.[82]

The possible liability of the creditor in tort should be mentioned, since this does not exist in English law. The creditor may, where the failure of the principal debtor to pay the principal debt is attributable to the actions of the creditor, either by irresponsible lending or by irresponsible withdrawal of credit, be unable to recover, in full or in part, from the guarantor.[83]

A relatively new development has been the use of the requirement for good faith. This is commonly given as an additional reason for striking down a guarantee where *dol* (particularly *dol par réticence*) has been found to exist, but the courts have also invoked it where there is no *dol*. Professor Legeais has written that it would not be surprising if the courts were to use good faith in order to establish proportionality between the guarantee obligation and the property of the guarantor.[84]

In contradistinction to English law,[85] where rules on the lapse of the guarantee are used mainly in order to protect the guarantor, in French law these rules relate mainly to the question of co-extensiveness of the gurantee with the principal contract. Two such rules are, however, relevant to the question of protection.

Detriment to the subrogated rights of the guarantor (for historical reasons misleadingly called "cession of actions")[86] negligently or intentionally caused by the creditor, discharges the guarantor. Article 2037,[87] which regulates this matter, covers all rights, not just those relating to security, and, although Article 2037 only refers to the "act" of the creditor, case law makes it clear that it is only the fault of the creditor which brings about the discharge of the guarantor. Article 2037 now specifically provides that it is not possible (unlike the situation in English law) to contract out of the rule.[88]

Fairly recently (1984), another cause of lapse has been "discovered" by case law.[89] If the creditor fails to prove in the liquidation of the principal debtor, the principal debt is deemed to be extinguished. Since the principal debt and the guarantee are co-extensive, the guarantee liability is extinguished. One can consider this rule as some protection for the guarantor.

---

[81] Simler and Delebecque, *Droit civil. Les sûretés*, §108; Legeais, *Le cautionnement*, pp. 42; and Philippe Delebecque, "Forme et preuve du cautionnement", Juris-classeur périodique, *La semaine juridique, Cahiers de droit de l'entreprise*, Supplément 2, 1992, p. 5.

[82] Delebecque, "Forme et preuve du cautionnement", p. 6.

[83] Simler and Delebecque, *Droit civil. Les sûretés*, §112.

[84] Legeais, *Sûretés et garanties du crédit*, §91.

[85] A partial renunciation of the principal debt, for example, gives rise simply to a corresponding reduction in the amount guaranteed.

[86] For this reason, Simler and Delebecque avoid the expression, preferring "the rule in Article 2037": see Simler and Delebecque, *Droit civil. Les sûretés*, §190 and footnote 1. See also for the historical aspects Caney, *The Law of Suretyship*, pp. 121–122. On English law, see Malek, "A critical review", pp. 14–17.

[87] "La caution est déchargée, lorsque la subrogation aux droits, hypothèques et privilèges du créancier, ne peut plus, par le fait de ce créancier, s'opérer en faveur de la caution. Toute clause contraire est réputée non écrite" ["The guarantor is discharged, when the subrogation to the rights, mortgages and preferential rights of the creditor, cannot, by the act of that creditor, operate in favour of the guarantor. Any clause to the contrary is deemed unwritten".]

[88] Inserted by Art. 49 Law of 1 March 1984.

[89] Simler and Delebecque, *Droit civil. Les sûretés*, §176; Art. 53, alinéa 3, Law 25 January 1985; and Cass. com. 19 June 1984, *Bull. civ.* IV, No. 198, D. 1985, 140, note Honorat.

In addition to these rules two rights exist which are unknown to English law: the benefit of discussion (or excussion) and the benefit of division, both of which have their origins in Roman law.[90] At first glance these seem to constitute a significant difference in approach. The benefit of discussion is a right which the guarantor enjoys to demand that the creditor sue the principal debtor before suing the guarantor. The benefit of division is the right of one of several guarantors to demand that the creditor only sue that guarantor for a proportionate part of the principal obligation. The difference between the English and French systems is here more apparent than real.

The benefit of discussion, contained in Article 2021 and elaborated in Articles 2022–2024, only grants a right to the guarantor to demand, in very restricted circumstances, that the creditor proceed first against the principal debtor. These circumstances include the effective requirement that the principal debtor be solvent. These requirements remove much of the procedure's usefulness, except that of being an irritant to the creditor.[91]

The benefit of division, contained in Article 2025, only applies to solvent co-guarantors.[92]

These weaknesses of the rules pale into insignificance, however, when one realizes that both benefits may be excluded by contrary agreement; that neither apply to joint-debt guarantees, which constitute by far the majority of guarantees in practice;[93] and that neither applies, by commercial custom recognized by case law, to commercial guarantees.[94]

Generally, the extension of the protection of guarantors has been very great in recent years, and has been exacerbated by the insolvency legislation, to such an extent indeed that many commentators have talked of a "crisis" of the traditional forms of security in general and of guarantees in particular. Potential beneficiaries of guarantees have looked to other, new forms of guarantee type mechanism in an attempt to escape the protective regime. In recognition of the fact that the law had become over-protective, the courts and the legislature have retreated from their very protective stance, with the courts limiting a (less extreme) regime to lay guarantors, and with the legislature amending such legislation as the Law of 25 January 1985 relating to insolvency in order to make business life somewhat easier.[95]

---

[90] Caney, *The Law of Suretyship*, Chapter IX ("The benefit of excussion"); and Chapter X ("The benefit of division amongst sureties").

[91] Simler and Delebecque, *Droit civil. Les sûretés*, §§127–130, particularly §128 and §129.

[92] *Ibid.*, §§131–134.

[93] But note that Art. 47 of the "Madelin" Law of 11 February 1994 provides that, where an individual guarantees the debts of an individual entrepreneur, the guarantee may only be a joint-debt guarantee if the guarantee is limited in amount.

[94] Commercial guarantees are presumed to be joint-debt guarantees: Simler and Delebecque, *Droit civil. Les sûretés*, §99.

[95] For an account of the history, see Legeais, *Sûretés et garanties du crédit*, §§6–16 and see below (section 6.1 "Comparative analysis").

3.3.7 *The extent of the guarantee*

All debts, present and future, can be guaranteed, and the guarantee may be limited or unlimited, the only general limitation being that the guarantee liability may not go beyond the amount of the principal debt.[96] The amount of the principal debt can be unlimited.

3.3.8 *The relationship between the contracts*

As seen above, French practice does not include an indemnity in the guarantee, but a joint-debt guarantee, which is regarded as a type of guarantee, and therefore still a dependent contract. All the logical consequences of an intimate link between the guarantee and the principal contract therefore exist, even for well drafted documents, and this is one of the reasons behind the greater recent reliance upon demand guarantees.

Therefore the principal contract must be valid,[97] and nearly all events which affect the principal liability affect the guarantee liability as well. Accordingly, such events as the reduction or extinction of the principal debt, statutory and non-statutory composition with creditors,[98] prescription and novation of the principal contract, the fusion of creditor and principal creditor, all have effects upon the guarantee which follow logically from the connection between the two contracts: for example, the guarantee liability is reduced *pro tanto* or discharged, the guarantor is discharged upon novation of the principal contract, and so forth.

3.3.9 *The relationship between the guarantor and the principal debtor: the right to indemnity*

The right to indemnity and the right to subrogation are seen as sub-categories of the right of recourse by the guarantor against the principal debtor. Article 2028 deals with the general right of indemnity (or personal recourse);[99] Article 2029 with the

---

[96] Art. 2015. See below (section 3.3.5 "The gratuitous nature of the guarantee") for a discussion of the effect of the "Madelin" Law and of the interpretation of Art. 1326 on all-money guarantees0

[97] There is a significant exception where it "might be annulled by an exception purely personal to the obligee" ["encore qu'elle pût être annulée par une exception purement personnelle à l'obligé"], (Art. 2012, with particular mention being made of the case of a minor), therefore avoiding the well-known problem of English law guarantees which was a major factor in the inclusion of an indemnity in those documents. Art. 2013 provides that the amount due under the guarantee cannot exceed the amount due under the principal contract; generally, see Simler and Delebecque, *Droit civil. Les sûretés*, §§75–77.

[98] *Ibid.*, §§164–177. The situation concerning statutory composition with creditors is rather complex: *ibid.*, §170.

[99] Intriguingly, Art. 2028 specifies that the right of indemnity applies whether the guarantee is granted with or without the knowledge of the principal debtor, in terms which recall the *shari'a* discussions.

right of subrogation (or subrogatory recourse). In principle, both take effect only upon payment, but the guarantor may, in certain circumstances set out in Article 2031 (including when the guarantor is being sued by the creditor, when the principal debtor has become insolvent and when the principal debt has become due and payable at the end of its term), take action against the principal debtor before payment has been made under the guarantee.

3.3.10 *The relationship between the guarantor and the creditor: the right of subrogation*

Article 2029 is no more than a confirmation of the general right of subrogation to be found in Article 1251. As discussed above, any detriment to the guarantor's subrogated rights arising out of the fault of the creditor discharges the guarantor.[100] In a typical contrast between English and French methods, Article 1252 (not applicable in the case of an indemnity) removes the possibility of competition between the guarantor and the creditor in the case of partial payment; something which in English law is dealt with in the standard form guarantee, the basic position being the opposite, that competition is possible in this situation.

3.3.11 *Co-guarantors*

Co-guarantors have a right of contribution against each other, granted by Article 2033. The benefit of division has been dealt with above.[101]

3.3.12 *Enforcement*[102]

The creditor sues the guarantor in the normal way for a contractual debt. As seen above, the benefit of discussion is not of particular relevance in practice.

3.4 The *shari'a* approach to the law of guarantees[103]

As with many subjects, it is difficult to give an accurate picture in a short space of the *shari'a* position on guarantees because of the variety of views among the differ-

---

[100] See above (section 3.3.6 "Protection of the dependent and the imprudent").
[101] *Ibid*.
[102] Simler and Delebecque, *Droit civil. Les sûretés*, §§164–185.
[103] See generally Book III, *Majalla* for *kafala* and Book IV for *hawala*; also in B. Lewis, Ch. Pellat and J. Schacht (eds.), *Encyclopaedia of Islam*, new edition, Leiden, E.J. Brill, 1965, entry for *kafala* (Y. Linant de Bellefonds), which is useful in that it succinctly discusses the variations among the schools; Joseph Schacht; *An Introduction to Islamic Law*, Oxford, Clarendon Press, 1964, pp. 148–149, 158–159; Frank E. Vogel and Samuel L. Hayes, *Islamic Law and Finance: Religion, Risk and Return*, The Hague, Kluwer Law International, 1998, pp. 106–107; David Santillana, *Istituzioni di diritto musulmano malichita: con riguardo anche al sistema sciafiita*, Istituto per l'Oriente, 1938, provides a full account of the Maliki law, with some discussion of the Shafi'i position.

ent schools, and sometimes in the same school. Given the concordance between the UAE law and the *Majalla*,[104] the *Majalla* position is often given below as "the *shari'a* position". This is purely for the sake of convenience and nothing more should be read into it.

3.4.1 General characteristics

The Qur'an and the *hadith* contain little of relevance. The concept of guarantee is mentioned in the Qur'an, although only one of the places where it is mentioned actually uses a word of the same root as *kafala*.[105] Several *hadith* exist, but seem to be quoted only in order to give some legitimacy to the existence of the idea of guarantee.[106]

Given the general tenor of the *shari'a* attitude, which stresses fairness, and, as a means of achieving that fairness, certainty of obligation, the law of guarantees is surprisingly liberal.

3.4.2 Basic forms

Arabic has two words in common use for guarantee – *kafala* and *daman*.[107]These are interchangeable. Historically, the Hanafi school used *daman*, the other schools used *kafala*.[108] *Kafala* will be used here, especially since this is the word used in the UAE legislation. However, as in English law an account of guarantee would be in-

---

cont.

The *Encyclopaedia of Islam* entry on *hawala* (A. Dietrich) is misleading, in that it only refers to an assignment of a right to receive money by the assignor to the assignor's creditor, which is the exception, and does not mention the primary characteristic, that of transfer of an obligation to pay – this is a common error, induced by various texts only dealing with the assignment of the right to receive money.

[104] *Majallat-i Akhami Adliye*, the Book of Rules of Justice, the Ottoman code, formulated at the end of the nineteenth century; the text in Arabic, with a commentary, can be found in Ali Hayder's commentary (*Durer Al-ahkam, An interpretation of Majalat al-ahkam al-adlia*, Maktaba Al-Nahda, undated) and in Salim Rustam Baz al-Lubnani, *Sharh al-majalla*, Al-Matba'a Al-'adabiyya, 1923; an English translation is C. A. Hooper, *The Civil Law of Palestine and Trans-Jordan*, Azriel Printing Works, 1933, serialized in *Arab Law Quarterly* 1986–1990, with an introduction by W. M. Ballantyne in *Arab Law Quarterly*, 1986 p. 364; an annotated edition (in French) is contained in George Young, *Corps de droit ottoman*, 1906, vol. VI, Clarendon Press. Ebül'ula Mardin, "Development of the Shari'a under the Ottoman Empire" in Majid Khadduri and Herbert J. Liebesny (eds.), *Law in the Middle East*, vol. 1 ("Origin and development of Islamic law"), The Middle East Institute, 1955, p. 279 provides a history of, and commentary on, the *Majalla*. The *Majalla* should be used with care, as it only represents the Hanafi school.

[105] This is the passage at 16:91; the other two passages are in 12:72 (where the word is *zai'm*) and 17:92 (where the word is *qabil*).

[106] Al-Bukhari (trans. Muhammad Muhsin Khan), *The Translation of the Meanings of Sahih Al-Bukhari*, 6th edn., Kazi Publications, 1986, pp. 271–273.

[107] Others exist: see Averroes (1126–1198), *Bidayat al-mujtahid wa-nihayat al-muqtasid*, vol. 2, Cairo, 1935, p. 291.

[108] Lewis *et al.*, *Encyclopaedia of Islam*, entry for *kafala*. The word *daman* has a variety of meanings, including that of "liability".

complete without mentioning indemnity, so an account of the *shari'a* position would be incomplete without discussing assignment (*hawala*), which was often used as a guarantee.[109]

3.4.2.1 *Kafala*

Kafala is defined as "the addition of an obligation to an obligation in respect to a demand for a particular thing".[110] In other words, a guarantee is an accessory obligation, just like an English guarantee or French *cautionnement*. *Kafala* is divided into two:[111] the *kafala bil-nafs*[112] (guarantee of the person), in which the guarantor assures the presence of the defendant in court; and the *kafala bil-mal*[113] (guarantee of the property), in which the guarantor promises to pay the creditor if the principal debtor fails to do so. Only the *kafala bil-mal* is dealt with here. Guarantees can be of all sorts: contingent, unconditional or limited in time or amount.[114]

3.4.2.2 *Hawala*[115]

Hawala is usually translated as "assignment" (of debt), but is primarily the transfer of the obligation to pay, like the French *délégation*.[116] The English-style assignment of a right to receive payment was, with the exception of the case where the

---

[109] Vogel and Hayes, *Islamic Law and Finance*, p. 108. Art. 648 provides: "If there is a condition in the contract of guarantee whereby the principal debtor becomes freed from his liability, the contract is changed into a transfer of debt". Art. 649 of the *Majalla* provides: "A transfer of debt subject to a condition that the debtor shall not be freed from liability is a contract of guarantee. Consequently, if a creditor instructs his debtor to transfer the sum he is owing to some other person on condition that the debtor is to guarantee payment, and he does so, such person may demand payment from whichever of the two he wishes."

[110] Art. 612 *Majalla*.

[111] Arts. 613 and 614 *Majalla*. Arts. 615–617 also provide for a guarantee for delivery, a contingent guarantee and an unconditional guarantee.

[112] Art. 614 and 643–658 *Majalla*.

[113] Art. 613 and 642 *Majalla*.

[114] Arts. 616–617 and 624–625 *Majalla*.

[115] For more detail, see Arts. 673–700 *Majalla*; Nicholas Dylan Ray, "The medieval Islamic system of credit and banking: legal and historical considerations" (1997) *Arab Law Quarterly*, p. 43, especially pp. 60–80; Emile Tyan, "Cession de dette et cession de créance dans la théorie et la pratique du droit musulman (d'après le madhab hanafite)", (1946) *Annales de l'école française de droit de Beyrouth*, p. 23; Santillana, *Istituzioni*, §78–83 is a full account, but considers *hawala* only as a transfer of the right to receive, and should therefore be read with care; Sélim Jahel, "L'adéquation du droit musulman classique aux procédés modernes de financement et de garantie" (1985) 38 *Revue trimestrielle de droit commercial et de droit économique* 483; and Foster, "Commercial security over movables in the UAE", at p. 41. A *hadith* on the subject relates that the Prophet said: "Procrastination in paying debts by a wealthy person is injustice. So, if your debt is transferred from our debtor to a rich debtor, you should agree": Al-Bukhari, *The Translation of the Meanings of Sahih Al-Bukhari*, vol. III, §487.
 The whole subject of *hawala* is one of considerable complexity and divergence between the schools, and the account herein is much simplified.

[116] Art. 673 *Majalla*. See footnotes 12 and 13 in Young, *Corps de droit ottoman*, 262. Lane's *Lexicon* (Edward William Lane, *An Arabic–English Lexicon*, London, Williams and Norgate, 1865) defines it as the "transfer of a claim, or of a debt, by shifting the responsibility from one person to another".

assignor was already indebted to the assignee, forbidden.[117] As in French law, the procedure more resembles an English law novation, in that it involves the consent of all parties, and the debtor can either be released from the obligation to pay, or remain jointly liable with the assignee. Again as in French law, the *hawala* was commonly used in order to create the same effect as a guarantee: by the debtor assigning the obligation to pay, but not being released thereby, a third party was introduced into the situation who is obliged to pay the creditor if the original debtor does not pay (or indeed if the creditor simply chooses to sue the assignee rather than the original debtor). This is precisely the same situation as that of a guarantee, the assignee being the guarantor, the only difference being in the route taken to reach the destination.

There were two types of *hawala*, the limited and the absolute: the limited type is defined as a *hawala* where "the transferor limits the payment by the transferee to property of his owing by the transferee or in his possession"; the absolute type one where no such limitation is agreed.[118] The true distinction though is that the limited type allows the transfer of a right to receive payment, whereas the absolute is the original kind, which transfers an obligation to pay. By using the limited type, where the transferor (C) of the obligation to pay was also owed an obligation to pay by the transferee (B), by transferring to B his obligation to pay A, C was effectively transferring his right to receive payment from B to A.

Articles 648 and 649 of the *Majalla* highlight the connection between the *hawala* and the *kafala*, providing that a *kafala* where the principal debtor is discharged is a *hawala* (or in French terms, a perfect *délégation*) and that (again in French terms) an imperfect *délégation* is a *kafala*. This is a simplification of a knotty point, on which there was a range of opinions in classical *fiqh*, deriving, according to Jahel, from some authors considering *hawala* as the transfer of the obligation to pay, others considering it as a *délégation imparfaite*, although the basic principle was that the *hawala* discharged the debtor.[119] This rule could be displaced by contrary agreement.[120]

The degree of independence of the *hawala* from the original contract was another matter of controversy, with some maintaining that defences available to the original debtor were transferred, others that they were not. What was certain, however, was that, whereas the discharge of the principal debtor automatically discharged the *kafala*, in the *hawala* (*délégation imparfaite*), this was not the case, and this was probably the reason for creditors preferring the *hawala* to the *kafala*.[121]

The *Majalla* requires the consent of all three parties. Other authorities state that the consent of the original debtor is not required.[122]

---

[117] See Imam Malik ibn Anas (trans. Aisha Abdurrahman Bewley), *Al-Muwatta*, London, Kegan Paul International, 1989, §85: "Malik related to me from Musa ibn Maysara that he heard a man say to Sa'id ibn al-Musayyab, 'I am a man who sells for a debt'. Sa'id said, 'Do not sell except for what you take directly to your camel'."

[118] Art. 678 *Majalla* (limited), Art. 679 *Majalla* (absolute).

[119] Jahel, "L'adéquation du droit musulman classique", pp. 491–493.

[120] *Ibid.*, pp. 492–493.

[121] *Ibid.*, p. 494 and Art. 662 *Majalla*.

[122] Art. 680 *Majalla*; Santillana, *Istituzioni*, §80.

The rest of the discussion refers only, except where otherwise stated, to *kafala* rather than *hawala*.

3.4.2.3 *Haml*

Indemnity exists in the *shari'a* under the name of *haml*. The intention to create an indemnity must usually be expressly stated (but there is a presumption of indemnity in certain exceptional cases). The indemnity has the effect of completely releasing the principal debtor, even from an indemnity claim by the indemnifier, who is assumed to have wished the indemnity to be an act of charity.[123] *Haml* does not have anything like the same importance in the *shari'a* as indemnity in English law, since the equivalent function to that of indemnity in English law was performed by *hawala*.[124]

3.4.3 Civil and commercial law

There is no distinction between civil and commercial law in the *shari'a*, so the question of a different treatment of civil and commercial guarantees does not arise.[125]

3.4.4 Validity and proof

Generally, written documents did not have much importance in the *shari'a*, overwhelming importance being given to oral testimony, and this is reflected in the law of guarantees, where no particular form is required.[126] In this spirit, the *Majalla* only requires an offer, which is valid until declined by the creditor.[127] The guarantor must be of age, of sound mind and not interdicted.[128] A bankrupt cannot grant

---

[123] Santillana, *Istituzioni*, §280.

[124] This lack of importance is indicated by the absence of an entry in Lewis, Pellat and Schacht (eds.), *Encyclopaedia of Islam*. The cognate word *hamala* is a synonym for *kafala*.

[125] Some claim that different considerations applied to commercial transactions and point out that the *hiyal* (stratagems, i.e. devices that used one mechanism in order to achieve another aim, mainly in order to circumvent the prohibition on *riba*) were devised in a commercial context. See Noel Coulson, "Muslim custom and case law" (1959) *Welt des Islams*, new series VI, 13–24; and Robert Brunschvig, "Fiction légale dans l'Islam médiéval" (1970–1971) 32 *Studia Islamica*, 41.

[126] Santillana, *Istituzioni*, §275; A. L. Udovitch, "Les échanges du marché dans l'Islam médiéval. Théorie du droit et savoir local", (1986–1987) 65 *Studia Islamica* 5, 24–25. This is despite the Qur'anic verse which recommends writing (2.282).

[127] Art. 621 provides *inter alia*: "A guarantee may be concluded and become executory by the mere offer of the guarantor". Art. 622 provides: "The offer of the guarantor, that is, words used importing guarantee, are any words which by custom are evidence of an undertaking to be bound". The consent of the principal debtor is not required: Santillana, *Istituzioni*, §273.

[128] Art. 628 of the *Majalla*. "Interdiction" is a state of lack of capacity, used to protect prodigals and others from the consequences of their acts. Special provisions apply to the gravely ill and the bankrupt, on which see below (section 3.4.7 "Protection of the dependent and the imprudent").

a guarantee without the consent of his creditors.[129] No such requirements apply to the creditor, who is regarded as a donee.[130]

3.4.5 The gratuitous nature of the guarantee

Unlike French and English law, the *shari'a* does not permit the grant of a guarantee against payment; the rationale is that, as the guarantor has a right of indemnity against the principal debtor upon payment, the guarantor who has received a fee for the grant of the guarantee would receive an unfair advantage, thus infringing the prohibition of *riba*.[131]

The question of the *vires* of the corporation to enter into a guarantee did not arise in the *shari'a*, which did not have corporations, only partnerships. At most, a question might have arisen as to the authority of the person purporting to bind the partners, and this would have been dealt with as a question of the authority granted to that person either expressly or by custom.

3.4.6 Protection of the dependent and the imprudent

The validity requirements provide some protection, but it is to be noted that the contractual options, such as that of the contractual session, do not apply.[132] However, the *shari'a*, quite surprisingly given the general requirement for certainty in contracts, allows a *kafala* of future debts of whatever amount. Also, apart from the Maliki school, it allows the creditor to proceed immediately against the guarantor, who has no right to demand that the creditor proceed first against the principal debtor – in French law terms, there is no benefit of discussion.[133]

The *Majalla* makes no specific mention of the position of the dependent or imprudent, apart from the validity requirements. Women in the *shari'a* are not able to provide a guarantee beyond a third of their property, except where the principal debtor is their husband. The rationale for this is that imposing the one third rule in this case would backfire, since the woman might suffer at the hands of her husband as a result of her inability to grant the guarantee.[134] Someone who is mortally ill can also only provide a guarantee up to a third of their property, so long as the

---

[129] Santillana, *Istituzioni*, §273.

[130] Lewis *et al.*, *Encyclopaedia of Islam*, entry for *kafala*.

[131] Santillana, *Istituzioni*, §275.

[132] Abu Ishaq al-Shirazi, *Kitab et-Tanbih. Ou le livre de l'admonition touchant la loi musulmane selon le rite de l'Imam Ech-Chafe'i*, (al-Tanbih fi al-fiqh al-shafi'i) (trans. G-H Bousquet), La maison des livres, 1949, vol. II, §36.

[133] Art. 644 *Majalla*: "The person claiming under the guarantee has the option of claiming either against the guarantor or against the principal debtor. The exercise of his right against the one in no way destroys his right of claiming from the other. He may claim first from the one and then from the other or from both simultaneously." The majority Maliki view is practically the same as Roman law, even down to an exception from the benefit of discussion for a joint-debt guarantee: Santillana, *Istituzioni*, §276.

[134] Santillana, *Istituzioni*, §273.

principal debtor is a stranger, but is incapable of granting a valid guarantee for the debts of his heirs.[135]

3.4.7 *The extent of the guarantee*[136]

The basic principle is the same as in English and French law, that of co-extensiveness.[137]

Article 612 of the *Majalla* defines the guarantee as: "A guarantee consists of the addition of an obligation to an obligation in respect to a demand for a particular thing. That is to say, it consists of one person joining himself to another person, and binding himself also to meet the obligation which accrues to that other person".

So the guarantee obligation cannot be greater than the principal obligation. As *kafala* is of broader ambit than the English law guarantee, the *fuqaha'* felt it necessary to specify that the guarantor can only be bound to perform non-personal obligations, so obligations arising under criminal law, or talion, for example, cannot be guaranteed.

The performance of the obligation in the principal contract must in general be "binding on the principal debtor";[138] however, a guarantee which relates to a principal contract concluded by a madman or a minor is valid.[139] The guarantee can cover a very wide range of property. It can cover principal debts due at a future date as well as those that are immediately due and payable, guarantees of guarantee obligations[140] and partial guarantees are possible, as well as guarantees which expire before the due date of the principal obligation.[141] Future debts, which should, according to general *shari'a* principles of contractual uncertainty, be incapable of being the object of a valid contract, may be validly guaranteed. All-money guarantees are allowed.[142]

It follows from the principle of co-extensiveness that a valid guarantee may not be granted in respect of an invalid principal contract. Therefore a guarantee of a contract to provide wine or pork, or one which is tainted by *riba*, for example, is not valid.[143]

---

[135] Art. 1605 *Majalla*.

[136] Santillana, *Istituzioni*, §274.

[137] Art. 631 *Majalla*. See also Art. 1565 *Majalla*, which provides specifically for the release of the guarantor where the creditor grants the principal debtor a general release from liability.

[138] Art. 631 *Majalla*.

[139] Art. 629 *Majalla*. This is very similar to the French law position: Art. 2012 French Civil Code; see above (section 3.3.8 "The relationship between the contracts").

[140] Art. 626 *Majalla*.

[141] Arts. 652–654.

[142] Art. 630 *Majalla*. This is not allowed by the Shafi'i school: Santillana, *Istituzioni*, §274.

[143] See Santillana, *Istituzioni*, §274. The *Majalla* itself only provides (Art. 631) a list of principal contracts which can, and which cannot, be the subject of valid guarantees, such as (valid) "the price of a thing sold, rent and other proved debts" and (invalid) "property sold before the receipt thereof, because if the property perishes while in possession of the vendor, there is no obligation upon him to deliver the actual property sold".

3.4.8 *The relationship between the contracts*

In the *shari'a* there is no general principle of the lapse of the guarantee upon changes to the principal contract. The release of the debtor releases the guarantor but, if the creditor grants a reduction of liability to the principal debtor, the guarantee liability is therefore presumably reduced, but not destroyed.[144]

3.4.9 *The relationship between the guarantor and the principal debtor: the right to indemnity*

The guarantor has a right similar to the English law right of indemnity if the creditor asked the guarantor to grant the guarantee, but not otherwise (except in the Maliki school, when the guarantor always has this right provided that payment has been made under the guarantee).[145] This right consists of the ability to take possession of the principal debtor's goods. In the *Majalla*, the guarantor is given a general right of recourse by Article 657, which preserves the requirement that the creditor must have requested the guarantor to grant the guarantee.

3.4.10 *The relationship between the guarantor and the creditor: the right of subrogation*

The question of subrogation is not dealt with by the *Majalla*, but the *shari'a* does grant the guarantor who has paid under the guarantee all the rights of the principal creditor.[146]

3.4.11 *Co-guarantors*

If there is more than one guarantor, and they have become guarantors separately, then each guarantor is liable for the entire amount guaranteed (in French law terms, there is no benefit of division), but if they become guarantors at the same time, each is only liable for his share (unless they have cross-guaranteed each other's obligations).[147]

---

[144] The *Majalla* does provide that, where there is a settlement between the creditor and either the guarantor or principal debtor or both, then it is presumed that the guarantee is released. If the guarantor alone is released, then the creditor may claim the settlement amount from the guarantor and the rest from the principal debtor, or, at the creditor's option, the entire debt from the principal debtor: Art. 668 *Majalla*.

[145] Santillana, *Istituzioni*, §278.

[146] *Ibid.*

[147] Art. 647 *Majalla*. The Maliki school does have the benefit of division: Santillana, *Istituzioni*, §276.

3.4.12 Enforcement

As noted above, the creditor could choose as to whether to sue the guarantor or
the principal debtor, and could make a demand on the guarantor as long as an obligation was due under the principal contract.

The guarantor benefits from all defences available to the principal creditor, apart
from those which are purely personal to the principal creditor.

4 GENERAL BACKGROUND TO THE UAE LAW OF GUARANTEES

In the UAE, two codes co-exist, the Civil Code[148] (of principally *shari'a* inspiration)
and the Commercial Code[149] (derived from Western (French) models). This is a
compromise solution to the tension created by the need for the legislator to respect the *shari'a* tradition and at the same time allow business to be conducted along
Western lines.

However, *shari'a* concepts do have to be taken into account even in commercial
matters for three main reasons: (a) the Commercial Code is an adjunct to the Civil
Code, which contains the basic rules, (b) *shari'a* concepts play a significant role in
the interpretation and enforcement of the law, and (c) although the Commercial
Code is the main repository of provisions dealing with solely commercial matters,
many issues of relevance to commerce are dealt with in the Civil Code.

The law of guarantees itself provides an example of the last point, for most of
the relevant law is contained in the Civil Code, but important, albeit brief, provisions are to be found in the Commercial Code.

It is also worth mentioning that the lack of a formal system of precedent might produce different results from cases with similar facts.[150] Although some cases are cited
below, it is as well to remember that the role of precedent is restricted in the UAE.

---

[148] *Qanun al-mu'amilat al-madaniyya* (the Law of Civil Transactions), enacted by Federal Law No.
5 of 1985, UAE Official Gazette, December 1985, came into force on 29 March 1986. See also
amendment enacted by Law No. 1 of 1987. For an English translation, see J. Whelan and M. J.
Hall, *The Civil Code of the United Arab Emirates: The Law of Civil Transactions of the State of the
United Arab Emirates*, London, Graham and Trotman, 1987; for an overview see W.
Ballantyne, "The new Civil Code of the United Arab Emirates: a further reassertion of the
shari'a", *Arab Law Quarterly*, 1986, p. 245. This article will refer to it as "the Civil Code". The
translation used is Whelan and Hall's.

[149] *Qanun al-mu'amilat al-tijariyya* (the Law of Commercial Transactions), enacted by Federal Law
No. 18 of 1993, UAE Official Gazette dated 20 September 1993, came into force on 20
December 1993. For an English translation, see Dawoud S. El-Alami (trans.) *The Law of
Commercial Procedure of the United Arab Emirates*, London, Graham and Trotman, 1994; for an
overview see Neil McNeill, foreword to Al-Alami; Richard Price, "United Arab Emirates", in
vol. 1 of this *Yearbook*, pp. 307–329; and Clifford Chance, "The UAE Commercial Transactions
Law" (1995) 2 *Middle East Commercial Law Review*, p. 41. This article will refer to it as "the
Commercial Code". The translation used is that prepared for Clifford Chance, Dubai.

[150] For more detail, see Foster, "Commercial security over movables in the UAE", pp. 23–24. It
should, however, be noted that a very useful collection of case reports has been published,
namely Richard Price and Essam Al-Tamimi, *United Arab Emirates Court of Cassation Judgments
1989–1997*, The Hague, Kluwer Law International, 1998.

Although there is some difference of opinion on the matter, the better view is that precedent has at most a role as a general indication of what judgments might be handed down. This aspect needs to be considered together with the fact that Dubai and Ras al Khaimah do not form part of the federal court system, which could produce further uncertainty in the form of differences in practice between different emirates.

5 GUARANTEES IN THE UAE

5.1 General characteristics

The banking environment in the UAE has been, and still remains, considerably less sophisticated than in France or England. In this environment the basis of many transactions has been trust and personal knowledge. These factors are reflected in the law of guarantees. It should also be remembered that the UAE is a very young state, which has had little opportunity to develop a legal regime complex enough to cover most eventualities.

The UAE law derives almost entirely from the *shari'a*, with many provisions lifted virtually verbatim from the *Majalla*. Articles 1056–1105 of the Civil Code constitute the main body of rules concerning guarantees.[151] A few provisions, such as Article 1087, which refers to guarantees "imposed by a provision in the law or by an order of the court", and Article 1089 (lapse of the guarantee upon failure to prove in insolvency procedure), derive from French law.[152]

Articles 73 and 74 of the Commercial Code provide for guarantees in commercial transactions.

Before the enactment of the Commercial Code, the common law had considerable relevance in Dubai and Ras Al Khaimah, which had contract laws codified from English principles.[153] Article 1 of Federal Law No. 5 of 1985, which enacted the Civil Code, provided that the Civil Code applied to all civil transactions until a federal commercial law was promulgated; with the promulgation of the Commercial Code, the Dubai Contract Law was repealed, so that the common law is no longer formally of any relevance.[154]

---

[151] All references in this section to articles without identification are references to the UAE Civil Code. The Explanatory Memorandum to the Civil Code (the Explanatory Memorandum to the Law of Civil Transactions, Law No. 5 of 1985, as amended by Law No. 1 of 1987, prepared by the Ministry of Justice) gives the precise provenance of the provisions and the comparable provisions in the Codes of other Arab countries.

[152] It is noteworthy that the Constitution of the UAE, Art. 7 of which provides that the *shari'a* is the main source of law of the UAE, which was formerly provisional, is now permanent.

[153] The laws were translations of the Trucial States Contract Law Regulation, 1961 (Queen's Regulation made under Art. 77 of the Trucial States Order, 1959, No. 1 of 1961), itself taken from the Indian Contract Act. In Sharjah, there was no equivalent statute, but the contract law provisions applied as a matter of practice.

[154] But the common law remains significant in commercial practice, see for example the discussion below on the English-style indemnity (section 5.2 "Basic forms"). There is some debate about whether the Dubai Contract Law has been fully repealed. If it is still applicable to some degree, it could, for example, be used to fill lacunae in other legislation such as the Commercial Code. It is not otherwise relied on by lawyers in Dubai.

Like the *shari'a*, the UAE law is surprisingly "commercial" in the lack of protection it provides for guarantors.

5.2 Basic forms

The basic form is the *kafala*, the guarantee. As in the *shari'a*, two forms of guarantee are provided, the *kafala bil-nafs* (the guarantee of the person) and the *kafala bil-mal* (the guarantee of the property). In case of doubt, Article 1073 provides a presumption that it is a guarantee of the property. A specialized guarantee, the *darak* guarantee giving an indemnity to the purchaser if goods sold are not in fact owned by the vendor, is also provided.[155]

The definition of the guarantee derives from the *shari'a*; it is very similar to that of the *Majalla* and can be found in Article 1056: "Suretyship is the joining of the liability of a person called the surety with the liability of the obligor in the performance of his obligations."

The UAE legislation also follows the *shari'a* in the place accorded to *hawala*, which is very similar to the *Majalla* mechanism.[156] Article 1106 defines *hawala* as "the transfer of a debt and claim from the liability of the transferor to the transferee".[157]

As in the *Majalla*, two types of *hawala* exist, limited and absolute.[158] The limited *hawala* is "one the execution of which is restricted to a (particular) debt by way of trust or guarantee";[159] the absolute *hawala* is one which is not so restricted. By Article 1109 a *hawala* needs the consent of all three parties. Article 1113 sets out a list of requirements for a valid *hawala*, failing which the *hawala* is void.[160] It must be absolute, or in the words of the statute, "completed and dependent on no condition other than an appropriate or customary condition";[161] its completion must be certain ("not be deferred to an unknown future date");[162] "it must be limited in time to a specific time limit";[163] and the obligation transferred "must be a known debt".[164] Article 1113(e) requires that in a limited *hawala*, the transferred property has to be "a debt or specific property which cannot be compounded, and both types of property must be equal in type, amount and description".

Echoing the *Majalla*,[165] Article 1065 provides: "Suretyship conditional on the discharge of the principal obligor is an assignment. An assignment which provides that the assignor should not be discharged is a suretyship."

---

[155] Arts. 1075–1076. This guarantee only takes effect upon judgment that "a third party right subsists in the thing sold and the seller is ordered to return the price": Art. 1076.

[156] Arts. 1106–1132 contain the main rules. The link between *hawala* and *kafala* is emphasized by the placement of these provisions in the section of the Civil Code (Chapter V) entitled "Contracts of personal guarantee".

[157] Art. 1106. "Debt" is the obligation to pay, not the right to receive payment.

[158] Art. 1108.

[159] Art. 1108(2). The Arabic words are *amana* (trust) and *madmuna* (guaranteed).

[160] Art. 1114.

[161] Art. 1113(a).

[162] Art. 1113(b).

[163] Art. 1113(c).

[164] Art. 1113(d).

[165] Arts. 648 and 649 *Majalla*.

The Commercial Code makes statutory provision in Articles 411–419 for demand guarantees, but only with respect to banks, so differentiating the UAE rules from English and French law.[166] These are defined in a non-restrictive way, with three examples being given. These examples are of guarantees given by way of: *aval* (although that word is not itself used) for commercial paper;[167] separate contract of guarantee;[168] and "letter of guarantee" (in other words a demand or bank guarantee), addressed by the bank to the beneficiary, guaranteeing the performance of the obligations of the bank's customer.[169] They may be conditional,[170] they may be assigned if the bank consents,[171] and the bank is expressly subrogated to the rights of its customer.[172]

An intriguing question which remains is the effectiveness of the English habit of including an indemnity in the guarantee document.[173] As seen above, the *shari'a* did have an equivalent to the indemnity, but it was an obscure and minor mechanism, the function of the indemnity in English law being fulfilled in the *shari'a* by *hawala*. There is no mention of *haml* in the UAE codes. If a document drafted along English lines, including an indemnity, were to come before the UAE courts, the judge would have to consider the matter of the indemnity from first principles, since it seems clear that an indemnity would not fall within the definition of *kafala* contained in Article 1056, as the essence of an indemnity is the independent nature of the obligation, which is the opposite of "the joining of the liability of . . . the surety with the liability of the obligor". For the same reason, the provisions of the Civil Code on joint liability are unlikely to be relevant.

Given the absence of directly applicable provisions, one turns to Article 1 of the Civil Code, which provides that, in the absence of provision in the Civil Code, the judge should look to the *shari'a*. As seen above, the institution of indemnity (*haml*) exists in the *shari'a*[174] and, in addition, it may well be that such indemnities would be upheld by UAE courts in any event on the basis of the accepted fundamental principle of *shari'a* freedom of contract, based on the *hadith* which provides that "Moslems are bound by their covenants except those that allow a prohibited matter or prohibit an allowed one".[175] Article 1 goes on to provide that, in the absence of anything in the *shari'a*, the judge may look to custom, so that, even if the argument based on the *shari'a* were to fail, one could argue that, since both international and local banks have adopted internationally recognized guarantee standard forms containing indemnities, such indemnities have become customary mechanisms, the validity of which should therefore be recognized.

---

[166] See above (section 3.2.2 "Basic forms" and section 3.3.2 "Basic forms").
[167] Art. 412(1).
[168] Art. 412(2).
[169] Arts. 412(3) and 414.
[170] Art. 414.
[171] Art. 416.
[172] Art. 419.
[173] One needs to distinguish between two types of "indemnity": the mechanism (a principal liability fulfilling the same basic function as a guarantee) and the right of a guarantor to reimbursement from the principal debtor. The former is the meaning used here, the latter is used in section 5.9 "The relationship between the guarantor and the principal debtor: the right to indemnity".
[174] See section 3.4.2 "Basic forms".
[175] This is Sabah Mahmoud's opinion (advice given to the author in his comments on this article).

For a commercial guarantee, the starting point would also be the Civil Code, but one can also look to the consecration of the freedom of contract contained in Article 2(1) of the Commercial Code, in the hope that the UAE courts would reason in the same way as did the French courts when sanctioning the demand guarantee.[176] Article 2(2) of the Commercial Code, although not of direct relevance because it deals with the situation where there is no specific agreement, does recognize the importance of the role of commercial custom, and the case for validity could be strengthened by this.

5.3 Civil and commercial law

UAE law does distinguish between civil and commercial law, and this is one of the main differences between UAE law and the *shari'a*.[177]

In addition to the provisions dealing specifically with guarantees, Article 72 deals with a guarantee-like liability, by stating that where two people assume liability for a commercial debt,[178] they are jointly liable[179] unless the law provides, or they agree otherwise.

Article 73 of the Commercial Code lays down the circumstances in which a guarantee is to be commercial. A guarantee is commercial in three situations:

(a)   if it is granted in respect of a debt which is commercial *vis-à-vis* the principal debtor. The article provides for two exceptions, one is an exception for specific provision to the contrary by law, the other allows contracting out, so that the parties may agree that such a guarantee is civil;

(b)   where the parties agree that the guarantee is to be commercial; or

(c)   the guarantor has the status of a merchant[180] and has an interest in guaranteeing the debt.

In the same way in which the UAE legislature has simplified other areas of the civil/commercial distinction, Article 73, although deriving from the French experience, does away with much of the complexity associated with French law on this subject.[181] The basic French rule, which has caused much litigation and case law because of its vagueness, is amended and relegated to a sweep-up provision, while the fundamental rule simply links the nature of the guarantee to the nature of the principal debt (a bank loan, as defined by Article 409 of the Commercial Code is by Article 410 of the Commercial Code deemed to be a commercial transaction

---

[176] See above section 3.3.2 "Basic forms".

[177] The difficult situation of the application of the Civil Code to commercial transactions before the coming into force of the Commercial Code had considerable repercussions on the law of guarantees, on which see Isam Ghanem, "The impact of the UAE Civil Code on commercial litigation", *Arab Law Quarterly*, 1990, p. 143.

[178] Commercial debt is not specifically defined, but it seems reasonable to conclude that it denotes an obligation to pay money incurred in the course of commercial business, as that term is defined by Arts. 4 and 5 Commercial Code.

[179] The Arabic word is a derivative of *daman*.

[180] Defined in Arts. 11–25 Commercial Code.

[181] See above (section 3.3.3 "Civil and commercial law").

whatever the capacity of the borrower or the purpose of the loan, therefore all guarantees of bank loans as defined by Article 409 of the Commercial Code are commercial). At the same time, Article 73 allows the parties the contractual freedom to determine that a guarantee is to be commercial if they so wish.

The commercial status of a guarantee results in its being governed by the general rules applicable to commercial transactions, which are more liberal than those applicable to civil transactions, and in the specific consequences of joint liability set out in Articles 72 and 74.[182] As noted below, it has been held by the Court of Cassation that Article 1092 (discharge of the guarantee if the principal debt is a claim is not made in respect of the principal debt within six months of the due date) does not apply to commercial guarantees, which includes all guarantees of bank lending.[183]

General rules applicable to commercial transactions include the principles of freedom of contract and the application of commercial customs and practices contained in Article 2 of the Commercial Code, the ten-year prescription period of Article 95, the flexible means of proof in Article 94, the prohibition on any respite for payment to a debtor except with the creditor's consent or in exceptional circumstances laid down in Article 86, the ability to charge interest granted by Article 76 and the obligation to pay interest on late payment set out in Article 88,[184] as well as other general consequences contained in Articles 72–95 and the possibility of contracting out of Civil Code rules, so long as such contracting-out does not infringe public policy.

Article 74 introduces by statute the French acknowledgement of commercial custom by providing that the guarantor in a commercial guarantee is jointly liable with the debtor, making it a French-style joint-debt guarantee.[185] This has somewhat less significance than in French law, since there is no benefit of discussion or division to dispose of, but it does mean that, where the principal contract is invalid for some reason which affects only the principal debtor, but not the guarantor as joint debtor, it is quite clear that the guarantee is not affected by such invalidity.

5.4 Validity and proof

There are no special requirements as to the form of a guarantee, the Civil Code simply provides that "suretyship may arise through use of that word, or words indicating a guarantee",[186] and, as in the *shari'a*, the guarantee may be constituted by the mere offer of the guarantor,[187] who must have the capacity to make gifts.[188] An in-

---

[182] The commercial rules are mainly derived from French law.
[183] Section 5.7 "Protection of the dependent and the imprudent".
[184] See also Arts. 89–91 Commercial Code.
[185] It also provides a rule relating to the liability of co-guarantors, discussed below (section 5.11 "Co-guarantors").
[186] Art. 1057(1).
[187] Art. 621 *Majalla* and Art. 1057(2) Civil Code.
[188] Art. 1058. Various types of guarantee are specifically prohibited or allowed by Arts. 1062–1064.

terdicted bankrupt is unable to make dispositions over "his existing and future property", which would seem to preclude the grant of guarantees by such a person.[189] A guarantee granted in respect of a person suffering from a terminal illness is not valid if the debt of the principal debtor is greater than the amount of his property.[190]

The guarantee may be conditional or unconditional, but an option to make it conditional renders the guarantee void.[191]

5.5 The gratuitous nature of the guarantee

Article 1098 adopts the *shari'a* position that the guarantee must be gratuitous; if it is not, it is invalid.[192] This will not cause problems in most cases, as guarantees are usually gratuitous. However, it may be that a guarantor might wish to charge a fee in a commercial context. One could argue that the freedom of contract granted in Article 2 of the Commercial Code operates to override Article 1098 for commercial guarantees (but query whether one can validly argue that this applies to the unlikely case of a civil guarantee of a commercial debt) as Article 2 of the Commercial Code contains an exception to this freedom where an overriding *commercial* text exists, and Article 1098 is not a commercial provision.[193] The decisive point would therefore be whether the court considered Article 1098 to contain a rule of public policy, out of which contracting is not permitted.

In provisions which are somewhat reminiscent of section 238 of the (English) Companies Act 1985 (transactions at an undervalue), a debtor may not make dispositions detrimental to his creditors. Article 396 provides that if the sum of the debtor's obligations "exceed or are equal to the assets" of the obligor, then he may not make any gift he is not bound to make or which custom does not dictate that he must, and an obligee may ask for an order declaring that such disposition is ineffective as against him. There is a time limit of three years from the date on which the obligee learnt of the relevant disposition, and an absolute time limit of fifteen years from the date of the relevant disposition.[194]

As far as the power of companies to enter into guarantees is concerned, the Commercial Companies Law deals with the question of the power of the management to bind the company in each of the types of company allowed by that law.[195] Various types of "company" (Arabic *sharika*) exist in the UAE, following the pattern of French law in which *société* denotes what English law regards as com-

---

[189] Art. 406.

[190] Art. 1064.

[191] Art. 1060 and 1059.

[192] But Art. 1096 gives the guarantor a right of recourse against the principal obligor for expenses incurred by the guarantor in carrying out obligations under the guarantee.

[193] It is of some interest that a commercial guarantee, like all other commercial transactions, is presumed to have been made for consideration, unless the contrary is proved: Art. 75 of the Commercial Code. This adds weight to the argument for commercial guarantees being valid if granted against consideration.

[194] Art. 400.

[195] The Commercial Companies Law is Federal Law No. 8 of 1984, as amended. For a translation, see Mahmoud, *UAE Company Law*, pp. 177–238; for the different types of companies and their characteristics, see Mahmoud, *ibid.*, Part 1 ("Classification of companies").

panies and partnerships. This discussion only deals with the equivalent of the French SA, the joint stock company, and the equivalent of the French SARL, the limited liability company, which is the most popular type of company used by entities investing in the UAE.

Article 103 of the Commercial Companies Law provides that, in the case of joint stock companies, "the board of directors shall assume all the necessary authority to perform the business required in the company objects", with the exception of certain excluded matters of considerable importance to the company, such as the sale of the company's real estate and long-term loan agreements (over three years). Article 104 equates the chairman with the board. It is clearly important then to ascertain that the company objects contain a reference to the grant of guarantees, or to obtain the approval of the general assembly, contemplated by Article 103. The authority of mere managers is questionable in this regard.[196]

Article 237 of the Commercial Companies Law gives the manager of the limited liability company "full authority to manage", but only if no limitations are expressed in the memorandum.[197] His actions bind the company, but only if "they are corroborated by stating the capacity for his actions".

It should be noted generally that, although the law as just described does not seem to be that different from other jurisdictions in its letter, the whole question of the authority of officers to bind the company is a rather difficult one in UAE law, where a high degree of formality is often required, both as a matter of business practice and the application of the law, and where the directors of the company run a high risk of being found personally liable. Guarantees are not registrable.

5.6 The extent of the guarantee

The Civil Code does not deal specifically with the main questions relating to the extent of the guarantee, namely the guarantee of principal obligations which are uncertain, such as future debts and all money obligations, and principal obligations contrary to (Islamic) public policy, including *riba* debts. All that is stated is that "the principal debtor must be indebted to the obligee in respect of a debt or property or a known person".[198]

It is specifically provided that the guarantee shall "cover the incidentals of the debt and costs of claiming unless the contrary has been agreed".[199]

There seems to be no problem in principle with the principal debt being a revolving amount rather than a fixed sum, but a case before the Dubai Court of Cassation showed the importance of proper wording, which also applies to any attempt to limit the amount of the guarantee.[200] Despite some difficulties in interpreting the statutory provisions regarding bank loans (defined by Art. 409 of the

---

[196] See Mahmoud, *ibid.*, pp. 51–52.
[197] Limited liability companies have partners (the equivalent to shareholders) and managers (the equivalent to directors).
[298] Art. 1061.
[199] Art. 1067.
[200] Dubai Court of Cassation Case No. 87/97, reported in *Yearbook of Islamic and Middle Eastern Law*, vol. 4 (1997–1998), pp. 352–353.

Commercial Code), the court's judgment made it clear that a guarantee could cover revolving facilities or a fixed-sum loan, even if such loans did not fall within the Article 409 definition, but the guarantee had to provide for this specifically. In this case, the court found that the intention was to guarantee a revolving amount limited to a specific sum, not a higher amount which was agreed between the creditor and the principal debtor at a later date. Significantly, the court held that this later agreement was a new principal contract which was not covered by the guarantee.[201]

5.7 Protection of the dependent and the imprudent

The validity requirements provide some protection. Article 1092 provides some protection by stipulating a maximum period of six months for the creditor to claim the principal debt. If this is not done within this period, the guarantee is deemed to have been discharged.[202] However, the parties may contract out of this provision,[203] and the Court of Cassation has held that it does not apply to commercial transactions, including, specifically, commercial guarantees.[204]

Unlike the *shari'a*, UAE law does not make any special provision for female guarantors.

In a rare provision of French inspiration, Article 1089 provides that the creditor "must prove for his debt in the bankruptcy otherwise his right of recourse shall lapse to the extent of the loss sustained by his not having so done". Unlike French law, it is not specifically provided that contracting-out is forbidden.

5.8 The relationship between the contracts

The general rules for termination of the guarantee, contained in Article 1099, reveal much of the relationship between the guarantee and the principal contract. The guarantee is terminated, *inter alia*, "upon the satisfaction of the principal obligation", when "the contract in which the duty was enjoined on the principal obligor termi-

---

[201] Purely as a matter of logic, it is perfectly possible to justify this conclusion by reference to the *shari'a* idea of the guarantee as an accessory contract, but it may well be that there is an echo here of the English notion of the lapse of the guarantee upon a change in the principal contract, a legacy of the Dubai Contract Law 1971, now repealed.

[202] See Dubai Court of Cassation Case No. 86/95, 13 November 1995, reported in Price and Al-Tamimi, *United Arab Emirates Court of Cassation Judgments*, p. 193.

[203] Court of Cassation Case No. 65/97, 13 April 1997, reported in the *Yearbook of Islamic and Middle Eastern Law*, vol. 4 (1997–1998), pp. 353–354 and in Price and Al-Tamimi, *United Arab Emirates Court of Cassation Judgments*, p. 199.

[204] Court of Cassation Case No. 140/18, 19 November 1996, reported in Price and Al-Tamimi, *United Arab Emirates Court of Cassation Judgments*, p.167. The Dubai Court of Cassation has held that, where the principal debt is a loan which has no specified time period for payment, Art. 1092 does not apply even if the creditor has not made a demand upon the principal debtor within six months: Dubai Court of Cassation Case No. 356/97, reported in Price and Al-Tamimi, *ibid.*, p. 63. This case is somewhat curious, since the arguments of the parties as described in the case report do not reflect judgments of both the Federal Court of Cassation and the Dubai Court of Cassation cited above in which it was decided that Art. 1092 does not apply to commercial guarantees.

nates"; and "upon the release of the surety debtor from the guarantee or of the principal obligor from the debt". If the whole or any part of the principal obligation is assigned, then the guarantor is released *pro tanto* from the guarantee obligation.[205]

5.9 The relationship between the guarantor and the principal debtor: the right to indemnity

Article 1096 grants the guarantor a right to indemnity from the principal debtor in the following terms: "The surety has the right of recourse against the principal obligor with regard to what he has paid in order to fulfil the requirements of the guarantee".

Article 1097 deals with the case of joint principal debtors, giving the guarantor the right to proceed against any of them. The mark of the *shari'a* is clear in Article 1090(1), which provides: "The surety shall not have any right of recourse against the principal debtor in respect of any obligation which he has discharged on his behalf unless the suretyship arose at the request or with the consent of the principal obligor, and the surety has discharged the obligation."

The derivation from the *shari'a* and the similarity to the "school" (i.e. over-theoretical and largely irrelevant) discussions on this subject in French doctrine[206] are the most interesting points to be made here, since it would only be in the rarest of situations that a guarantee would be granted without the consent of the principal creditor.

There seems to be no difference between a civil and a commercial guarantee here, unless the parties can contract out of this provision pursuant to Article 2 of the Commercial Code.

5.10 The relationship between the guarantor and the creditor: the right of subrogation

The equivalent to the English right of subrogation is given (somewhat obliquely, because it follows the *shari'a*) by Article 1091, which, rather than providing that the guarantor stands in the shoes of the creditor upon payment under the guarantee, requires the principal debtor to give to the guarantor all papers in order for the guarantor "to exercise his right of recourse against the principal obligor"; and, if the principal debtor enjoys the benefit of real security, the principal debtor must either hand it over (if the property is a chattel) or transfer his rights (if the property is real estate).

---

[205] Art. 1105(1).
[206] Art. 2014 French Civil Code; see Simler and Delebecque, *Droit civil. Les sûretés*, §§53 and 143.

5.11 Co-guarantors

The provisions as to the liability of co-guarantors to the creditor are the same as in the *Majalla*. The basic rule is that, where there are co-guarantors, their liability is joint and several, so the creditor may proceed against any one for the whole debt.[207]

The right of contribution among co-guarantors is provided for in Article 1086.

Co-guarantors of a commercial debt are jointly liable unless the law provides, or they agree, otherwise.[208] This situation is to be distinguished from that of a commercial guarantee (it is possible, pursuant to Article 73 of the Commercial Code, to have a civil guarantee of a commercial debt), in which case Article 74 provides that commercial guarantors are jointly liable with each other. There is no provision for an exception provided by law, nor for contracting out, which is specifically mentioned in the other two articles dealing with guarantees. On the other hand, freedom of contract in commercial matters is enshrined in Article 2 of the Commercial Code, making it difficult to reach any definitive conclusion as to whether contracting out of this provision is possible, the essential question being whether such contracting-out would be held to be against public policy.

5.12 Enforcement

Article 1077 states that the guarantor "must discharge his obligation when the time falls due", and it is expressly provided that, in the case of a conditional obligation, the time of discharge of the obligation is the time when the condition is fulfilled. If either the principal debtor or the guarantor dies, the obligation is payable out of the deceased person's estate.[209] Specific provision is made in Article 1079 for the discharge of the guarantee obligation to be made out of property of the principal debtor deposited with the guarantor, so long as the creditor agrees.

As in the *Majalla*, there is no benefit of discussion. This is clearly provided for by Article 1078(1), which states: "The obligee may claim against the principal obligor or the surety, or may claim against them both."

Although not specifically allowed by the Civil Code, it is possible to contract out of this provision. This conclusion derives from general principles of freedom of contract in the absence of express provision to the contrary, and is reinforced by Article 1082, which mentions the possibility of the guarantor making a "condition that recourse should be had against the principal obligor first".[210] In the usual situation of a bank guarantee, of course, this would be highly unlikely.

---

[207] Art. 1085. There is an exception where they have all become guarantors under one contract in the absence of an express provision to this effect (Art. 1085), in which case each guarantor is only liable for that guarantor's share of the liability. Guarantors under guarantees imposed by law or by court order are jointly liable (Art. 1087).

[208] Art. 72 Commercial Code.

[209] Art. 1084.

[210] Art. 1083 provides specifically that a sub-guarantor of the guarantee obligation may "make it a condition that the obligee should have recourse against the other surety first".

If this is the case, Article 1082 provides that a debt secured by a real security before the grant of the guarantee shall be satisfied first out of the real security, and only after realization of this security by execution against the property of the guarantor.

Article 1094 imposes an obligation of notification upon the principal debtor if he pays the debt before the guarantor pays it, or "if he learns of any reason preventing the obligee from making a claim". If the principal debtor fails so to notify the guarantor, then the guarantor may choose to pursue the creditor or the principal debtor.

6 CONCLUSION

6.1 Comparative analysis

The most striking general conclusion which appears from a comparative study of the law of traditional guarantees in the jurisdictions studied is their similarity, both on the fundamental level of the basic concepts and on the degree of similarity of result even where the rules seem quite different.

On the more specific level of the French and English regimes, no simple conclusion can be reached.

As regards the general principles and the basic mechanisms, starting from a point of reasonable agreement on the basic characteristics of guarantees, but with some differences, French law has (rather surprisingly, given the fairly strong contrast between English and French law in the area of real security)[211] followed a reasonably similar path to that taken by, and arrived at a position which is quite similar to that of, English law.[212] Such differences as the quirks of the English general law, like the rules relating to the lapse of the guarantee on variation of the principal contract, or the benefits of division and discussion in French law, have in both jurisdictions been rendered all but irrelevant by the use of standard forms. In French law the existence of special rules pertaining to commercial contracts contributes to the similarity (in most cases) between the two jurisdictions. There are, of course, numerous differences of detail.

Another similarity is the parallel development of the distinction between lay and commercially experienced guarantors, with a severe regime being applied to the commercially experienced guarantor, and a protective regime being applied to the lay person in both jurisdictions, with an increase in litigation and a more protective attitude of the courts in recent years. This is of particular interest given the existence in French law of the formal divide between civil and commercial matters, which has shown itself to be less than perfect in this context, leading to the establishment of the new, English-style, distinction.[213]

---

[211] See Foster, "Commercial security over movables in the UAE", at pp. 11–18 and 60.

[212] With some important differences, such as the absence of a doctrine of undue influence in French law.

[213] This similarity is somewhat masked by the difference in style between the two jurisdictions: learned writing in England tends to ignore the distinction, whereas it is openly discussed in the French doctrinal works.

This conclusion must be qualified, however, since substantial differences do exist between the English and French regimes as far as the protection of the guarantor is concerned. Apart from the (admittedly important) doctrine of undue influence where lay guarantors are concerned, English creditors have little to concern them if they have well-drafted documentation (and, in the case of lay guarantors, have strictly followed the procedures necessary to enable them to escape from the consequences of the doctrine of undue influence), which renders the protection enjoyed by the guarantor merely theoretical.[214]

French law is very similar in many ways to English law in the means which it uses to circumvent the protection theoretically available to the creditor and, as just mentioned, it has (after a period considered to be of excessive protection for the guarantor) applied the protective regime to lay guarantors only. However, more technical pitfalls remain than in England where lay guarantors are concerned. The use of the vices of consent, the good faith requirement, the interpretation of Article 1326 of the Civil Code on manuscript acknowledgements, the effect of the "Madelin" Law on guarantees given in respect of entrepreneurs, the necessity to prove in the insolvency proceedings of the principal debtor, the need to exercise particular care in ensuring the validity of any other security held, together with the discretionary two year maximum grace period for payment by any debtor, including guarantors[215] and, where the guarantor is insolvent, the restrictive effect of the insolvency legislation,[216] all add up to a regime which is still substantially more onerous in practice for banks in France than in England.[217] A further qualification must be added to this conclusion – it relates only to the substantive law, not to the law as applied. The English courts have restricted their protective activities to the extension of the doctrine of undue influence/unconscionability to lay guarantors, whereas the French courts have been more prepared to be creative in the interests of the lay guarantor, using the broad range of techniques mentioned above to attempt to protect lay guarantors, leading to a great amount of litigation and a great increase in the use of alternative techniques.[218]

As regards the *sharīʿa*/UAE and the Western regimes, the similarity is remarkable, with the *sharīʿa* traditional guarantee rules bearing an even greater resemblance to

---

[214] A few exceptions remain, such as the doctrine of unconscionability applied in *Credit Lyonnais Bank Nederland NV v. Burch* [1997] 1 All ER 144, CA, but generally the recent tendency is for the lay guarantor to be less protected: *Royal Bank of Scotland v. Etridge (No. 2)* [1998] 4 All ER 70, CA.

[215] Art. 1244-1. The judge must take into account the situation of the debtor and the needs of the creditor.

[216] Law of 25 January 1985, as amended by Law of 19 of January 1994; see generally Legeais, *Sûretés et garanties du crédit*, §§14–16.

[217] In addition to the pitfalls referred to above, which are relevant during the pre-formation and formation period, banks and other financial institutions are, during the life of the guarantee, obliged to inform the guarantor of a principal debt owed to an enterprise of the amount of the total principal sum outstanding once a year. The sanction for non-compliance is the loss of interest between the last notification and the next. See Law of 1 March 1984; Simler and Delebecque, *Droit civil. Les sûretés*, §114; see also the "Neiertz" Law of 31 December 1989.

[218] See the concern of French bankers in this regard, as shown by Jean-Michel Calendini, "Le point de vue du banquier sur le cautionnement", Juris-classeur périodique, *La semaine juridique, Cahiers de droit de l'entreprise*, Supplément 2, 1992, p. 1.

those of English law even than to those of French law (and surprising by being considerably less sympathetic to the guarantor than one might expect).

How does one explain this? Two possibilities exist: parallel evolution and borrowing/mutual influence.[219] Parallel evolution should certainly not be discounted, as the legal problems produced by the guarantee situation are essentially the same in all the societies whose law has been considered, and the number of different solutions limited. The way in which undue influence and *dol* have developed in similar ways without, presumably, much or any interaction between the two legal systems, certainly provides evidence for parallel evolution.[220] It is unlikely, however, that parallel evolution is the whole story. If one compares the four systems under study to, for example, Roman law,[221] although the fundamental issues remain the same, the diversity of the Roman mechanisms presents a strikingly different picture to that obtaining in the four systems examined herein. We need, then, to look at the possibility of borrowing between the systems. Unfortunately, the paucity of evidence and scholarly studies constitutes a problem with the history of commercial law, so what follows is necessarily speculative and more in the nature of ideas for further research than definitive answers.[222]

To begin with, it seems likely that at least some of the *shari'a* law was borrowed from other sources. As seen above, some of Maliki law is clearly influenced by Roman law.[223] Moving slightly beyond traditional guarantees, *hawala* and *délégation* look very much like each other, especially when one compares them to the English way of doing things, with the similarity extending to the division into two types with similar names,[224] and this may well be as a result of the borrowing by the *shari'a* of the mechanism of *delegatio* from Roman law.[225]

---

[219] The concept of "borrowing" is not intended in a crude sense, but is meant to include direct and indirect borrowings, borrowings in both directions and mutual influence. It may be that the *shari'a* was influenced to some degree by Roman law: the majority Maliki view on the benefit of discussion, for example, is remarkably similar to Roman law.

[220] The way in which all the legal systems have devised alternative mechanisms in order to circumvent the problems associated with the link between the guarantee and the principal contract, resulting in the nullity of the guarantee where the principal contract is avoided, may also be evidence for parallel evolution.

[221] Donnellan, "Historical: the Roman law".

[222] William H. Loyd, "The surety" (1917) 66 *University of Pennsylvania Law Review* 40 states at p. 55 that "[n]o part of the history of English law is more obscure than that connected with the Law Merchant".

On the historical aspects, see, for example, Ray, "The medieval Islamic system of credit and banking" (*shari'a*); O'Donovan and Phillips, *The Modern Contract of Guarantee*, 3–7 (England); Pollock and Maitland, *The History of English Law*, pp. 185, 190–192, 210–211, 224–225 (England); Loyd, "The surety", especially pp. 40–43 (general), 43– 46 (Rome) and 46–55 (England); Holdsworth, *A History of English Law*, vol. II, pp. 83–84, vol. III pp. 414–416 and vol. V, p. 112 (England); Willis D. Morgan, "The history and economics of suretyship", (1927) 12 *Cornell Law Quarterly* 153 (England); Philip K. Jones, "Roman law bases of suretyship in some modern civil law codes" (1977) 52 *Tulane Law Review* 129 (some civil law codes, including the French).

[223] See section 3.4.6 "Protection of the dependent and the imprudent".

[224] As seen above (section 3.3.2 "Basic forms" and section 3.4.2 "Basic forms"), the distinction between the types is not the same, but this does not reduce the significance of the same categorization being used.

[225] On the Roman law see Henry John Roby, *Roman Private Law in the Times of Cicero and the Antonines*, vol. II, Cambridge University Press, 1902, pp. 42–45.

Another possible source of the *shari'a* law is Jewish law and practice. Some scholars have argued that Jewish law "manifestly did contribute to the formation of the *shari'a*".[226] A further possibility is that not only did some form of borrowing between Jewish and Islamic law of guarantees take place in the early period of Islamic law, but that borrowing by the *lex mercatoria* took place from both the *shari'a* and Jewish law, facilitated by some similarities between them.

Second, it is quite probable that (re?-)borrowing took place by Europeans from the *shari'a* into the *lex mercatoria*.[227] The Arabs and the Italian city-states were in constant commercial contact for hundreds of years and there is linguistic evidence of the borrowing by Europeans of *hawala* (as *aval*) and *mukhatara* (as *mohatra*) as well as "irrefutable evidence of a vast and profound migration of philosophical, medical, astrological, and scientific knowledge" which leads Ray to consider it "almost certain that significant aspects of medieval Islamic finance were transmitted to medieval Europe".[228] Various aspects of the systems have an uncanny resemblance to each other, such as the simplicity of the basic guarantee mechanisms and their operation, the ease with which both the *shari'a* and the French system accept the guarantee of future debts, and the similarity between the concepts of *hawala* and *délégation* and their use as substitute mechanisms for guarantees. This similarity extends to such points as the sub-division of both mechanisms into two categories and the consideration in French doctrine and case law of whether a *délégation* is possible where the assignee of the obligation is not the creditor of the assignee, which resembles the situation in the *shari'a* where the assignment of the right to receive payment is only admitted in those circumstances (the conclusion reached is the opposite in the two systems, but this does not affect the resemblance between the thought processes).[229] If one compares the French and *shari'a* positions with the quite basic Roman law position, one is led to conclude that *délégation* did not simply evolve naturally from Roman law *delegatio*, but was transformed by the *shari'a* before being borrowed back via the *lex mercatoria*.

---

[226] Patricia Crone, *Roman, Provincial and Islamic Law: The Origins of the Islamic Patronate*, Cambridge University Press, pp. 2–3. See Chapter 1 ("The state of the field") of this work for a general discussion of the extent to which the *shari'a* derived from influences external to Islam. See also Ray, "The medieval Islamic system of credit and banking" for a discussion of the historical background of the commercial aspects of Islamic law; Yaakov Meron, "Points de contact des droits juif et musulman", (1983–1984) 60 *Studia Islamica* p. 83, especially pp. 88–93 for a consideration of the *kafala*; and Gideon Libson, "Sefer Ha'arevuth ('Book of Surety') of Rav Shmuel Ben Hofni Gaon and its relationship to Islamic law" (1991) 73 *Studia Islamica* p. 5.

[227] On the law merchant, see Leon E. Trakman, *The Law Merchant: The Evolution of Commercial Law*, Fred B. Rothman, 1983, Chapter 1 ("The medieval law merchant") and Chapter 2 ("The modern lex mercatoria").

[228] Ray, "The medieval Islamic system of credit and banking", p. 80. It may be that the name of the bill of exchange (*lettre de change* in modern French, *lettera di cambio* in medieval, *cambiale* in modern, Italian, both *cambio* and *cambiale* being related to the word for "change": see Francesco Galgano (ed.), *Dizionario Enciclopedico del Diritto*, CEDAM, 1996) is also an indication of borrowing. The name is usually explained by the use of the mechanism to make payments across currencies, but it may be that this is a popular etymology, the real source being a translation of the word *hawala*, which derives from the root *hwl*, meaning change.

[229] Simler and Delebecque, *Droit civil. Les sûretés*, §255.

The *lex mercatoria*, which derived from the law and practice of the Italian city-states, was a significant factor in the development of commercial law both of France and England.

Germanic customary law had a form of guarantee mechanism, known in England as *frithborh* (the guarantor was the *borh*) or frankpledge, but this was a form of legalised hostage-taking.[230] The story told in the literature is that this body-pledge slowly evolved into the modern law, with no mention being made of the possibility of influence external to Western law.

In France this is supposed to have taken place by the adoption of Roman law as the base of the modern law, but with the core mechanisms simplified by the codification process (in the broad sense of that term, including the preceding work of jurists such as Pothier).[231] This seems rather unlikely, since the codification process clarified and derived general principles rather than making changes to basic mechanisms. The fact that *délégation* was illogically preserved along with *novation* is indicative of this tendency.

Another possibility is that the simplification derived from the Germanic law. The problem with this is that in Germanic law, although the mechanism was simple, the rule was that the guarantor entirely took the place of the principal debtor, who was freed from liability, a solution completely different from that in fact adopted. An equally, if not more, plausible explanation is that it came from the *lex mercatoria*.

In England the development of the law of guarantee is acknowledged to have been influenced by the *lex mercatoria*, as well as by the actions of the courts: guarantees were known in the Middle Ages and there are records of actions concerning them in the rolls of the fair courts,[232] which enforced the *lex mercatoria*.[233] In the courts of law, guarantees and indemnities were not enforceable at law until the reign of Henry VIII and so it was the court of Chancery, which was influenced to some extent by civil law doctrine, which played a major role in devising the basic rules.[234] The *lex mercatoria* was received into the common law in the sev-

---

[230] See O'Donovan and Phillips, *The Modern Contract of Guarantee*, pp. 4–7 and above (section 2 "Terminology and scope").

[231] Philip K. Jones, "Roman law bases of suretyship in some modern civil codes", (1977) 52 *Tulane Law Review*, p. 129 maintains (at p. 154) that "earlier codes [this includes the French Civil Code] merely systematized and simplified the applicable Roman common law of *fideiussio* and *mandatum credendae pecuniae*"; on a similar view in Roman–Dutch law, see Donnellan, "Historical: the Roman law" at p. 21, who attributes the simplification of the Roman mechanisms into one as the work of Roman–Dutch law, the implication being that this was achieved without any outside influence. Loyd, "The surety" states: "the growth of European law was partly through the natural development of native institutions to meet new conditions, and partly through the absorption of Roman law owing to its intrinsic merits and through the overpowering influence of Latin culture upon the mediaeval mind" (at p. 46).

[232] Holdsworth, *A History of English Law*, p. 112.

[233] See Gerard Malynes, *Consuetudo, Vel, Lex Mercatoria: or, the Ancient Law-merchant*, London, 1685 (reprint 1981, Professional Books Limited), Chapter X ("Of suretiship and merchants promises") (sic), where the author discusses the question of guarantees in terms of civil law, common law and custom of merchants, and recounts a case where the custom of merchants was too diverse, so the civil law determined the matter.

[234] See Loyd, "Surety" at p. 54. Even after the courts of law enforced guarantees, the "continuing relations between the three parties to the contract gave rise to equities arising out of their conduct which only the court of Chancery could enforce". Holdsworth, *A History of English Law*, p. 298.

enteenth and eighteenth centuries, and among the bodies which played a significant role in the reception process were the civil law court of Admiralty and, to a
lesser extent, the court of Chancery.[235]

It is likely, therefore, that the basic mechanism and some other characteristics of
both English and French law owe much to the *lex mercatoria*/civil law and, more dis-
tantly, but to some degree at least, through the intermediary of the *lex mercatoria*/civil
law, to the *shari'a*, which was itself to some degree influenced by Roman law and
Jewish law.

6.2 The UAE regime and legal transplants

Despite the fact that the very idea of codification which gave rise to the *Majalla* is
itself a foreign import from (continental) Europe, it is inappropriate to talk in
terms of "transplants" in the ususal sense of that word with regard to the UAE regime
of traditional guarantees, as it is derived from the *shari'a* through the medium of
the *Majalla*.[236] A more pertinent point is whether the *shari'a* as adopted by the UAE
legislator provides a reasonable set of rules for commercial transactions. Some scholars maintain that the *shari'a* is a "work of pure scholarship"[237] and was never really
applied as such; others argue that the evidence, such as it is, points, in commercial
law at least, to a reasonable correlation of the academic with the practical.[238] To make
an amalgam of the work of scholars taking the latter view, custom, specifically commercial custom, was a source, although formally unacknowledged, of the *shari'a*;[239]

---

[235] Holdsworth, *A History of English Law*, pp. 129–154 ("The reception of foreign doctrines of
commercial and maritime law"), see especially p. 135 *et seq.* on the roles of the various courts
and institutions in the reception.

[236] However, it should be noted that this depends on a restrictive interpretation of the words
"transplant" and "reception". On the role of the *Majalla* in the modern legislation, see
Ballantyne, "The new Civil Code of the United Arab Emirates" at pp. 245–246; on the
reception of foreign law into Islamic countries, see Muhammed Farouq Al-Nabhan, "The
learned academy of Islamic jurisprudence", *Arab Law Quarterly* (1985–1986) p. 389. The
other types of guarantee (to be found in the Commercial Code) are of course imports.

[237] Crone, *Roman, Provincial and Islamic Law,* p. 18.

[238] Generally, see A. L. Udovitch, "The 'Law Merchant' of the medieval Islamic world", in G. E.
von Grunebaum (ed.), *Logic in Classical Islamic Culture*, Wiesbaden, 1970, p. 113: a summary of
the arguments is set out at pp. 113–115 and Professor Udovitch states (at p. 128) that "there is
an almost one-to-one relationship between the importance of problems as reflected in the
Geniza papers, and the amount of space and attention they receive in the law books"; *hawala* is
specifically mentioned in A. L. Udovitch, "Reflections on the institutions of credits and
banking in the medieval Near East", *Studia Islamica*, 41 (1975), p. 5; see also A. L. Udovitch,
"Theory and practice of Islamic law: some evidence from the Geniza", (1970–1971) 32 *Studia
Islamica*, p. 289, at pp. 290–291, who maintains that "Hanafi commercial law, especially that
portion of it dealing with institutions of commercial association, had a very close relationship
to actual practice" (p. 290). It is certainly the case in the UAE that the *shari'a* has a practical
impact on commercial matters, given its importance as a source of law, especially as reinforced
by the now permanent Constitution.

[239] The "back door" through which custom slipped is said to be *istihsan*; see Gideon Libson, "On
the development of custom as a source of law in Islamic law", (1997) 4 *Islamic Law and Society*
132. The relevant *Majalla* article is Art. 45. See also Udovitch, "The 'Law Merchant'" at
121–126.

this custom was sanctified by the practice of the courts, another formally unacknowledged source of the *shari'a*;[240] and in this picture, *hiyal* "stratagems" played an important role in making the law more useful for merchants.[241]

In areas where the letter of the *shari'a* is clearly impractical, the controversies just outlined could be of great importance, since, if the first view is correct, a kind of reception might occur, constituted by the application as positive law of a purely theoretically conceived system, and this could cause considerable practical problems. However, in the area of guarantees, it is submitted that, although they do need to be borne in mind, these controversies do not need to be considered in depth, for the *shari'a* law of guarantees, whatever its origin, is prima facie a practical regime.

The precise way in which the UAE system will work remains, however, to be seen, especially if it continues to be used to a significant degree by Western (mainly common law trained) lawyers, most of whom are either, at worst, unfamiliar with the *shari'a* background to the law, or, at best, have some knowledge of the *shari'a*, but still tend to think along English law lines and use English law documents. The resulting interaction between two different mentalities and legal traditions will provide intriguing material for further comparative study.

---

[240] Coulson, "Muslim custom and case law".
[241] On *hiyal* generally see Robert Brunschvig, "Fiction légale dans l'Islam médiéval" (1970–1971) 32 *Studia Islamica*, 41.

Kuwaiti, Jordanian and Omani Securities Markets: a Comparative Study

Lu'ayy Minwer Al-Rimawi*

1 INTRODUCTION

A wider comparative study of Arab securities regulation is still needed to address many issues at doctrinal, legal and epistemological levels, as the question of financial regulation in the Arab world poses both "functionalist" and "ideologist" challenges. Yet it is hoped to see a methodological approach of analysis that contrasts Arab securities regulation (in a collective and divisible sense) with British and European minimum standards, as enshrined in many European directives. Moreover, such analysis would also benefit from visiting international standards as agreed in multilateral treaties. This examination is also justified on the grounds that, given their high desire to attract foreign investors, Arab countries are keen to adopt international standards of regulation. However, comparative studies *vis-à-vis* securities regulation in the Arab world should not necessarily be vacuous, as *shari'a* principles are not completely dissimilar from Western concepts, especially Islam's doctrinal stance against fraud. In this context, Islam is strongly for the elimination of fraud and uncertainty in contracts' subject matters. *Shari'a* principles encourage equity trading, as Islam supports trade and is assertively against idle money. In addition, many Islamic financing instruments (and Islamic finance in general) can be seen as equity financing. (Though, due to prohibiting interest charge, Islam is traditionally seen as averse to debt financing and interest bearing instruments.) It is hoped that this article will give a brief legal insight into the regulation of securities markets in Kuwait, Jordan and Oman, assessing in its conclusive remarks their aptitude for comparative studies in securities regulation.

---

* LLB (Jordan University); LLM (Cambridge University); MSc (LSE). The author is a part-time lecturer in public international law and researches financial regulation at the London School of Economics and Political Science/University of London.

When looking at securities regulation in the Arab world, some important questions should be raised. For example, "Why should Arab countries want to regulate their securities markets?" Such a question is highly relevant, as, thus far, Arab securities regulation has not been born out of an organic development, as is the case in most Western countries. Second, "Whom does such regulation attempt to protect?" This question is pertinent as there is still ambivalence about whether the aim of Arab regulation is to address problems aimed at protecting small investors or instead ameliorate the overall investment ambience for western fund managers. Third, "How 'cosmetic' or 'substantive' is Arab securities regulation?" The author argues that much of such regulation is only calculated to give the appearance that Arab countries are doing something to make their markets more efficient and transparent. However, as will be seen, Kuwait has followed a more organic approach, basing its regulation in response to the many setbacks that it had to encounter. This was especially the case after the market collapses of 1977 and 1982. Jordan, with its modest economy and avid desire to receive foreign portfolio investment, can be seen as rushing into more advanced securities regulation without proper assessment of underlying basic laws. For its part, Oman, with its nascent securities markets, can be seen as a good example of an Arab country that has prioritized its commercial regulation and made marked headway in accommodating modernist legal requirements.

2 SECURITIES MARKETS AND ISLAMIC SECURITIES

2.1 Securities markets

From a microstructure point of view,[1] securities markets are often a composite of broker–dealer firms, physical (or electronic) exchanges, clearance and settlement houses, agents for issuing securities and institutional underwriters of securities, etc.[2] Securities markets can be subdivided (though not mutually exclusively) into dealer or auction, periodic (call) or continuous, exchange or over-the-counter (OTC), and floor or electronic markets.[3] A broker acts as an agent (with no financial interest) buying and selling on behalf of their clients. Dealers, on the other hand, are principals making their profit from a "mark-up" on the securities sold and a "markdown" of the securities purchased (with often an inventory in which they take long or short positions).[4] In dealer-markets (or quote-driven markets) investors represented by their brokers trade with jobbers (market-makers), where random arrival of orders is often bridged by such jobber providing two-way (bid and offer)

---

[1] Briefly, microstructure theory examines how trading systems and traded security influence market behaviour. See J. Glen, *An Introduction to the Microstructure of Emerging Markets*, Discussion Paper No. 24, IFC, Washington, (November 1994) p. 2.

[2] See J. Norton and H. Sarie-Eldin's article, "Securities law models in emerging economies", in J. Norton and M. Andenas (eds.), *Emerging Financial Markets and the Role of International Financial Organisations*, Kluwer, 1996, pp. 344–349.

[3] See H. Stoll, *Regulation of Securities Markets: An Examination of the Effects on Increased Competition*, Monograph Series in Finance and Economics, New York University, 1979, pp. 5–6.

[4] See E. Willett, *Fundamentals of Securities Markets*, New Century, New York, 1971, p. 21.

quotations.[5] Auction-agency markets facilitate buying and selling through a centralized auction or agency process, often referred to as "order-matching" or "order-driven", relying on natural order flow to maintain market trading.[6] In periodic (or call) markets, trading occurs at "discrete" intervals, allowing buying and selling interests to build, therefore increasing the number of traders present at each session, which ultimately leads to enhancing markets' liquidity and depth.[7] An exchange market is one with a fixed physical location, while an OTC is a non-physical one with an often-automated communications network.[8] In an OTC market securities traders do not meet physically, and rather deal through telephone, computers or other automated means.[9] For their part, electronic securities markets refer to exchanges (or OTC systems) which are aided by automated (trading, clearing, monitoring, netting, quoting, executing) systems. In this respect, the computer assisted trading system (CATS), which is an order-driven continuous auction market, has contributed significantly to the development of both emerging and developed securities markets including Korea, Malaysia, Taiwan, Tokyo, São Paulo, Paris and Lyon.[10] In a floor-based market, price discovery is interactive, enabling floor-based traders to react to submissions of orders thereby forming their own trial prices before the market is set.[11]

Securities markets are also generally divided into money, capital, primary or secondary markets. In money markets, trading takes place in financial debt securities such as treasury bills and notes such as commercial papers, which are unsecured short-term promissory notes issued at a discount in bearer form.[12] Capital markets on the other hand, facilitate trading in securities with a longer maturity span with no fixed time limit to distinguish between money and capital markets. However, it is generally accepted that securities traded on money markets mature within one year or less, while securities which mature in more than one year are traded on capital markets.[13] Primary markets simply refer to markets of newly issued securities, while secondary markets refer to markets on which securities are traded. Primary markets are of vital importance to the issuers (financial or non-financial cor-

---

[5] See P. Dattels, *The Microstructure of Government Securities Markets*, Monetary and Exchange Affairs Department, IMF, WP/95/117 (November 1995), p. 6.

[6] *Ibid.*, pp. 6–7.

[7] This is technically referred to as "intertemporal consolidation of order flow". On the other hand, continuous trade execution allows more flexible trading strategies, providing "contemporaneous" information on price, transactions and overall general market condition. See *ibid.*, p. 6.

[8] See Stoll, *Regulation of Securities Markets*, pp. 5–6.

[9] See Willett, *Fundamentals of Securities Markets*, p. 61.

[10] See R. Pardy, *Regulatory and Institutional Impacts of Securities Market Computerization*, Country Economic Department, World Bank, WPS 866 (February 1992), p. 5.

[11] Such a definition refers to an open-outcry call auction. In this context, "price discovery" refers to finding the price at which trades are made or "equilibrium value". Equilibrium value means that the price of a security reveals fully the underlying demand and supply conditions. See Dattels, *The Microstructure of Government Securities Markets*, pp. 45, 46, 51.

[12] Commercial papers (CPs) are often used as a close substitute for bank borrowing by large corporations which enjoy high credit ratings. See T. Smith, *Markets for Corporate Debt Securities*, Research Department, IMF (July 1995), pp. 3–4.

[13] See F. Fabozzi, *Capital Markets: Institutions and Instruments*, Prentice Hall, New Jersey, 1996, p. 12.

porations) as a source of liquidity. For their part, secondary markets are of more importance to investors as they facilitate converting securities into cash, thus transferring property rights between investors *inter se* providing them with liquidity.[14] In the Arab world, securities markets are generally a floor-based, auction-agency. It is also worth mentioning at this early stage that it is secondary markets that are the most active in Arab equity markets. However, with the proliferation of specialized securities firms, Arab securities markets are moving towards electronic, dealer-market systems especially given that there is no specific Arab statutory prohibitions on dual-capacity for market makers.[15]

2.2 Islamic securities

2.2.1 General reference to the US and UK definitions

Equity securities generally refer to securities "which are an evidence of ownership" comprising common stocks (shares with voting rights, whose dividends do not have priority over other claims), and preferred stocks (shares, whose dividends have priority claim over common stocks).[16] Debt securities are generally referred to as debentures issued (generally at a discount) by a corporation, a public body or even individuals, in which the issuer promises interest and full redemption of the instrument upon maturity.[17] A difference between them can be seen in that the former entitles the holder to an ownership share in the company, while the holder of the latter is generally simply a creditor.[18] Having said this, it should be pointed out that due to continued market innovations the definition of "securities" cannot be fixed by statute. To shed light on its connotations it is helpful to examine its meaning in some developed economies and then look briefly at its Islamic meaning. Accordingly, references are made to the US and UK understanding of securities. In the UK it is important to look at the Financial Service Act 1986 which uses the term "investment" when referring to securities instruments, defining it as "any asset, right or interest falling within any paragraph in Part I of Schedule I to this . . . Act".[19] For its part, Schedule I, *inter alia*, refers to shares and stocks in the share capital of a company, debentures, government and public securi-

---

[14] See K. Garbade, *Securities Markets*, McGraw-Hill, United States, 1982, p. 1.

[15] Most notable markets that are moving in this direction are the Kuwaiti, Moroccan, Egyptian and Lebanese.

[16] See Willett, *Fundamentals of Securities Markets*, pp. 89, 96.

[17] On the definition of debentures and an exposition of relevant UK Companies Act 1989 provisions, see P. Davies, *Gower's Principles of Modern Company Law*, Sweet & Maxwell, 1997, pp. 321–326. Generally speaking, however, upon the liquidation of the corporation debt instrument claims have priority over share claims.

[18] *Ibid.*, p. 299.

[19] Cf. para. 4.02 of Gower, *Review of Investor Protection*, Part I (January 1984), Cmnd. 9125, where "all types of property except physical objects over which the purchaser has exclusive control after their acquisition" were included in the definition. However, the definition of "investment" and "investment business" (FSA 1986 Sched I, Part I and parts II–III respectively) is seen as "prolix", though such definitions can be easily altered by secondary legislation. See E. Lomnicka *et al.* "The UK Model of Securities Regulation", in J. Norton and M. Andenas (eds.), *Emerging Financial Markets and the Role of International Financial Organisations*, Kluwer Law International, 1996, p. 455.

ties, instruments entitling to shares or securities, certificates representing securities, units in collective investment schemes, options, futures, etc.

In the US the statutory definition of securities can be assumed to be broader than in the UK due the fact that the US Securities Act 1933 and the US Securities Exchange Act 1934 have opted for catch-all and often, open-ended definitions.[20] For example, section 2(1) of the US Securities Act 1933 gave the term "security" a loose definition. Under this Section securities were defined as any "note, stock, treasury stock, bond, debenture, evidence of indebtedness, certificate of interest or participation in any profit-sharing agreement, collateral-trust certificate". Such definition was also repeated in the Investment Advisors Act 1940, the Investment Company Act 1940, and the Exchange Act 1934.[21] However, despite the fact that the Exchange Act 1934 departed from earlier definitions, the American Supreme Court held that both were functionally "equivalent".[22] Though, the occasional generic definition of US securities and their apparent inability to keep up with market innovation has often spurred courts to develop an elaborate system of jurisprudence in order to deal with evolving definitional challenges. This has enabled US courts to add their interpretations, deploying a variety of tests in order to determine whether or not a transaction involves a security. Such court interpretations have been studied extensively by Loss. One can point to landmark US cases such as *SEC v. Joiner Leasing Corporation* (1943) (the first definition of "security" by the US Supreme Court), *SEC v. Howey & Co.* (1946) (on the "investment contract" concept and the economic reality test), *United Housing Foundation v. Forman* (1975) (on real estate and "stock"), and *Landerth Timber Co. v. Landerth* (1985) (on the sale of part of a business).[23]

2.2.2 Islamically

Islamically, the term "securities" is significantly less complex than the UK and US definitions. This is mainly due to Islam's general prohibition of interest (subsequently excluding interest-bearing instruments) and prohibition of contracts the subject matter of which is uncertain or futuristic (in principle, eliminating derivatives and currency hedging instruments). However, in order to present a comprehensive understanding of the term "securities" Islamically, this subsection:

(a)   briefly assesses sources of *shari'a* and the historical relationship between it and Arab Civil Codes;
(b)   looks briefly at the main financing mechanisms under Islam and assesses the limitations of *shari'a* on equity financing;
(c)   considers the relevance of *shari'a*'s limited interpretation of securities; and

---

[20] See Lomnicka, "UK model".
[21] See R. Hameed, "Some comparative aspects of securities regulation in the United Kingdom and the United States", unpublished PhD thesis, University of London, 1993, pp. 68–69.
[22] See *Tchereonin v. Knight* (1967) 389 US 332, 336; *United Housing Foundation Inc. v. Forman* (1975) 421 US 837, 847, Hameed, "Some comparative aspects", note 12. For its part, the Exchange Act 1934, *inter alia*, did not contain a reference to "evidence of indebtedness" as a security. Neither is the certificate of interest or participation extended to any oil, gas or other mineral royalty or lease.
[23] (1943) 320 US 344, (1946) 328 US 293, (1975) 421 US 837, (1985) 471 US 681, respectively. See L. Loss, *Fundamentals of Securities Regulation*, Little Brown, Canada, 1988, pp. 165–202.

(d) presents an Islamic definition and the statutory Jordanian and Kuwaiti definition of the term "securities".

2.2.2.1 Sources of Muslim law and relationship between *shari'a* and Arab Civil Codes

The term *shari'a* refers generically to Muslim law. This Muslim law is not unified, though, and there can be quite noticeable differences in its application depending on sectarian divisions and geo-political Islamic variations. Furthermore, it is unrealistic to speak of a uniform Islamic legal system on a practical level that represents identical procedural and substantive legal rules all over the Islamic world.[24] For their part, Muslims are broadly divided into Sunni and Shi'ite sects. These two sects are in turn subdivided into sub-sects, with each often adhering to distinct interpretations of *shari'a*. It is therefore not unusual to observe that, in light of diverse readings as to what constitutes *haram* (illegal) or *halal* (legal), different sects reach irreconcilable conclusions.[25] Sunnis can broadly be subdivided into four sects or schools: the Hanafi, Hanbali, Shafi'i and the Maliki.[26] (The majority of Sunnis belong to the Hanafi school.) For their part, Shi'ites are subdivided into three major sub-sects: the Athna-Asharias, Ismailyas and the Zaidyas.[27] However, most Islamic jurists concur that sources of law under *shari'a* are subdivided into revealed and non-revealed as follows:[28]

(a) The revealed:
    (i)   the Qu'ran;
    (ii) *sunna* and *hadith* (Prophet's deeds and proven sayings);
(b) The additional non-revealed:
    (i)   *ijma'* (the consensus of the community of scholars);[29]
    (ii) *qiyas* (reasoned analogy by Islamic jurists deducing what the above-mentioned three sources would have said in a similar question);[30]
    (iii) *istihsan* (seeking the most equitable solution according to Islamic jurists);[31]

---

[24] See W. El-Malik, *Mineral Investment under the Shari'a Law*, Graham & Trotman, 1993, p. 4.

[25] The clearest example is Sunni and Shi'ite diametrically opposed views on the legality of temporary marriage, which is predetermined from the outset to last for a specific time. While Sunnis condemn it as illegal bordering on prostitution, Shi'ites on the other hand accept it as legitimate.

[26] For a brief explanation of these Islamic legal schools see El-Malik, *supra* note 24, pp. 34–37.

[27] See M. Mannan, *Mulla's Principles of Mahomedian Law*, Pakistan edn., PLD Publications, Lahore, 1991, pp. 30–33.

[28] There are often some variation in the enumeration of these sources. See for example J. Burton, *The Sources of Islamic Law: Islamic Theories of Abrogation*, Edinburgh University Press, 1990, pp. 9–18, where he enumerates sources of Islamic law as the Qu'ran, Sunna, Islamic sciences and *usul al-Fikh* (Islamic jurisprudence).

[29] See N. Ray, *Arab Islamic Banking and the Renewal of Islamic Law*, Graham & Trotman, 1995, p. 27. The meaning of *ijma'* has varied over the years. It originally meant the consensus of the Islamic nation. Some writers have even unconvincingly argued that *ijma'* refers to the concurrence of the Prophet's companions on a solution to a particular question that was not addressed in revealed sources. See, for example, M. and A. Hidayatullah, *Mulla's Principles of Mahomedan Law*, Bombay, NM Tripathi Private, 1990, s. 33.

[30] Hidayatullah defines *Hadith* as: "precepts, actions and sayings of the Prophet Mahomed . . . not written down during his lifetime, but preserved by tradition and handed down by authorized . . . persons."

[31] See D. Dwyer, *Law and Islam in the Middle East*, Bergin & Garvey, 1990, p. 2.

(iv)   *istislah* (seeking the best solution for the general interest according to Islamic jurists or public interest);[32]

(v)   *taqlid* (precedents);[33] and

(vi)   *istishab* (presumption of continuity).[34]

The importance of *shari'a* in Arab countries does not stem only from its relevance as being a major source of many present pieces of legislation. For, such purported importance implies that *shari'a*'s influence has been transfixed in a merely historical backdrop. Rather, with the rising and ebbing of underlying populist adherence to Islam, the impact of *shari'a* could equally gain or lose noticeable momentum.[35] Historically, many Arab countries, at one stage or another, relied on Ottoman civil laws which were largely embodied in *Majallat el-Ahkam el-Adliyya* or *Majalla*, which was promulgated in the late nineteenth century and was influenced by *shari'a*. For its part, the Ottoman Empire did not rely exclusively on *shari'a* to govern all its commercial transactions. French models influenced the Ottoman 1850 Commercial Code and the 1861 Commercial Code Procedures.[36] The *Majalla* was relied upon heavily by Egyptian judges and is still a source of civil law in many Arab countries including Jordan and Iraq.[37] (For its part, the Egyptian Civil Code of 1949 has influenced the formation of many Arab civil codes especially in the Arab Gulf.) Moreover, most Arab civil codes share much in common, as they were promulgated in the latter half of the twentieth century and include, for example, Syria,[38] Iraq,[39] Jordan,[40] Kuwait[41] and the United Arab Emirates.[42] However, despite the fact that *shari'a* still constitutes an important legal source to Arab civil codes, most Arab countries have adopted French and continental distinctions between civil law and commercial law, often prescribing distinct rules for commercial dealings. Moreover, commercial laws in Arab countries can be particularly distinguished by offering more flexible rules of evidence,

---

[32] Dwyer, however, defines *Sunna* as "the model behavior . . . of the Prophet" and *qiyas* as "analogic reasoning". *Ibid*.

[33] *Taqlid* literally translates to imitation. See R. Sharma and N. Maheshwari, *Key to Islamic Law*, Baroda Law House, India, 1988, p. 1.

[34] See M. Kamali, "Methodological issues in Islamic jurisprudence", *Arab Law Quarterly*, 1996, p. 3. For other interesting work on Islamic legal theories see generally W. Hallaq, *A History of Islamic Legal Theories: An Introduction to Sunni Usul Al-Fiqh*, Cambridge University Press, 1997; A. Ibrahim, "Sources and development of Muslim law", *Malayan Law Journal*, Singapore, 1965; A. Rahim, *Muhammadan Jurisprudence*, Lahore, 1970; J. Schacht, *The Origins of Muhammadan Jurisprudence*, Clarendon Press, 1979; and N. Coulson, *Conflicts and Tensions in Islamic Jurisprudence*, University of Chicago Press, 1969.

[35] Many learned writers acknowledge this fluid state of affairs. See for example, M. Khan, "Islamic interest-free banking: a theoretical analysis", in M. Khan and A. Mirakhor, *Theoretical Studies in Islamic Banking and Finance*, IRIS Books, United States, 1987.

[36] See generally A. Buang *The Prohibition of Gharar in the Islamic Law of Contracts: A Conceptual Analysis with Special Reference to the Practice of Islamic Commercial Contracts in Malaysia*, PhD thesis, London University, 1995, section dealing with relationship between *shari'a* and Arab civil codes.

[37] Note that Egypt had its own Civil Code of 1875 which is often seen as a hybrid of *shari'a* and Western laws.

[38] In 1949.

[39] In 1951.

[40] In 1976.

[41] In 1980.

[42] In 1985.

imposing shorter statutory limitations, addressing wider issues in bankruptcy, presuming solidarity among debtors in a manner seen as more protective of debtors.[43]

2.2.2.2 Permissible financing techniques under *shari'a* and legal limitations posed by *riba* and *gharar* on the definition of Islamic securities

What makes Islamic economy distinct is its value system, which has significantly shaped Islamic saving, investment, consumption and production decisions.[44] Key features of the Islamic economic system are its respect for private property, encouragement and reward for work (private and public), aversion towards hoarding/monopoly, social solidarity through its tax system (*zakat*) and the prohibition of *riba* (interest or usury).[45] Islamic writers have suggested two broad objectives for Islamic development, namely narrowing the distributional gap in the state and maximizing the utilization of economic resources.[46] It is this emphasis on the utilization of economic resources that gives equity financing a distinguished place in Islamic economic and social justice theories. Yet, although stock exchange trading was known in the West since the late seventeenth century, equity trading on recognized exchanges in most Arab and Islamic countries was, until very recently, almost unheard of. In the Islamic context equity trading on recognized exchanges must be distinguished from equity financing by a means of having a share in the enterprise. While the former was not practised, most Islamic financing principles are based on equity holdings. Indeed it has even been argued that the Islamic financial system, while averse to debt financing, actually encourages equity financing in a manner that likens it to a "purely equity-based financial system" that, in addition to equity securities, boasts many more financing techniques.[47] This in a loose sense can be seen as a corollary to prohibiting charging interest or trading in interest-bearing instruments (including investing in leveraged debt enterprises) in favour of equity capital.[48] Moreover, Islamic banking can itself be broadly seen as an equity-based system in which depositors are treated as shareholders, where Islamic commercial banks are largely similar to mutual funds or investment trusts.[49]

To understand the role of equity holdings in Islam, a general appreciation of traditional Islamic financing mechanisms is necessary. Islamic financing can be seen through a number of contemporary financial techniques, which are deeply

---

[43] See N. Saleh, "Financial transactions and the Islamic theory of obligations and contracts", in C. Mallat (ed.), *Islamic Law and Finance*, Graham & Trotman, 1988, p. 26.

[44] For an account of Islam's value system influence on saving, consumption, investment and production decisions see M. Arif, *Monetary and Fiscal Economics of Islam*, King Abdulaziz University Press, Saudi Arabia, 1982, pp. 2–7.

[45] See M. Zineldin, *The Economics of Money and Banking: A Theoretical and Empirical Study of Islamic Interest-Free Banking*, Almqvist & Wiksell International, Stockholm, 1990, pp. 43–51.

[46] See A. El-Ashker, *The Islamic Business Enterprise*, Croom Helm, 1987, p. 60.

[47] See P. Moore, *Islamic Finance: A Partnership for Growth*, Euromoney Publications, 1997, pp. 15, 69.

[48] See M. Chapra, "Money and banking in an Islamic economy", in M. Arif, *Monetary and Fiscal Economics of Islam*, p. 152.

[49] Private enterprises are encouraged in Islam and even envisaged to participate on an equal footing with public enterprises in fulfilling the objective of economic development. See M. Khan, "The financial system and monetary policy in an Islamic Economy", in M. Khan and A. Mirakhor (eds.), *Theoretical Studies in Islamic Banking and Finance*, IRIS Books, United States, 1987, pp. 163–164.

rooted in Islamic practice and legal jurisprudence.[50] *Murabaha* (cost plus financing) involves a deferred sale in which a bank, for example, purchases the goods and sells them to the customer for a pre-arranged price. In this sense *murabaha* has been seen as suitable for a variety of financial purposes such as financing real estate investments and forming an important component of project financing.[51] Payments for the items purchased by the bank can be settled immediately, but it is often the case that parties to a *Murabaha* transaction choose to effect payments by instalments taking into account the customer's financial ability.[52] *Musharaka* (venture capital) entails a partnership whereby the parties put up capital, sharing profit and loss according to a pre-agreed ratio. In Islamic banking, equity participation is referred to as "permanent *musharaka*", entailing three modes of equity participation:[53] first, direct equity participation for the purpose of financing enterprises that yield short- or medium-term returns; second, participation in the equity capital of a given project in order to enhance its equity base; third, lines of equity for the purpose of a development finance institution (fund) in order to finance small entrepreneurs.

Mudaraba (or trust financing) is another important mode of Islamic financing.[54] It involves a partnership in which the owner of the capital (*rab el mal*) invests with a partner (*el mudarib*) who manages the investment, providing expertise as his/her share in the project. In other words, *mudaraba* is also often referred to as commenda, which is basically an arrangement between one or more investors (*rab el mal*) with an agent-manager (*el mudarib*) with whom they entrust their capital. The agent-manager is expected to trade with the capital, returning the principal and a pre-determined share of the profit.[55] It differs from *musharaka* in that only one party provides capital while the other strictly provides managerial skills. The agent-manager, however, does not get paid a salary for providing skill or management, as such skill or management is his/her contribution to the project. Both agree to share the profit according to a pre-arranged percentage. If loss occurs, the capital owner (*rab el mal*) risks losing part or all of his/her profit plus principal, while the agent-manager (*el mudarib*) loses only his/her efforts. *Al-qard el-hassan* (benevolent interest free loans), is another mode of financing which is either paid back at the end of the loan period without any increment, or converted into an equity share in the project. *Ijura* (leasing) is another Islamic financing technique, which is no different from the contemporary legal meaning of leasing, whereby the lessor retains title of the equipments and the lessee retains possession and usage for a pre-agreed period in lieu of a pre-determined rent. *Ijura-wa-iktina'* (hire-purchase) is the same

---

[50] See Moore, *Islamic Finance*, pp. 32–42 and Butterworths Editorial Staff (ed.), *Islamic Banking and Finance*, Butterworths, London, 1986, pp. 86–88. For a Western perspective on Islamic banking in general and Islamic financing techniques see for example, *European Perceptions of Islamic Banking*, a collection of articles issued by the Institute of Islamic banking and Insurance, London, 1996, particularly the article by J. Martin, "Security in Islamic Banking", pp. 69–76.

[51] See C. Price *et al.*, "Legal aspects of Islamic banking and finance", in Moore, *Islamic Finance*, p. 113.

[52] *Ibid.*

[53] See A. Bananga *et al.*, *External Audit and Corporate Governance in Islamic Banks*, Athenaeum Press, UK, 1994, pp. 15–16.

[54] For an interesting study of the legal liabilities arising from *mudaraba* contracts See M. Siddiqi, *Partnership and Profit-Sharing in Islamic Law*, The Islamic Foundation, London, 1985.

[55] See El-Ashker, *The Islamic Business Enterprise*, p. 75.

as leasing, but with the option at the end of the leasing period for the lessee to own the leased equipment.

It is argued that the first three options comprise the most used mechanisms for Islamic financing contracts with *murabaha* occupying 70 per cent, and *musharaka* and *mudaraba* occupying 20 and 10 per cent respectively.[56] Writers on Islamic finance have differentiated between these instruments' original mediaeval conceptual framework and their modern applications.[57] Yet the aim of enumerating these instruments in this subsection is to mention their relevance to modern equity financing and not to reconstruct a conceptual analysis. Such analysis necessitates examining in detail the highly diversified legal views of each Islamic school (i.e. Hanafi, Maliki, Shafi'i, Hanbali, Ja'fari,[58] Ibadi),[59] something which is outside the remit of this brief analysis as principles governing Islamic financial mechanisms find their roots in Islamic contract law.[60] My discussion of *shari'a* and Arab finance will be limited accordingly, especially as a wave of Islamic legal revivalism has also explained Islam's position *vis-à-vis* modern financial issues such as insurance[61] and commercial litigation.[62]

From the viewpoint of *shari'a*, one can attribute the legal problems that could potentially limit the definition of Islamic securities to *riba* and *gharar*. It is therefore necessary to turn to discuss briefly these two Islamic concepts.

Riba In its basic linguistic usage, *riba* often generically refers to charging interest on money loans. Juridically, the term *riba* refers to an exchange or a contractual relationship that leads to an unlawful benefit gained either by means of excess in the same genus, or by means of deferment in delivery.[63] Islamic scholars have traditionally subdivided *riba* into two main broad technical types, with elaborate rules

---

[56] Leasing, lending and hire-purchase contracts are here seen as not substantially different from equivalent Western mechanisms of financing. See Ray, *Arab Islamic Banking*, p. 37.

[57] For a comprehensive account of mediaeval and modern variations of Islamic financing mechanisms see *ibid.*, pp. 37–83.

[58] It is a Shi'ite sub-sect dominant in Iran and largely present in Kuwait, Bahrain, Lebanon, and Iraq.

[59] Largely the majority sub-sect in Oman.

[60] See generally S. Al-Kuhaimi, "Contract law and the judicial system in Saudi Arabia", PhD thesis, London University, 1982; I. Edge, "Comparative commercial law of Egypt and the Arabian Gulf", *Cleveland State Law Review*, 34, 1985–1986; S. Mahmasani, *The General Theory of the Law of Obligation and Contracts under Islamic Jurisprudence*, 2 vols. Beirut, 1972; P. Owsia, *Formation of Contract: A Comparative Study under English, French, Islamic and Iranian Law*, Graham & Trotman, 1994; N. Anderson, "The *shari'a* and civil law: the debt owed by the new civil codes of Egypt to the *shari'a*", *The Islamic Quarterly*, vol. 1, 1954; and N. Saleh, "Definition and formation of contract under Islamic and Arab laws", *Arab Law Quarterly*, May 1990. See also generally J. Schacht, *An Introduction to Islamic Law*, Oxford 1964, and N. Coulson, *A History of Islamic Law*, Edinburgh, 1964.

[61] See generally, F. Moghaizel, "Insurance in the light of Islamic legal principles", PhD thesis, London University, 1991; M. Al-Zarqa, *Nazam Al-Ta'min* [Insurance System], Beirut, 1984; M Muslehuddin *Insurance and Islamic Law*, New Delhi, 1982; A. Rahman, *Banking and Insurance*, London, 1979; M. Siddiqi, *Insurance in an Islamic Economy*, The Islamic Foundation, 1985; and M. Billah, "A model of life insurance in the contemporary Islamic economy", *Arab Law Quarterly*, 1997, pp. 287–306.

[62] See for example, I. Ghanem, "The role of Islamic law in commercial litigation in North Yemen", PhD thesis, University of London, 1987.

[63] See N. Saleh, *Unlawful Gain and Legitimate Profit in Islamic Law*, Graham & Trotman, 1992, p. 17. On works that have touched on *riba*, see for example C. Mallat, "The renaissance of

governing their conditions. The first is *riba al-fadl*, which takes place when identical or similar items are exchanged (or borrowed) with a stipulation that they should be exchanged (or paid back) with an increase in their original value or weight[64] (for example lending one kilogram of sugar and stipulating that it should be returned as 1.250 kilogram). The second is *riba al-nasi'a*, which put simply refers to delaying (or deferring) the completion of delivering the countervalues or exchange.[65] (This for example takes place when two items are exchanged but instead of handing both of them over on the spot, the delivery of one or both of them is deferred.)

Riba is prohibited on economic and religious grounds. Among the reasons advanced in support of the economic reasons is that it encourages idle money and deprives the wider society from prospects of growth associated with employment and engagement in risk-sharing enterprises. Furthermore, some Islamic writers exclusively attribute the rationale behind prohibiting *riba* to an Islamic legal maxim which states that "financial gain must be earned against taking risk".[66] Religiously, charging interest (or *riba*) has been evidenced by many Qur'anic verses and Prophet citations which condemned and outlawed such practice.[67] However, unlike the historical linguistic variations of the nuances of the English term "usury", mainstream traditionalist Islamic opinion on the topic of *riba* has remained consistent in not differentiating between *interest* and *usury*, proscribing both.[68]

Gharar   The prohibition of *gharar* can be evidenced from a number of Qur'anic verses and Prophet citations, though as a legal concept, *gharar* has traditionally

---

cont.

Islamic law: constitution, economics and banking in the thoughts of Muhammad Baqer As-Sadr", PhD thesis, London University, 1990; S. Madi, "The concept of unlawful gain and legitimate profit in Islamic law", PhD thesis, London University, 1989; N. Thani, "Legal aspects of the regulatory framework of the Malaysian financial system", PhD thesis, London University, 1993, especially pp. 278–320; E. Kazarian, "Finance and economic development: Islamic banking in Egypt", PhD thesis, Lund University, Sweden 1991; A. Kharrufa, *Al-Riba Wa'l-Fa'ida* [Usury and Interest], Baghdad 1962; A. Qureshi, *Islam and the Theory of Interest* Lahore, 1974; M. Siddiqi, *Banking without Interest*, The Islamic Foundation, 1983; S. Siddiqui, *Islamic Banking*, Royal Book Company, 1994, especially pp. 1–25; S Homoud *Islamic Banking*, Arabian Information, London, 1985, especially pp. 47–181; and M. Zineldin, *The Economics of Money and Banking: A Theoretical and Empirical Study of Islamic Interest-Free Banking*, Almqvist & Wiksell International, Stockholm, 1990. For articles, see: A. Mayer, "The regulation of interest charges and risk contracts: some problems of recent Libyan legislation", *International and Comparative Law Quarterly*, vol. 28, 1979, especially pp. 541–553; N. Cagatay, "Riba and interest concepts and banking in the Ottoman empire", *Studia Islamica*, 32, 1970; and R. Wilson, "The issue of interest and the Islamic financing alternative", *Journal of International Banking*, 1998, especially pp. 23–25.

[64] *Fadl* literally means excess.
[65] See Saleh, *Unlawful Gain and Legitimate Profit in Islamic Law*, pp. 16–17.
[66] See S. Amin, *Islamic Banking and Finance: The Experience of Iran*, Vahid Publications, Iran, 1986, p. 25.
[67] Main Qur'anic verses are found in *Suret Ar Rum, Suret An Nissa', Suret Al Imran, Suret Al-Baqara*. Main Prophet Citations (or *Hadith*) are found in citations on debt-usury and citations on sale-usury. For an excellent synopsis of these Qur'anic verses and citations see Homoud, *Islamic Banking*, pp. 64–85.
[68] See Moore, *Islamic Finance*, p. 17.

been more difficult to construct.[69] In the context of a contract of sale it has generically been referred to as any element that introduces lack of knowledge (*jahel*), excessive risk or uncertaintity. From the Qur'anic verses one can also point out that *gharar* embodies elements of wagering, speculation and betting. Further, it has been argued that an elimination of want of knowledge regarding the characteristics, identification, existence, date of future performance of the subject-matter, together with exercising control over the countervalues, will all generally avoid vitiating an Islamic contract of sale on grounds of *gharar*.[70] In this context, it is not unusual to come across Islamic legal writers who argue that the legal concept of *gharar* can exclusively be equated with want of knowledge (*jahel*) of the subject matter of the contract.[71]

The rationale behind prohibiting *gharar* can, ironically, in a sense be seen as a rather cumbersome form of protection designed to protect the weaker party in a transaction. Such protection is made through providing that contracts should not contain uncertaintity, thereby ensuring that the weaker party has perfect knowledge of the subject matter.[72] For, in a contract of sale under *shari'a* (and generally under most Arab civil codes) the subject matter must be licit or *Mashru'*, necessitating the fulfilment of four conditions:[73] first, the existence of the subject matter when contracting; second, the possibility of delivering the subject matter; third, the subject matter should be legitimate, not contravening public order and morality; finally, its genus, specie, value and quality must be determined. However, in order to bring more clarity into this brief legal-historical debate, it is beneficial to interject and allude to the subtle differences between Islamic jurists (*shari'a* contracts) and Arab scholars (Arab civil law contracts) definitions of contract of sales. The former defines contracts of sales as "legally sound combinations between offer and acceptance in such a manner that its effect leaves its marks on its subject matter".[74] The latter defines contracts as "agreements between two wills to establish, transfer or terminate a right".[75] The difference here is seen through emphasizing the word "combination" in the *shari'a* definition, which denotes the presence of offer and acceptance and a legally "sound" tie between the parties.[76] Yet vitiating Islamic contracts on the grounds of *gharar* can, on many occasions, be quite overreaching due to the vagueness and pervasiveness of such concept, the interpretation of which has tested the legal acumen of Islamic scholars to the limit. However, after the seminal work of Islamic legal scholars like Ibn Qayyim and Sanhuri, future contracts (which previously would have been viti-

---

[69] For an account of such Qur'anic verses and Prophet citations see A. Buang, "The prohibition of *gharar* in the Islamic law of contracts: a conceptual analysis with special reference to the practice of Islamic commercial contracts in Malaysia", PhD thesis, London University, 1995, pp. 129–165.

[70] See Saleh, *Unlawful Gain and Legitimate Profit in Islamic Law*, pp. 66–105. See also Buang, "The prohibition of *gharar* in the Islamic law of contracts", pp. 233–252.

[71] See Buang, "The prohibition of *gharar* in the Islamic law of contracts", pp. 233, where, although he qualifies his evidence with later juristic "refinements", he nevertheless mentions the acceptance of such interpretation by notable Islamic jurists such as Ibn Rushid, Ibn Hazm and Baji.

[72] See Saleh, *Unlawful Gain and Legitimate Profit in Islamic Law*, p. 62.

[73] See N. Comair-Obeid , "Particularity of the contract's subject matter in the laws of the Arab Middle East", *Arab Law Quarterly*, 1994, p. 335.

[74] Definition by the Islamic jurist Al-Zarqa as quoted in M. Zahraa, "Negotiating contracts in Islamic and Middle Eastern laws", *Arab Law Quarterly*, 1998, p. 265.

[75] Definition by Al-Ssbouni, *Ibid*.

[76] *Ibid*.

ated on grounds of *gharar*) have been validated with the *caveat* that they do not involve material elements of uncertainty, risk or speculation, though admittedly, clarifying the confusion often made between the non-existence of the subject matter of
the contract of sale and the uncertainty of its future existence is largely credited to
Ibn Qayyim.[77] In this context it can be added that as a result of limiting the voidness of contract of sales only to cases of "material" *gharar*, Islamic law now divides
sale of goods contracts into two broad classes. One which is a "common contract",
applicable to all transactions transferring delivery and risk with contemporaneous
effect called *bai'*, while the other provides for future delivery called *Sallam*, which is
seen as an exception to the general rule of immediate delivery.[78]

For their part, Arab civil codes have adopted relatively similar approaches to defining contractual subject matter. For example, the Jordanian Civil Code (Arts.
159–161) and the Iraqi Civil Code (Arts. 127–130) display great similarity, lean-
ing more towards "juridico-moral" Islamic teachings concerned with the object of
obligation in an attempt to protect the parties from all risks that may prejudice the
contractual benefits.[79] The Kuwaiti (Arts. 167–175) and United Arab Emirates
(Arts. 199–205) Civil Codes, on the other hand, are viewed as identical in strictly
demanding that the subject matter protect the parties against any risk of aleatory
elements. This is seen through indeterminability, adversely affecting the parties
through procuring an illicit gain for one, while causing unforeseen loss to the other.[80]

Finally, although the ensuing subsection will demonstrate that *shari'a*'s prohibition of *gharar* and *riba* is being limited by modern Arab statutes, it is nevertheless
pertinent to mention the theoretical general limitations that *shari'a* can impose on
equity and debt trading, thus indirectly limiting the Islamic definition of "securities". These limitations can be summarized as follows:

(a) Limitations related to Islamic theory of social justice and economic activity,
     as acquisition of corporate shares is not allowed in companies that transact in
     illegitimate business. Such illegitimate business includes companies that trade
     in alcohol, pornography, pork, gambling, prostitution and any other illegal ac-
     tivity prohibited by Islamic values.
(b) Limitations related to the potential voidness of a contract of sale because of the
     element of *gharar*, which from the above discussion is understood to refer to
     want of knowledge, uncertaintity in the subject matter. Additionally, under
     the concept of *gharar* one can include wagering and betting, something which
     renders pure speculation of securities markets illegal under *shari'a*. This of
     course involves inherent problems faced when dealing with Islamic contracts
     of sale, when the subject matter of the contract is uncertain or impossible to
     determine. In this context, futures and derivative contracts should be void in

---

[77] See Saleh, "Financial transactions and the Islamic theory of obligations and contracts",
      p. 21 and *Unlawful Gain and Legitimate Profit in Islamic Law*, pp. 63–64.
[78] See D. Hill *et al.*, "Comparative survey of the Islamic law and the common law relating to the
      sale of goods", *Journal of Islamic and Comparative Law*, vol. 2, Ahmad Bello University, Nigeria,
      1968, p. 90.
[79] See Comair-Obeid, "Particularity of the contract's subject matter in the laws of the Arab
      Middle East", pp. 344–345.
[80] *Ibid.*

most Arab countries. But as will be seen when looking at the definition of securities, Arab statutory definitions have accepted the validity of these securities and did not adopt the narrow Islamic interpretation.
(c) Limitations related to the Islamic prohibition of dealing in interest. Interest or usury, which is known in *shari'a* jurisprudence as *riba*, is prohibited under Islamic law. This can be manifest in the following:
  (i) receiving fixed interest income on shares through dividends;
  (ii) buying equities in companies leveraged (wholly or partially) at interest (i.e. investing equity in companies that borrow at interest to finance its activities);[81]
  (iii) when shares are issued/underwritten by financial intermediaries that use interest in their transactions.

2.2.2.3 Influence of *shari'a* today over Arab civil codes *vis-à-vis* limiting the definition of securities

From the above discussion follows the need briefly to consider the influence of the Islamic limitation on acceptable "securities", especially in light of the fact that most Arab constitutions hold *shari'a* to be either *the* or *a* principal source of law.[82] However, it must be pointed out at the outset that these limitations are seen as religious rather than legal (from a secular perspective that is), despite the afore-mentioned historical-legal relationship between *shari'a* and Arab civil codes. Yet this is not to suggest that such limitations can be ignored completely. For, the impact of *gharar* and *riba* has created an overall reluctance among the wider public to commit substantial sums of its funds to local equity markets despite the fact that the Islamic financial system favourably encourages equity holdings over debt instruments. It is worth mentioning in this respect that in the securities markets of the Middle East and North Africa, only 3 to 4 per cent of all Islamic assets are invested in equities.[83]

However, this article is concerned only with the legal effect of *shari'a* limitations. Accordingly, despite the above historical-legal account of *shari'a* and Arab civil codes, neither a detailed examination of *gharar* is relevant in the context of this article, nor is it necessary to discuss *shari'a*'s archaic technical rules proscribing *riba*. This is largely due to two broad reasons. The first is that Arab statutes and civil codes have, on many occasions, ignored strict *shari'a* rules proscribing *riba* and *gharar*. Second, an overwhelming majority of Arab statutory definition of "securities" has eschewed *shari'a*'s aforementioned limitations.[84] Concerning the former, most Arab civil codes do not have absolute rules prohibiting contracts the subject matter of which is not in existence at the time of contracting, thus exhibiting relative flexibil-

---

[81] For a discussion on this see for example "Islamic equity investment", *The Arab Banker,* vol. IV, No. 4, 1997, London, pp. 26–30 and "Legal structure of Islamic finance and privatisation", *Yearbook of Islamic and Middle Eastern Law*, vol. 2 (1996), pp. 32–50.
[82] For example as an indication of the rising importance of *shari'a* in some Arab countries, Art. 2 of the Egyptian Constitution was amended in 1980 to make *shari'a the* principal source of law. See Ballantyne, "A reassertion of the Shari'ah: the jurisprudence of the Gulf states", p. 157, in N. Heer, *Islamic Law and Jurisprudence*, University of Washington Press, 1990.
[83] See Moore, *Islamic Finance*, p. 75.
[84] See subsection dealing with the Arab definition of securities.

ity towards validating future contracts. For example, under Article 131 of the Egyptian Civil Code, the contracting parties may contract on a subject matter that shall exist in the future.[85] Most Arab civil codes of today have also adopted Ibn Qayyim's distinction between material and non-material *gharar,* permitting parties to contract on non-existent subject matters that will exist in the future. Examples which come to mind are Iraq (Art. 129(1)), Qatar (Art. 33), Jordan (Art. 160(1)), the United Arab Emirate (Art. 202(1)), and Kuwait (Art. 168) providing the existence of the future subject matter does not rely on mere chance.[86]

The author further argues that *shari'a*'s limitations are also especially ignored by modern Arab commercial legislation. *Shari'a*'s prohibition of interest is no longer fully adhered to by Arab banking regulations, most of which now specify a legal limit to chargeable interest.[87] Moreover, Arab commercial courts are exhibiting more willingness to enforce interest accruing from banking obligations, civil or tortuous liabilities. For example, in the United Arab Emirates, the Dubai civil courts now even uphold fully agreed commercial interest regardless of the principal. Such a position is also upheld in other parts of the UAE especially after the 1987 Abu Dhabi Law No. 3 (though under the 1987 Abu Dhabi Law No. 4 interest is prohibited if it exceeds the principal).[88] In late 1997 even the traditionally conservative Saudi central bank introduced floating rates notes (FRNs) paying 15 and 30 basis points respectively over floating inter-bank deposit rates.[89] Moreover some Arab countries have also specifically excluded the dealings on securities markets from the limitations posed by *gharar* by special legislation. An example is Egypt's Special Law No. 23 of 1909, which permitted forward dealings on the stock exchange despite the fact that the Commentary of the Egyptian Civil Code admitted that these sales contain elements of betting and *gharar*.[90] One may finally conclude this subsection by referring to examples from the case study countries (Kuwait, Oman and Jordan) that demonstrate the non-compliance with *shari'a*'s limiting precepts in regard to *riba* in commercial dealings. For example, Article 543 of the 1980 Kuwait Civil Code stipulates that, in a civil context, a loan should be repaid without any increase on its value or quantity.[91] Furthermore, Article 547 of the same Civil Code adds that a loan cannot generate interest or secure an advantage to the lender.[92] However, we can observe that the situation differs considerably in commercial dealings. Article 102 of the Kuwaiti Commercial Code makes it perfectly legitimate to charge interest on commercial loans and even refers to a legal rate of interest which is esti-

---

[85] See Buang, "The Prohibition of Gharar in the Islamic Law of Contracts", pp. 223–224.

[86] See Saleh, "Financial transactions and the Islamic theory of obligations and contracts", pp. 20–21.

[87] This is normally no more than 12 per cent. Such a limit is imposed for example in Jordan and Egypt.

[88] See R. Turner, "Security and enforcement in Dubai and the other United Arab Emirates", *Arab Law Quarterly*, 1991, p. 312.

[89] See Moore, *Islamic Finance*, pp. 155–156.

[90] See Buang, "The Prohibition of Gharar in the Islamic Law of Contracts", p. 338.

[91] Article 534 reads: "A loan is a contract by which a lender undertakes to give to the borrower a sum of money or any other fungible thing on condition that the latter will return a thing equal in kind, quality and amount".

[92] Article 547 reads: "(1) Lending shall be without interest; every stipulation otherwise shall be null without prejudice to the contract of the loan itself. (2) Every advantage stipulated by the lender is deemed tantamount to interest."

mated at 7 per cent.[93] Also it is within the capacity of the Kuwaiti Central Bank to fix minimum and maximum chargeable rates of interest for bank deposits.[94] In the context of Oman, Articles 80–81 of the 1991 Omani Commercial Code also allow the creditor of a commercial loan to charge interest.[95] Such interest (which is chargeable on a yearly basis taking into account the purpose, risk and duration of the loan) is determined by the parties within the limits permitted by the Ministry of Commerce and Industry in collaboration with the Omani Chamber of Commerce and Industry. Receiving interest is not also exclusively limited to commercial loans, and is legitimate in other commercial contexts such as share dividends. In Jordan for example, it is acceptable for corporations to distribute dividends with pre-determined interest. A recent example on such distribution of dividends was the Jordan Insurance Company (JIC), which distributed dividends for the financial year ending in March 1998 reaching 12 per cent.

2.2.2.4 Islamic and Arab statutory interpretation of the term "securities"
It is appropriate to mention that the legality of many financial instruments is still undetermined even by some Islamic banks. Even financial instruments used currently by the more liberal of Islamic banks are either still subject to controversy or should be banned altogether according to less liberal Islamic legal opinion. Such controversy can, however, be largely attributed to the inherent vagueness of the concept of *gharar* and the differing perspectives in interpreting the concept of *riba*. For example, among the instruments subject to controversy are letters of credit (due to charging interest), while unacceptable instruments still used by liberal Islamic banks include financial future dealings (due to the element of *gharar*) and discounted commercial papers, factoring, documentary credit (all due to the element of pre-determined interest).[96]

In a broad yet pure jurisprudential Islamic context, "legitimate" securities can be deemed to include non-interest bearing notes, stocks (that do not yield interest-based dividends) and certificates of participation in profit-sharing arrangement.[97] For their part, the examined Arab jurisdictions have given varying definitions for financial security, generally not complying with strict Islamic interpretations. For example, various Jordanian Acts and regulations (prior to the new Jordanian Securities Act of 1997) gave less adequate definitions. For example, Article 2 of the Rules Covering Trading in Financial Papers on the Amman Financial Markets defines securities as: "Shares, bonds and debentures issued in the Kingdom by government corporations or municipalities or Jordanian public or private shareholding

---

[93] Article 102 reads: "(1) A creditor is entitled to charge interest on commercial loan, save where otherwise agreed; where the rate of interest is not stated in the contract, interest which accrues shall be the legal rate (i.e. 7 per cent). (2) Where the contract stipulates a rate of interest and the debtor delays payment, the delay interest shall be computed on the basis of the agreed rate."

[94] See Saleh, *Unlawful Gain and Legitimate Profit in Islamic Law*, p. 7.

[95] *Ibid.*, p. 9.

[96] G. Attia, "Financial Instruments Used by Islamic Banks", in *Islamic Banking and Finance*, pp. 103–113.

[97] See L. Errico *et al.*, *Islamic Banking: Issues in Prudential Regulations and Supervision*, Monetary and Exchange Affairs Department, IMF (March 1998), p. 24.

companies, or any negotiable financial paper". Article 2 of the Internal Regulations of the Amman Financial Market also gives an identical definition.[98] Neither
does Article 3 of the new Securities Act 1997 follow the strict Islamic understanding of the term securities. It for example enlists financial securities as ordinary shares;
investment units issued by investment funds; securities deposit receipts issued by
financial services companies; equity option bonds; futures contracts, call and put options; and any other local or international security which is internationally considered as such. Kuwait has also not conformed to the strict Islamic view that, among
other things, excludes bonds. Article 2 of the Degree Regulating the Kuwait Stock
Exchange, for example, defines securities as shares and debentures of Kuwaiti joint-
stock companies. It also adds bonds issued by the government, a government body
or Kuwaiti public institutions, together with Kuwaiti or non-Kuwaiti securities licensed by the Kuwait Stock Exchange Market Committee. Furthermore, Article 1
of the Rules Pertaining to Listing and Dealing in Market Securities on the Kuwait
Stock Exchange also adopts verbatim the definition forwarded by the afore-
mentioned Article 2 of Degree Regulating the Kuwait Stock Exchange.

3 ARAB REGULATORY DEFICIT IN SECURITIES
REGULATION: LEGAL SURVEY OF CASE STUDY AND
IMPLICATIONS

3.1 Arab regulatory deficit

3.1.1 *What is securities regulation?*

Regulation of securities markets is not a discrete discipline. Nor can it be isolated
from wider related legal externalities such as transfer of legal property rights, corporate and civil liabilities of directors and fund managers or contractual relations.[99]
In its basic form, regulation of securities markets attempts to regulate primary trading activities such as new issues markets, secondary trading activities, together with
market policing and regulation of market participants.[100] Such regulation should
provide an appropriate balance between considerations of competition and market
goals, through promoting fairness and efficiency[101] by improving transparency

---

[98] The same definition is also repeated by Art. 2 of the Amman Financial Market Law of the year
1976. And again the same definition is given in Art. 2 of the Amman Financial Market Law No.
31 of the year 1992.

[99] See H. Blommestein *et al.*, *The Role of Financial Institutions in the Transition to a Market
Economy*, Research Department, IMF, WP/93/75 (October 1993), p. 23. See R. Pardy,
Institutional Reform in Emerging Securities Markets, Country Economic Department, World
Bank, WPS 907 (May 1992), pp. 2–3.

[100] See generally M. Chuppe *et al.*, *Regulation of Securities Markets*, World Bank, WPS/829 (January
1992).

[101] For studies examining efficient market theories and their implication see for example S. Keane,
Stock Market Efficiency: Theory, Evidence and Implications, Philip Allan, Oxford, 1983;
W. Baumol, *The Stock Market and Economic Efficiency*, Fordham University Press, New York,
1965; M. Firth, *Share Price and Mergers: A Study of Stock Market Efficiency*, Saxon House, 1976;
I. Asimakopoulos *et al.*, *Stock Prices, Exchange Rate and Market Efficiency*, Research Paper No.
97/4, Institute of European Finance, University of Wales, 1997.

and building a framework within which markets function.[102] However, one must add here that the concept of "fairness" in securities regulation has not yet been settled and could refer to various meanings including creating a level playing field, protecting investors from abusive market practices, and resolving potential conflict of interest between market participants.[103] A highly prominent theme in securities regulation is to provide a system of adequate investment protection and maintain investors' confidence in the integrity of securities markets through, for example, eliminating insider trading, fraud and market manipulation.[104] Such a theme accounts for the heavy reliance on disclosure of material information as a salient technique of securities regulation in Western developed countries. In this context, public disclosure of material information in the course of securities trading, together with prudential regulation of intermediaries, is vital for price efficiency and market confidence.[105] Accordingly, disclosure (as a regulatory device) has aided in the enforcement of laws, discouraged acts disproved by the larger public and has had an inherent informative value.[106] In this respect one can further argue, that a statutory duty to disclose material information on securities markets stems from either anti-fraud or mandatory provisions.[107] Other important techniques of securities regulation include authorization through licensing and recognition.

From the above-mentioned discussion one observes that there is often not much practical difference between attempts at protecting investors and responding to what economists term as "market failure".[108] This is even more the case as although avoiding market failure is an important rationale for regulation, it is nevertheless not the overriding one.[109] Preventing dishonesty, addressing informational problems and systemic risk are all necessary for the welfare of both markets and investors.[110] In this context, general legal rules (especially in light of the principle of *caveat emptor*) are not adequate and additional specific intervention of the law is needed to protect unsuspecting financial investors. Increasing legal protection from fraud, enhancing market rules on supplying and evaluating information, and tightening extra measures to control risk undertaken by institutions (the failure of which may lead to the collapse of the overall financial system) are all deemed in the interest of financial investors too.[111] It is accordingly pertinent to add that the theme of investor pro-

---

[102] See Dattels, *The Microstructure of Government Securities Markets*, pp. 27–28.

[103] See M. Long, *et al.*, *Financial Regulation: Changing the Rules of the Game*, Country Economic Department, World Bank, WPS 803 (Nov. 1991), p. 13.

[104] See Norton and Sarie-Eldin, "Securities law models in emerging economies", p. 338.

[105] See Pardy, *Institutional Reform in Emerging Securities Markets, Country Economic Department*, p. 5.

[106] See generally, Note, "Disclosure as a Legislative Device" 76 (1962–1963) *Harvard Law Review* 1273, as quoted in Hameed, "Some comparative aspects of securities regulation in the United Kingdom and the United States", p. 42.

[107] *Ibid.*, p. 44.

[108] Broadly speaking, market failure occurs when markets are not efficient. See A. Page *et al.*, *Investor Protection*, Weidenfeld & Nicolson, London, 1992, p. 35.

[109] See D. Vittas, *Policy Issues in Financial Regulation*, Country Economics Department, World Bank, WPS 910 (May 1992), p. 5.

[110] See Page, *Investor Protection*, pp. 35–39.

[111] On the prevention of dishonesty, it is argued that "sharp" fraudulent practices will not normally be sufficiently addressed by general law and that "prevention is better than cure". With regard to informational problems, it is assumed that information (as a public good) will often be

tection still occupies high prominence even in the regulatory discourse of Western securities markets, which are often dominated by institutional and professional investors which do not require high protection levels. Such a theme was, for example, specifically highlighted in the influential 1995 Securities and Investment Board's report *Regulation of the United Kingdom Equity Markets*.[112] The report stated that in order to achieve and retain investor confidence, a regulatory system must meet three basic criteria. First, market users must be confident that they are treated equitably in the sense that no one group of market participants should use the market to the disadvantage of another. Second, they must have confidence in the integrity of the price formation processes. This means that regardless of the method by which market users choose to deal, they must be able to do so in the confidence that quoted prices, so far as practicable, reflect the full extent of market activity at the time of the transaction. Third, market users should always be confident that all reasonable steps will be taken to maintain the safeguards against market abuse and that adequate measures (effective and timely) will be undertaken in order to punish abusers.[113] More recently, however, the Financial Services Authority (FSA) has set amongst its main objectives to monitor and enforce high standards of financial soundness and enhance customers' confidence in its strength and probity.[114]

A word must also be added on governments' involvement in regulating securities markets in emerging economies. Although self-regulation through market forces is accepted to go hand in hand (if not on many occasions to outweigh) governmental regulation in advanced economies, an overwhelming literature favours governmental involvement in regulating securities markets in emerging economies.[115] Yet this should not be seen as a glib advocacy for an overall bureaucratic involvement in all aspects of securities trading in emerging economies. Notwithstanding this caveat, empirical evidence from emerging markets have demonstrated that a "key" to enhancing securities markets' development was the "tightening" of the prudential

---

cont.

    insufficiently supplied, justifying intervention to "compel" disclosure to enable investors to make informed calculations on risk and return. Moreover, as "experience goods" (which differ from "search goods" such as clothing), information in an investment context cannot generally be evaluated in advance by lay investors, rendering them particularly vulnerable to the skill and probity of financial advisors. See Page, *Investor Protection*, pp. 35–38.

[112] See *Regulation of the United Kingdom Equity Markets: Report by the Securities and Investment Board*, the Securities and Investment Board, June 1995, London.

[113] For a follow-up on this report, see also *Regulation of the United Kingdom Equity Markets, Market Views: A Digest of Responses to SIB's Discussion Paper*, the Securities and Investment Board, June 1995, London.

[114] See generally http://www.fsa.gov.uk/. For an interesting perspective in the pre-launch era of the FSA see "Perspectives in the FSA", *The Financial Regulator*, vol. 2, no. 3, December 1997, pp. 24–36.

[115] See for example K. Kalotay, *Emerging Markets and the Scope for Regional Cooperation*, United Nations Conference on Trade and Development, UNCTAD/OSG/DP/79, (February 1994), pp. 24–26 and 37–41, Norton and Sarie-Eldin, "Securities law models in emerging economies", pp. 444–445, Long, *Financial Regulation*, pp. 5–7, and Pardy, *Institutional Reform in Emerging Securities Markets, Country Economic Department*, pp. 22–27. For an interesting discussion on government and regulation, see J. Barth *et al.*, *Financial Regulation and Performance: Cross-Country Evidence*, Development Research Group, World Bank, WPS2037 (January 1999), pp. 7–13 and Page, *Investor Protection*, pp. 78–84. For a recent general account of the changing role of the state in economic matters, see V. Tanzi, *The Changing Role of the State in the Economy: A Historical Perspective*, Fiscal Affairs Department, IMF, WP/97/114 (September 1997).

regulatory environment.[116] Yet although governmental involvement is primarily prudential, it can also be exercised through setting up the exchanges, exercising supervisory and enforcement powers or laying down the core laws regulating securities trading. Moreover, initial official regulation has even been called upon to complement market governance and market goals.[117] In this context, certain regulatory objectives such as limiting competition between decentralized markets in order to achieve a concentration (or depth) of supply and demand of securities can be achieved through governmental involvement. Such a task was, for example, undertaken in Poland where securities regulation stipulates that capital markets instruments should be traded on a centralized exchange, prohibiting OTC trading.[118]

3.1.2 Arab regulatory deficit in securities regulation

It must, however, be stressed that it would virtually be impossible to identify and address all Arab deficits in securities regulation in the scope of one article. Yet the aim here is to present a more articulate account of the types of legal problems currently encountered by the majority of Arab countries which have operable securities markets. When examining Arab securities markets one can generally speak of four distinct groups of Arab countries:[119]

(a) Djibouti, Mauritania, Somalia, Sudan, Iraq[120] and Yemen: these countries simply lack the requisite macroeconomic foundations necessary for securities markets. They are all unlikely to establish credible stock exchanges in the short and medium term.

(b) Algeria, Libya and Syria: due to near complete state monopoly over the economy, a meaningful private sector role has so far been excluded, dashing hopes for erecting equity markets in the short or medium run. Syria is, however, implementing tentative steps towards reforming its company laws in a manner that would facilitate a better role for its private sectors.[121] Moreover, the

---

[116] In addition of course to boosting investor confidence and market growth. See generally "Private market financing for developing countries", *World Economic and Financial Survey*, IMF (December 1993).

[117] See Blommestein, *The Role of Financial Institutions in the Transition to a Market Economy*, pp. 24–26.

[118] See Dattels, *The Microstructure of Government Securities Markets*, pp. 27–28.

[119] See A. Abisourour, "The emerging Arab capital markets: Status, role and development prospects", in S. El-Naggar, *Financial Policies and Capital Markets in Arab Countries*, IMF, 1994. pp. 65–66.

[120] Iraq opened a formal stock exchange in 1992, though. However, at the end of September 1997 Iraq promulgated new Companies Law No. 21 of 1997 which came into effect on 28 December 1998. The new law identifies four types of companies: public, private (limited liability), partnership and sole trading companies. See S. Al-Mukhtar's survey of Iraq, p. 269, in the *Yearbook of Islamic and Middle Eastern Law*, vol. 4 (1997–1998). Iraq, however, has a semi-functioning stock exchange regulated by the Baghdad Stock Exchange Law No. 24 of 1991. In January 1997, new listing and admission regulations were promulgated (in accordance with Art. 26 of Law No. 24 of 1991).

[121] Syria does not have a formal stock exchange, although informal trading in shares is on the increase. However, draft Art. 337 of the Syrian Commerce Code is being debated in Syria in order to introduce holding companies on a par with Arts. 232–236 of the 1989 Jordanian

fact that Syria does not have an official stock exchange has not prohibited it
from establishing an active debt (government) securities market that has often
been used to finance domestic public borrowing.

(c) The six Gulf Co-operation Council (GCC) countries.[122] These capital-surplus
Arab countries enjoy operational (albeit limited) securities markets, stable
economies and freely convertible currencies.

(d) Jordan, Tunisia, Lebanon, Egypt and Morocco: these capital-deficit Arab countries now boast the most legally regulated Arab capital markets underpinned by
relatively stable macroeconomic conditions and openness to foreign investors.
These securities markets are also active in facilitating the privatization process.

For their part, financial regulators in Arab countries have thus far focused on setting
up physical exchanges and trading systems for equity and debt, neglecting to address
important issues of investor protection. In this context, it is widely acknowledged
that even recent attempts at modernizing Arab commercial laws have overlooked
addressing many important investor protection concerns.[123] For example, the new
Kuwaiti Law No. 13 of the year 1996 (which prohibits illegal competition and
monopolistic practices) has been criticized on the grounds that it lacks effective teeth
to underpin its provisions in a manner that would be meaningful in protecting small
investors. In addition, this law neither creates specific authorities to receive complaints from retail investors, nor addresses determining a reasonable price for products.[124] The overlooking of investor protection is also widespread in modern Arab
banking regulations, which tend to be prudential in orientation. For example, while
the Saudi Arabian Investment Fund Regulations of the year 1993 contain prudential regulations necessary for smooth operation of banking, they noticeably ignore
the resulting questions of investor protection.[125]

Arab disregard of investor protection is, however, hard to justify – especially in
light of the fact that *shari'a* and Arab civil codes are not conceptually averse to in-

cont.

Companies Act or the Lebanese legislative degree No. 45 of 24 of June 1983 on holding
companies. See J. el-Hakim's survey of Syria, in the *Yearbook of Islamic and Middle Eastern Law*,
vol. 3 (1996), pp. 186–188. However, although it has rejected World Bank and IMF economic
structural adjustment programmes, since the early 1990s Syria has been adopting more liberally
orientated economic policies, such as Law No. 10 of 1991, which grants productive
investments (by Syrians and non-Syrians) tax exemptions and regulatory privileges. These
"productive investments" are expected to "create employment, promote import substitution
and exports, and lead to transfer of technology and managerial expertise." See H. Azzam, *The
Emerging Arab Capital Markets: Investment Opportunities in Relatively Unplayed Markets*, Kegan
Paul International, 1997, p. 60.

[122] GCC countries comprise Saudi Arabia, Kuwait, Bahrain, Qatar, United Arab Emirates and
Oman. However, it must be cautioned that GCC revenues have declined sharply due to record-
low oil prices.

[123] See A. Al-Melhem, "Privatisation and protection of investors in Kuwait: Reality and ambition",
Arab Law Quarterly, 1998, p. 195.

[124] *Ibid.*

[125] These regulations known as Regulations for Investment Funds and Collective Investment
Schemes, Ministerial Decision of the Minister of Finance and National Economy No. 2052 (17
January 1993) addressed issues relating to: management of funds, capital adequacy, limitation
of investment in other funds, etc. See R. Meyer-Reumann, "The banking system in Saudi
Arabia", *Arab Law Quarterly*, 1995, p. 227.

vestor protection and that Arab countries have adopted Western models of capital markets. Indeed as has been observed from earlier discussion of *shari'a*, the prohibition of *gharar* and *riba* was in large respect seen as overstretching the concept of investor protection and rendering it cumbersome and rather paternalistic. However, this Arab regulatory lack of attention to investor protection and proper market policing in not necessarily the case in other Islamic countries which have adopted western models in regulating their securities industries.[126] For example, parts VI and XI of the 1983 Malaysian Securities Industry Act authorizes the Securities Commission to supervise and investigate market manipulation and abuse. Moreover such authorization has been backed up by extensive judicial involvement which has expanded on the letter of the law.

Manipulative practices also still go undetected on Arab financial markets. "Wash sales",[127] "pooling"[128] and "matched orders"[129] are among such practices. Furthermore, "cold calling" and investment advertisement also remain under-regulated. Barring limited *ad hoc* regulations, few Arab countries have laid down specific and detailed rules prohibiting such fraudulent or manipulative practices. Yet even when Arab regulatory authorities lay down specific provisions to ban such practices, their statutory provisions fall short of providing adequate protection on par, for example, with the overreaching US 1934 Securities Exchange Act. Provisions in mind here are section 10(b) and its subsections 10(b)1, 10(b)2, 10(b)3, 10(b)6, 10(b)18 (on market manipulation) and 10(b)5(2) (prohibiting directly or indirectly making/omitting misleading statements of a material fact in the course of a purchase or sale of registered securities).[130] Also, Arab countries do not have specialized anti-fraud legislation on historical par, for example, with the UK Prevention of Fraud (Investments) Act 1958.[131] For example, the Kuwaiti Law Concerning the Combating of Fraud in Commercial Dealings (amended substantially in 1989) fails to contain even a single general provision on prohibiting fraud on financial markets.[132]

---

[126] However, the afore-mentioned does not imply that Arab countries did not pay adequate attention to their investment legislation, which is becoming highly orientated towards attracting regional and international investors. Jordan, for example, has passed a number of laws that aim at promoting domestic investment. These include the 1955 Encouragement and Guidance of Manufacturing Act (No. 27), the 1955 Encouragement of Foreign Capital Act (No. 28) and the 1967 Provisional Act for Investment Promotion (No. 1). The 1972 Investment Promotion Act (No. 53) and the 1987 Encouragement of Investment Act (No. 11) are also among such laws. However, one of Jordan's investment laws which aims at promoting Arab and foreign investment in Jordan is the 1992 Act Regulating Arab and Foreign Investments. This Act has been instrumental in facilitating foreign and Arab investment in Jordan. A follow-up to this Act were the 1992 Regulations Organizing Arab and Foreign Investments. In addition, the 1995 Investment Promotion Act (No. 15) was modified and offers customs and income tax exemptions.

[127] Transactions that involve no change in beneficial ownership.

[128] Concentrated buying of securities by a syndicate or a group of people that is then followed by attempts to raise the price by falsely stimulating public interest. The group disposes of its securities once a satisfactory appreciation in the prices has occurred.

[129] Transactions that involve sale or purchase of security in the knowledge that a matching order will be entered into by the same person or their associates at substantially the same price.

[130] See Loss, *Fundamentals of Securities Regulation*, pp. 702–709.

[131] See especially ss. 13–14 of this Act. An earlier version of this Act was embodied in the Prevention of Fraud (Investments) Act 1939.

[132] Law No. 20 of 1976 Concerning the Combating of Fraud in Commercial Dealings.

It is also pertinent to add in this context that on the rare occasions that Arab regulators have prohibited market manipulative practices, no mention has been made of appropriate remedies for the injured parties. This, for example, is noticeable in the Jordanian legislation. For example, Article 68(d) of the new Jordanian Securities Act for the year 1997 prohibits a number of practices. These include giving the public a false information of real or fictitious dealing in securities, to influence the prices of securities and adversely affect the capital market in any form. Despite proscribing manipulative practices no mention was made to concomitant remedial compensation for the benefit of injured parties who might suffer as a result of such manipulation. This prohibition can be seen as similar to the prohibition mentioned in section 47 of the Financial Services Act 1986 which, *inter alia*, prohibits conducts that create a false or misleading impression to the market in or the price or values of any investment.[133] In this context "false" is seen as something that is objectively incorrect, while "misleading" indicates a (subjective or objective) effect that is likely to induce an investor into erroneous belief.[134]

Further, civil remedies are generally ignored in Arab legislation as emphasis is placed on criminal sanctions, which are not particularly reputed to have a high degree of efficacy in the face of complex commercial crimes.[135] For example, in the area of Arab insider dealing anti-fraud provisions have received little or no attention to civil remedies. Instead, Arab regulators focused on criminal law when addressing abuse of price sensitive information. For example, Article 67 of the 1997 Jordanian Securities Act defines inside information as any information which has not been made public and that if advertised is expected to affect the price of one security or more. Article 68 prohibits insiders such as members of the Board of Directors of the Jordanian Securities Commission (JSC), members of the Securities Deposit Centre and the executive managers and staff to exploit inside information. Article 70 of the same Jordanian Act imposes hefty penalties on violations of the provisions of the Act. Such penalties vary between up to JD20,000 and/or of a fine not less than twice and not more than five times the profit made or loss avoided by the violator. In addition to the fine, violators of Article 68 can expect a prison sentence of up to three years and up to one year for violation. Similar criticisms can be levelled when looking at insider dealing prohibition in Kuwait. Under Article 140 of the Companies Act No. 15 of 1960, the legislator prohibited members of the boards of directors from misusing information that they had obtained by virtue of their position. One may also add in this context that attempts at fusing "company secrets" with the "confidential information" protected (by penal imprisonment of up to three years) under Article 13 of the Kuwaiti Public Fund Protection Act proved to be unrealistic.[136] Such discussion of insider trading inevitably leads to a wider inquiry of the basis of fiduciary duty in the Arab corporate context. Neither have Arab courts satisfactorily delineated the boundaries of the concept of fiduciary relationships and the various

---

[133] See subs. (2) of s. 47 of the 1986 Financial Services Act.
[134] See *CRW Ltd v. Senddon* (1972) 72 AR (NSW) 17, as cited in K. Au, "Major issues in securities regulation in the 1980s: a comparative study", PhD thesis, University of London 1994, p. 119.
[135] For views in support of giving more role to civil penalties see *Securities Markets in OECD Countries: Organisation and Regulation*, OECD Documents (1995), p. 10.
[136] See A. Al-Melhem, "Insider dealing in the Companies Act of Kuwait No. 15 of 1960", *Arab Law Quarterly*, 1998, p. 14.

grounds for consequent civil liability. For example, Article 322(7) of the United Arab Emirates Companies Act restricted the prohibition to "company secrets", regardless of the existing of a fiduciary relationship rather than widening the definition to encompass price sensitive information. In addition, although the position of the theory of "misappropriation" of inside information in Arab securities dealings has never been raised before Arab courts, it is still also not fully addressed even in the public arena such as when divulging "state secrets". Nor have Arab courts addressed the position of "tippees" as insiders.[137] However, this situation can be contrasted with other Muslim countries with more advanced economies such as Malaysia. In Malaysia, the courts have been involved in delineating the boundaries of sections 89 and 90 of the 1983 Malaysian Securities Industry Act that prohibit insider trading. In this respect, cases like *PP v. Ghoudhury, Green v. Charterhouse, Ryan v. Triguboff* and *Waldron v. Green* were instrumental in broadening the concepts mentioned in section 89 and 90 of the 1983 Securities Industries Act.[138]

3.2 Survey of relevant laws in the Arabic jurisdictions

In its case study, the article will focus on three Arab countries: Jordan (a capital-deficit Arab country, with relatively advanced securities regulation). Kuwait (a surplus-capital Arab country, which has the oldest securities markets in the Gulf) and Oman (a surplus capital Arab country, with relatively newly established securities markets). In addition to the various stages of regulatory development these countries portray, they also provide interesting examples to study financial regulation in light of *shari'a*'s impact on their respective civil codes. While Jordan represents a case where there is a "clear" influence of *shari'a* on its civil code, Kuwait represents an example where an Arab civil code has been "considerably" influenced by *shari'a*. For its part, Oman represents one of the few Arab countries which still does not have a civil code and therefore still relies heavily on *shari'a*. Before considering in more detail the market conditions and regulatory structure of Kuwait, Jordan and Oman it is pertinent to mention at the outset that these three countries have marked differences in their respective regulatory environments. For example, as will be seen in this subsection, the severe micro-credit crises and excessive speculation on Kuwaiti stock markets has meant that much of Kuwait's financial regulation was directed at addressing issues outside the strict realm of securities regulation like the ramifications of payments with post-dated cheques. Jordan never suffered from such chronic speculation, mainly due to its less endowed economic resources and better corporate governance. For its part, Oman's securities industry is still relatively very nascent and it appears that its regulators (at least theoretically) have taken into account market collapses in Kuwait. However, one must point to a peculiarity of the Kuwaiti

---

[137] In this context, note the recent development in the US where the Supreme Court ruled that the SEC could apply Rule 14e-3(a) on non-corporate insiders. Rule 14e-3(a) prohibits trading on inside information in a tender offer situation, notwithstanding the absence of a duty to disclose. See US Department of Justice, FBI "White-Collar Crime: Facts and Cases", Chapter III (Securities Fraud), 1997.

[138] See N. Thani, "Legal aspects of the regulatory framework of the Malaysian financial system", PhD thesis, London University, 1993, pp. 353–356.

financial system that often resulted in Kuwait's ignoring regulating its domestic securities markets. As will be seen in the context of this subsection, Kuwait invested substantial sums of its oil wealth (under official policy) in European and north Atlantic securities. This indirectly reduced governmental attention to its own domestic corporate and securities regulation. Lack of effective securities regulation was also (up until the early 1980s) fuelled by a moral hazard associated with the Kuwaiti government's complete readiness to step in in 1979 and 1982 to bail out the market.[139]

3.2.1 Kuwait

3.2.1.1 Introduction

Kuwait has traditionally occupied a unique position in the Arab Gulf, seen through the maturity and relative independence of its legal institutions. Its position in the Arabian Peninsula has often been marked with more organized governance, with the finances of the central government separate from those of the ruling family.[140] Most Arab countries have adopted French and continental distinctions between civil law and commercial law, prescribing more flexible rules for commercial dealings.[141] Kuwait, too, follows the French Civil Law model and has both a Civil Code[142] and a Commercial Code,[143] which lay down different rules for commercial and non-commercial activities. In this respect Kuwait made *shari'a* the first source of Law No. 15/1996, which replaced custom as it was then the first source of law of the Civil Code. Article 2 of the Kuwaiti Constitution states that Islam is "a principal source of legislation".[144] In this respect, the Civil Code follows a similar vein and asserts that in the absence of adequate provisions, the judge should rule first according to custom and failing that according to his independent judgment "guided by the principles of Islamic jurisprudence".[145] The Kuwaiti legal system has also adopted different rules for commercial and civil activities in the procedural and evidential spheres, exemplified by the Civil and Commercial Procedure Law of 1980[146] and the Proof (Evidence) in Civil and Commercial Matters of

---

[139] Though, due to falling oil prices, the government of Kuwait may not be prepared to play as a prominent role in bailing out the market as it has done in the past. We now turn into looking at these three jurisdictions in more detail.

[140] R. Wilson, *Banking and Finance in the Arab Middle East*, Macmillan, 1983, p. 101.

[141] Commercial law in Arab countries is distinguished by offering more flexible rules of evidence, imposing shorter statutory limitations, addressing wider issues in bankruptcy, presuming solidarity among debtors, etc. See N. Saleh, "Financial transactions and the Islamic theory of obligations and contracts" p. 26 in C. Mallat (ed.), *Islamic Law and Finance*, Graham & Trotman, 1988.

[142] See Amiri Decree No. 67 of 1980, Pertaining to Enacting the Civil Code, promulgated in Official Gazette No. 1335, dated 5 January 1981.

[143] This law repealed the earlier Law of Commerce (Amiri Decree No. 2 of 1961). See Amiri Decree No. 68 of 1980 Enacting the Law of Commerce. Enacted on 15 October 1980 and came into force on 25 February 1981. See Art. 1.

[144] See A. Ballantyne, *Legal Development in Arabia*, Graham & Trotman, 1980, p. 110.

[145] See Art. 1(2) of the Kuwaiti Civil Code.

[146] See for example Amiri Decree No. 38 of 1980, Enacting the Civil and Commercial Procedure Law, promulgated in Official Gazette No. 1307, dated 25 June 1980.

1980.[147] Kuwait has recently also shown consistent sensitivity to the legal needs of commerce, as it now upholds arbitration bodies by statutory recognition.[148]

3.2.1.2 Company laws
In its Commercial Companies Act of 1960,[149] Kuwait has adopted the types of company prevalent in the Arab world. To elaborate on such types, it is pertinent to recount Ballantyne's general summary of Arab companies.[150] These are: *sharika musahama*[151] (joint stock company); *sharika masoulya mahdouda*[152] (private limited company); *sharika tawsiya*[153] (limited liability partnership without shares); *sharika tawsiya bil ashum*[154] (limited liability partnership with shares); *sharika tadhamun*[155] (simple partnership); and *sharika muhasa* (joint venture). For its part, Kuwait has the following types of business associations:

(a) Simple partnerships are formed by two or more persons in order to carry on commercial activities. The partners are jointly liable for all the obligations of the partnership.[156]
(b) Commandite partnerships are formed either by active partners who manage the partnership (whose liability is unlimited), or sleeping partners (whose liability is only to the extent of their contribution).[157] Commandite partnerships are however subdivided into (a) simple commandite partnership and (b) commandite partnerships by shares.[158]
(c) Joint ventures are commercial partnerships formed between two or more persons and are not valid *vis-à-vis* third parties.[159] They cannot be registered,[160] nor do they have legal personality.[161] They are not allowed to issue negotiable shares or debentures.[162]
(d) Joint stock companies are formed by a number of persons, who subscribe for negotiable shares, who are liable only to the value of their respective shares.

---

[147] See for example, Amiri Decree No. 39 of 1980, Pertaining to Proof (Evidence) in Civil and Commercial Matters, promulgated in Official Gazette No. 1307, dated 25 June 1980.
[148] See Ministerial Resolution No. 33 of 1992, Creating Arbitration Bodies, promulgated in Official Gazette No. 50, dated 10 May 1992.
[149] See Amiri Decree No. 15 of 1960, Pertaining to Commercial Companies, enacted on 12 May 1960.
[150] See W. Ballantyne, *Legal Development in Arabia*, p. 54.
[151] *Société Anonyme.*
[152] *Société à responsabilité limité.*
[153] *Société en commandite simple.*
[154] *Société en commandite par action.*
[155] *Société en nom collectif.*
[156] See Art. 4 of the 1960 Kuwaiti Commercial Companies Act (KCCA).
[157] See Art. 42 of 1960 KCCA.
[158] See Arts. 44–55 of the 1960 KCCA.
[159] See Art. 56 of the 1960 KCCA.
[160] See Art. 57 of the 1960 KCCA.
[161] See Art. 58 of the 1960 KCCA.
[162] See Art. 62 of the 1960 KCCA.

(e) Limited liability companies are formed by a number of persons not exceeding thirty, all liable only to the value of their respective shares.[163] The incorporation, increase of capital, or borrowing may not be affected by public subscription; neither can such companies issue shares or negotiable debentures.[164]

(f) Holding companies aim at appropriating shares in Kuwaiti or foreign joint stock companies, as well as shares of Kuwaiti or foreign limited liability companies.[165]

3.2.1.3 Securities markets and laws

Although share dealing in Kuwait started in earnest in the early 1960s, one can trace the beginning of equity trading to the 1950s, when the National Bank of Kuwait,[166] the Kuwait National Cinema Company,[167] Kuwait National Airways,[168] and the Kuwait Oil Tankers Company[169] were established.[170] However, the overwhelming majority of Kuwaitis then invested their wealth in real property, as shares issued by the aforementioned companies were limited and covered a narrow base.[171] The years 1960–1962 witnessed a staggering rise in domestic equity trading, as thirteen new public shareholding companies were incorporated. Of particular importance was the Kuwait Investment Company (incorporated in 1961), which took equity holdings in the projects it supported and occasionally even underwrote entire issues.[172] Between 1963 and 1970 enthusiasm abated, resulting in the incorporation of only eight new public shareholding companies.[173] Spearheaded by the Kuwaiti International Investment Company in 1974, Kuwait also became an important regional centre for publicly quoted bond issues, inducing large international institutions to come to Kuwait to borrow funds denominated in Kuwaiti dinars.[174] But due to rising interest rates abroad and fears of collapse in Kuwaiti bond markets (in light of Kuwaiti interest rates), the government in 1979 enforced a temporary moratorium on issuing bonds.[175] However, it has traditionally been institutional investors who dominated Kuwaiti bond markets, as individual investors turned their energies to investing on the more lucrative equity markets.

During the boom years, which extended into the early 1980s, Kuwaiti financial policy encouraged borrowing[176] and injected huge sums of governmental funds into

---

[163] See Art. 185 of the 1960 KCCA (as amended by Law No. 28 of 1995, promulgated in the Official Gazette No. 216, dated 23 July 1995).
[164] See Art. 186 of the 1960 KCCA
[165] See Art. 227 of the 1960 KCCA (as amended by Law No. 28 of 1995, promulgated in the Official Gazette No. 216, dated 23 July 1995).
[166] This was Kuwait's first shareholding company, incorporated in 1952.
[167] Incorporated in 1954.
[168] Incorporated in 1956.
[169] Incorporated in 1960.
[170] See A. Abdel Hadi, *Stock Markets of the Arab World: Trends, Problems and Prospects for Integration*, Routledge, 1988, p. 19.
[171] *Ibid.*, p. 20.
[172] Private Kuwaiti families later held 50 per cent of this initially publicly held company. See Wilson, *Banking and Finance in the Arab Middle East*, p. 102
[173] The promulgation of the Kuwaiti Commercial Companies Act in 1960 had a significant impact on the proliferation of Kuwaiti public shareholding companies. See M. Al-Yahya, *Kuwait: Fall and Rebirth*, Kegan Paul International, London, 1993, pp. 20–21.
[174] These include Mitsubishi Heavy Industries, Banque Nationale de Paris, etc.
[175] See Wilson, *Banking and Finance in the Arab Middle East*, pp. 107–108.
[176] For example, through the subsidised funds provided by the Industrial Bank and the Real Estate Bank.

the local economy, capping interest rates while not imposing any income tax what-soever.[177] Limited avenues for domestic investment meant that Kuwaiti citizens could only invest their capital either in real estate or on under-regulated stock mar-kets. Phenomenal surpluses in petrodollars, coupled with weak corporate gover-nance led to equity trading becoming a highly speculative tool, where the value of shares never reflected underlying corporate assets or commercial potential. Inherent legal loopholes that permitted forward dealing in shares on the basis of post-dated cheques further aggravated (and facilitated) the intensity of share speculation. In this respect, it is pertinent to add that earlier scant official interest in regulating domes-tic Kuwaiti securities markets can also be attributed to Kuwait's official active in-terest in investing substantial funds abroad through amassing equity and bond hold-ings. For, over the past two decades, 96 per cent of the total of Kuwait's revenue has come from oil exports and investments abroad, as Kuwait has long implemented a policy of setting aside 10 per cent of its oil income in the Reserve Fund for Future Generations.[178] Moreover, as early as 1966, Kuwait had officially set up the Lon-don-based Kuwait Investment Office (KIO) for the purpose of holding minority stakes in Western key financial institutions and industries.[179] Indeed, Kuwaiti over-seas investment institutions have long been considered among the most sophisti-cated in the Middle East. In the 1980s for example they issued large numbers of straight dollar bonds, floating rate notes (FRNs), Kuwaiti dinar bonds, US dollar convertible bonds and zero coupon US dollar bonds, together with leading issues for General Motors Acceptance Corporations, European Coal and Steel Commu-nity and Bank of Tokyo.[180] However, one must add that Kuwait did not neglect reg-ulating its domestic equity markets altogether and interfered on many occasions (1963, 1973, 1975 and 1977) to stabilize share prices that often inflated at alarm-ing rates.[181] Moreover, Chapter Six of the Commercial Code is of relevance as it briefly touched upon brokerage and stock exchanges, explaining the nature of bro-kerage contracts[182] and laying down general rules on the exchanges' juristic per-sonalities.[183]

However, spiralling levels of speculation and excessive forward transactions ul-timately led to the first market collapse in early 1977, when on average shares value dropped by nearly 20 per cent.[184] This collapse spurred the government to take radical steps to remedy the situation. In December 1977 it opened and regulated

---

[177] See Al-Yahya, *Kuwait: Fall and Rebirth*, pp. 16–17.
[178] See N. Chalk, *Fiscal Sustainability with Non-Renewable Renewable Resources*, IMF, WP/98/26, Fiscal Affairs Department (March 1998), p. 17. See also generally N. Andrew *et al.*, *Kuwait: From Reconstruction to Accumulation for Future Generations*, IMF, Occasional Paper No. 150 (1997).
[179] The KIO, however, was superseded by the Kuwaiti Investment Authority, which since 1982 has had overall responsibility for Kuwait's foreign investments. See for example *Middle East Economic Digest* (London) 14 September 1985, p. 4.
[180] The Kuwait Foreign Trading Contracting and Investing Company (KFTCIC), Kuwait Investment Company (KIC) and Kuwait International Investment Company (KIIC) largely executed these operations. See J. Seznec, *The Financial Markets of the Arabian Gulf*, Croom Helm, 1987, pp. 96–97.
[181] *Ibid.*, p. 56.
[182] See Art. 306.
[183] Art. 323 stipulates that the Stock Exchange is a legal person with a capacity to litigate and dispose/manage its property.
[184] See Al-Yahya, *Kuwait: Fall and Rebirth*, pp. 19–20.

an official Stock Exchange and even instructed the KFTCIC[185] to intervene to maintain share prices and public confidence in the market.[186] The collapse also led to the establishment of a Securities Commission to regulate the market more efficiently.[187] For its part, the Ministry of Trade and Industry introduced measures to suspend registering new public holding companies and prohibited any increase in company capital except as already agreed.[188] Ironically, though, due to stricter regulation of trading on the official market and tighter corporate rules for registering Kuwaiti companies, the public circumvented these measures by setting up Gulf shareholding companies,[189] trading their equity on an *ad hoc* non-official local Kuwaiti market known as Sook Al Manakh. Excessive speculation, lack of listing rules for Gulf shareholding companies (on a par with Kuwaiti shareholding companies) and forward dealing based on post-dated cheques persisted. This predictably resulted in a dramatic market crash in 1982 with aggregate bad debt amounting to US$7.7 billion.[190] The collapse of Sook Al Manakh (and the colossal financial bailout that the Kuwaiti government undertook in its aftermath) sent shock waves beyond Kuwaiti domestic markets and made the more conservative of Arab Gulf governments become even more sceptical about equity markets.

It is, however, notable to observe that the Kuwaiti legal response to this collapse took two distinct forms:

(a)   The first were regulatory measures concerned with resolving the huge debt problem that posed a systemic risk that threatened Kuwaiti economy as a whole. Such problems were largely addressed by an Amiri decree issued in late 1982,[191] followed up by intricate *ad hoc* regulations to resolve some of the legal repercussions ensuing from ill regulated forward trading in shares.[192] (However, forward share dealing was recently revisited by regulations issued by the Stock Exchange Commission, which permitted it, though stipulating, *inter alia* that it has to be practised through registered market jobbers.)[193] However, an indirect result of the extensive financial

---

[185] Kuwait Foreign Trading Contracting and Investing Company.
[186] See Seznec, *The Financial Markets of the Arabian Gulf*, p. 56.
[187] See generally Ministry of Commerce and Industry Resolution No. 61 of November 1976.
[188] See Al-Yahya, *Kuwait: Fall and Rebirth*, p. 20.
[189] These companies where mostly registered in Bahrain or the United Arab Emirates.
[190] See Seznec, *The Financial Markets of the Arabian Gulf*, p. 61.
[191] Amiri Decree No. 57 of 1982, Pertaining to Forward Rate Dealing in Company Shares, promulgated in Official Gazette No. 1436, dated 20 September 1982.
[192] See for example Minister of Justice Resolution Order No. 46 of 1982, Pertaining to the Regulation of the Business of Arbitration Bodies in Regard to Forward Rate Dealings of Company Shares (promulgated in Official Gazette No. 1439, dated 10 October 1982. Amiri Decree No. 59 of 1982, Pertaining to Transactions in Company Shares on the basis of Forward rates and Securing the Rights of Creditors Relevant Thereto (promulgated in Official Gazette No. 1446, dated 28 November 1982.) Council of Ministers Resolution No. 57 of 1982, Regulating Security Instruments of Forward Shares (promulgated in Official Gazette No. 1505, dated 13 November 1982.) Council of Ministers Resolution No. 14/21 of 1983, Pertaining to the Settlement of Forward Dealings in Company Shares (promulgated in Official Gazette No. 1478, dated 23 May 1983.)
[193] See for example Arts. 1 and 2 of Stock Exchange of Kuwait Order No. 2 of 1996, Pertaining to Forward Rate Dealings in Company Shares, promulgated in Official Gazette No. 279, dated 20 October 1996.

bailout which the government undertook in the aftermath of the two market collapses (especially the 1982 one), was that state-owned companies held between 48 and 50 per cent of the traded shares.[194] This fact has often impeded the growth of the Kuwaiti Stock Exchange and marginalised the role of individual investors, as it is now estimated that the Kuwait Investment Authority and commercial banks alone account for more than 80 per cent of equity annual trading.[195]

(b)   The second response was regulatory measures aimed at introducing more regulation into Kuwait's financial markets by a number of Amiri[196] Decrees, Ministerial Resolutions and Orders by the Stock Exchange Commission. In this context, a leading piece of legislation was the Amiri Decree of 1983.[197] This Decree established the Kuwaiti Exchange as an autonomous, juristic person[198] and defined "stock" as shares and debentures of Kuwaiti joint stock companies and/or debentures issued by the government or public bodies.[199] It was followed up by the1983 Ministerial regulation enacting the bylaws of the stock exchange, which was an extensive piece of legislation addressing important areas like registration of securities, market membership, negotiation of securities, etc.[200] According to the 1983 Amiri Decree, the stock market was also to be managed by a market committee under the chairmanship of the Minister of Trade and Industry[201] and to have arbitration[202] and disciplinary[203] committees. During 1984–1985 the Stock Market Committee issued numerous orders regulating share dealings,[204] establishing arbitration[205] and disciplinary[206] com-

---

[194] It is estimated that by May 1983, the Kuwaiti government injected US$2 billion in order to prop up share prices. See Azzam, *The Emerging Arab Capital Markets: Investment Opportunities in Relatively Unplayed Markets*, p. 194.

[195] *Ibid.* Though government domination over the corporate sector is diminishing as Kuwait is embarking on a privatisation programme.

[196] Amiri is an Arabic adjective relating to the royal prerogative issued by the Emir of Kuwait.

[197] Amiri Decree Regulating the Kuwait Stock Exchange Market, 1983, promulgated in the Official Gazette No. 1492, dated 14 August 1983.

[198] Art. 1.

[199] Art. 2. However, Art. 31 of the Ministerial Resolution No 35 of 1983, for some reason, excepts from the definition "inheritance, wills or such other cases as are approved by the market".

[200] Ministerial Regulation No 35 of 1983, Pertaining to Enactment of the Bylaws of the Stock Market of Kuwait, promulgated in the Official Gazette No. 1505, dated 13 November 1983. This resolution is subdivided into the following chapters: Ch. 1 (Objective of the market); Ch. 2 (Registration and acceptance of securities); Ch. 3 (Market membership); Ch. 4 (Negotiation of securities); Ch. 5 (Market management); Ch. 6 (Budget and accounts of the market); Ch. 7 (Disputes and arbitration); Ch. 8 (Disciplinary action); Ch. 9 (General and transitory provisions).

[201] Arts. 5–8.

[202] Art. 13.

[203] Art. 14.

[204] Stock Exchange of Kuwait Order No. 1 of 1984, Pertaining to Rules and Regulations of Dealing in Shares in the Market, promulgated in the Official Gazette No. 1567, dated 8 July 1984.

[205] Stock Exchange of Kuwait Order No. 2 of 1984, Pertaining to the Formation of an Arbitration Commission and Procedures before it, promulgated in the Official Gazette No. 1583, dated 21 October 1984.

[206] Stock Exchange of Kuwait Order No. 3 of 1984, Pertaining to the Formation of a Disciplinary Commission and Procedures before it, promulgated in the Official Gazette No. 1583, dated 21 October 1984. Also, Stock Exchange of Kuwait Order No. 1 of 1985, Pertaining to the Formation of a Disciplinary Commission, promulgated in the Official Gazette No. 1595, dated 13 January 1985.

missions. The Stock Market Committee has also issued orders regulating list-ings[207] and the work of jobbers on the exchange.[208] Other Amiri decrees in-clude legislation regulating settlement[209] and the listing of brokers and their assistants.[210]

In 1986 Kuwait took measures to restrict speculation by adjusting share prices of Gulf joint stock companies through correlating the price to the value of assets and liquidating non-viable companies. In a further attempt to stem speculation, bro-kerage firms were also expected to produce share lists with their commissions pegged to the value of the shares traded daily. In addition, daily price increases were not allowed to exceed 5 per cent of value and circumventing price fluctuations by di-viding shares into units of 500 to 100,000 shares.[211] Moreover, a particularly im-portant decree was in 1990 licensing investment funds and the negotiation of se-curities thereof,[212] which was followed by a ministerial resolution,[213] *inter alia* elaborating on the conditions required for granting a licence to invite the public to subscribe for Kuwaiti shares[214] and debentures.[215] It also dealt with the conditions pertaining to offering non-Kuwaiti shares,[216] the conditions for inviting the public to subscribe to non-Kuwaiti shares,[217] as well as the conditions for offering and mar-keting units in foreign investment funds.[218] There is also a Commission order pre-scribing different procedures for bulk sales, which comprise no less than 5 per cent of a company's capital.[219]

---

[207] Stock Exchange of Kuwait Order No. 4 of 1985. The Rules for Listing and Dealing in Securities in the Stock Market of Kuwait, promulgated in the Official Gazette No. 1600, 17 February 1985.
[208] Stock Exchange of Kuwait Order No. 16 of 1985. The Conditions for Listing and Regulation of the Work of Jobbers of the Stock Exchange Market of Kuwait, promulgated in the Official Gazette No. 1688, 12 October 1986.
[209] Amiri Decree Regulating Settlement of Stock on the Clearing House of the Stock Exchange of Kuwait, promulgated in Official Gazette No. 1699, dated 28 December 1986.
[210] Amiri Decree Concerning Listing of Brokers and Their Assistants on the Stock Exchange Market of Kuwait, promulgated in Official Gazette No. 1574, dated 19 August 1984.
[211] See Abdel Hadi, *Stock Markets of the Arab World: Trends, Problems and Prospects for Integration*, pp. 30–31.
[212] See Amiri Decree No. 31 of 1990, Pertaining to the Regulation of Securities and Creation of Investment Funds, promulgated in Official Gazette No. 1874, dated 6 May 1990. This decree repealed Amiri Deree No. 32 of 1970, Regulating the Negotiation of Companies' Securities and consolidated relevant provisions found in the Commercial Companies Law, the Decree Regulating the Stock Exchange Market, the Decree Pertaining to listing jobbers and their Assistants, the Decree Pertaining to Settlements. (See Preamble to Decree Amiri Decree No. 31 of 1990.)
[213] See Ministerial Resolution No. 112 of 1992 Enacting the Implementing Regulations to Decree No. 31 of 1990, Pertaining to the Regulation of Securities and Creation of Investment Funds, promulgated in Official Gazette No. 50, dated 10 May 1992.
[214] See Art. 3
[215] See Art. 13, as amended by Ministerial Resolution No. 16 of 1995.
[216] See Art. 9
[217] See Art. 10
[218] See Art. 15, as amended by Ministerial Resolution No. 16 of 1995.
[219] However, these rules apply only when "one natural or juristic person owns the bulk shares on the date preceding that of offering them". See Art. 1 of Stock Exchange of Kuwait Order No. 1 of 1996, Pertaining to the Exclusion of Big Quantities of Shares from Certain Negotiation Rules, promulgated in Official Gazette No. 263, dated 30 June 1996.

There has been a marked expansion in securities trading on the Kuwait Stock Exchange, especially since 1996 and early 1997 where the volume of trading is double that of all other Arab Gulf countries (with institutional investors executing nearly 60 per cent of the transactions).[220] For the time being the main listed securities are common stocks issued by joint-stock companies,[221] but there are plans to introduce trading in convertible bonds and warrants. In 1999, there are sixty-five actively traded companies on the official Kuwaiti Stock Exchange, most of which are Kuwaiti joint stock and Arab companies that satisfy listing requirements. These can be broken down to eight commercial banks, thirteen investment financial institutions (which include mutual funds and securities firms), four insurance companies, thirteen manufacturing companies, nine services companies, five food-processing companies and six non-Kuwaiti companies.[222] In late 1996, the Kuwait Stock Exchange had the first equity futures market in the Arab world, with futures contracts maturing in three, six, nine or twelve months.[223]

3.2.2 Jordan

3.2.2.1 Introduction
Given its small size and high receptiveness to external regional influences one cannot understand Jordanian legal and financial systems fully without grasping Jordan's geo-political setting. However, one must hasten to add that it has traditionally been less liberalized than the Lebanese system and freer than the semi-centralized economies of Egypt and Syria. As a civil law country, Jordan's legal system has been influenced heavily by other regional civil law states like Syria, Egypt and Lebanon. These countries were, during different historical periods, under direct French colonial rule and subsequently heavily influenced by the French legal system.[224] In this respect, one can easily discern almost identical similarities between Jordanian commercial, shipping, penal and administrative codes and their Egyptian, Syrian and Lebanese counterparts. Yet, although historically Jordan was under British rule from 1921 until 1946, its tribal laws and Ottoman codes were almost kept intact. This, however, can be contrasted to British mandated Palestine where the British pursued domestic policies, which influenced substantially its legal system. Like Kuwait, Jordan has separate civil and commercial codes that regulate its commercial and non-commercial activities. *Shari'a*'s role in Jordan, though important, is nonetheless not overriding in matters outside the remit of personal status laws. Article 2 of the 1952 Jordanian constitution stipulates that Islam is the religion of the state. Article 2(1) of the Jordanian Civil Code[225] stipulates that

---

[220] See *Financial Systems and Labour Markets in the Gulf Cooperation Council Countries*, IMF, Middle Eastern Department, November 1997, p. 15.

[221] Though, in 1981 Kuwaiti regulations allowed for the first time closed joint-stock companies to trade their shares on the official market.

[222] See daily Arab stock markets bulletin in *Al-Hayat* (London) 1 April 1999.

[223] The market is called El-Wa'ad Financial Investment Service, covering a limited number of stocks on the Kuwaiti Stock Exchange. See Azzam *The Emerging Arab Capital Markets: Investment Opportunities in Relatively Unplayed Markets*, p. 188.

[224] Syria and Lebanon until the late 1940s and Egypt during the late eighteenth century.

[225] Known as Law No. 43 of 1976, promulgated in Official Gazette No. 2645 dated 1 August 1968.

statutory shortage should be plugged by recourse to Islamic jurisprudence, failing which the court must apply general principles of *shari'a*. Paragraph 3 of the same Article adds that if there were still no applicable rules, then the court applies custom and general principles of justice. However, Articles 2, 4 and 5 of the Jordanian Commercial Act No. 12 of 1966[226] state that sources of commercial legislation in Jordan include the Commercial Code, the Civil Code and trade custom. With regard to the Civil Code being a legislative source of commercial practice, Article 2(1) of the Jordanian Commercial Act states that, if there is no adequate legislation available, then the rules of the Civil Code should be applied.

3.2.2.2 Company laws

Company law in Jordan is considered part of commercial regulations. Many early Jordanian company laws find their roots in corporate legislation enacted in neighbouring Arab countries. For example, the Companies Act No. 12 of the year 1964, in its provisions dealing with limited liability and foreign companies, re-enacted earlier Palestinian company law. In respect of publicly held companies, this Act followed rules adopted by the Syrian trade law. Before the Companies Act of 1964, companies in Jordan were subject to the Provisional Companies Act No. 33 of the year 1962, which replaced the Ottoman trade law which in itself was adapted from the French Trade Law of 1807.[227] The most important company Acts in Jordan are the Companies Act No. 12 of the year 1964, the Provisional Companies Act No. 1 of the year 1989 and the Companies Act No. 22 of the year 1997.[228] Article 6 of the 1997 Companies Act divides Jordanian companies into the following categories: general partnerships,[229] limited partnerships,[230] limited liability companies,[231] limited partnerships in shares,[232] and public shareholding companies.[233] Part 8 also regulates holding companies,[234] while Part 9 regulates mutual fund companies or joint investment companies[235] and Part 10 regulates offshore companies or exempt companies. The 1997 Jordanian Companies Act also introduced a new breed

---

[226] This Act which comprised 480 Articles was published in the Official Gazette No. 1910, 30 March 1966.

[227] See Aziz Akili, *Commercial Companies under Jordanian Legislation: A Comparative Study with Company Laws in Iraq, Lebanon, Saudi Arabia and Egypt*, Amman, 1995 at p. 23 (in Arabic).

[228] The Companies Act No. 12 of the year 1964, all its subsequent amendments, and all other legislation which may contravene were abrogated by Art. 285 of the Companies Act No. 22 of the year 1977 and Art. 320 of the Provisional Companies Act No. 1 of the year 1989. The Provisional Companies Act No. 1 of the year 1989 was published in the Official Gazette No. 3596 dated 1 January 1989. The Companies Act No. 22 of the year 1997 was published on page No. 2038 of the Official Gazette No. 4204 dated 15 May 1997.

[229] Arts. 9–40.

[230] Arts. 41–48.

[231] Arts. 53–76.

[232] Arts. 77–89.

[233] Arts. 90–203. These forms of companies are also found in company laws in a number of Arab countries including Egypt, Syria, Lebanon and Saudi Arabia.

[234] Arts. 204–208.

[235] Arts. 209–210.

of companies called "civil companies", which basically refer to partnerships between professionals such as lawyers, doctors, accountants, etc.[236]

3.2.2.3 Securities markets and laws

Before the establishment of the Amman Financial Market (AFM), trading in stock took place through brokers and estate agents. The AFM, which started its operations on 1 January 1978, was initially set up jointly by the Central Bank of Jordan (CBJ) and the IFC. In this respect, it is warranted to mention that in addition to its monetary role, the CBJ exercises regulatory and supervisory roles over commercial banks and other financial institutions in Jordan.[237] The Control of Foreign Currency Act No. 6 of the year 1959 extended supervising all matters related to foreign currency to the executive committee of the CJB.[238] Moreover, as a tool of central government planning, the CBJ has been instrumental in injecting funds into the AFM[239] and setting up financial institutions undertaking public services.[240] In addition, CBJ regulations allow banks to grant loans for the purpose of investing in the AFM.[241] Since its establishment, the number of listed companies traded on the AFM has almost doubled. Since 1980, the AFM has had a share price index. This indicator was developed to represent market trends. In 1992, the index was revised and updated in cooperation with the IFC. Companies in the index are based on their market capitalisation, liquidity and price. The index currently comprises the top sixty Jordanian companies. In the past few years, Amman has witnessed a burgeoning of brokers and securities firms, with investment banks taking a more visible role in issuing and underwriting shares. Equities, bonds (commercial and governmental), bank certificates of deposits are traded on the AFM and settlement among brokers takes place on a spot basis.[242]

Jordan also has a parallel market established in 1982, which requires less stringent listing requirements. Trading on the parallel market started on 20 February 1982.[243] Traditionally, the AFM has been subject to the Articles of Associations of the AFM, the

---

[236] Art. 7.

[237] The Central Bank of Jordan Act No. 4 for the year 1959 mandated that a central bank should be established. In addition, the Jordanian government also issued the Supervision of Banks Act No. 5 of the year 1959 extending the supervisory role of the CBJ to all other operating banks in Jordan.

[238] All these acts were published in the Official Gazette No. 1413 issued in April 1959. However, this Act was amended by the Act No. 33 of the year 1960.

[239] The CBJ demands that commercial banks invest at least 20 per cent of their paid-up capital and reserves in stocks, 4 per cent of their deposits in bonds of public holding companies, and 4 per cent of their deposits in government bonds and bills.

[240] The CBJ has also been instrumental in setting up the Housing Bank, which is the largest bank in Jordan specializing in giving loans for housing purposes. The CBJ has also been instrumental in setting up the Jordanian pension fund The Social Security Corporation.

[241] For example, from 30 December 1995 the CJB raised the level of credit facilities granted to individuals for investment in the AFM from JD150,000 to JD500,000. With regard to corporations and other juristic legal personalities, the ceiling was raised from JD300,000 to JD1 million. Though, should the amount requested exceed the JD150,000 or JD300,000, the prior consent of the CBJ is required. See the *Central Bank of Jordan Annual Report*, No. 31 for the year 1994, p. 48.

[242] See P. Cashin *et al.*, *Informational Efficiency in Developing Equity Markets*, WP/95/58, Research Department and Middle Eastern Department, IMF (June 1995), p. 3.

[243] By the end of the same year (1982), the parallel market was capitalized JD16 million.

Amman Financial Market Act No. 31 of the year 1976 and its amendments and the Amman Financial Market Act No. 1 of the year 1990 as amended by the Act No. 31 of the year 1992. Other directives and regulations have also governed the AFM, including; the Directives for Listing and Suspension of Jordanian Public Shareholding Companies;[244] the Rules Covering Trading in Financial Papers on the Amman Financial Markets;[245] Regulations No. 26 of the year 1980;[246] and the Draft Regulations on Listing and Accounting Principles of the year 1998 (Disclosure and Transparency Regulations).[247] Jordan has also recently promulgated a new securities act called the Provisional Financial Papers Act No. 23 of the year 1997.[248] This new Act separates the supervisory role of the AFM from its management branch. Traditionally, the AFM has been given mandate to regulate the activities of member firms dealing in securities such as underwriters, brokers and investment advisors. The 1997 Securities Act sets up a Jordanian Securities Commission and a Securities Deposit Centre,[249] regulates financial ser-

---

[244] These Directives comprise 39 articles. Part One defines a number of terms including "The regular market", "The parallel market", "The trading floor", "Delisting" and "Suspension". These directives also deal with "Listing requirements for public shareholding companies at the regular and parallel markets" (Part Two), "Transfer and delisting of public shareholding companies at the regular market" (Part Five) and "Suspension of public shareholding companies from the parallel market and the regular market" (Part Six).

[245] Issued in accordance with Arts. 3 and 87 of the Articles of Association of the Amman Financial Market. These Rules comprise over 255 articles. Part One deals with definitions. Part Two deals with procedures for trading in financial papers on the floor of the market. Part Two is subdivided into three chapters and thirteen sections dealing with: management and administrative procedures, execution procedures and procedures for follow-up on the execution of purchase and sale orders. Part Three deals with "Procedures regarding the transfer of title and the trading of financial papers outside the market floor" Part Three is subdivided into two chapters and four sections dealing with transfer of title of financial papers which are not subject to trading on the market floor through the legal department and trading in shares issued by companies which are not listed on the market. Part Four deals with "Settlement procedures", subdivided into 4 chapters dealing with settlement procedures between brokers, settlement procedures for returned agreements, settlements' procedures between brokers and clients and settlement procedures between brokers and the AFM.

[246] Known also as the Internal Regulations of the Amman Financial Market, which were issued in accordance with Arts. 34 and 51 of the Amman Financial Market Act No. 31 of the year 1976. These Regulations comprise eighty-seven articles. Part One deals with various definitions. It defines financial paper as "negotiable shares, bills and bonds issued in the Kingdom by the government, governmental institutions, municipalities, or public and private Jordanian shareholding companies, or any other negotiable financial papers". It also defines securities transactions as "buying and selling financial papers directly or through brokers". Part Two deals with the "Management of the AFM". Part Three deals with "Membership", "Duties of public shareholding companies" and "Conditions for membership of public shareholding companies". Part Four deals with "Brokers" and "Conditions of admission". Part Five deals with "Functions of brokers", "Duties and rights of brokers", "Actions by persons and Brokers" and "Securities transactions on the floor". Part Six deals with "Market resources", "Membership and brokers fees" and "Market commissions". Part Seven deals with "The general assembly". Part Eight deals with "Authorities of the disciplinary council".

[247] This draft comprises 38 articles.

[248] Art. 77 of this Act abrogates (after the passing of the specified period mentioned in Art. 73) the Amman Financial Market Law No. 1 of the year 1990 and all its amendments. In addition, Art. 80 also abrogates all other laws and regulations which may contravene this Act.

[249] Arts. 29–34. However, Art. 7 states that the Jordanian Securities Commission shall regulate and monitor issuance and dealing in securities and monitor business operations of entities which fall under its supervision. In addition it shall regulate disclosure of information

vices companies,[250] together with investment funds and investment companies[251] and imposes rules on disclosure.[252] It also addresses insider dealing and deals with violations and penalties.[253]

3.2.3 Oman

3.2.3.1 Introduction

Oman is an interesting example of an Arab country that still has no Civil Code; yet has managed to respond very well to commercial needs in the regulatory sphere.[254] Such success however is due to the fact that, before the discovery of oil, Oman was historically a trading nation. Moreover, its independence from direct foreign colonization has also meant that its local trade customs were developed in an organic manner that reflected its commercial needs. Theoretically, however, Oman's legislation has its origins from the *Ibadi*[255] sect of Islam, though lack of a Civil Code and the need to consult *shari'a* has not stultified Oman's civil justice system or rel-

---

cont.

  concerning securities and issuers and dealing of insiders, and regulate public tenders to purchase joint stock companies. However, Art. 20 states that the following are subject to the monitoring of the SEC: the Exchange, The Securities Deposit Centre, financial services companies, joint stock companies, investment funds and certified financial professionals.

[250] Arts. 35–43. Art. 35 states that financial services companies can invest as trustees, practice investment management, engage as financial advisors and financial brokers. They may also manage primary issues.

[251] Arts. 44–52. Art. 46, however, divides investment funds companies into "variable-capital investment funds" (open-ended), or "fixed-capital investment funds" (closed-ended.) Art. 50, states that an "investment company" means a public joint stock company which primarily undertakes or intends to undertake the business of investing and trading in securities, or owns or intends to own securities equal in value to more than 50 per cent of its total assets. The definition also excludes banks, insurance companies, financial services and holding companies.

[252] Arts. 53–66. Art. 55 stipulates that an issuer or an affiliate of an underwriter may not sell a security before the approval of the prospectus. Art. 56 states that the prospectus shall contain the following: adequate description of the issuer, adequate description of the security, the financial position of the issuer and any other information required by the SEC or authorized by it.

[253] Arts. 67–72. Art. 67 defines inside information as any information which has not been made public and that if advertised is expected to affect the price of one security or more. Art. 68 prohibits insiders including members of the Board of Directors of the SEC, and members of the Securities Deposit Centre and the executive managers and staff to exploit inside information. Paragraph (d) also prohibits a number of practices. These include giving the public a false information of real or fictitious dealing in securities, to influence the prices of securities and adversely affect the capital market in any shape or form. Art. 70 imposes hefty penalties on violations of the provisions of the Act. Such penalties vary between up to JD 20,000 and/or of a fine no less than twice and not more than five times the profit made or loss avoided by the violator. In addition to the fine, violators of Art. 68 can expect an imprisonment sentence of up to three years and up to one year for violating provisions 35(b), 36(b) and 45(c).

[254] For an exhaustive account of Oman's economy and prospective growth, see generally World Bank, Report No. 12199-OM entitled *Sultanate of Oman: Sustainable Growth and Economic Diversification* (May 1994).

[255] Sources of law according to the *Ibadi* sect are the Qur'an, *sunnah* (the prophet's deeds and unspoken approvals), *ijma'* (consensus of opinion), *qiyas* (analogy) and *istidlal* (juristic reasoning). See N. Saleh, *The General Principles of Saudi Arabian and Omani Company Laws: Statutes and Shari'a*, Namara Publications, London, 1981, pp. 28–31.

egated it to jurisdictional anachronisms. For, the fact that Oman does not have a Civil Code (with the implication that problems in civil dealings are to be referred to *shari'a*) has in practical terms meant that judges there would invoke modernist Arab civil jurists, most notable of which is Al-Sanhoury's *Al-Wasit*.[256] Needless to say, much of the Western-inspired commercial legislation in Oman, which peaked between 1971 and 1976, witnessed minimalist reliance on *shari'a*.[257]

3.2.3.2 Company laws

Like Kuwait and Jordan, Oman has a Commercial Act[258] and draws a distinction between civil and commercial activities. It also has a Commercial Register Law (No. 3/74),[259] which adopts the Latin tradition in setting aside special rules for commercial activities and traders. This distinction between commercial and non-commercial activities was further addressed in the Sultani Decree No.79/81, establishing the Authority for the Settlement of Commercial Disputes.[260] In large resemblance with Kuwait, Omani business associations are general partnerships,[261] limited partnerships,[262] joint ventures,[263] joint stock companies,[264] and limited liability companies[265] (or private limited companies). All Omani commercial companies (except joint ventures) possess juristic character.[266] Shares in joint-stock companies are required by law to have a nominal value, and offered to the public through public subscription.[267] Joint stock companies are also authorized to issue nominate or bearer negotiable bonds through public subscription, giving their owners the right to receive fixed rate interest.[268]

3.2.3.3 Securities markets and laws

The stock exchange in Oman (known as the Muscat Securities Market) started its activities in 1989, with sixty-eight joint stock companies.[269] However, the number of listed companies has risen substantially since then, sub-divided into banking, services, insurance and industrial (manufacturing) sectors. Oman also has a parallel market which trades stocks of companies that do not qualify for listing in the Muscat Securities Market (MSM), together with a third market. Number

---

[256] See A. Hirst's introduction to *Business Laws of Oman*, Graham & Trotman, 1988, p. 1.0–4.
[257] See Saleh, *The General Principles of Saudi Arabian and Omani Company Law*s, p. 32.
[258] Law No. 4/74 of May 15, 1974. Promulgated in Official Gazette No. 56 dated 1 June 1974.
[259] Ministerial Resolution No. 121/86, promulgated on 29 December 1986 implemented this law.
[260] Issued on 19 September 1981.
[261] See Art. 28 of Omani Commercial Companies Act (OCCA).
[262] See Art. 46 *ibid*.
[263] See Art. 51 *ibid*.
[264] See Art. 56 *ibid*.
[265] See Art. 136 *ibid*.
[266] See Art. 3 *ibid*.
[267] See Art. 85 *ibid*.
[268] See Art. 86 *ibid*.
[269] See Azzam, *The Emerging Arab Capital Markets: Investment Opportunities in Relatively Unplayed Markets*, p. 169.

of companies traded on the Parallel Market has also increased, allowing more joint-stock companies to tap into equity markets. Like Jordan, Oman has an elaborate recent Securities Act, which separates the regulatory responsibilities from the Exchange. Equity trading in Oman has been open to foreigners apart from the Arabs of the Gulf Co-operation Council, as foreigners can own up to 49 per cent of corporations. Also as in Kuwait, foreigners can own shares by investing in mutual funds. In a similar vein, Oman in its capital market laws has followed the Jordanian and Kuwaiti approach. For example, Article 87 of the Omani Commercial Companies Code accepts bonds as legitimate security. Furthermore, under Article 1 of the 1998 Omani Capital Market Law No. 80/98, the term "securities" refers to shares, bonds and "any" tradable security. It is, however, interesting to observe that the meaning of securities under this Code was literally copied from the earlier definition mentioned in Article 1 of the now repealed Muscat Securities Law No. 53/88.

3.3 Implications for comparative study

The subsection on the legal background of Kuwaiti, Jordanian and Omani securities laws has demonstrated that these countries can be the subject matter of a comparative study in securities regulation. For, despite the influence of *shari'a,* they follow commercial and civil code models which are not too dissimilar from continental law models. Further these Arab jurisdictions, *inter alia,* have adopted regulatory systems and market structure similar to Western models, albeit imperfect copies. Such similarities can also be seen through designating their exchanges as non-governmental (juristic) entities, operating on the same principles with strong emphasis on listing and disclosure. Their rules for share offering to the public (through using universal banks as underwriters of securities) are similar to those of Europe, though the mechanisms may vary. Moreover, the composition of participants in the markets is akin to participants on Western markets (commercial banks, broker-dealers, investment companies, insurance companies, etc.)[270] It follows that comparative aspects are viable, especially in the areas that have witnessed regulation. This means that a comparative study, which contrasts and compares the systems in certain market aspects, would be feasible.[271]

The choice of a comparative study with EU regulations is, however, not arbitrary. It can be justified on the following grounds. First, the overwhelming majority of Arab countries follow the EU and UK models of universal banking, as opposed to the US banking system under the Glass–Steagall Act of 1933 which separates commercial and investment banking activities. Second, with recent Arab (political and

---

[270] However, the presence of local and international institutional investors is less in Arab securities markets (partially due to restrictions imposed on nationality), which has effectively meant that unit trust schemes have become popular.

[271] I.e. listing rules, mechanisms of share offering, regulation of brokerage and securities firms, financial intermediation, regulation of fraud, etc. In this respect, (as was mentioned in the previous chapter) another area that would benefit greatly from a comparative legal examination would be civil remedies available for fraudulent activities and insider dealing, especially given the heavy reliance of Arab legislators on often-ineffective criminal law approach.

economic) attempts at creating an Arab Community markets, there is an increasing willingness on Arab securities markets' regulators to consider harmonizing their
regulations. The EU experience in this context would be important to reflect upon,
especially as such harmonization of entry requirements (on a par with EU "minimum" or "equivalent" standards) is already under way in the Gulf Co-operation
Council. In addition, there is also evidence of collective desire to link Arab securities markets in order to increase their depth through many multi-listing agreements.[272] Thirdly, looking at the EU is relevant due to the many recent association
agreements which Arab countries have signed with the EU. The European Union
has so far signed association agreements with a number of Arab countries including Egypt, Jordan, Tunisia and Morocco, which are expected to lead to the establishment of a free trade zone by the year 2010.[273] Such Arab–EU association agreements, though at the moment not directly related to financial services, are tying more
Arab markets with Europe in an unprecedented manner that is very likely to expand in the future to encompass many aspects of financial services.

Yet one must hasten to add that although comparative law has traditionally
been used as a tool for bringing about institutional change, it is inconceivable em-
pirically to tailor a regime of securities regulation that would address *all* regulatory
requirements in *all* countries.[274] Different institutional structures, varying scales of
economic development and political ideology, all inevitably lead to different methods of regulating securities industries.[275] Needless to say, securities regulation can
also often be influenced by pure domestic financial scandals.[276] It could equally depend on the peculiarity of the historical relationship between the central government
and the financial sector, as was the case in the self-regulatory system of the City of
London before the Big Bang.[277] Here the unique importance of the City as a financial centre, that had even occasionally financed expensive Crown activities, resulted
in regulatory autonomy favouring the City and its operators[278] (though, after the

---

[272] These mainly comprise multi-listing agreements inside the Gulf Co-operation Council.
[273] See L. Al-Rimawi, "Jordan's Association Agreement with the European Union: Comment",
Yearbook of Islamic and Middle Eastern Law, vol. 4, p. 486.
[274] See Norton and Sarie-Eldin, "Securities law models in emerging economies", pp. 339–441.
[275] See generally, M. Moran, *The Politics of the Financial Services Revolution: The USA, UK and
Japan*, Macmillan, London, 1990.
[276] Well-known historical English examples in this sense are the *1697 Act to Restrain the Numbers
and Practices of Brokers and Stock Jobbers* (passed after the damning report of the Royal
Commission of Trade in England) and the 1720 Bubble Act (enacted after the collapse of the
share price of the South Sea Company). See G. Gilligan "The origins of UK financial services
regulation", *The Company Lawyer*, vol. 18, no. 6, 1997, pp. 171–174. See also generally
G. Robb, *White-Collar Crime in Modern England: Financial Fraud and Business Morality,
1845–1929*, Cambridge University Press, 1992.
[277] The financial self-regulatory system of the City of London is also often attributed historically to
decentralization and lack of strong state interference. In more recent times, however, the lobbying
efforts of City professionals, its developed internal structures which were averse to public models in
regulation, together with its unique links with the Treasury and the Bank of England, have all
helped maintain the City's regulatory independence. See Gilligan, "The origins of UK financial
services regulation", pp. 167–174. See also C. Goodheart, "Structural Changes in the British
Capital markets" in C. Goodheart *et al.*, *The Operation and Regulation of Financial Markets*,
Macmillan, London, 1987, pp. 32–36.
[278] See Gilligan, "The origins of UK financial services regulation", p. 169.

Big Bang, the self-regulatory structure became two-tiered).[279] Moreover, in the context of much of the literature on emerging markets securities' regulation, it is accepted that there is no "unique blueprint" that can be transplanted from advanced economies into emerging markets regulatory systems.[280] However, one must add here that the role of the legal elite in transplanting foreign legal systems has, on a few occasions, proved influential.[281]

Nevertheless, underlying macroeconomic and institutional differences between developed and emerging economies should not undermine the intrinsic value of comparative legal studies in securities regulation for two main reasons. First, although a choice between civil or common law may justifiably present itself in choosing between "basic" commercial and contract law models, more sophisticated legal areas such as banking and securities laws do not necessarily lend themselves exclusively to the civil or common law models.[282] Second, comparative studies in securities regulation are particularly relevant due to increasing internationalization of securities markets, in the sense of less restrictive market barriers and complete liberalization of exchanges and currency convertibility. It can be further argued that recent flows of funds from industrial countries have inadvertently created a "worldwide allocation of savings", which makes financial regulators receptive to developing international supervisory standards that would promote the "robustness" of financial systems in industrial and emerging economies alike.[283] In this respect one can also justifiably add that the recent tendency to internationalize emerging securities markets can achieve three major benefits.[284] First, it reduces the cost of unfavourable international price developments by enhancing emerging markets' ability to utilize market-based risk management techniques. Second, it brings about external improvements resulting from the involvement of sophisticated institutional investors from developed countries in emerging securities markets, producing a bet-

---

[279] For the impact of the Big Bang on regulation in the UK see for example, L. Gower, "Big bang and city regulation" (1988) 51 *Modern Law Review*. See also on UK financial regulation generally, B. Rider *et al.*, *Guide to the Financial Services Regulation*. CCH Publications, 1997. For general books on the subject of securities regulations see L. Loss, *Fundamentals of Securities Regulations*, Little Brown, Boston, 1983. However, following the institutionalisation of the FSA, SROs are expected to continue their regulatory responsibilities until the regulation transferring their responsibilities to the Financial Services Authority becomes a law in early 2000. See *CCH Financial Services Newsletter*, No. 4, April 1998, p. 1.

[280] See for example Blommestein, *The Role of Financial Institutions in the Transition to a Market Economy*, p. 3, and generally Norton and Sarie-Eldin, "Securities law models in emerging economies", and B. Rider, "Blindman's bluff: a model for securities regulation", p. 351, in J. Norton and M. Andenas, *Emerging Financial Markets and the Role of International Financial Organisations*, Kluwer, 1996.

[281] See A. Watson, *Legal Transplants: An Approach to Comparative Law*, University of Georgia Press, 1993. His most salient example was Turkey's adoption of the Swiss Civil Code, largely due to its minister of Justice having studied law in Switzerland, pp. 115–116.

[282] See Norton and Sarie-Eldin, "Securities law models in emerging economies", p. 440.

[283] See generally J. Heimann, "Global institutions, national supervisions and systemic risk", *Financial Stability Review*, No. 3, pp. 82–91 (Autumn 1997). See also M. Knight, *Developing Countries and the Globalization of Financial Markets*, Monetary and Exchange Affairs Department, IMF, WP/98/105 (July 1998), p. 25.

[284] See M. Kumar *et al.*, *Emerging Equity Markets in Middle Eastern Countries*, Middle Eastern and Research Departments, IMF, WP/94/103 (September 1994) p. 14.

ter financial intermediation process and transfer of expertise and technology. Third, greater integration with international markets can result in enhancing policy credibility of emerging economies and provide an indirect effective disciplinary policy-making instrument. Admittedly, the internationalization of securities markets brought with it the associated problems of "regulatory arbitrage" in which investors seek out less regulated markets. Yet this state of affairs has been largely responsible for the development of transnational standards in securities regulation through attempts at harmonizing securities regulations on regional and international bases, together with increased co-operation between international enforcement agencies.[285] Moreover, transnational trading in securities has (since the mid 1980s) resulted in the development of international regulatory agencies working at achieving common standards in areas such as international equity offerings and international capital adequacy – albeit there is still a "long way to go" before achieving truly international securities markets.[286]

The internationalization argument for justifying a comparative study is relevant in the Arab context. For, as it was demonstrated in the previous subsection on the Arab region's recent macroeconomic developments, there is an ever-increasing Arab awareness of the need (and indeed active steps are being made) to internationalize Arab securities markets. Budgetary and fiscal constraints and limitations on external borrowing are all forcing Arab countries not only to rely on (and equally enhance) securities markets when raising capital, but also to even open them up to foreign investors.[287] Additionally, in light of Arab desire to integrate their economies and financial markets with the wider international financial system it is difficult to argue, nor is it even propitious to advocate a purely Islamic financial model of regulating capital markets. From the contemporary legal debate considered in the subsection on *shari'a*, one can further add that financial markets *per se* do not engender the same ideological and theologian concerns that have long accompanied the topic of Islamic banking. Furthermore, the recent proliferation of a generically distinct (or even paradigmatic) Islamic system of banking is not matched by a proliferation of Islamic financial markets that necessitates distinct Islamic models of regulation.[288]

---

[285] Such regional and international cooperation is, however, more prominent especially when confronting cross-border market manipulation. See OECD Documents (1993).

[286] For example the International Organization of Securities Commissions (IOSCO), established in 1986 with its membership comprising official securities markets' regulators from developed and developing countries. It strives to enhance the international integration (and harmonization) of domestic securities markets. See generally G. Underhill, *Keeping Governments out of Politics: The Internationalisation of Securities Markets and the Question of Regulation*, Working Paper No. 118, University of Warwick (August 1993).

[287] See generally P. Alonso-Gamo, *Globalisation and Growth Prospects in Arab Countries*, Middle Eastern Department, IMF, WP/97/125 (September 1997). However, such internationalization is taking place through cross-regional listings arrangements, listings of American depository receipts (ADRs) and global depository receipts (GDRs) in domestic equities, giving foreign investors and fund managers substantially freer access to domestic securities markets, etc.

[288] It is estimated that in the last few years Islamic banking has grown by an average of 15 per cent per annum and that market size is projected to reach US$100 billion by 2000. Moreover, 84 developing and emerging countries are, in varying degrees, now involved with Islamic banking. See Errico, *Islamic Banking: Issues in Prudential Regulations and Supervision*, p. 4.

Doing Business in Egypt

Tarek Riad *

Egypt presently has a promising legal environment in which to do business and the Egyptian government is doing its utmost to encourage foreign investment. The scope of the incentives and guarantees provided for investments has expanded in recent years as detailed below.

1 INVESTMENT

The present Law No. 8 of 1997 on Investment Guarantees and Incentives[1] – which replaced the previous Investment Law No. 230 of 1989 – offers incentives for Egyptians and foreigners for investment in certain fields of activities, specifically for:

(a) reclamation or cultivation of barren and desert lands;
(b) animal, poultry and fish production;
(c) industry and mining;
(d) hotels, motels, hotel flats, tourist villages and tourist transport;
(e) refrigerated transport of goods in refrigerators for storage of agricultural products, industrial products and food stuffs, container stations and silos;
(f) air transport and the services directly connected therewith;
(g) overseas maritime transport;
(h) oil services, assisting digging and exploration operations, and transport and delivery of gas;
(i) housing projects, the units of which are wholly leased empty for non-administrative housing purposes;
(j) the infrastructure, including drinking water, drainage, electricity, roads and communications;

---

* Partner at Kosheri, Rashed & Riad, Special Legal Adviser to the Speaker of the Egyptian People's Assembly.
[1] The law is fully set out in *Yearbook of Islamic and Middle Eastern Law*, vol. 4 (1997–98), pp. 517–530.

(k)   hospitals and medical and treatment centres which offer 10 per cent of their capacity free of charge;
(l)   financial leasing;
(m) guaranteeing subscription in securities;
(n)   risk capital;
(o)   production of computer software and systems; and
(p)   projects funded by the Social Fund for Development.

The law allows the Council of Ministers to add other fields to those mentioned above.

The Investment Guarantees and Incentives Law guarantees Egyptian as well as foreign companies and establishments against nationalization and confiscation.

There are no controls on the prices of the products of companies and establishments subject to this law or on their profits, and those companies and establishments have the right to own buildings, land and build real estate which is necessary for exercising and expanding their activities, whatever the nationality or place of residence of the partners or the percentage of their participation.

Moreover, these joint stock companies are exempted from the obligation to distribute 10 per cent of their profits to their employees and their boards of directors may be composed of foreigners.

The tax exemptions provided in the above-mentioned law include exemption from the tax on revenues of commercial and industrial activity of individuals, or the tax on profits of corporations as the case may be, for a period of five years, starting from the first financial year subsequent to the start of production or exercise of the activity.

This exemption shall be for a period of ten years with respect to companies and establishments set up in the new industrial zones, the new urban communities and in the remote areas determined by a decision by the Prime Minister.

In addition, profits of companies and establishments exercising their activities outside the Old Nile Valley and the partners' shares therein, shall be exempted from the tax on revenues of commercial and industrial activity or the tax on profits of corporations as the case may be, for a period of twenty years, starting from the first financial year subsequent to the start of production or exercise of the activity. A decision of the Cabinet of Ministers determines the areas to which this provision applies.

A percentage of the paid up capital equivalent to the Central Bank of Egypt's lending and discount rate for the accounting year shall also be exempted from the tax on profits of corporations, provided that the company is a joint stock company and its stocks are registered at one of the stock exchanges.

Yields of bonds and finance share warrants, and other similar securities issued by joint stock companies shall also be exempted from the tax on revenues of movable capital, provided they are offered for public subscription and are registered at one of the stock exchanges.

The Law on Investment Guarantees and Incentives also provides for subjection of all imported machines, equipment and instruments that are necessary for the projects to a reduced customs tax of 5 per cent.

Finally, this law provides that settling investment disputes in connection with the implementation of the provisions of this law may be carried out in the manner agreed upon with the investor, which may be reached between the concerned parties on settling these disputes within the context of the Conventions in force between the Arab Republic of Egypt and the country of the investor, or within the context of the Agreement on Settlement of disputes which arise in respect of investments, between the countries and the nationals of the other countries, which the Arab Republic of Egypt adhered to by virtue of Law No. 90 of the year 1971 (i.e. the Washington Convention of 18 March 1965, creating ICSID), according to the conditions, terms and in the cases where these agreements apply, or according to the provisions of the Egyptian Law on Arbitration in Civil and Commercial Matters promulgated by Law No. 27 of the year 1994.[2]

Agreement may also be reached on settling the afore-mentioned disputes by arbitration before the Cairo Regional Centre for International Commercial Arbitration.

2 FOREIGN EXCHANGE

There are no controls on import and export transactions of foreign exchange through the banks and other establishments that are authorized to deal in foreign exchange.

3 IMPORT AND EXPORT

Only Egyptian nationals and fully Egyptian owned and managed companies may engage in importation into Egypt for trade on condition of registration in the Register of Importers.

Nevertheless, Law No. 8 of 1997 on Investment Guarantees and Incentives provides that all companies and establishments subject to this law may import by themselves or via third parties what they need for their establishment's expansion or operation, including production necessities, materials, machines, equipment, spare parts and means of transport, without it being recorded in the Register.

Registration in the Register of Exporters is needed for engagement in export from Egypt and no restrictions are imposed on foreigners in this respect. Moreover, companies and establishments subject to Law No. 8 of 1997 have the right to export their products by themselves or through a third party without a licence and without the need for their registration.

4 COMMERCIAL AGENTS AND INTERMEDIARIES

Entry into the Register of Commercial Agents and Intermediaries is a condition for engagement in these activities, and only Egyptian nationals and fully owned and managed Egyptian companies may be inscribed in this Register.

---

[2] The law is fully set out in *Yearbook of Islamic and Middle Eastern Law*, vol. 1 (1994), pp. 500–517.

5 CHOICE OF LEGAL BUSINESS FORMS

The Egyptian law provides for the existence of full partnerships, limited partnerships, partnerships limited by shares, limited liability companies and joint stock companies, all of which are more or less modelled on the classical European continental style.

The Companies Law No. 159 of 1981 used to provide for the need to obtain an administrative licence in order to establish partnerships limited by shares, limited liability companies and joint stock companies, but since the promulgation of Law No. 3 of 1998[3] in January 1998, such requirement is no longer necessary and the administrative authority now has only to be informed, *a posteriori*, of their establishment.

However, an administrative licence is still needed from the Investment Authority in order to establish companies subject to Law No. 8 of 1997 on Investment Guarantees and Incentives.

The following details concerning limited liability companies and joint stock companies is worth mentioning.

6 LIMITED LIABILITY COMPANIES

The Egyptian limited liability company has a minimum of two founding members and a maximum of fifty whose responsibility is limited by the value of their shares in the company. The company may not engage in the activities of insurance, banking, savings, receive deposits or invest funds on behalf of third parties. No partner in the company may transfer a share in it to a third party without first offering it to existing members.

The minimum issued capital of a limited liability company is LE50,000 which must be fully paid up at incorporation. The issued capital may be 100 per cent foreign owned and is divided into equal parts, all of which must be subscribed on formation.

Limited liability companies are directed by one or more directors (at least one of whom must be Egyptian) and by their general assemblies. If the company has more than 10 partners it must also have a supervisory council.

7 JOINT STOCK COMPANIES

The responsibility of the shareholder of a joint stock company is limited by the number of his shares in the company. In general, the issued capital of the Egyptian joint stock company whose shares are not offered for public subscription is LE250,000 and the minimum issued capital of the company whose shares are offered for public subscription is LE500,000.

---

[3] The law is fully set out in *Yearbook of Islamic and Middle Eastern Law*, vol. 4 (1997–1998), pp. 531–535.

Ten per cent of the issued capital has to be paid at formation and it has to be increased to 25 per cent within three months from the date of formation of the company, and the rest has to be paid within a maximum of five years from this date.

Moreover, the issued capital of the company may be 100 per cent foreign owned and directed.

The company may also specify in its articles of association an authorized capital which may not exceed ten times the issued capital.

The members of the board of directors of the joint stock company are appointed and dismissed by the shareholders in an ordinary general meeting of the shareholders. The board of directors and the general meetings of the shareholders should be held in Egypt and the shareholders may vote in person or by proxy to other shareholders. Resolutions are passed by a simple majority of the shares represented at the meeting, unless the articles of incorporation require a greater majority. In extraordinary meetings, resolutions are passed by a two-thirds majority, unless the resolution relates to an increase or decrease of capital, dissolution of the company, a change of its purpose, or a merger, in which case the majority is three-quarters of the shares represented in the meeting.

Every company must appoint an independent auditor who is licensed to practice in Egypt.

Moreover, the employees of the company play a role, by virtue of the law, in management of the company, usually through an administrative committee, that views the subjects relating to the employees, and whose chairman is entitled to attend and vote in the meetings of the boards of directors of the company, and 10 per cent of the profits of the company, on condition of not exceeding the yearly salaries of its employees, has to be distributed to the employees of the company. The above rule relating to distribution of 10 per cent of employees does not apply to companies subject to Law No. 8 of 1997.

A foreign company may establish a branch in Egypt provided it is registered in the Egyptian Commercial Register and in a special register in the Egyptian Companies Department. Every year, the company's branch must submit to the Companies Administration, a copy of its balance sheet, profit and loss account and auditor's report, along with details concerning managers, personnel and salaries together with its profits and the employees part in it as stated above.

The branch must also abide by Egyptian legislation including the laws governing companies, taxation, labour, social insurance and foreign exchange, and must also employ an Egyptian auditor.

It should also be noted that partnerships limited by shares, limited liability companies, joint stock companies, and branches of foreign companies operating in Egypt may not employ foreigners representing more than 10 per cent of their work force, or pay them more than 20 per cent of the total payroll unless they receive an exemption by the concerned minister.

Representative offices of foreign companies may also be established in Egypt. They may not engage in any commercial activity and their sole purpose is to study the markets and the potentials of production for foreign companies in Egypt. They also have to be registered at the Egyptian Companies Department.

8 INCOME TAXES

The major taxes imposed on income in Egypt as follows:

(a)   personal income tax, imposed on individuals usually residing in Egypt and on non-residents' income derived in Egypt;
(b)   from movable capital;
(c)   from the commercial and industrial activity of individuals;
(d)   on salaries and wages;
(e)   from non-commercial professions;
(f)   from immovable property; and
(g)   corporate income tax.

We shall investigate this last tax further, due to its importance for foreign business in Egypt.

9 CORPORATE INCOME TAX

Joint stock companies, partnerships limited by shares and limited liability companies incorporated in Egypt are subject to corporate income tax as well as foreign banks, companies and establishments operating in Egypt (whether as principals having their main offices abroad or as branches) concerning their profits realized from their activities in Egypt. The taxable profits of those companies consist of the total revenue, including gains from the sale of fixed assets, after deducting all legitimate costs, expenses, exempt income, various allowances and relief for losses brought forward.

The standard rate of corporate income tax is 40 per cent. The rate is 32 per cent on profits arising from industrial and export activities and a noteworthy exemption from this tax is that joint stock companies listed in the stock market are allowed to deduct a sum equal to a percentage of their paid up capital, equal to interest income that can be earned on bank deposits (as decided by the Egyptian Central Bank). Moreover, all industrial joint stock companies with fifty employees or more and maintaining proper books of accounts are granted a tax holiday for a five-year period.

10 SOCIAL INSURANCE CONTRIBUTIONS

Social insurance must be paid by the employers to the Social Insurance Authority on behalf of their Egyptian employees. Expatriate staff are not liable for Egyptian social insurance unless their employment contracts are for longer than a year and on condition of reciprocal treatment for Egyptians working in the concerned foreign state.

The social insurance contributions cover old age, incapacity, death, work accidents, sickness and unemployment. The total employer's contribution amounts to 26 per cent of the employees' salaries and the employee's contribution amounts to 14 per cent.

11 LABOUR LAW

A work permit is required for foreigners who intend to work in Egypt. The present Egyptian Labour Law of 1981 provides for a probation period for the employee for up to three months and the employment contract may be either for a definite or an indefinite period of time.

Renewal of Egyptian employees' definite period employment contracts are considered *de jure* renewals for an indefinite period of time.

The legal maximum working hours are eight per day or forty-eight hours per week excluding overtime and meal periods, and employees must get weekly rest which must not be less than twenty-four hours.

Employees have the right to fifteen days of paid annual holiday during the first year of service, twenty-one days after working for one year and 30 days after working for ten consecutive years or at reaching the age of fifty.

The employee is entitled to six months of sick leave per year with pay between 75 and 85 per cent of the normal wage.

The minimum overtime premiums are 25 per cent of normal pay for overtime work during daylight, 50 per cent for work at night, and 100 per cent for work on rest days and holidays.

Dismissal of the employee is legal if he commits a serious offence as defined by law. However, it is quite difficult to dismiss employees for other reasons, including redundancy, without being liable to legal action for damages based upon unfair dismissal.

In all cases, dismissal of the employee has to be preceded by a presentation of his case to a special advisory committee. Employers may not change the work volume of the establishment or its activity that affects the number of employees without the approval of a committee whose members are appointed by a decision of the Prime Minister.

Finally, it should be noted that the present Egyptian labour law was promulgated in 1981, in a totally different social and economic climate than that which prevails today, and the Egyptian government, taking this factor into consideration, has prepared a new draft labour law which will be presented to the People's Assembly for approval in the near future.

12 PATENTS, TRADEMARKS AND COPYRIGHT

12.1 Patents and industrial designs

The law allows investors to obtain patent protection for fifteen years from the date of application and it may be extended for an additional five years in cases defined by the law. Exceptions are chemical inventions related to pharmaceuticals, medicines and food products generally, for which the patent period is currently ten years.

It is the patent holder's exclusive obligation and right to fully exploit the invention, otherwise the patent holder may be subjected to compulsory licensing in favour of a third party for failure to do so, as detailed in the law.

A separate office and register is maintained for industrial designs, and the protection period in this respect is for five years from the date of registration.

12.2 Trademarks

The Trademark Law provides owners with a protection period of ten years, subject to renewals for similar periods. The owner of the trademark is the person who effects the registration and that ownership cannot be challenged if the registered owner has used the trademark for five consecutive years from the date of registration without a legal action being successfully brought against him.

12.3 Copyright

Copyright protection includes, *inter alia*, architectural designs, speeches, musical works, theatrical pieces, maps, photographic and cinematographic works, works for broadcast on television or radio, video tapes and computer software.

Protection extends to fifty years after the death of the author. If the author is a legal entity then the protection begins on the date of first publication. In the cases of non-creative photographic and cinematographic works, the protection period ends after fifteen years from the date of first publication and the computer works protection is for twenty years from the date of deposition.

12.4 International conventions

Egypt is, *inter alia*, a signatory to the Paris Convention for the Protection of Industrial Property, the Hague Agreement on Industrial Designs, the Madrid Agreement on the International Registration of Trademarks and the International Patent Classification Agreement. Egypt is also a signatory of the final acts embodying the results of the Uruguay Round of multilateral negotiations at Marrakesh on 15 April 1994 (i.e. the WTO Agreement).

13 FINANCIAL LEASING

Egypt has a modern financial leasing law that was promulgated in 1995[4] and which provides for the necessity to register the financing lessors and the financing leases.

The foreign financing lessors are allowed to register themselves in the register of importers, mentioned above, concerning imports of goods destined for financial leasing, and are exempted from the conditions of Egyptian nationality and management provided for in the above-mentioned laws regulating the registration of

---

[4] The law is fully set out in *Yearbook of Islamic and Middle Eastern Law*, vol. 2 (1995), pp. 517–530.

importers. Moreover, the foreign lessor inscribed in the register of lessors has the right to be entered into the commercial register.

14 GOVERNMENTAL TENDERS AND AUCTIONS

A new law concerning governmental tenders and auctions was promulgated in 1998[5] and it clears up some of the ambiguities found in the previous law. The new law explicitly provides for the right of the private contractor to claim damages from the government before the Egyptian courts in cases where it contravenes its contractual obligations, unless the parties agree to arbitration in accordance with the Egyptian Law on Arbitration in Civil and Commercial Matters, No. 27 of 1994 as amended.

15 SETTLEMENT OF DISPUTES IN CIVIL AND COMMERCIAL MATTERS

Egypt modernized its arbitration law in 1994 by adopting the UNCITRAL Model Law with very limited modifications. The new law, No. 27 of 1994,[6] applies to all arbitrations which take place within the country, with the possibility of obtaining assistance from the judicial courts to implement the arbitration agreement, to secure the proper functioning of the procedures, together with the enforcement of the awards rendered thereunder. Awards rendered abroad are enforceable under the New York Convention of 1958 to which Egypt has adhered since 1958.

In this respect, it is important to note that the setting aside of a foreign award is subject only to the grounds provided for under Article 5 of the New York Convention, but an award rendered in Egypt under the new legislation can be amended for an additional ground which is the failure by the Arbitral Tribunal to apply the law chosen by the parties to govern their contract. Equally, the request for enforcement becomes admissible only after the expiration of the period required for lodging an annulment plea, i.e. the requesting party has to wait ninety days before submitting a request for enforcement in front of the competent court which is, in principles, the Cairo Court of Appeal.

Finally, we note the transformation of the classical French concept of the "concession contract" in the field of construction, administration and management of public services, as well as electricity, roads and airports. Under the new Anglo-Saxon abbreviations of "BOOT and "BOT", the new generation of governmental contracts dominate the trend towards privatization and the transfer to the private sector of initiatives which were formerly in the domain of the public sector.

---

[5] Law No. 89 of 1998, see Part II, pp. 196–197.
[6] See note 2 above.

A Note on the Theory and Practice of Islamic Banking

*John J. Donohue**

1 INTRODUCTION

On 28 March 1997 the daily *al-Hayat* carried a report from Kuwait that the Kuwaiti House of Finance intends to found an Islamic Bank in Lebanon.

The following day the Beirut *Daily Star* carried a report of Agence France Presse that Islamic banks in Egypt are under attack as hypocritical operations taking advantage of people's religious conviction to amass their own wealth. Shaikh al-Azhar has joined in the attack by stating that Islamic banks should erase the word '*Islamic*' from their title, as it suggests that other banking establishments are not Islamic. He claims that banks paying fixed interest rates in advance are actually closer to Islam than the so-called Islamic banks. The Shaikh's position is rather more nuanced than the AFP report would give us to understand, but there is no doubt that the banks are appearing in a bad light because of the bankruptcy of some Islamic investment companies such as Rayyan in Egypt, and because of their connection with the financing of Muslim extremist groups. At the same time, Islamic banks are on the increase, and their profits outstrip those of traditional banks.[1]

There is no doubt that the Islamic aspect, i.e. obeying religious injunctions, can serve to mobilize funds, especially those of people who may not have confidence in large banks, and who see doing things the Islamic way as an assertion of identity.

---

* Director, Centre d'Etudes du Monde Arabe Moderne (CEMAM), Professor, St Joseph University.
[1] Examples of the worldwide interest in the phenomenon of Islamic banking appear in e.g. Special Advertising Section on Islamic Banking, *Newsweek*, 17 May 1993; Diarmid O'Sullivan, *Special Report on Islamic Banking*, MEED, 12 July 1996. In *Al-Bunuk al-islamiyya hawl al-'alam*, Dar al-Afaq al-Jadidah, Beirut, 1996, Suha Ma'ad goes so far as to consider Islamic banking as a solution for Lebanon's reconstruction efforts, through non-interest loans (provided that the country's banking laws are changed).

Saudi Arabia's al-Rajhi Banking and Investment Corporation reported an 8 per cent rise in net income for 1996 to $322 million. Banque Audi of Lebanon had an increase of 50 per cent over 1995, for a total of $19.8 million.[2]

The Emirates has announced plans for creating the world's largest Islamic bank. The Emirates already have the Dubai Islamic Bank, which is the second in the world after the Egyptian Faysal Islamic Bank. In May 1996, Kazakhstan became the fiftieth member country in the Jedda-based Islamic Development Bank, and in July 1997 Citibank of New York opened an Islamic bank in Bahrain. The Dutch bank ABN AMRO is also opening an Islamic division to its offshore unit in Bahrain. Two of London's merchant banks, Kleinwort Benson and ANZ International, have Islamic divisions.

2 HISTORY

The history of Islamic banks is recent, but concern with Islamic economy dates at least from the beginning of the twentieth century.

The economies in Islamic countries functioned effectively for several centuries and developed casuistic solutions to avoid interest. However, in the nineteenth century Islamic countries were incapable of mobilizing the capital necessary for the development of modern societies. They had to borrow and finally ended up in a state of indebtedness to Western banks and states.

Can equity-based financing function well in a modern state? In the Middle Ages, Mediterranean trade (Muslim and non-Muslim) was based largely on equity-based forms of financing. Is it merely an accident that the decline of Middle East trade in history coincided with the gradual replacement of equity financing with debt financing in other regions of the world?

That is a question for historians. Here we try to put the practical dimension in a contemporary perspective.

The focus of concern has been usury (*riba*).[3] The central question is whether the interest paid on deposits in a traditional bank is usury or not. In 1903 Muhammad Abduh declared that the interest paid by the Postal Savings Fund (*Sunduq al-Tawfir*) in Egypt was *riba* and should not be accepted.[4]

However, in the Egyptian Civil Code drawn up by Abd al-Razzaq al-Sanhuri which became law in 1949, usury is defined as interest in excess of 7 per cent (on the European model).

The use of the banking system introduced from Europe does not appear to have bothered the majority of the people who had money to bank. But the political and economic situation of Islamic countries caught between the capitalist and the socialist models of the West sent some Muslims in search of a third way.

---

[2] MEED, 14 March 1997.
[3] Qur'an, II, 275.
[4] Cf. Chibli Mallat, *The Renewal of Islamic Law*, Cambridge, 1993, p. 159.

We have writings on Islamic economy by the Iraqi jurist Muhammad Baer al-Sadr dating from the 1960s.[5] The interest in establishing Islamic banks followed. The brief histories available focus on Arab contributions, but the real impetus may have come from Pakistan which was to be a fully Islamic state. In the bibliographies I have seen, the literature dates from the late 1960s and early 1970s.

For the Arab world, the first modern Islamic bank was created by Dr Ahmad al-Najjar at Mit Ghamr in Egypt in 1962. He sought to mobilize the savings of the peasants for development of their own rural areas. His experiment was short lived but inspired the formation of the Nasir Social Bank in September 1974, a government-sponsored institution with social aims. Also in 1974 in Jedda, a group of Islamic countries formed the Islamic Development Bank pursuant to a conference of Islamic Finance Ministers in 1973. In February 1976, the first World Congress on Islamic Economy was held in Mecca, organized by the University of King Abdul-Aziz.[6]

The influx of petro-dollars in the wake of the October War certainly played a part in the spread of Islamic banks. The first Islamic bank with the functions of a commercial bank (service and investment), the Islamic Bank of Dubai, was founded in the Emirates in 1975. The Kuwaiti House of Finance followed in 1977, the Egyptian Faysal Islamic Bank also in 1977. This led the way to the establishment of the Barakah Islamic Bank in Bahrain in 1983 with a Barakah International Bank in London, the Jordan Islamic Bank in 1989 and the Tunisian-Saudi House of Finance.

There are presently over 100 Islamic banks and financial institutions.

3 CLASSICAL LAW TRANSACTIONS AND MODERN PRACTICE

The various transactions usually listed for Islamic banking run as follows:

(a) *mudaraba*: one party provides money, the other an asset (land, machinery, etc.) or expertise. They agree on the division of profits beforehand. Any losses are borne by the lender;

(b) *musharaka*: partners invest in a project and manage it jointly having decided on the division of profits beforehand. The bank provides equivalent venture capital;[7]

(c) *murabaha*: a bank buys goods on behalf of a customer who then buys them at a mark-up at a later date or by instalments; .

(d) *ijara*: the bank buys an asset and leases it to someone who pays the bank a fixed fee. One version is a lease which leads to final ownership by the lessee.

Less important transactions include:

(a) *muzara'a*: this is a transaction for agriculture. The bank purchases the equipment and seeds, the farmer provides the land and labour;

(b) *musaqat*: the finance of irrigation projects, etc., concerning land.

---

[5] Cf. Mallat, *The Renewal*, and J. Donohue, "Notre Economie", *Les Cahiers de l'Orient*, Paris, 1987, pp. 8–9, 179–202.

[6] CEMAM Reports (Beirut), 1976, pp. 25–40.

[7] See *Arab Law Quarterly* (1999) no. 3, which is devoted to *musharaka* financing.

These transactions have not been used equally, and most remain theoretical. Two decades into the spread of Islamic banking, we analyse comments by some of the writers on the subject.

For Professor Mannan, in the light of the prohibition of usury in the Qu'ran, money cannot be conceived as a commodity. Profit or gain must come from work or risk. For him, the Islamic economy is the subject of an integrated social science with a constant exogenous variable (the will of God).[8]

Here are, according to Mannan, the targets and sectoral priorities set by the IDB (Islamic Development Bank) in 1975:

Table 1 IDB targets and priorities in 1975

The functional targets	*Actual results 1985*
1 Investment in profit-sharing projects 40–45%	Only one profit sharing deal foreign trade financing 80% loan leasing 11% equity assistance 9%
2 Equity participation 30–40%	
3 Loans for social and infrastructure 2–25%	
Sectoral priorities	*Actual (%)*
1 Agriculture 30–40%	16.35
2 Industry 25–35%	34
3 Public utility 10–15%	13.8
4 Transport and communications 10–15%	20
5 Social sectors 10–15%	12
6 Others 5–10%	1.2

As an example of how money can make money in Islamic ventures, Mannan dedicates two pages to Dar al-Mal al-Islami (DMI) which in 1986 was the largest Islamic investment company.[9] The bank was formed in 1981 by indenture under the laws of the Commonwealth of the Bahamas as a distinct legal entity with authorized capital of US$1 billion; under the terms of the indenture, all trust assets are held by the fiduciary custodian and investments are administered by the trust administrator, DMI SA, Geneva – a wholly owned Swiss subsidiary.

Thus was established a multinational holding company with a worldwide network of banks, insurance companies and investment firms operating in accord with the *shari'a*. Five types of account were considered for the planned twenty-eight Faysal Islamic Banks, nine investment companies and five insurance firms:

---

[8] Muhammad Abdel-Mannan, *Islamic Economics: Theory and Practice*, Boulder, Colorado, Westview Press, 1986, pp. 9–11. To this is added a brief comment on how the Christian Church lost its battle to the secularists on the question of usury (interest).

[9] *Ibid.*, p. 206.

(a)   a so-called fourth *mudaraba* – at least US$500, 3 per cent retained, yield similar to traditional companies;
(b)   an institutional account – US$90,000, 1 per cent retained, with a better yield;
(c)   an investment account – US$500,000, 1 per cent retained, yields up to 30 per cent;
(d)   an Islamic current account – US$20,000, no profit; and
(e)   a so-called seventh *mudaraba* – an insurance, savings and investment account.

It is not clear how the multinational Islamic venture has fared, but Mannan noted that achievements may fall short of expectations – progress in this area depends on the political will of leaders. In that particular case, the operation, which was conceived by Prince Muhammad Al-Saud, the son of the late King Faysal, did not curry much favour with the Saudi authorities.

    In a study on Islamic banks in Sudan, published in the journal *al-Liwa*,[10] it is clear that these banks prefer *murabaha* to *musharaka*.

Table 2 Comparison of *musharaka* with *murabaha*[1]

Name of bank	Total financing	% partnership	% resale	Profit by resale (%)	Profit by partners (%)
Bank Faysal	138,459	28	72	26	64
Sudan Islamic Bank[2]	121,712	46.4	52.4	42.7	56.6
Barakah[3]	47,601	35	65	15	18
Islamic Bank West Sudan[4]	12,157	35.9	63.8	6.9	6.4
Development Bank[5]	73,827	16.5	55.1	–	–

Notes:

[1]   Information for 11 months of 1406 (1986), twelve-month estimate
[2]   Operations in form of commenda reached £1,460,000; 0.5% of total. Return of 0.7%
[3]   Estimation
[4]   Operations in commenda 40,000 or 0.2% of total, return of 30%
[5]   Operations in commenda of £20,947,000, 28.4% of total

---

[10] "New study on Islamic banks in Sudan", *al-Liwa* (journal) 15 December 1989 and 22 December 1989.

Table 3 Investment operations contracted between 1980 and 1986 according to the *sharīʿa* form followed in Faysal Islamic Bank in Sudan

	Murabaha (£000)	%	*Musharaka* (£000)	%	*Mudaraba* (£000)	%	Other (£000)	%	Total (£000)
1980	11,380	41	16,185	59	55	–			27,620
1981	16,951	30	38,987	69	565	1			56,503
1982	10,433	14	56,405	77	5,773	8	112	1	72,723
							1		
1983	42,145	31	86,844	64	6705	5			135,694
1984	45,874	62	27,376	37	740	0.3			73,990
1985	70,210	65	37,879	35	260	0.3			108,350
1986	84,876	61	54,265	39	–	–			139,141

For Muhammad Abduh Yamani,

the experiment on the whole is an attempt to imprint (*tanzil*) the Islamic rules of transactions on contemporary banking activity. It has brought Muslim money back into an economic role. In commercial banks with interest money lies idle and is lost to Islamic countries. The Islamic bank has put new blood into economic activity and has given little people the possibility of getting finance for home industries.[11]

However the experiment is young, barely twenty years old, and the author makes a point that the attempt to create Islamic banking is a human action, so there are errors and shortcomings. What are the problems?

Among the external factors, he mentions the insufficiency of existing legislation organizing banking in Islamic countries;[12] the relations with the Central Bank which sets credit ceilings and legal reserves; the fact that the Central Bank does not act as lender of last resort if an Islamic bank is short on liquidity; the problem of taxes, as interest is free of tax, but the investment activities of Islamic banks are highly taxed. In addition, the countries with the greatest absorption capacity for long-term investment lack the infrastructure favourable to investment. The Islamic bank has hesitated to enter here, though according to its philosophy it should. Finally, there is the moral problem: successful *mudaraba* operations depend on the fidelity, honesty and good intentions of the *mudarib* (agent). Islamic banks incurred losses because of bad faith of many *mudaribs* and since has turned away from these contracts to *murabaha*.

As for internal factors, they have mostly been problems of expertise, and appear in the lack of appropriate banking structure; or appropriate codified instruments; of coordination among Islamic banks; and of trained cadres who understand Islamic banking. Each bank has a *shari'a* committee to approve or disapprove of transactions, but there are differences of opinion between committees.

Not only have *murabaha* contracts come to dominate but Islamic banks also engage in buying and selling currency to avoid the risk of fluctuations. They calculate a margin of gain in reference to interest rates on loans between London banks (LIBOR). they also deal with shares of companies which still work with usurious interest.

The Islamic banks also favour the profits of shareholders at the expense of depositors. The return to a depositor should be higher than that of traditional banks. In fact, it is usually lower.

---

[11] *Al-Hayat*, 4 February 1996.

[12] Egypt passed a law in 1988 regulating the operation of Islamic investment funds and requiring them to comply with standard banking regulations. In Jordan, Islamic banks are licensed, regulated and supervised by the Central Bank to avoid malpractice and to ensure that these investment companies are subject to the same interest rate restrictions as other banks. ESCWA *Report on Housing Finance*, E/ESCWA/HS/1992/2, 8 and 20.

In March 1998, rumours of difficulties in the Dubai Islamic Bank provoked a rush on withdrawals. The government of the Central Bank intervened to quiet fears and imposed a blackout on news of the Bank, after the press revealed that the director and two of his partners had embezzled between US$15 and 150 million. The Bank had earlier problems because of investments in the International Bank of Credit and Commerce which collapsed in the early 1990s.

In a 1996 report for the *Newsletter of the Economic Research Forum for the Arab Countries, Iran and Turkey*, the telling data shown in Table 4 were presented.[13]

Table 4 The financing operations of Islamic banks in Iran and other countries 1981–1994

	1981–85 %	1986–90 %	1991–93 %
Profit–loss sharing techniques			
Iran	38.2	33.3	32.7
Other	8.4	7.6	6.5
Mark-up financing techniques			
Iran	50.5	56.2	60.1
Other	82.9	88.9	90.1

Table 5 The structure and distribution of investment in Islamic banks 1984–1992

Term structure of finance	(%)
Short term	75.4
Medium term	5.4
Long term	2.1
Real estate	15.4
Sectoral distribution of finance	
Agriculture	7.2
Real estate	15.4
Trade and commerce	82.1

The author concludes that the ascendancy of *murabaha* and debt creating contracts which form 60–80 per cent of investments, does not fit the original vision of Islamic banking, and the man on the street cannot see the difference between Islamic banks and those which are traditional. Islamic banking investments are short term. Only 10 per cent of Islamic banks' assets had maturities of more than five years.

4 RECENT DEVELOPMENTS

Recently, several Islamic banks have launched independent funds, but this raises religious problems. Can a Muslim invest in the stock of a company that has borrowings or interest income?

---

[13] Tarik M. Yousef, "Islamic banking, financial development and growth", *Newsletter of the Economic Research Forum for the Arab Countries, Iran and Turkey*, September 1996.

Three schools of thought exist. The first school is strict, and rejects any such investment. The second school, such as adopted by Dallah al-Barakah, purifies gains of interest. Dallah made a five-year study of 19,000 companies in developed economies and chose 560 which met its Islamic criteria. The third school, which is based on some precedents in classical law which accept the receipt of interest in *dar al-harb*, sees no problem in interest-bearing investments.

Some observers, such as Adnan al-Bahar of the *International Investor*, Kuwait, are optimistic, predicting that Islamic banking will attract 80 per cent of Muslims. Others, such as an official of the Arab Banking Corporation, explain that Islamic banks will have to adapt some basic Islamic requirements to those of monetary agencies. The Governor of the Bank of England, who suspended the banking licence of al-Baraka International Bank in 1993, has raised questions about three areas: the role of the *shari'a* committees, the problem of risk management in the absence of interest rates, and the appropriate levels of capital for Islamic banks.

There is a certain satisfaction in the fact that the Islamic banks have survived despite difficulties. However, it would appear that there is a need for more serious evaluation and research if they are to play the role they propose for themselves.[14]

Finally, one should concur with Tarik Yousef, who remarks that the phenomenon of Islamic banking will stand out as an intriguing chapter in the history of international finance in the twentieth century, if only because it has managed to survive and grow under the pressures of today's global market while at the same time being governed by religious principles dating back to the seventh century.

---

[14] Yousef proposes interdisciplinary historical research into the reasons for the eighteenth- and nineteenth-century collapse of the classical Middle East trade financing system.

The 1998 Proposed Civil Marriage Law in Lebanon: the Reaction of the Muslim Communities

*Nadia M. El-Cheikh**

1 INTRODUCTION

The personal status of the Lebanese is governed by the respective laws of the country's eighteen recognized religious communities. Article 9 of the Lebanese Constitution states that the State shall "safeguard for the citizens of whatever religion or sect, due respect to their personal status code and their spiritual interests".[1] In addition to the Christian and Jewish communities, the Lebanese Constitution recognizes three main Muslim communities, the Sunni, the Shi'ite and the Druze. Each of these communities possesses its own jurisdiction and sole competence in all matters of personal status.[2] Personal status rules are primarily *shari'a* based in that *shari'a* courts have jurisdiction with regard to the Sunni Hanafi and Shi'ite Ja'fari sects, while the Druze have a Codified Personal Status Law promulgated in 1948 and amended in 1959. The various confessional laws, both Muslim and Christian, contain fundamental differences. Complications arising from the variety of laws regulating the same issue are particularly acute in the context of marriage between persons belonging to different sects. In order to provide some remedy to this situation, the president of the republic presented the Cabinet with a detailed draft of a facultative civil personal status code in February 1998.

---

* Assistant Professor of History, American University of Beirut, Lebanon. The author woudl like to thank the Institute for Women's Studies in the Arab World (LAU), Mona Khalaf, Myriam Sfeir, Ghena Ismail, Hisham Shehab and Fadi Moghaizel for providing documentation for this paper.
[1] In Jamal Nasir, *The Islamic Law of Personal Status*, London, 1990, p. 32.
[2] Edmond Rabbath, *La formation historique du Liban politique et constitutionnelle*, Lebanese University, Beirut, 1973, p. 125.

The supporters of the law argued its necessity in Lebanon by pointing to the fact that couples are forced to travel abroad to contract the civil marriages denied to them by local laws. This was deemed to be an infringement of the country's sovereignty, as the national civil courts are thus forced to apply foreign laws under whose auspices such marriages take place. Those Lebanese who choose not to marry outside Lebanon are forced to undergo conversion in order to comply with religious marriage requirements.[3] Furthermore, the proposed law, in some of its articles, was designed to be advantageous to the juridical status of women, since to varying degrees the prevalent religiously based personal status rules are detrimental to women.[4] The preamble to the law also stressed the beneficial impact that such a law could have on national cohesion.

In this article, I will review the proposed law and reconstruct the reaction to it by the three principal Muslim sects in Lebanon, namely the Sunnis, the Shi'ites and the Druze. I will outline the arguments, actions and reactions of different Muslim constituencies, namely the clerics, the politicians and the intellectuals and activists.

2 THE PROPOSED LAW

The question of civil personal status has a relatively long history in Lebanon. On 28 April 1936, a decree by the French Mandate authorities entrusted the civil courts with personal status litigation, reducing the juridical competence of the religious courts to actions relating to marriage. However, the protests of all the communities, particularly the Muslims, were so violent that the French High Commissioner was forced to postpone the decree indefinitely.[5] After independence in 1943, discussions concerning the introduction of an optional personal status law occurred during a debate surrounding the law of 2 April 1951 which gave Christian religious courts powers similar to those enjoyed by Muslim religious courts. It is significant that, at the time, both Muslim and Christian clerics exerted strong pressure to institute the above-mentioned law. In reaction to the extension of the powers of the religious courts, the Order of Lawyers proclaimed a strike that lasted for six months. The strike was called off only after the lawyers received a promise that Parliament would discuss civil personal status law sometime in the near future. As in the 1950s, debates over a civil personal status law burst out intermittently in the 1960s and early 1970s. One of the most serious proposals preceding the current one was elaborated by the Democratic Party in 1971. In 1997, the Syrian National Socialist Party also proposed such a law in Parliament.

The proposed bill of 1998 is mainly confined to issues pertaining to marriage and its effects without delving into issues of inheritance and testaments; thus it does not include all aspects of personal status. By not discussing the religious affiliations of the parties involved, the proposed law implicitly permits the marriage of a Muslim woman to a Christian man, a union forbidden by the *shari'a*. More explicitly, a

---

[3] *The Daily Star*, 6 February 1998.
[4] Laure Moghaizel, "Les textes juridiques: vers l'élimination de la discrimination", paper presented at a conference entitled *Les droits de la femme au Liban. Situation et perspective dans le cadre de la réconstruction nationale*, Beirut, 1993.
[5] Violette Daguerre, "Droit et nécessité", *Le Liban citoyen* 42 (April–June 1998), pp. 15–20.

number of articles are in clear contradiction to Muslim religious laws on personal status. Article 9 infringes Muslim men's legal rights to marry more than one wife by clearly stating that "it is illegal to contract a marriage between two persons, if one of them is already bound by an existing marriage". Article 25 establishes the equality of the sexes in divorce by granting equal rights to women and men in initiating a divorce. The law also allows a marriage prohibited in Islam, namely the marriage between two persons connected through the relationship of *rida ʿah* (suckling). Another article in the proposed law which is fundamentally contrary to the *shariʿa* recognizes the principle of adoption.

The proposed law has been criticized by supporters of civil marriage as being wanting in secular spirit in that it allows religious marriages to be subject to religious laws. Indeed, the proposed law does not aim at abolishing the religious courts.[6] Moreover, the proposed law follows current legal practices with regard to other legal areas, such as child custody, guardianship and inheritance. Thus, following a divorce, custody of the children is automatically given to the mother until the son reaches the age of seven and the daughter the age of nine (Art. 42). As for guardianship, it is given to the father and reverts to the mother in the cases of the ex-husband's death, disappearance or loss of sanity (Art. 86). Finally, the law relinquishes the regulation of inheritance and testaments to the current religious personal status laws of the concerned parties (Art. 110).[7]

3 THE SUNNIS

3.1 The religious establishment

As soon as the actual text of the optional personal status law was made public, the clamour which had been going on for a few months intensified. Rumours that it was impending had already aroused vocal opposition. The polemic had started more than a year earlier when, on the occasion of Lebanon's Independence Day (22 November 1996), the President announced his intention to present and support this proposal. A statement by the Sunnite Islamic Council rapidly followed which denounced the future project with a rare virulence.[8] The campaign was spearheaded by the Sunni Grand Mufti of Lebanon, Shaykh Muhammad Rashid Qabbani. The Sunni clerical establishment, headed by Qabbani, was the most categorical in its rejection of the law. The arguments offered against it were based upon the grounds that it opposed legal provisions in the *shariʿa*; that it introduced further secularism at the expense of the religious authorities and religious courts; and that it endangered the well-being of the family.

The Sunni establishment's position concentrated on a number of legal rejections. The first concerned the illegality, from an Islamic perspective, of a contract of marriage between a Muslim woman and a non-Muslim man. Under the *shariʿa* and all

---

[6] Fadi Mughayzil, "al-Zawaj al-madani al-ikhtiyari min mindhar huquq al-insan", unpublished paper.

[7] Dalal al-Bizri, *al-Nahar*, 20 March 1998, p. 19.

[8] Georges Corm, "Mariage civil. Inverser le problème", *Le Liban citoyen* (April–June 1998), pp. 1 and 25–6.

modern Islamic laws, both for the Sunnis and the Shi'ites, the marriage of a Muslim women to a non-Muslim is null and void.[9] This view is so pervasive that even one of the most moderate of Shi'ite clerics, Muhammed Hasan al-Amin, confirmed that there is a consensus among Muslim jurists that such an act is forbidden.[10] A second major issue pertained to the prohibition of polygamy. The Sunni position on this matter was clearly enunciated by the judge Muhammad Kan'an, who stated that the stipulation in Article 9 preventing a Muslim man from marrying more than one wife would be contrary to the Qur'an, the Sunna and the *ijma'*. Moreover, Article 61 defined as illegitimate progeny children resulting from the relationship between two persons one of whom married another under this law. Thus, a Muslim man who married in accordance with the civil law, and then contracted a Muslim marriage with another woman would find his progeny resulting from the second marriage to be illegitimate. Article 61 was understood by the Muslim establishment as a law outlawing polygamy.[11]

Another criticism concerned the articles pertaining to divorce. Muslims contended that the religious courts take rapid decisions concerning such lawsuits in order to ensure a quick stabilization of the lives of the persons involved. One critic asserted that in light of the situation prevalent in the Lebanese civil courts, divorce lawsuits were likely to last for many years, thus possibly impeding the resumption of a normal life for the parties concerned.[12] On a more substantial level, the Muslims criticized Article 26 which prohibits divorce by mutual consent. Objections were also raised concerning the length of time required to lapse before a divorced woman is allowed to remarry (*al-'idda*). Article 34 states that a woman can remarry only 300 days after the nullification of the previous marriage. This makes the *'idda* three times longer than what the *shari'a* stipulates. People related to each other via "suckling" are allowed to marry under the proposed law, thus contradicting Article 18 of the Law of the Rights of the Family of 16 July 1962, which states "Marriage of women to a man where there is a relationship by suckling between them shall be permanently forbidden."[13] The article which legitimizes adoption was also deemed to be in clear defiance of the *shari'a*.

It is clear from the official and unofficial objections to the proposal that the main problem did not only lie with the contract of marriage *per se*, but with its effects on personal status in general. One commentator stated that

civil marriage is contrary to the *shari'a* as well as are its effects on child custody, support, divorce, *'idda*, adoption, the law of succession and guardianship . . . Many of the details pertaining to civil marriage and its effects are clearly in contradiction to the Qur'an and Sunna.

---

[9] Nasir, *The Islamic Law of Personal Status*, p. 84.

[10] Interview with cleric Muhammed Hasan al-Amin, *al-Nahar*, 11 March 1998.

[11] Shaykh Muhammed Kan'an, *Mashru' qanun al-ahwal al-shaksiyya al-madani*, Beirut, 1998, 2nd edn., pp. 9–10.

[12] Nabil Jamil al-Husami, "Limadha nu'arid mashru qanun al-ahwal al-shakhsiyya al-ikhuyari", *al-Nahar*, 2 February 1998.

[13] Dawoud El Alami and Doreen Hinchcliffe, *Islamic Marriage and Divorce Laws of the Arab World*, Kluwer, London, 1996, p. 150.

Sami Khadra concluded by exclaiming

How is it possible to turn one's back on a divine *shari'a* . . . and replace it with human laws? . . . And what is the Muslim left with in a country that forbids the implementation of Islamic laws in all areas except personal status?[14]

The view that personal status was the last bastion in which the *shari'a* could manifest itself was reiterated on various occasions, reflecting an almost existential concern.

Another reason for the opposition, as the Mufti of Mount Lebanon remarked, is that the bill "presupposes the drafting of unified civil laws for marriage, divorce, guardianship, financial compensations, child custody . . . in other words, it pre-supposes the establishment of secularism and the relegation of the religious au-thorities to the sidelines".[15] Thus, in addition to trespassing on territory covered by the Muslim *shari'a*, the law was seen to pose a major threat to the Muslim reli-gious authorities. Indeed, at an early stage of the debate, Qabbani had stated:

We have been following with apprehension suggestions concerning optional civil marriage, the elimination of the religious courts, and the transfer of their powers to the civil courts. The Muslim religious court is not subject to give and take. It is an established institution and its competencies cannot be entrusted except to the *'ulama* who are specialists in Islamic jurisprudence and its *ahkam*.

Sunni religious leaders in al-Kharrub district highlighted this issue in a statement condemning the bill and its author, the President: "In his recent speeches on civil marriage, the president is undermining the authority of the religious leaders and is making a mockery out of them."[16] A civil law on personal status thus represented a direct threat to the clerics' autonomy in their relationship to the state and, equally important, to their legitimacy in regulating the personal matters of their commu-nities.

That the law threatened the family was one of the underlying themes of the cler-ics' attack. Tripoli's Sunni Mufti, Shaykh Taha Sabunji, said that the bill was likely to undermine the family as society's nucleus, stating that "civil marriage heralds the end of the family".[17] One of the arguments used by the Higher Shar'i Muslim Council to discredit civil marriage claimed that "countries that have turned their back on religion have reaped nothing but anxiety, dissolution, and social and psycho-logical crisis". The argument, presented in a statement by the Council, focused on the dissolution of the family and the resulting "illegal cohabitation in the name of personal freedom". According to the statement, another result of the rejection of re-ligion was that the "phenomenon of illegitimate children has become widespread . . . until matters came to [the point of] legitimising homosexual marriages".[18] This view equated civil marriage with the utter dissolution of traditional "family val-ues"; in countries where civil marriage exists, cohabitation rather than marriage is

---

[14] Sami Khadra, "As'ila 'an al-zawaj al-madani: al-tafakkuk a-usari", *al-Nahar*, 3 March 1998.
[15] Mustafa al-Juzu, "Tawhid qawanin al-ahwal al-shakhsiyya wa mushkilatih", *al-Nahar*, 16 May 1998.
[16] *The Daily Star*, 28 March 1998.
[17] *Ibid.*, 10 February 1998.
[18] Statement of the Higher Shar'i Muslim Council, *In Rejection of the Optional Status Law*, n.d.

the rule, illegitimate children roam the streets and legal homosexual relations are tolerated. The statement reflects a real fear of the degradation of a certain ideal model and paints a picture of that degradation by describing the worst features of Western society from the perspective of religious Muslims. What results is an apocalyptic picture of what Lebanese society could become if it were to go beyond the bounds set by the Muslim culture.

All of the above objections were clearly expressed by the Grand Mufti, who presided over the Council, on various previous occasions. Marriage in Islam is governed by Islamic rules and "if these rules, which were set by the prophet Muhammad, were jeopardized, our lives will be sacrificed to defend them".[19] On a later occasion, Qabbani stated that the proposed law "is an insult to the Muslims and the *shari'a* which was dictated by God and upheld by the constitution". The Mufti said that he would campaign with all spiritual leaders to confront "this dangerous proposal which we will not accept under any condition".[20] The attitude of the Sunni clerics was one of defiance and escalation as Qabbani reiterated that "there are limits that we will never allow anyone to trespass . . . Religion and family are red lines . . . our position is clear and irrevocable".[21] On 2 February, in a Friday sermon, Qabbani said that he would not allow "secular-minded people to cultivate the germ of civil marriage and other secular ideas in Lebanon so it spreads to Arab and Islamic countries".[22] The passing of the law in Lebanon was, thus, seen as constituting a dangerous precedent for the other Arab countries. Lebanon was to be the first and last battlefield in the confrontation between religion and secularism on a regional level.

By the time the position of the Sunni religious establishment was published in the official statement referred to above, the intensity of the reaction had reached a fever pitch. The statement reminded the Muslims that "for more than fifty years, some have tried to introduce the subject of civil marriage, arousing great controversy, and each time the Muslims stood against it in absolute rejection". Observing that "Muslim personal status laws are the epitome of perfection and equilibrium", the statement reiterated that "civil marriage is considered to be a violation of Islamic rules . . . and of the Qur'an and Sunna . . . and that following its rules is a sin that leads to apostasy".[23] Once the term apostasy was used, it spread and was repeated by the Sunni and, later, the Maronite clerics. This was one of the practical intimidating actions undertaken by the religious establishments to halt any further discussion of the proposed law.

On a more popular level, the Dar al-Fatwa stepped up action by mobilizing the man in the street. Demonstrations against the bill spread and intensified to such a degree that the Interior Minister declared that street protests would be strictly banned. Moreover, he accused the clerics of fomenting unrest in their calls for demonstrations. Sunni clerics remained defiant, maintaining that it was their duty to oppose the draft bill publicly, and to mobilize the masses against it.[24] By mid-March, Muslims around the country who were opposed to civil marriage used the opportunity given

---

[19] *The Daily Star*, 2 February 1998.
[20] *Ibid.*, 20 March 1998.
[21] *Ibid.*, 21 March 1998.
[22] *Ibid.*, 2 February 1998.
[23] Higher Shar'i Muslim Council, *In Rejection of the Optional Status Law.*
[24] *The Daily Star*, 21 March 1998.

by Friday prayers to hold peaceful protests and to attack verbally those political leaders who were pushing ahead with the bill. In Tripoli, Islamic associations and movements staged a sit-in after Friday prayers in the Mansouri mosque. In Sidon, around 2,000 people gathered at the Zaatari mosque to hear sermons against the proposal. They shouted that the proposal would be passed "only over our dead bodies".[25] Delegations of women went to Dar al-Fatwa to express their objections to the proposed bill.[26] The following Friday, stirred up by fiery clerical sermons, several thousand worshippers poured into the streets of both Beirut and Tripoli after noon prayers to protest against the civil marriage proposal. In Tripoli, protesters burned a banner which read "civil marriage".[27] By 30 March, the newspapers were still reporting delegations to Dar al-Fatwa supporting the Grand Mufti's categorical rejection of the civil marriage bill.[28]

3.2 The Sunni politicians

The religious dignitaries counted on the political leadership to support them. Qabbani said that he trusted the Sunni prime minister, Rafiq Hariri, "to take measures to block this dangerous precedent and act in accordance with God's wish".[29] The head of the Sunni Muslim religious courts expressed his further conviction that Muslim MPs would vote down any bill on the matter: "I am sure the proposal will not see light because Muslim members of Parliament are fully aware of its dangers".[30]

A number of interlocking political factors influenced the subsequent reaction by various political forces in Lebanon. The most significant of these factors was the distribution of power between the Maronite President, Elias Hrawi, the Sunni Prime Minister, Rafiq Hariri and the Shi'ite Speaker of the House, Nabih Berri. The personal and political interaction between these three men known as the "troika" among the Lebanese, was of pivotal importance in determining their reactions to the proposed bill. Another variable included the specific relations of each member of the troika to his own religious community. Moreover, the timing of the proposition by the President of the republic was indicative of political motivation since it coincided with the last year of his term in office. Thus, the reaction to his proposal was closely linked to this perception that politics, and not the national welfare, was behind the president's initiative.

On 2 February 1998, the proposal was presented to the Council of Ministers. During the Cabinet's session of 18 March, it was adopted by a majority of twenty-two ministers out of thirty. Prime Minister Rafiq Hariri, who rejected the bill, pointed out that the Cabinet had only endorsed the principle of an optional personal status law, and that it would need to study the draft, article by article, before endorsing it.[31] Insisting that his objections mainly concerned the timing of the debate,

---

[25] *The Daily Star*, 21 March 1998.
[26] *Al-Nahar*, 30 March 1998.
[27] *The Daily Star*, 28 March 1998.
[28] *Ibid.*, 30 March 1998.
[29] *Ibid.*, 20 March 1998.
[30] *Ibid.*, 26 January 1998.
[31] *Ibid.*, 20 March 1998.

Hariri added that the law not only needed the approval of the Christian community, but in depth discussion – yet a heated debate over the proposal would only divert attention from Israel's manoeuvres to avoid implementation of UN Resolution 425.[32] Consequently, Hariri refused to sign the bill, thus preventing its presentation to Parliament. As the Lebanese Constitution does not bind the Prime Minister to a deadline for his signature, the bill was for all practical purposes shelved.

The Higher Shar'i Islamic Council, nonetheless, expressed its disapproval that the bill had been submitted to the Cabinet before consultation had taken place with the religious authorities.[33] The struggle between the religious and political establishments over spheres of influence was now out in the open. Indeed, the tension between the two forces reached dangerous levels when the Higher Shar'i Islamic Council declared that "anyone who calls for the proposal, or agrees with it, is going against the will of the Muslims and loses all capacity to represent them in any position".[34]

Although the majority of Cabinet ministers voted for the proposed law, the reaction of politicians in general, including deputies and ministers, was largely cautious and evasive. As the religious establishment became increasingly vocal, a number of Muslim deputies, particularly those who had previously been absent from the debate, demanded a suspension of any discussion of the proposed law.[35]

Ministers who opposed the bill hinted at political machinations which had surrounded its introduction to the Cabinet. The Minister of Information spoke of an "act" of infiltration, while Minister 'Umar Misqawi stated that the issue was "an open bazaar between president Elias Hrawi and speaker Nabih Berri with the aim of confronting the prime minister". The former Prime Minister and current MP 'Umar Karami emphasized that political disagreements between the members of the troika had constituted the real context for the bill's approval.[36]

No prominent Sunni politicians spoke in favour of the bill, while quite a number took the line argued by the religious authorities. For example, Karami considered the civil marriage proposal to be a call for people to deviate from their various religions. In one statement, he equated secularism with atheism, saying: "This law is rejected by all except for the few who call for atheism and secularism".[37] Even moderate Sunni politicians such as MP Salim al-Hoss evaded the question by pointing out that the conditions prevailing in the country were not propitious for any discussion of the subject:

All indicators suggest that the proposed law will fail in parliament. In order to avoid sharp discussions in the country we ask that it may be withdrawn, because further discussions will be followed by a demand that confessionalism be abolished completely on both the political and administrative levels. Is the country ready for such a probability at the moment?[38]

---

[32] *Ibid.*, 24 March 1998.
[33] Higher Shar'i Muslim Council, *Statement Concerning the Optional Personal Status Law: Civil Marriage*, 24 March 1998.
[34] *Ibid.*
[35] *Al-Hayat*, 3 March 1998.
[36] *The Daily Star*, 21 March 1998
[37] *Al-Nahar*, 21 March 1998.
[38] *Ibid.*, 23 February 1998.

Al-Hoss was hinting at what many considered to be the crux of the problem: namely, that civil marriage was inextricably linked to the issue of political sectarianism.

The support that the Sunni religious clerics received from the leading Sunni politician, Hariri, and obversely, the Sunni clerics' backing for Hariri's opposition to the bill resulted in a unified position on the part of the Sunni community. This partly explains the strength and virulence of Sunni opposition to the civil marriage bill.

4 THE SHI'ITES

4.1 The religious establishment

Initially, the position of religious Shi'ites was slightly ambivalent. It gained in intensity only gradually, perhaps in conjunction with the fierce Sunni attack on the proposed legislation. On 21 January, one of the leading Shi'ite religious scholars, Muhammad Husayn Fadlallah, denied having given his full approval to civil marriage. The occasion was the publication of an interview with Fadlallah in the London-based *al-Mouharrir* which quoted him as stating that civil marriage was compatible with Islamic law under certain conditions. He subsequently explained that:

> ... the Muslim marriage is a civil marriage in the sense that a religious cleric does not need to be present during the contraction of marriage. However the Muslim marriage includes provisions that are not found in the civil marriage ... Thus, we can say, from a Muslim point of view, that if a marriage does not include the provisions in the *shari'a*, it is considered invalid and illegal.[39]

He confirmed that Islamic religious courts should govern the personal affairs of the Muslims.[40] A month later, a prominent Shi'ite cleric, 'Abd al-Amir Qabalan, demanded that the President of the republic withdraw the proposal for civil marriage before a Cabinet vote in order to allow Christian and Muslim spiritual leaders to examine it first.[41]

While the head of the Higher Shi'ite Council, Muhammad Mahdi Shams al-Din, at one point stated that "civil marriage is a critical issue ... it is not negotiable under any circumstances",[42] on another occasion he maintained that the Muslim marriage contract was similar to civil marriage, and that Islam had no problem with the latter.

Throughout the subsequent debate, Shams al-Din behaved with caution and prudence. Despite his principled rejection of the proposed bill, he was careful not to declare its supporters apostate, as did Sunni and Maronite spiritual authorities. Shams al-Din's moderate tone was influenced by the political stance taken by major Shi'ite politicians.

Speaker Nabih Berri, and almost all the Shi'ite ministers of the Cabinet voted for the bill. Shams al-Din's circumspection is to be understood in the context of his need to carefully balance his religious position with that held by his political al-

---

[39] *Nahar al-shabab*, 17 March 1998.
[40] *The Daily Star*, 22 January 1998 and 27 January 1998.
[41] *Al-Nahar*, 23 February 1998.
[42] *The Daily Star*, 3 January 1998.

lies. But a clear shift in his position occurred on the second day following the Cabinet vote, when he proclaimed his solidarity with the Sunni religious authorities. Thus the positions of the Sunni and Shi'ite clerics were fully brought into alignment. A meeting at Dar al-Fatwa which included Shams al-Din and Qabbani produced a joint statement condemning the civil marriage proposal.[43] By taking this stand, Shams al-Din was closing the door to potential accusations that the Shi'ites had tacitly accepted the bill, a necessary move due to a perceived lack of intensity by the Shi'ites when contrasted with the Sunnite opposition.[44]

Gradually, then, Shi'ite clerics rejected the proposed law in clear and unequivocal terms. Shams al-Din stated that "civil marriage is in violation of the core of Islamic thought and belief, and for this reason cannot gain any legitimacy, and should be dropped immediately".[45] Fadlallah attacked the bill repeatedly, stating that the civil marriage bill would legalize adultery.[46]

On Friday 21 March, the Shi'ite clerics reiterated in their weekly sermons their opposition to the proposed law. Shams al-Din advised its withdrawal while Fadlallah repeated that "a Muslim who embarks upon a marriage that is not bound by Islamic legal provisions is living in adultery".[47] By the end of the month of March, Shams al-Din's tone became threatening. As he reiterated that both Muslims and Christians opposed the proposal, he hinted that "had the spiritual authorities wished to bring the people into the streets to express their opposition to the proposal, they would have brought everyone capable of moving". He added that he had had no idea that the situation was going to last so long since the idea should have been withdrawn the moment it was voiced.[48]

The advisor to the Ja'afari court, Muhammad Hasan al-Amin, was the only divergent voice among both Sunni and Shi'ite clerics. He considered the discussion surrounding legal marriage to be comic and insisted on the necessity of working toward the achievement of a completely secular state:

I thought that Christian clerics would be more adamant in their rejection of civil marriage, since for them marriage is a sacrament . . . while in Islam, it is possible to contract a marriage in front of a civil board, and it can be righteous if it conforms to the conditions of the Muslim *shari'a* . . . The civil marriage contract resembles the Muslim marriage contract in that both parties can conclude it based upon conditions to which they agree . . . Since the Muslim marriage contract allows for the stipulations of conditions, what is the need for civil marriage? It is possible to come to settlement of the problem by amending a few articles in the proposed law.[49]

Thus, the one Shi'ite religious cleric who tried to reconcile the clerical and secular positions, nevertheless, found the option of civil marriage to be superfluous.

---

[43] *The Daily Star*, 21 March 1998.
[44] *Al-Nahar*, 27 March 1998.
[45] *The Daily Star*, 25 March 1998.
[46] *Ibid.*, 20 March 1998.
[47] *Al-Nahar*, 21 March 1998.
[48] *Ibid.*, 30 March 1998.
[49] *Ibid.*, 11 March 1998.

4.2 The Shi'ite politicians

On a popular TV talk-show, Shams al-Din expressed the wish, as early as January, that parliamentarians avoid discussing the civil marriage issue, since he argued, "we have not elected members of Parliament so that they may take decisions concerning such matters, which bring temporal authority into spaces which do not belong to it".[50] The message was clear: if support for the religious position was not to be expected from politicians, then the politicians were not to get involved at all. Nevertheless, and in spite of this warning, a number of Shi'ite ministers and deputies openly supported the bill.

Shi'ite speaker Nabih Berri expressed the view that optional civil marriage would not contradict religious teachings.[51] He endorsed the Cabinet's approval and considered that particular Cabinet session to be "the most important of all ministerial meetings in recent history" for daring to tackle the issue of sectarianism. Berri accused the opponents of civil marriage of fearing the demise of political sectarianism: "The cause of the controversy lies in the call to annul sectarianism. The real battle isn't that of introducing a civil marriage law. Civil marriages made abroad are recognised here . . . The problem is political sectarianism."[52] The Shi'ite political community was divided between Berri and his strong Amal party, heavily represented in Parliament and the Cabinet on the one hand, and Hizbullah, backed by a group of religious clerics and some popular circles on the other. The Hizbullah, the main political rival to Berri, rejected the bill repeatedly. On one occasion, a Hizbullah spokesman rejected civil marriage as "it would only lead to further moral degeneration among the young".[53]

The introduction of the optional civil law was understood by many, both opponents and supporters, as the first battle for the progressive dismantling of the confessional system, but the activists pushing for the civil marriage bill soon came to regret the association of the two issues. Indeed, one prominent journalist lamented the situation and expressed his incomprehension as to why civil marriage needed to be connected with the abolition of political sectarianism. He suggested that the connection between civil marriage and such a complicated national question aimed, as was usually the case, at the paralysis of any project capable of benefiting citizens.[54] The obvious and tacit link between the two issues led the information office of Fadlallah to take a defensive position stating that "the elimination of political sectarianism does not mean the elimination of [religious] personal status because the latter is related to culture, not politics".[55]

---

[50] *Ibid.*, 24 January 1998.
[51] *The Daily Star*, 24 March 1998.
[52] *Ibid.*, 21 March 1998 and 30 March 1998.
[53] *Ibid.*, 19 January 1998.
[54] Jibran Twayni, "al-zawaj al-madani shay' wa ilgha al-taiffyya shay'akhar", *Nahar al-shabab*, 24 March 1998.
[55] *Al-Nahar*, 20 March 1998.

5 THE DRUZE

5.1 The religious establishment

The Druze religious establishment held a distinctive position which initially endorsed the optional secular marriage law. The fact that the Druze, alone among the Muslim communities, have a codified personal status law coloured their reception of the new law, and their reaction to it. For instance, Article 10 of the law of 24 February 1948 (Pertaining to Personal Status for the Druze Sect) states that "polygamy is prohibited and a man shall not be permitted to have two wives at the same time. If he does so the marriage to the second woman shall be void." Moreover, Article 12 does not include the relationship resulting from suckling among those precluding marriage.[56] Indeed, the main points of disagreement between the Druze personal status law and the proposed civil law were only two. First the Druze personal status law does not allow a divorced woman to return to her ex-husband in a subsequent remarriage, and second, it does not allow mixed marriages.[57]

Acting Druze spiritual leader, Shaykh Bahjat Ghayth, said that civil and religious marriage contracts should both be allowed concurrently: "As long as the proposal is for voluntary civil marriage, we have no say in the matter."[58] The advisor to the Druze High Court of Appeal, Judge Shaykh Sulayman Ghanim, answered a question on whether civil marriage contradicted Muslim provisions in the following way:

> If there exists any contradiction between civil marriage, on the one hand, and Muslim and spiritual religious provisions on the other, the contradictions, in any case, remain much less than those found between the legal provisions of one sect and those of another sect . . . Civil marriage remains a common denominator between the various religions and sects.

He added that the Druze personal status law has a civil and secular character that he "as a judge, saw nothing harmful in legislating an optional civil law".[59] The gap between the Druze code and the proposed law was not so wide as to warrant a strong reaction. Nevertheless, and in light of the intense rejection of the bill by other Muslim and Christian religious dignitaries, the Druze religious hierarchy realigned its position accordingly.

5.2 The Druze politicians

From the beginning, the Druze political leader, Walid Jumblat, announced that he was backing the civil marriage proposal because the move would be "a step to-

---

[56]   El Alami and Hinchcliffe, *Islamic Marriage*, p. 173.

[57]   The other spiritual courts oblige a Druze to change his or her religion, when marrying a non-Druze. Since the Druze forbid conversion to their own religion, mixed marriages are practically impossible.

[58]   *The Daily Star*, 22 January 1998.

[59]   *Nahar al-shabab*, 19 February 1998.

wards building a true civil society and annulling political sectarianism".[60] Three months later, Jumblat renewed his support for the bill: "I fully support the optional civil marriage because I have had three civil marriages myself."[61] The controversial bill also received the backing of Druze MP, Ayman Shuqayr, who is a member of Jumblat's Progressive Socialist Party. He stated: "The bill's approval by the Cabinet is a positive move and is likely to enhance national accord and achieve a unified society".[62] A number of Druze politicians supported the bill in clear terms. Others, who were not equally vocal, did not reject it outright.

6 POLITICAL PARTIES, ORGANIZATIONS, ACTIVISTS AND INTELLECTUALS NOT REPRESENTING MAINSTREAM MUSLIM IDEOLOGY

Supporters of the civil marriage proposal included members of the Syrian Social Nationalist Party, the Communist Party, the National Bloc Party, the Wa'ad Party, the Progressive Socialist Party, the Baath Party, the Arab Democratic Party and followers of former general Michel 'Aoun. By and large, all of these parties have a secularist agenda. Other prominent parties with more confessional characters did not support the bill.

Many NGOs, including the Committee for Women's Rights, as well as lawyers and groups supported the proposed law. A considerable number of intellectuals and academicians also announced their support for a civil personal status law. The daily newspaper, *al-Nahar*, interviewed thirty writers, artists and intellectuals belonging to various religious sects. On the whole, all supported the proposed law, declaring that it is a basic human right.[63]

'Asim Salam, the president of the Order of Engineers, denied that civil marriage stood in contradiction to religious dogma. He argued that religion had to respect the individual.[64] The president of the human rights' organization, Ibrahim al-'Abdallah, stated that the details of the proposed law could be subject to debate, but that his organization accepted the law in principle because it would give Lebanese citizens freedom of action and freedom of belief.[65] The Women's Rights Council organized a series of events to discuss the proposed law. The People's Right Movement undertook an active campaign, and organized a one-day forum at the American University of Beirut. Speakers complained that those in favour of civil marriage were being branded as non-believers.[66]

More conservative organizations and institutions had more difficulty in taking a position. This was exemplified by the controversy triggered among leaders of al-Maqassid, a Sunni philanthropic association which runs schools, clinics and a hospital. When the head of its alumni league, Sami Sha'ar, welcomed the notion of

[60] *The Daily Star*, 5 January 1998.
[61] *Ibid.*, 7 April 1998.
[62] *Ibid.*, 25 March 1998.
[63] *Al-Nahar*, 21 March 1998, 21.
[64] *Ibid.*
[65] *Ibid.*
[66] *The Daily Star*, 9 March 1998.

optional civil marriage, it caused a reaction from the association's president, Tammam Salam, who demanded consultations with the highest ranking Muslim clerics before taking a position on the matter.[67]

It is important to note that an organized campaign encompassing intellectuals, activists and local NGOs did not crystallize until late in April when more than fifty non-governmental associations and political parties joined forces to campaign in support of a civil status law. Participants announced the formation of a group called the Meeting for an Optional Secular Personal Status Law.[68] However, by that time, the bill had been politically shelved and on the whole, the reaction of the NGOs and activists was modest when compared to the vociferous response of the religious establishment. The level of coordination, and the hesitant and slow response reflected the weakness of civil society in Lebanon.

The reaction of the population at large can be partly measured through a reading of a number polls that were conducted at the time of the debate. It should be pointed out that the reaction of the population was not directed at specific articles in the bill but, more generally, toward the very idea of an optional personal status law. A questionnaire that circulated in late 1997 gave the following results: 26 per cent of the Muslims polled knew nothing about the proposed bill; a majority of 83.83 per cent preferred religious marriage; and support for the bill was highest among members of the upper classes, the young and holders of university degrees.[69] Another questionnaire conducted among university students in late January of 1998 revealed that the proportion of those who approved of civil marriage within this category was much higher (64.48 per cent). A difference between the principle behind the bill and its practical application was highlighted when students were asked: "If the law permits it, are you ready to contract a civil marriage?" The answers tended to be more negative than previously because the question no longer involved a theoretical possibility, but a more likely practical prospect. Only 44.62 per cent expressed their willingness to marry under civil law. However, here again, the overwhelming majority of those unwilling to do so was constituted of Muslims (34.81 per cent). It is significant that young women showed less willingness than young men to contract a civil marriage.[70] In March, a probe carried out by *al-sharika al-dawliyya li al-maʿlumat* revealed that half of those polled did not have a clear idea of the details of the proposed law. The proportion of those who approved of the bill was almost the same within the Muslim and Christian communities. Of the Muslims polled, 31.5 per cent supported the bill. This figure rose to 36.8 per cent for the Christians. The notable exception was the high rate of approval prevalent within the Druze community (72.7 per cent). Whereas there were no significant differences between the opinions expressed by men and women, the bill was more popular with the young and among educated citizens.[71]

---

[67] *Ibid.*, 2 February 1998.
[68] *Ibid.*, 24 April 1998.
[69] *Al-Nahar*, 1 January 1998.
[70] *Nakar al-shabab*, 27 January 1998. Questionnaire conducted by *Nahar al-shabab*.
[71] *Al-Nahar*, 25 March 1998.

7 CONCLUSION

Lebanon offers the example of a country which has proved unsuccessful in bringing about a unified personal status law for its Muslim and Christian communities.[72] The latest attempt at introducing a civil personal status law revealed the enormous obstacles that such attempts have to face.

The controversy that surrounded the civil marriage bill exposed, moreover, the weakness of civil society and the strength of confessional institutions following twenty years of civil war. The tension between the secular and the religious spheres was revealed in all its magnitude during the debates over civil marriage. The absence of a real dialogue was evident not only in the campaign that was organized by the clerical establishment, but also by the complete estrangement of secular and religious discourses. Indeed, the negative responses demanding that the proposed law be withdrawn from circulation represented an obvious attempt at silencing secular voices and stifling democratic discussion.

Although religious dignitaries belonging to the various sects condemned the proposed optional law, the Sunni clerical establishment was the most categorical in its total rejection. Only four political leaders supported the proposed law in clear terms: the Maronite President Elias Hrawi, his co-religionist the ex-general Michel 'Aoun, the Druze leader Walid Jumblat and the Shi'ite Speaker of the House Nabih Berri. The voices of ordinary people were drowned out by the debate between politicians and clerics.

The reaction of each community to the bill was informed by a number of factors. While the responses of the Sunni political and religious leadership were concurrent, the Shi'ite responses reflected divergent opinions among clerics and politicians. The Druze position was informed by their community's divergent legal practice in questions of personal law while displaying a generally unified stance among the religious, political and popular elements of their community.

Although discussion on the political level has subsided, the debate is still alive. The Meeting for an Optional Secular Personal Law has been organizing an awareness campaign that has included seminars and discussion groups, as well as a petition which has collected 38,000 signatures. In September of 1998 this group organized a celebration for five couples who had recently contracted their civil marriages outside Lebanon.[73] In the unwavering confessional atmosphere still prevalent in Lebanon, civil marriage constitutes a most meaningful political act.

---

[72] Chibli Mallat, "Introduction: Islamic law variations on state identity and community right", in Chibli Mallat and Jane Connors (eds.), *Islamic Family Law*, London, Graham & Trotman, 1993, pp. 1–7.
[73] *The Daily Star*, 13 and 14 September 1998.

The Status of Children and their Protection in Algerian Law

*Yamina Kebir**

1 INTRODUCTION

The situation of children in Algerian society is quite pre-eminent. Young people under the age of 15 represent 41 per cent of the total population. All the expectations of the nation are focused on its children and youth.

The State's concern for them continues the Algerian cultural tradition according to which the lack of offspring is regarded as being a curse. This concern for protection is evidenced by a number of laws specifically related to the protection of children, but it is also reflected in various provisions of the most important laws in Algeria.

The Constitution states that "the family enjoys the protection of the State and of society". In effect, since the obligation to protect children is primarily incumbent upon their parents, these duties are set out in the Family Code and in the Civil Code – the Criminal Code states the punishment for not fulfilling such obligations.

The obligation to protect children is also incumbent upon the State and on society as a whole, and a series of laws ensure that children's rights are safeguarded. Such legislation includes the Ordinance of 1972 relating to the Protection of Children and Youth, the laws on apprenticeship, the decrees relating to education, the Labour Code, the Code of Public Health, the Code of Information, the Nationality Code and various decrees relating to the organization of social services and youth centres.

---

* Attorney-at-law, Algiers Bar, admitted to appear before the Supreme Court of Algiers. See also the country survey of Algeria covering the year 1997 in this *Yearbook* at p. 417. This article covers Part I of the study; Part II will be published in the next volume of the *Yearbook*.

© Kluwer Law International 2000

As a consequence, in addition to the provisions of the Family Code, the protection of children is ensured by a specific legislation relating to childhood and youth and numerous provisions scattered among various laws such as the Civil Code, the Nationality Code, the Criminal Code, the Code of Public Health and the Labour Code to state only the most important and significant ones.

Algerian laws relating to childhood are primarily directed towards the protection of minors, the goal being the promotion of children. However, this legislation is characterized by a certain complexity which is mainly due to the diversity of sources of Algerian law.

This point will be the first topic to be considered in this article. It will then give way to an analysis of the means of protection of minors within the family through the Family Code, the responsibility of the state and society being defined by specific laws related to the protection of the youth.

2 THE SOURCES OF ALGERIAN LEGISLATION RELATED TO CHILDREN

Algerian laws concerning the protection of children originate in different sources, which in fact are coexistent with one another. These sources are the following: Islamic law, the *shari'a*, French laws which were applicable to Algeria under colonial rule, Algerian legislation which has developed since independence in 1962 and last, but not least, the international treaties which have been ratified by Algeria.

The diversity of sources of the Algerian legal system which in turn accounts for the complexity of the legislative system can be explained in the light of history.

From the Islamization of Algeria to the French conquest, Algerian society was totally and exclusively ruled by Islamic law. In colonising the country in 1830, France introduced its own legislation. However, with regard to the personal status, the Islamic law was not to be challenged, at least officially. Under the terms of the agreement of 5 July 1830 signed between the Dey of Algiers and the Commander-in-chief of the French army, the "practice of the Muslim religion [will] remain free".

The Decree of 1 October 1854 further specified the scope and application of the Islamic law. According to this decree, the *shari'a* was to be applied to all civil and commercial disputes arising between Muslim natives, as well as to questions relating to the personal status.

The jurisdiction of the Algerian *qadis* was restricted to the disputes relating to personal status and inheritances. But they did not have jurisdiction for the appeal of their decisions. The appeals were brought to the Muslim Appeals Division of the Court of Appeal of Algiers which followed the French judicial system. It was through that means that the French courts distorted and mutilated the Islamic law as applied to personal status of Algerians by adjudicating according to the principles and standards of the French legal system.

It would be interesting to compare the interference of the French jurisdictions with the Algerian Islamic law system with the influence of the British jurisdictions in India and the role played by the Privy Council in the carrying out of an Anglo-Muslim law.

Other texts, such as the Senatus Consulte of 14 July 1865 and subsequent decrees contributed to shape or rather to amputate the extent of application of the *shari'a*. This decree gave prevalence to local customs (Ibadite in the Mzab and Berber in Kabylie) over the *shari'a*. The lawyers of the time justified these measures by the need "to limit the scope of application of Islamic law" which was considered too extended and "strengthen the local customs".

The Islamic law did not only suffer from the courts during the colonial period – a set of laws were enacted, among which the most important deeply modified personal status, including the law of 1882 establishing civil status, the law of 1957 reforming guardianship and absence and, above all, the Ordinance of 1959 regulating marriage and its dissolution.

Even though family law was partly untouched, it became inevitably infiltrated with this legislation.

All these statutes remained in force after independence in 1962 in pursuance of Law No. 62-157 of 31 December 1962 which reconducted the previous legislation except in cases "where it attained at the sovereignty of the nation". This law was abrogated in 1973 and with it all the legislation in force before independence.

In regaining its sovereignty, Algeria developed its own independent legal system in harmony with its political and social realities as well as the society it has shaped.

A specific Algerian secular legislation has been gradually enacted (Civil Code, Criminal Code, Code of Commerce, Code of Civil Proceedings, Code of Criminal Proceedings, Nationality Code, tax laws, intellectual property laws, etc), superseding the colonial legislation. This legislation breaks with the Islamic law, giving a wide place to Western patterns with a slight survival of some Islamic principles in the Civil Code.

With regard to personal status, it was not until 1984 that the Family Law was finally enacted. This is due to the tough conflicts which emerged between those who favoured a law based on the strict *shari'a* and those who wanted to depart from such rules and from a religious inspiration by adopting a secular law.

In the meantime, however, the system did not suffer from a legal vacuum since Islamic law regulated, though not totally, personal status as well as inheritance, testaments and donations. Consequently, the courts applied the *shari'a*. In doing so they were also in strict conformity with the Constitution and the Civil Code which provide that in the absence of a law, the courts must adjudicate in compliance with the principles of Islamic law; the judges made their decisions on the basis of Islamic law, more specifically the Maliki doctrine as it was codified by Sidi Khalil since Algeria follows the Maliki rite.

However, the courts also applied the Hanafi doctrine at times when its rules appeared to be more appropriate or better adapted to the social evolution, making use of the *talfiq* method.

At the same time, legal rules which were enacted since 1962 were to be applied in this matter; such is the case for the requirement to celebrate a marriage before the Registrar, this being a condition for its validity or the legal capacity for marrying.

Law No. 84-11 of 9 June 1984 establishing the Family Code unified these rules. The principles of the *shari'a* have been codified in the law with some exceptions. If the rules of the *shari'a* with regard to inheritance are totally embodied in the Family Code, some secular provisions have been incorporated in the other chapters of the law. Moreover, the law states that in the absence of a provision in the law, reference is to be made to the *shari'a* (Art. 222, Family Code). It is to be noted that the same provision exists in the Civil Code of 1975 (Art. 1, Civil Code).

The Family Code has been and still is the subject of hot debate within Algerian society and it is being much criticized for various reasons. First, the Islamic law system is a global system, having its own logic and coherence, and which was quite adapted to the traditional patriarchal society. In the Family Code, some of the concepts of the *shari'a* have been modified and distorted if not suppressed, which ruined the original coherence of the system, balance and adaptation of the *shari'a* to the society from which it originates.

And the necessary adjustments which were to be brought about are still lacking. In addition, some provisions of the Family Code, in particular those related to the rights and duties of spouses and to divorce, contradict the principles set forth by the Constitution according to which all citizens are equal before the law and which prohibit any discrimination of grounds of birth, race, gender, opinion, or any other social or personal circumstances.

In line with this principle, the fundamental laws of Algeria forbid all kinds of discrimination between sexes and claim that women's promotion is an intangible principle. In effect, this principle is embodied in the main Algerian laws such as the Civil Code, the Code of Commerce and the labour laws to cite only a few. Discrepancies of the Family Code with these laws are blatant and often lead to distressing situations.

As a result, the Family Code is bitterly attacked on one side by the orthodox Islamists who claim that this law does not convey the letter of the *shari'a* and on the other by those who request its abrogation on the grounds that the principle of equality of all citizens before the law should also be reflected in the Family Code and that the Family Code should not contain any reference to the *shari'a* but depart from it.

Between these two irreconcilable positions, the adaptation of the *shari'a* to a modern society by the means of *ijtihad* is making its way to try and address some core issues. Such is the case when a decree relating to *kafala* was passed in 1992 with the aim of circumventing the strict prohibition of adoption set out in the Family Code according to the *shari'a*. The reformation of the Code by recourse to *ijtihad* is in view with the support of the Islamic High Committee.

Last, but not least, Algeria ratified the Convention on the Protection of Children. It is to be noted that all the principles set out in the Convention already existed in Algerian legislation, which even goes further.

The coexistence of two types of legal rules possessing radically different conceptions and techniques and dedicated to a subject as delicate as the family law in a rapidly changing society, in fact creates extremely serious problems.

3 THE PROTECTION OF THE CHILD WITHIN THE FAMILY

Legal personality starts for a person with their birth and ends with their death. The child enjoys civil rights at the time it is begotten under the condition that he is born alive.

The natural framework within which the child will enjoy his rights and be protected is the family, the family being described by the law as "the fundamental unit of the society" (Art. 2, Family Code).

In order to allow the parents to efficiently ensure this protection, Algerian law grants the parents with mutual rights and duties towards their children provided the legal bond of paternity is established.

The Constitution imposes on the parents the duty of protection and education of their offspring (Art. 65). These duties are devolved to both parents who are jointly under the obligation to contribute to their protection and education.

As long as the parents are united by the bonds of marriage, those rights which virtually belong to both father and mother are virtually intertwined.

The situation is totally different in the case of divorce of the parents where the respective rights and duties of each parent are distinctly determined and exercised; these being the paternal authority for the father and the right to custody (*hadana*) which is devolved to the mother. The father remains in all circumstances the sole holder of the paternal authority; as for the mother, she is, by principle and as a rule, automatically entitled to the *hadana* (custody) of the children.

3.1 Paternal rights and duties

3.1.1 Duty to provide maintenance to the children

The paternal duties primarily consist of the maintenance of the children. The father is under the obligation to maintain his family by ways of *nafaqa* which is defined by the law as including food, clothing and lodging. The duration of this obligation to the children varies according to the sex of the child; the father is obliged to provide maintenance to his children until they reach majority at the age of nineteen for male children (majority is determined in the Civil Code); this duty is extended until his child completes his studies or if the child is physically or mentally handicapped; as for the girl, she remains the responsibility of her father until her marriage, at which time she is taken in charge by her husband.

3.1.2 Paternal power: wilaya

This is the most important duty devolved to the father by law under which he is the legal guardian of his children. *Wilaya* or guardianship is considered a religious duty and a pious act on the part of the person who assumes this responsibility.

According to classical Islamic laws, this protection extends to any child whether having his parents or whether he is an orphan. Algerian law specifies that the minor is put in a guardianship regime, from his birth to his coming of age; the *wilaya* is carried out on the person as well as on his property regardless of the marital status of his parents.

The paternal power which is in fact a "protection power" consists in a general authority to represent children under age, to manage their property and more generally, vests him with the control of their upbringing, education and welfare.

The father, being the legal representative of his child is entitled to represent him in all actions of his civil life (Art. 74, Civil Code) as well as to manage his property. He is, moreover, "responsible for damages caused by [his] minor children living under his roof" (Art. 135, Civil Code).

Another aspect of the paternal authority is very important – as a guardian, the father is also expected to give his consent to the marriage of his minor child and to his daughters, irrespective of their age.

This attribute of the paternal authority differs from the matrimonial constraint, *djabr*, according to which a father could compel his children having not yet reached puberty, to marry. This prerogative on the part of the father or other *wali* has been abolished by Algerian law. The law also prohibits the *wali* to prevent a person under his guardianship from getting married.

The paternal power is exercised solely by the father and is exclusively connected to him regardless of the course of marital life. He can neither renounce it, nor liberate himself from it, nor trust it to another person, even to his wife; the judge alone has the right – having regard to the welfare of the child – to deprive him of his power.

The father forfeits his paternal authority when he commits a serious offence or when his behaviour threatens his children physically or morally (Art. 24, Criminal Code).

In the case of the father's death, the guardianship of the children is automatically transferred, *by law*, to the mother (Art. 87, Family Code). The mother's role is thus strengthened by the law since she becomes, on the death of her husband, the legal guardian of her children. She also becomes the legal guardian of her children where the father is bankrupt, or in the absence of a guardian specified in the will. As a result, she is entitled to all the rights and obligations which constitute the paternal authority. There is no objection to her managing the property of her minor children, since she has the total capacity to do so. There is one limitation, however, to this guardianship in the fact that the mother can never consent to the marriage of her children.

An interesting aspect also is that the law provides that the guardianship can be exercised by the *wasi*, or testamentary guardian appointed by the father or the grandfather to act after their death. However, departing from the Maliki doctrine, this can only be effected in the case where the mother is deceased or if she is not fit to be the guardian of her children.

3.2 The mother's right of custody: *hadana*

In line with the *shari'a*, the mother's prerogatives *vis-à-vis* her children are included in the specific right of *hadana*. It consists in trusting the mother or in default the maternal kinship, with the physical and material custody of the child, with all that this responsibility implies in terms of care, affection and education and, as set out in the law, "education in his father's religion". The *hadana* exists from the child's birth to the benefit of the mother when the parents are linked by the bond of marriage, but it only acquires its full meaning and effect when the parental couple split.

It is then the wife's proper right established with an aim to counterbalance the very large powers of the father over his offspring. The fact is that it is almost always incumbent on the mother, the father being in all cases entitled to the paternal authority.

During the parents' common life, the child's custody is in fact shared and exercised by both parents; it is only when the parents part that their specific rights and obligations are clearly separated – the mother has the material responsibility of her children, the father having all the obligations resulting from the paternal authority. It is to be noted that under Algerian law divorce may only be established by a court judgment, this judgment granting to each spouse respective rights with regard to their children.

The law states that the boys are under the care of their mother until the age of 10. As for girls, they remain in the custody of their mother until they are married.

All legal systems recognize a natural right to the mother to have custody of her children. However, under the *shari'a* this right is so strong that the granting of this right is effected almost automatically by the courts provided the mother is of sound mind and of good morality.

The *hadana* is a right indeed but it nevertheless involves obligations. In reality and generally speaking, the mothers consider it rather as a right that they fiercely claim, in the interest of their children but also because once they are deprived of the custody, they can no longer take part in their upbringing.

The courts also admit that "in order to get a divorce, a woman can validly waive her right to custody", custody being considered a right of the mother and not an obligation. Consequently, she cannot be compelled to exercise it nor can she receive any payment for it.

Forfeiture of custody is decided by the judge in very limited and precise cases which are determined by the law. If the mother be married again to a man who is not nearly related to the child, she loses her right to custody. A mother's immorality and notorious misconduct are another reason for the forfeiture of custody.

In such a case, the *hadana* is transmitted down to the women on the mother's side and in default, to the women on the father's side. And yet it is admitted that this order can be disregarded in the cases where husband and wife agree upon custody of their children when they divorce by mutual assent.

A third reason for the mother being deprived of her right to custody may result from the fact that the mother moves too far away from the father, thus preventing him from controlling his children and their education. The law provides that in such a situation, the court may decide to maintain the mother in her right or to withdraw it having regard to the child's interest. In practice the courts are inclined to favour the father.

It is a principle codified by the law that the husband is responsible for the maintenance of his wife and children, no matter what the the circumstances are and regardless of the financial condition of the wife. The father is not freed from this obligation towards his children after the divorce. In reality, most often, it is the mother who maintains the children who are under her custody. It is a fact that the sums allocated as alimony by the courts, taking into account the revenues of the debtor, are shamefully low, except in cases where parents agree within a divorce procedure by agreement on a more substantial sum.

On the other hand, this obligation is not always carried out. Although the Criminal Code sanctions the offence of abandoning the family and imprisonment sentences and fines are imposed on parents who evade their moral or material obligations, fathers too often fail to comply with the law and court orders. The situation of mothers is more precarious in that after the dissolution of marriage they find themselves, if they do not work, deprived of any resources and in all cases of the marital home. If the *nafaqa* due to the wife is a must, by all means, during the marriage, it ends naturally after the divorce, or rather after the viduage period (*idda*).

The dividing up of the parental rights and duties according to criteria as rigid as those which aim to confer to the mother only the physical and affective custody of the child while the paternal authority is incumbent solely upon the father does not correspond to the realities or to the declared ideals of the promotion of the individual, more particularly that of the child. In reality, the custody of a child implies material care, tenderness too, but also an active contribution of both parents to his education. It so happens that the traditional conception of custody in as far as it excludes the total responsibility of the person who has the custody, deprives him at the same time of the legal means to exercise it. This leads to some painful situations and serious problems arising from the fact that the person who has the custody cannot act even for the simple acts of the child's life without the authorization of the father, and results in a permanent confrontation of the parents where the interest of the child is unfortunately forgotten and even denied. This dichotomy was conceivable at a time when the respective roles of the man and woman within the couple were defined and limited. The transformation of society, the participation of women in all spheres of social life and above all, new relations within the marriage based on equality and cooperation cannot be consistent with these solutions. The protection of the child requires an equal share between parents in their responsibility towards their children.

4 PATERNITY

Parents are entitled rights and obligations to their legitimate children provided the parental bond is established.

As a principle, the *nasab*, or paternity, is established towards the father. This principle is reinforced by the fact that, under the Civil Code, the father transmits his name to his children.

Paternity results from the lawful marriage of the parents. The law fixes the duration of pregnancy at 6 months with a maximum of 10 months (Art. 42, Family Code). As a consequence, a child born within 10 months from the date of divorce of the parents or of the father's death is related to his father (Art. 43, Family Code).

However, although the law considers only legitimate children, this principle is not intangible. The jurisprudence developed by the *fuqaha* was very tolerant in considering the validity of a marriage in order to grant it full legal effect with regard to children, and more generally their approach toward paternity was prompted by a humanitarian concern for children begotten out of wedlock and for women exposed to public reprobation. In line with the solutions developed by the *fuqaha*, the law provides that paternity is established in various circumstances.

Consequently, paternity is established when it results from an irregular or a void marriage or from any marriage annulled after its consummation and by the proof of the marriage.

Paternity is also established by acknowledgement of paternity by the father. It is worth noting that in such cases, the child is treated as a legitimate child.

An interesting aspect is that the law contains provision for the acknowledgement of maternity in cases where the father is unknown. Although maternal affiliation has a subsidiary role compared to paternity, the children are connected to the mother's *nasab*, and consequently they take her name. The mother is then vested with all the rights and obligations of both parents. Material affiliation is also being considered by the Nationality Code. Algerian citizenship is determined by the *jus sanguinis*. A child whose father is Algerian automatically acquires Algerian citizenship. However, Algerian citizenship is only transmitted by the mother to her child born of unknown father, or of a stateless father.

5 *KAFALA*

In line with the position of Islamic law with regard to adoption, the law provides that "Adoption is prohibited by the *shari'a* and by the law" (Art. 46, Family Code).

But this does not imply that children deprived of a family are left without a home and the protection of a family. The law provides for a substitute to adoption which is the *kafala*. The *kafala* is defined by law as the commitment of a person (*kafil*) to benevolently provide maintenance, education, care and protection to a minor child (*makfoul*) as would a father do for his son. The purpose of *kafala* is to vest the *makfoul* with legal guardianship of the *kafil* who will be treated for familial or educational purposes as though he were his legitimate child.

The child put under *kafala* may be a child whose paternity is established or of unknown paternity. *Kafala* must be effected by official deed or by a court order and is subject to the child's wishes when he has a mother or father.

With regard to the effects of *kafala*, these exclude any paternity link of the *makfoul* towards the *kafil*. Where the child's parents are known, the child retains his original paternity, where the parents are unknown, he will remain deprived of paternity.

The *makfoul* cannot inherit the *kafil* but may receive one-third of his property by way of donation or legacy. Finally, the *kafala* may be revoked by the *kafil* by judicial action and upon the *kafil*'s death the *kafala* is transmitted down to his heirs.

However, the most important innovation of Algerian law has been brought by Decree 92-24 of 19 January 1992 amending Decree 71-157 of 3 June 1971. By the provisions of this Decree, the *makfoul* whose parents are unknown may be given the name of the *kafil* by concordance of names. The child is given the name of this *kafil* but this does not imply that he enjoys any of the effects attached to paternity and his status remains governed by the general rules of *kafala* considered above.

Nevertheless, the solution brought by this Decree to the dramatic problem of the children of unknown paternity and deprived of a home is very interesting. The aim was to help these children overcome their identity problems and to reinforce their psychological and social adaptation: *kafala* is thus made closer to adoption. And in fact the *kafala* has known a considerable success pursuant to the Decree.

It is also interesting from a legislative point of view in that this pattern allows flexibility in the adaptation of the *shari'a* and could be followed in eliminating the other discrepancies existing within the Family Code.

The Concept of *Wilaya* in Hanafi Law: Authority versus Consent in *al-Fatawa al-'Alamgiri*

*Mona Siddiqui**

1 INTRODUCTION

From the earliest twilight of human society, every woman was found in a stage of bondage to some man. Laws and systems of polity always begin by recognizing the relations they find already existing between individuals. They convert what was a mere physical fact into a legal right and give it the sanction of society (John S. Mill)

The verb *wilaya* may be translated as having legal power, friendship or guardian-ship. In legal texts, *wilaya* denotes the abstract right of guardianship and the *wali* is the guardian so empowered.[1] The position of the *wali* forms one of the most inter-esting areas of *ikhtilaf* in classical Hanafi legal texts. This is mainly because of the tension arising between paternal authority and legal autonomy, so that a woman may legally contract herself in marriage but the social and legal imperative of obtaining pa-ternal consent ensure that she still remains subordinate to the wishes of her *wali*. The discussions on *wilaya*, along with *kafa'ah*[2] and *mahr*,[3] form some of the longest sections in the *fiqh* texts with the arguments revolving around themes of female pro-tection or subjugation, social stability and social hierarchy and the fundamental but problematic issue of legal autonomy. In this article, I will discuss how *wilaya* was elab-orated in *al-Fatawa al-'Alamgiri* as a major issue in marriage and the problems ju-rists faced in defining the parameters and nature of this authority.

---

* PhD, Faculty of Divinity, University of Glasgow.
[1] In Islamic law, *walis* are divided into three categories: *wilayat al-nikah* (guardianship of marriage), *wilayat al-hadana* (guardianship of person) and *wilayat al-mal* (guardianship of property).
[2] *Kafa'ah* refers to the principle of compatability/equality between husband and wife.
[3] *Mahr* is commonly known as the dower, property or wealth which the groom legally owes the bride. For a detailed discussion of this issue, see M. Siddiqui, *"Mahr*: legal obligation or rightful demand?"* (1995) 6 *Journal of Islamic Studies*, pp. 14–24.

The texts are riddled with various overlapping issues, but one of the most interesting areas lies in allowing women a legal right to contract, ensuring that they at the same time respect the wishes of the *wali* and, finally, recognizing that in marriages arranged by *walis* themselves, the consent of the woman is imperative. While all this is theoretically valid for the adult female, the situation of minors is quite different. The manner in which these two different positions are juxtaposed is an excellent reflection of how juristic logic and social reality came together in *fiqh* works.

The translation of *wali* as guardian implies in it the concept of guardianship found in archaic or Roman jurisprudence. Roman law, however, distinguished two forms of guardianship, the *patria potestas* and the *tutores*. *Patria potestas* was defined as:

The people within our authority are our children, the offspring of a Roman law marriage. Our authority over our children is a right which only Roman citizens have. Nobody has such extreme control over children. Any child born to your wife is in your authority. The same is true of one born to your son and his wife, i.e. your grandson and grand-daughter are equally within your authority.[4]

Tutores, however, is defined as follows:

Guardianship as defined by Servius, is a right of authority granted and permitted by the law of the State over the person of a freeman with the object of safeguarding him while he is too young to look after himself. Guardians are those who exercise this power and authority. They take their names from what they do. Thus they are called "tutores" . . . Where the head of the family has children within his authority below the age of puberty, he is allowed to appoint guardians for them by will.

The concept of guardian as implied in *tutores* is a type of authority over children or minors which may be either acquired through the state or given by the head of the family. *Patria potestas* is an inherent right that runs through the male line. It is an institution which allows a son or grandson (once he has reached 15) to become the head of a new family on the death of his father. As head of the family, he may exercise parental powers and enjoy full personal rights. The woman, however, does not seem to have any capacity of this kind. It is this institution of Roman law which Maine describes as:

The perpetual tutelage of women, under which a female, though relieved from her parent's authority by his decease continues subject through life to her nearest male relations, or to her father's nominees as her guardians. The perpetual relationship is neither more nor less than an artificial prolongation of the *patria potestas*.[5]

By Justinian's epoch, legislation ended guardianship for both boys and girls when they reached puberty. Within the sphere of the marriage, this relative independence from her guardians permitted a woman to contract herself in marriage to whomsoever she wished without recourse to either the *tutores* or the authority of the *patria potestas*.

---

[4] The original Latin for this quote and the following are from P. Birks and G. Mcleod, *Justinian's Institutes*, 1:20-24, "De auctoritate tutorem", London, 1987.
[5] Henry S. Maine, *Ancient Law*, London, Dent, 1906, p. 158.

The power exercised by the *wali* of marriage of Islamic jurisprudence appears to bear a closer resemblance to the institution of *patria potestas* as it existed before Justinian's legislation than to the position of the *tutores*. Nevertheless, his status does contain capacities from both categories and this is perhaps more clearly understood if we define the concept of *jabr*. *Jabr* or force allows a *wali* to impose a marriage on a minor (*saghir*) and all those people whose consent is not legally required as they themselves are legally deficient, for example, a lunatic or an idiot. It also allows a father to give his virgin daughter in marriage without her consent. In Hanafi law, *jabr* terminates at puberty. When this *jabr* is exercised by the father or the grandfather, there is conflict as to whether their authority is binding on the minor even after reaching puberty. Thus, it is a form of *potestas* that is absolute and where the attainment of puberty does not change the legal position of the child.

Tutores implies that it was necessary to maintain a chain of guardianship in order to secure control over the minor's welfare. This is similar in some respects to the Islamic hierarchy of *walis* which ensures a system of intervention in the girls' private affairs. As for the boy, he achieves legal independence on reaching puberty and is not subject to the interference of his guardians in his choice of marriage.

2 *WILAYA* AND THE HANAFI ARGUMENT

The issue of guardianship in Islamic law deals with several categories of people who are subject to protection and authority from their families and relatives. These include both male and female minors, male and female adults, i.e. those who have reached puberty, adult female virgins, adult non-virgins, widows, divorcees and the mentally deficient. The texts are confusing because they often jump from one category to another, principally in trying to establish common ground between the minors and the female virgin when it comes to the issue of consent in marriage and whether these two categories of people can be forced into marriage by their nearest male relatives.

One of the primary areas of interest lies with the adult female virgin and the necessity of obtaining her consent if she has been entered into a contract by her paternal relatives. In addition to this, there are also the legal arguments concerning her right to choose her partner in marriage. Maliki and Shafi'i law do not permit a virgin woman to contract herself in marriage without a *wali*. Hanafi law stands apart in that it does allow such a woman the right to give herself in marriage without recourse to her *walis*. However, this relative freedom is restricted by the factor of *kafa'ah*, which if not present, gives the *wali* the right to interfere and demand that the couple be separated.[6] It should be noted here that in dealing with guardianship in marriage, the issues centre on the female who reaches puberty (*bulugh*); the male on attaining *bulugh*, is fully competent to act on his own interests and is not answerable to the possible interference of any guardians.

---

6 Cf. 2 above. The complexities surrounding this debate have been discussed in M. Siddiqui, "Law and the desire for social control: an insight into the Hanafi concept of *Kafa'ah* with reference to the *Fatawa 'Alamgiri*", in M. Yamani (ed.), *Feminism and Islam*, Ithaca Press, 1996, pp. 49–68. See the review of this book in *Yearbook of Islamic and Middle Eastern Law*, vol. 4 (1997–1998), pp. 617–618.

This seemingly significant right which Hanafi law accords a woman, is thus not of paramount importance in legal texts, since the organization and distribution of arguments does not lend itself to this principle. An explanation for this is that the social and cultural fabric of societies in which *fiqh* developed, was a society in which the relation of a female to the family in which she was born, was much more strict and closer than that which united her male kinsmen. Therefore, Hanafi law subordinates the woman to her blood relations in the agnatic line, i.e. a son, a son's son (in the case of a mother), the father, the father's father, the full brother, etc., her maternal relations and finally the *qadi*. This chain of authority ensures that a woman's legal right to marry of her own accord may be restricted by the dual forces of power and protection exercised by her *walis*.

Two of the most celebrated Hanafi sources, *al-Bahr al-Ra'iq* and the *Fath al-Qadir* state plainly the right of the woman to marry without a *wali*: "The marriage of a free, adult, sane woman without a *wali* is operative";[7] and "A woman who is free, sane and adult may be married by virtue of her own consent, even though the contract may not have been made by the guardian."[8] *Al-Fatawa al'Alamgiri* also cites *al-Tabyin*: "The marriage of a free, sane woman is operative without a *wali* according to Abu Hanifa."[9]

There is however no explanation in the above text as to why the woman has this right. The *Hidaya* and *al-Bahr al-Ra'iq* elaborate:

In marrying, the woman has acted with regard to a right that concerns her exclusivity. For this, she is fully competent, being sane and capable of distinction. These very reasons which allow her to act for herself in matters of property, permit her to choose a husband. She only requires a *wali* to marry her off so as not to be associated with shamelessness/immodesty.[10]

And again from *al-Bahr al-Ra'iq*: "Everyone whom the law permits to dispose of their property acting as their own guardian, it also permits them to marry acting as their own guardian."[11]

This is the logic behind this legal principle. For in Islamic law, the highest legal capacity is that of the free Muslim who is sane (*'aqil*) and of age (*baligh*). A person belonging to this category has the capacity to contract and dispose; thus the woman who acts as her own guardian in marriage is competent to do so by virtue of an inherent right, irrespective of the social or personal constraints.

Al-Fatawa al'Alamgiri at the outset discusses that a suitable *wali* must have the four factors of kinship (*qaraba*), guardianship (*wila*), leadership (*imama*) and pos-

---

[7] Ibn al-Humam, "'Abd al-Wahid" (1970) 3 *Fath al-Qadir*, 257.
[8] Sheikh Nizam Burhanpur, *Al-Fatawa al'Alamgiri*, 3rd edn., Beirut, 1973, p. 287. All references to *al-Fatawa al'Alamgiri* are from the third edition. A comprehensive analysis of the text is to be found in M. Siddiqui, "The Juristic Expression of the Rules of Marriage as Presented in the Fatawa al'Alamgiri", unpublished thesis, University of Manchester, 1992. The text is also known as the *Fatawa Hindiyya*. There were various scholars involved in the compilation of the book which took place between 1664–1672, but Sheikh Nizam Burhanpur was the chief jurist; thus references to the text in this article will have his name as the "author".
[9] Nizam, *al-Fatawa al'Alamgiri*, p. 287.
[10] Al-Marghinani, Abu al-Hasan, 'Ali b. Abi Bakr b. 'Abd al-Jalil, *Al-Hidaya, Sharh Bidayat al-Mubtadi*, vol. 1, Cairo, 1908, p. 196.
[11] Ibn Nujaym, *al-Bahr al-Ra'iq*, Cairo, 1968, vol. 3, p. 117.

session (*milk*). These four aspects are the legal criteria necessary to establish the right of guardianship. Moral behaviour or good conduct is not a legal requirement. A person's character is not only difficult to assess legally but it would appear that any defects in character do not bear disadvantages for the purpose of guardianship: "Bad character (*fisq*) does not prevent guardianship."[12]

The order of hierarchy is essential to guardianship so that the nearest *wali* to a minor or a woman are the *'asaba* – her male relatives. In the default of any paternal relations, guardianship devolves upon the maternal relatives, the *dhawu'l arham*. There is, however, disagreement as to whether cognates should be considered as guardians: "Muhammad says, *wilaya* is not accorded to the maternal relations whilst Abu Yusuf's words are confused [insufficiently supported]."[13]

This disagreement is not resolved and it is interesting to note that Schacht does not mention the maternal relations in his discussion on *wilaya*.[14] Guardianship is also invested in the *sultan* and the *qadi*, with the *sultan* preceding the *qadi*: "Then the *sultan* and then the *qadi* according to *al-Muhit*."[15]

In effect, this chain of guardians means that in the absence of one, the right of *wilaya* devolves upon the other. Depending upon legal competence of the subjects, the limits of guardianship vary, but generally speaking, a female who is a minor or an adult is very likely to be answerable to the wishes or authority of her *wali*. The superior rights of the paternal male relatives reflects a system of agnation that is not based on the marriage of father and mother, but on the authority of the father, a patriarchal structure that is perpetual.

There are two categories of *walis*: those who may not act as *walis* at all and those who may act as *walis* on behalf of certain people only. In the first category, we have slaves, minors (*saghir*) and lunatics (*majnun*); these people do not possess any rights of *wilaya* as they are all legally incompetent. The slave is subject to his master and therefore not responsible. The child before discretion and the adjudged lunatic are subject to extrinsic control on the grounds that they do not possess the faculty of forming a judgement on their own interests; thus they are wanting in the first essential of an engagement by contract. In the second category, we have the relationship between unbelievers (*kafirs*) and Muslims. The former do not have any rights of guardianship over the latter and vice versa: "a *kafir* does not have any rights of *wilaya* over a Muslim man or woman . . . a Muslim does not have any rights of *wilaya* over a *kafir* man or woman. A *kafir* has rights of *wilaya* over another *kafir*".[16]

Al-Bahr al-Ra'iq however, modifies this: "They say 'and it is imperative that it be said, except if the Muslim is owner of a *kafir* slave-girl or [if he is] a *sultan*' according to *al-Bahr al-Ra'iq*".[17]

---

[12] Nizam, *al-Fatawa al'Alamgiri*, p. 284.
[13] *Ibid.*, pp. 284–285.
[14] J. Schacht, *Introduction to Islamic Law*, Clarendon Press, Oxford, 1964, p. 161.
[15] Nizam, *al-Fatawa al'Alamgiri*, p. 284. The position of the *qadi* is of some significance and will be dealt with later on in this article.
[16] *Ibid.*, p. 284.
[17] *Ibid.*

The authority of a Muslim master and the sultan's right of authority reflects the political and social situation of the Mughal period. The close connection between religion, law and politics ensured that this political situation was given juristic sanction.[18]

The relevance of discussing lunacy or insanity (*junun*) is that its presence renders the person affected wanting in the first essential of a contractor. Therefore, when lunacy is present in a person, the person is barred from acting as *wali*. There are two types of lunacy – complete lunacy (*junun mutbiq*) and intermittent lunacy. If a person suffers the first type of insanity, then his capacity for guardianship ceases. In the second case, a person's authority as a *wali* does not end and any decisions he makes during those periods of sanity will be held as operative: "If the guardian suffers from complete madness, his authority of guardianship ceases; if he becomes mad and then sane, his authority does not cease and the decisions he makes during those periods of sanity will be held as operative according to *al-Dhakira*."[19]

The jurists do not define how madness is established nor why there is no need for a juridical decision to confirm lunacy in a person. Sanity is a fundamental criterion of legal competence and similarly, if a boy attains maturity, but he is mentally handicapped or insane, he does not gain autonomy over his person: "[Owing to the presence of lunacy/handicap, a son on reaching puberty, who would otherwise no longer need a *wali*], is still subordinate to the authority of his father with respect to both his person and his property according to the *Fatawa al-Qadi-Khan*".[20]

A direct conflict of opinion on a related theme is cited in *al-Fatawa al-'Alamgiri* on the authority of *Dhakhira*. If a son grows up sane and then becomes insane, Abu Yusuf maintains that *wilaya* appertains to the *qadi* by *qiyas* and Shaybani states that *wilaya* reverts to the father by *istihsan*. Abu Yusuf's argument is that since the boy has reached puberty, he is free from his father's authority and therefore the only person who may legally carry out any decisions on behalf of the boy on account of his insanity is the *qadi*. Shaybani's view based on *istihsan* acknowledges the continuance of the father's authority since the independence the boy acquires from reaching puberty is restricted and cancelled by the presence of insanity. Thus, it would be as if the father's guardianship had never ended.

Although the authority of *wilaya* may be an inherited right, it is not absolute to just one *wali*. This is apparent by the discussion of "near" (*'aqrab*) and "distant" (*'ab'ad*) *walis*, which suggests that a woman may have more than one *wali* to act on her behalf. The *wali* who is "near" is the one who has prior rights of guardianship as opposed to the *wali* who is "distant". However, if the "near" *wali* is absent, this would entail a transfer of rights and authority. This absence is known as *ghayba munqati'* and may be interpreted as the type of absence of a guardian which results in communication being cut off. There is much *ikhtilaf* as to what constitutes this absence, but three points emerge:

---

[18] Interestingly, the apostate (*murtadd*) does not have any rights of guardianship over anyone else including a fellow *murtadd*.

[19] Nizam, *al-Fatawa al-'Alamgiri*, p. 284.

[20] *Ibid*.

(a)   if the *wali* is travelling to such a distance as permits him to substitute for nor-
      mal prayers the traveller's prayers;
(b)   if the *wali* is absent at such a distance that there is a risk of losing a suitable
      match for the girl while his opinion is being sought; or
(c)   if the *wali*'s location cannot be traced at all or his travelling is such that he has
      no fixed address or even if he is deliberately hiding.

A minor girl may have two "equal" *walis*. If they both contract her into marriage one
after another, then the first contract is valid but not the second. If one were to marry
her off without the other's knowledge, this marriage is also valid. This is a situation which is compared to the position of the slave-girl, who if owned by two masters can only be married if they both consent. The regular comparison between slave-
girls and minors illustrates their common status – they are both legally and socially
subservient to the authority of another. The fundamental difference however, is that
the slave-girl is the property of both her masters and their complete ownership of
her makes it imperative that they both consent to any decisions affecting her. The
minor girl on the other hand, is never the property of any one of her guardians.

The balancing of authority between two guardians is controversial because it is
not only their authority but also the rights of the girl which have to be taken into
consideration. Thus, the Hanafi jurists are not invalidating the position of any one
particular *wali* but ensuring a more flexible approach to the whole question of
guardianship. This they achieve by allowing guardianship in marriage to be distributed among several people so that a stringent adherence to the consent of the
nearest guardian does not result in the girl forfeiting the opportunity of a suitable
marriage in the former's absence.

The guardianship of the distant one is made void by the nearer one, but not so the contract [he may have made] for he executed that on the basis of complete *wilaya* according to
al-Tabyin.[21]

The conflict over this issue arises as a result of absent *walis*: "If he marries her off
from wherever he is, there is no tradition on this; but is should not be permitted
since his authority as a *wali* has been cut off according to *al-Muhit* of Sarakhsi."[22]

But the *Hidaya* argues that absence should not be destructive of a right: "The
wilaya of the nearer one subsists for it is established as his right secured by kinship;
thus, it does not become void by absence. Therefore, if he marries her from wherever he is, it is permitted."[23]

The fact that a *wali* may reserve the right to carry out a contract of marriage
from wherever he is, illustrates two fundamental points concerning the marriage
of minors. First, a minor girl may be married off by her *wali* without her having
knowledge of the marriage. Second, the minor's consent is not necessary for the
completion of the marriage contract. Along with the minor boy and girl, the insane and the idiot hold a similar position, i.e. in Islamic law, they are considered as
persons of "defective" capacity and therefore unable to act in their own interests.

---

[21] Nizam, *al-Fatawa al-'Alamgiri*, p. 285.
[22] *Ibid.*
[23] Al-Marghinani, *al-Hidaya*, vol. 1, p. 200.

Although they may be legally bound by the wishes of the *wali* as minors, on reaching puberty, both the male and the female have the option of puberty (*khiyar al-bulugh*). This entitles the minor to have the marriage annulled or cancelled by the *qadi* if he or she so wishes. If, however, the marriage was contracted by the father or the grandfather, then the jurists argue that the marriage would be binding without the option of puberty. This is because the law raises a presumption in their favour that they must have acted in the best interests of the minor: "If the father or grandfather marry them then they have no option after reaching puberty; if someone other than the father or grandfather has married them, then each of the two has the option after reaching puberty – if they wish to consent to the marriage or cancel it according to the *Hidaya*."[24]

The issue of paternal authority is not exclusive to Islamic law, but as Maine writes:

Many of the cases which helped to mitigate the stringency of the father's powers over the persons of his children are doubtless amongst those which do not lie upon the face of history. We cannot tell how far public opinion may have paralysed an authority which the law conferred or how far natural affection may have rendered it endurable.[25]

If the authority of the father was binding in classical law, allowing no option of puberty, and we assume that most marriages of minors were contracted by their fathers, then why is the *khiyar al-bulugh* of such juristic importance? My hypothesis is that this issue is essentially one of juristic "idealism". It is an area of Islamic law where rights and options are distributed so as to create the impression of careful and logical administration. Because of the very nature of a society where a minor may be married off by a guardian, the jurists formulated a series of rules under the option of *khiyar al-bulugh*, protecting the interests of the minor by allowing him/her legal autonomy on reaching puberty. Thus the jurists present the option, the minor exercises this option and finally it is the *qadi* who represents the judicial process whereby this option can be put into social effect. The debate in *al-Fatawa al'Alamgiri* illustrates how the jurists and the *qadi* have created a systematic and organized procedure of cancelling an unwelcome marriage contract.

The role of the *qadi* in such a situation is of great significance since it is only he who can use his authority to bring about the cancellation (*faskh*) of the contract. *Faskh* is a legal term implying a type of separation. It is translated as a cancellation of a contract which in effect means that the marriage never actually took place.[26] Along with *tafriq* and *talaq*, it is just one of the many forms of terminating a marriage contract in Islamic law.

Although *al-Fatawa al'Alamgiri* uses the term *faskh* with respect to both the boy and the girl, it continues to state that *faskh* is more specifically the name given to a type of separation initiated by the girl as opposed to *talaq*, i.e. divorce which is

[24] Nizam, *al-Fatawa al'Alamgiri*, p. 285. Also, Quduri "al-Mukhtasar", in G. Bousquet and L. Bercher (eds.), *Le Statut Personnel en Droit Musulman Hanefite*, Tunisia, Institut des hautes études de Tunis, 1950, p. 21. Fyzee explains the amendment to this law: "By the older law, a minor girl contracted in marriage by her father or grandfather could not exercise this option of puberty. This restriction has now been removed by statute", in A. A. A. Fyzee, *Outlines of Muhammadan Law*, 3rd edn., London, Oxford University Press, 1964, p. 91.
[25] Maine, *Ancient Law*, p. 147.
[26] Schacht, *Introduction*, pp. 148 and 165.

solely a male prerogative: "Every separation that is initiated by a woman with no cause from the man is a cancellation [*faskh*] like the option of emancipation and the option of puberty. Every separation that is initiated by the man is a divorce."[27]

The discussion also states that if separation takes place under the option of puberty and the marriage has not been consummated, the woman is not entitled to her *mahr*; if the marriage has been consummated, she is entitled to a full *mahr* whether it is the woman or the man who initiates the separation. What is clear is that the judicial decree of the *qadi* is imperative. In fact the role of the *qadi* concerning the various forms of separation in Islamic marriages illustrates the considerable extent of his judicial powers. Another example is: "If the boy or girl choose separation after reaching puberty and the *qadi* has not separated the two when one of them dies, they have mutual rights of inheritance. The husband is permitted to have intercourse [with his wife] until the *qadi* separates the two according to *al-Mabsut*."[28]

Several points emerge from this. First, it is the boy or girl who directly demands separation; the *qadi* however is under no obligation to separate them on demand. Second, until the *qadi* separates the two, both partners enjoy mutual rights of inheritance and the man may continue to have intercourse until the *qadi* separates the two. Finally, it would appear that the option of puberty implies a right of cancellation that does not drop whether or not the marriage has been consummated.[29]

The *qadi* may also act as a *wali*: "And if the *qadi* or the *imam* contracts a marriage, the right of the contractors to rescind the contract is secure according to *al-Kafi*."[30]

The implication is that at the time of the contract, the *qadi* is carrying out the duties of a *wali* only and therefore his authority is not binding. On reaching puberty, the boy and the girl could approach the same *qadi* to have the contract confirmed or cancelled. This time, the *qadi*'s authority would be binding as he is acting within the power of judicial decree and not the authority of *wilaya*.

Khiyar al-bulugh is an option that may be exercised or lost. However, the manner in which this option comes into effect depends largely on the sexual status of the woman. This reveals a particular feature of female status within Islamic law, i.e. female status is discussed through female sexuality and female sexuality is approached via marriage. The two categories of women are (a) women who are living in matrimony, and (b) women who are not living in matrimony. Women who have not been married are known as *bikr* or virgins.[31] Those who have been married but whose marriage no longer subsists either through divorce or the husband's death are known as *thayyib*. The common factor between women who are *thayyib* is that they are no longer virgins. Tahir Mahmood comments: "Islamic law placed both *bikr* and *thayyib* women

---

[27] Nizam, *al-Fatawa al-'Alamgiri*, p. 286.

[28] *Ibid.*, pp. 285–286.

[29] The present text suggests clearly that if intercourse takes place prior to a judicial separation, then the demand for separation is subsequent to the choice of the minor who has reached puberty. However, this is a point of *ikhtilaf* among various Hanafi texts, with arguments that this right drops after consummation.

[30] Nizam, *al-Fatawa al-'Alamgiri*, p. 286.

[31] The term *bikr* also applies to those women who may have lost their virginity through any form of exercise or injury. Abu Hanifa extends this application to a woman who has lost her virginity through fornication as long as it is not made public; his two students, however, refute this.

in the general category of *ghayr mutazawwija* [women not living in matrimony] and does not differentiate between them in any respect."[32]

In the discussion on the marriage of minors, however, *bikr* and *thayyib* are carefully distinguished. In the area of legal consent the manner in which the option of puberty is exercised and its subsequent consequences are determined by the sexual status of the female in such marriages. The major difference is that the right belonging to the virgin is lost if she is silent, i.e. if she does not rescind the marriage on reaching puberty, the marriage becomes binding. The status of the *thayyib* is that on reaching puberty, her right is not lost through silence, i.e. silence does not mean consent; rather she must provide a more demonstrative expression of her approval or rejection: "If she were a *thayyib* at the time of the marriage, or if a virgin and her husband had consummated with her and she arrives a puberty whilst living with him, her option would not be cancelled by silence."[33]

In fact the *thayyib* must consent to the marriage either expressly (*sarihan*) or show her consent through an action such as allow her husband intercourse or ask about maintenance. Thus, the argument in *al-Fatawa al'Alamgiri* is that puberty is the time when *khiyar* is to be exercised, and sexual experience the criterion that determines how this *khiyar* is exercised.

A curious but interesting exception to this argument concerns the consideration of the girl who has lost her virginity not just through any form of strenuous exercise but also through fornication outside of marriage. In such a case, Abu Hanifa argues that the girl is not to be treated as *thayyib* but as a virgin and her silence should suffice as consent to a marriage. However, his two students refute this, as does al-Shafi'i who argues that she is to be treated as *thayyib* on the grounds that sexual intercourse has taken place and thus, she be allowed to speak out regarding her marriage. Abu Hanifa's reluctance to disclose the sexual status of such a girl reflects a desire to protect women in this situation and to ensure that an act of sexual intercourse, in whatever circumstance it should have taken place, does not injure a girl's prospects of securing a good marriage.[34] This would not be the case, however, if the woman had lost her virginity in an invalid marriage, for there the observation of *'idda*, payment of *mahr* and establishment of any paternity would be evidence of the law recognizing her status as a married woman.

The time and place when a girl (who has been contracted into marriage by her *wali*) reaches maturity, i.e. her menstrual cycle begins, enabling her to exercise the option of puberty, is called *majlis*. The legal significance of this *majlis* lies in the fact that it is at this very *majlis* that a girl must show either her consent or rejection of the marriage contract; if she delays, the marriage may become binding. A *thayyib* does not lose her *khiyar* if she were merely to get up and leave the *majlis* and her right to accept and reject the marriage remain intact. The jurists do not specify any time limitations to how long she can think about the option. As remaining silent does not render her *khiyar* void, this situation remains until she shows an explicit approval of the marriage, i.e. asking for maintenance or having intercourse.

---

[32] Mahmood Tahir, *Muslim Personal Law*, Delhi, Vikas, 1977, p. 295.
[33] Nizam, *al-Fatawa al'Alamgiri*, p. 286.
[34] Charles Hamilton, *The Hedaya*, India, 1982, p. 99.

For a virgin, it is imperative that she exercise her *khiyar* as soon as she sees any blood: "When she reaches her periods, she must exercise her choice as soon as she sees blood."[35]

The complexities that arise from translating a private and biological process into public and legal autonomy are manifest by the various *ikhtilaf* on this issue: "If she sees blood at night and says 'I cancel the marriage', she may bring forward two witnesses in the morning and say, 'I have only just now seen the blood'. [This is because] she would not be believed if she were to say that she saw the blood at night and cancelled the marriage. This is mentioned in the *Majmu 'al-Nawazil*."[36]

The jurists acknowledge that this is a lie but add "A lie is permissible in some situations according to the *Khalasa*."[37]

Though the jurists say that deception is permissible in the interests of the girl, there is *ikhtilaf* over who is to be believed should there be a dispute between the husband and the wife: "If there is dispute over the option of puberty, and the woman were to say 'I have chosen, and I rejected the marriage when I reached puberty', but the man were to say, 'No, rather you were silent and your option is dropped', then the words of the husband are to be believed according to the *Muhit*."[38]

This would imply that the woman's words are to be superseded by her husband's; the burden of proof is cast upon the woman. If, however, the issue is of the news of the marriage itself, the burden of proof lies on the husband. Thus, if a guardian has contracted his ward into a marriage without formerly consulting her, and subsequent dispute arises about the woman's agreement to the marriage, the woman is to be believed. The onus is the husband to prove that the woman was silent at the time she received the news of the marriage; if he can do so, she is his wife, if not then there is no marriage between them. The difference is that reaching puberty and knowing about the marriage may not necessarily coincide with relation to time, but conceptually, they carry the same significance, i.e. the woman may exercise her option.

If a female minor on reaching puberty is not aware of the *khiyar al-bulugh* as her right, and she remains silent, she forfeits her right to contest the marriage. It is a silence of ignorance of the law rather than a silence of consent, but it would not exempt her from the consequences, i.e. the marriage would become binding. If she is ignorant of the marriage itself, then she retains her option until such a time that she becomes aware of the marriage.

Because minors in a marriage contract can actually consummate the marriage, the discussion moves on to determine the criteria for determining when a female minor is deemed suitable for sexual intercourse. They focus on the age and physique of the girl and estimate that nine is the minimum suitable age for the act of intercourse; others specify the arrival of puberty as the appropriate time. *Al-Fatawa al'Alamgiri* cites *al-Muhit*:

If the girl is stout and fat, able to endure [intercourse with] a man, and there is no risk or fear of danger to her health, the husband is allowed to consummate with her, even if she

---

[35] Nizam, *al-Fatawa al'Alamgiri*, p. 286
[36] *Ibid*.
[37] *Ibid*.
[38] *Ibid*.

should not have reached nine years. But if she be weak and slender, not able to endure intercourse and there is fear of injury to her health, the husband is not permitted to have intercourse, even if she exceed that age; this is sound.

As the contract of *nikah* is based on the fundamental act of intercourse, physical ability to carry this out becomes a matter of legal debate. There is however, no discussion in these texts of any mental or emotional preparation, or even if that features as part of the sexual act.

It was established at the beginning that the Hanafi tradition allowed a free, sane, adult woman to contract herself in marriage without the consent of a *wali*. However, if the *wali* himself has contracted her in a marriage, her consent is imperative. The fact that a guardian may enter an adult woman into a marriage without her knowledge, places this woman in the same category as a minor girl, i.e. they can both have the status of marriage imposed upon them. However, whereas the minor girl must wait for the option of puberty in order to confirm or cancel the contract, the woman must show her approval or disapproval of the marriage as soon as she is informed and the marriage will only become operative pending her decision. The contract is neither dissolved nor becomes binding until she has made her choice:

It is not permitted for anyone whether a father or sultan to impose marriage on a woman of sound mind without her consent whether she is a virgin or not. If someone does this, then the marriage is dependent on her consent, according to the *Siraj al-Wahaj*.[39]

The *sultan*'s political strength therefore allows him to act as *wali* according to the succession of male *walis*, but he must also recognize the legal rights of the woman which makes her consent imperative. This consent may be given in a manner of ways and particular sets of words and gestures carry a decisive force. The arguments, however, become somewhat confusing for they change from seeking consent from the girl before any marriage has taken place to asking her consent after the guardian has already entered her into a contract. The discussion of the effect of tears and smiles reflect the creative power of *fiqh* as certain human norms are taken as the prevailing criteria for legal analysis. Thus we have laughter divided into laughter of happiness and laughter of derision in order to assess what constitutes a confirmation of a contract and what constitutes its rejection. The jurists distinguish the following gestures as reflecting acceptance by the girl on news of her marriage: laughter, silence, smiles, weeping without tears, talking about unrelated subjects on hearing the news, having sexual intercourse.

The issue of sexual intercourse is again problematic: "If she was a virgin and her husband has had intercourse with her, she is not to be believed if she says, 'I did not consent', for allowing him to consummate is itself consent."[40]

The problem is of establishing whether sex took place with consent or by force. If the husband has forced the woman to have sexual intercourse with him, then her claim to reject the marriage stands valid, for in such a case, intercourse would be no proof of consent. However, since it is difficult to establish whether force

---

[39] *Ibid.*, p. 287.
[40] *Ibid.*, p. 289.

took place or not, the legal ruling concludes that in most cases where the couple are found to have had sexual intercourse, it will be presumed that it was with the woman's permission and thus, consent to the marriage is established. Proof of virginity appears to be the crucial factor in defence for a woman to reject an unwanted marriage contract. The expressions which the jurists define as signifying rejection of the marriage are express refusal, such as "I do not want so-and-so", laughter of derision and weeping with tears.

Any financial legacy or inheritance is also dependent on the clarity of distinction between acceptance and refusal. Thus, if a man gives his adult daughter in marriage without first obtaining her permission , the death of her husband may allow her to inherit. Those inheriting from the husband may protest that the woman's ignorance of the marriage cancels out her right to inherit. In such a case, the woman may say, "my father married me with my permission", her words are to be believed and furthermore, she would have to observe the *'idda*. Despite the apparent deception, the jurists entitle her to some form of financial protection on the basis of a public disclosure of her marriage, irrespective of whether or not her consent was given.

In as much as the words of the woman determine the outcome of a marriage contract, so are the words of the *wali* important in giving her sufficient information on which to base any decision. The relevance of revealing the quantity of *mahr* and the identity of the husband becomes an obligation on the guardian. Thus, if he says to a woman "I marry you to . . ." without mentioning the two, her subsequent silence is not to be construed as a silence of consent. In such a situation, even if he has already entered her into a contract, her silence is not a silence of consent. This is explained in the following citation:

> If the father asks her permission before the marriage and says "I am going to enter you into marriage", and he does not mention the *mahr* or the husband's name; if she is silent, her silence is not a silence of consent and she reserves the right to reject the contract.[41]

Conversely, if both the identity of the *mahr* and the quantity of the *mahr* have been mentioned, the girl's ensuing silence is interpreted as a silence of consent. It is also pointed out that should the husband's name have been mentioned, but not the quantity of the *mahr*, the girl's subsequent silence is a silence of consent. The explanation for this is that the girl has consented to a form of marriage in which the *mahr* may not have been specified, but it was still implied on the basis of the *mahr al-mithl*.

In short, the Hanafi jurists recognized the legal capacity of an adult female to form her own decision concerning her marriage. In order to do this, she was entitled to know about the *mahr* and the identity of the husband from her guardian. *Ikhtilaf* on this subject centres on determining just how much knowledge of her marriage is a girl's legal right as opposed to how much information the social and legal structure obliges the *wali* to disclose. The *wali* cannot be deprived of the significant right of entering either a minor or an adult female into marriage of the social structure balances on this right and authority. But the Hanafi juristic logic made it imperative to accord a woman her legal capacity which not only made her consent to the marriage essential to the continuance of a marriage contract, but rendered her

---

[41] *Ibid.*, p. 288.

eligible to enter a marriage without a guardian. Despite the possible intervention on the basis of *kafa'ah*, a contract made willingly by the two people would still be valid recognizing all rights of inheritance, *mahr* and paternity. The guardian's opposition to such a marriage would not lead to any separation unless the *qadi* alone separate the couple. This itself would be a form of rescission of the contract and not tantamount to divorce for that can only come about with the express words of the husband.

Many of the *fiqh* texts do not actually discuss whether or not guardianship is one of the conditions necessary for the validity of the marriage. The rules and stipulations define the parameters of behaviour and relationships between the guardian and his ward from which a variety of options can be inferred. *Al-Fatawa al'Alamgiri* does not provide us with the principle behind guardianship and it is interesting to read by way of comparison a text such as the Maliki *Bidaya al-Mujtahid*[42] of Ibn Rushd, which presents the reasons behind the conflict of opinion on this matter. There are two narrations in the Maliki school, one saying that there is no marriage without a guardian, based on the Qur'anic verse, "When they reach their term, place no difficulties in the way of their marrying their husbands". The argument is that this verse is basically addressed to one who has the right of looking after the interests of a woman. The most significant tradition used by the proponents of this view is narrated by al-Zuhri from 'Urwa from 'Aisha, "The Messenger of Allah said, 'Any woman who marries without the consent of her guardian, her marriage is void, void, void, and if the wedding takes place she is entitled to dower according to her status. And if they should disagree, then the sultan is the guardian of whoever is without a guardian'".

The verse that is used to justify a woman's right to contract is "There is no sin for you in that which they do of themselves within their recognized limits." Ibn Rushd comments that it is difficult to assess how important the involvement of the guardian is, but that there is insufficient evidence to conclude that his presence or consent is essential to the validity of the contract.

3 CONCLUSION

In conclusion, it would appear that Hanafi juristic logic made it imperative to accord a woman her legal capacity. This then not only made coercion impossible but also her consent absolutely essential.

Entering a marriage without a *wali* means that she is responsible for her own actions and rejecting a marriage contract on the basis of the *khiyar al-bulugh* again signifies the ability and expectation that she will make her own decision. Ghada Karmi argues in her discussion of the patriarchal nature of Islamic societies, that women are "infantilised in the Qur'an. They are to be protected and economically provided for by men, but admonished and punished if they are disobedient".[43]

---

[42] Ibn Rushd, *Bidaya al-Mujtahid*, translated by Imran Nyazee, *The Distinguished Jurist's Primer*, vol. 2, Garnet Publishing, pp. 9–11. See the review of both volumes of *The Distinguished Jurist's Primer*, in Part V of this volume of the *Yearbook*, pp. 560–563.
[43] Ghada Karmi, "Women, Islam and Partriarchalism", in *Feminism and Islam*, note 6 above, p. 79.

I would argue that this is not the case in the *fiqh* texts. The compilers of these texts are ultimately aware of the limits set in the Qur'an, the various *hadith* that provide dimensions to the basic laws of the Qur'an, and the nature of the society in which their literature grew and was debated.

If systems of patriarchy formed the background to these texts, then it is inevitable that this will be reflected in the law itself and perhaps no more so than in the laws of guardianship in marriage. But it should also be acknowledged that these texts are witness to an elite who were struggling with what they saw and explored. The fundamental precepts in the sacred sources are stretched as far as possible so that if possible, a just and equitable system could be established. In the laws of marriage and divorce, women very often appear the victims, the minorities in societies, with rights granted to them but not many avenues for realizing these rights. The Hanafi notion of *wilaya* however, illustrates the importance of accepting and respecting a woman's right in some of the fundamental issues of marriage. The jurists establish that irrespective of whether a female is responsible for the inception of a marriage contract, she should be given the choice over the continuance of such a contract; quite simply, this is a right that cannot be taken away from her.

Part II

Country Surveys

Egypt

Kosheri, Rashed and Riad*

1 CONSTITUTIONAL LAW AND CASES

1.1 Law No. 168 of 1998

The Supreme Constitutional Court's Law No. 48 of 1979 – as applied by the Court – provided that all judgments declaring the unconstitutionality of articles of laws and regulations had an automatic full retroactive effect from the date of their entry into force, except for cases which were the subject of final judgments. This resulted in huge financial losses for the public treasury when it had to repay sums of money in implementation of judgments declaring laws, in particular tax laws, unconstitutional with retroactive effect.

In order to resolve this problem, Law No. 168 of 1998 was promulgated. It provides that the judgment of the Supreme Constitutional Court declaring the constitutionality of a law or regulation has a retroactive effect unless the Court decides otherwise and that in all cases, judgments declaring the unconstitutionality of tax provisions shall not have retroactive effect except for the party that brought the legal action before the Supreme Constitutional Court.

1.2 Cases

1.2.1 Judgment dated 7 February 1998 in Case No. 77 of the 19th judicial year: see Mr. Hassan Moustapha Kamel Aly and Another v. The Prime Minister and Others

Section C of Article 36 of the Labour Unions Law promulgated by Law No. 35 of 1976 provides that a lapse of one year from the date of membership of the union

---

* Legal Consultants and Attorneys at Law, Cairo, Egypt.

is a condition for candidature for the board of directors of the union's organisation. This article, together with the corresponding article of the Minister of the Labour Force's Decision No. 146 of 1996 concerning the procedures for candidature and election to the labour union organizations, as well as other articles of the above-mentioned Labour Union Law, were the subject of a recourse for unconstitutionality.

The Court in this case mentioned that the right of employees to establish their trade union organizations and the freedom of the trade unions to manage their affairs were an indivisible part of their adoption of democracy as the only means of regulating their activity, and the establishment of their formation in accordance with the free will of their members without heed to their beliefs, opinions and inclinations.

The Court added that, in particular, labour trade unions should not be subjected to restrictions that hindered their activity, that their establishment should not be subject to an authorization from the public authority, and that the public authority should not substitute itself for the trade union organization in deciding what was best for the interests of its members.

This means that the trade union organization must be based upon free will and that the public authorities may not dominate or control it, as is confirmed by Article 56 of the Constitution.

The Court went on to say that freedom of opinion is a supreme value to which democracy is linked, that freedom of opinion is the way to establish democratic organizations having multiple decision-making centres that tolerate their opponents and propose alternatives through discussion with a view to adopting the best solutions.

In a sense this means that different opinions may not be suppressed even though others do not like or accept them, and that the legislature may not interfere without reason with a view to restricting presentation of specific opinions, and that a person should not be obliged to accept or adopt opinions which he or she dislikes.

The Court then stressed that the right to vote is a form of expression of opinions aiming at the choice of representatives, that the Constitution guarantees to every citizen the right to vote in accordance with the conditions provided by the legislature without overstepping its essence by imposing limitations on this right which deforms or transforms the votes, or limits the basis of choice of candidates for elections.

The Court reminded that the right of the candidates to win elections for the membership of the board of directors of the trade union organizations is not separate from the right of the electorate to vote and choose those in whom they have faith, and that therefore no limitation may be imposed on either of them that is not linked to completion of the election process and to the guarantee of its credibility.

The Court added that all electoral systems should provide for balanced presentation of the views of the candidates and for the defence of their opinions, and that the conditions imposed by the legislature – which had no objective basis – relating to who should be accepted as candidates for the electorate campaign were a negative factor that obstructed the opportunity of the electorate to express its opinions concerning the choice of the right candidates.

Finally, the Court mentioned that section C of Article 36 of the Labour Union Law and the corresponding article in the Ministry of Labour Force's Decision No. 146 of 1996 provide that a lapse of one year from the date of membership of the union is a condition for candidature for membership of the board of directors of a union organization, that the right of the worker to exercise the rights deriving from democracy of labour action – whether in voting or in candidature – is linked to the necessary conditions for joining the labour organization to which a worker adheres, that multiplicity and interaction of opinions inside each union's organization is the basis, that the condition subject of the recourse restricted freedom of exchange of opinions and the workers' choice from a wide base of candidates, that it contravened the basis of democracy of the labour action and was contrary to Articles 47, 54 and 56 of the Constitution which respectively guaranteed freedom of opinion, the right of assembly and the right to create syndicates and trade unions on a democratic basis.

The Court ruled that section C of Article 36 of the Labour Unions Law promulgated by Law No. 35 of 1976 was unconstitutional and lapse of its corresponding provisions in the above-mentioned Minister of the Labour Force's Decision No. 146 of 1996.

1.2.2 Judgment dated 7 March 1998 in Case No. 162 of the 19th judicial year: see Mr Adel Attia Abd Elmaksoud v. the President of the Republic and Others

Article 25 of the State Advocates Authority Law No. 75 of 1963 provides that the Disciplinary and Complaints Committee shall be composed of the Head of the States Advocates Authority or his replacement and ten members from among the vice presidents, deputies or counsellors according to their seniority.

This committee shall be responsible for disciplining the members of the Authority and it shall decide upon requests to abrogate administrative decisions concerning its affairs and the requests for damages resulting therefrom which were originally part of the jurisdiction of the judiciary. The committee shall also rule on the above-mentioned subjects after hearing the member and reviewing his comments.

Moreover, Article 26 of this law specifies the disciplinary penalties that may be imposed on the members of the State Advocates Authority and it also provides that the disciplinary action has to be brought by the Minister of Justice at the request of the Head of the Authority. The third paragraph of this article adds that the request may only be made after a criminal investigation or after an administrative investigation made by a deputy of the Authority.

Article 25 and the third paragraph of Article 26 of the above-mentioned law were subject of a recourse for unconstitutionality brought by a member of the State Advocates Authority who was expelled from it by a Decision of the Disciplinary and Complaints Committee.

The Supreme Constitutional Court in this case recalled that independence of the judicial authority is a necessary condition to ensure subjection to the law, and that its impartiality is a crucial factor in preserving its mission, of no less importance than its independence and which complements it.

The basic principles relating to the independence of the judiciary adopted by the General Assembly of the United Nations in its two Decisions dated 29 January 1985 and 13 December 1985 clearly confirm that disputes viewed by the judicial authority have to be decided upon in an impartial way.

The independence and impartiality of the judicial authority are two guarantees that together ensure the efficiency of administration of justice and therefore have the same constitutional value. Moreover, the guarantee of a fair trial provided in Article 67 of the Constitution applies to all judicial disputes including disciplinary ones, which have to be investigated by a Court of Justice or by another authority which, by law, has to be guaranteed independence and impartiality and which may only pronounce judgments after ensuring that the guarantees of a fair trial have been respected, including, *inter alia*, the right of each party to present its case and to comment on the other party's allegations on an equal basis and in a manner which provides for a progressive notion of justice that is compatible with the prevailing criteria as applied in civilized states.

The Court then mentioned that the right to litigation provided in Article 68 of the Constitution means that every dispute must have a joint solution which ensures judicial satisfaction necessitated by the need to redress aggression against the alleged rights, and that this satisfaction presupposes that its content must be in accordance with the Constitution.

This does not apply if the decision is taken by an authority lacking the independence and or impartiality which are two guarantees that limit the discretionary power of the legislature to organize rights, and annulment is the sanction for all legislation concerning the organization of a judicial dispute that does not respect those guarantees.

The Court then affirmed that the disciplinary action brought against a member of the State Advocates Authority had to be preceded by a full and objective investigation that ensured hearing the views of the person subject of the investigation, that the body that had to decide upon the case had to take the judicial form in its composition and guarantees, and that its members must not include a person who was connected with an action taken before its convocation, whether it took the form of an investigation or an accusation.

The Court added that the disciplinary action was brought, in accordance to Article 26 of the above-mentioned law, by the Minister of Justice at the request of the head of the State Advocates Authority, and that such a request can only be made after investigation of the case, its review and consideration by the head of the Authority, which in essence affects the guarantee of his impartiality towards the parties of the case and is in this respect unconstitutional.

Moreover, Article 26 of the law does not prohibit the deputy or the counsellor who took part in the investigation from being a member of the Disciplinary and Complaints Committee that is judging the state advocate who is the subject of this same investigation, and this renders the constitution of the Committee unconstitutional for lack of impartiality of one of its members.

The Court mentioned finally that the Constitution guarantees the right of defence as a cornerstone of supremacy of the law, that the third paragraph of Article 26 of the State Advocates Law does not provide for the necessity to hear the statement of the advocate subject of the investigation, and that the investigation in such circumstances may not result in an accusation.

The Court decided first that Article 25 of the above-mentioned law was unconstitutional in:

(a)   providing that the Disciplinary and Complaints Committee shall be presided by the head of the authority who requested from the Minister of Justice to bring the disciplinary action;

(b) providing for the right of the Committee to decide upon the disciplinary case even though one of its members was a party to the investigation or the accusation.

Second, that the third paragraph of Article 26 of this law was unconstitutional in not mentioning the necessity to hear the statements of the member of the State Advocates Authority at the stage of the investigation.

As a basis of their contravention, the following articles of the Constitution were cited:

– Article 40, which provides for equality of citizens before the law;
– Article 65, which provides for subjection of the state to the law;
– Article 68, which provides for the inalienability of the right to litigate;
– Article 69, which guarantees the right of defence.

1.2.3 Judgment dated 9 May 1998 in Case No. 41 of the 19th Judicial Year: see Mr. Hussein Mohamed Osman v. the Prime Minister and Others

Section (9) of Article 1 of Law No. 308 of 1955 concerning administrative attachment allows for application of the administrative attachment procedures provided in this law to recover the sums due to the banks in which the government owns the majority of their capital. The plaintiff in this recourse alleged that this section was unconstitutional.

The Court in this case mentioned that banks in Egypt take the form of joint stock companies that are considered private law persons, that ownership by the state of the majority of their capital has no effect on the nature of the banks' operations or the way of their management which are distinct from the public services provided by the Administrative Authority to the citizens.

The Court added that the rule in compulsory recovery of rights is to refer to the enforcement procedures provided for in the Civil and Commercial Procedures Law, which require obtainment of an executory deed, and that this is not the case in accordance with the Administrative Attachment Law which allows the representatives of the administration to issue by themselves orders which are considered equivalent to executory deeds.

The Court then mentioned that the organization, management and rules applicable to public law persons differs from those applicable to private law persons and that the nature of the service, the public interest aim, and the usage of public law procedures have to be relied upon in defining the public service. In other words, the public interest aim is not sufficient in defining the public service and it is necessary to rely in this respect upon the object, nature and organization of the service.

The Court then recalled that banking operations rely upon savings, investment and on the provision of credit whose very nature subject them to private law rules, even when the banks that carry out those operations are fully or partially owned by the state, because there is no relationship between the body owning their capital and the subject of their activities, their methods of operation and their final "profit" – and not "public service" – aims.

The rules provided in the Administrative Attachment Law aim at allowing public law persons simplified means of recovery of their rights as an exception to the rules of enforced execution provided in the Civil and Commercial Procedures Law and those rules render the creditor in a preferential position in relation to the debtor. This exceptional nature of the rules of administrative attachment necessitates linkage of their application to their aims and to the management of the public services.

Therefore, their application to banking operations in relation to the debts claimed by the banks from the clients – which have to be ascertained in equality – means that banking operations are considered in this light as public services, which is not the case, and this subjects recovery of banking debts to a type of procedure that is alien to the flexible commercial activities and to the needs of the clients of the banks to obtain credit in security.

The Court finally stated that subjection of the state to the law provided in Article 65 of the Constitution presupposes that private law persons have to abide exclusively in their banking activities by the rules and means of the private law, that derogation of this rule may only be accepted in exceptional cases and within their scope.

The Court thus ruled that Section 9 of Article 1 of the above-mentioned Law No. 308 of 1955 was unconstitutional.

1.2.4 Judgment dated 6 June 1998 in Case No. 28 of the 6th judicial year: see Mr. Mohamed Fadel El-Margoushy v. the President of the Republic, the Prime Minister and others

Article 5 of the Decree Law No. 178 of 1952 concerning the agricultural land reform, provides that the person whose land is taken over by the government in accordance with this Decree Law has the right to compensation amounting to ten times the rental value of the land, and that this rental value shall be evaluated at seven times the original tax on the land. Article 6 of this decree law provides that this compensation shall be paid in the form of thirty-year state bonds.

Article 4 of the Decree Law No. 127 of 1961 amending Law No. 178 of 1952 provides that the person whose land is taken over by the government in accordance with the Decree Law No. 127 of 1961 has the right to compensation as prescribed in the Decree Law No. 178 of 1952.

Article 5 of the Decree Law No. 127 of 1961 provides that this compensation shall be paid in the form of fifteen-year state bonds.

The plaintiff in this recourse alleged that the compensation provided in accordance to the above-mentioned two decree laws contravened Article 34 of the Egyptian Constitution which protects private property, Article 36 which prohibits general confiscation of property and also prohibits partial confiscation except by judicial judgments, Article 40 which provides for equality before the law and Article 65 which provides for subjection of the state to the law.

The Court in this case recalled its jurisprudence concerning the unconstitutionality of expropriation except for the general utility, and against compensation.

The Court mentioned that although the legislature has the right to organize the rights, nevertheless organization of the right of property may not include destruction of its elements and termination of the attributes.

It added that any restriction on the right of property has to be compared to the aims of this restriction, that the legality of expropriation is linked to acceptance of the lesser harm in view of preventing a greater one, that although the Constitution allows for limitation of property of land in view of abolishing feudality, such limitation necessitates compensating the persons whose land has been taken over by the state, on the basis of the market values of those lands at the time of the takeover.

The Court then stressed that the just compensation cannot be evaluated by rigid criteria, that the assumption that the value of lands is equal is a fallacy, that such value has to take into consideration all the elements linked to the land including, *inter alia*, the logical possibility of its investment, the servitudes imposed on it, its location, its linkage to roads, the nature of its soil, the types of crops grown on it, the ways of its irrigation, etc., which essentially necessitate *ad hoc* factual inquiries.

In essence, compensation for agricultural land is not based upon the benefits to the government derived from expropriation of those lands from their owners, but is based upon the profits of which they have been deprived and the losses that they have suffered as a result of expropriation of their properties.

The Court then mentioned that evaluating the compensation on the land that is taken over by seventy times the original land tax imposed on it is a lump sum estimation that is unrelated to its true market value.

The Court added that subjection to the agricultural land reform law does not constitute a penalty imposed on owners of excessive property, that distribution of this land to dispossessed farmers and improving their conditions may not violate the terms of justice that have to prevail for all people, nor prevent those whose agricultural lands have been taken over from the right to obtain full compensation for them, as is the case for those whose properties are otherwise expropriated in accordance to the general rules of law.

The Court also ruled that Article 5 of the above-mentioned Decree Law No. 178 of 1952 was unconstitutional, that Article 6 lapsed in relation to its applicability to compensation based upon the land tax, that likewise Article 4 of the above-mentioned Decree Law No. 127 of 1961 was unconstitutional and that Article 5 lapsed in relation to its applicability to compensation based upon the land tax.

2 LAWS RELATING TO THE PRIVATIZATION PROGRAMME

In order to liberalize Egypt's economy, a number of new laws were promulgated during 1998 which demonstrate the will to speed up implementation of the privatization programme and the reduction of administrative involvement in the private sector. The following laws are relevant in this respect.

2.1 Law No. 3 of 1998 amending the (private sector) Joint Stock Companies, Partnership Limited by Shares and Limited Liability Companies Law No. 159 of 1981

This law abrogated the previous system which necessitated the need for obtaining an administrative permit before establishment of joint stock companies, and replaced it with a new system based upon the right of the administration to object against the companies' establishment – after their creation – if their articles of association were contrary to the law, or if one of their founders does not have the needed capacity for participating in their foundation.

Moreover, this law provides for the right of the interested parties to bring legal actions against the government before the concerned court of the Council of State in case of winding up the company as a result of the administration's objection to its establishment.

2.2 Law No. 19 of 1998

This law transformed the National Authority for Wire and Wireless Communications into a private joint stock company subject, in general, to the above-mentioned Law No. 159 of 1997, and which allows the Council of Ministers to sell the minority of its shares to the private sector through public subscription.

2.3 Law No. 155 of 1998

This law regulated the private sector's participation in the capital of public sector banks, which explicitly allows for such participation and provides for the general regulation of those banks to the above-mentioned Law No. 159 of 1981.

2.4 Law No. 156 of 1998

This law amended some rules relating to the public sector insurance and reinsurance companies, which also explicitly allows for the private sector's participation in the capital of those companies and for their subjection to Law No. 159 of 1987.

2.5 Law No. 161 of 1998

This law aims at the protection of the national economy against the effects of harmful practices in international trade and is a result of Egypt's adherence to the Agreements contained in the final Act of the Uruguay Round of multilateral trade negotiations. The law provides that the Ministry of Trade and Provisions shall have the right to take the necessary actions and decisions for the protection of the national economy against the dangers resulting from subsidies, dumping and unwarranted increase in imports, within the limits provided by those Agreements.

3 TENDERS AND AUCTIONS RELATING TO ADMINISTRATIVE AUTHORITIES

The new Law No. 89 of 1998 concerns the organization of tenders and auctions relating to the administrative authorities.

This law does not introduce any major changes in the previous practices in this respect based upon transacting by way of general and limited tenders, negotiated tenders and by direct order.

Nevertheless, the new law explicitly provides – for the first time – for the right of the party that claims non-fulfilment by the Administrative Authority of its contractual obligations, to bring a legal action for damages against the Administrative Authority before the courts, unless the parties agree to resolve their disputes by arbitration.

4 CRIMINAL LAW: MARRIAGE PURSUANT TO RAPE

Article 290 of the Egyptian Penal Code provides that anyone who kidnaps a female by deception or duress, whether by himself or through others, shall be punishable by life imprisonment and by death if this felony is linked to the felony of rape.

Article 291 of this law provides that if the kidnapper legally marries the kidnapped, he will be exempted from all punishments.

This last article had not been subject to close scrutiny until the last few years, due to the limited cases in Egypt of kidnapping linked with rape.

However, a series of such crimes recently horrified the Egyptian public, who felt that the death penalty was the right punishment for the crime of kidnap linked with rape, and that the loophole provided by Article 291 of the penal law – which originally aimed at correcting the wrong committed against the victim of rape – enabled the perpetrator of a horrible crime to evade any and all punishment, by the easy expedient of marrying his victim, who in many cases had to accept such a marriage in order to avoid the negative social effects of the crime in the deeply conservative Egyptian society.

Therefore, the Egyptian People's Assembly recently reacted to the public outcry and passed Law 14 of 1999 which simply provides that "Article 291 of the Penal Law is abolished".

In other words, Article 291 of the Egyptian Penal Code has been abolished in its entirety as of 23 April 1999 by the promulgation of Law No. 14 of that year.

A NOTE ON RAPE IN EGYPT

*Khaled Mohammed Al Kady**

Rape, in some of its cases, involves physical compulsion in the form of the beating or wounding the criminal inflicts upon the victim. But the act of compulsion does not form a separate crime. Therefore, they both form a single crime.

---

* Deputy Attorney-General, Master of Law.

However, if the action leads to the death of the victim, death is considered to be an incident separate from rape. The punishments to which the criminal will be sentenced do not add because the two crimes have one purpose. The severest of the two punishments is executed.

Rape by its nature involves ravishing because it involves severe violation of the victim's bashfulness, but the two crimes do not add. The case is one of dispute over articles as the article on rape is a special one if compared with the article on indecent assault, which, *inter alia*, includes rape.

If rape is committed openly the two crimes of obscene action in public add with regard to meaning.

If the victim is married, rape and adultery do not add. Rape excludes the element of adultery which is the incidence of sexual intercourse with the consent of the two parties. There is a contention of two articles one of which negates the assumptions of the other.

If the criminal adds murdering the victim on purpose to the act of copulation it will be necessary, as the case is, to differentiate between two situations:

–   If he committed copulation first and then killed the victim to evade the responsibility of his crime, he will be responsible for murder accompanied by a crime.
–   If he commits murder first and then violates the corpse of the victim, he will be responsible for murder only and will not be considered responsible for rape. One of the necessary conditions of a complete crime of rape is that the victim should be alive at the time of committing the action.

It is also the case with regard to kidnapping accompanied by rape. This case is exemplified in kidnapping a female by contrivance or compulsion. This means the necessity of the presence of the elements of the kidnap crime defined in Article No. 290 in the Penal Code.

In order for the punishment to be executed, kidnapping should be accompanied by copulation. To put the severity circumstance defined in Article No. 290 in the Penal Code into effect the following conditions should be present:

–   First, the crime of kidnapping a female by means of contrivance or compulsion is committed.
    (i)   Kidnapping means taking the victim away from the site of the kidnap whatever it is with the intention of violating her by means of an act of deceit and delusion, something which deceives the victim or using any concrete or literary means which deprives her of her own will.
    (ii) Contrivance means any act of deception and fraud that enables the criminal to deceive the victim or her custodian. If the means which the kidnapper has used are no more than mere words, which do not amount to fraud or what he did was mere lying, contrivance is not present. Therefore, it could be stated that contrivance in a kidnap crime has the same meaning which other contriving methods have.
    (iii) Compulsion means that kidnapping is committed against the victim's will or without her consent. This is the case whether compulsion is concrete or literary. Compulsion is realized by any means that deprives the victim of the expression of her will such as giving her narcotic materials or when the kidnapper takes advantage of the victim's unconsciousness when she is asleep, made asleep under hypnosis, drunk, or in a faint.

It is enough for contrivance to be present in the kidnap crime when it happens to the one in whose custody the victim is. It is not necessary that it happens to the victim herself, so long as this contrivance has enabled the criminal to kidnap the victim.

- Second, Article No. 290 in the Penal Code necessitates the presence of a special criminal intention. This is the kidnapping with the intention of violating the victim. In other words, the criminal's purpose of kidnapping the female is to copulate with her.
- Third, infliction of rape on the kidnapped female means that a complete rape crime happens in the absence of the consent of the victim to the copulation. If the criminal has kidnapped the victim and then copulated with her consent the severity circumstance defined in Article 290(2) is not applicable. However, Article 290(1) in the Penal Code is applied and his punishment is a life sentence with hard labour. The condition of the incidence of a complete rape crime is deduced from the clause "however the doer of this crime – a kidnapping crime . . . if it happened together with copulating with the victim without her consent". The severity circumstance is not present if the crime accompanying kidnapping is an attempt to rape.
- Fourth, the kidnapping crime is accompanied by the rape crime. This means the simultaneity of the two crimes. As the kidnapping crime is an on-going one, the case is the same whether the rape is committed during the kidnapping or when it went on. If the kidnapped restored her freedom and then met the kidnapper and he copulated with her against her will, the severity circumstance defined in Article 290(2) in the Penal Code is not present. He is sentenced according to the punishment defined in Article 267(1) which is temporary hard labour.

It is worth mentioning that the execution sentence the legislator legislated for the crime of rape accompanied by kidnapping with its afore-mentioned conditions is applied even if the kidnapper married the person he kidnapped. This was the case under Article 291 in the Penal Code which exempted the criminal from punishment if he married the one he kidnapped. After a juridical dispute in legislative and judicial circles and which went on at the People's Assembly, Law No. 14 of 1999 cancelling this article was passed on 22 April 1999.

Iraq

*Sabah Al-Mukhtar**

The complete disregard of the rules of international law by the US backed by the UK in respect of Iraq (while accusing Iraq of such disregard) persist unabated. Both countries continue to bomb Iraq on an almost daily basis. They insist that they are enforcing the "no-fly zone" and that the bombing is in self-defence. In fact there is no single UN Resolution which refers to, imposes or permits the establishment of the so-called "no-fly zone". This is the illegal division of Iraq into the three *wilayah*s into which the Ottoman Empire divided Iraq. These were Mosul *wilayah* (north of the 36th parallel), Basra *wilayah* (south of the 32nd Parallel) and Baghdad *wilayah*. This illegal attempt to dismember Iraq is also preventing its government from exercising sovereignty over its own territory as guaranteed in the UN Charter. Meanwhile, the US and the UK are giving themselves the right to fly into the Iraqi airspace without any right other than brute force and fire power. Their disregard for international law is further compounded by the absurd claim that when the almost defunct Iraqi air defence even switch on its radar, the US and UK are entitled to bomb Iraq again under the further absurd claim of "self-defence".

A more disturbing phenomena is the UN's silence in the face of this naked aggression against a sovereign member country by other Member States despite the continuing muted protest. While the other three permanent members of the Security Council of the UN (as well as other countries within the UNSC and outside) condemn the US and UK action as illegal, nothing is being formally said or done. Irrespective of who rules a country or the history of illegal actions of its regime, the rules of international law must be preserved and adhered to by all, especially by the major powers such as the US and UK and, more importantly, by the UN itself. When the law enforcer sinks to the level of the criminal, aside from becoming the worst culprit, law is replaced by thuggery. It will be difficult in the future to convince others not to follow the leaders or to convince students of international law

---

* Member of the Iraqi Bar and Arab Lawyers Federation; Legal Consultant in Iraqi, Arab and Islamic Law; Founding Member and Partner of Arab Lawyers Network, London; Chairman, Arab Lawyers Association, London.

that there really are rules of law which the UN apply and are applied equally to all states irrespective of their leaders.

On the other hand, the killing of the weaker members of the Iraqi civilian population by the siege of the middle ages called "sanctions" as highlighted by the UNICEF report dated July 1999 continues unabated.

1 CONSTITUTIONAL AND ADMINISTRATIVE LAW

1.1 Military service

A new department in the Presidential Office was established by RCC Resolution No. 36 of 1998. Retired army and police officers who took part in training volunteers in the past to defend the country are now returned to service in that department. This is aimed at increasing their period of pensionable service which will, in turn, result in increased income as well as being able to obtain the benefits that are normally conferred on those in active service. The statutory instrument implementing the law (1 June 1998) set out the details of the rights and privileges as well as the mechanics and logistics involved.

1.2 Defence of the realm

In anticipation of the February 1999 bombing of Iraq by the US and UK forces (Operation Desert Fox), which lacked any legitimacy in international law, Iraq was divided into four military zones. Presidential Decree No. 98 gazetted on 4 January 1999 provides that the five northern governorates be under the control of the Deputy President of the RCC, Mr Izat Al-Douri. The four central governorates (including Baghdad) are under the control of the Minister of Defence, the five governorates of the Central Euphrates zone are under the control of Mr Muhammed Hamza (member of the RCC) and the four southern governorates (including Basra) are under the control of Mr Ali Hassan Al-Majeed (member of the RCC).

All military services within each zone were brought under the direct and immediate control of the designated governor of the zone. Each of them had a deputy who was a member of the national leadership of the governing Ba'ath Party with the highest military officer in the zone as the second deputy, except the central zone. The governor of each zone was given full powers to enlist all national resources within the zone to defend Iraq against American and British forces. However, orders in respect of air defences, rocket launchers and the airforce remained centralized and remain under the direct control of the president of the Revolutionary Command Council.

1.3 National military service

All male citizens over the age of 18 have to undergo military training as part of their national service under the Military Service Law of 1969. Those who are in full-time education are called for service after completion of their studies. However, the 1969 law allows the making of monetary payment in lieu of service in certain years and the amount is dependent on whether the conscript is a university graduate or not. The monetary payment has over the years been changed to reflect the value of the currency on the one hand and the need for conscripts on the other. In the 1960s when the currency was relatively strong and the need for conscripts was low, the amount was ID100. In 1996, when the currency lost its value and the need was greater, the amount was ID1.5 million for those who were not university graduates and ID2 million for those who were. Those amounts were subsequently halved.[1]

RCC Resolution No. 31 of 1999 increased the amount from ID1 million to ID1.5 million for university graduates and from ID750,000 to ID1 million for those who were not. Additionally, following the call-up of those who were born in 1981 (RCC Resolution No. 195 of 1998), RCC Resolution No. 25 of 1999 gave those living in the Autonomous Region of Iraq (Kurdish area) the right to seek postponement of their service or to enlist immediately.

1.4 War veterans

RCC Resolution No. 201 of 1999 provides that veterans who, as a result of the war, are deformed or handicapped will be granted ID0.5 million each to enable those wishing to get married to do so. Prisoners of war and those lost in action will be deemed to continue to be in active service as long as they are not back home. POWs who return will continue to enjoy the benefits of those in active service for five years following their return.

1.5 Cabinet reshuffle

The Minister of Labour and Social Security, Abdul Hamid Aziz Al-Saigh was relieved of his post by Presidential Decree on 18 May 1998. He was replaced on 6 July 1998 by Field Marshal Saadi Toma Abbas.

1.6 Ministry of Information

Statutory Instructions No. 2 of 1998 were gazetted by the Ministry of Information (8 June 1998) to facilitate the implementation of the Ministry of Culture and Information Law No. 94 of 1981. The Statutory Instrument sets out the objectives and structure of the Department of Information within the Ministry. The objectives are:

(a) to promulgate information about Iraq's culture, history, art as well as political views; and

---

[1] See Sabah Al-Mukhtar, "Iraq", in *Yearbook of Islamic and Middle Eastern Law*, vol. 3 (1996), p. 194.

(b) to enhance the understanding of Iraq's position by others and also to document such information that would assist researchers in cultural, social and economic matters.

The Department is empowered:

(a) to arrange conferences, seminars and other activities to achieve its objectives;
(b) to facilitate visits by foreign media representatives, grant licences and permits to print books magazines and newspapers; and
(c) to censor imported matter, films and other media material.

It is run by a board of management composed of the director-general of the Department and the heads of the various desks within it. The Department is divided into fourteen desks including: Arab, international, informatics, publications protocol, treaties and conventions, and censorship.

1.7 Iraqi passports

The fee for obtaining a new passport was increased fivefold from ID 2000 to ID10,000. This was effected by a decision of the Economic Committee of the Council of Ministers No. 50 of 1998 which became effective as of 11 January 1999.

1.8 Working abroad

The Ministry of Foreign Affairs published Statutory Instrument No. 1 of 1998 (1 June 1998) to facilitate the implementation of the Revolutionary Command Council Resolution relating to this matter No. 15 of 1998.[2] The Instrument provides that the Commission (which is an independent body with juridical personality) is empowered to contract out Iraqi nationals to work outside Iraq on secondment basis. The Commission is to collect information about work opportunities that exist outside Iraq which are open for Iraqi nationals. This includes working for international and regional organizations such as the UN and its agencies, the Arab League and its agencies, associations, federations and other organizations and NGOs of which Iraq is a member. The Commission is also required to collect data of Iraqi professionals who have the requirements and qualifications and who are interested in working abroad and is charged with the determination of applications received from individuals to work outside Iraq. More important, it deals with the request for nominations of Iraqi representatives in international and Arab organizations. It is also charged with dealing with expatriate Iraqis, assisting them in their relationship with Iraq and generally representing their views and interest both to the legislature and the executive.

[2] See Sabah Al-Mukhtar, "Iraq", Yearbook of Islamic and Middle Eastern Law, vol. 4 (1997–1998), p. 265.

1.9 Travel and exit visas

Iraq, which is suffering from shortage of manpower in every discipline due to the unbearable living conditions in Iraq under the UN siege, is continually revising travel and exit visa rules. As in most countries in the world, citizens need an exit visa to leave the country. However, in the case of Iraq the government is trying to make it extra difficult to stop the "brain drain". It imposes a very high exit visa cost (ID400,000), and requires a variety of permissions from the employer, security services, Income Tax and National Service Department of the Ministry of Defence. Additionally, Iraq bans the travel of various categories of citizens, which include single women, ex-military officers, doctors and scientists.

On 15 June 1998 an additional amount of ID500 was imposed on those leaving and entering the border with Syria at the point of Al-Waleed. Students studying privately outside Iraq have to pay the exit fee of ID400,000. The amount is refundable with interest if the student returns after graduation in accordance with RCC Resolution No. 90 of 1998. The amount government scholarship students have to pay as security to fulfil their contract is refunded with interest in addition to compensation against depreciation of the currency by linking the amount of the deposit to the price of gold. Further, Statutory Instrument No. 116 of 1998, published on 21 December 1998, provided for the setting up of a special bank account into which the interest is credited on monthly basis. The Statutory Instrument also provides for the possibility of extending the study period and specifies the additional guarantee needed.

1.10 Nationality and national identity

Citizens have, *inter alia*, two important documents in Iraq. These are the Iraqi nationality certificate and the national identity certificate. These documents used to be freely provided as they are the property of the state and have to be carried by the citizens. However, RCC Resolutions 73 and 74 of 1998 have now empowered the Nationality and the Civil Status Departments to make a charge for providing these certificates. Fifty per cent of the revenue is paid to the National Treasury; the remainder is divided between the employees of the departments who receive 30 per cent of the revenues while the remaining 20 per cent goes into the Department's account. RCC Resolution 89 of 1998 authorized the Ministry of Finance to advance the amount of ID200 million to the Nationality Department and the Civil Status Department for the purpose of issuing certificates on the basis that the amount advanced will be recovered from the charge to be made by these departments. The amount of charge was set out at ID150 per certificate. Printing of the forms, which cost almost ID10 million, was in fact carried out in accordance with RCC Resolution 108 of 1998. The Ministry of Interior subsequently issued instructions on 24 September 1998 to facilitate the implementation of the Resolutions containing a list of the documents concerned.

1.11 National Statistics Authority

The National Statistics Authority Regulation No. 1 of 1987 was amended on 11 May 1998. The amendment is aimed at increasing the role and influence of the National Statistics Authority Offices in the governorates. These offices are now empowered to require public bodies to take into consideration statistical findings when implementing the various economic sectors projects in the National Development Plan. Offices in the governorates are obliged to collect statistics in four sectors: agriculture, industry, construction and a further set for the remaining sectors of economy.

1.12 Official forms

The Ministry of Interior has issued an announcement setting out the fees that must be paid for using the various official forms needed by the public to obtain services. These were normally given free of charge as they are imposed by the state. The forms listed in the announcement principally relate to personal and family matters such as, registration of births, deaths and marriages, naturalization, nationality certificates, civil identity cards and the like. The fees range between ID250 and ID3,000 depending on the type of form. This was imposed in accordance with the provisions of RCC Resolution No. 108 of 1998.

1.13 The oil industry

RCC Resolution 76 of 1998 (3727) replaced RCC Resolution No. 800 of 1987 which incorporated the State Establishment for Oil and Gas Industrialization (South). The new Resolution, which is an absolute reversal of the situation just ten years earlier, provides for the creation of two separate entities. Though attached to the Ministry of Oil, each has a full legal capacity and independent juridical personality. These are the state establishment for Oil Refining (South) and the State Establishment for Gas Industry (South).

In May 1987, a series of Revolutionary Command Council Resolutions purged the Iraqi Oil Industry when the Iraq National Oil Company was dissolved and the whole oil industry was centralized under the direct control of the Ministry of Oil. At present, and for the last ten years, the structure of oil industry may be summarized as follows.

The Ministry of Oil is the supreme central authority with a number of entities attached to it. However each of these entities has an independent juridical personality. They include:

- North Oil Company;
- South Oil Company;
- Northern Refining Company;
- Central Refining Company;
- Southern Refining Company;
- Oil Drilling Company;

- Oil Projects Company;
- Oil Installation and Facilities Company;
- Oil Products Transport Company;
- Oil Products Distribution Company;
- Oil Marketing Company.

1.14 Antiquities

There is a dramatic increase in organized crime causing the destruction and pilferage of Iraqi antiquities. This is the result of the inability of the Department of Antiquities to protect almost 3,000 historical sites with less than 300 wardens and guards to do the job, coupled with the increase of incidents of theft as a direct result of the blockade which has reduced most of the Iraqi population of 22 million people to well below the poverty line.

A variety of measures have been tried over the last few years, including dramatically increasing the penalty for such crimes to include the death sentence, and increasing the powers of the security services and other authorities to combat this phenomenon. In 1998 it is reported that nine people were hanged to death for stealing and destroying antiquities. The government has made many pleas and representations to the UN and its specialized agencies and to the usual states where these antiquities end up such as the US, the UK and other European countries. These pleas have met with very little support despite the fact that Iraqi antiquities are in fact being openly auctioned in well-known auction houses in London and other capitals. One of the exceptions is Jordan where a number of smuggled antiquities were returned to Iraq and formally handed over by the Jordanian Minister of Information. RCC Resolution No. 82 of 1998 amended RCC Resolution No. 111 of 1996 by empowering the security services in the governorates to confiscate the assets of the thieves and smugglers including vehicles and other means of transport.

1.15 Iraqi Nuclear Authority

Having been deprived of all of its installations, facilities and infrastructure, the hundreds of Iraqi nuclear scientists who are still working for the authority have now been authorized to offer their services to others. RCC Resolution No. 125 of 1998 have empowered INA to enter into contracts with Iraqi state-owned entities as well as with the private sector to undertake research and offer their scientific knowledge and services on a commercial basis.

1.16 National Centre for Planning and Management

Instruction No. 10 of 1998 established a consultative authority within the National Centre for Planning and Management to consider the laws and regulations in force and the means of effectively enforcing same. The instructions set out the various objectives and matters that may or need to be considered.

1.17 National Planning Authority

The internal structure of the National Planning Authority (established by Law No. 24 of 1994) is set out in the Statutory Instructions No. 11 of 1998 (3747). The Authority is made up of eighteen divisions including the Central Statistics Agency, the Central Standards and the Quality Control Agency and National Centre for Planning and Management. The other divisions are sectorially based (agriculture, housing, industry, manpower, etc.), in addition to management oriented ones (accounts, audit, administration, legal, etc.). The instructions set out the qualifications of the cadre, functions, objectives and rights and powers of the divisions.

1.18 Academy of Science

The General Assembly of the Academy voted to approve the new internal regulations and structure which were prepared in accordance with Article 29 of the Academy of Science Law No. 3 of 1995 (replacing the earlier Law No. 163 of 1978).

The Regulations set out the powers of the President, executives, departments, committees and the general assembly. It sets out the rules for election, quorum and the procedures governing meetings and decision making process. It deals with publications, archives and local non-Arabic languages used in the Academy.

1.19 Civil Service

Civil Service Law No. 1 of 1991 amending Law No. 24 of 1960, was gazetted on 1 February 1999. The amendment annuls the appointment orders of a civil servant if a post is not taken up by an appointed civil servant within ten days. It also provides that a civil servant who does not commence work within five days of a transfer order without lawful reason will be dismissed from service. Otherwise, any civil servant who absences himself from work without lawful reason is deemed to have resigned his post. This is a clear indication that the state is trying to streamline the civil service and to avoid the burdens which it places on the treasury.

1.20 Civil defence

The Ministry of Interior reorganized the National Civil Defence Authority by a Ministerial Decision gazetted on 5 April 1999. The NCDA is headed by the Minister and made up of the under-secretaries of the Ministries of Interior, Communications, Health, Agriculture and Information. Additionally, there are other members of front line services such as the police, army, fire, water, electricity, telephone and red crescent. Each governorate has its own local civil defence authority. The Ministerial Decision details policy, functions and objectives which are to be put into effect in emergency situations. The categories of emergencies are listed and the measures to be adopted are set out in each case. They include emergencies of nuclear, chemical and biological contamination, unexploded munitions, protection of civilians, government buildings, food and water supplies, animal welfare, etc. A number of services are listed where the competent authorities are empowered to undertake exceptional measures to deal with emergencies, including traffic authorities, ambulance, security, fire and others.

1.21 Scouts and cubs

Law No. 12 of 1998 was published on 22 June 1998 to regulate the rights and duties of the members of the movement. They must be between twelve and fifteen years of age, in full-time education and in good health; willing and able to be members and who produce written parental approval. They must observe a strict code of conduct and display qualities of bravery, perseverance, honesty and patriotism. The movement is structured on a geographical basis. The law sets out the relationship which the movement has with other voluntary organizations, such as student unions and youth organizations. The members are given priority in admission to specialized schools and later in the police and military academies. The law grants Mr Udday Saddam Hussein the authority to issue rules and regulations to achieve the objectives of the law.

1.22 The handicapped

To facilitate the implementation of the Social Benefits Law No. 116 of 1980, the relevant Statutory Instructions were amended on 18 January 1999. They impose further qualifications on those establishing institutions or homes for the handicapped. The instructions further tightened the requirements in respect of safety and building in which they are established as well as staffing level and qualification.

2 JUDICIARY AND JUDICIAL SYSTEM

2.1 Court fees

RCC Resolution No. 69 of 1998 levies a further fee of ID250 to be paid for the service of proceeding through the Bailiff Service. To improve the performance of court bailiffs and servers of proceedings, a performance bonus based on a points system was introduced by the Justice Department on 31 August 1998

Law No. 17 of 1998 amended the provision of the Judicial Fees Law No. 114 of 1981. It sets out new fees to be paid by claimants when the judge or other court officers have to make visits outside their office or working hours for the purposes of evidence by deposition or as examiners of the court.

2.2 Judicial courses

The Judicial Institute is the professional body charged with training lawyers to become judges. RCC Resolution No. 52 of 1998 has now empowered the Institute to hold and charge for legal training courses to improve the legal understanding of the Civil

Service Cadre. These courses may also be available to employees of the public sector and even the private sector. The fees for these courses are to be paid for by the employer.

2.3 Limiting courts' jurisdiction

During the first three years following the Gulf War, municipalities leased some of their property to third parties at the then prevailing rent. These rents have by now become almost worthless due to the collapse of the Iraqi currency. As contracts under Iraqi law continue to be binding for their term irrespective of economics, the municipalities have sought to annul such lease contracts but failed. To remedy this situation it became necessary to legislate to revoke such contracts. Therefore RCC Resolution No. 77 of 1998 provides that all property leases between the municipalities and third parties which were signed without public auction during the years 1992–1994 shall be terminated. Each property is to be revalued and offered to the same tenant on a new contract with the new rent. If the tenant declines to sign the lease contract then the municipality may lease the property to others in accordance with the Sale and Lease of State Property Law No. 32 of 1986. The Resolution further prohibits the courts from hearing cases brought as a result thereof.

Another instance where the state has sought to curb the courts' jurisdiction is in the case of RCC Resolution No. 86 of 1989 expressly prohibiting the courts from hearing a specific class of suits. This involved preventing the courts retroactively from obliging the government to pay more than 50 per cent of the amounts it owes to persons (natural or juridical). This was an incredible decision, as aside from being iniquitous, it was unethical and indeed strategically harmful. Such a step is bound to discourage people from working within government departments.

2.4 Civil Procedures Code

The Civil Procedures Code No. 83 of 1969 was amended by Law No. 16 of 1998. The Law amends a number of articles relating to the deposit to be paid by the parties in litigation at different stages and instances. The deposits were increased by fourfold and in certain instances by twentyfold.

Further amendments to the Code were gazetted on 20 July 1998 (3731). The penalties prescribed in Articles 28, 63, 96, 200, 288 and 291, by virtue of the provisions of RCC Resolution No. 206 of 1994, were dramatically increased, some by as much as a hundred-fold.

2.5 Membership of the Iraqi Bar

RCC Resolution No. 174 of 1998 bans anyone from practising as a lawyer or having his name on the roll of the Iraqi Bar to practise as such if he has been dismissed from a civil service job which he used to hold or if he was dishonourably discharged from such post or if he was sentenced for a crime that was contrary to morality. The Resolution applies to those who are already members of the bar. Such persons were granted a three-month period to hand over the cases they were handling.

2.6 Juveniles Law

Law No. 76 of 1983 concerning the protection of juveniles was amended by Law No. 31 of 1998. The amendment relates to Article 54 which now provides that juvenile courts will be presided over by a judge and two other members, one a lawyer and the other a specialist in a field relating to juveniles, and that the court shall have the power to uphold or overturn decisions of investigative judges. Article 76 of the 1983 Law was amended to provide that if a child commits a crime for which a prison sentence is normally handed down, then the court may decide to put him in custody in accordance with the law, commit him to a rehabilitation institution for six months to five years or may hand him over to a parent or a guardian whom the court is convinced will be able to guarantee the child's proper behaviour for a period of one to three years. However, if the crime committed calls for the death sentence then the juvenile must be committed to a rehabilitation institution for a period not exceeding ten years. A similar provision was amended to deal with the case of teenagers. The amendment further calls for social reports to be produced in order to determine the proper penalty. The amendment also dealt with the case where the juvenile reaches the age of 18 at the time of sentencing.

2.7 Enforcement law

Enforcement Law No. 45 of 1980 was amended by Law No. 32 of 1998. The amendment dealt with a number of provisions with a view to facilitating and simplifying enforcement procedures. They are aimed at balancing the interests of the creditor and debtor when the defendant makes a payment into the Enforcement Department. They are aimed at making it easier for a divorcee to obtain the dowry specified in the marriage certificate. The amendment also dealt with the repossession of impounded properties.

2.8 Notary public

The Notary Public Law No. 27 of 1977 was repealed and replaced by Law No. 33 of 1998. The *raison d'être* of the law provides that the new law is aimed at reflecting the changes in the needs, activities and functions of the notary public as a result of the social, economic and legal changes over the last quarter of a century. The law is made up of seven chapters, the first dealing with the principles, objectives and jurisprudence. The second details in ten articles the structure of the notary public (which is part of the judiciary) in the legal system of Iraq. Chapter 3 details the powers and authorities of the notary and the legal value of work performed by notaries. The fourth chapter details the procedures to be followed to notarize documents. The fifth deals with registration of machines and equipment. This used to be covered by the Machines Registration Law No. 31 of 1939, which is also now repealed. Chapter 6 confers on the documents and the registers of the notary public the legal effect of being unquestionable public documents that may not be disputed except in the case of forgery.

2.9 Release of prisoners

The Revolutionary Command Council resolved that prisoners who have completed at least half their prison term would be eligible for release against payment of money in lieu. The amount payable is set at ID2 million for each year or part of a year remaining to be served. Twenty per cent of the money collected is to be distributed to the orphans and the old, 30 per cent to the officers in the police, prison and social services, 20 per cent to members of the Public Prosecution Service and the judiciary and the remaining 30 per cent goes to the treasury. RCC Resolution No. 13 of 1999, which was gazetted on 15 February 1999, has a ninety-day validity period. Certain categories of prisoners are excluded from the provisions of this Resolution. They include those who have committed crimes against the state, whose sentence was already reduced from death to imprisonment, drug dealers and dangerous thieves.

2.10 Detention of women

RCC Resolution No. 47 of 1999 prohibits the detention of women who are waiting for or who are on trial. They must be released on bail until they are sentenced to imprisonment and the sentence is final.

2.11 Customs Appeal Court

Customs Law No. 23 of 1984 was amended by Law No. 21 of 1998. Article 250 of the law now provides that an appeal bench be especially established to deal exclusively with appeals against judgments of the Customs Court. The bench, in addition to the high court judges, is to have a representative of the Ministry of Finance. He may not be the commissioner of customs. The period of appeal is thirty days from service of the judgment of the Customs Court and it is now open to the commissioner of customs to appeal against lenient sentences.

3 COMMERCIAL LAW

3.1 Duty free zone

Law No. 3 of 1998 established the General Authority of Duty Free Zones ("DFZ"). The zone is attached to the Ministry of Finance and has independent juridical personality. Its objectives and powers are to operate and promote DFZ areas within Iraq in the national interest and for the public benefit and to control matters of customs and excise within the bonded areas. It has a nine-member board of directors including representatives of the Ministries of Trade, Oil, Transport and Industry. The stated aim is to attract foreign capital, facilitate trade and give national capital investors a window on the outside world.

The Minister of Finance issued Internal Regulation No. 3 of 1999 (22 March 1999) setting out the management structure of the DFZ, authorities and powers vested in the board, management and divisions.

Statutory Instructions No. 4 of 1999 were gazetted on 24 May 1999, setting out the criteria and rules under which investors may operate within the DFZ. They include applications, deposits, licences and leases relating to their activities within the zone. The instructions set out the duties and powers of the Authority.

3.2 Road tax

Traffic Law No. 48 of 1971 was amended by RCC Resolution No. 51 of 1998. The amendment imposes a variety of financial burdens in the form of taxes and licensing fees. Such levies relate to the registration of new vehicles, transfer of registration permits to enter restricted areas and driving across governorate jurisdictions. They also affect licensing of car mechanics and repair centres, parking garages and driving schools.

A further special tax is imposed by RCC Resolution No. 36 of 1999. This tax is to be paid once every five years by all road users for the purpose of maintaining the road network. The tax ranges from ID1,000 to ID10,000. The Resolution specifies the percentage to be allocated for local roads within the built up areas, national roads and bridges and for traffic improvement and research.

3.3 Income Tax Law

Income Tax Law No. 113 of 1982 was amended by RCC Resolution No. 55 of 1998. The amendment provides that 75 per cent of the income resulting from the sale of immovable assets shall be exempted from income tax if the property was held for at least five years.

A further amendment was affected by RCC Resolution No. 5 of 1999. The Resolution announced a six-month amnesty for those who notify the Income Tax Department of any breach of the law. The six months begins from the effective date of the Resolution which is 1 February 1999. The effect of the amnesty is to drop all charges in any reported case that has not been judged or where the judgment is not yet final.

Deduction at source of tax from contractors has been imposed by the Ministry of Finance Instructions No. 6 of 1998 (amending Instructions No. 4 of 1993): 7.5 per cent of all monies due to contractors (foreign and national) must be deducted and withheld by government departments, public sector entities and private persons. The amounts must be immediately paid to the Treasury and final account submitted when the final acceptance certificate is issued.

3.4 Contractors' Federation

Iraqi Contractors' Federation Law No. 97 of 1988 was amended by Law No. 10 of 1998 to enable the General Assembly of the Federation to determine the membership fee. The fee was fixed in the law, which requires an amendment of the law every time the membership fee has to be changed.

3.5 Privatization of holiday resorts

Lake Habania is one of the main holiday resorts west of Baghdad. It was a mixed sector entity (owned by the government and the private sector) that suffered such neglect and lack of investment that it almost became derelict. RCC Resolution No. 83 of 1998 authorized the State Establishment of Tourism to buy the shares of the private sector and to directly upgrade the public facilities and services in the resort. Thereafter, it is to lease these facilities and services to the private sector to be run on commercial basis. Residential units and houses in the resort, on the other hand, are offered to the private sector for a seven-year period against investing in the refurbishment and furnishing the houses and units. Once the resort is in operating condition, 49 per cent of the shares will be offered to the public to subscribe to.

3.6 Income from holy shrines

RCC Resolution No. 88 of 1998 repealed RCC Resolution 227 of 1978 regarding the distribution of income which the holy shrines in Iraq receive. The income is usually generated from three sources: the Islamic *waqf* (trust) normally attached to the shrine, donations and charities by the believers, and a state contribution. The new RCC Resolution provides that 20 per cent of the income is to be allocated for repair and maintenance, 20 per cent for administration and 20 per cent is to be distributed to the needy in the surrounding area. The remaining 40 per cent is paid to those who work in these shrines or their dependants if they become unable to work, or die.

3.7 Customs and excise

Customs and Excise Law No. 23 of 1984 was amended by Law No. 15 of 1998, granting the Ministry of Finance certain powers. In accordance with the amendment, the Ministry may divide the penalties and liabilities imposed by the court between those sentenced, in such a manner as to lighten their burden for rehabilitation purposes.

Custom duties on cars from American and German sources have been reduced from 20 to 10 per cent. Cars from other sources are reduced from 10 to 5 per cent according to the Council of Ministers Announcement published in the Official Gazette No. 3767.

3.8 Illegal imports

RCC Resolution No. 30 of 1993 imposed the death penalty on imports into Iraq of banned goods. The same penalty was also imposed when a person was found in possession of goods which were not on the official import list. The aim was to discourage tradesmen from importing goods other than those which were essential at the time immediately following the war. This Resolution was repealed by RCC Resolution No. 96 of 1998 indicating that businessmen may import consumer goods and non-essential imports rather than confining private imports to foods, medicine and basic essentials.

3.9 Companies' profit distribution

Income Tax Law No. 101 of 1964 provides that companies have to allocate a certain percentage of their profit for distribution to their employees. Additionally, further allocations have to be made for pensions and other benefits. The law was amended by Law No. 9 of 1998 to exempt banks, investment companies and other financial institutions from these requirements. However, these companies are required instead to pay the equivalent of 10 per cent of their net profit to the Department of Labour and Social Security.

3.10 Industrial Investment Law

Law No. 20 of 1998 (repealing No. 25 of 1991), was gazetted and came into effect on 3 August 1998. It is aimed at encouraging investment in industry by the private sector alone or in association with the public sector (termed "mixed sector"). The law defines the industrial projects covered by its provisions and sets out a licensing system. It provides for a five-year tax holiday for those projects which were established prior to the law coming into force and a ten-year tax period for those established after the law came into effect. The tax holiday is progressive and dependent on the type of industry, size of investment and location of the project (rural/urban). Further, land and infrastructure are to be made available on easy terms. Town planning, safety, environmental consideration and other policies and rules must be observed and adhered to before a licence is granted. The law also has provisions dealing with the situation of upgrading and expanding existing projects and affording them incentives.

3.11 Investment companies

The Council of Ministers approved Statutory Regulations No. 5 of 1998 regulating investment companies. The Regulations were published in the Official Gazette No. 3735. They empower the Central Bank of Iraq to license public companies incorporated in accordance with the Companies Law No. 21 of 1997 to exclusively undertake financial investment activities. The minimum capital of such companies must be no less than ID15 million and no juridical person may hold more than 5 per cent of its share capital. Such companies may undertake all investment activities including sale and purchase of shares, stocks and bonds, manage portfolios, issue debentures and participate in existing companies as shareholders or extending loans to them. The Central Bank shall determine the reserves, cover and investment rules for the protecting of investors. The companies are obliged to make full and regular disclosure to the Central Bank, which has supervisory and inspection powers. Should the company lose 25 per cent of its capital and reserves, then the Central Bank will intervene and take the measures it deems necessary. Companies accounts must be annually published and are subject to the National Audit Office supervision.

3.12 Cooperative Law

Cooperative Law No. 15 of 1992[3] was amended by Law No. 27 of 1994[4] and then by Law No. 7 of 1999. The present amendment aims at removing the difficulties that became evident following the experience of the last few years. There was a wider participation of cooperative entities and restructuring of the distribution of the income of the cooperatives. The amendment imposes penalties in cases of abuse by members and executives of the cooperatives as well as of persons illegally claiming to be involved in cooperative work.

3.13 Non-resident bank account

Foreign exchange control regulations issued in accordance with Article 78 of the Central Bank Law No. 64 of 1976 are amended from time to time. The twenty-sixth amendment was published in the Official Gazette as Central Bank Instructions, on 17 May 1999. The amendment provides that Iraqis, who are not resident in Iraq, and their agents, may withdraw any amount of money from their non-resident bank accounts that are held by banks in Iraq. This right did not extend to the "agents" of the depositor before the amendment.

3.14 Insurance

RCC Resolution No. 192 of 1998 designated the Ministry of Finance as the Regulatory Body for the purposes of the Companies Law No. 29 of 1997 in respect of insurance and re-insurance activities. Insurance outside Iraq for risks within Iraq is banned by the Resolution. Insuring such risks must be placed with domestic insurance companies. The Ministry of Finance is charged with setting out the rules and regulations for the insurance sector. More important is that the Insurance Brokers and Agents Law No. 49 of 1960 was repealed by this Resolution.

3.15 Quality control markings

Statutory Instructions No. 16 of 1998 were issued by the Planning Board and gazetted on 18 January 1999. They were issued in accordance with requirements to facilitate the implementation of the Central Board of Standard and Quality Control Law No. 54 of 1979. The instructions define the product, Iraqi standards, quality control certification, markings, licences and inspection. They set out the procedures to be followed and conditions to be satisfied before certification is given and before markings are placed on the product. The instructions detail the breaches and penalties as well as complaint procedures.

---

[3] See *Yearbook of Islamic and Middle Eastern Law*, vol. 1 (1994), p. 177.
[4] See Sabah Al-Mukhtar, "Iraq", in *Yearbook of Islamic and Middle Eastern Law*, vol. 2 (1995), p. 135.

3.16 Trade Mark Registration Agents Law

The Registration Agents Law No. 60 of 1955 was repealed and replaced by Law No. 4 of 1999. The provisions of the law apply to persons who undertake company registration, trade mark and patent registration and commercial names registration agency work. The Ministry of Trade is to establish a new register of such agents. The agent must be Iraqi national, member of the Iraqi Bar and have his own office to practice from. A licensing committee is to be established by the Ministry of Trade that would vet applicants and place names of successful ones on the Register of Agents. The law came into effect ninety days after publication (15 March 1999) and existing agents must register within ninety days of the effective dates.

3.17 Public sector companies

Article 6 of the Public Sector Companies Law No. 22 of 1997[5] provides that the Registrar of Companies shall publish in the Bulletin the Memorandum of Association or a notice thereof and the incorporation certificate of each registered public sector company. A notice of the Memorandum of Association is also published in the Official Gazette. Over the period of this survey (March 1998–May 1999) the Memoranda of Association of 133 publicly owned companies were published in the Official Gazette. They are principally companies that are attached to the Ministries of Trade, Industry, Housing, Transport, Oil, Irrigation, and Finance. They include banks, insurance, trade, manufacturing, construction, import, export, power, phosphate, and sulphur mining, as well as the oil sector companies. The Memorandum of Association of each set out the objectives of the companies, their capital, and the ministry to which they are attached. The capital of the companies surveyed range from ID10 million to ID2 billion. Typically trading, consultancy and other service companies have a capital in hundreds of millions. Asset holding companies and major industries have a capital in billions or hundreds of thousands of millions.

3.18 Slaughterhouses

The Baghdad Municipality is empowered by RCC Resolution No. 33 of 1998 to levy a further fee on the slaughter of each animal. This levy is over and above the normal fees and charges, due to the need of the almost five million inhabitants of Baghdad.

4 LABOUR LAW

4.1 Work related disability

A new Employees Medical Inability Law No. 11 of 1999 in respect of ill health and work-related illness and disability was promulgated and became effective fifteen

---

[5] See *Yearbook of Middle Estern and Islamic Law*, vol. 4 (1997–1998), pp. 269–272.

days after publication (24 May 1999). The law repeals certain provisions of the Civil Service Pension Law No. 33 of 1966. It combines legal provisions in a variety of legislation into one law as well as introducing important changes for the protection of those who serve the nation. The law defines and distinguishes between illness that is not related to work and illness or disability resulting from or during work. In the first case, the employee is entitled to free treatment, and paid leave for up to three years. Thereafter, he may be given work commensurate with his ability or given a pension. If the illness or disability relates to work, then the paid leave is not limited by time. Compensation is also paid, and if necessary the employee who is no longer able to work, irrespective of his period of service, will be entitled to a pension that is higher than that he would be entitled to otherwise. The law provides for the establishment of medical committees and provides for an appeal procedure.

4.2 Overtime for civil servants

Until this year civil servants and employees of public sector entities could not be paid for working outside normal working hours. RCC Resolution No. 1 of 1999, which came into effect on 18 January 1999, authorizes the ministries and other entities to request their staff to work outside working hours against overtime payments. No one may work for more than an additional sixty hours per week. The pay is set at one and half times the hourly rate of the employee.

4.3 Labour card

Labourers and employees in the private sector were obliged to carry a labour card in accordance with the provisions of the Labour Card Law No. 64 of 1983. Law No. 30 of 1998 repealed that law on the basis that such card is no longer necessary since each individual has other identity cards which may be relied on.

4.4 Incentives

The policy of distributing part of the revenue of state entities to employees and staff[6] continues to spread to other entities. RCC Resolution No. 162 of 1998 provides that 2.5 per cent of income tax collected by the Inland Revenue is to be paid to the staff and employees. Statutory Instructions Nos. 18 and 19 of 1998 (12 October 1998), for example detail the distribution of incentives to the employees in the nationality department. Statutory Instructions No. 16 of 1998 (5 October 1998) details this matter in respect of the Central Bank. RCC Resolution No. 54 (8 June 1998) provides the payment for the employees of the Ministry of Transport.

---

[6] See *Yearbook of Islamic and Middle Eastern Law*, vol. 3 (1996), p. 194 and vol. 4 (1997–1998), p. 274.

218 Country Surveys

4.5 Social security

Social Security Law No. 39 of 1971 was amended by Law No. 22 of 1998. The amendment provides for the increase of the deposit referred to in Article No. 90 of the 1971 Law. That deposit must be made by the employer when it appeals against the decision of the Director General of the Department of Labour or when disputing a decision of the Pension Fund in respect of pension disputes. The amount of deposit which is now ID 5,000 will be refunded or credited to the Pension Fund depending on the outcome of the appeal.

4.6 Disabled soldiers

Members of the armed forces who suffer 100 per cent disability (loss or paralysis of both legs, etc.) are entitled to the same benefits as those paid to the heirs of martyrs. RCC Resolution No. 28 of 1998 provides that in addition to other benefits, they will be entitled to a special monthly allowance of ID10,000.

4.7 Inventors and Innovators Law

Law No. 1 of 1998 provides that each Ministry and public sector entity must establish a committee to encourage, identify and nominate inventors and innovators within the entity. The Central Board of Standards and Quality Control set up a committee in respect of the private sector. Annexed to the law are standard forms to be used for these purposes. In addition to awards and commendations, the inventor/innovator is entitled to 50 per cent of the benefits that the invention generates and the remaining 50 per cent is for the employer. The Council of Ministers gazetted instructions on 4 January 1999 (3755) to facilitate the implementation of the law.

4.8 Iraqi Ports Authority

A very detailed statutory instrument relating to the operation and use of Iraqi Ports was gazetted on 20 July 1998, containing 358 articles divided into two parts, the first dealing with maritime matters and the second with cargo. Each part is divided into chapters and sub-chapters. The instructions deal with such matters as arrival and departure of vessels, notices, communications, navigational channels, draught, speed, personnel, crew, tow, jetties, piloting, collision, flag, search and rescue, handling, stevedoring, transit and penalties.

5 LAW OF PROPERTY

5.1 Property tax

Property Tax Law No. 162 of 1959 was amended by Law No. 5 of 1998. The amendment introduces performance linked incentives for the staff of the Department. The incentives are also offered to assessors, valuers and members of committees in accordance with delegated legislation to be introduced by the Ministry of Finance.

5.2 Property Rent Act

Property Rent Act No. 87 of 1979 provides, *inter alia*, for security of tenure. It also set out the cases where the landlord may seek the eviction of the tenant. Law No. 3 of 1999 amends the 1979 law by adding a new ground for eviction. The right to demand eviction is now granted to prisoners of war who return from captivity. If the prisoner of war was the owner of the property or if the property is in the name of his wife then returning to the city where the property is situated is a proper ground for seeking determination of a secured lease.

5.3 Town planning

The Ministry of Finance issued Instructions No. 3 of 1998 to facilitate the provisions of RCC Resolution No. 150 of 1997 which was gazetted on 25 May 1998 but came into effect on 27 October 1997. The Instructions deal with the allocation of residential areas in towns and villages and also with agricultural land. They set out the procedures for distribution of land to farmers for government-subsidized prices. The instructions empower the Ministry of Agriculture to take certain measures in respect of right of use and leases when the Ministry is the owner of the land. Each governorate is to establish a committee to deal with the various types of land within its jurisdiction. These committees shall have among their members representatives of the governorate, Municipality, Town Planning, and Land Registry Departments. Those who qualify to purchase the land, the consideration to be paid, payment conditions, etc., are set out in these Instructions. They also set out the construction specifications that must be used as a minimum standard for building on the lands.

RCC Resolution No. 66 of 1998 imposes fees for services rendered by the Ministry in respect of plans, drawings and details provided to local governments, municipalities and other state-owned entities. The Resolution lists, in a schedule attached thereto, the applicable fee scale. Only 50 per cent of the fees is payable to the treasury, the remainder is distributed to the staff of the relevant departments.

5.4 Compulsory purchase

The Compulsory Purchase Law No. 12 of 1981 was amended by Law No. 6 of 1999. The amendment removes mixed sector entities from those empowered to seek compulsory purchase of real property. The right is now confined to ministries, government departments and public domain entities. The amendment also permits the purchaser to agree a substitute property to be given in lieu of payment of money. In the case where the property needed by a state entity is owned by another, then the transfer of title may be affected by administrative decision rather than by purchase under the law. In emergencies (such as natural disasters and wars) the relevant state entity may temporarily take over any property that is necessary to deal with the emergency. Such takeover may not exceed a maximum period of two years in any event.

5.5 Pavements

Instructions No. 23 of 1998 was gazetted (11 January 1999) to facilitate the enforcement of RCC Resolution No. 184 of 1997.[7] Municipalities and local governments are charged with the improvement and repair of pavements. They may do so by their own employed labour force, or through outside contractors by means of tender and charge the benefiting properties with the cost of such improvement and repair. Owners on the other hand, may now be obliged to do the work required in accordance with details and specifications that are prepared by the municipality and pay the cost.

5.6 Small industries

In 1990 RCC Resolution No. 64 authorized municipalities to lease to the public, plots of land that they own at designated industrial areas to build small industries and services on them. The Resolution prohibited sub-leasing to others. RCC Resolution No. 38 of 1999 removed such prohibition by providing that the use of the land is not changed and the rent agreed does not exceed the value of the land.

6 CRIMINAL LAW

6.1 Law and order

In an attempt to encourage public officials to inform the authorities about theft, forgery and misappropriation, RCC Resolution No. 41 of 1998 extended the rewards which were offered in 1995 by RCC Resolution No. 103 to include all officials in addition to those in the security services.

Persons impersonating civil servants or members of the armed forces, police or security services, will be subject to a ten-year prison sentence in accordance with RCC Resolution 102 of 1998. The same penalty will be imposed on those who obstruct the measures undertaken by the competent authorities. The use of a forged identity, or document in the commission of offence will be deemed as an aggravating circumstance.

RCC Resolution 175 of 1998 provides that 30 per cent of the value of the assets recovered in case of misuse shall be paid to the informers whose information leads to the arrest of the culprit. The confidentiality of the information and investigation shall be maintained until it is put before the investigative magistrate to decide if proceedings are to commence. The Criminal Court should consider the case

---

[7] See *Yearbook of Islamic and Middle Eastern Law*, vol. 4 (1997–1998), p. 275.

as soon as possible but within period not exceeding two months of the date when the person is charged.

A further Resolution No. 29 of 1999 was promulgated increasing the percentage of the value of the recovered property that should be paid to informers. The Resolution additionally provides for the reward to be shared by the law enforcement agencies in addition to the informers. The shares of the various authorities are detailed in the Resolution.

6.2 Amendment of the Penal Code

The provisions of Article 384 of the Penal Code No. 111 of 1969 were amended by Law No. 8 of 1999. The amendment provides that the person who is ordered to pay maintenance to his wife or any of his issue or parents or any other person that he is obliged to pay for their maintenance but fails to do so within thirty days he shall be imprisoned for one year. The penalty increases to two years in case of repeated failure. Such action can only be commenced by the public prosecutor at the request of the beneficiary. Should the beneficiary abandon the claim or be willing to forgive then the penalty shall be immediately suspended.

6.3 Death sentence

RCC Resolution No. 61 of 1999 was promulgated following the bombing of Iraq by the US and UK during the operations code named Desert Fox. The Resolution provides that any one assisting the enemy or causing harm to military installation which is likely to affect the security and safety of the national communications network or which enables the enemy to listen to communication or to target communication system and equipment will be sentenced to death. If the action is the result of negligence then the penalty shall not exceed seven years of imprisonment. If the above crime is committed in other than a state of emergency, then the penalty will be no longer than one year in case of negligence.

6.4 Vehicles owned by foreign companies

To further protect the property and assets of foreign companies which used to be in Iraq from being used by officials of the departments which used to employ the foreign companies, RCC Resolution No. 18 of 1998 was promulgated. The Resolution provides that any official who utilizes a vehicle that is owned by a foreign company that has left Iraq will be deemed to have stolen the vehicle. As such, he will be sentenced to at least two years of imprisonment.

6.5 Illegal export of gold

RCC Resolution No. 136 of 1998 empowers those in charge of customs and excise at the points of exit on the Iraqi border to confiscate any gold which is being taken out of Iraq without the need to charge the accused with smuggling. This exception from the provisions of Law No. 78 of 1983 Regulating the Movement of Gold is limited to the case where the gold does not exceed 50 grammes. In such instance the gold must be confiscated in accordance with the procedure laid out in the Resolution. However, when the gold exceeds 50 grammes then the person must be criminally charged.

6.6 Fines on flour mills

Due to the importance of the control and availability of flour under the circumstances in Iraq, harsh penalties are imposed on flour mills which violate government regulations. RCC Resolution No. 37 of 1999 imposes on-the-spot fines if the mill does not adhere strictly to the instructions and announcement made by the government from time to time. In the case where the mill does not adhere to the production policy in respect of the quantity and quality of production then the Ministry of Trade may order the seizure of the mill for a period of no longer than one year and lease it to third parties to ensure production of flour. In case of serious violation, then the Council of Ministers at the proposal of the Ministry may order the confiscation of the mill. Finally, the Resolution suspends the applicability of any provision of law contrary to this Resolution as well as denying the ordinary courts jurisdiction to consider any legal action in this regard.

6.7 Scales and measures

Certain provisions of the Metering of Scales, Measurements and Standards Law No. 42 of 1978 were amended by Law No. 10 of 1999. The penalties for tampering with metered equipment were increased. Prison sentence and fines in addition to confiscation of the equipment were imposed by the amendment and added to the penalties. Those involved in the forgery of seals and stamps relating to scales and measurements will receive heavier sentences when caught. Persons preventing or obstructing official inspectors from carrying out their duties will also receive a prison sentence.

6.8 Smuggling of petrol

Since the Gulf War almost all commercial road vehicles travelling across the Iraqi borders have been modified by their owners to carry more petrol. The fuel tanks were dramatically enlarged and more tanks, visible as well as hidden, were added. In some instances ordinary passenger cars were modified to carry as much as 1,000 litres of petrol or more. The reason being the difference in the petrol prices between Iraq and the neighbouring countries. Drivers used to fill up their vehicles at the last petrol station on the Iraqi border with Jordan and Turkey only to sell it at about 500 times the price on the other side. Lorries obviously carry more petrol than passenger cars and these vehicles became illegal fuel tankers and were extremely dangerous in cases of accidents. Many people were burnt to death as a result of being involved in collisions. To put an end to this, RCC Resolution No. 72 of 1999 came into effect fifteen days after its publication in the Official Gazette on 24 May 1999. The Resolution declared the modification of fuel tanks or adding further tanks of any sort not consistent with the design capacity of the vehicle a crime. This prohibition applies not only to Iraqi registered vehicles but also to foreign ones. The Resolution further prohibits the unauthorized transport of any fuel, be it the same that the vehicle uses or not. Violation of the provisions of this Resolution is deemed as a serious crime aimed at undermining the national economy for which a ten-year prison sentence may be handed down. If the violation is carried out when the country is in a state of war, then this will be an aggravating circumstance. The vehicles will be confiscated and the driver and his accessories detained and tried before special courts. The Resolution finally provides that any provision of law contrary to its provision shall not apply.

6.9 Judicial powers to Registrar of Companies

RCC Resolution No. 110 of 1998 grants the Registrar of Companies powers of a magistrate to try offences committed under Articles 213–217 of the Companies Law No. 21 of 1997. These articles provide for penalties to be imposed in cases of failure to register a company, not in possession of proper books or late in paying penalties already imposed. The RCC Resolution has a retroactive effect to the effective date of the Companies Law itself, which in fact may be unconstitutional.

6.10 Food crimes

RCC Resolution No. 146 of 1998 imposes a ten-year prison sentence on those selling meat which is unfit for human consumption. This harsh penalty has become necessary as some traders were caught mixing the meat of dogs and donkeys with beef and lamb.

7 INTERNATIONAL LAW

7.1 Iraq–UN relationship

The relationship between UN and Iraq has, over the last twelve months, received further setbacks and is now almost non-existent. In December, 1998 the UNSCOM inspection work came to halt, when the inspectors were withdrawn by the UN (subsequently revealed to be at the behest of the US). The work of UNSCOM was further discredited when some of the senior inspectors[8] testified that that they were in fact spying for the US, thereby confirming Iraq's protestation for the last four years to that effect.

---

[8] Especially Mr Scott Rieter.

In January 1999, Russia and France submitted a draft resolution for lifting the sanctions if Iraq complies with UN resolutions, which is in fact a restatement of paragraph 22 of UN Resolution 986[9] that provides sanctions contained in Resolution (661) of 1990 "shall have no further force or effect". That draft was not acceptable to the US as it refuses to even discuss the lifting of the sanctions as long as Iraq has Saddam Hussein as its president under the Liberation of Iraq Act.[10] France then suggested some "guidelines" for a draft resolution which takes into consideration some of the US concerns but has an inducement to Iraq by making a reference to the lifting of the sanctions. That was not acceptable to the US supported by the UK. Nine months later and now the permanent members of the UNSC cannot even agree on a paper to be discussed so as to be able to reach a draft resolution on Iraq's plight to be agreed by UNSC. The UK submitted a draft resolution with the support of the Netherlands, which the US does not agree with but do not object to, but the other permanent members do object to. The death of almost 6,000 children every month in Iraq solely as a result of action of the UN itself which began some nine years ago, will have to continue because the UNSC cannot agree a Resolution to stop it. History will no doubt show that 200 babies died every day while the UN considered whether to lift the blockade it imposed or not.[11]

Two Security Council resolutions were, however, adopted within two weeks in November 1998 namely 1205 and 1210 on 5 and 24 November.[12] The first condemned Iraq for refusing to cooperate with UNSCOM (after the UN's decision to withdraw the inspectors and the disclosure that they were spying for the US) and the second to grant Iraqi Muslims the right to go to Mecca for pilgrimage.

7.2 Iraqi Fund for Foreign Development

Iraqi Fund for Foreign Development ("IFFD") was established by Law No. 77 of 1974. At the time Iraq was one of the wealthy nations, therefore it established the IFFD to assist in the development of poorer nations by giving aid and extending soft loans. Some thirty-six countries in Asia and Africa benefited from the fund including some of the Arab countries. Iraq is now unable to recover the loans it extended to others under the pretext of UN sanctions. For the same reason it is even denied the benefits from its participation in numerous international and regional organizations, funds, companies and other associations.

For the purposes of grouping all of Iraq's foreign financial assets and interests in the hands of one entity the IFFD Law was amended by Law No. 2 of 1998. In accordance with the amendment IFFD is now charged with following up, liaising and coordinating Iraq's foreign financial interests, assets and rights in international and regional organizations and entities. Further, the value of all Iraq's participation in the capital of all of the pan-Arab companies is now added to and forms part of the capital of IFFD.

---

[9] See *Yearbook of Islamic and Middle Eastern Law*, vol. 1 (1994), p. 528.
[10] Iraq Liberation Act 1998 is reproduced in Part III of this *Yearbook* at p. 474.
[11] UNICEF Iraq Child and Maternity Mortality Surveys, http://www.unicef.org.
[12] Reproduced in Part III of this *Yearbook* at pp. 469 and 471.

7.3 Treaty with China

Law No. 13 of 1998 is the enabling Act to ratify the Economic, Trade and Technical Cooperation Treaty with China. The Treaty was signed in Peking between the two countries on 6 August 1997.

7.4 Treaty with Algeria

Law No. 27 of 1998 is the enabling act to ratify the Treaty on Agricultural Quarantine and Protection of Plants Against Diseases. The Treaty was signed in Algiers between the two countries on 23 July 1996.

7.5 Arab Convention

Iraq has acceded to and ratified the Arab Convention on Rehabilitation of Handicapped Persons. The Convention was concluded by the 22nd session of the Arab Labour Organization's Conference held in Amman, Jordan in April 1993. The enabling Act is Law No. 28 of 1998.

8 EDUCATION

8.1 Ministry of Education

The law establishing the Ministry of Education No. 124 of 1971 after more than a quarter of a century was replaced by Law No. 34 of 1998. The new law sets out the policy of education as being based on principles of patriotism, Arabism and Islam. The objectives of the Ministry are listed in some fourteen paragraphs ranging from the preparation of educational plans, training of teachers, building new schools, enhancing reading, numeracy and religious education, extra-curricular activities, research to cooperating with national, regional and international bodies on matters of education. The Ministry is made up of twenty divisions. Each is charged with a specific function such as programmes, infrastructure, buildings, technology, kindergartens, primary and secondary schools, vocational and part-time education, teachers, training, etc. The law provides that students have to go through six years of compulsory primary education from the age of six. Secondary school is another six years before qualification to enter universities. Education is free at all stages including university level. The Ministry of Education is charged with holding three national exams at the ages of twelve, fifteen and eighteen years based on national curriculum. Special education requirements for those with learning difficulties, handicapped and also for those with exceptional ability and extreme intelligence must be met by the Ministry. Private education is regulated through a licensing system.

8.2 Academic secondment

Members of the teaching staff of Saddam University (established by Law No. 17 of 1993), may be seconded to other universities in Iraq. They may also be seconded to universities outside the country for no more than three years. They may be given sabbatical leave for no more than one year. Their services may also be loaned for short periods not exceeding three months to other educational institutions. These limitations, procedures and other details were set out in Statutory Instructions No. 5 of 1998 (8 June 1998).

8.3 No free education

RCC Resolution No. 38 of 1998 amended Resolution No. 82 of 1997[13] by enabling medical colleges and institutes to charge fees depending on the stage and specialization. The fees are to be spent on the maintenance and development of the facilities. This has become necessary to raise public funds to meet the costs which the state is no longer able to meet due to the sanctions that Iraq is subject to.

8.4 Cooperation with academia

RCC Resolution No. 78 of 1998 provides that ministries and government departments should carry out training programmes, rehabilitation courses and seminars for their employees. These programmes are to be undertaken by lecturers drawn from academic institutions which teach the subjects that are relevant to the work of these ministries and departments. The lecturers will be paid fees by the inviting ministry or department at the rates set out in the Resolution.

RCC Resolution No. 109 of 1998, on the other hand, authorizes technical and vocational colleges and institutes to establish and run evening courses and programmes to train government employees and staff. The fees received from these courses is to distributed between the colleges and institutes on one hands and the treasury on a 60:40 per cent basis respectively.

8.5 Medals for teachers

RCC Resolution No. 119 provides that all teaching staff who have remained in service for the last eight years are awarded bravery medals. This is aimed at recognizing the suffering of teachers in the face of hardship (low salary, lack of facilities and difficult circumstances) since the impositions of sanctions on Iraq. Holders of such medals are normally entitled to certain material benefits, including some financial rewards.

---

[13] See *Yearbook of Islamic and Middle Eastern Law*, vol. 4 (1997–1998), p. 281.

8.6 Religious schools

Statutory Regulations No. 2 of 1993 establishing religious schools were amended by Regulations No. 4 of 1998. A number of articles of the regulations were amended, including the composition of school boards to include learned religious preachers. The qualifications of the school head and teachers were raised and the rules on discipline of students and staff were amended.

8.7 Children's Education House

The Ministry of Culture and Education gazetted Statutory Instructions No. 3 on 10 August 1998 to establish the Children's Education House. This is a publishing house specializing in children's books and other education learning aids. It is charged with the production and procurement of books, magazines, newspapers, videos, films, toys, etc. It is to coordinate its activities with the Ministry of Education and professional teaching bodies. The House is exempt from all taxes and duties.

8.8 National Symphony Orchestra

The Ministry of Culture and Education gazetted Statutory Instructions No. 4 on 24 August 1998 to amend the 1985 Instructions establishing the National Symphony Orchestra. The amendments are aimed at distributing part of the revenue received by the Orchestra among its members. The point system adopted takes into consideration seniority, commitment, enthusiasm, performance as well as absenteeism, late arrival for practice sessions and the like.

8.9 Names of schools

RCC Resolution No. 155 of 1999 provides that educational authorities should begin consultation with local authorities, municipalities, local Ba'ath Party branches and the governor of each of the eighteen governorates. The aim is to review names of all schools which have no patriotic, national or historical significance with the view of changing such names. Such schools should be re-named after recent national martyrs (those killed during the two Gulf wars 1979–1999).

8.10 Saddam University

The Council of Ministers gazetted Statutory Instructions No. 9 on 19 October 1998 in accordance with Saddam University Law No. 17 of 1993. The Instructions deals with the procedures to be followed in respect of the academic promotion of the teaching staff. Generally speaking, the Instructions expect each member of the teaching staff to produce at least one original research paper every year in his own field of knowledge. The committee of academics will select the papers and research work for the purpose of publication and, if relevant, register the copyright and patent any discovery. The committee may seek the help of experts from outside the country to assess the research work. Thereafter, the board of the college makes the necessary application to the university senate for consideration before promotion is granted.

8.11 Teacher training college

Due to the severe shortage of teachers in Iraq, RCC Resolution No. 169 of 1998 establishes an open university-type training college for teachers. The college is to be attached to the Ministry of Education but be under the direct supervision of the Ministry of Higher Education and Scientific Research. The Resolution empowers the board of the College to determine the subjects they teach and the other rules relating to the running of the college. To ensure the consistency of the level of education, the students of the college will have, at the end of each academic year, to sit the same exams that are held by full-time teacher training colleges at the various universities of Iraq.

8.12 Scientists and intellectuals

Statutory Instructions No. 10 were gazetted on 2 November 1998 in accordance with the provisions of Law No. 1 of 1993 in respect of scientists and intellectuals. The Instructions relate to the awards that are given annually to scientists and intellectuals who are nominated by various authorities including ministries and universities. The Instructions set out the criteria which must be met and attaches to it standard forms to be used in that respect.

8.13 Support for researchers

Statutory Instructions No. 1 were gazetted on 17 May 1999 to grant support and financial rewards for scientists, academics, researchers and others who are involved in intellectual work. The Instructions set out the amount to be paid to those who produce original work. The awards range from ID1,500 to ID30,000 depending on the type of research, its value and originality. There is a further support which relates to the volume of the work in terms of the number of pages and the type of the work which ranges from ID25 to ID100 per page. The Instructions provide that the copyright of the work will be that of the university for the first five years reverting thereafter to the author himself. The Instructions also detail the processes and procedures to be followed in selecting the work including establishing academic and scientific committees.

9 HEALTH

9.1 Registration of medicine

The Ministry of Health issued Statutory Instruments No. 13 (3714) under which pharmaceutical companies are obliged to register medicine before it is allowed to be sold in Iraq. The instructions imposed a nominal fee of ID 300 for each brand name registered.

9.2 Heart surgery

Arabs and foreigners have since 1990 been banned from having heart surgery in the official heart centres in Baghdad except where the patient has been referred by the official panel of specialists. However, according to Presidential Instructions (3720) they may now have operations if they are referred by their own doctors. This is to avoid having to be referred to the panel of specialists before undergoing surgery. In such instance, they will have to pay the cost in hard currency.

9.3 Training and development centre

RCC Resolution No. 56 of 1998 established an independent training and development centre with independent juridical personality. It is charged with improving the medical knowledge among the medical staff in Iraq. This has become necessary due to the embargo on medical knowledge imposed by the US and UK, which formally prohibits the supply of even medical journals and books to Iraq. The internal regulations of the centre were ratified by the Ministry of Health on 30 November 1998.

9.4 Medicine

A series of RCC Resolutions were gazetted to regulate certain aspects of the manufacturing and supply of medicine to deal with the acute need of Iraq. These include RCC Resolution No. 59 of 1998 empowering the private pharmaceutical industry to buy Arab and foreign know how, after obtaining the necessary licence from the Ministry of Health.

RCC Resolution No. 60 of 1998 empowered the Union of Pharmacists to grant licences for the establishment of offices for the promotion of medicaments, in accordance with the provisions of the Pharmaceutical Law No. 40 of 1970. It authorizes such offices, along with privately owned pharmacies and hospitals, to import medicine and medical needs through licences issued by the State Company for Imports and Exports after the approval of the Ministry of Health.

Instructions No. 4 of 1998 were gazetted on 11 January1999 and detailed the conditions for establishing the medical promotion offices. The licence granted to these offices must be in the name of a registered and practising Iraqi pharmacist. The specifications of the office are detailed, as well as the books and records to be kept.

The office functions are limited to the provision of samples and literature as well as representing no more than five foreign manufacturers. The employees must be qualified Iraqi nationals who do not have a conflict of interest if they were working on part time basis. There are rules on inspection, penalties and appeal procedures.

RCC Resolution No. 61 of 1998 provides that medicine that is imported by the State Company for Import and Export may be made available to privately owned pharmacies at commercial prices which are determined by a special committee to be established by the Ministry of Health. Half of the difference between the commercial price and that which is paid by state owned hospitals and pharmacies is to be allocated for maintenance of hospitals. The remaining half is to be distributed as incentive to the staff of the health sector. Fund holding hospitals, popular medical poly-clinics and social security hospitals will continue to receive medicine at prices subsidized by the state.

Pharmaceutical Law No. 40 of 1970 was amended by Law No. 14 of 1998. The amending law removed the restriction on the size of pharmacies, their locations and some of the strict conditions on opening outlets. Each pharmacy must have at least one pharmacist present whenever it is open. The law also lifts the ban on pharmacists who own their own pharmacy from owning pharmaceutical production facilities at the same time.

Instructions No. 5 of 1998 were gazetted on 11 January 1999 and detail the specifications that must be met by any property before it is licensed as a pharmacy. These include minimum conditions in respect of area, content, display, partitioning, hygiene and general cleanliness. There are rules on inspection, penalties and appeal procedure.

Statutory Announcement No. 49 of 1998 (3754) by the Pharmacist Union contained a list of non-prescription medicaments which pharmacies are authorized to sell over the counter. The new list is to replace that which was published in the Official Gazette No. (3415) dated 20 July 1992.

The Ministry of Health published Statutory Instructions No. 4 (26 April 1999) detailing the procedures, licences and conditions to be met and followed before the establishment of pharmaceutical factories. The instructions list the information that must be submitted for approval prior to licensing, which includes the site, location, plan, design, method, products, process, storage and quality control, the owners, and management qualifications and lay down operating rules, inspection, penalty and appeal procedures.

Announcement No. 60 by the Ministry of Health on 7 September 1998 sets out the procedures for the importation of medicine into Iraq. The importer must be a practising pharmacist, who has given the necessary undertakings to obtain an import licence. He must be resident and actually practising in Iraq (as evidenced by his national identity card, domicility certificate and his food ration identity card). The Announcement set out an appeal procedure, determining the licence period, specifying the source of funding, and permission of the Foreign Exchange Department of the Central Bank of Iraq. No medicine will be released from the customs warehousing until samples are tested, a certificate of suitability and quality is issued by the Ministry and a report to that effect is produced. Iraq is extremely concerned about the medicine it is receiving because it has limited control over what the UN allows into the country. There has been instances where the medicine supplied was in fact not safe to use for a variety of reasons.

9.5 Research in medicine

More pharmacists are to be recruited as full-time researchers in Iraqi Universities. Law No. 2 of 1999 amended the provisions of the Pharmacists Law No. 15 of 1982 providing that up to 2.5 per cent of the top graduates of each year may be recruited by their universities to be employed as researchers. This is an attempt by Iraq to reduce its dependence on the international pharmaceutical companies which is seen as using the supply of medicine to apply political pressure on behalf of their home governments.

9.6 Mentally disturbed persons

The increase in the number of people suffering from depression, psychological problems and mental illness in Iraq is estimated to have increased by 800 per cent since the 1991 war. The health institutions and hospitals are no longer capable of dealing with the patients. Social rehabilitation and care in the family and in the community is seen as the only way to reducing the numbers of in-patients. RCC Resolution No. 70 of 1998 charges the Ministry of Health with the responsibility of establishing social rehabilitation centres. They are to be financed from the amounts made available by the Baghdad Municipality, contributions and donations and proceeds from the sale of goods produced by the rehabilitation workshops and farms. Statutory Instruction No. 3 was published on 19 April 1999 to facilitate the implementation of the Resolution to assist the families and society to help themselves.

9.7 Saddam Cancer and Genetic Research Centre

There is an eight-fold increase in cancer cases and dramatic rise in genetic malformation. These are thought to be the result of the use of depleted uranium by the US and UK forces during the 1991 war. Law No. 11 of 1998 therefore established the Cancer and Genetic Research Centre which is to be attached to the Ministry of Scientific Research and Higher Education. The centre has independent juridical personality and is managed by a board of directors composed of specialists in the field. It is financed from the central state budget as well as from the revenue it is able to generate from the service it renders. The law sets out the scope, objectives and services that the centre is to work to achieve.

9.8 Disability

In accordance with the provisions with the Public Health Law No. 89 of 1981, the Minister of Health published in the Official Gazette No. 3748 Statutory Instructions No. 2. These are detailed instructions defining disabilities and the degrees of disability. The determination is normally made by medical committees based on the details contained in the instructions. More than eighty-five categories of ailments causing disability are listed. Many thereafter are divided into stages of illness or parts of the body afflicted. In each instance, a range for disability is set out for the medical committee to determine.

9.9 Skin treatment centres

In accordance with the Public Health Law No. 89 of 1981, the Minister of Health published on 10 May 1999 Instructions No. 5 dealing with private skin treatment centres. The instructions provide that such centres are only permitted to work under the direct supervision of a physician who must be a qualified dermatologist. The centres are subject to licensing system and are obliged to keep records and be subject to inspection.

9.10 Ambulance service

The Minister of Health published on 24 May 1999 Announcement No. 39. Accordingly an ambulance service may be provided against the payment of fees in certain instances. These include cases where the use of ambulance is at the request of patient or his family (not the hospital). The cost of transport is according to a scale which depends on the distance travelled and if the patient is having state medical care or private care. Emergencies and necessary transport by ambulance, however, continue to be free.

Iran

M. A. Ansari-Pour*

During 1997 and 1998 a number of very important pieces of legislation were passed by Parliament, together with a number of interesting judgments. In 1997, the seventh presidential election was held and one of the programmes of the present government is to campaign more than before for the rule of law. Such a policy includes the adoption of new laws and regulations as wells as the improvement of the legal system. In addition, the Eighth Islamic Summit Conference was held in Tehran in 1997. Several important issues were considered at the Summit and these issues have been reflected in the "Islamic Summit Conference: Tehran Declaration".[1]

This survey highlights the most important legal developments which occurred in Iran during 1997, 1998 and early 1999.[2]

1 CONSTITUTIONAL LAW

1.1 Interpretation of laws

Under Article 73 of the Constitution the interpretation of ordinary laws, i.e. parliamentary statutes, is vested with Parliament. Such an interpretation is to be considered law as well, thus any interpretation of the law must be ratified by the Council of Guardians (hereinafter cited as the CG).[3] A question had been put forward to the CG by the then President as to whether or not the interpretation of law would have retrospective effect. In his question, the President, *inter alia*, stated that under Article 73 of the Constitution, ordinary laws are interpreted in cases of ambiguity and vagueness. In most cases there is a long interval between the adoption of the law

---

[*] Chairman of the Iranian Law Institute. Former Iranian judge. I would like to thank Mr M. Kitabi of the Sanat Yadak Company in Tehran for providing some of the material for this survey.
[1] See the text of the Declaration in *International Legal Materials* (37), 1998, pp. 938–941.
[2] I.e. From 10.10.1375 to 15.11.1377 according to the Iranian calendar.
[3] CG, decision of 24.5.1362, No. 9404, in *Majmuʻi-yi Nazariyyat-i Shura-yi Nigahban*, vol. 1, Tehran, 1369 (1991), p. 410.

itself and its interpretation. Before the interpretation and during the enforcement of the law, some rights may be established for people and these rights may be transferred to others or they may be inherited. He then added that when a law is interpreted the following questions arise: to what extent can the interpretation have retrospective effect and to what extent can it negate the rights established by the law itself and which group of rights can be overridden by the interpretation?

A number of examples were mentioned for this issue and in the end the President asked the CG, on the basis of Articles 73 and 94 of the Constitution, to give its opinion on the question: "is it possible to deny the rights and conditions which have been established for people in accordance with laws . . . by the interpretation of the laws?" Four examples were then given of cases where an interpretation might affect the pre-interpretation rights established by the relevant law. They consisted of (a) when the interpretation extends the application of the law in such a way that it creates some obligations for the pre-interpretation period; (b) when the interpretation restricts or rejects the employment rights which have been established in the past; (c) when the interpretation affects past contracts and transactions and other decisions which have created some rights for non-government employees; and (d) when the interpretation extends directly or indirectly the application of criminal law provisions to an action or omission committed in the past.[4]

In response to the above question, the CG stated that:

1. the purpose of interpretation is to state the intention of the legislature. Therefore restricting or extending the application of a law, in cases where it is not made in order to remove the ambiguity of the law, is not regarded as interpretation. 2. The interpretation, from the date of stating the intention of the legislature, is binding in all cases. Therefore, the interpretation does not apply to cases which relate to the past and the executives, while having different understanding from the law, had enforced it.

In short, the interpretation of the law does not have retrospective effect.[5]

1.2 The administration of ministries

Under Article 114 of the Constitution, the period of each presidency is four years. When the period of presidential office comes to an end, the first thing which the President-elect must do is to introduce his Cabinet Ministers to Parliament for a vote of confidence. This process, as has happened, may take a few weeks. The question was who should run the government departments during this time. The following five specific questions were presented to the CG:

(a)   Can the ministers, from the date of termination of the presidential office until the introduction of new ministers and a vote of confidence by Parliament, remain in their position as before?

---

[4]   *Ruznami-yi Rasmi*, 8.4.1376, No. 15239; *Majmu'ah Qawanin*, 1376, pp. 241–242. *Ruznami-yi Rasmi* (hereinafter cited as RR) means "Official Gazette". It is published by the Organization of the Official Gazette which is part of the judiciary. *Majmu'ah Qawanin* (hereinafter referred to as MQ) means the "collection of laws", which is published annually by the same organization.
[5]   RR, *ibid.*; MQ, *ibid.*, p. 243.

(b)   If existing ministers are competent to run their relevant departments during the above period, can the Council of Ministers meet and decide under the supervision of the new President?

(c)   Can the President's deputies who, under Article 126 of the Constitution, are appointed to administer the plan and budget affairs and administrative and employment affairs after the termination of the presidential office, continue their work or must they be re-appointed?

(d)   Are the decisions of the special representatives of the President, who are appointed according to Article 127 of the Constitution,[7] enforceable during the said period?

(e)   Is the convening of the commissions consisting of Cabinet ministers, the subject matter of Article 138 of the Constitution,[8] permissible during the afore-mentioned period? Are their decisions, following the approval of the new President, binding?

The CG replied to the above questions one by one:

(a)   The ministers remain in their position as before from the date of the termination of the presidential office until the vote of confidence by Parliament to the new Cabinet ministers.

(b)   The existing ministers, during that period, keep their position and the Cabinet can convene and decide under the supervision of the new President.

(c)   The President's deputies can continue their work, but with respect to the administration of the plan and budget affairs and the administrative and employment affairs, the continuation of their office depends on the agreement of the new President.

(d)   Decisions of the special representatives of the President, who have been appointed according to Article 127 of the Constitution, are not enforceable during the afore-mentioned period.

(e)   With regard to the last question, the decision of the above commissions, with the approval of the new President, are binding.[9]

---

[6] Art. 126 of the Constitution provides: "The President is directly responsible for the plan and budget affairs and administrative and employment affairs and he can entrust somebody else with the management of these". It should be noted that there are two government departments for the administration of the above affairs. They consist of the Plan and Budget Organisation and the Administrative and Employment Affairs Organization respectively.

[7] Art. 127 of the Constitution states: "The President can, in special circumstances, where necessary, with the approval of the Council of Ministers, appoint one or more special representatives with specific powers. In such cases, the decisions of the representative(s) will be considered as those of the President and the Council of Ministers."

[8] Art. 138 of the Constitution, *inter alia*, provides: "The government can delegate the approval of some matters relating to its tasks to the commissions consisting of several ministers. The decisions of these commissions within the limit of law and after the ratification of the President are to be enforced."

[9] RR, 3.6.1376, No. 15287; MQ, 1376, pp. 440–441.

2 LEGAL PROFESSION

2.1 The periodic transfer of judges

Article 164 of the Constitution, *inter alia*, provides that:

a judge's place of service or post cannot be changed without his consent, unless the interest of society determines otherwise, in accordance with the decision of the Head of the Judiciary after consultation with the Chief Justice of the Supreme Court and the Prosecutor General. The periodic transfer and rotation of judges will be in accordance with general rules to be established by law.

Parliament adopted the Periodic Transfer of Judges Act 1997 in order to implement this constitutional principle (Art. 1).[10] Under Article 2 of the Act, every judge who is appointed after the adoption of this Act, must work in each justice administration classified as class 3, 2 or 1 for five years. However, observing the order in working at the above classes respectively is not necessary. The transfer of any judge to Tehran is dependent on fifteen years of work in each of the above three classes of justice administration and also on the existence of a bench (i.e. a judicial post) in Tehran. However, those judges who have worked longer in classes 3 and 2 have priority over other judges. The provisions of this Act are also applicable to the existing judges who have worked less than fifteen years.

Under Article 3 of the Act, the classification of the departments of justice administration will be determined, on the basis of privation, bad weather conditions and remoteness from the capital, by a regulation to be prepared by the Minister of Justice and is to be ratified by the Council of Ministers.

Following this Act, the Council of Ministers classified the departments of the judiciary around the country into three classes, starting from the lowest class, as class 3, class 2 and class 1.[11]

2.2 Attorneyship licence

The first comprehensive law since the revolution regarding attorneyship-at-law, i.e. joining the bar association, was adopted by Parliament in 1997.[12] The Act, which can be translated as the Manner of Taking the Attorneyship Licence Act, consists of seven articles. Some of the cardinal provisions of this Act are briefly examined here. Under Article 1, every bar association in the country must hold an examination for those who have applied for the attorneyship licence at least once a year. Within a maximum of six months from the date of examination, when notifying the exam results, the licence of "attorneyship trainee" for those who have passed the bar examination must be issued. The number of attorneys required for each bar association will be determined by a commission consisting of the head of the provin-

---

[10] RR, 14.1.1376, No. 15170; MQ, 1375, pp. 1158–1160.
[11] RR. 8.4.1376, No. 15239; MQ, 1376, pp. 258–275.
[12] RR. 4.2.1376, No. 15188; MQ, 1376, pp. 25–29.

cial administration of justice, the Chief Justice of the Islamic Revolution Court and the president of the relevant bar association.

Article 2 deals with the educational and general qualifications of the applicants. With respect to the educational qualifications, the Act states that applicants must hold an LLB or higher degree in law, or hold a BA in Islamic law or its equivalent from the Islamic seminaries.[13]

According to *tabsirah* 5 (translated as "note")[14] of Article 2 the "attorneyship licence" is valid for three years. The validity of the licence can be extended at the request of the applicant. If an attorney misses one of the qualifications mentioned in Article 2 and becomes disqualified, the bar association concerned must notify the issue and the reasons concerned to the disciplinary court of attorneys and ask for an examination. The court, after examining the case, decides on the extension or non-extension of the licence. The licence of the attorney concerned, until the final judgment of the court, is valid unless the court decides that it is necessary to suspend his membership.

Article 4 deals with the membership of the board of directors of each bar association. Members of the boards are elected for a period of two years and the candidates must, in addition to having the general qualifications stated in Article 2, have a number of other qualifications for nomination.

Article 6 provides that attorneys-at-law cannot establish an office outside the place for which they have received their licence. In addition, they cannot practise their attorneyship activities outside the said place. A number of disciplinary punishments have been stated for those who violate this provision. A few exceptions to this rule have been made in note 1 of Article 6. The boundaries of each bar association will be determined following the proposal of the Minister of Justice and the approval of the Head of the Judiciary.

2.3 The competence of judges

In 1997, Parliament adopted an Act which can be translated as "the Examination of Judges' Competence Act". This Act deals with the competence of existing judges.[15] The examination of judges' competence which, according to Islamic and legal principles, has been called into question by the authorities stipulated in this Act, rests with the Supreme Disciplinary Tribunal of Judges, which consists of three judges who are all appointed by the Head of the Judiciary.

Under Article 2, the competence of a judge may be called into question by a number of authorities including the Head of the Judiciary, the Chief Justice of the Supreme Court (hereinafter cited as the SC), the Prosecutor General, the presid-

---

[13] It should be noted that lawyers who join the bar can plead and argue a case in lower courts as well as in the Supreme Court. The division of lawyers into solicitor, barrister and QC does not exist under the Iranian legal system.

[14] *Tabsirah* is an Arabic term which is frequently used by the Iranian legislature. According to the *Hans Wehr* dictionary, it literally means "enlightenment, instruction and information". Under Iranian law it means a "note" (which is added to an article) or a "sub-article".

[15] RR, 24.3.1376, No. 15227; MQ, 1376, pp. 187–189.

ing judge of each branch of the Supreme Disciplinary Court of Judges and the head of the National Inspection Organization.

Under Article 3, when the competence of a judge is called into question by one of the authorities mentioned in Article 2, the issue is first dealt with by a commission consisting of the judicial deputy of the Head of the Judiciary, the legal deputy of the Minister of Justice, the judicial deputy of the Chief Justice of the SC, the judicial deputy of the Prosecutor General and the disciplinary prosecutor of the judges. The commission considers the case and will report the result, within three months at the maximum, to the Tribunal. Under Article 4, if the majority of the judges decide that the judge concerned is not competent, then he will be sentenced to one of the several penalties stipulated in this article. In accordance with Article 5, the judgment of the Tribunal is final. If the act for which the judges' competence is called into question is a crime, then he will also be prosecuted by the competent court in this regard (Art. 6). If the Supreme Disciplinary Tribunal of Judges or the Supreme Disciplinary Court of Judges,[16] when considering the competence of a judge, finds out that judgments given by him are in conflict with Islamic precepts, then these judgments will be sent to the appeal courts for reconsideration (Art. 7)

2.4 Appointment of judges

In early 1998, the Head of the Judiciary passed an executive regulation on the basis of several Acts of Parliament regarding the appointment of judges and their training before commencing work.[17] It should be noted that before being appointed as judges, the qualified applicants are appointed as "judicial trainees". After completing a period of training they are appointed as judges. Article 1 states that through annual examination, held by the judiciary, the "judiciary trainees" are selected from among those applicants who hold an LLB or a higher degree in law, or hold a BA or a higher degree in Islamic law and from those who have studied in the Islamic seminaries according to law. Under Article 2, the number of the judges required is notified annually, by the judicial deputy of the Head of the Judiciary, in cooperation with the Ministry of Justice to the education department of the judiciary. Article 3 deals with the procedure for the selection of the judicial trainees and their general qualifications. Articles 4 and 5 concern the subjects of examination and the minimum grade allowed for passing the examination.

Articles 6 to 27 generally relate to the procedure of selection and method of training, subjects taught during training, examination, etc. One important provision among them is Article 9, which states that training is by teaching and practice. The minimum and the maximum periods for training are one and two years respectively. According to Article 28, judicial trainees at the end of their training and before being

---

[16] If a judge commits an offence then the Supreme Disciplinary Court of Judges is the competent authority to deal with it. If on the other hand he does not commit an offence but loses his competence to work as a judge (e.g. when he lacks one of the qualities that a judge must have) or he is unable to work properly, then the Supreme Disciplinary Tribunal of Judges is the competent court to examine the case. For details see *Mushruh-i Mudhakarat-i Majlis-i Shura-yi Islami*, Fifth Period, Session 74, 5.12.1375, published in RR, 23.12.1375, No. 15159.

[17] RR, 22.10.1376, No. 15406; MQ, 1376, pp. 1025–1031.

appointed as judges must, in the presence of the Head of the Judiciary or his representative, swear the oath as stated in this article.

3 LEGAL SYSTEM

3.1 Family courts

After the adoption of the Establishment of General and Revolution Courts Act 1994 (hereinafter cited as the EGRCA),[18] which provided that cases relating to marriage and divorce would be dealt with by those general courts which had been authorized by the Head of the Judiciary,[19] the above cases were considered by a number of general courts.

One of the developments concerning the Iranian legal system is the establishment of a new family court. In 1997, Parliament adopted a single article Act by which a number of present courts were empowered to work as "family courts"; the subject matter of Article 21 of the Constitution. Article 21 first provides that "the government must ensure the rights of women in all respects, in conformity with Islamic criteria, and accomplish the following goals". In paragraph 3 it is then stated: "the establishment of a competent court to protect and preserve the family".

The new Act provides that within three months, the Head of the Judiciary has to allocate at least one branch of the general courts in the jurisdiction of each city to deal with family disputes. The number of branches required to deal with family disputes must be in proportion to the population of each city jurisdiction. After the establishment of the family court, the general courts cannot adjudicate these disputes.

The jurisdiction of the family court includes disputes relating to the following issues:

(a) permanent and fixed-term marriage;
(b) divorce and cancellation or annulment of marriage (*faskh*)[20] and waiving the remaining period or termination of the term of marriage (in fixed-term marriage);
(c) dower;
(d) dowry;
(e) reasonable compensation (*ujrat al-mithl*) and gift (*niḥlah*) for the work done during the marriage by the wife;
(f) unpaid maintenance and present maintenance of the wife and those close relatives for whom maintenance must be paid;
(g) custody of children and their visits;
(h) lineage;

---

[18] For details, see M. A. Ansari-Pour, "Iran", in *Yearbook of Middle Eastern and Islamic Law*, vol. 1 (1994), pp. 392–395.
[19] See Art. 3 (note 3) of the EGRCA.
[20] Under Art. 1120 of the Civil Code, a marriage can be dissolved, *inter alia*, by cancellation. This happens where, for example, either of the spouses are insane or they suffer from some specified diseases or where a special quality has been stipulated for either of the spouses, such as having higher education, and after the marriage it becomes clear that the spouse concerned lacks the stipulated or implied quality, then the other spouse can annul the marriage. See for details Arts. 1121–1126 and 1128 of the Civil Code.

(i)   recalcitrance (*nushuz*)[21] and obedience or compliance (*tamkin*) by the wife;
(j)   appointment of guardian and supervisor, attachment of a trustee (*damm amin*)[22] and their dismissal;
(k)   prudence;
(l)   remarriage; and
(m)   conditions incorporated into the marriage contract.

This Act also includes three notes. Note 1 provides that the judges of the family court must be married and must have a working experience of at least four years. Note 2 states that in the districts' jurisdictions the general court will replace the family court. Note 3 provides that each family court starts adjudication, where possible, in the presence of women counsellors. The judgments will be given following consultation with the women counsellors.[23]

3.2 Basis of overruling

Article 18 of the EGRCA[24] provides three bases for the overruling of judgments of the general and revolution courts. It states that a judgment can be quashed in the three following cases:

(a)   where the judge, who has given the judgment, realizes his own mistake;
(b)   where another judge discovers the mistake in such a way that if he reports it to the judge, who has given the judgment, the latter will accept the mistake; and
(c)   where it is proven that the judge had no competence to consider the case and to give judgment.

With respect to the interpretation of the second case, two conflicting judgments had been given by two branches of the Appeal Court (branch 6 and 20). The question was whether or not when another judge discovers the mistake of the judge who has issued the judgment, it is necessary to inform the latter of his mistake, and whether or not when he was informed, he must confirm his mistake. The case, under Article 3 of the Articles Added to the Criminal Procedure Code in 1337 (1958),[25] was referred to the Plenary Assembly of the Supreme Court (hereinafter cited as the PASC).[26] The PASC (by an overwhelming majority), *inter alia*, held that:

---

[21] Art. 1108 of the Civil Code, without referring to the term *nushuz*, indirectly defines this term and states that " if the wife without any legitimate excuse refuses to fulfil her conjugal obligations she will not be entitled to maintenance". In other words, *nushuz* means failure on the part of the wife to fulfil conjugal duties.
[22] Under Art. 1184 of the Civil Code, for example, if the natural guardian cannot mange the property of the ward properly or he misappropriates the property of the ward, a trustee is attached or added to the guardian by the court for the management of the property.
[23] RR, 3.6.1376, No. 15287; MQ, 1376, pp. 443–444.
[24] For the text of the EGRCA, see RR, 3.5.1373, No. 14383; MQ, 1373, pp. 309–317.
[25] In 1337 (1958), six articles were added to the Criminal Procedure Code 1290 (1911). RR, 17.6.1337, No. 3951; MQ, 1337, p. 512.
[26] RR, 29.1.1377, No. 15476; MQ, 1376, pp. 1232–1235.

The provisions of Article 18 of the EGRCA adopted in 1373 are a guarantee to secure the accuracy of courts' judgments and to ensure that the judgments are devoid of mistakes. What is gathered from paragraph 2 of Article 18 of the above Act . . . is that the mistake in the judgment given should be so obvious that if it is reported to the judge who has given the judgment he will realize that mistake. But the necessity of informing the judge and his confirmation [of the mistake] cannot be established from the above paragraph. When another judge who, from the point of view of rank and law, is in a position to supervise the correct implementation of laws, finds out that the judgment is incorrect, and he reports this in writing and in a substantiated way [to the Appeal Court], it binds the Appeal Court to implement the provisions of the note of Article 18.

According to the note of Article 18, the Appeal Court must quash the judgment and reconsider the case.

3.3 Official translators

The first Act relating to the translation of statements and documents in the courts and in the offices of notary publics was adopted in 1316 (1937). This Act consisted of three articles.[27] Article 1 of the Act relates to the translation of statements and, *inter alia*, provides that when one of the parties to a dispute, or witnesses and experts in courts and government departments, and the contracting parties or witnesses in the offices of notary publics do not know the Persian language, their statements will be translated by an official translator. Article 2 deals with the translation of documents and provides that the translation of the following documents must be approved by the official translators or by Iranian diplomats and the officials working in Iranian consulates abroad:

(a) documents which have been drawn up in a foreign country or have been drawn up in Iran but in a foreign language and these documents are to be used in courts or government departments; and
(b) documents which have been drafted in Iran and its translation is needed in a foreign country.

Article 3 of the above Act was amended and six new articles were added in 1998.[28] Article 3 includes the qualifications of those people who apply for the licence of official translation. Article 4 deals with the period of the validity of the licence and its renewal. Articles 5 to 7 relate to offences committed by official translators and their disciplinary punishments. Under Article 8, the establishment of an office or institution and the translation of documents and statements without regard to the provisions of this Act is illegal and the wrongdoer is to be sentenced to the punishment of a swindler.

---

[27] See the text of the Act in *Majmu'i-yi Saliyanih*, 1316, pp. 43–44.
[28] RR, 3.6.1376, No. 15287; MQ, 1376, pp. 445–447.

4 CIVIL LAW

4.1 Family law

4.1.1 Medical examination before marriage

In 1997, and following the proposal of the Foundation of Special Diseases Affairs (*Bunyad-i Umur-i Bimarihayi Khass*), the Council of Ministers made a resolution (*taswibnamah*) by which the medical examination of the potential spouses, for determining whether or not they carry the *thalassemia* disease, was made compulsory before marriage. The notaries have also been instructed to demand from any couple the relevant certificate and then to proceed with the conclusion of the marriage and its registration.[29]

4.1.2 Presumed death

Article 1023 of the Civil Code of Iran (hereinafter cited as the CC) provides that with respect to the cases mentioned in Articles 1020–1022 of the CC regarding missing persons, the court can only issue a judgment of presumed death of a missing person when a notice has been published in one of the local newspapers and in one of the widely circulated newspapers of the capital for three consecutive times at monthly intervals, inviting those people who may have news of the missing person to convey their information to the court. If one year passes from the date of the first notice and the life of the missing person is not proved, then the judgment of presumed death of the missing person will be given. The same procedure has almost been articulated in Article 155 of the *Umur-i Hisbi* Act.[30]

Parliament, by legislation, made an exception to the above general rule in 1376 (1997). It provides that, with respect to those people who have been missing in the course of the Islamic revolution and the sacred defence (the Iran–Iraq war), the announcement in the newspapers according to Article 1023 of the CC and Article 155 of the *Umur-i Hisbi* Act is not necessary and the certificate issued by the highest executive authority in the Shahid Foundation[31] is sufficient for the court to give judgment of presumed death.[32]

---

[29] RR, 9.2.1376, No. 15191; MQ, 1376, p. 44

[30] *Umur-i Hisbi*, under Art. 1 of the *Umur-i Hisbi* Act 1940, consists of cases where the courts have to take action and decide without being dependent on the existence of a dispute between people and taking legal action by them. They include, *inter alia*, the appointment of a guardian for minors and other interdicted people, the appointment of trustee for the administration of inheritances, the appointment of a trustee for the administration of the property of a missing person, etc. See also A.K.S. Lambton, "Hisba: iii.- Persia", *The Encyclopaedia of Islam*, vol. 3, new edn., 1971, pp. 490–491.

[31] A charity foundation which provides cover for the families of those martyred for the cause of the Islamic revolution.

[32] RR, 30.2.1376, No. 15208; MQ, 1376, p. 74.

4.1.3 Guardianship

In 1997, Parliament adopted a single article Act with respect to the guardianship of children, who are covered by the government department which looks after the disabled, orphans, those who are destitute and the like, known as *Saziman-i Bihzisti*, which can be translated as "Welfare Organization" (hereinafter cited as "the Organization") before the appointment of a guardian by court. It provides that when the Organization begins to cover for and protect an interdicted person (minors, lunatics and prodigals) for whom a guardian must be appointed, it must report the case to the relevant court for the appointment of a guardian. Before the appointment of a guardian, where necessary, the head of local administration of justice can temporarily appoint the president of the Organization or the head of the local branch of the Organization as the legal representative of the interdicted person. This guardian enjoys all powers and responsibilities which a guardian has under law, and who can delegate this authority to another person as his representative. The determination of necessity rests with the Organization.[33]

4.1.4 Indexation of dower

Dower (*mahr*)[34] is one particular aspect of Islamic and Iranian law that is fixed for the wife in the marriage contract. Generally speaking, dower can be anything which has market value and can be owned and it must be certain.[35] Article 1082 of the CC provides that by the conclusion of the marriage contract, the wife becomes the owner of the dower and can make any disposition that she wishes. It also implies that the wife can ask the husband to pay the dower. A time limit can be fixed for the payment of the dower and it can even be paid by instalments (Art. 1083).

Women do not usually ask their husband to pay the dower. However, in some minor cases and especially in divorce proceedings, the question of dower becomes one of the central issues between the spouses. In the majority of cases until now, the dower has been determined in Iranian currency. Money, because of inflation, loses it purchasing power. The question is whether the obligation of the husband is to pay the specified amount of the dower at its face value or to pay the purchasing power of the dower when the marriage was concluded.

This question was debated in Parliament in 1375 (1996).[36] Following this debate, a very important piece of legislation was adopted in 1997. The legislation was the addition of one note to Article 1082 of the CC. It provides:

---

[33] RR, 27.5.1376, No. 15281; MQ, 1376, pp. 426–427.
[34] For an introduction to the concept of *mahr* under Islamic law, see J. J. Nasir, *The Islamic Law of Personal Status*, 2nd edn., London, 1990, pp. 86 *et seq.*; J. Nasir, *The Status of Women under Islamic Law and under Modern Legislation*, pp. 46–62; M. Siddiqui, "*Mahr*: legal obligation or rightful demand", *Journal of Islamic Studies* (6), 1995, pp. 14–24; O. Spies, "Mahr", in *The Encyclopaedia of Islam*, vol. 6 new edn., 1991, pp. 78–80; D. Pearl and W. Menskie, *Muslim Family Law*, 3rd edn., London, 1998, pp. 178–181.
[35] See generally Arts. 1078–1080 of the CC.
[36] *Mashruh-i Mudhakarat-i Majlis-i Shura-yi Islami*, Fifth Period, Session 49, 20.9.1375, published in the RR, 17.10.1375, No. 15105; *Mashruh-i Mudhakarat-i Majlis-i Shura-yi Islami*, Fifth Period, Session 50, 21.9.1375, published in the RR, 19.10.1375, No. 15106.

If the dower is the currency it will be calculated *in proportion to* the annual change of the price index at the time of payment, as compared with the year when the marriage was concluded, which will be determined by the Central Bank of the Islamic Republic of Iran, and will be paid [to the wife], unless the spouses have agreed otherwise at the time of the conclusion of marriage.

In other words, the rate of inflation based on the change of the price index can be demanded by the wife from her husband. It covers the depreciation of money as a result of changed circumstances and where there exists a normal rate of inflation.

It was stated that the executive regulation of this Act had to be prepared by the Central Bank in cooperation with the Ministry of Justice and the Ministry of Economic and Financial Affairs and had to be ratified by the Council of Ministers within three months, at the maximum, from the date of the adoption of the Act.[37]

The executive regulation of the above Act was ratified by the Council of Ministers on 13.2.1377 (1998). The regulation consists of seven articles.[38] Article 1 almost repeats the provisions of the Act. Article 2 deals with the method of calculating the dower. It states that the average price index of the previous year is divided into the average price of index of the year when the marriage was concluded and the result will be multiplied by the amount of dower. Article 3 states that where the dower must be paid from the property of the dead husband, the date of death is the date of the calculation of the dower. Under Article 4, the Central Bank has been instructed, first, to prepare the price indexes of the years before the implementation of this Act and present it to the judiciary and second, to prepare the price index of each year until the end of the third month of the year (*Khordad*), at the maximum, and to present it to the judiciary. According to Article 5, all courts and offices of the Department for the Registration of Documents and Properties must calculate the amount of the currency–dower in accordance with Article 2, and in determining the change of price index of the dower, they must act according to the indexes stated in Article 4 of this regulation. Article 7 provides that if the husband asks the court for a divorce, the court must fix the dower according to this regulation and other relevant laws and criteria.

4.1.5 Custody of children

Article 1173 of the CC was amended by Parliament in 1977. The former text of this article provided that if, as a result of lack of care or moral degradation of the parent who has custody of the child, the physical health or moral upbringing of the child is endangered, the court could, following the demand of the child's relatives or his guardian or the Public Prosecutor, make any decision appropriate for the custody of the child.

Since the *parquet* system was abolished in 1994,[39] the new text of Article 1173 replaces the Public Prosecutor by the head of the local administration of justice, Sec-

---

[37] RR, 3.6.1376, No. 15287; MQ, 1376, p. 442.
[38] RR, 24.2.1377, No. 15497; MQ, 1377, pp. 3–4.
[39] The *parquet* system was abolished by the EGRCA. See for details, Ansari-Pour, "Iran", pp. 392–395.

ondly, it provides five examples of lack of care or moral decline of each of the parents, including:

(a) addition to alcohol, drugs or gambling;
(b) being renowned as having immoral behaviour and obscenity;
(c) suffering from psychiatric disorders;
(d) abusing the child or compelling him/her to enter into immoral professions such as obscene acts, begging or drug-trafficking; or
(e) beating and injuring the child repeatedly beyond what is reasonable.[40]

4.1.6 *Certificate of impossibility of reconciliation*

One of the procedures before the execution of divorce, under the Iranian legal system, is to obtain a certificate from the court which can be translated as the "certificate of impossibility of reconciliation"[41] or "certificate of irreconcilability". This procedure was introduced into Iranian law for the first time by the Family Protection Act 1967.[42] Although the necessity of the issuance of the certificate before the execution of divorce had not been abolished,[43] it was reiterated again in the Amendment of Divorce Provisions Act in 1992 (hereinafter cited as the ADPA).[44] The ADPA had fixed no time limit for the validity of this certificate; however, under Article 19 of the Family Protection Act 1967 and Article 21 of the Family Protection Act 1975,[45] the certificate was valid for three months.

In 1997, Parliament by legislation, limited the validity of this certificate as before to three months from the date of issuance until its presentation to the divorce registry. It should be added that when the certificate is presented to the divorce registry within the time limit, the notary (who is in charge of the divorce registry) must inform the spouses to attend for the execution of divorce and its registration. If one of the spouses does not attend at the specified time, they are invited for the second time within one month, after which the following procedure occurs. First, if the wife refuses to attend for the execution of the divorce, the divorce is executed by the husband and after the registration of the divorce, the wife is notified by the registry. Secondly, if the husband refuse to attend and to execute the divorce, the divorce registry confirms this refusal and notifies it to the court which has issued the certificate. At the request of the wife, the court summons the husband. If the husband does not attend, then the court, while complying with Islamic criteria, executes the divorce and orders the divorce registry to register it and notify the spouses. Thirdly, if the husband attends the divorce registry, but refuses to execute the divorce, then the procedure adopted in the second case is to be followed.[46]

[40] RR, 9.9.1376, No. 15370; MQ, 1376, p. 683.
[41] This is the translation which has been adopted by D. Hinchcliffe. See D. Hinchcliffe, "The Iranian Family Protection Act", 17 (1968), ICLQ, pp. 516–521.
[42] For the Persian and English text of this Act, see *Islamic Studies* 6 (1967), pp. 250–255 and 256–261 respectively.
[43] Plenary Assembly of the Supreme Court, Judgment 21-30.7.1363, in MQ, 1363, pp. 380–384.
[44] For the text of this Act, see RR 19.9.1371, No. 13914; MQ, 1371, pp. 490–492.
[45] For the text of the 1975 Act, see RR 12.12.1353, No. 8785; MQ, 1353, pp. 302–310.
[46] RR, 26.9.1376, No. 15384; MQ, 1376, pp. 698–699.

4.2 Exempted properties

Article 65 of the Execution of Civil Judgments Act 1356 (1977)[47] lists a number of properties which cannot be attached in order to recover the judgment debt. In other words, they are regarded as exempted properties. However, nothing is mentioned about the debtor's place of residence in that whether or not it is among the exempted properties. This lacuna provided an opportunity for the creditor to ask the court for the sale of the debtor's residence in order to recover the judgment debt from its price. In 1997, the Head of the Judiciary asked the CG to give its opinion with respect to the provisions of Article 65 of the above Act in that whether or not it is consistent with Islamic law.

The CG replied that Article 65 of the Act only deals with movable or personal property. It does not apply to the place of residence. Nevertheless, a needed and suitable residence, under Islamic law, is among the exempt properties.[48] In other words, no creditor can ask for the attachment of the debtor's residence and recover the judgment debt from its price if that residence is commensurate with the needs of the debtor and his family.

4.3 Endowment

The CG had been asked in 1987 to give its opinion on the question of whether or not clay, gravel and sand in the endowed properties are part of the properties concerned or if they are regarded as *anfal*[49] and come under public ownership. In that case, the CG stated that these things are part of the land and therefore they are part of the endowed properties.[50] The same question was put forward to the CG again in 1997 with respect to industrial soil, i.e. clay, since the Ministry of Mines had interpreted the above decision not to be applicable to industrial soil. The CG, by referring to its earlier decision, stated that industrial soil is like ordinary clay and therefore it is to be considered part of the endowed properties.[51]

---

[47] For the text of this Act, see RR 26.9.1356, No. 9610.
[48] RR, 31.3.1376, No. 15233; MQ, 1376, pp. 227–229.
[49] *Anfal* literally means booty or spoils and addition or increase. Under Shi'ite law, *anfal* consists of properties, such as uncultivated and abandoned lands, minerals and the like, which belong to the Prophet, in the first place, due to his divine leadership, and after him they belong to the Shi'ite Imams because of their leadership and *Imamate*. However now, as Article 45 of the Constitution states, *anfal* are regarded as public wealth and property and they shall be at the disposal of the Islamic government for it to use in accordance with the public interest. For details regarding the literal and legal notion of *anfal*, see S. Abu-Habib, *Al-Qamus al-Fiqhi*, Damascus, 1982, p. 358; R. M. Khomeini, *Tahrir al-Wasilah*, vol. 1, 3rd edn., Beirut, 1981, pp. 368–369; M. H. Najafi, *Jawahir al-Kalam*, vol. 16, 7th edn., Beirut, 1981, pp. 115–134; *Mu'jam Fiqh al-Jawahir*, vol. 1, Beirut, 1996, pp. 507–512.
[50] Council of Guardians, decision of 28.3.1366, No. 8444. See the decision in RR, 31.3.1376, No. 15233; MQ, 1376, pp. 223–224.
[51] RR, 31.3.1376, No. 15233; MQ, 1376, pp. 222–223.

4.4 Nationality Law

In 1997, Parliament passed legislation by which every Iranian national, whether legal or natural, must have a national number and postal code. The Act consists of six Articles. The main provisions have been enshrined in Articles 1–4. Under Article 1, the Ministry of the Interior and the Ministry of Post, Telegraph and Telephone have been instructed to allocate these.[52]

All persons whether legal or natural, ministries, organizations, companies and government institutions or those affiliated with government, universities, banks, municipalities, Islamic revolution institutions, armed forces and all other companies and institutions must use and employ these numbers, which consist of ten digits and will be allocated by the Department for the Registration of Personal Status (in the form of an identity card) in cooperation with the Post Company[53] for the recognition of individuals and their addresses: workplace or residence (Art. 2).

Under Article 3, the above card is to be regarded as the document for recognizing Iranian nationals and it is subject to all relevant civil and criminal laws and it must always be carried by the person to whom it belongs.

According to Article 4, the issuance of any administrative or professional identity card or driving licence and the like after the implementation of this Act, without inserting the national number and postal code, is illegal.

4.5 Mortgage

In a mortgage contract, the ownership of the mortgaged property remains intact for the mortgagor. However, a right is created for the mortgagee in that he is given preference over other creditors to recover his claim from the price of the mortgaged property if it has not been stipulated in the mortgage contract that the mortgagee can recover his claim from the mortgaged property itself or from its price in case of the mortgagors' default.[54] Under Article 793 of the CC the mortgagor cannot bring about changes in the mortgaged property except with the latter's consent. With respect to the extent of the right of the mortgagor over the mortgaged property two conflicting judgments had been given by two branches of the SC. The case was finally decided by the PASC as follows.

In one case, the mortgagor whose property (several shops) had been mortgaged to a bank, transferred the key money of one shop by a lease agreement to a third party without seeking the permission of the bank. The creditor, i.e. the bank, asked the court to rule on the annulment of the transfer, arguing that it was in conflict with the rights of the creditor. The court invalidated the transfer.

After appeal against the judgment, branch 21 of the SC held that, under Article 7 of the mortgage agreement, after the conclusion of the mortgage, the mortgaged property had been returned by the creditor to the mortgagor in order to benefit from its usufructs. Therefore, the object of the mortgage had been the property itself, not

---

[52] RR, 24.3.1376, No. 15227; MQ, 1376, pp. 189–190.
[53] Part of the Ministry of Post, Telegraph and Telephone.
[54] See Arts. 777 and 780 of the CC.

its usufructs. The court went on to say that the mortgagor did not transfer the property to the third party but the usufructs of the property, which he had owned. Therefore the disposition of the usufructs was not in conflict with the provisions of Article 793 of the CC. Consequently, the judgment of the trial court was objectionable.[55]

In the second case, the mortgagor transferred the key money of part of the mortgaged property (one of several shops) to a third party through a lease agreement. The mortgagee, which was a bank, sued the mortgagor, arguing that when the mortgage contract was made, the property had not been leased, but after the conclusion of the mortgage the mortgagor, without regard to the content of the mortgage document, had leased it to the third party. The creditor then, on the basis of Article 793 of the CC, asked the court to annul the lease agreement and to dispossess the mortgaged property. The court, on the basis that the transfer of the key money without the consent of the mortgagee had no justification and, by referring to Article 793 of the CC, ruled on the annulment of the agreement and the dispossession of the mortgaged property.

The debtor then made an appeal against the judgment and the case was referred to branch 14 of the SC. This court dismissed the appeal and ratified the judgment of the trial court.

As is clear, the transfer of the key money of the mortgaged property by a lease agreement to a third party by the mortgagor without the consent of the mortgagee was regarded as valid by branch 21 of the SC while being regarded as invalid by branch 14. The dispute, as a result, was considered by the PASC, who by a majority, *inter alia*, held:

> In accordance with the Articles of the CC, although the mortgage contract does not cause the transfer of ownership from the mortgagor but it creates a priority right over the mortgaged property for the mortgagee by which he can recover his claim from the price of the mortgaged property. If the transactions of the mortgagor with respect to the mortgaged property are in conflict with the right of the mortgagee they will not be effective regardless of whether the transaction actually or potentially is in conflict with the right of the mortgagee. Therefore, where . . . the mortgagee gives the mortgaged property to the possession of the mortgagor, the mortgagor's action in selling and transferring the key money of the mortgaged shop to a third party without the permission of the mortgagee is a disposition which is in conflict with the right of the mortgagee and is not effective.

4.6 The Landlord and Tenant's Relations Act

An important piece of legislation was passed by Parliament in 1997 which can be translated as the Landlord and Tenant's Relations Act (or as the Lessor and Lessee's Relations Act).[56] The Act consists of 13 articles. Before the adoption of this Act, two pieces of legislation were applicable to tenancy agreements. The first one was the

---

[55] Plenary Assembly of the Supreme Court, Judgment 620-20.8.1376, in RR, 22.10.1376, No. 15406; MQ, 1376, pp. 860–862.
[56] RR, 17.6.1376, No. 15299; MQ, 1376, pp. 498–500.

1356 Act (1977)[57] and the second was the 1362 Act (1983).[58] Generally speaking, the first Act was applicable to commercial premises and the second one to residential places.

The most important difference between the first two Acts and this one is that the tenancy agreements, except for a few cases, with respect to commercial premises and residential places were governed by the 1356 Act and the 1362 Act respectively. However, the new Act governs all tenancy agreements, without exception, together with the provisions of the CC and the stipulations agreed upon by the parties. In other words, the private aspect of the tenancy agreement has been strengthened in the new Act, contrary to the previous Acts in which the public aspect was strong.

The new Act consists of two chapters. The first (Arts. 1–5) covers the landlord and tenant's legal relations. The second (Arts. 6–10) deals with the issue of key money or premium. Since the examination of all the above laws is beyond the scope of this survey, only the prominent provisions of the new Act are highlighted here.

4.6.1 Landlord and tenant's relations

Article 1 states that from the date of the implementation of this Act, the lease of all places including residential, commercial and educational places, whether concluded by a formal agreement (i.e. by deed) or by an informal agreement will be governed by the provisions of the CC, the provisions of this Act and the conditions agreed upon by the contracting parties.

Article 2 states that the informal tenancy agreements must stipulate the period of tenancy and they must be written in two copies and signed by the contracting parties. The agreement must also be certified by two trustworthy people as witnesses.

After the expiry of the tenancy, following the demand of the landlord or his legal representative, the eviction of the tenant from the property in tenancy agreements with the formal documents (i.e. deed) will be carried out within one week by the Department of Execution.[59] With respect to the tenancy agreements with an informal document, the eviction will be carried out by a court order within one week after taking legal action (Art. 3).

If the landlord has received an amount of money as a deposit, or a guarantee or loan, or has taken a legally binding document or the like from the tenant, vacating the property and giving its possession to the landlord depends on the restitution of the amount or the document to the tenant or depositing them with the Department of Execution. If the landlord claims that his property has been damaged by the tenant or the tenant has not paid the rent or the tenant owes him on account of telephone, water, electricity and gas bills and demands compensation for the damage, or demands the recovery of the above debts from the amounts mentioned above

---

[57] RR, 1.6.1356, No. 9518.
[58] RR, 5.3.1362, No. 11140; MQ, 1362, pp. 12–16.
[59] The Department of Execution is part of the Department for the Registration of Documents and Properties and deals with the execution of deeds and binding documents. The procedure employed by this office to recover the creditor's claim from the debtor is simpler and quicker than taking legal action before a court.

(i.e. the deposit, guarantee or loan) he must, when depositing the money or the document with the Department of Execution, submit a certificate from the office of the competent court, in that he has taken legal action asking for compensation and damages to the extent of the claim, to the Department of Execution. In this case, the Department, to the extent of the landlord's claim, deducts from the amount or the document and returns the rest to the tenant. After legal proceedings if the court rules in favour of the landlord and the amount kept by the Department of Execution is more than the landlord's claim, the excess will be paid to the tenant.

If the tenant, with respect to the content of the contract presented by the landlord, claims any right against the latter while complying with the order of eviction, he can take legal action before the competent court (Art. 5)

4.6.2 *Key Money*

Article 6 provides that when an owner leases his commercial premises he can receive from the tenant an amount as key money or premium. Also, if the tenant transfers his right of possession during the tenancy, he can receive an amount from the owner or the next tenant as key money, unless it has been stipulated in the contract that the tenant cannot transfer the object of the tenancy to another person.

Article 6 also has two "notes". The first states that if the owner has not received any key money and the tenant in return for the key money has transferred the property to another person, after the expiry of the tenancy, the second tenant cannot ask the owner to pay the key money. The second note states that if the landlord transfers the key money to the tenant, according to a valid procedure under Islamic law, when vacating or being evicted, the tenant can ask for a fair price of the key money at that date.

When it is stipulated in the agreement that, as long as the object of the tenancy is used by the tenant, the owner has no right to increase the rent or to evict the tenant; and/or he undertakes to lease the object of the tenancy to the tenant every year for the same amount of rent, in this case the tenant can, for waiving his rights, ask an amount as key money from the landlord or from the next tenant (Art. 7).

When it is stipulated in the agreement that the owner must not lease the object of the tenancy agreement to anyone other than the tenant, and every year he must lease it to the tenant for a reasonable amount of rent, the tenant can, for waiving his right or for vacating the property, ask for an amount as key money (Art. 8).

Under Article 9, if the period of tenancy expires or the tenant has paid no key money to the landlord and/or the tenant has enjoyed all the rights stipulated in the contract, when vacating the property he has no right to ask for the key money.

Article 10 provides that in cases where, according to this Act, the taking of key money is permissible, if the parties do not reach an agreement concerning the amount of the key money it will be fixed by court. It is added that the taking of any amount in tenancy relations, not permitted by the above provisions, is illegal.

Article 11 provides that the places which have been rented before the adoption of this Act will not be governed by this Act and they will be subject to the relevant laws. Article 12 states that the executive regulation of this Act will be prepared by the Ministries of Justice and Housing and will be approved by the Council of Ministers. Article 13 categorically abrogates all laws and regulations which are inconsistent with this Act.

5 COMMERCIAL LAW

5.1 The law of cheques

Two articles of the Issue of Cheques Act 1976 (as amended in 1993)[60] were amended in 1998. First, a note was added to Article 2.[61] It provides that the holder of the cheque can ask the court, whether before the delivery of judgment or after, to adjudge the drawer to pay all damages and expenses borne directly and indirectly and usually for recovering his claim. If the holder asks for the damages and expenses mentioned above after the judgment is given, he must lodge his petition before the court that issued the judgment.

The second article was Article 14.[62] Note 1 of this article was rephrased, however the content has not changed. It formerly stated "in the case where the beneficiary orders for the non-payment". It now provides "in the case where the non-payment is ordered according to this article". Second, another note was added to Article 14. It now has three notes. Under note 3, the payment of certified and travellers' cheques cannot be suspended unless the issuing bank claims that they have been forged. In this case, the right of the holder regarding taking legal action in the judiciary will remain intact.

5.2 Commercial arbitration

On 26.6.1376 (1997), Parliament passed legislation with respect to commercial arbitration, which is the first comprehensive law in this area. The Act, which can be translated as "the International Commercial Arbitration Act", consists of thirty-six articles divided into nine chapters.[63]

Chapter 1 includes the general provisions (Arts. 1–6). In Article 1, arbitration, international arbitration, arbitration agreements, arbitrator and court are defined. The domain, i.e. the cases to which this Act applies, the method and the authority for notifications, the commencement of the arbitration proceedings, giving up the right of protest and the authority for supervision are considered in this chapter.

Chapter 2 deals with the arbitration agreement (Arts. 7–9). The form of arbitration agreement, taking legal action before court with respect to the subject matter of the agreement and the issue of interlocutory injunction and judgment by court, before or during arbitration proceedings, have been enshrined in this chapter.

---

[60] The Act consists of 23 Articles. For the text of the Act, see RR, 19.5.1355, No. 9120.
[61] RR, 16.4.1376, No. 15246; MQ, 1376, pp. 289–290.
[62] RR, 25.11.1376, No. 15432; MQ, 1376, pp. 1118–1119.
[63] RR, 28.7.1376, No. 15335; MQ, 1376, pp. 593–604.

Chapter 3 concerns the formation of the arbitration board or tribunal (Arts. 10–15). The number of arbitrators, appointment of arbitrators, cases where an arbitrator's position can be challenged, formalities of the challenge, failure or impossibility to function as an arbitrator and the appointment of succeeding arbitrator are dealt with in this chapter.

Chapter 4 relates to the competence of the arbitrator (Arts. 16 and 17). Making a decision by the arbitrator about his/her own competence to proceed with the arbitration and the validity of the arbitration agreement as well as the cases where an arbitrator can exercise his power to issue a provisional award are the main focal points of this chapter.

Chapter 5 concerns the method of arbitration proceedings (Arts. 18–26) and includes equal treatment of the parties, the place and language of arbitration, petitioning and defence, hearing and proceedings, failure to petition or to provide defence or failure of the parties to attend the hearing, referring the case to experts and the cases where a third party can enter into the arbitration proceedings.

Chapter 6 deals with the end of arbitration proceedings and the arbitration award (Arts. 27–32). Issues such as the applicable law, conciliation, the decision-making process of the arbitration board, the form and the content of the award, end of proceedings, amendment and the interpretation of the award, as well as complementary awards are included in this chapter.

Chapter 7 deals with the protest to the arbitration award and its annulment (Arts. 33 and 34) and Chapter 8 relates to the execution of the award (Art. 35).

Finally, Chapter 9 incorporates the miscellaneous provisions (Art. 36). Article 36 is divided into three paragraphs. Paragraph 1 states that the arbitration of an international commercial dispute has been excluded from being governed by the arbitration rules of the Civil Procedure Code and other laws. Paragraph 2 provides that this Act has no effect with respect to the laws according to which certain disputes cannot be referred to arbitration. Paragraph 3 stipulates that if in the international conventions, to which Iran is a party, different arrangements and conditions have been provided for commercial arbitrations, the provisions of those conventions are to be followed.

5.3 Interest on bonds

The Council of Ministers, by referring to Article 12 of the Issue of Treasury Bonds and Debenture Bonds Act 1348 (1970),[64] had made a resolution regarding the issue of treasury bonds and debenture bonds. The resolution provided that the Ministry of Economic Affairs and Finance can, in order to repay the principal sum and the prizes of the debenture bonds issued, issue new bonds with the observance of relevant regulations and previous arrangements.

---

[64] For the text of this Act, see RR, 23.7.1348, No. 7193.

The CG stated that since the resolution referred to Article 12 of the above Act[65] and its implementation is dependent on the observance of the relevant regulations and arrangements mentioned in that Act, and that Act allows the charge of interest on debenture bonds, it is inconsistent with Islamic law. The CG further stated that Articles 6, 7, 8, 12, 20–24, 27 and 28, which legalize the charge and payment of interest on debenture bonds, are inconsistent with Islamic law and, under Article 4 of the Constitution, they are to be abrogated.[66]

5.4 Late payment damages

One of the issues which the CG has been repeatedly asked about is the legality or illegality of "damages for non-payment of debt" or "interest on debt". The CG had, on many occasions since the revolution, stated that the charge of such damages, as a rule, is illegal. Nevertheless, the CG was asked again in 1977 about the legality of these damages provided in Article 12 of the Issue of Cheque Act 1976 (as amended in 1993). The Council referred to a number of its earlier decisions and stated that these apply to the dishonoured cheque as well.[67]

It should be noted, however, that the damages for non-payment of debt can be stipulated into the contract as "liquidated damages" or as a "penalty clause". In such a case, the above damages can be recovered from the debtor if he does not pay the debt on time. This issue had been approved earlier by the CG[68] and it was also allowed by a parliamentary legislation in 1997.[69]

6 CRIMINAL LAW

In 1997–1998, several developments occurred with respect to criminal law. The most important event was that the implementation of the Islamic Punishment Code (hereinafter referred to as the IPC) was extended for ten years and a number of its provisions were affected by these developments. For example, Article 252 was announced by the CG to be inconsistent with Islamic law. One note was added to Article 19, Articles 38 and 729[70] were amended and a new article (62-1) was added.

---

[65] Art. 12, *inter alia*, provides that: "the amount and the date of issue, rate of interest and the type of each series of debenture bonds are considered by a council . . . and will be proposed to the Minister of Finance".

[66] RR, 24.2.1377, No. 15497; MQ, 1377, pp. 8–9.

[67] RR, 31.3.1376, No. 15233; MQ, 1376, pp. 224–227.

[68] For example, see Council of Guardians, decision of 11.12.1361, No. 7742, in MQ, 1362, p. 419.

[69] RR, 11.4.1376, No. 15242; MQ, 1376, pp. 236–237.

[70] The former text of Art. 729 provided that all laws inconsistent with this Act are to be abrogated. Art. 729 now provides that all laws inconsistent with this Act, including the Public Penal Code of 1304 (1925) are to be abrogated. In other words, the former text of Art. 729 did not refer specifically to the abrogation of the 1304 Code.

6.1 Extension of the IPC

The IPC was adopted by the Judicial and Legal Affairs Committee of Parliament, under Article 85 of the Constitution,[71] in 1991 for five years on a probationary basis.[72] The implementation of the IPC was extended by Parliament in 1997 for a further ten years.[73] It should be noted that the extension only applies to Articles 1–497 of the IPC, but not to Articles 498–729 since the latter articles were adopted by Parliament itself.

6.2 Abrogation of Article 252

Articles 231–256 of the IPC deal with the ways and evidence by which a murder can be proved. One of them is "oath".[74] Article 252 of the IPC, which relates to oath, provides that "If the number of defendants is more than one person the plaintiff must, for proving his claim, swear fifty oaths with respect to each defendant. If the plaintiff does not swear, then each of the defendants must swear fifty oaths."

In 1997, the CG announced that Article 252 was inconsistent with Islamic law.[75] In fact, the problem related to the first sentence of this Article. Under Islamic law, if there is more than one plaintiff, swearing fifty oaths for all of them will be sufficient even if there are several defendants.[76]

6.3 Restraining the offender

Article 19 of the IPC, *inter alia*, provides that a court can prevent an offender from living in a certain place or places or order him to live in a certain locality. A new provision as a note was added to Article 19 in 1998. It provides that where an offender is sentenced to live in a certain place, such a place is to be determined by the Ministry of Justice and the State Security Council[77] and then it is notified to the judiciary.[78]

---

[71] Art. 85 of the Constitution, *inter alia*, provides: "The Assembly [Parliament] cannot delegate the power of legislation to an individual or to a group of people. But, where necessary, it can delegate the power of legislating certain laws to its own committees, in accordance with Article 72. In such a case, the laws will be implemented on an experimental basis for a period specified by the Assembly, and their final approval will rest with the Assembly [as a whole]."

[72] RR. 11.10.1370, No. 13640; MQ, 1370, pp. 593–656.

[73] RR, 3.2.1376, No. 15187; MQ, 1375, pp. 1272–1273.

[74] J. Pedersen [Y.L. De Bellefonds], "Kasam", in *The Encyclopaedia of Islam*, vol. 4, 1978, pp. 687–690, especially pp. 689–690.

[75] RR, 3.2.1376, No. 15187; MQ 1375, pp. 1273–1275.

[76] For example, see R. M. Khomeini, *Tahir al-Wasilah*, vol. 2, 3rd edn., Beirut, 1981, p. 530.

[77] It is part of the Supreme Council for National Security. See Art. 176 of the Constitution.

[78] RR, 28.3.1377, No. 15525; MQ, 1377, p. 119.

6.4 Conditional release of prisoners (parole)

Articles 38–40 of the IPC relate to the release of prisoners on parole. Article 38 was amended in 1998. Apart from some changes in the wording,[79] the amendment relates to the main paragraph of the above article.

Previously, it had been provided that anybody who, because of the commission of a crime, was sentenced for the first time to imprisonment, under certain conditions[80] could be released from prison after serving two-thirds of his sentence in respect of the crimes whose punishment is more than three years' imprisonment, or after serving half of the sentence with respect to the crimes, the punishment of which is up to three years' imprisonment.

The main paragraph of Article 38 now generally provides that a person who, because of the commission of a crime is sentenced for the first time to imprisonment, after serving half of the sentence, under the same conditions, can be released on parole.[81] Under the new provision, serving half of the sentence is sufficient for the release of a prisoner on parole if the conditions stated in the above article are met. It does not matter whether the punishment of the crime committed is more than three years' imprisonment or less.

6.5 Deprivation of civil rights

Articles 49–62 of the IPC deal with the "limits of criminal responsibility". A new article has been added to the provisions of this part as Article 62-1,[82] which provides for the deprivation of certain offenders of civil rights. Under this article, the criminal conviction of an offender in deliberately committed crimes, mentioned below, deprives the convict of civil rights. After the expiry of certain periods specified in this article, following the execution of the sentence, the effects of the conviction are negated and the convict can exercise those rights again.

Convicts who are deprived of civil rights include:

(a) convicts who have been condemned to amputation as a result of committing crimes to which the *hadd* [83] applies (such as theft and robbery under certain conditions), five years after the execution of the sentence;

---

[79] Since the *parquet* system had been abolished and the responsibilities of the judges of this office had been transferred to the judges of court the relevant provisions in this article were amended accordingly.

[80] Three conditions have been stated in Art. 38(1), 38(2) and 38(3) for the release of a prisoner on parole: (a) if he has consistently behaved well during his imprisonment; (b) If it can be expected, from the circumstances concerned, that the convict would not commit any crime after his release; (c) if he, as much as he can, pays the damages which have been awarded by court or agreed by the private claimant, or he promises to pay. In cases where punishment includes imprisonment as well as a fine, he pays the fine, or with agreement of the head of local administration of justice, he makes an arrangement for its payment.

[81] RR, 28.3.1377, No. 15525; MQ, 1377, p. 119.

[82] *Ibid.*, p. 120.

[83] Under Art. 12 of the IPC, *hadd* consists of a punishment the type, quantity and particulars of which have been fixed in Islamic law. *Hadd* has been defined in *The Encyclopaedia of Islam* as "the technical term for the punishments of certain acts which have been forbidden or sanctioned by

(b)   convicts who have been sentenced to flogging because of committing crimes to which *hadd* applies (such as fornication), one year after the execution of the sentence; and

(c)   convicts who have been sentenced to more than three years (*ta'ziri*) imprisonment, two years following the execution of the sentence.

The above article has five notes. The first defines the civil rights. They consist of the rights which the legislature has provided for Iranian nationals or those who live within the Iranian territory and the negation of those rights is possible only by law or by the judgment of a competent court.

These rights include:

(a)   the right of being elected as a member of Parliament and the Assembly of Experts, membership of the Council of Guardians and being elected as the President;

(b)   membership of all associations, councils and assemblies whose members are elected according to law;

(c)   membership of juries and boards of trustees;

(d)   entry into teaching professions and journalism;

(e)   employment in the ministries, government departments, companies and institutions affiliated with the government, municipalities, institutions which provide public services, the administrative section of Parliament and the Council of Guardians and in the revolutionary institutions;

(f)   membership of the bar and working as notary public;

(g)   being selected as an arbitrator or as an expert in government departments; and

(h)   the use of governmental medals and honorary titles.

Note 2 provides that if the execution of the death penalty is cancelled, no matter on what ground, in this case its subordinate consequences come to an end, after the expiry of seven years from the date when the execution was cancelled.

Note 3 states that with regard to crimes which are forgivable, if after the pronouncement of the final judgment the execution of punishment is stopped because of the private claimant's pardon, the effects of the criminal conviction will be removed.

Note 4 provides that the pardon of the criminal does not obliterate the consequences or effects of the punishment unless it has been stipulated.

Note 5, *inter alia*, states that in cases where a prisoner is released on parole, the effects of conviction are negated after the expiry of the specified period from the date of release.

6.6 Compensation for breaking a bone

Under Article 367 of the IPC for injuring an organ of the body for which no *diyah* (specified amount of compensation) has been fixed,[84] the criminal must pay com-

---

cont.

punishments in the Qur'an". See B. C. De Vaux [J. Schacht], "Hadd", in *The Encyclopaedia of Islam*, vol. 3, new edn., 1971, pp. 20–21.

[84] *Diya* means "a specified amount of money or goods due in cases of homicide or other injuries to physical health unjustly committed upon the person of another". See E. Tyan, "Diya", in *The Encyclopaedia of Islam*, vol. 2, new edn., 1965, p. 340.

pensation (*arsh*).[85] Article 442 of the IPC state that the *diyah* for breaking the bone of an organ, for which a *diyah* has been fixed, is one-fifth of the *diyah* for that organ, and if it is cured perfectly then its *diyah* is four-fifths of the *diyah* for its breaking. The *diyah* for crushing the bone of an organ is one-third of the *diyah* of that organ and if it is cured soundly then its *diyah* is four-fifths of the *diyah* for it crushing. Under Article 477 of the IPC, if a criminal act causes the loss of or defect and deformity in some bodily functions, such as sleeping and sense of touch, or causes illness for which no *diyah* has been fixed, then the culprit must pay compensation.

With respect to the award of compensation for breaking a bone as a result of careless driving, two conflicting judgments had been given by two different branches of the Appeal Court. In the first case, the trial court, in addition to the payment of *diyah*, had ordered for the payment of compensation as well. After appealing against the judgment, the case was referred to branch 1 of the Appeal Court, which ratified the judgment of the trial court. In the second case, the trial court had again ruled for the payment of *diyah* as well as compensation. After the appeal, the judgment with respect to the payment of compensation was quashed by branch 12 of the Appeal Court. The case was sent to the PASC,[86] who held, *inter alia*, that:

Under Article 367 of the Islamic Penal Code adopted in 1370, compensation is awarded only in cases where in law no *diyah* has been fixed for the injuries inflicted on the organs of the body. In Article 442 of the above Act for the breaking of a bone whether it is cured perfectly or it is left defective and deformed, *diyah* has been fixed [and] . . . the same amount [i.e. *diyah*] must be paid. Awarding an additional amount over the *diyah* is inconsistent with the above Article.

6.7 Punishment for the drawing of a dishonoured cheque

Article 47 of the IPC provides that in cases where the culprit has committed several crimes, if the crimes committed are different, then a separate punishment must be given for each of them. However, if they are not different, then only one punishment will be fixed. In the latter case, the numerousness of the crimes can be one of the causes to intensify the punishment. If all the crimes committed can be classified under a specific crime in law, then the culprit will be sentenced to the punishment fixed in law.

In the Issue of Cheques Act, the drawing of a dishonoured cheque and post-dated cheque have been forbidden. For each of these offences from six months to two years imprisonment have been fixed. However the pecuniary punishment, i.e. fine for each of them is different.[87] The question was whether for the commission of both offences one punishment should be given or the offender should be sentenced to two punishments. Two trial courts had given separate punishments which were quashed by two branches of the Appeal Court. A third trial had also fixed two pun-

---

[85] *Arsh* has several meanings. In this context it is the compensation for an injury for which no *diyah* has been fixed. See Abu-Habib, *Al-Qamus al-Fiqhi*, p. 19; *Mu'jam Fiqh al-Jawahir*, pp. 308–310.

[86] RR, 22.10.1376, No. 15406; MQ, 1376, pp. 1019–1021.

[87] For the punishment of a dishonoured cheque, see Arts. 7 and 10, and for the punishment of a post-dated cheque see Art. 13 of the Issue of Cheques Act.

ishments for the same crimes, but when the case was reconsidered by one branch of the Appeal Court, it ratified the judgment and held that since the drawing of a dishonoured cheque and post-dated cheque were two different crimes, under Article 47 of the IPC two separate punishments had to be given.

Since there was a conflict between the judgments of two branches of the Appeal Court in the first scenario and one branch in the other, the case was referred to the PASC[88] which held, *inter alia*, that:

If the dishonoured, post-dated . . . cheque the subject matter of Articles 3, 7, 10 and 13 of the Issue of Cheques Act 1355, as amended in 1372, has been drawn by a single person, they are not regarded as separate crimes which, following the waiver of the private claimant or the payment of the amount of the cheque, the legal proceeding against the defendant is ended. Therefore the punishment for the accused . . . must be fixed according to part 2 [second sentence] of Article 47 of the Islamic Penal Code. Consequently, fixing separate punishments for each of the above crimes is in conflict with the intention of the legislature.

6.8 Financial convictions

In 1998, Parliament passed legislation[89] which literally means the "Method of Execution of Financial Convictions Act".[90] It consists of seven articles. The main provisions of the Act have been enshrined in Articles 1–4.

Article 1 states that if anybody who has been sentenced by court, in a criminal case, to pay a fine and does not pay it and no property (other than the exempted properties) can be obtained from him, he will be detained by the order of the judge, in lieu of an amount of 5,000 *tumans* or less for one day. If the financial conviction is passed together with a jail sentence, the detention which substitutes the fine will begin from the date of the termination of imprisonment and it will not exceed the maximum period of the imprisonment provided for that crime by law. In any case, the maximum period of imprisonment in place of a fine must not exceed five years.

There is a note for Article 1 which, *inter alia*, states that the amount of 5,000 *tumans* will be adjusted every three years following the proposal of the Minister of Justice and the approval of the Head of the Judiciary.

Article 2 of the Act states that if a person who is adjudged to transfer a property to another person, whether it is the restitution of a tangible property or the payment of its price or the transfer of its equivalent or he is ordered to pay the damages resulting from a crime or to pay *diyah* and he does not transfer or does not pay it, the court will order him to transfer or to pay it. If he has any property available, the court will attach it and will recover the judgment debt from that property. If he has no property available, the court, at the request of the creditor, will detain him until the time of payment, provided that he is not insolvent.

---

[88] RR, 26.8.1375, No. 15064; MQ, 1375, pp. 645–648.
[89] RR, 16.9.1377, No. 15666; MQ, 1377, pp. 469–471.
[90] By this Act, two previous Acts, i.e. the Method of Execution of Financial Convictions Act 1351 (1972) and the Prohibition of Detaining Individuals for Non-Fulfilling Financial Obligations Act 1352 (1973) were repealed. For these two Acts, see RR, 5.5.1351, No. 8013 and RR, 14.9.1352, No. 8415 respectively.

There is also a note for Article 2 which generally provides that if the subject matter of this article is merely a debt (i.e. the payment of a debt) the court, in its judgment, will take into account the properties exempted from attachment for the recovery of the debt. In other words, these properties are not attached by the court to recover the debt. With respect to the restitution of a tangible property the above provisions apply only if the property is not existing.

Under Article 3, when the judgment debtor claims that he is insolvent (during detention), his claim will be considered with priority. If his insolvency is proved, he will be released from detention. If he is able to pay the debt by instalments, the court will order the debt to be paid in this way in proportion to his financial situation.

This article also has a note which declares that if the judgment debtor is ill in a way that his detention aggravates his illness or delays his treatment, the detention will be deferred until the treatment of the illness.

Article 4 states that if anybody with the intention of avoiding the payment of a debt or avoiding the fulfilment of financial obligations, the subject matter of binding documents and all financial convictions, transfers his property to another person in a way that the rest of his assets are not sufficient for the payment of his debt, the transfer will be regarded as a crime and the transferor will be sentenced for a minimum of four months or a maximum of two years' imprisonment. If the transferee also knowingly accepts the transfer, he will be considered to be an accomplice. In this case, if the property is in the possession of the transferee, the property itself, or its price or its equivalent will be recovered from the transferee's properties in order to pay the debt.

7 ADMINISTRATIVE LAW

In 1983, Parliament passed legislation by which female employees in the ministries, public institutions, government corporations and the like can apply for part-time work (i.e. half of the usual working period) if the highest authority in the department concerned gives his consent.[91]

Parliament added one note to the Act in 1997. Under the new provision, a female employee can, following the agreement of the highest authority in the relevant government department, apply for three-quarters of the normal time of work.[92]

8 MEDIA LAW

Article 6 of the Press Act 1364 (1986)[93] deals with the exceptions to the general rule of the freedom of the press. Article 6 included nine paragraphs and one note. Two new provisions were added to the above article in 1998.[94] The first provision was adopted as paragraph 5 of Article 6 and the following paragraphs were renumbered accord-

---

[91] RR, 11.10.1362, No. 11316; MQ, 1362, p. 433.
[92] RR, 25.2.1376, No. 15205; MQ, 1376, p. 71.
[93] RR, 24.1.1365, No. 11976; MQ, 1364, pp. 665–674.
[94] RR, 15.6.1377, No. 15590; MQ, 1377, p. 257–258.

ingly. Article 6(5) now prohibits the press from using individuals (male or female) as tools in pictures and in content, from degrading and offending females, and from propagating unlawful ceremonies and luxuries.

The second new provisions is now the second note of Article 6. It provides that those who violate the provisions of Article 6 are subject to the punishments provided for in Article 698 of the IPC,[95] and in case of a repeated violation their punishment may be intensified and their licence may be invalidated.

9 SOCIAL SECURITY LAW

In 1997, Parliament added a note to Article 76 of the Social Security Act 1354 (1975).[96] This article deals with the conditions for the use of a retirement pension. The first condition under this article is the payment of an insurance premium for at least ten years before applying for retirement. The second condition, with respect to women, is to be 55 years old. Under the new provisions, female workers who have worked for twenty years and are now 42 years old, can retire from work with a salary of twenty days out of one month, provided that they have paid the insurance premium.[97]

10 LABOUR LAW

In 1997, Parliament passed legislation by which it made compulsory the training of technical and professional skills for those who are unemployed.[98] The Act consists of a single article with five notes. First, it provides that in order to profit as much as possible from the investments made, to improve the quality of products and to organize existing skills, all employers of industrial, productive, service and business sectors must ask job applicants to provide the "technical and professional skill certificate" issued by the competent authority. In addition, they must also provide an opportunity for their existing unskilled and semi-skilled workers to improve their skills through training.

Under note 1, training alongside work for those workers who are already employed by the above sectors will be according to the programmes timetabled by the Technical and Professional Training Organization (hereinafter cited as TPTO).[99]

---

[95] Art. 698 of the IPC provides that: "He who, with the intention of harming others or confusing public opinion or the officials, by letter or complaint or correspondences or statements or reports or distribution of any kind of printed material or handwriting with signature or without signature, asserts some lies; or with the same intention, contrary to the facts, attributes directly or quoting from other some acts to a natural or legal person or to the officials expressly or impliedly . . . in addition to the rehabilitation, if possible, [the culprit] will be sentenced to from two months to two years in prison or to flogging up to 74 lashes."

[96] RR, 25.4.1354, No. 8894; MQ, 1354, pp. 232–263. See also *Majmuʻi-yi Qawanin wa Muqarrarat-i Kar wa Taʼmin-i Ijtimaʻi*, 5th edn., Tehran, 1990, pp. 529–570.

[97] RR, 28.7.1376, No. 15335; MQ, 1376, p. 606.

[98] RR, 11.4.1376, No. 15242; MQ, 1376, pp. 230–231.

[99] Part of the Ministry of Labour and Social Affairs.

According to note 2, all relevant organizations must, for the issuance of a work permit, ask the applicant to provide a professional skill certificate issued by centres for technical and professional training affiliated with the Ministry of Labour and Social Affairs or by universities, technology schools and the like.

Note 3 states that within six months from the adoption of this Act, the list of professions and occupations in which training has not been feasible, or compulsory training without prior planning causes some problems in the production and fluctuations in the labour market, is to be prepared by the TPTO and after the approval of the Supreme Council of Labour is ratified by the Minister of Labour and Social Affairs.

Note 4 provides that the TPTO must, by using the existing facilities and in order to resolve the difficulties which may exist for women who look for work, pave the way for technical and professional training for women, in proportion to the job opportunities, in all centres in the provinces and cities.

Note 5 deals with the announcement of training programmes at the beginning of each course in the media and the registration of those employees, who are introduced to the TPTO by the employers, applying for training.

In the final provisions, pecuniary punishment has been provided for those employers who do not observe the provisions of this Act.

11 ENVIRONMENTAL LAW

The first comprehensive law regarding the environment was adopted in 1995.[100] Article 6 of the above Act states that "municipalities, police and relevant ministries and departments must provide a plan for the use of motor vehicles and the municipal transport system, which in addition to the decrease in air pollution, meet daily transport needs". For the implementation of the above article, the Council of Ministers adopted its executive regulation.[101]

The regulation consists of fourteen articles divided into three chapters. Chapter 1 includes the general provisions defining the areas of the cities and the times when the passage of motor vehicles has been restricted and also the cities to which such restrictions can be applied (Arts. 1 and 2). Chapter 2 deals with the issuance of an entry permit for motor vehicles within the restricted areas and the method for supervising the implementation of restrictions (Arts. 3–6) and Chapter 3 deals with organizing and improving municipal transport (Arts. 7–14).

In addition, the Iranian Parliament ratified or allowed the government to accede to a number of international conventions concerning the environment which will be referred to in section 13 below. As a result, the above conventions are now part of the Iranian domestic law.

---

[100] For details, see M. A. Ansari-Pour, "Iran", *Yearbook of Islamic and Middle Eastern Law*, vol. 2 (1995), pp. 251–256.
[101] RR, 18.3.1376, No. 15222; MQ, 1376, pp. 138–142.

12 FOREIGN INVESTMENT

Under Article 81 of the Constitution, the granting of a concession to foreigners for the formation of companies in Iran is, as a general rule, forbidden. In 1997, Parliament passed legislation by which foreign companies, which are regarded as lawful companies in their own countries can, in the fields specified by the Iranian government and within the framework of Iranian laws and regulations, register their branch or their agency, provided that the national state of the companies concerned recognize reciprocal rights for Iranians. It is stated that the executive regulation of this Act will be proposed by the Ministry of Economic and Financial Affairs in co-operation with other relevant authorities and will be approved by the Council of Ministers.[102]

13 INTERNATIONAL LAW

During 1997–1998, the Iranian government entered into a number of bilateral and multilateral treaties. The most significant of these treaties are as follows.

13.1 Environment

(a) On 28.9.1375[103] Parliament ratified the Adjustments and Amendments to the Montreal Protocol on Substances that Deplete the Ozone Layer (London, 29 June 1990),[104] and the Montreal Protocol on Substances that Deplete the Ozone Layer: Adjustments and Amendments (Copenhagen, 25 November 1992).[105]

(b) On 11.10.1375 Parliament allowed the government to accede to the United Nations Convention to Combat Desertification in those Countries Experiencing Serious Drought and/or Desertification, Particularly in Africa (17 June 1994).[106] The Convention, in addition to the preamble, consists of forty articles and four annexes.[107] However, one reservation was made with respect to paragraph 2 of Article 28 regarding the settlement of disputes. According to this reservation, the government can use the procedures mentioned in that paragraph if Parliament approves.

(c) On 7.11.1375, Parliament permitted the government to accede to the International Convention relating to Intervention on the High Seas in Cases of Oil Pollution Casualties (Brussels, 29 November 1969)[108] and to the Proto-

---

[102] RR, 26.9.1376, No. 15384; MQ, 1376, p. 697.

[103] RR, 17.11.1375, No. 15131; MQ, 1375, pp. 881–894.

[104] For the English text of the Adjustments and Amendments, see *International Legal Materials* (30) 1991, pp. 537–554. For the text of the Montreal Protocol itself, see *International Legal Materials*, (26), 1987, pp. 1550–1561.

[105] For the English text of the Adjustments and Amendments, see *International Legal Materials* (32), 1993, pp. 874–887.

[106] RR, 29.11.1375, No. 15139; MQ, 1375, pp. 992–1038.

[107] For the English text of the Convention and its annexes, see *International Legal Materials* (33), 1994, pp. 1328–1382.

[108] RR, 21.12.1375, No. 15157; MQ, 1375, pp. 1121–1131. For the English text of the Convention see *International Legal Materials* (9), 1970, pp. 25–44.

col Relating to Intervention on the High Seas in Cases of Marine Pollution by Substances Other than Oil (London, 2 November 1973).[109] Parliament also stated that referring to the disputes resulting from the enforcement of this Convention to conciliation or arbitration depends on the approval of the legally competent authorities.

(d) The fourth convention to which the Iranian government acceded and also relates to the environment was the International Convention on Oil Pollution Preparedness, Response and Cooperation (London, 30 November 1990).[110]

13.2 Customs

On 20.3.1376, Parliament allowed the government to accede to the International Convention on Mutual Administrative Assistance for the Preservation, Investigation and Repression of Customs Offences (1977).[111]

13.3 The ECO

On 23.6.1376, Parliament adopted an Act by which it ratified the Treaty of Ezmir. The first Treaty of Ezmir was adopted in 1977 and only three countries were party to it, i.e. Iran, Pakistan and Turkey. This treaty was amended in 1990 and 1992 as the charter of the Economic Cooperation Organization (ECO). Under the new treaty, which was adopted in Ezmir in 1996, ten countries became parties to it which include, in addition to the above three countries, Afghanistan, Azerbaijan, Kazakhstan, Kirghizia, Tadzikistan, Turkmenistan and Uzbekistan.[112] This treaty now, in addition to the preamble, consists of sixteen articles. The Secretariat of the ECO, under Article 9 of the treaty, is in Tehran.[113]

13.4 Law of the Sea

On 23.7.1376, Parliament ratified the Agreement for the Implementation of the Provisions of the United Nations Convention on the Law of the Sea of 10 December 1982 Relating to the Conservation and Management of Straddling Fish Stocks and Highly Migratory Fish Stocks (1995).[114]

---

[109] RR, 21.12.1375, No. 15157; MQ, 1375, pp. 1131–1140. For the English text of the Protocol see *International Legal Materials* (13), 1974, pp. 605–610.

[110] RR, 3.6.1376, No. 15287; MQ, 1376, pp. 447–460. For the English text of the Convention see *International Legal Materials* (30), 1991, pp. 733–747.

[111] RR, 23.4.1376, No. 15252; MQ, 1376, pp. 321–333.

[112] The name of the last six countries are spelled differently in different texts and world maps. The above spellings have been borrowed from *The Times Atlas of the World*, 7th edn., 1985.

[113] RR, 20.7.1376, No. 15328; MQ, 1376, pp. 581–589.

[114] RR, 29.8.1376, No. 15362; MQ, 1376, pp. 641–676. For the English text of the Agreement, see *International Legal Materials* (34), 1995, pp. 1542–1580.

13.5 Chemical weapons

On 5.5.1376 Parliament allowed the government to accede to the Convention on the Prohibition of the Development, Production, Stockpiling and Use of Chemical Weapons and on their Destruction (Paris, 13 January 1993).[115] Parliament also stated that the Ministry of Foreign Affairs must, in all negotiations and within the framework of the Convention, try for the unbiased and complete implementation of the Convention, especially in the field of inspection and the transfer of technology and chemicals for peaceful purposes. If the above conditions (i.e. unbiased and complete implementation of the Convention) are not met following the proposal of the Council of Ministers and the approval of the Supreme Council for National Security, the procedures for the withdrawal of Iran from the Convention will be put into effect.[116]

13.6 Intellectual property

On 17.8.1377 (1998), Parliament allowed the government to accede to the Stockholm Revision of the Paris Convention for the Protection of Industrial Property (14 July 1967).[117] However, Parliament made two reservations as well. The first relates to paragraphs 3 and 4 of Article 1 and paragraph 2 of Article 2. The second reservation concerns paragraph 1 of Article 28.[118]

14 ISLAMIC SUMMIT CONFERENCE

As noted above, the Islamic Summit Conference was held in Tehran in 1997. A number of very important issues relating to general international law or to the Islamic countries themselves, were discussed at the Summit and which have been incorporated into the Tehran Declaration. Participation of the Organization of Islamic Conferences (hereinafter cited as the OIC) in international affairs, promotion of solidarity, peace and security within the Islamic world as their priority, the establishment of an Islamic Common Market, condemnation of terrorism while distinguishing terrorism from the struggle of peoples against colonial or alien domination or foreign occupation and their right for self-determination, rejection of unilateralism and extraterritorial application of domestic law or sanctions, and urging the Member States to accelerate the completion of the ratification procedure for the International Islamic Court of Justice are among the principal issues in the Declaration.

One of the most important issues of this Summit, as stated in the Declaration, was to press for one permanent seat in the Security Council of the UN for the OIC as a whole. Paragraph 23 of the Declaration, *inter alia*, provides for "stress . . . on

---

[115] For the English text of the Convention, see *International Legal Materials* (32), 1993, pp. 800–873.
[116] RR, 11.10.1376, No. 15397; MQ, 1376, pp. 721–855.
[117] For the English text of the Revision, see *International Legal Materials* (6), 1967, pp. 806–826.
[118] RR, 18.9.1377, No. 15668; MQ, 1377, pp. 481–495.

the need for a more effective and equitable role and representation of the OIC membership in the UN organs, particularly the Security Council".[119] It was argued at the opening of the Summit that the OIC, as the representative of fifty-five Islamic countries and a population of one billion and several millions, must become a permanent member of the UN Security Council and to be the sixth member with the right of veto as long as this right exists. Such a demand has been made repeatedly by the Iranian authorities since then on behalf of the OIC as the presidency of the OIC belongs to Iran at present.[120]

15 CONCLUSION

The majority of the above legal developments occurred in 1997. Some of these laws constitute the cornerstone of each legal system, such as the laws relating to joining the bar association, the establishment of a new family court, the landlord and tenants' legal relations and international commercial arbitration. Part of these developments affect the economy as a whole. For example, the law relating to the indexation of dower may have far-reaching effects in other areas of law. It may be used by courts as a basis for awarding the rate of inflation, in other financial obligations, in favour of creditors. Or the legislation which permits foreign companies to register their branches or their agencies in Iran removes one of the impediments to foreign investment.

It is interesting to note that most cardinal legislation adopted during 1997–1998 were Members' bills introduced to Parliament, under Article 74 of the Constitution, rather than government bills. For example, the legislation relating to the establishment of the family court, indexation of dower, bar association membership, examination of judges' competence, financial convictions and the legislation which makes the learning of technical and professional skills compulsory for job applicants were Members' bills.

---

[119] See the statement in *International Legal Materials* (37), 1998, pp. 938–941.
[120] For example, see *Kayhan* (newspaper) of 19.2.1377.

Jordan

*Hamzeh A. Haddad**

1 JUDICIAL AND LEGAL SYSTEM

No major legislative changes have occurred under this title.

2 CONSTITUTIONAL, ADMINISTRATIVE AND CIVIL LAW

No major legislative changes have occurred to these branches of the law.

2.1 Court of Cassation (Civil Division) No. 121/98, p. 49 of 1999

The High Court of Justice is empowered to give a decision for ceasing the effect of any Order (Regulation) which is in contradiction with the Constitution or the laws, though this court has no power to abolish such an Order.

3 CIVIL PROCEDURE AND EVIDENCE

No major legislative changes have occurred under this heading.

3.1 Court of Cassation (Civil Decision) No. 903/96, p. 2961 of 1997

A lawyer's authentication of a client's signature shall be in the presence of the client in person and before the lawyer. Otherwise, the power of attorney is null and void.

---

* Minister of Justice, Jordan.

4 COMMERCIAL LAW AND ARBITRATION

A new law called the Law of Industry and Trade No. 18 was enacted in 1998 under which the Law of Supply No. 17/1992 was abolished. According to the new law, all rights and responsibilities of the Ministry of Supply provided for in the previous laws have been moved to the Ministry of Trade.

4.1 Court of Cassation (Civil Division) No. 227/97, p. 3589 of 1997

A depository bank may send a cheque outside Jordan for collection and, in doing so, the bank is considered as an agent of its client. Therefore, a contractual clause that the bank may not be liable in the event the cheque is lost is a valid and operative clause.

4.2 Court of Cassation (Civil Division) No. 1786/97, p. 3545 of 1998

An arbitration clause granting the arbitrator a power to impose reconciliation on the disputant parties and providing that an award to this effect is decisive and binding if rendered within three months of the first hearing is a valid clause. Hence, an award complying with these conditions is enforceable at law.

5 THE SECURITIES LAW

According to Article 73 of the Securities Law No. 22 of 1997, certain parts of the law may not become operative unless this is decided by the Council of Ministers. On the basis of this, the Council has decided to bring Articles 23–28, 29–34, 35–43 and 44–52 of the Law relating to the Stock Exchange, Securities Deposit Centre, and the Financial Services and Investment Fund, respectively, into operation as of 1 May 1999.

New regulations concerning the licensing of financial services and commission have been adopted and became operative as of 1 May 1999.

A new kind of protection for Jordanian productions has been given in the law No. 4 of 1999. Such protection includes, *inter alia*:

(a) imposing and increasing customs duties on imported commodities;
(b) limiting the quantity of imported commodities;
(c) cancelling or decreasing customs duties on imported commodities whenever they constitute an integral part of local products.

6 LABOUR LAW

Article 12 of the Labour Law of 1997 has been amended by Law No. 12 of 1998. The amendment considers the employment of non-Jordanians as a violation of the law in certain cases, such as employment without a licence or if the work given to the employee was different from that which is provided for in the licence.

7 PROPERTY LAW

No major legislative changes have occurred under this title.

8 INTELLECTUAL PROPERTY

A new Law, No. 14 of 1998, amended the Copyright Law No. 22 of 1992.

8.1 High Court of Justice No. 121/97, p. 799 of 1998

The rejection of the Minister of Tourism to renew the licence of a hotel having a trade name similar to an international famous name without permission is correct even though the famous name was not registered among the trade names in Jordan.

8.2 Berne Convention

Jordan has become, since 2 May 1999, a party to the Berne Convention for the Protection of Literary and Artistic Works 1971.

9 FAMILY LAW AND SUCCESSION

No major legislative changes have occurred under this title.

10 CRIMINAL LAW AND PROCEDURE

No major legislative changes have occurred under this title.

11 PUBLIC INTERNATIONAL LAW

11.1 Bilateral agreements

The following are some of the most important conventions that Jordan has joined:
(a)   the Comprehensive Prohibition of Nuclear Experiments;
(b)   the Arab Convention for Anti-Terrorism; and
(c)   the Convention of Distorting and Prohibiting the Usage, Storage, Production and Transportation of Anti-Personnel Mines.

12 PRINTING AND PUBLICATIONS

A new law called the Printing and Publications Law No. 8 of 1998 was enacted and has came into force on 1 September 1999.

In Decision No. 226/97 (BAJ, 1998, p. 389), the High Court of Justice froze the (provisional) law No. 27 of 1997 relating to printing and publications enacted by the government, for the law was in violation of the Constitution. The Court stated that the conditions for enacting a provisional law by the government, as provided for in the Constitution, had not been met.

Palestine

*Anis Al-Qasem**

1 CONSTITUTIONAL LAW

The Basic Law for the Interim Period, which was passed by the Legislative Council on 2 October 1997 and submitted to the President of the PNA for promulgation on 4 October 1997, has yet to be promulgated. The President has given no official reason for his inaction and, unfortunately, there is no constitutional mechanism in place to force him to act. The Legislative Council complains but, so far, has failed to act in a meaningful manner to bring about a closure of this very sad chapter.

The failure of the President to promulgate the Basic Law has left Palestine without a proper constitutional framework of government for the whole of the Interim Period. The powers of the various organs of government have remained undefined, with the result that the Executive, chiefly the President, has held supreme power even in the legislative field, as exemplified by the number of laws passed by the Legislative Council which still await promulgation by him. No proper system of accounting has been developed, and the no confidence procedure has proved ineffective – mainly because of the reluctance on the part of the Legislative Council to pursue this procedure with serious vigour.

The problem is compounded by the fact that the Interim Period of five years has expired, together with the term of office of both the President and the Legislative Council. It will be recalled that both were elected for a definite term, and with the expiry of this term a vacuum would be created unless some transitional measures were taken. A meeting of the PLO Central Council was called for on 27 April 1999 to deal, *inter alia*, with the situation. However, no decisions were taken and it seems there was general agreement that the problem was only imaginary. On constitutional matters, the Council decided to ask the Secretary General of the Arab League to form an Arab committee, chaired by him, to help draw up a draft constitution for the state

---

* Barrister, Consultant on the Laws of the Middle East (London), former Chairman of the Legal Committee of the Palestinian National Council (PNC).

of Palestine. The Council, as is apparent from its resolutions, did not discuss the Basic Law that was passed by the Legislative Council, nor did it ask the President to account for his failure to promulgate it. Thus, the PLO accountability machinery has failed to materialize.

It would appear that the thinking that prevailed at the Council was the absence of any vacuum, as no declaration was made acknowledging the expiry of the transitional period. Presumably, it was deemed extended. It is questionable whether the mandate of the elected President and Legislative Council can be tacitly extended in this manner. The interim period was not to exceed five years from a certain date under the Declaration of Principles and the elections were held expressly for a mandate covering the interim period. However, no action was taken to remove these doubts about the continued authority of the President and the Legislative Council.

The PLO Central Council was convened mainly for another reason. President Arafat has been, for some time, touring world capitals to win recognition of the state of Palestine which was to be declared on the expiry of the interim period, and the Central Council was convened to take a decision, particularly since most world heads of state had advised postponement of the decision. I was of the opinion that the state of Palestine was created by the Declaration of Independence made in 1988 by the Palestine National Council. After that declaration, the majority of states recognized the state of Palestine and exchanged diplomatic representatives. The Palestine National Authority was exercising sovereign powers over most of its population in the occupied territories. What remained were the recovery of the territory, which remained under Israeli control, and the termination of the occupation. Under the circumstances, there was no need for another declaration: what was needed was the termination of the occupation and the recognition of the state of Palestine by those states which had, so far, refrained from according such recognition. It seems that this view has prevailed. No reference is made to the issue of declaration in the resolutions of the Central Council and discussion of the issue does not take the priority it once took in the statements of President Arafat.

A boost in that direction came from Europe in the European Council Presidency Conclusions of 24–25 March 1999. In part, these Conclusions reaffirm the European Union "continuing and unqualified Palestinian right to self-determination including the option of a state and looks forward to the early fulfilment of this right . . . The European Union declares its readiness to consider the recognition of a Palestinian State in due course in accordance with the basic principles referred to above."

2 LEGISLATION

Fifteen laws were passed and published in the Official Gazette between November 1997 and December 1998. Publication indicates that the legislative process was complete. The laws were:

(a) Law No. 1 of 1997 on Palestinian Local Authorities;[1]

---

[1] Official Gazette (OG) No. 20 of November 1997.

(b) Law No. 2 of 1997 on Palestinian Currency Authority;[2]
(c) Law No. 1 of 1998 on Encouragement of Investment;[3]
(d) Law No. 2 of 1998 on Firearms and Ammunitions;[4]
(e) Law No. 3 of 1998 on Civil Defence;[5]
(f) Law No. 4 of 1998 on Civil Service;[6]
(g) Law No. 5 of 1998 on Hallmarks and Precious Metals;[7]
(h) Law No. 6 of 1998 on Correction and Rehabilitation Centres;[8]
(i) Law No. 7 of 1998 on Public Budget and Fiscal Affairs;[9]
(j) Decree Law No. 1 of 1998 on the Coming into Force of Tourism Law.[10]
(k) Decree No. 3 of 1998 on Consecration of National Unity and Prohibition of Enticement;[11]
(l) Law No. 8 of 1998 on Protection of Animal Wealth;[12]
(m) Law No. 9 of 1998 on Public Purchases;[13]
(n) Law No. 10 of 1998 on Industrial Cities and Free Industrial Zones;[14] and
(o) Law No. 11 of 1998 on Higher Education.[15]

A Public Assemblies Law was passed and promulgated on 28 December 1998.[16] The Judicial Authority Law, which was passed by the Legislative Council on 25 November 1998 has not been promulgated. Laws which have been passed by the Legislative Council and sent to the President for promulgation since 1997, but not promulgated, include the Basic Law, the Law on the Ownership of Immovable Property by Foreigners in Palestine and the Palestinian Petroleum Authority Law. Laws passed in 1998 and awaiting promulgation include the Charitable and Non-Governmental Organizations Law, the Public Tenders Law and the Natural Resources Law. A Civil Affairs Law was passed in 1999 anf is still awaiting promulgation by the President.

The President issued Resolution No. 15 of 1998, extending the jurisdiction of the Security Court to include specific offences that have been within the jurisdiction of the normal criminal courts. This resolution did not amend existing legislation on jurisdiction, and possible conflicts of jurisdiction between this court and ordinary courts may arise.

It is obvious from the above that the Legislative Council has been active in considering and passing legislation. However, it is also clear that the President not only controls the legislative process through his refusal to promulgate laws already

---

[2] OG No. 21 of January 1998.
[3] OG No. 23 of June 1998.
[4] *Ibid.*
[5] OG No. 24 of July 1998.
[6] *Ibid.*
[7] *Ibid.*
[8] *Ibid.*
[9] OG No. 25 of September 1998.
[10] OG No. 26 of November 1998.
[11] *Ibid.*
[12] *Ibid.*
[13] *Ibid.*
[14] OG No. 27 of December 1998.
[15] *Ibid.*
[16] The Official Gazette in which this Law was published was not available at the time of writing.

passed, but also legislation independently from the Legislative Council. The legality of the Security Court, which was created by a presidential resolution, was challenged, and now, by another resolution, its jurisdiction has been widened at the expense of ordinary courts. Similarly, Decree No. 3 of 1998 on the Consecration of National Unity and Prohibition of Enticement was a presidential legislative act that criminalized certain activities. Such measures are normally beyond the powers of the Executive. The absence of a Basic Law defining the authority and powers of the President and the relationship between him and the Legislative Council helps to create further confusion.

It will be noted that the legislation so far enacted has not tackled some of the basic legislative requirements. Apart from the recently enacted Judicial Authority Law yet to be promulgated, no major legislation has been passed to unify the laws in the two territorial sectors of Palestine, the Gaza Strip and the West Bank.

3 THE JUDICIARY[17]

The judiciary suffered a severe set-back in its independence through the forced retirement of the Chief Justice. Although when appointed to the post he had reached retirement age, he was retired by fax sent to him by the head of the civil service on 17 January 1998 with effect from 15 February 1998. The head of the civil service has no legal powers regarding the judiciary. Nevertheless, the Chief Justice was retired through an illegal act, and more than a year passed before a successor was appointed.

Security forces have continued to refuse to enforce decisions of the High Court affecting human rights of detainees, and the High Court itself has, on occasions, failed to provide protection. The action of the security forces led to the resignation in protest of the newly appointed Attorney-General, Fayez Abu Rahma, a former president of the Palestinian Bar. He had succeeded the much criticized first Attorney-General on 19 July 1998 and resigned in late March 1999. His successor was not appointed until June 1999.

There is still a severe shortage of judges at First Instance level and no remedial measures have been taken. For a total population of about 2 million there are twenty-two judges of courts of First Instance and twelve judges of the High Court.

The new Judicial Authority Law(when promulgated by the President) opens the door for the appointment of lawyers and law teachers to the bench, as well as on secondment from other Arab countries, and give the High Judicial Council the power to regulate judges' training.

Under this Law, a High Judicial Council oversees the judiciary. This Council is composed of the president of the High Court as chairman, the most senior judge of the High Court, two of the most senior judges of the High Court elected by the general assembly of the Court, presidents of the Courts of Appeal of Jerusalem, Gaza and Ramallah, the Attorney-General and the under-secretary of the Ministry of Justice.

The courts authorized by the Law are:

---

[17] For a more detailed general view, see *Fourth Annual Report*, 1 January 1998 – 31 December 1998, published by the Palestinian Independent Commission for Citizens' Rights, pp. 71–95.

(a) *shari'a* and religious courts;
(b) the High Constitutional Court;
(c) ordinary courts, comprising:
     (i)   the High Court as a court of cassation and high court of justice;
     (ii) courts of appeal;
     (iii) courts of first instance; and
     (iv) magistrate courts.

It is interesting to note that the Law has no provision for the creation of special courts, such as security courts.

It remains to be seen whether this Judicial Authority Law willbe promulgated or whether it will suffer the same fate as the Basic Law and other unpromulgated laws.

4 PEACE PROCESS

The peace process with Israel stalled completely in 1997 and 1998 despite continued efforts from Washington and the European Union to move Mr Netanyahu. Finally, on 22 October 1998, the Wye River Memorandum[18] was signed which provided for further redeployments of Israeli forces from the West Bank so as to transfer to the Palestinian Authority – 13 per cent from Area C, viz. 1 per cent to Area A and 12 per cent to Area B. Optimism was short-lived however, as having redeployed from the 1 per cent, Mr Netanyahu decided that there would be no further redeployment. Soon afterwards, he announced that there would be Israeli General Elections in May 1999 and the Wye River Agreement could not be implemented.

Hopes were revived in May with the defeat of Mr Netanyahu and the election of Mr Barak. In September the Sharm el-Sheikh Agreement was signed to implement the Wye River Memorandum and to make an immediate start on the final status talks on Jerusalem, border settlements and refugees with a view to completing a Framework Agreement by February 2000 and a Final Agreement by September 2000.

5 RULE OF LAW DEVELOPMENT

This was referred to in last year's *Yearbook*.[19] The Office of the United Nations Special Coordinator in the Occupied Territories has now published a *Survey of the State of the Development Effort* (May 1999) in the Rule of Law Domain which lists and explains the fifteen projects involving the international effort to provide development support, focusing on strengthening the Palestinian legal sector and justice system. Of special interest is the Law Reform Project aimed at the unification and harmonization of the laws of Gaza and the West Bank through law committees aided by regional and international consultants.[20]

---

[18] The full text is set out in Part III of this volume, pp. 479–486. See also the full text of the Sharm el-Sheikh Memorandum, pp. 487–490.
[19] *Yearbook of Islamic and Middle Eastern Law*, vol. 4 (1997–1998), pp. 295–296.
[20] The author and Judge Eugene Cotran, the general editor of this *Yearbook*, are involved as international consultants to this project funded by the British Department of International Development. Work has already started.

Lebanon

*Nayla Comair-Obeid**

1 INTRODUCTION

In November 1998, Lebanon democratically elected a new President of the Republic. In his investiture speech, the new President, Emile Lahoud, insisted that the law is above each and every citizen.

A number of administrative reforms have been adopted by the government composed, in its majority of technocrats, in order to fight corruption on all levels. Ministers and high-ranking state employees were placed under arrest by the judiciary for their fraudulent management, forgery and embezzlement of public funds, in an effort to rehabilitate public finances and reinstate the rule of law.

The new government, in the face of a very considerable public debt, was obliged to adopt an austerity policy. It has also encouraged new investors by the promulgation of legislation favourable to investment.[1]

The Law on the Budget, promulgated with a certain delay, and published recently in the Official Gazette,[2] adopted a number of provisions intended to encourage taxpayers, whether individuals or legal entities, liable for the income tax on built properties, registration rights, and all direct and indirect taxes including stamps rights, to

---

* Attorney-at-Law, Beirut, Professor of Law, Lebanese University, Beirut; author of *The Law of Business Contracts In The Arab Middle East*, Kluwer Law International, 1996, and *Arbitration In Lebanese Law, A Comparative Study,* Delta 1999. For a review of *The Law of Business Contracts in the Arab Middle East*, see this volume of the *Yearbook*, pp. 580–581.

[1] Several laws have been promulgated authorizing the government to conclude agreements in order to protect and encourage investments between Lebanon and Canada (Law No. 52 of 31 March 1999), between Lebanon and Greece (Law No. 53 of 31 March 1999), between Lebanon and Tunisia (Law No. 55 of 31 March 1999), between Lebanon and Italy (Law No. 51 of 31 March 1999), between Lebanon and Iraq (Law No. 58 of 31 March 1999), between Lebanon and France (Law No. 60 of 31 March 1999), between Lebanon and United Arab Emirates (Law No. 61 of 31 March 1999), between Lebanon and the Azerbaijan Republic (Law No. 64 of 31 March 1999).

[2] Law No. 107, published in the Official Gazette No. 36 on 30 July 1999.

pay their taxes. Paragraph 55 of this law provides that exemption from penalty shall apply for the period of two months for all delays in payment concerning the years 1988–1998.

Paragraph 56 stipulates that the increase by 10 per cent of the tax, usually applied to non-Lebanese, on the registration rights for purchased apartments, is no longer required if the buyers have paid their registration rights before the end of 1999.

In addition, several new laws have been promulgated, and will be discussed in greater detail below. First, a detailed overview of specific case judgments involving an important decision on matters of principle, where a reversal of jurisprudence should be noted, will be presented. The last part will feature the new projects of laws.

2 LEGISLATION

2.1 The Intellectual and Artistic Property Protection Law

On 3 April 1999, Law No. 75 was promulgated concerning the protection of intellectual and artistic property, based on the most recent and updated international laws on the subject.[3] This new law abrogated Articles 137–180 (inclusive), of Decision No. 2385 of 17 December 1924, concerning commercial and industrial property rights. In the new law, the legislator approved additional rights to the beneficiaries, and increased the penalties.

The legislator defined by virtue of this law the works included under protection. These refer to the whole of a person's intellectual work, whether written, drawn, or sculpted, or verbally transmitted, whatever its value, or importance, or purpose, and whatever the modality or the form of their expression. The law mentions the works included under protection as examples, and not restrictively. It also refers to all the works that are not included such as the daily news, laws, decree by laws, judgments, speeches delivered in public meetings, reflections, abstract scientific data and facts, and all artistic folk activities.

The legislator defined the beneficiary of an author's copyright, and he stipulated that the person who creates a literary or artistic work as his own creation shall have the absolute author's copyright on such work without the necessity to mention it, to preserve the author's rights, or to carry out any formal procedures.

The legislator also determined the scope of the legal protection concerning the author's nationality (Lebanese or non-Lebanese) or residence (in Lebanon or abroad). The legislator enumerated the rights enjoyed by the beneficiary of the author's copyright, both material and moral.

The legislator also mentioned the authors of similar rights, such as the producers of audio recordings, television and radio broadcasting companies and establishments, publishing houses, artists such as actors, musicians, singers, members of musical orchestras, dancers, puppet-masters and artists performing in a circus.

The legislator also provided cases where protection is granted to each of the authors of similar rights in the areas mentioned above.

---

[3] Published in the Official Gazette No. 18 on 13 April 1999, and in force on 13 June 1999.

The legislator defined the period of protection granted, provided that the author's material rights fall under the protection mentioned in this law during his entire life, in addition to fifty years after the author's death.

The legislator made a distinction between the different kinds of intellectual and artistic property, for example between common and collective works; audiovisual works and works published without mentioning the author's name, or those published under an author's pseudonym.

As for the moral rights of an author or an artist, the legislator stipulated that such rights shall be under unlimited protection which will not lapse by any prescription, and will devolve upon third parties through wills or succession laws.

The legislator discussed the case where an author and the beneficiary of similar rights or their specific successors, or sole legatees, delegate the management of their rights and the collection of all the indemnities due wholly or partially, to associations or civil companies constituted between them, by virtue of a power of attorney. Consequently, the legislator set the rules to be followed in the execution of the said power of attorney, and the conditions required from associations and companies of management of collective rights, as well as the control exercised by the Ministry of Culture. The legislator mentioned the modality of distributing the amounts collected by the beneficiaries.

The legislator required the work or the audio recording, or the performance, or the radio or television programmes, to be desposited with the Department of Private Property Protection, at the Ministry of Trade and Commerce. Deposition of the work clearly involves a presumption of the depositor's right of ownership of the work, audio recording, performance, or radio or television programme. However, various forms of evidence may be advanced to refute this presumption.

The legislator provided the possibility to register each contract concluded on a work, or an audio recording, or performance, or radio or television-recorded programme, at the Department of Private Property mentioned above.

The legislator discussed the cases of possible breach of an author's copyright and similar rights, allowing the beneficiary of such rights, or his sole legatees or special successors, particularly the associations or companies of management of collective rights, to take all the provisional measures, to prevent the breach of such rights. The legislator also granted the competence to take all these provisional measures to the judge of summary procedure, and to the competent president of the civil court or to the competent prosecution. The penalty for breaching an author's copyrights or similar rights consists of the payment of a fair indemnity for the material and moral damage incurred, also for his loss of missed profit and for the material profit obtained by the offender. It shall also be possible to decide on a penalty of imprisonment varying between one month to three years, and a fine of L5 million (approximately US$3,300) up to L50 million (approximately US$33,300), or both penalties, in cases detailed by the legislator.

As for bringing the legal action in the said violations, it shall be automatically incumbent on the prosecution, or upon the request of the party injured, or decided by the president of the Department of Private Property Protection.

The legislator prohibited unconditionally the import or entry into a warehouse or free zone, and the passage by transit, of all recordings and works that enjoy the legal protection in Lebanon, thereby ordering their seizure wherever found. The legislator enumerated the persons entitled to determine objects suspected of infringing the law and to take samples of those objects. These persons are official employees, such as police commissioners, customs officers.

The legislator provided also that the judgment issued in the said suits will always require the application of the following subsidiary penalties:

(a) affixing the judgment in the places determined by the court, its publication in two daily newspapers, also designated by the court which issued the judgment, and the expenses shall be borne by the defendant; or

(b) if the party condemned represents a newspaper or a magazine, or a radio, or television station, then it shall always be required to publish or broadcast the judgment in this newspaper or magazine, or radio, or television station, in addition to publishing the judgment in two daily newspapers chosen by the court.

The law also included transitional and temporary provisions covering protection of all works created before the date of enforcement of this law, whether or not they have been published, and the period of protection mentioned in the same law, provided that they should have entered the public realm on the date of enforcement of this law; the protection period, which lapsed at the promulgation of this law, will be deducted from the period of protection provided therein.

2.2 Judicial court costs law

2.2.1 Law No. 710 of 15 November 1998, concerning the amendment of the law on judicial court costs,[4] abrogating the law of 10 October 1950, and amended Law No. 98[5]

The law on judicial court costs mentions two kinds of legal expenses in legal suits: fixed and proportional expenses. In 1991, some of the fixed legal expenses were increased due to the depreciation of the national currency. The average costs of proportional legal expenses were increased in 1981 and 1991.

The proportional cost which is 4 per cent of the suit's value is imposed on each degree of the three degrees of courts, and the proportional cost of 5 per cent is incumbent on the execution of the judgment.

The proportional costs previously imposed before the amendment were very high in comparison with the averages applied in other countries, especially since a number of countries do not impose proportional costs on suits. Moreover, imposing high legal expenses is not compatible with the rule of free proceedings and providing justice to all at lower cost.

Many litigants have resorted to coming to monetary arrangements among themselves when the new judgment was issued, in order to avoid paying the due costs.

The law on judicial courts costs No. 710 was approved according to the following bases:

---

[4] Published in the Official Gazette No. 51 on 12 November 1998.
[5] Published in the Official Gazette Annex No. 37 on 12 September 1991.

(a) The reduction and unification of the proportional costs to the level which previously applied in 1950, meaning 2.5 per cent before the courts and before the execution offices (instead of 4 per cent and 5 per cent).

(b) Submitting some suits to the fixed costs, because of their nature, which were formally subject to the proportional costs. These include suits resulting from expropriations and demands to grant the executory formula to arbitration decisions, and lawsuits ensuing from bankruptcy.

(c) Raising the value of the fixed costs and some other judicial fees (copy and photocopy fees) so that the fixed costs are calculated on the basis of the three degrees of court: the first instance court, the court of appeal, and the Court of Cassation (L25,000 – approximately US$17; or L50,000 – approximately US$34).

(d) The guarantees provided in Article 78 of the law on judicial court costs, initially reduced and in the national currency, shall be multiplied by five.

(e) The legal expenses provided in Article 36 of the law on judicial court costs (penal legal expenses) which are also symbolic and in the national currency, shall be multiplied by ten. The cost for the execution of the will has become a fixed cost of L10,000 (approximately US$7).

(f) Finally, fixed costs before the State Council has been amended to L50,000 – approximately US$34.

3 CIVIL LAW AND PROCEDURE

3.1 Abrogation and amendment of certain legal texts concerning notices of provisional registration of real estate suits in the Registers of the Land Office[6]

Law No. 76 was promulgated on 3 April 1999. It abrogated or amended certain legal texts related to the noting in the Land Register of provisional registration and law suits involving real estate. It had previously been required by virtue of the provisions of Article 47 of Decision No. 188 issued on 15 March 1926 to register the mention of any suit concerning real estate on the Land Register, otherwise the suit would not be admitted.

The new law grants the president of the competent civil court freedom to decide whether to order mention of a real estate lawsuit in the Land Register, or whether to order it to be written down against a guarantee.

In the event of the refusal of the demand, the president of the civil court shall decide to make a provisional registration mention for one month, which registration shall be crossed off after the said period has elapsed.

Any person who suffers injury as a result of this decision may submit an appeal within eight days from the date of his notification. If the Court of Appeal considers the motives of the appeal to be well founded, it will decide whether mention of the lawsuit should be deleted from the Land Register, or inscribed without guarantee, or against a financial or bank bond. In the latter case, mention should be made of the deadline for its presentation, and the value of the guarantee; however, the

---

[6] Official Gazette No. 18 of 3 April 1999.

mention inscribed will be deleted if the guarantee is not submitted within the period indicated. The decision of the court of appeal shall not be liable to any ordinary or extraordinary means of appeal, and shall be executed by writing or crossing off the mention on its minutes without the necessity of notification. Without complying with Article 47 of Decision No. 188 issued on 15 March 1926, the crossing off of the mention shall not prevent the lawsuit examination from continuing; the plaintiff shall have the right, when necessary, to claim for indemnity (in cash).

The courts have already started to apply these texts, and some decisions have recently been handed down admitting the attachment of a mention to an item of real estate, but this time against a guarantee providing the injured party with a right to indemnity and execution when there is proof of injury.

3.2 Civil procedure

Decree No. 13440[7] has amended the competence of the first instance courts, according to the value of the suits submitted before the said courts.

The court is now made up of one civil judge with the authority to examine suits with a value that does not exceed L100 million (approximately US$66,666) instead of the previous system whereby only suits of L10 million (approximately US$6,666) were referred to one civil judge. It is provided that the personal suits, as well as those related to movable and immovable property, shall be transferred administratively to one competent judge, when their value is equal or less than L100 million (US$66,666).

This excludes suits where proceedings have ended.

4 PENAL LAW

4.1 Law No. 7 of 20 February 1999, amending Article 562 of the Penal Code

Article 562 of the Penal Code has been amended to allow extenuating circumstance for the perpetrator of murder or involuntary injury to a spouse or member of his/her family when such a person has been caught in a flagrant act of adultery or illegal sexual relations.

This article replaces the previous absolution for any such act, allowed on a plea of extenuating circumstances. So the amended law provides severer penalties, based on social considerations with a view to limiting crimes within the family.

---

[7] Decree No. 13440 of 5 October 1998; this decree is published and enforced as of 1 February 1999.

5 JURISPRUDENCE

5.1 Parliamentary immunity

A decision issued by the penal Court of Cassation (Chamber Seven), examining publication[8] cases, has decided for the first time in Lebanon to remove the parliamentary immunity of a deputy for acts of libel he has committed.

The Court of Cassation considered that Article 39[9] of the Constitution concerns two different kinds of parliamentary immunity:

(a) a complete privilege, such as irresponsibility covering the opinions and ideas issued by the deputy during his mandate;
(b) a limited privilege restricting freedom for the prosecution to bring a public action against a parliamentary deputy for penal offences of which he is accused. Prosecution for such offences is possible only after authorization from Parliament, except in the case of *flagrante delicto* according to Article 40 of the Constitution.[10]

The decision is seen as very important in setting the limits separating the scope of each of both those articles, in knowing the place of the offence the deputy is accused of, and in defining the track of proceedings according to the rules. Therefore, the decision provides that the complete immunity granted by Article 39 of the Constitution to the deputy is a real privilege. Such an immunity shall include two conditions in order to produce its effect. The first condition is that the said immunity shall be related to the purpose it is granted for, which is the exercise of his function by the deputy, as representative of the nation, in freedom, peace and objectivity, and not from personal motives. If he deviates from such representations, he is no longer entitled to the immunity of Article 39 of the constitution, and his prosecution is allowed.

The second condition considers Article 39 of the Constitution as an exception to the general rule and as not susceptible to any extension in its interpretation which would limit the general rule according to which all citizens are deemed equal before the law.

Accordingly, the Court of Cassation considers the parliamentary immunity of the deputy ensuing from the opinions and ideas he issues during his mandate, provided in Article 39 of the Constitution, as not absolute and not including all the opinions and ideas he expresses, but limited to the opinions and ideas he issues when related to Parliament, as well as related to public national matters and interests he is invested to treat by virtue of his parliamentary representation without abuse. This clearly defines the immunity included in Article 39; the decision also considers that the delegation of the deputy and his popular representatives grants him

---

[8] No. 5/1999, 3 June 1999, unpublished.
[9] Art. 39 of the Lebanese Constitution stipulated that it shall not be allowed to bring a penal action against any member of the Parliament because of the opinions and ideas he expresses during his mandate.
[10] Art. 40 stipulates that: "it shall not be allowed during the sessions, to take penal proceedings against any member of the parliament, nor to arrest him, if he commits a penal infraction, unless there is a parliamentary authorisation, and except for the case of *flagrante delicto*".

the right of control by legal and regular means, but also imposes on him the obligation of respecting other people's dignity and reputation, such as those stipulated in the matters raised, otherwise he will forfeit his right to enjoy the provisions of said Article 39.

It is worth noting that this decision led to a violent reaction from parliamentarians, and the Speaker of Parliament, who considered that the parliamentary immunity should not be removed, unless by Parliament, and by virtue of a demand submitted by the State Prosecutor, to the Minister of Justice, who should submit it to Parliament, the latter deciding whether or not to remove the parliamentary immunity of the deputy.

6 REDUCTION OF ATTORNEYS' FEES

A preparatory judgment[11] was issued by the Beirut Court of Appeal, examining the matter of opposing the formality of execution related to an attorney's fees. The Court of Appeal considers it has the right to reduce an attorney's fees in a case whereby the client has to pay his attorney's fees of up to 20 per cent of the indemnity value on his property, in a case involving the restitution of family property.

The judgment has decided that the Court shall have the right to change the attorney's fees, even if an agreement defining those fees exists. It will reduce them if the remuneration is not commensurate with the service provided, in application of the principle reciprocity of obligations.

The judgment also considered that equity and justice were not the sole basis for the amendment of agreements and contracts; therefore the court shall always have the right to amend the attorney's fees, even in the case of a previously existing agreement determining their value.

The application of this right means that the courts now control the fees when they exceed 20 per cent of the value of litigation, when it deems that fees demanded by the attorney exceed the value of the services he provides. This refers to Article 69 of the attorneys' professional code, which sets a presumption concerning the attorney's fees when they exceed 20 per cent of the litigation's value, in civil matters allowing the courts to reduce the said fees when they exceed the services performed by the attorney on behalf of the client.

7 LIABILITY FOR MEDICAL MALPRACTICE

A judgment[12] issued by the civil judge of Beirut was considered courageous and rare in the history of Lebanese jurisprudence, as it provided for a doctor's liability for malpractice, when resulting from a surgical operation where neither medical, nor technical procedures were followed. The case concerns a patient who had entered hospital in order to undergo medical examinations due to stomach pains; the at-

---

[11] Preparatory judgment, dated 14 July 1999, Beirut Civil Court of Appeal, 10th Chamber, unpublished.
[12] Decision No. 1068/98 of 10 November 1998, published in *al-ʿAdl* review 1999, No. 1, p. 136.

tending physician suspected the presence of a malignant tumour, and decided to operate without requiring further necessary tests. This led to the patient's death.

It was later proved by the post mortem carried out on the deceased patient that the organs removed were not affected by any malignant tumour, contrary to the doctor's diagnosis. The experts appointed by the court certified also that the surgical operation was made without justification and the organs removed were not affected by any malignant tumour.

The judgment decided that the liability of the doctor for his malpractice was based on the causality between the doctor's negligence and the prejudicial result. The judgment also ruled that although the doctor had the freedom and right to choose a treatment for his patient, this freedom is limited by the requirement of awareness and care for the patient's health in choosing a course of treatment and embarking on it.

Finally, the judgment considered the existence of the causality between the doctor's negligence in diagnosing and the prejudicial result by the occurrence of death. The court therefore decided that liability of the doctor for his negligence exists, and ordered him to pay indemnity, as a result of the said negligence.

8 DIVORCE AND CUSTODY

The Court of Appeal of Beirut (Third Chamber) issued a decision[13] concerning the custody of two children, resulting from a divorce between a Lebanese national and a French national. The civil marriage had been concluded in the state of New York. This decision ruled on two matters, the first related to the competence of the court, the second related to application of the law on litigation.

Concerning the first matter, the Court of Appeal decided that it was within the competence of the Lebanese civil courts to rule in this matter. This is according to Articles 79, 104 and 106 of the Civil Procedure Code and Decree No. 109 issued on 14 May 1935, when one of the spouses is Lebanese and the marriage is civil and concluded abroad.

As for the second matter, the Court of Appeal considered that the law applicable to divorce is the law pertaining to the place where the marriage was held, in this case, the state of New York, referring therefore to Article 25[14] of Decree No. 60 LR of 13 March 1936, amended by Decree No. 146 of 18 November 1938, without any justification and based on a special interpretation of Article 25 of Decree No. 60 LR. The judge considered that in this case this was one of the many interpretations of Lebanese jurisprudence.[15]

---

[13] Decision No. 1056 of 17 August 1988, unpublished.
[14] Art. 25 of Decree No. 60 LR stipulates that "if a marriage is concluded abroad between a Lebanese or between a Syrian or Lebanese, or between a Syrian or a Lebanese and foreigner it shall be valid if celebrated according the procedures followed in that country". "If the personal status regulation to which the spouse is subject does not admit the form neither the effects resulting from the law of the marriage celebrated, then, the marriage shall be subject in Syria and Lebanon to the civil law."
[15] Court of Cassation, all the Chambers, No. 36, on 19 December 1964, *Bar Bulletin*, 1964, p. 149. Civil Court of Appeal of Mount Lebanon, first Chamber, No. 27, on 22 March 1998, *al-Adl* review, 1989, t. 1, p.109 and 115 High Court of Beirut on 5 April 1968, Judicial publication 1970, p. 996.

Since there are various interpretations of the said Article 25, some courts have applied that chosen by the consent of the two spouses. Other courts have applied the law of the religious community of the husband, while yet others have applied the religious law common to both parties, when this is possible, even when a civil marriage has been concluded abroad, but followed by a religious one.[16]

Consequently, and according to the afore-mentioned, the said decision applied the provisions of Article 10, paragraph 17 of the New York Civil Law, which examines the consequences of the severe treatment, and the commission of adultery, considering both as grounds for divorce.

The decision implied two rules. First, it is not allowed that either spouse should change by hisor her sole will the marital home place, moving to another country without the consent of the other spouse.

Second, both spouses shall be considered responsible for the divorce between them, which shall influence the children's custody conditions, and since the children had been separated for a number of years between the parents, the judge ruled that neither spouse should have sole custody for both children, and that the children should remain with the parents they had been living with until now.

This was the first time a judge differentiated his interpretation of the law on custody of children from a specified law. In this case, his judgment took into consideration the humanitarian condition of the children.

Normally, Lebanese courts submit the custody of children to one law, whereby one parent is given the custody of the children.

9 ARBITRATION

In the new Lebanese Code of Civil Procedure of 1983, there is a chapter devoted to internal and international arbitration, comprising a reform which takes as its model the new French Code of Civil Procedure and adopts most of the latter's dispositions concerning such arbitration. The influence of French legal thinking is also to be seen in the distinction the former makes between internal arbitration on one hand and international arbitration on the other.

Recently, the parties began to adopt in their contracts arbitration clauses, in order to provide rapidity in the examination of their cases. This is seen as a more efficient and rapid way of settling disputes, especially commercial ones.

The whole question is of particular concern now that reconstruction in Lebanon is in full swing, with the Lebanese authorities concluding important agreements every year with international companies for carrying out major infrastructure projects. In nearly all these contracts the agreed means of settling disputes is by arbitration.

Lebanese universities are now aware of the importance of arbitration, and have accordingly included arbitration in their curriculum.

Lebanese courts have also widened the domains where arbitration is accepted as a way of settling disputes.

---

[16] Decision of Mount Lebanon Civil Appeal court, First Chamber, No. 114 issued on 29 November 1988, Civil Court of Cassation, Chamber 2, No. 13, issued on 14 March 1991 (unpublished). The said decision has been approved by the Court of Cassation.

9.1 Arbitrability of disputes

9.1.1 *Concerning lease law*

A judgment[17] was issued by the civil court of Jdeidet-El-Metn; the court considered itself competent in a litigation concerning lease law. The first instance court considered the possibility of submitting the case to an arbitrator according to the arbitration clause included in the contract.

However, the first instance court considered itself incompetent to examine the suit when an arbitration clause is provided to settle the dispute, except in cases involving public policy.

This decision is the first of its kind in Lebanon; it defined the scope of admitting arbitration in a major matter, in this case lease law, which is normally within the competence of ordinary judicial courts.

9.1.2 *Concerning contracts for commercial representation*

Article 5 of Decree-Law No. 34 of 5 August, 1967 lays down that the court of law of the locality where a commercial representative operates is competent to judge differences arising over his contract for representation, and this despite any agreement to the contrary.

An argument arose when it became nessecary to know whether the exclusive competence of the courts of law could be upheld in matters concerning commercial representation because of the said Article 5 involving public policy and concerning protection of the rights of representatives. This would mean that disputes arising out of contracts for representation could not be settled by arbitration. The decree of the Court of Cassation, First Chamber, of 17 July 1988, considered when giving its reasons that agreement for arbitration derived from the autonomy of the will, and that the text of Article 5 "non-obstant any contrary agreement" excluded agreement for arbitration as it constituted a distinct entity outside the framework of Article 5, and therefore it was not contrary to public policy or interest.

After a recent about-turn of jurisprudence expressed in the judgment of a lower court,[18] subsequently confirmed in the court of appeal,[19] it was considered that Article 5 gave exclusive competence to the jurisdictions of the state as it was a regulation concerning public policy aimed at protecting the interests of Lebanese commercial agents and should therefore be interpreted restrictively. The Court of Cassation issued a judgment of principle deciding the question, giving among its reasons that the contract binding the parties was a contract of commercial representation coming under Article 5 of Decree-Law No. 34. This makes the ordinary court of law for the district where the agent operates competent to settle disputes relating to the execution of his contract. Consequently, the Court of Appeal, by declaring

---

[17] Judgment No. 49/98 on 1 April 1998.
[18] Beirut Court of First Instance, 3rd Chamber, case of *Kombo and Co.* dated 21 January 1997.
[19] Beirut Appeal Court (2nd Chamber), dated 29 October 1998, unpublished.

itself competent to settle the dispute in question, had correctly applied the law concerning commercial representation, it being one concerning public policy. The agreement for arbitration could not therefore be applied.[20]

9.1.3 *The possibility of admitting a judge as arbitrator*

The Lebanese Code of Procedure of 1933 had allowed the judge of summary procedure to act as an arbitrator. However, Article 6 of the former code for judicial organization had forbidden a judge to act as an arbitrator, even unpaid. This solution was confirmed by the judge for summary procedure on the grounds that the said code had forbidden a judge to be an arbitrator.[21] In the absence of any explicit text in the 1983 Civil Code of Procedure, Article 120 about challenge to a judge is to be applied; in paragraph 4 one of the causes allowed for challenging a judge is his previous designation by one of the parties as arbitrator in another affair. The New Code of Judicial Organization in Article 47 of Legislative Decree No. 150 of 16 September, 1983, forbids a judge to exercise any other function involving paid work. This implies that a judge may not be paid for acting as an arbitrator. It should be noted that the Civil Code of procedure allows a judge to be appointed conciliator between parties. May one conclude that by not explicitly mentioning the possibility of a judge being appointed arbitrator, whereas it does for conciliation, the Code does not allow a judge competency for arbitration?

A decision has been issued by the Beirut Court of Appeal, which was also unique of its kind. The Court's decision considered that the litigants, by including an arbitration clause in the contract, agreed to resolve their litigation by arbitration. The contract included the clause stating that in the case of a dispute, a submission for arbitration should detail the points of litigation, as well as appointing arbitrators.

Such submission provides that the judge of summary procedures in Beirut, shall be the final arbitrator. The Court of Appeal has considered that the judge of summary procedure is competent to settle disputes. This refers to Article 763[22] of the Civil Procedure Code concerning the modalities of appointment of an arbitrator. The clause provides that, under pain of nullity, the arbitration clause should include the designation of the arbitrator or arbitrators, either in their person, or in their quality, or it should fix their designation.

The Court of Appeal considered that since the parties had fixed the modality of the designation of the arbitrator, in this case the judge of summary procedure, therefore, the arbitration clause was valid and the judge of summary procedure of Beirut would be competent to settle the dispute as an arbitrator.

The question here is whether the judge of summary procedure has to accept the decision of the Court of Appeal and act as arbitrator, or whether he can refuse this

---

[20] Beirut Court of Cassation 19 March, 1998, judgment 6/98, unpublished.

[21] The Judge of summary procedure of Zahleh, 17 July 1959, Judiciary Review, 1956, p. 879.

[22] Art. 763 stipulated that: "the arbitrator clause will be the principal contract in writing in the principal contract or in a document to which this refers. It should under pain of nullity include designation of the arbitrator or arbitrators either in their person or in their quality, or it should fix their designation."

role, as no explicit and clear text is found in the 1983 Civil Code of Procedure. This matter raises several questions that jurisprudence has not yet settled.

9.1.4 The right of individuals to include arbitration clauses on behalf of their companies

Article 381 of the Civil Code of Procedure demands that the authorized agent should be provided with special power allowing him to sign an agreement for arbitration in the name of his mandator and on his account.

In a recent judgment of the Beirut Court of First Instance,[23] Lebanese jurisprudence rejected a demand for annulment of an agreement for arbitration signed by the managing director of a joint stock company despite the absence of specified powers to make such an agreement. It was considered that the prior authorization given by the board of directors gave him the right to sign any contract in the interest of the company.

9.2 Annulment of an arbitration award

9.2.1 Absence of previous deliberation

The Civil Court of Appeal of Beirut has issued a decision[24] annulling an arbitration award because there was no deliberation between the members of the arbitration tribunal.

The court considered that even though an arbitration award and minutes of court proceedings are considered as instruments of written proof, these contents are taken into consideration until the allegation of its forgery is proven. According to the court, Article 201 of the Civil Procedure Code stipulates explicitly that the court is allowed to decide whether to reject any instrument or consider it void, if it suspects clearly that they are forged. The Court will have to justify its decision.

The Court of Appeal decided that in this case, since no deliberation had taken place between arbitrators, in compliance with Articles 788 and 528 of the Civil Procedure Code, that the arbitration award was void, as it did not comply with public policy.

This ruling has cut short the usual proceedings, as it has entitled the Court of Appeal to consider the arbitral award was void, since no deliberation between arbitrators had taken place and the instruments were seen as forged. Normally, the Court of Appeal would have had to await the decision of the Penal Court concerning the forgery of the arbitration proceedings minutes, then make its ruling. The Court now directly applies Article 201 of the Civil Code of Procedure to settle the matter.

[23] Beirut Court of First Instance, 29 October, 1998, unpublished.
[24] Decision No. 670 on 20 May 1999, 3rd Chamber.

9.2.2 Free debate and confrontation

In a case of recourse for annulment of an arbitrator's award, the Beirut Court of Appeal decided that the arbitrator had respected the principle of debate and the rights of the defence, and that the appeal against his award on the grounds that he had failed to respect these two principles could not be accepted. The Beirut Court of Appeal considered that doctrine and consistent jurisprudence viewed that in arbitration it is possible to hear the parties separately without this constituting failure to respect the principal of free debate, provided that the order party be informed and be allowed to discuss each document: "The right to confrontation differs from the right to free debate; and the fact of one of the parties renouncing his right to confrontation does not authorise him to oppose recourse against the judgment delivered by the arbitrators on the grounds of failure to respect the right of debate."[25]

Recourse for annulment of an arbitral award is considered a matter of public policy, and neither party may renounce the right to it; any renunciation therefore is considered null and void and rejected.

10 NEW PROJECTS OF LAW

Parliamentary committees are now reviewing the Code of Commerce, the Penal Code and the Penal Procedure Code. In addition, a new electoral law is under consideration and will be adopted before the next round of parliamentary elections, expected in the second half of the year 2000.

The Committee for the Updating of Laws, appointed by the Minister of Justice, is considering reforming the law of public adjudication, the Labour Law and the law of administrative decentralization.

---

[25] Second Chamber, 15 July, 1998, No 104/98 unpublished.

Libya

Mustafa El-Alem*

1 CRIMINAL LAW

1.1 Falsification of passports

Article 350 of the Penal Code has been amended by virtue of Act No. 5/1428 (1998) in order to increase the punishment for falsification of passports, passes or permissions or the like. The punishment was either imprisonment for a period not exceeding three years or a fine not exceeding LD50. After this amendment, the punishment has been extended to imprisonment for a period not exceeding five years. The same penalty is to be applied for use of such false documents without participation in their falsification.

1.2 Execution of death sentence

Act No. 14/1428 (1998) has amended Article 19 of the Penal Code so that an offender who is sentenced to death must be executed by shooting and no longer by hanging.

1.3 Adultery

Act No. 10/1428 (1998) has added a new article, 6bis, to Act No. 70/1973 establishing the penalty for adultery. According to this new article, the crime of adul-

---

* Attorney at Law before the Libyan Supreme Court.

tery may be proved either by confession, by testimony of four witnesses or by any other scientific means of proof.

1.4 Larceny

Article 2 of the Larceny and Robbery Act prescribed the amputation of the offender's right hand as a penalty for larceny. Article 3 of this Act prevented the application of this penalty in five cases where the general provisions of the Penal Code may be applied instead. Among those is the case where ownership of the stolen property is transferred to the offender after the larceny and before the issuance of the final judgment. This case (or exception from the application of the penalty) has been abolished by virtue of Act No. 1/1428 (1998).

1.5 Smuggling

According to Article 122 of the Customs Law No. 67/1973, smuggling and attempted smuggling were punishable by either one of the following two penalties or both of them:

–   a fine not exceeding three times the amount of the due customs tax, in addition to three times the price of the goods subject to smuggling, or alternatively, the amount of LD100, whichever is bigger;
–   imprisonment for a period not exceeding six months.

Moreover, the smuggled goods, the means of transport and the equipment used therefor may be confiscated.
    Article 122 has now been amended by Act 13/1428 (1998) amending some articles of the Customs Law. Accordingly, the penalty for smuggling and attempted smuggling has now become:

–   the amount of the alternative fine has been increased to LD300;
–   both penalties, i.e. fine and imprisonment, must be applied together;
–   the smuggled goods shall always be confiscated.

2 ROAD TRANSPORT

Act No. 18/1428 (1998) on Road Transport provided for the following rules:

(a)   Road transport means the carrying of passengers and goods by vehicles and trains from one place to another inside and outside the country.
(b)   Such activity must be performed by companies, partnerships and individuals with an official permission. Monopoly of any type of road transport is prohibited.
(c)   Exceptionally, individuals, private and public moral persons may be allowed to carry their own goods and passengers by their own means of transport.

(d) Without prejudice to provisions of the agreements to which Libya is a party, foreign carriage of goods and passengers shall be subject to Libyan laws and regulations during passage through Libya.

(e) Non-Libyans are not allowed to perform road transport inside Libya. Exceptionally, and in application of the principle of reciprocity, a non-Libyan may be so allowed by permission of the Secretariat of Transport.

(f) There must be insurance against any damage that may be sustained by a third party's property because of road transport.

3 STAMP DUTY LAW

The Stamp Duty Law No. 65 of 1973 has imposed a fixed or proportionate stamp duty on papers, documents, deeds, notices, registers, and any other written matters. Stamp duty is also imposed on dispositions, transactions and affairs. Duty must be paid according to the provisions of this law and in the manner and rates stated in the table attached thereto [not included in this survey].

Act No. 16/1428 (1998) has amended the Stamp Duty Law. The most important amendments are:

(a) The table (schedule) attached to the law stating the rates and manner in which the stamp duty must be paid has been abolished and replaced by a new table attached to the Act.

The new table provides generally for higher rates. For example, item 29(a) of the old table used to impose a rate of 1 per cent of the contract price on import, transport, concession and public works contracts to be paid by the contractor. This rate has become 2 per cent in the new table.

(b) Articles 15 and 18 have been amended to read as follows:

Article 15
Without prejudice to prescribed penalties the Department may estimate the value of a written matter, disposition, or other material in case the person fails to mention it or to submit an additional declaration thereof.

The department may also estimate the value in cases where the value contained in the written matter, disposition or other material, or that declared by the person concerned, is inferior to the standard prices prevalent at the time of composition of the written matter or conclusion of the transaction.

Article 18
Persons concerned may lodge a protest against the Department's resolution regarding the application of the provisions of this law within 30 days as from the date on which the resolution is duly notified. The protest shall not be accepted unless a fee amounting to 10 per cent of the disputed duty is paid.

The provisions relating to conciliation and settlement of income tax disputes shall be applied to the conciliation and settlement of stamp duty disputes.

4 SOCIAL CARE FUND

The Social Care Fund is an independent institution established by Act No. 20/1428 (1998). This institution has the status of a public juridical person. It is charged with the organization of matters relating to social security pensions and social care services including:

–   health, education, housing and any other social services;
–   financial lump sum grants and aids;
–   administration of social care institutions such as rehabilitation centres, kinder-gartens, and care homes for women, juveniles or the older generation;
–   relief grants in case of natural disasters;
–   basic pensions;
–   exceptional and additional pensions and gratuities that may be granted to citizens who have rendered distinguished services to the country.

Those benefits provided by the social care system are enjoyed by the following persons:

–   those persons who are deprived of tutelage "guardianship";
–   beneficiaries of basic pensions;
–   handicapped and invalids;
–   large poor families;
–   those for whom a pension scheme is not sufficient;
–   beneficiaries of lump sum gratuities;
–   victims of natural disasters.

Sudan

*John Wuol Makec**

1 CONSTITUTIONAL LAW

1.1 Freedom of Association and Organization

Article 26(1) of the Constitution authorizes the creation of *huria el tawaaly* and *tanzim* (freedom of association and organization). Article 26(1) states:

(a) Citizens shall have the right of association and organisation for cultural, social, economic, professional or trade union purposes without restriction save in accordance with the law.

(b) There shall be guaranteed for citizens the right to organise political associations, and shall not be restricted save by the conditions of the consultative decision making (*shura*) and democracy in the leadership of the organisation, and use of propagation not material force in competition and abiding by the fundamentals of the constitution that as regulated by law. [English translation]

Under this article citizens are entitled to form ordinary voluntary associations and political parties. Previously, ordinary associations (non-political) and political parties were treated separately. However, now the words "political party" have acquired a new terminology which brings them into the same category as ordinary private and voluntary associations.

What is more significant in this terminological play is the meaning of the word *tawaaly*. The meaning of this word has created much confusion among reputed Islamic jurists and scholars of the Arabic language.

However, when a protracted inquiry ultimately fails to achieve a satisfactory meaning, people question what motivated the Constitution policy-makers to deliberately choose the most confusing terminology in lieu of the known or com-

---

* LLB; LLM; Justice of the Supreme Court of the Sudan.

mon phrase (i.e. "political party"). In other words, what is being avoided by the use of this terminology?

The translators of the Arabic version of the Constitution into English selected the word "association" to represent *tawaaly*. However, many scholars doubt the correctness of this translation. Critics of this choice question whether the Constitution really permits the formation of political parties as an exercise of democracy.

The provisions of Article 26 of the Constitution were implemented by means of a statute which we investigate further below.

1.1.1 *Organization of* Tawaaly El Siyyasia *(Political Associations) Act 1998*

Towards the end of 1998 the National Assembly, in its endeavour to implement the Constitutional Provisions, enacted one of thirty new laws entitled Organization of *Tawaaly El Siyyasia* Act 1998. It came into force on 1 January 1999. This Act repealed no previous Act as the law which regulated political parties was one of the laws repealed by the Salvation Government when it came into power on 30 June 1989.

Article 3 of this Act lays down principles or conditions which must be observed by political parties. An association must observe the principles of freedom, *shura* (consultation) and democracy. Accordingly, the following conditions must be observed:[1]

(a)   The choice of any person to join an association must be free and voluntary. Further, the members of an association must freely confer among themselves when they are directly or indirectly choosing the organs of the association and its local, regional and national leadership.

(b)   Membership of an association must not be induced through coercion or temporary material benefits or loyalty of a traditional group. Again, membership of an association must not be determined by religious, colour, heritage or class discrimination. Reference to "loyalty to a traditional group" includes traditional religious sects, such as the *Ansaar*, or the followers of Mohammed Ahmed El Mahdi, who form the core of the *Umma* party or the *Khatimiyya* religious sect which is the focal centre of the Democratic Unionists Party (DUP). However, this provision seems to have been purposely overlooked in practice when the political associations were formed under this Act.

(c)   The third condition is that an association must be bound by the basic fundamental principles of the state Constitution of 1998 and the law. No association shall adopt as a way or method of implementation or fulfilment of the objectives of a religious book any means or measures intended to amend those basic fundamental principles of the Constitution and the law. Any amendment of the basic principles shall be made in accordance with the provisions of the Constitution and the law.[2] It follows that no association is entitled to compromise or adjust the basic fundamentals of the Constitution and the law to suit or conform with religious concepts. This provision seems to be directed towards religious political associations or parties based on religious sects.

---

[1]   S. 3(1), Organization of *Tawaaly El Siyyasia* (Political Associations) Act 1998.
[2]   S. 3(2), *ibid.*

Critics of this law contend that the provisions of sections 3(2) and 11 are aimed at obligatory subjection of any political association to the adoption of the political objectives of the ruling National Congress.

(d) The fourth condition is aimed at preventing unfair and hostile competition between political associations. Relations between political associations should be based on the disclosure of how each of them would best rule the country if it took power. Political competition must be limited to peaceful means and good interaction. Under no circumstances should such competition involve the use of physical violence or treacherous activities or abuse (or use) of power for the achievement of political victory or gain over other associations.

Sections 4 and 5 deal with the conditions for the formation of associations. Under section 4, every 100 citizens qualified to vote in general elections are entitled to form an association.

Further, every citizen is entitled to join an association, provided that he is not at the same time taking part in the formation of another association or in the leadership of more than one association if he has been politically disqualified according to law.[3] Every association must have a constitution which has been drawn up in conformity with the state Constitution and the law.[4]

Specifically, the constitution of an association must contain the following:

(a) the name of the association, provided that it is not the same as another registered association;
(b) indication of the location of the association's headquarters in the Sudan;
(c) conditions of membership, procedure for joining associations and removal of a member from it, or unilateral withdrawal from membership;
(d) the procedure for formation of association and its structure; and
(e) the principles (or objectives) and policies of the association and ways of carrying out its work in conformity with the provisions of section 3(2) and (3).

The application of a group of citizens for registration of a special association follows a specific procedure. There are also special conditions which must be fulfilled before the procurement of registration,[5] namely:

(a) presentation of application for registration. An application must be presented to the Registrar;
(b) attachment of the constitution of the proposed association; and
(c) attachment of a declaratory document accepting that the association will be bound by the provisions of the state Constitution and the law.

The Registrar is an appointee of the President of the Republic and his appointment must be confirmed by the National Assembly. The Registrar is a powerful man on whom the registration and continued survival of any political association depends entirely. His qualifications for appointment are his personal integrity and sufficient experience.

---

[3] S. 5, *ibid.*
[4] S. 6, *ibid.*
[5] S. 9, *ibid.*

Upon receiving the application for formation and registration of an association, the Registrar will proceed to announce it publicly. He will begin to make its examination or investigation in order to ascertain whether it is made in accordance with the provisions of Articles 3, 4, 5 and 6 of the Act. The Registrar must also investigate the persons (or founding members) who present the application with the constitution of the association. The Registrar will also receive and make decisions on any objections raised by others against the registration of the association.[6]

When the Registrar, after the completion of his investigation, concludes that the application satisfies all the conditions required by the state Constitution and the law, he makes a decision to register the association and issues a certificate to this effect. However, if he believes that the application does not satisfy the required conditions, he must reject the application.

The Registrar will give another opportunity for the applicant to comply with the required conditions within a period of two weeks. At the end of one month, commencing from the date the application for registration was presented to him, the Registrar must make a decision and inform the applicants of that decision. He will then publish his decision publicly, together with the reasons for the association's admission or rejection in a newspaper two weeks after its announcement, and if no objection is submitted against it to the Constitutional Court in accordance with the provision of section 18 of this Act.

1.1.2 Objection against application for registration

Any citizen is entitled to object to the registration of an association, provided that he submits his application to the Registrar within two weeks from the date of publication of the application.[7] The Registrar must communicate the contents of the objection to the applicants so that they are able to prepare and submit their defence against the objection within a further two-week period and thereafter, the Registrar will make his decision on the objection.

1.1.3 Conditions of leadership in associations

The law protects associations from the participation of convicted persons. However, there is no absolute or definitive preclusion of such persons from taking part in the leadership of a political association. It is a temporary exclusion or disqualification until the lapse of the period of conviction.

Section 11 of the Act provides that any person in the leadership of an association must not have been convicted of misappropriation of funds, causing violence in public political relations, using force against the Constitution, or of any crime affecting his honour or trust. No leadership post, whether at a national or state level, may be held by a person convicted of the above-mentioned crimes or offences un-

---

[6] Art. 10, *ibid.*
[7] S. 10, *ibid.*

less seven years have passed from the date of his conviction or unless he has been granted an amnesty by the President of the Republic.

1.1.4 Sources of funds and control of associations

The Act under review implicitly prohibits political associations from acquiring funds for their political activities from abroad.

The most likely fear of law makers is that such an acquisition of funds from abroad may lead to an unfair political advantage, as some associations may have no link or relations with foreign donors. However, it seems that the greatest fear is that any government formed by a political association where funds come from abroad is likely to be influenced by foreign institutions or persons, which might jeopardize national interests. Hence under the provisions of section 12 of the Act, funds of any association must be obtained only within the Sudan and in accordance with the law.

Although the law prescribes that the funds of an association must be locally obtained, it is very doubtful that all the political associations depend only on their local sources. Clandestine arrangements for acquisition of funds abroad may be adopted by any political party.

Section 12 also provides that an association must deposit its funds in any bank in the Sudan and keep its accounts properly. The deposit of association funds in a bank in the Sudan enables the Registrar to monitor them more easily and effectively.

The provisions of the Act vest extensive power in the Registrar in his control of political associations in nearly every aspect of their activity. For example, wherever he thinks fit, he may make a revision to the basic principles of the constitution of an association, the position of the leadership of that association, its accounts, income and expenditure. He may also inspect the documents of associations.[8] More of these extensive powers have already been surveyed in the earlier provisions of the Act.

Punitive measures may be brought against an association where the Registrar has requested it to submit to him a report related to the fulfilment of all its obligations or its conformity with the provisions of this Act, but it fails to respond within fourteen days. The penalty leads to the suspension of the functions of the association. The Registrar must inform the leadership of the association of such suspension. Further, the Registrar has power to declare a dissolution of a political association where the majority of its leadership are severally or jointly convicted of an offence under section 11 of the Act. Of course, a fairer alternative could be the removal of the disqualified political leaders, while the association continues to exist and to be run by members who are qualified.

Where the Registrar has declared a dissolution of an association or suspension of its functions, its accounts and activities are frozen.[9]

The decision of the Registrar remains binding unless it has been quashed by a decision of the Constitutional Court after an objection has been presented to it within

---

[8] S. 15, Organization of *Tawaaly El Siyyasia* (Political Associations) Act 1998.
[9] S. 16, *ibid.*

14 days from the date it was taken.[10] The assets of the association must be confiscated if the decision of the Registrar remains binding.

1.1.5 *Annual Report*

Each political association is required to prepare in detail and publish annual reports and deposit a copy with the Registrar with regard to:

(a)   any amendment of its constitution;
(b)   the names of its leaders who hold senior posts at national and state level; and
(c)   its total income and expenditure at national and state level.[11]

Any citizen is entitled[12] to submit his objection to the Registrar against the choice of any political leader, or the correctness of any statement published in the report (in compliance with the provisions of section 13), or the functions of the administrative unit of the association, management of finance or political activities which violate the Constitution and the law.

In conclusion it should be noted that there may be some justification for conferring a right on any citizen to object to the choice of any other citizen in the leadership post of an association. However, it must also be stated that the conferment of this right conflicts with the rights of others. First, any citizen has a right to be appointed to the leadership post of an association. Second, other citizens have a right to appoint a person of their own choice to any leadership post of an association after they are satisfied that he has no legal disqualification. There is also a possibility that the leaders of one political association may incite a citizen to submit an objection against the choice of any person they fear politically in a rival political association.

Further, the independence and survival of a political association appears to be very uncertain where extensive authority is vested on the judgment of one person. Although there is a right to appeal to the court against the decision of the Registrar, experience shows that many cases for constitutional or administrative review are often dismissed in the preliminary stages because of the existence of numerous and complex procedural requirements to be fulfilled by the applicants before the courts approach the merits of those cases.

1.2 Public Grievances and Correction Board Act 1998

Article 130(1) of the Constitution of the Republic of the Sudan, 1998 authorizes the creation of a body to be called the Public Grievances and Correction Board. This is an independent body whose chairman and members are appointed by the President of the Republic with the approval of the National Assembly among the persons of efficiency and propriety. The board is responsible to the President and the

---

[10] S. 18, *ibid.*
[11] S. 13, *ibid.*
[12] S. 14, *ibid.*

National Assembly. The state law, if any, establishes a state Public Grievances and Correction Board, and the Governor takes the place of the President. On 14 December 1998, the National Assembly, in execution of the provisions of Article 130 of the Constitution, enacted an Act called the Public Grievances and Correction Board Act 1998. This Act repealed the previous laws, namely the Bureau (Board) of Public Control and Administrative Reforms and Evaluation Act, 1995, and the Bureau (Board) of Public Grievances Act 1996. Nevertheless, all regulations and decisions already made under these laws remain valid until they are revoked by the National Assembly.

1.2.1 Creation of the Board, its composition and vacancy of office

The Act provides under section 4 for the formation of a body called the Public Grievances and Correction board as "an independent institution, as prescribed under Article 130(1) of the Constitution", with its principal office in Khartoum. The Act also provides, as the Constitution prescribes, for the Board to be responsible to both the President of the Republic and the National Assembly.

The Board[13] consists of a Chairman and two members whose qualifications and appointment are the same as provided under Article 130(1) of the Constitution. Their tenure of office is five years from the date of appointment and this period is subject to renewal. The President of the Republic defines their conditions or terms of service.

The office of the chairman and members may fall vacant[14] in any one of the following ways:

(a) loss of capacity;
(b) acceptance of resignation by the President of the Republic; or
(c) removal by the President of the Republic on grounds of health, or conviction of an offence affecting reputation or honour by a court.

1.2.2 Jurisdiction and powers of the Board (ss. 7 and 8)

1.2.2.1 Jurisdiction
Section 7 of the Act deals with the jurisdiction of the Board. The objectives of the boards which are stipulated under Article 130(2) of the Constitution constitute the preamble of section 7 of the Act.

The provisions of sections 7 and 8 of the Act are the most important because they confer the administrative and legal control of the whole machinery of the government on the Board. In other words, its jurisdiction ranges from administrative to legal and non-legal matters. The Board may be viewed as the watchdog of the whole government machinery. However, although the chairman and the members of the

---

[13] S. 5, Public Grievances and Correction Board Act 1998.
[14] S. 6, *ibid.*

Board are vested with these wide-ranging legal and administrative powers, there is
no requirement in the conditions of their appointment that they must possess sufficient qualifications and experience in law or any other specified subject. Section 7
provides:

Without prejudice to the jurisdiction of the judiciary, the Board shall work at the federal
level to remove obvious grievances, ensure efficiency and purity in the practice of the state
and in systems or the final executive or administrative acts, and also to extend justice after
the final decisions of the institutions of justice[15] and without prejudice to the generality of
what has been abovementioned, the Board in cooperation with various state organs
determines and makes decisions on matters stated hereunder. It must:

(a)   settle public grievances related to state organs;
(b)   remove obvious detriments arising out of final judicial decisions or excesses of these
       decisions without prejudice to their finality;
(c)   find a solution to detriments arising out of abuses of power or corruption
       committed by the state organs, provided that the complainant has exhausted all
       administrative remedies available to him;
(d)   solve hardships resulting from acts of governors, ministers, and holders of leadership
       posts in the state other than judges;
(e)   consider any law whose application provides obvious injustice and thereafter makes
       a submission to the concerned authorities to undertake remedial action. The
       concerned authorities include the Attorney-General, the Council of Ministers, the
       President of the Republic and the National Assembly;
(f)   settle any other public grievances arising out of acts of state organs as a result of
       obvious injustice which remains unsettled;
(g)   ascertain that state organs work with sufficient ability, efficiency and purity in a way
       which conforms with the general state policy;
(h)   inspect performances of the state organs in a way which facilitates scientific
       evaluation and exposes aspects of failure and achievements or success;
(i)   ascertain the usage of available material and human resources by the state organs;
(j)   ascertain effective and just application of laws and regulations which govern and
       organise administrative activity and the relations of the employees within the state
       organs;
(k)   conduct administrative investigations in respect to any form of failure and loopholes
       which it discovers during the exercise of its supervisory functions;
(l)   dispose of any public complaints submitted to it by individuals against regulations in
       the performance of any federal organ;
(m)   consider any other duty assigned to it by the President or National Assembly.

1.2.2.2 Powers of the Board
In the execution of its jurisdiction prescribed under section 7, the Board exercises
the following powers:[16]

---

[15] Under the Constitution of the Republic of the Sudan, the judiciary is classified as one of the
    institutions of justice in Part V, Chapters I and II of the Constitution. It follows from this
    preamble that this organ of the executive has power to review final decisions of the Supreme
    Court. Of course, its predecessor had power to review final decisions of the Supreme Court (ref.
    Constitutional Decree No. 13 of 1996).
[16] S. 8, Public Grievances and Correction Board Act 1998.

(a)   request for any information and documents which are relevant to the problem referred to it by any other state organ;

(b)   summoning any person whose appearance before it is deemed necessary for questioning in the resolution of the pending problem;

(c)   directing the taking of any necessary corrective measures for all forms of failure or loophole exposed during the exercise of supervisory role or activities;

(d)   directing estate organs to adopt necessary and practical administrative guiding principles (*tadabiir*);

(e)   preparation of the Board's budget and its submission to the President. It is not shown whether the President is required to present this budget to the National Assembly for a decision and approval.

The Board makes its reports and recommendation and submits these to the President of the Republic or National Assembly or other relevant state organ.

To summarize, the board plays the role of an overseer or controller of all the executive organs and justice institutions of the state. Its responsibility is not limited to the enforcement of efficiency, and the execution of state policies and plans but it must also ensure high standards in the practice of public responsibilities in the state. Implicitly, the executive or administrative functions of the state organs must imperatively reflect or conform with religious virtues or values. Promotion of religious virtues or purity finds authority in the Constitution. For example, Article 4 of the Constitution bestows the *hikimia* (governance) in the state on Allah (God). Under this article, state sovereignty which is vested in the people of the Sudan is practised as worship of Allah. Provisions of Articles 16 and 18 of the Constitution entrench the purity of the state. Public officials must be dedicated to religious worship of God and this must be reflected in the discharge of state functions and private life of every individual in society.

The objectives of the Act under survey therefore, are aimed at the implementation of Articles 4, 16 and 18 of the Constitution. Decisions of the Board on administrative irregularities or injustice or failures in the discharge of public responsibilities which it has discovered during its supervisory role, must be executed by the concerned organs or administrative authorities. However, wherever there is any disobedience, or neglect of the Board's decisions, the concerned authorities must directly be reported to the President of the Republic who is entitled to take any necessary action to ensure the execution of the Board decision. Under section 14, refusal or neglect of the decision of the Board without any reasonable ground by any body constitutes an offence which may invite penalty under any other law.

It should also be mentioned that the Board is the most powerful administrative and judicial organ of the state. Its decisions are final and eligible for immediate execution.[17] The finality of its decisions, together with its power to review final decisions of the justice institutions leads to the belief by many persons that the power of judicial review has been precluded by Article 10 because justice institutions include the courts. Nevertheless the Supreme Court contends that its inherent power of judicial review still survives the promulgation of the provisions of section 10.

---

[17] S. 10, *ibid.*

1.2.3 Employees Justice Chamber

Article 127(2) of the Constitution authorizes the establishment by federal legislation or state law an organ called the Employees Justice Chamber. This organ has competence to determine the grievances of public service employees. The appointment of the president of the Chamber must be made by the President of the Republic who supervises him. In the state, the appointment and supervision of the president of the Chamber must be carried out by the state governor. The decisions of the Chamber are final and are not reviewed by courts.[18]

The Sudanese courts have always held that statutory provisions which prescribe the finality of the decisions of certain executive organs or authorities merely preclude appellate jurisdiction but do not extend to the preclusion of the inherent power of judicial review. The English version of Article 127(2) of the Constitution appears to show that what has been precluded is the "review" jurisdiction of the court. However, the Arabic version, which is the original, uses the word *nazar* which means "seen" but not "review" or "revision".

2 PRESS AND PUBLICATIONS

2.1 Press and Publication Act 1996

The Press and Publication Act of 1996 repealed the Press Act of 1993. Both Acts were enacted at short intervals by the same government and there are currently preparations to make another Act to replace the existing one. It is probable that the new Act will come into existence before the end of 1999.

It is not the objective of this survey to consider whether the provisions of this Act guarantee freedom of the press or not. It is up to the reader to draw his own conclusions. The objective is to analyse the most important provisions of the Act.

2.2 The National Council for Press and Publications

As will be discussed regarding the provisions of the Act, the National Council for Press and Publications is a very powerful institution. It has been vested with all the powers for the regulation and control of the press and publications. For example, the members of this institution have the power to frame or formulate press and publication policies. Second, it has power to grant licences for press and publication. Third, it authorizes the registration of journalists and, finally, it has the power to play a supervisory role over press and publications. It determines whether the journalists conform with a standard of journalism and the law in their writing. More of these powers are embodied in various sections of the Act.

The President of the Republic who appoints some council members is the patron of the Council. The composition of the Council is constituted under section 8(1) as follows:

---

[18] Art. 127(2), state Constitution.

(a) seven members appointed by the President of the Republic from the persons of high integrity upon a recommendation made by the Minister of Culture and Information. One of them becomes the Secretary General of the Council;[19]

(b) two members representing owners of printing presses who are elected by the Chamber of Printers in the Union of Businessmen;

(c) seven members representing journalists and who are elected by the General Assembly of the General Union of the journalists; and

(d) five members representing the National Assembly who are elected from its members.

The President of the Council represents the law[20] and he supervises the Council's meetings. The Secretary General on the other hand is vested with the administrative authority of the Council. He executes the Council's decisions.[21]

2.3 The Jurisdiction of the Council (s. 5)

The jurisdiction of the Council covers the following powers:

(a) the framing of general policies for the regulation of the press and publications which must conform with social values, objectives and the general strategies of the state. It seems probable that these are the ones now reflected in the present Constitution. Moreover, the press and the Constitution policies and objectives lie at the root of the current trend of thought in the Sudan;

(b) promotion of the standard of journalism;

(c) supervision of the public performance of the press corporation, companies, and the role of the printing, publication and centres of press services; and

(d) supervision of the organization and development of publication work.

2.4 Powers of the National Council (s. 6)

The National Council has been vested with the following powers under section 6 of the Act:

(a) granting of press companies and corporations and the role of printing publication, press services and government news agencies;

(b) registration of journalists, the setting of professional examinations and the issuing of certificates to those who practise journalism; and

(c) ascertainment of conformity with principles prescribed under this law by the press corporations and companies. The Council requests these corporations

---

[19] The Secretary, who is the President's appointee, is the most powerful member of the Council, since he is vested with all executive powers and the execution of Council decisions.

[20] S. 10 of the Press and Publications Act (1996).

[21] S. 11 *ibid.*

and companies to submit reports of their general performance, especially in relation to the meetings of its administrative councils, their budgets and audited accounts.

The National Council under this Act is not only entitled to know the activities of the press institutions, but also their budgets and accounts;

Further, since the President of the Republic is the Patron of the National Council, and is also the head of the state and the government, it follows that the National Council is the eye of the government which must ensure the conformity of the press institutions with the principles embodied in the provisions of the Press Act, 1996. It means that the government is indirectly (through the National Council) entitled to know the performances, accounts and expenditures of all press institutions;

(d) The offering of the necessary assistance for the facilitation of the work and activities of the press companies;

(e) the formation of any specialized branches and the organization of their work;

(f) authentication of the offices and new agencies of the foreign press and the registration of foreign correspondents who are resident in Sudan without prejudice to the jurisdiction of the Ministry of Culture and Information in exercise of its general supervision;

(g) settlement of complaints and problems submitted to it by persons from a publication of injurious falsehood, by the press, against them;

(h) participation in the settlement of the disputes between the press organization but without prejudice to the provisions of the Constitution of the General Union of Journalists;

(i) imposition of penalties prescribed under this Act.

The Council may delegate its powers, for example power to grant licences for small publication press services centres in any state, whenever necessary to any authority concerned in the state or state assembly.

2.5 Restrictions on the right to press ownership

Every Sudanese citizen is entitled, under Article 18 of the Act, to acquire ownership of press and publications anywhere in the Sudan. Right of ownership of press and publications is not restricted to natural persons alone, but it extends to entities such as companies which are registered under the Companies Act 1925. However, monopoly of press and publications companies for the interests of certain individuals, families, tribes or religious sects or any other body which works for its private interests is prohibited. These named bodies may own shares in press and publication companies, but they must not be allowed to own shares exceeding 20 per cent in each company. Any social institution, international corporation or government unit is entitled to press ownership or ownership of other publications related to the development of the international activities of that body or corporation or government unit provided that a highly qualified editor-in-chief holds responsibility for publications.

It is obvious from this legal provision that the influence of religious sects, such as the *Ansaar* (the followers of Mohammed Ahmed El Madhi) and the *Khatimiyya* (the other major religious sects) or the families of El Madhi or Mirghani, over the press and publications is seriously limited.

Complete ownership of a press company is denied to these bodies but each of them has a limited number of shares in the press company. This limitation of shares is aimed at reducing or eliminating the influence and control of these bodies in the determination of the nature of material for publication in the press.

2.6 Press and publication licences and conditions for the granting of them

The provisions of section 19 of the Act confer on the National Council the power to grant licences for the press and publications. No newspapers or publications must be established and work before it has been licensed by the Council. The granting of licences requires the fulfilment of specific conditions which are:

(a) The establishment of a newspaper or publication or information communi-cation must be the basic objective of the body or company seeking to obtain a licence. It follows that no licence shall be granted where the main objective or the function of this body is something else.
(b) The company (or body) must deposit an amount of money fixed by the Na-tional Council in the regulations for the development of press work. The com-pany must make an undertaking that it will not use or withdraw the deposited amount for different purposes.
(c) the press company must contract with sufficient number of well-qualified and experienced journalists to carry out the profession of journalism.

2.7 Registration of journalists and conditions for appointment of editor-in-chief

Before a person becomes a journalist, he must apply to the National Council to be registered as a such. He must be a person who has obtained qualification above the level of general education.[22] An editor-in-chief must also:

(a) be a Sudanese of not less than 35 years of age;
(b) have practised the work of journalism for a period not less than ten years;
(c) be a university graduate;
(d) have been released (if he is a working person) to carry out the work of jour-nalism.

The National Council may exempt a candidate for the post of editor-in-chief from the conditions which require him to be a university graduate with experience if such a candidate has other distinguished type of qualifications and experience. These provisions gives wide discretion to the National Council to determine persons who must be required to fulfil certain legal conditions. Of course, the possibility of abuse of this discretionary power in favour of some candidates seems to be rampant.

---

[22] S. 21, *ibid*.

2.8 Rights of journalists

The rights of journalists are provided for under section 22 of the Act under review. These rights are related to the protection of journalists against undue pressures and intimidation that may result in the disclosure of their sources of information. However, the claims of these provisions have not yet been properly tested in courts.

Section 22 enumerates these rights and duties of other bodies as follows:

(a) A journalist enjoys the following rights:
    (i)   no journalist should be subjected to any undue or unlawful pressure for the purpose of influencing his fairness or his commitment to his professional duties;
    (ii) a journalist has a right to the protection of his sources of information;
    (iii) he is not responsible for the comments or opinion he makes or expresses on the material he has obtained except in accordance with the law;
    (iv) he cannot be arrested in respect of a charge which relates to his practice of the profession of journalism except after the notification of the journalists' General Union.
(b) Any public official and every person who is in possession of some information related to the state and society is under duty to communicate it to a special journalist and the public unless the law or regulation prohibits its publication.
(c) The National Council takes appropriate measures to guarantee the rights and privileges of the journalists.

Of course, the protection of the rights of journalists becomes realistic if these provisions are strictly observed by the concerned authorities.

2.9 Duties of a journalist

Section 23 of the Act describes the duties of a journalist. Some of these duties are negative because they constitute limitations of rights or public functions. Under these provisions:

(a) A journalist must be fair, honest and committed to the ethics of his profession.
(b) He must not publish any material which is confidential or related to the security of the state or military affairs.
(c) Where he is making a report which is related to a crime or some civil irregularity, he must not exaggerate it.
(d) A journalist must not make comments on any investigation or judicial proceeding unless a final decision has been made thereon.
(e) He is prohibited from making any publication which conflicts with a religious information. Further, he must not publish harmful or destructive rumours. A provision of this nature, though it has its own merits, is liable to be misused to curb the freedom of journalists.
(f) A journalist is not allowed to publish any material which may be deemed to undermine the morals of society. However, it is not shown who will be the judge for what may be deemed to be a violation of the general ethics of soci-

ety. It is however, more probable that the government may be the guardian or the protector of the ethics of society.

(g)   He must conform with the general professional standards and regulations of good conduct contained in the charter of the General Union of Journalists.

All these duties of a journalist also apply to every person who deals or takes part in printing publications and distribution of any published material.

While journalists are entitled to inform the public through their publication of news, there is also a great fear that if they have an unlimited right to publish any material or information, individuals' reputations may suffer from injurious false-hoods. Hence the Act embodies section 24 of the protection of people against injurious publications or circulation of injurious material.

First, where an individual claims that he has been injured by published material or comments in a newspaper or any publication, the editor must upon request of that person publish a correction or comment on the same subject and in the same paper in which he printed the injurious material or comment.

Second, the correction must be published within three days from this date of the receipt of the complaint in the case of a daily newspaper, or in the first volume after the receipt of the complaint, in the case of a weekly, monthly or quarterly newspaper.

However, there is a limitation period for the publication of correction of injurious material or comment. No correction can be published more than sixty days after the publication of injurious material or comment. The presumption is that the injured person must receive the notice of such publication within a period of sixty days from the date it was made. Further, no publication of the correction can be made where the editor has already published the correction before the complaint was submitted. The journalist must refrain from making such correction where it adversely affects or injures another person or where it is likely to be a sort of propaganda or commercial notice or advertisement or where the contents of the correction would amount to a violation of law.

2.10 Duties of a publisher

The publisher of a newspaper or other printed material is also burdened with a number of duties.[23] Some of these duties are aimed at the protection of rights or conditions of journalists working with the publisher.

Under these duties the publisher must set aside a specific amount out of income to be spent for the training of journalists. This amount must be fixed by the Council (i.e. National Council) to ensure the adequacy of that amount for training. To be more precise, this legal provision guarantees the training of journalists by their employers. This training services public interest when more efficient and responsible journalists exercise their public duty to inform people.

---

[23] S. 25, *ibid.*

The second duty imposed on a publisher or publishing company is that the conditions of service of journalists whom it employs must be made in accordance with the standards prescribed by the Labour Act 1997.

Third, the publisher in his newspaper must write in block letters either on the first page or the last page the name of the contributor (writer of a given material) and printer, their addresses and date of publication. These particulars are essential for reference or the identification of the contributor of the published material and the date of publication. This information will be relevant in future if, for example, the published material injures the reputation of another person or where another person wishes to reply to that publication or printed material.

The fourth duty of a publisher is that he must supply the Secretary General of the National Council with a specified number of copies of every publication. The number of copies to be delivered to the Secretary-General is fixed by the National Council. This condition or publishers' duty enables the Secretary-General, the National Council and ultimately the government to monitor the nature of information published.

Finally, the publisher must make financial statements related to its accounts to be audited by the Auditor General. There appear to be three objectives for which this duty was imposed on the publishers. In the first place, it may reassure the shareholders that their money in the company is not lost when the accounts are regularly audited by the Auditor-General with a statement of accounts made thereafter. Second, the rights of a company's employees, such as the journalists, are protected where the accounts are regularly audited. This may ensure that their salaries will not be curtailed through the liquidation of the company due to becoming insolvent as a result of misappropriation or lack of accountability or mismanagement of funds. Third, it provides the National Council and ultimately the government, with full knowledge of the company's funds and accounts. Section 26(1) imposes a duty on owners of printing presses and centres of press services to obtain licences before they start their work. These licenses are subject to renewal annually upon the payment of fees.[24] Finally, section 28(1) referred to above imperatively requires anybody to obtain a licence before he or it imports any foreign printing press. Further, anybody who imports printed foreign materials is under an obligation to deposit a fixed number of copies with the Secretary General.[25] The number of copies is determined by the National Council.

2.11 Penalties (section 29)

The Act prescribed penalties against the violators of its provisions. The duty is conferred on the Chief Justice to set up a court which must try the offences under the Press Act.[26] Notwithstanding the generality of the provisions of clause 1 of this section, the Press Court must try offences under sections 19(1), 26(1) and 28(1).

---

[24] S. 26(2), *ibid.*
[25] S. 28(2), *ibid.*
[26] S. 29(1), *ibid.*

Where the court passes conviction under any of these sections, it may impose a sentence of a fine which does not exceed a sum of D250,000. However, where the accused repeats the same offence, the court is entitled to order, in addition to a fine, confiscation of the printing machines subject of the offence. The court is also entitled to withdraw the licence of any printing press which has been suspended twice according to the provisions of section 30(2)(b) of the Act and the matter shall be referred to the court according to the provisions of section 30(5).

Any party who feels aggrieved by the conviction, sentence and orders passed under the provisions of section 19 is entitled to appeal to a concerned appellate court within thirty days from the date he obtained notice of the court decision. Cases related to press and publication offences are deemed to be urgent matters and must be summarily tried.

2.12 Penalties imposed by the National Council

Apart from penalties which are imposed by the court, the National Council also has power under section 30 to pass certain types of penalties under section 29.[27] These penalties are specified under section 30. The National Council has power to try an offence where the law has not conferred jurisdiction on the court under section 29.

The National Council may impose the following sentences:

(a) warning or reprimand;
(b) suspension of the work of printing for a period not exceeding two months; or
(c) suspension or cancellation of the licence of the printing press or centre of press services where any one of the conditions for granting a licence has been contravened.

The National Council must hear the defence of the accused before it passes any penalty under section 30 and is also obliged to inform the accused of any provision of the Act which it believes has been contravened by the publication.

Where the work of the printing press has been suspended twice before in accordance with provisions of clause 2(b) of section 30, the National Council shall, under section 24(5), refer the third violation to the court to try the offence under the provision of section 29(3). The National Council is entitled to delegate its powers under section 30 to any of its concerned committees.

2.13 Power to make regulations

The National Council is entitled to make its internal regulations for the organization of its work and the execution of the provisions of this Act.[28] In this respect, it may pass regulation on the following matters:

---

[27] S. 30(1), *ibid.*
[28] S. 31, *ibid.*

(a)   conditions for the granting of licences, their renewal and their surrender;
(b)   organization of the Council's business and the business of its specialized committees;
(c)   conditions for the practice of journalism;
(d)   procedure of penalties;
(e)   conditions of the employees of the Secretary-General; and
(f)   monetary procedures.

2.14 Application of the law

The provisions of this Act cover the proceedings of the repealed Act which remain incomplete at the time this Act came into force. Further, its provisions also apply to proceedings which had been completed prior to its coming into force but only for the purpose of correction.

3 LOCAL GOVERNMENT

3.1 Local Government Act 1998

Under Article 2 of the Constitution of the Republic of the Sudan, the Supreme Authority of the government is divided into three departments, namely (a) central government, (b) states' governments, and (c) local government. On 5 December 1998, the Sudanese Legislature passed an Act entitled the Local Government Act 1998. This Act constitutes the implementation of the provisions of Article 2 of the Constitution which states that the Supreme Authority of the government will be administered at the base by local government in accordance with the law. The Act repealed previous laws, namely:

(a)   Native Administration Act 1990;
(b)   People's Committee's Act 1992; and
(c)   Local Government Act, 1995.

3.2 Organs of local government

There are seven organs of local government and these are (a) commissionership, (b) security sommittee(s), *mahaliat* or counties (tiers), (c) council, (d) people's administration, (e) native administration, and (f) local government chamber. These bodies are assigned various responsibilities.

3.2.1 Commissionership (ss. 4–6)

The Constitution provides for a federal state in the Sudan.[29] The government is divided into central government, with its headquarters in Khartoum, and state

---

[29] Art. 2, Local Government Act 1998.

governments. The country is divided into twenty-six states and each state has legally defined boundaries. Further, each state has been divided into a specific number of provinces or commissionerships with legally defined boundaries.

3.2.1.1 Creation of commissionership (Art. 4)
The commissionership is created when the President of the Republic issues a Presidential Order or decree after his consultation with the state government and the state assembly. The creation of commissionership is based on the following standards or requirements:

(a) sufficient number of people in the *Mahaliat* or counties;
(b) sufficient political consciousness and security; and
(c) the boundaries of a commissionership must be based on social groupings and economic interests.

The income of a commissionership is part of the state budget.

3.2.1.2 Appointment of a commissioner (Art. 5)
There must be in every commissionership a commissioner who is appointed by the President of the Republic in consultation with the state governor, provided that the person appointed must be of sound mind and high integrity and familiar with the conditions of the area. The state law must regulate the administrative structure of the commissionership. Furthermore, the federal law regulates emoluments and privileges of the commissioner.

3.2.1.3 Jurisdiction and powers of the commissioner (s. 6)
The commissioner's responsibilities are general in nature; however, routine administration is the responsibility of the ordinary government officials. Section 6 of the Act provides for the jurisdiction and powers of the commissioner as follows:

(a) chairing the meetings of the security committee of the commissionership;
(b) general mobilization of the people and the heading of people's collective development work;
(c) supervision of native administration of the commissionership;
(d) submission of reports of general conduct of work in the commissionership; and
(e) any powers assigned to him by the state or federal government.

3.2.2 Security committee (Art. 7)

The security power in the commissionership is vested in a security committee. This committee, in its exercise of this power, is entitled to take any necessary legal action. The committee submits its recommendation to the State Security Committee. However, section 7 of the Act, which confers security power on the security committee, is silent about its composition. The practice, however, is that it is the commissioner who is always the chairman of this committee with the membership of the commanders of the organized forces and a legal counsel.

3.2.3 Mahaliat *(counties) (Arts. 8–10)*

The state government is entitled to create *mahaliat* or counties by means of warrants of establishment. The state assembly must confirm the creation of a county,[30] which requires the existence of certain criteria, namely:

(a) sufficient population in the area; and
(b) people's homogeneous cultures, social values and economic prosperity;
(c) adequate security and availability of suitable administrative resources for development and the rendering of services to the people.

Every county is an entity which is entitled to sue and be sued. The geographical boundaries, the number of its council's members, its jurisdiction and powers are prescribed by state law through a warrant of its establishment that must conform with concurrent powers (of the federal and states) and the state powers which are provided in the Constitution.[31]

3.2.4 *Council (Art. 11)*

Every county must have a council whose members are elected as follows:

(a) 75 per cent through direct general election from the geographical constituencies; and
(b) 25 per cent through direct or indirect election to represent women, students, and members of pensionable professions.

The tenure of office is four years from the date of election, but the state government may at anytime dissolve the council after approval by a majority of the state assembly, provided that the declaration for the dissolution of the council contains a decision for the formation of an interim body to discharge the functions of the council. The elections of the new council members must be conducted within sixty days after the dissolution of the outgoing council.[32] The warrant of establishment specifies the council's sessions.[33]

The council must have a chairman who is elected by members among themselves during its first meeting after the general election.[34] The chairman of the council presides over its meetings, signs the minutes of its meetings and makes a timetable of such meetings after consultation with the director of the council.[35] The chairman leads the council's social and political functions as well as anything else delegated by the council to him. He officially represents the county during religious or national occassions.[36]

---

[30] Art. 8, *ibid.*
[31] Art. 10, *ibid.*
[32] Art. 11(3), *ibid.*
[33] Art. 12, *ibid.*
[34] Art. 30(1), *ibid.*
[35] Art. 13(2), *ibid.*
[36] Art. 13(3), *ibid.*

The council must set up a number of specialized committees in accordance with state law (if any) and these must include a committee for the council's affairs.[37] The council's affairs committee must be headed by the chairman of the council and all the heads of the other specialized committees shall be members of this committee while the director is its secretary.[38] The committee for the council's affairs discharges the functions of the council and prepares (or drafts) the county's laws. It presents its decisions to the council in its first meeting. Chairmanship of each of the other specialized committees is determined through election by the committee's members among themselves. Its secretary must be one of the members of the executive organ who has been chosen by the director.[39]

The council's jurisdiction includes:[40]

(a) the making of the county's laws as prescribed under the warrant of establishment and in any other law;
(b) the passing of the county's budgets;
(c) supervision of the performance or functions of the executive organs of the county; and
(d) the making of recommendations to the state government to form people's administrative bodies whose functions it must supervise.

The council also gives approvals for proposals of the budgets of people's administrative bodies (committees). The council lays down any general political plans of the county. It has power to exercise other functions referred or delegated to it by law.[41]

Article 16 of the Act creates an executive organ which is headed by a director (formerly known as the executive officer) who is assisted by heads of departments.[42] The director is appointed by state government from the professional administrators, in the state or at federal level. The government also appoints a number of professional administrators to head the departments in the county. By virtue of his authority, he becomes the council's secretary and also the finance secretary.

The county makes its own charts or segment of posts with the approval of the state government. The county is entitled to fill vacant posts in the chart through direct appointment or secondment from different state organs in conformity with the Public Service Law. All the employees of the county are responsible in their performances to the director.

The council's members – members of the executive organ and heads of native administration in the county, together with their residences and assets – enjoy legal protection. No criminal proceedings (except in cases of *hudud*) can be taken against them unless after the notification of the chairman of the council or the commissioner in certain circumstances.

The law guarantees the council members' freedom of thought or opinion during the council's meetings or council's committee's meetings. The state law prescribes

---

[37] Art. 14(1), *ibid.*
[38] Art. 14(2), *ibid.*
[39] Art. 14(4), *ibid.*
[40] Art. 15, *ibid.*
[41] Art. 15, *ibid.*
[42] Art. 16(1), *ibid.*

the renumerations and privileges of the council's leaders and members as well as the leaders of native administration.[43]

Article 18 confers power on the council to make laws for the county within the sphere of its jurisdiction. The council must report this immediately to the state government and deposit copies of the law in the state assembly.

The local law comes into force on the date of its enactment by the council and its signature by the chairman. The state government may order its cancellation or within thirty days from the date it obtained notice of the enacted law, or order its return to the council for amendment. The state assembly may, within thirty days from the date of the deposit of the county's laws, quash or amend them.[44] It seems that if thirty days pass before the state government or state assembly quash or annul the county's laws they can no longer do so.

3.2.5 *People's administration*

There must be a people's administration in every residential quarter, village or tribal area.[45] This body is created by means of a warrant of establishment issued by the state government in accordance with a recommendation of the county. The members of the people's administration are directly elected by the citizens. This organ exercises powers delegated to it by the county's council or the executive organ.

3.2.6 *Native administration (ss. 20–22)*

The formation and organization of the native administration, its structure, qualification of its leadership, its jurisdiction, powers and the standards of its relations must conform with state law.[46] Selection of the leaders of the native administration is made through a process of election which is regulated by the rules of *shura* (consultation) and local customs in accordance with law.[47] The tenure of office of the leaders of the native administration is seven years from the date of their election and this period is subject to renewal.[48]

The system of native administration was established by the Condominium Government based on Millner's report on the experience of Nigeria (which was based on the recommendations of Lord Lugard, a British expert). Prior to the advent of the Condominium rule in Sudan, each community ruled itself through its own traditional leaders. The British officials found that it was a cheaper system to follow since it enabled one or two British officers to rule vast areas while the traditional leaders effectively controlled their people and administered their local affairs. It is a

---

[43] Art. 17, *ibid.*
[44] Art. 18, *ibid.*
[45] Art. 19(1–2), *ibid.*
[46] Art. 20, *ibid.*
[47] Art. 21, *ibid.*
[48] Art. 22, *ibid.*

system of indirect rule; the local people rule themselves through their own leaders to whom they owe more allegiance than the government officials.

During the early years of General M. Nimeriri's rule, the influence of left-wing elements in his government led to the abrogation of the system of Native Administration in the northern Sudan. However, the system continued to exist in Southern Sudan because the southern leaders objected to its liquidation. The traditional leaders in the northern Sudan, however, continued to pressure Nimeriri's government for the restoration of the system but to no avail. It was after the overthrow of Nimeriri's government in 1985 that the elected government restored the system of native administration and it has continued to survive. The major political parties, *Umma* and the National Democratic Party (NDP), restored the system because it was always the basis of their political power.

3.2.7 *Local government chamber*

The law creates an organ within section 23 of the Act known as the local government chamber, which falls under the supervision of the state government. The chamber executes local government policy through making contacts, training, conferences and cooperation between the people's and native administrations, in coordination with the state government and state institutions.

3.3 County's financial regulations (s. 25)

3.3.1 *Sources of finance*

The county's sources of income are many and include:

(a) taxes on immovable (assets) and sales;
(b) fees from local land and river transport;
(c) 60 per cent of income from agricultural and animal husbandry of which 40 per cent of this goes to the state treasury;
(d) 40 per cent of business tax in the state;
(e) income from local investment projects;
(f) local share from the county's development fund;
(g) any share from the profits of state projects in the county according to state law (if any);
(h) any share from the profits of federal government projects; and
(i) any other source of income in the county, according to federal law.

3.3.2 *County's development fund (s. 24)*

The law creates a fund known as the county's development fund with contributions from the state and county's budgets. The fund is managed by boards of trustees which fall under the supervision of the local government chamber. Allocations from this fund are distributed equitably and fairly for development and discharge of services in the county.

3.3.3 *Management of accounts*

The county must keep correct accounts of its income and expenditure according to proper and accepted standards in the state. The county must submit its reports to the state government that its accounts have been closed.[49]

The county's fiscal year begins on 1 January each year and ends on 31 December of the same year.

Accounts of the county are audited yearly by the Auditor General who submits his reports to the state government and assembly.[50]

---

[49] Art. 28, *ibid.*
[50] Art. 29, *ibid.*

Kuwait

*Fadi B. Nader**

1 INTRODUCTION

There have been few legislative developments in Kuwait over the last two years (1997–1998). However, most of the significant changes occurred in May 1999, which has witnessed the promulgation of an Emiri order granting Kuwaiti women full political rights. The Emiri order, which was approved by the Kuwaiti Cabinet, will amend the country's election law, allowing women to vote and run for public office as of the year 2003. The Emiri decree will be presented to the newly elected Parliament in July 1999, which is widely expected to ratify it as its rejection would require a vote of two-thirds of the members.

Another noticeable change took place in 1999 with the promulgation of an Emiri Decree of the Foreign Investment Law which would allow foreigners to own up to 100 per cent of companies in Kuwait, compared with a current restriction of a maximum of 49 per cent. A law decree approved by the Council of Ministers had also permitted non-Kuwaitis to own shares of Kuwaiti limited companies and to trade these shares on the Kuwaiti Stock Exchange. Both pieces of legislation are expected to be ratified by Kuwait's new Parliament.

Similarly, during 1999 the Ministry of Commerce issued a ministerial resolution organizing the setting up and operation of the Free Zone in Kuwait.

I will attempt in this survey to highlight the main provisions of the legislation on direct foreign capital investment in the state of Kuwait, the principal feature of the law permitting non-Kuwaitis to own shares in Kuwaiti joint stock companies and the regulations related to the free zone law.

---

* Legal Counsel, The International Investor.

2 LAW DECREE REGULATING THE DIRECT INVESTMENT OF FOREIGN CAPITAL IN THE STATE OF KUWAIT

2.1 Article 1: Definitions

Foreign capital investment means:

(a)   Money, financial and commercial papers transferred to Kuwait;
(b)   Machinery, equipment/plant, means of transportation, raw materials, and mer-
       chandise requirements imported from abroad for investment purposes;
(c)   Intellectual rights like patents, trade marks, licences and registered trade names;
(d)   Foreign capital gains/profit increasing foreign capital investment or employed
       to set up new investment operations/projects.

Foreign investor means a natural or judicial (corporate) person who does not hold
Kuwaiti nationality. Foreign investment means the employment of foreign capital
in an activity licensed or authorized pursuant to the provisions of this law. Project
means any economic activity/operation governed by this law. Investment committee means a foreign capital investment committee formed under the fifth article of
this law.

2.2 First section: foreign capital investment

2.2.1 *Article 2*

The Council of Ministers may determine the economic/business projects which foreign investors may engage in within the state of Kuwait independently or with national local capital contribution, in a manner consistent with the overall policy of the
government and its economic development plans.

2.2.2 *Article 3*

A licence authorizing a foreign investor to engage in an economic/business project
shall be issued by a resolution endorsed by the Minister of Commerce and Industry, upon a recommendation from the Investment Committee. However, clause 1
of Article 23 and Article 24 of Law No. 68/1980 (relating to Commercial Law)[1]
shall not apply to such a licence.

---

[1] Clause 1 of Art. 23 of Law No. 68/1980 related to Commercial Law prohibits a non-Kuwaiti
     from engaging in commerce or commercial activities unless he has one or more Kuwaiti
     partners, provided that the Kuwaiti capital in the joint business is not less than 51 per cent.
       Art. 24 prohibits foreign companies from setting up branches in Kuwait, or from engaging in
     any commercial activities unless such activities are carried out through a Kuwaiti agent.

2.2.3 *Article 4*

As an exception to Article 68 of the aforesaid Law No. 15/1960 (relating to Commercial Company Law),[2] by a resolution form the Minister of Commerce and Industry, and a recommendation from the Investment Committee, foreign holdings
in Kuwaiti operations may be as high as 100 per cent of the company capital, subject to the terms and conditions laid out by the Council of Ministers.

2.3 Section two: foreign capital investment committee

2.3.1 *Article 5*

A committee shall be formed, chaired by the Minister of Commerce and Industry,
named the Foreign Capital Investment Committee. Its formation, by-laws, duration and compensation of its members shall be determined by a resolution to be
passed by the Council of Ministers.

   The chairman of the Foreign Capital Investment Committee shall act as secretary-general of the committee. The Minister of Commerce and Industry shall issue
a resolution regulating the committee's activities.

2.3.2 *Article 6*

The Investment Committee will take charge of the following:

(a) review of investment requests/applications, and giving relevant recommen-
     dations;
(a) promoting investment opportunities/potentials available in the country, and
     embarking on initiatives aimed at attracting foreign investments;
(b) offering investment incentives to foreign investors pursuant to Article 12 of
     the law, by liaising with the appropriate authorities, and ensuring that the
     Kuwaiti private sector is offered adequate incentives;
(c) facilitating project licensing and registration procedures, and overcoming rel-
     evant obstacles encountered in setting up such projects.

---

[2] Article 68 of law 15/1960 on Commercial Company law provides that: "Any joint stock
     company incorporated in Kuwait is of Kuwaiti nationality, and all its shareholders should be
     Kuwaitis, and the Company's principal address should be in Kuwait.
        However, an exception can be made to allow non Kuwaiti to became shareholders, if there is
     a need for a foreign capital investment or for a foreign expertise provided that the Kuwaitis
     holding in the share capital is not less than 51 per cent of the Company's capital and provided
     that an authorization is duly obtained from the competent governmental authority." The law
     also sets the minimum Kuwaiti participation in banks and insurance companies at 60 per cent of
     these entities' capital. Furthermore, foreign participation in insurance companies is subject to
     the approval of the Ministry of Commerce and Industries, whereas foreign participation in
     banks has to be approved by the Central Bank of Kuwait.

(d)   developing a mechanism to monitor foreign investment performance, iden-
       tifying and overcoming any obstacles they may encounter;
(e)   looking at and settling complaints of foreign investors and other concerned
       persons, or any disputes arising between them in connection with the imple-
       mentation of this law, and passing its recommendation in this regard to the
       concerned authorities;
(f)   imposing penalties provided for in Article 14 of this law;
(g)   preparing draft by-laws/regulations required for the implementation of this law;
(h)   examining issues referred to from the Minister of Commerce and Industry rel-
       evant to the implementation of this law;
(i)   preparing an annual report on incoming foreign investment, and major ob-
       stacles encountered, and ways of dealing with the same, to be put before the
       Council of Ministers.

2.3.3 *Article 7*

An office named the "Foreign Capital Investment Office" shall be set up to act as the
technical and administrative body of the Investment Committee. It will be formed
and its by-laws/activities outlined by a resolution from the Minister of Commerce
and Industry.
    The Office will handle licence applications and processing through the concerned
authorities, carry out studies and put forward the required recommendations relevant to same, for submission to the Investment Committee.
    The Office will also handle all issues related to foreign capital investment, and
in particular:

(a)   advise the international market of projects offered for investment, and ad-
       vantages/benefits available for foreign capital investments in the State of
       Kuwait;
(b)   provide information, clarifications and statistics/figures as requested by the for-
       eign investors;
(c)   monitor implementation of licensed projects, and overcome obstacles en-
       countered;
(d)   liaise with the concerned authorities to facilitate the foreign investor's entry
       and residence in Kuwait, as well as his representatives and any person whose
       presence in Kuwait is needed by the foreign investor;
(e)   prepare regular statistical reports on foreign investment, and an annual re-
       port to be presented to the Investment Committee on the activities of li-
       censed projects, before submission to the Council of Ministers.

2.4 Section three: secured guarantees for foreign investments

2.4.1 *Article 8*

No foreign project/operation authorized under this law shall be transferred to the
government unless a compensation is paid equivalent to the market value thereof.

Rights and benefits accrued to foreign investment authorized under this law will be not be subject to or be exposed to any harm or damage.

2.4.2 *Article 9*

This law applies to existing investments by foreign capital to the extent that the objectives of this law are achieved and provided that the benefits, exemptions and guarantees granted to such investments under this law are no less than those provided before, subject to the foreign investor applying for benefits stipulated by this law to the Foreign Capital Investment Committee for consideration as set out in Article 6.

2.4.3 *Article 10*

(a) A foreign investor may assign his investment to another foreign or local investor, or to his local partner in case of partnership, subject to the relevant laws and regulations applicable in the state of Kuwait, and the licence terms.
(b) In the event that a foreign investment is transferred to another foreign investor, such investment shall continue to be governed by the provisions of this law.

2.4.4 *Article 11*

A foreign investor may repatriate his profit abroad, as well as compensation stipulated in Article 8 herein. Furthermore, non-Kuwaiti employees in such projects or other foreigners associated with the ventures may also repatriate their savings and dues.

2.5 Section four: benefits and obligations of foreign investments

2.5.1 *Article 12*

The Investment Committee may offer foreign investors all or some of the following benefits, to the extent to which the project contributes in the implementation of the economic development objectives of the state of Kuwait:

(a) income tax, any other tax or charge exemption for a maximum of ten years from the actual commencement of project operations, as well as exemption of any new investment in the project from taxes and charges for a period equal to that given to the original investment upon the commencement of the project;
(b) benefits provided under agreements preventing double taxation, and investment enhancement and protection agreements;
(c) whole or partial customs duty exemption for the following imports:
  (i) plant/machinery, equipment and spare parts required for construction, replacement, expansion and development;

(ii) raw materials, semi-finished products, packaging and other materials required for production purposes;

(d)   exemption from all or part of export or import restrictions;

(e)   allocation of land and property required for the project's objectives in line with the laws and regulations applicable in the state of Kuwait;

(f)   foreign manpower recruitment required for the project's objectives in line with the laws and regulations applicable in the state of Kuwait.

2.5.2 *Article 13*

A foreign investor shall:

(a)   give priority to national manpower, if available, and train them to acquire the necessary skills;

(b)   protect the environment from pollution;

(c)   observe public order and the public code of ethics.

2.6 Section five: penalties

2.6.1 *Article 14*

If a foreign investor violates the provisions of this law, the licence terms, or the laws and regulations in force in the state of Kuwait, the Investment Committee may impose on him one of the following penalties:

(a)   issuance of a caution notice;

(b)   issuance of a warning notice;

(c)   deprivation from part or all of benefits provided. However, a foreign investor rectifying his violation may request that such deprivation be reconsidered;

(d)   administrative suspension of project for a certain period of time;

(e)   licence cancellation and termination of the investment.

A foreign investor and other concerned persons may complain to the Council of Ministers about penalties set out in 3, 4 and 5 above within thirty days of notification of the penalty imposed. If the complaint is rejected, such decision must be in writing accounting for reasons of rejection.

After the expiry of sixty days from the date the complaint was submitted, the complaint will be deemed to be rejected.

2.7 Section six: final provisions

2.7.1 *Article 15*

Agreement may be made to refer any dispute arising between foreign investment operations and third parties to a local or international arbitration panel.

Third parties for the purposes of this article shall mean government authorities, natural persons, and public and private entities.

2.7.2 *Article 16*

Foreign investment under this law shall benefit from the confidentiality of information, equality and the safeguarding of investment initiatives, in accordance with the relevant applicable laws.

2.7.3 *Article 17*

Foreign investment shall be governed by the laws and regulations in effect in the state of Kuwait with respect to any matter not specifically provided for in, and to the extent consistent with, this law.

2.7.4 *Article 18*

The Minister of Commerce and Industry shall issue the laws and regulations required for the implementation of this law.

2.7.5 *Article 19*

All concerned ministers are required to implement this law decree as of the date of its publication in the Official Gazette. This law decree shall be presented to the National Assembly.

3 LAW DECREE AUTHORIZING NON-KUWAITIS TO OWN SHARES IN KUWAITI JOINT STOCK COMPANIES

3.1 Article 1

Non-Kuwaitis are authorized to own shares in joint stock companies which are existing at the time this law enters into effect or in such other companies incorporated hereafter.

Non-Kuwaitis may also participate in the incorporation of Kuwaiti joint stock companies in accordance with the provisions of this law.

3.2 Article 2

The Minister of Commerce and Industry shall, by a decision taken with the approval of the Council of Ministers, determine the restrictions related to the participation of non-Kuwaitis in Kuwaiti joint stock companies, as well as the maximum limit of such participation and the rights resulting from it.

3.3 Article 3

The rules related to trading, settlement and clearance as in force on the Kuwaiti Stock Exchange shall apply to shares held by non-Kuwaitis in listed Kuwaiti joint stock companies.

3.4 Article 4

The provisions of this law shall not affect the rights and benefits granted to nationals of GCC countries by virtue of Law No. 33/1988 and its applicable directives, as well as any rights and benefits which they might be entitled to after this law enters into effect.

3.5 Article 5

This law shall be implemented by the concerned ministers, and shall enter into effect as of the date of its publication in the Official Gazette.

4 THE DIRECTIVES RELATED TO LAW NO. 26/1995 ON THE FREE ZONE, AS ISSUED BY THE MINISTER OF COMMERCE AND INDUSTRY (DECISION NO. 69/1999)

4.1 Section one: supervision and control of the free zone

4.1.1 Article 1

Free zones shall be under the control of the Ministry of Commerce and Industry, who shall set the general policies, and implement any decision it deems appropriate to fulfil the objectives for which the free zone is established, particularly:

(a) propose the setting up of new free zones, determining the locations thereof by liaising with the concerned government authorities;
(b) determine the way of running such free zones, whether by the Ministry itself or by engaging a private sector entity;
(c) liaise with other government authorities/bodies to implement the Free Zone Law;
(d) prepare plans and schemes relevant to the improvement and development of free zones;
(e) propose facilities which may need to be provided by the government authorities in accordance with law.

4.1.2 Article 2

The appropriate authority in charge of the free zone shall take all actions/procedures and decisions required for the running of the free zone, which shall consist, *inter alia*, of the following:

(a) authorizing the use and rent of land and property, and investment in third party owned free zone facilities;
(b) securing licences required for engagement in various activities within the free zone;
(c) entering into all contracts required with the free zone investors following approval of authority in charge of such contracts;
(d) developing international trade transactions and transit trade, embarking on promotion and marketing campaigns at the local, regional and international levels;
(e) providing the necessary plants/facilities for the operation of the free zone in line with the organizational structure thereof;
(f) facilitating the procurement of manpower required for investors to run their operations, to the business needs and requirements;
(g) preparing promotion plans aimed at encouraging investors into the free zone, and entering on its behalf into contracts with third parties;
(h) proposing directives regularizing operations within the free zone;
(i) securing residency permits and visitor/employment entry visas for free zone employees and investors, by liaising with the government authorities, pursuant to the applicable relevant rules, laws and regulations;
(j) regular check and control, and spotting any violations, in line with the law and the executive by-laws;
(k) securing approvals required for setting up manufacturing, banking and trading operations.

4.1.3 Article 3

The free zone authority shall assume the following obligations:

(a) handling its operations in line with the applicable law and directives;
(b) maintaining regular accounting books and records;
(c) maintaining all security steps, measures and precautions within the free zone;
(d) observing all contractual terms with the supervising authority if a private sector entity or organization is engaged to run the free zone.

4.2 Section two: licence conditions and procedures for free zone operations

4.2.1 Article 4

No entity may engage in any activity in the free zone unless it has obtained an operation licence from the free zone authority according to the terms and conditions set forth herein.

4.2.2 *Article 5*

An application to obtain an operation licence can be submitted to the free zone management authority and should be made in the form provided for such purpose, which includes the following information:

(a) name, nationality, address and elected domicile of applicant;
(b) particulars of the project/operation to be set up in free zone and its duration;
(c) size of the area to be occupied, and whether it is to be built out or a prefabricated unit;
(d) plant, machinery and equipment required for the project;
(e) capital, source of funds, legal status relevant to association or partnership with foreign organizations, if any;
(f) expected water and electricity consumption;
(g) manpower number, nationality, specialization, wage rates, and number of working days;
(h) amount of financial guarantee.

4.2.3 *Article 6*

The free zone authority shall issue its licence within two months from the date an application is properly submitted with the information and supportive documents required under the previous article. If the free zone elects to reject an application, or gives no reply within the aforesaid time period, the applicant may complain about such decision within sixty days from the date he is informed of such a decision or upon the expiry of the aforesaid period. A complaint is to be lodged with the concerned authority. In the event the approval is issued, a licence applicant shall be notified to sign the contract within one month from the date the approval is issued and shall provide the financial guarantee, failing which the applicant shall be deemed to have waived his application.

The rights and obligation of the licence applicant and the free zone management authority shall be set out in a contract conclude by both parties.

4.2.4 *Article 7*

A licence may be issued for more than one activity within the free zone.

4.2.5 *Article 8*

The supervising authority shall be notified of all the issued licences, and of the contracts entered into with investors, as well as of all the information related to licensed operations. The supervising authority or the free zone authority may not cancel any licence unless it is in violation of the law or its executive directives, or if the licencee commits any breach of the law or its executive directives or if he fails to fulfil his contractual obligations.

4.2.6 *Article 9*

A licence for a free zone operation/project must include all business information, legal status, nationality, capital, limits of site to be occupied, objectives of operation, value of financial guarantee to be provided by licensee, and the validity term of the licence. A licence is assignable under the same conditions subject to the approval of the free zone authority and the competent party issuing the licence. Such assignment shall not be valid unless the relevant fees have been paid.

4.2.7 *Article 10*

The free zone authority shall, with the investor's consent, determine the time required to commence the project's activities following the date a licence is issued, in the light of the investor's own circumstances and type of his activity. However, an investor who is contractually committed to occupy a parcel must complete the construction of his facility within the period specified by the free zone authority from the date a parcel is handed over to him, unless the free zone authority agrees to extend such period, in the light of the construction circumstances. If investor fails to commence operations following the expiry of the specified period or expiry of period specified for construction of the facility, the free zone authority may terminate the contract entered into with the investor. It may also terminate the contract of an investor who does not engage in any activity for a whole continuous period of one year without any acceptable excuse.

4.3 Section three: entry visas and residency permits rules for free zone personnel/employees and visitors

4.3.1 *Article 11*

The free zone authority shall, by liaising with the appropriate government authorities, arrange for the issuance of entry visas in favour of the free zone employees/personnel and visitors, in accordance with the relevant applicable rules and regulations.

4.3.2 *Article 12*

VIP visas shall be issued pursuant to the following procedures:

(a) If the free zone authority is advised beforehand of the visit, the free zone authority shall write to the airport entry post to issue a temporary visa for the visitor upon his arrival.

(b) If a visitor arrives without the prior knowledge of the free zone authority, the visitor shall contact the concerned entry post personnel, fill out a temporary entry visa form and the entry post personnel authorized by the Interior Ministry shall contact the Free Zone Authority seeking an approval for the visit. In this case, the free zone authority shall advise the entry port of its approval of the visit, and the entry post shall issue a temporary entry visa at the responsibility of the free zone authority according to the relevant applicable rules and regulations.

4.3.3 Article 13

The free zone authority shall, by liaising with the appropriate authorities, arrange visas and residency permits for authorized operation owners or their representatives and foreign employees, once their applications have been approved. The permit term shall be determined in line with the applicable rules and regulations in effect.

The free zone authority shall issue employment identification cards for the free zone employees, the validity of which shall be the same as the validity of the residency permit shown in the passport.

4.3.4 Article 14

All accommodation permits within the free zone shall be issued by the free zone authority. Such permits shall be only issued in favour of the free zone employees who are required, by the nature of their work, to work in the free zone area beyond the normal. The permits shall not entitle the employees' family members to stay within the free zone. Specific locations shall be assigned for the accommodation of the free zone employees.

4.3.5 Article 15

The provisions of the Kuwaiti Labour Law (private sector) and its executive directives shall apply to the free zone employees, without prejudice to any other benefits provided under the rules/regulations related to the licensed projects. Licensed projects should provide medical insurance to their free zone employees.

4.3.6 Article 16

Employment contracts executed between owners of licensed free zone projects and their employees should be made in four copies. One copy must be lodged with the free zone authority, and another copy with the Ministry of Social Affairs and Labour. The contract should cover all details required under the applicable laws and regulations.

4.4 Section four: free zone import/export

4.4.1 *Article 17*

The free zone authority shall be authorized to monitor the traffic of goods in and out of the free zone. It shall have access to books and records of the licensed projects, and to inspect any of their stocks in the free zone area. For this purpose, the free zone authority may have access to any area/locations within free zone to verify information and documentation provided in connection with such stocks.

4.4.2 *Article 18*

Goods shall be allowed to enter the free zone through the relevant free zone port, following submission by the concerned person of the required documents to the free zone authority. Goods entering the free zone other than through the relevant free zone port shall be handled as follows:

(a) the importer will have to submit the required documents to the free zone.
(b) the handling/shipping agent shall sort out the goods coming from abroad to the free zone on the manifest, and such goods shall be properly marked.
(c) customs shall stamp free zone goods according to the applicable laws and regulations.
(d) goods will be moved to the free zone area at the responsibility of the free zone authority.
(e) customs shall check the goods stamp/mark upon arrival to free zone entry gate.

4.4.3 *Article 19*

Goods entering the free zone from within the country shall be treated as goods exported from Kuwait to overseas. Such goods shall be accepted to the free zone after submission of the relevant documents evidencing ownership title. The same goods may be taken out of the free zone and into the country without incurring any custom duties or taxes.

4.4.4 *Article 20*

Licensed projects shall be under no restrictions to export any specific percentage of its goods abroad or to sell any specific percentage of its goods in the local market. The free zone authority shall be responsible for the issuance of a certificate of origin for the exported goods.

4.4.5 Article 21

Goods shall be exported overseas from the relevant free zone port in accordance with the following procedure:

(a) A free zone export application together with the required documents must be submitted to the appropriate authorities;
(b) Goods shall be loaded for shipment following review and approval of documents by the free zone authority.

The implementation of the above procedure shall be made without prejudice to the procedures, rules and regulations stipulated in the relevant laws and directives.

4.4.6 Article 22

Goods shall be entered from the free zone into Kuwait in accordance with the following procedure:

(a) the person concerned is required to arrange entry documents required by Kuwait customs officials;
(b) goods are to be checked and verified against documents. Goods shall be assessed and inspected by the relevant government authorities, customs and the free zone authority before entry.

4.4.7 Article 23

The export of free zone goods overseas shall be effected by air, land and sea through the relevant free zone port or any other free zone port, as follows:

(a) the free zone authority shall prepare the required export documents;
(b) goods shall be stamped/marked by the free zone authority;
(c) goods leaving the free zone shall be stamped/marked by customs.

The implementation of the above procedure shall be made without prejudice to the procedures, rules and regulations stipulated in the relevant laws and directives.

4.5 Section five: taking goods into/out of the free zone, trading and building works within the free zone

4.5.1 Article 24

The free zone goods and products may be traded within the free zone once the free zone authority is advised of the type of and volumes of such goods and products. Furthermore, goods and products may be traded between one free zone and another within Kuwait. In such event, the provisions of Article 22 of these Directives shall apply.

4.5.2 *Article 25*

Licensed projects may not dispose of plant, equipment, machinery and transportation equipment they use within the free zone unless they have satisfied all necessary procedures, secured the free zone authority approval and paid all customs taxes and duties.

4.5.3 *Article 26*

A construction licence or a licence to add on existing building in the free zone shall be obtained in accordance with the following procedure:

(a) an application form for construction or building expansion together with the required documents shall be submitted to the free zone authority;
(b) the application and documents, as well as conformity of specifications to the regulations of concerned government authorities shall be checked by the free zone authority, in line with a set of specifications agreed with the free zone authority and the supervising authority.

The free zone authority shall issue the licence pursuant to applicable relevant laws, rules and regulation. The supervising authority shall be advised of the same.

4.5.4 *Article 27*

Machinery, equipment and vehicles regarded as part of the project's assets may be transferred from and into the free zone in accordance with the following procedure:

(a) an application for transfer must be submitted to the free zone authority giving reason for entry, exit, time specified for such entry or exit, and whether it is for one or several times within a specific period of time;
(b) a description of such vehicles, equipment, as well copies of title and registration of same shall be submitted to the free zone authority;
(c) the free zone authority shall issue a temporary gate pass (entry/exit permit);
(d) customs and Interior Ministry shall be advised by the free zone authority;
(e) the free zone authority shall be advised by the applicant upon the return of such vehicles and equipment to their original locations.

4.6 Section six: permitted activity, prohibited activity and exemptions

4.6.1 *Article 28*

Without prejudice to the applicable relevant laws, rules and regulations, it is allowed to carry out the following acts in the free zone:

(a) storage and display of any type of goods of any origin and source;
(b) sorting out and checking goods upon delivery to warehouses;

(c)   sorting out, cleaning, mixing of goods, even if of local origin, repackaging and other similar activities, including changing form of goods existing at the free zone, for trade transactions and market requirements;

(d)   carrying out any other activity needed by the free zone employees, such as banking, postal services, insurance, shipping, loading and unloading, exchange and others.

4.6.2 *Article 29*

The entry, warehousing and display of the following goods is prohibited in the free zone:

(a)   goods of prohibited origin or goods which are prohibited locally or worldwide.

(b)   drugs and alcohol, save for pharmaceutical manufacturing requirements as prescribed by the Health Ministry, without prejudice to the relevant laws, rules and regulations;

(c)   fire arms, ammunition and explosives, save as expressly permitted by the appropriate security and defence authorities within the scope of the applicable laws and regulations;

(d)   perishable, readily inflammable and radiant material, as prescribed by the supervising and competent authorities.

4.6.3 *Article 30*

Subject to the relevant laws and regulations prohibiting the dealing in certain merchandise/good or materials, all equipment, machinery, plant and transportation equipment required for free zone licensed projects in line with the Free Zone Law shall be exempted from customs tax and duties.

The authority supervising the free zone may allow some local goods into the free zone on temporary basis for repair or transfer of free zone goods into the country on temporary basis for repair, free of customs tax and duties.

4.7 Section seven: service charges

4.7.1 *Article 31*

Free zone licensed projects shall be charged for administrative services pursuant to the rules and tariffs set out by the supervising authority, which are regarded as an integral part of, and as binding as, these directives, whereby the free zone authority shall charge a fee for the following services:

(a)   porterage;

(b)   insurance;

(c)   warehousing/storage;

(d)   transfer;

(e) occupancy;
(f) entry;
(g) other authorities' services and use of facilities and equipment.

4.7.2 *Article 33*

Service charges set out in the above article shall be calculated on the value of goods entering the free zone for storage and re-export, as well as on value of goods exiting the free zone for the projects' account.

4.7.3 *Article 34*

If no documents are submitted showing value of goods, or stated value not reflecting true value, the value shall be estimated based on the prevailing current value of the goods.

4.7.4 *Article 35*

A service charge on incoming or outgoing goods shall be due immediately upon arrival or departure of such goods.

4.7.5 *Article 36*

The Free Zone Authority shall carry out the porterage activities and charge owner of goods based on package/unit weight or actual weight, as the case may be, as set out by the supervising authority.

4.7.6 *Article 37*

The free zone authority shall provide insurance coverage for the free zone pursuant to the applicable laws, rules and regulations. Insurance beneficiaries shall be charged by the free zone authority on the basis of space/area and type of insurance, as the case may be, and as prescribed by the supervising authority.

4.7.7 *Article 38*

The free zone authority shall collect warehousing charges for goods stored in the free zone warehouses for the entire period of storage without any grace period. Warehousing charges shall be assessed based on gross weight, volumes or size as determined by the supervising authority.

An additional charge shall be also imposed on the occupancy of specific premises/facilities stated in contracts entered with the concerned person. A charge shall be also imposed for each assignment/transfer of goods, business occupancy contract or transportation equipment, as well as materials, services, certificates, copies of document provided, equipment and facilities used.

4.7.8 *Article 39*

A charge shall be due for all services set out in Article 31 herein. The free zone authority upon default of concerned person on payment of the due charge may deduct the relevant payment from the financial guarantee provided for the operation. The free zone authority may take the appropriate step or action to preserve its rights by seizing goods or assets of defaulting projects and selling such goods or assets by way of public auction, in accordance with the procedures provided in the applicable laws and regulations.

4.8 Section eight: free zone financial and administrative system security and safety measures

4.8.1 *Article 40*

The free zone authority should submit to the supervising authority the accounting/financial system applied and any amendments it elects to introduce for review and approval within thirty days from the commencement of the activity or from the date the amendment is effected. The free zone authority shall make available to the supervising authority all records and documents on such dates specified by the authority. The free zone authority shall provide the supervising authority with a copy of its balance sheet and closing accounts certified by a Kuwaiti auditor within three months of the end of the relevant financial year. The supervising authority may check and review the balance sheet and closing accounts in the presence of the supervising authority representatives.

4.8.2 *Article 41*

All projects/operations in the free zone should observe fire and explosive prevention measures, and should have an insurance coverage against the same. Insurance shall cover civil liability to the extent determined by the free zone authority, with insurance companies acceptable to the free zone authority. Such insurance shall be mandatory and at the cost of the free zone projects/operations.

4.8.3 *Article 42*

Occupants and owners of authorized free zone projects shall be responsible for all damage caused by them, their representatives, their operations goods or premises they set up within the free zone. Their compliance with the safety rules shall not relieve them from such responsibility.

4.8.4 *Article 43*

The free zone authority shall regularly check on free zone operations to ascertain compliance with the hygienic and residential safety of premises, facilities, safety of electromagnetic equipment, machinery, general conditions and premises/facilities maintenance, in accordance with specifications agreed with the appropriate authorities. The person in charge of a free zone operation commits to repairing any damage, fault or violation noted within a reasonable period of time to be specified by the free zone authority. Such an obligation shall be provided for in the contracts made with free zone operations.

4.8.5 *Article 44*

The free zone authority shall insure its own property existing at the free zone, as well as all other property used including machinery, buildings and electronic equipment, and shall also insure its own free zone personnel at its own cost. Each operation is to insure its own assets, property, equipment and premises at its own cost.

4.8.6 *Article 45*

The free zone authority shall take appropriate steps to keep and safeguard the safety and security of goods available at the free zone, to the applicable standards and specifications of customs security.

4.8.7 *Article 46*

The free zone authority shall liaise with various authorities for the following procedures:

(a) organization of overall in-house or external security at the free zone to prevent smuggling and theft;
(b) put in place all security, civil defence and fire protection steps and measures;
(c) set special security rules through special authorized security men at the cost of shipping operations or agencies.

4.9 Section nine: general rules and penalties

4.9.1 *Article 47*

The supervisory authority shall take the necessary steps and measures to monitor the free zone authority's implementation of law and directives. For such purpose, it may have access to the records, restrictions, entry/exit permits and bills offers for goods.

4.9.2 Article 48

Goods manufactured in the free zone shall carry a stamp indicating that they have been made in a Kuwait free zone.

4.9.3 Article 49

Government authorities may have access to the free zone to do their job by liaising with the free zone authority.

4.9.4 Article 50

Free zone licensed projects seeking to terminate their activities should express their desire in the manner specified by the free zone authority at least three months prior to the termination date. Such projects should provide an evidence confirming their fulfilment of all their local dues and a release from the Interior Ministry (General Disciplinary and Judgment Execution Department) before being allowed to dispose of their property.

4.9.5 Article 51

If tenants and owners of authorized free zone projects violate the Free Zone Law or these directives or commit any breach of their rent contracts, the free zone authority shall give them notice to rectify such violation. Should they fail to do so within the time specified, the free zone authority may ask the supervising authority to terminate their contracts, and specify a reasonable time for eviction, following which utilization of relevant premises/facilities shall pass to the free zone authority at no cost. Owners of operations failing to evacuate within the specified time shall give the free zone authority the right to arrange eviction at their own cost, and take possession of their property at their own cost at free zone warehouses.

4.9.6 Article 52

The provisions of Article 15 of Law 26 of 1995 on free zones shall apply particularly to the following violations:

(a) failure to provide a packing list or the same being missing, or providing multiple packing lists, or delay in providing the same beyond times specified in these directives;
(b) failure to provide any documents set out in these directives, or providing documents containing incorrect information;
(c) missing information which should be included in the packing list, warehousing or removal requests or warehousing records;

(d) shipping, unloading or transfer of goods from one transport to another of any type whatsoever without authorization from the free zone authority or its representative not attending;

(e) storage or packaging of goods in areas not designated for such purposes;

(f) failure to enable the free zone authority personnel to do their job, check, inspect and request documents and records;

(g) operations representatives or personnel not obeying these rules or directives given to them;

(h) failure to comply with the proper warehousing rules, or maintain the necessary records;

(i) failure to keep seals/stamps fixed on packages or transports, even if not leading to shortage in or alteration of goods;

(j) possessing or moving goods within the free zone contrary to the rules and regulations set out in these directives.

4.9.7 *Article 53*

These directives shall come into effect as of the date of their publication in the Official Gazette.

Saudi Arabia

Vernon Handley and Fares Al-Hejailan*

1 INTRODUCTION

A number of significant legal developments have recently taken place in Saudi Arabia. Several major and long heralded legislative changes in the fields of foreign capital investment law, companies law and agency law have, however, again failed to materialize.

2 JOINT STOCK COMPANIES

2.1 Conversion of corporate entities into public joint stock companies

Business entities in Saudi Arabia are governed by Royal Decree M/6 of 22/3/1385AH (corresponding to 20 July 1965) (the "Companies Regulations"). The principal forms of Saudi Arabian business entities as governed by the Companies Regulations are limited liability company, joint stock company and general partnership. Public joint stock companies are the only type of Saudi company whose shares can be offered for subscription to the general public.

As noted in volume 4, although the Companies Regulations anticipate that business entities established thereunder may convert from one permitted form to another, subject to certain restrictions, Ministerial Order No. 495 dated 25/3/1418AH (29 July 1997) introduced a number of restrictions on the ability of business entities to convert into public joint stock companies. These restrictions included requirements that the relevant business entity must:

(a) have achieved "significant" turnover and profitability in the financial year preceding the date of the conversion application;

* Solicitors, Law Firm of Salah Al-Hejailan, Riyadh, Saudi Arabia.

(b)   have net assets of not less than SR75 million (approximately US$20 million);

(c)   have had an annual rate of return on equity in each of the financial years preceding the date of the conversion application of not less than 10 per cent;

(d)   be projected (according to a feasibility study required to be submitted by the applicant) to achieve an annual rate of return on equity in each of the financial years succeeding the date of the conversion application of not less than 10 per cent;

(e)   have been established for not less than ten years; and

(f)   be able to demonstrate that it has management and internal controls appropriate for joint stock companies.

It was widely thought that the conditions specified in Ministerial Order No. 495 were overly restrictive and, consequently, the Minister of Commerce has now issued an order[1] relaxing the conditions by (a) reducing the required net asset value from SR75 million to SR50 million, (b) requiring that the rate of return on shareholders' equity in each of the three financial years preceding the application should not be less than 7 per cent, as opposed to 10 per cent over the preceding five years, (c) providing that the required feasibility study should confirm that the anticipated return on equity will not be less than 7 per cent per annum in each of the three financial years succeeding conversion, (d) requiring that the applicant must have been established for at least five years prior to the conversion and (e) providing that not less than 40 per cent of the shares in the joint stock company will be offered for public subscription.

The requirement that the applicant should be able to demonstrate that it has management and internal controls appropriate for joint stock companies remains in place.

Amended regulations have also been issued, dealing with the procedure for converting into a joint stock company. In particular, such regulations require that the application which must be submitted to the General Directorate of Companies at the Ministry of Commerce in relation to the proposed conversion should include the following:

(a)   the name, address and date of incorporation of the applicant;

(b)   the amount of bonuses and fees paid to directors and executive officers of the applicant, together with any financial or other material benefits enjoyed by any of them (including, *inter alia*, pension awards, etc.);

(c)   a description of any shares of significant value owned by its executive officers in any other company having a business relationship with the applicant;

(d)   a summary of the financial information in respect of each year of the three preceding financial years including, *inter alia*, sales, profits, operating capital, total assets and long term loans;

(e)   a description of legal proceedings against the applicant that are not finally settled;

(f)   a statement of plans made by the applicant's management for investment of the amounts resulting out of the transformation process;

---

[1]   Ministerial Order No. 1151 dated 22/9/1419AH (9 January 1999).

(g) a statement of the manner of determining the share price of the prospective joint stock company and the various factors taken into consideration for the determination of such price, description of the manner of transformation of the applicant either by the current subscribers as well as current share capital or otherwise, and a statement of prospective share capital and the rate allotted for the current subscribers and that allotted for subscription;

(h) a description of the value of the shares owned by directors and executive officers of the applicant and by any other persons associated with the applicant, the corresponding shares in the prospective joint stock company and a description of any significant differences in respect of the five years preceding the application for transformation; and

(i) a description of the subscription arrangements if the shares have not been fully subscribed for, the names of guarantor/guarantors of subscribers, the number of shares guaranteed by each of them and their respective fees, if any.

Furthermore, the application submitted by the applicant must be accompanied by the following documents:

(a) a copy of the memorandum of association of the company and any supplementary amendments;

(b) a letter confirming the current shareholders' consent to the proposed transformation;

(c) the audited financial statements of the applicant in respect of the three years preceding the date of application;

(d) a report by the applicant's auditor on the financial statements of the applicant in respect of the period commencing from the date of the last audit up to the date of the filing of the application, wherein the auditor confirms its non-awareness of any facts contradicting the financial statements that it has audited; and

(e) a feasibility study prepared by a firm licensed to operate in Saudi Arabia including an evaluation of the converted company, financial statements of the new company for the first three years, the price of the shares of the joint stock company and a description of the criteria for determining the said price in accordance with professional standards. The feasibility study must also include a summary of the statements and data included in the application.

Once the application is approved, the applicant's memorandum of association is required to conform with the specimen form for joint stock companies issued by the Ministerial Resolution No. 583 dated 1/5/1385AH (28 August 1965) (as amended) provided that the memorandum of association shall include provisions with respect to the following matters:

(a) the appointment of the first board of directors of the company for a period not exceeding three years and the nomination of an auditor for the first financial year;

(b) the transfer of dividends of the existing shareholders upon transformation to shares and a provision prohibiting transfer thereof prior to publication of the balance sheets and profit and loss accounts for two financial years of not less than twelve months each from the date of the resolution approving the transformation; and

(c)   a definition of maximum voting rights in general meetings, providing that a principal shareholder or a shareholder by proxy or a shareholder acting in both capacities shall not have a number of votes exceeding 5 per cent to 20 per cent (as the case may be upon transformation) with respect to all resolutions of general meetings, pursuant to Article 34 of the standard form of memorandum of association for joint stock companies[2] and Article 107 of the Companies Regulations.[3]

2.2 Feasibility study requirements

Any feasibility study submitted pursuant to Ministerial Order No. 495 (see section 2.1) must now, in accordance with Ministerial Order No. 563 of 10/4/1419AH (2 August 1998), be prepared by a consulting office or professional company licensed to do business in Saudi Arabia and be in the Arabic language. Ministerial Order No. 563 also applies to reports prepared pursuant to Article 52 (which deals with the requirement to submit a feasibility study when applying for the incorporation of a joint stock company to establish the probability of the new company) and Article 60 (which deals with the requirement to submit a report relating to the correct evaluations of non-cash capital contribution to joint stock companies) of the Companies Regulations.

2.3 Directors of joint stock companies

A Council of Ministers resolution has been issued amending paragraph 5 of subsection (iv) of Council of Ministers Resolution No. 17 of 20/1/1402AH (16 November 1981) by providing that no director should be a director in more than five boards of joint stock companies at any one time.[4] This requirement does not, however, apply to directors that are appointed by the government, governmental entities, joint stock companies or to directors of governmental institutions.

The Council of Ministers resolution repeals subsection III of Council of Ministers Resolution No. 80 of 30/4/1405AH (21 January 1985), which provided that a person, by way of exception to the restrictions referred to above, may be appointed simultaneously to hold the position of director in three boards of directors of joint stock companies, provided that none of such companies is a company that:

(a)   carries on banking operations;
(b)   manages a public facility; or
(c)   receives state subsidies.

---

[2]   Art. 34 of the standard form of memorandum of association for joint stock companies specifies the majorities which will have to be achieved in order to pass shareholder resolutions at general meetings.

[3]   Art. 107 of the Companies Regulations provides that the memorandum of association of a joint stock company may limit the number of votes exercised by a single shareholder.

[4]   Council of Ministers Resolution No. 17 of 20/1/1402AH provided for a maximum number of directorships in joint stock companies of four per person with the consent of the Minister of Commerce, but otherwise two per person.

3 DRAFT INVESTMENT BUSINESS REGULATIONS

The Saudi Arabian Monetary Agency ("the SAMA") (the central bank of Saudi Arabia) circulated in April 1998 draft regulations[5] (the "Investment Business Regulations") to Saudi Arabian banks. It is anticipated that the Investment Business Regulations will be issued by the SAMA pursuant to Article 16(3) of the Banking Control Law,[6] which permits the SAMA, with the approval of the Minister of Finance and National Economy, to issue general rules fixing the terms and conditions which Saudi Arabian banks should take into consideration when carrying out certain types of transaction.

Although the Investment Business Regulations are merely in draft form, we understand that the SAMA has indicated to Saudi Arabian banks that it expects Saudi Arabian banks to comply with the Investment Business Regulations in the interim period prior to their formal adoption.

The objectives of the Investment Business Regulations are stated to be as follows:[7]

(a) to establish a regulatory framework for the offering by Saudi Arabian banks of investment services in Saudi Arabia;

(b) to ensure Saudi Arabian banks are administratively organized and sufficiently proficient to offer such investment services;

(c) to ensure the accountability of Saudi Arabian banks;

(d) to contribute to the orderly growth and development of Saudi Arabian capital markets and the Saudi Arabian national economy; and

(e) to protect the customers of Saudi Arabian banks.

Although the provisions of the Investment Business Regulations are broad ranging (for example, dealing with the appointment of bank compliance officers, defining the responsibilities of banks to various categories of customer, prescribing certain documentation standards and such like), in the context of the relaxation of the restrictions on the conversion of corporate entities into public joint stock companies referred to above, the provisions of the Investment Business Regulations relating to the participation of Saudi Arabian banks as sponsors in relation to public and private placements of securities are of particular relevance. The requirements of the Investment Business Regulations in this regard can be broadly summarized as falling within four categories, namely:

(a) the requirement to obtain the SAMA's approval in relation to any prospectus;

(b) a requirement on banks to report to the SAMA in relation to distribution services;

(c) an obligation on issuers to pay damages to investors that are misled by misrepresentations contained in any prospectus; and

(d) various content requirements in relation to placement agreements, prospectuses and subscription agreements.

---

[5] Dated 19/4/1998.
[6] Promulgated in the Official Gazette No. 2136, dated 5/3/1386AH (24 June 1966).
[7] Paras. 1–3 of Schedule 1, Investment Business Regulations.

It is unclear as to when the Investment Business Regulations will be formally promulgated.

4 FOREIGN CAPITAL INVESTMENT

4.1 Advertising and publishing services

In Saudi Arabia, foreign equity investment is generally prohibited unless foreign investors first obtain a licence issued by the Ministry of Industry and Electricity upon the recommendation of the foreign capital investment committee (a "foreign capital investment licence"). In order to obtain a foreign capital investment licence pursuant to Royal Decree No. M/4 of 2/2/1399AH (31 December 1978) the foreign investor must demonstrate that it will invest its capital in a "development project".

Ministerial Order No. 11/W/D of 17/7/1410AH (12 February 1990) defined "development projects" to include the development of (a) manufacturing industry, (b) agricultural production, (c) health services, (d) the provision of services and (e) contracting.

Ministerial Order No. 7/2/D dated 1/3/1418AH (5 July 1997) permitted foreign capital investment in electric power generation facilities to qualify as development projects for the purposes of obtaining a foreign capital investment licence.[8] Consistent with the government's stated wish to extend foreign investment in Saudi Arabia, Ministerial Resolution No. 17/K/D dated 20/7/1419AH (9 November 1998) has been issued by the Ministry of Industry and Electricity adding "advertising and publishing services" to the projects that are to be regarded as development projects. Rather than constituting a new category of development project, the ministerial resolution is merely a clarification that advertising and publishing services can now be included in the services category of development project already specified in Article 5 of Ministerial Resolution No. 11/M/R dated 17/7/1410AH (12 February 1990). In addition to advertising and publishing services, business activities falling within the ambit of Article 5 include banking, hotels and tourism, training, maintenance and operation services which require higher technology, specialized technical workshops and refrigeration stores.

4.2 Aviation companies and travel, tourism and air cargo agencies

A new regulation[9] has been issued by the Minister of Defence and Aviation relating to aviation companies and travel, tourism and air cargo agencies operating in Saudi Arabia. In order to operate an aviation company or a travel, tourism and air cargo agency, the new regulation requires the promoters to obtain a licence from the Presidency of Civil Aviation (the "PCA"). Although the regulation applies to both Saudi and foreign investors, foreign investment will only be allowed in the aviation, travel, tourism and air cargo sectors on a reciprocal basis (i.e. the PCA will

8 See *Yearbook of Islamic and Middle Eastern Law*, vol. 4 (1997–1998), p. 334.
9 Official Gazette No. 3737 dated 17/11/1419AH (5 March 1999).

only permit investors from foreign countries to participate in the aviation, travel, tourism and air cargo sectors in Saudi Arabia if Saudi individuals and companies are permitted to invest in those countries). In addition to the licence issued by the PCA, in order for non-GCC investors to participate in Saudi companies operating in the aviation, travel, tourism and air cargo sectors, a foreign capital investment licence would also be required.

In order to obtain a licence from the PCA, the promoters are required to submit a bank guarantee, valid for two and a half years. A SR1,000,000 guarantee must be submitted to open a main office of a travel and tourism agency and a SR300,000 guarantee must be submitted to open a main office of an air cargo agency. The guarantee for each branch office is 25 per cent of the guarantee for the main office. There is provision for a 50 per cent discount in the required amount of the bank guarantee at the time of renewal of the relevant licence, provided that the office has operated satisfactorily for not less than five years.

Under the new regulation, aviation companies and travel, tourism and air cargo agencies are not allowed to publish any tourism programmes, pictures, advertisements or other printed materials without prior permission from the PCA. Aviation companies and travel, tourism and air cargo agencies are required to maintain records of their accounts and activities and to prepare annual budgets. These records must be certified by authorized chartered accountants. Agencies licensed by the PCA pursuant to the regulation are required to settle all their financial obligations in a timely manner.

The new regulation also requires travel, tourism and air cargo agencies to furnish details of ticket sales and bills of lading to the PCA on a monthly basis. The regulation also includes provisions relating to the powers of the PCA to carry out inspections and penalties for non-compliance. Each licence issued by the PCA is to be for a two-year period.

4.3 Amendment to procedures for obtaining tax holiday in relation to industrial expansions

The procedures for obtaining a tax exemption in respect of an expansion of industrial facilities falling within the foreign capital investment regime have been slightly adjusted. Provided that there is a minimum of 25 per cent Saudi capital participation, a foreign investor forming a Saudi limited liability company will be exempt from Saudi income taxes for a period of ten calendar years for industrial and agricultural projects and five calendar years for other development projects. The tax holiday covers only the share of the non-Saudi partner in the profits of the Saudi limited liability company. In order to encourage additional foreign investment to finance the expansion of existing industrial facilities, Ministerial Order No. 3/3170 dated 2/12/1413AH (23 May 1993) permitted a further tax exemption period to be granted in relation to the profits generated by an expansion of such facilities. Article 10(i) of the Ministerial Order (as amended) provided that the applicant should file an application for a new exemption from tax to the Department of *Zakat* and Income Tax within three months from the date of the issuance of the industrial licence relating to the expansion. This requirement has now been relaxed by Ministerial Resolution No. 2421 dated 28/10/1418AH (24 February 1998) and a related Department of *Zakat* and Income Tax (the "DZIT") Circular No. 118/1 dated 5/11/1418AH (3 March 1998) stating that only the notification relating to the expansion issued by the Foreign Capital Investment Committee is required to be forwarded to the DZIT. The Ministerial Resolution is stated to be retroactive.

5 LABOUR LAW

5.1 End of service benefits: deductibility

We understand that the DZIT has issued a circular providing that any end of service benefit paid in excess of the provisions of the Saudi labour law will not be deductible for the purposes of computing corporation tax. The circular reflects the existing practice of the DZIT.

5.2 Secondments and entitlement to end of service benefits

The Saudi Labour Court has recently ruled that an employee that is seconded to a Saudi Arabian company is not entitled to end of service benefits at the end of that employee's service in Saudi Arabia. The facts of the case were broadly as follows:

An employee ("E") worked for an American company ("X"). E was then seconded by X to a Saudi Arabian company ("Y"). Y was liable to pay a secondment fee to X in respect of E, together with certain payments as contribution to the premiums for professional indemnity insurance maintained by X and covering, in part, the activities of E. X assumed no responsibility for the payment of salary by Y to E. Although E remained listed in the internal directory of X as being an "associate" of X, E had little practical contact with X. E was issued with an *iqama* (work permit), permitting E to work in Saudi Arabia, which named Y as E's employer. E's salary was unilaterally reduced by X. E continued to work for Y following the reduction in salary, but then resigned and claimed end of service benefits from Y on the basis of constructive dismissal and an amount equal to the accumulated difference in salary following the reduction. The question arose as to whether E was entitled to receive end of service benefits from Y pursuant to the Saudi Labour Law and, if so, the amount of such benefits.

Article 87 of the Saudi Labour Regulations[10] provides that:

If a definite term work contract expires or if an employer rescinds an indefinite term contract, the employer shall pay to the worker a bonus for his term of service to be calculated on basis of half a month's wage for each of the first five years and the wage of one month for each subsequent year; the most recent wage shall be used for calculating bonus.

Article 88 of the Saudi Labour Regulations provides that:

---

[10] As implemented by Royal Decree No. M/21 of 6/9/1389AH (15 November 1969).

In indefinite term contracts, the worker shall be entitled to: one third of the bonus provided for in [Article 87], if he resigns from the work, after not less than two nor more than five consecutive years service; two thirds of the said bonus, if his service period exceeds five, but has not reached ten years; and full bonus, if he resigns after ten years.

The Saudi Labour Regulations define a "worker" as being "any person who, for wages, does work under the management or control of an employer, even when out of his sight" and define an "employer" as being "any natural or juristic person who employs one or more workers for wages".

The Higher Labour Commission[11] decided that E was not entitled to end of service benefits upon the termination of his contract of employment with Y. The reason behind the judgment appears to be that, although Y was named as the official employer of E for the purposes of his *iqama*, the actual employer of E was at all times X. Upon the termination of E's contract of employment, E should, therefore, seek redress against X rather than Y. The Higher Labour Commission appeared to conclude that E would, potentially, be entitled to two sets of benefits upon the termination of his contract of employment. The Higher Labour Commission does not appear to have considered the factual question of whether E was in fact entitled to any end of service benefit payment from X and it is unclear as to whether, had X been able to demonstrate that he would not have been entitled to any end of service benefits from X, the Higher Labour Commission would have held Y to be liable.

The Higher Labour Commission also rejected E's contention that he had been constructively dismissed on the grounds that E, by continuing to work for X, had impliedly consented to the reduction in salary (it has been generally assumed that it is unlawful to reduce wages under the Saudi Labour Regulations, even with the consent of the relevant employee, save in specific circumstances). Hence, even if E had been entitled to end of service benefits under the Saudi Labour Regulations, the benefits would only have been payable at the reduced levels of benefit provided in Article 88.

As the labour courts do not have any system of binding precedent, it is unclear as to whether the approach adopted by the Higher Labour Commission as described above will be followed in future cases.

6 CUSTOMS DUTIES: MANUFACTURED GOODS: REBATE UPON EXPORT

With a view to reducing the production cost of goods manufactured in Saudi Arabia, Ministerial Resolution No. 31/2431 dated 2/11/1418AH (28 February 1998) has been issued adding a new paragraph to Article 98 of the Customs Regulations[12] allowing the refund of customs duties paid on foreign materials used in the manufacture of exported goods in accordance with certain principles.

---

[11] On appeal from the Primary Labour Commission in Riyadh, that had determined that X was entitled to end of service benefits from Y.

[12] The Implementing Regulations to Royal Decree No. 425 dated 5/3/1372 (22 November 1952).

The refund will be limited to the actual amount of customs duty paid on the imported items and would not include storage and porterage fees. The customs duties will be refunded in accordance with a specified formula following the export of the finished products and subject to the submission of supporting documentation.

7 TEMPORARY COMMERCIAL REGISTRATION: DIRECTIVE RESTRICTING AVAILABILITY

The simplest way for a foreign company to establish a legal presence in Saudi Arabia so as to perform a contract made with the Saudi government or its agencies for the provision of services (for example, a construction or maintenance contract) is to obtain a temporary licence and commercial registration from the Ministry of Commerce.

By virtue of Ministry of Commerce Resolution No. 680 of 1978, a foreign company performing work under a contract (or a related subcontract) with the Saudi government or one of its agencies is required to apply to the Ministry of Commerce within thirty days of signing the contract for the issuance of a temporary licence to operate in Saudi Arabia in order to perform such contract or subcontract.

Although it was always a requirement that the relevant contract be with the Saudi government or a governmental entity, this requirement was loosely enforced and it was, for example, the practice of certain public joint stock companies in which the Saudi government was part owner to procure the issuance of temporary licences of their foreign contractors. However, the Minister of Commerce has now directed[13] that the Ministry of Commerce will no longer issue temporary licences other than where the contract is with the Saudi government or a governmental entity (for this purpose, we understand that a governmental entity could include a company that is wholly-owned by the Saudi government).

In addition, we understand from discussions with the Ministry of Commerce that subcontractors are entitled to apply for temporary licences where the prime contractor's contract is with a governmental entity, but that for this purpose a governmental entity would probably not include a company that is wholly owned by the Saudi government, although the rationale for this distinction between prime contractors and subcontractors is somewhat unclear.

As a result of such directive, foreign contractors, which may previously have been able to conduct business activities in Saudi Arabia pursuant to a temporary licence, will now have to apply to the Ministry of Industry and Electricity for the issuance of a foreign capital investment licence. For example, a foreign contractor could establish a branch in Saudi Arabia pursuant to a foreign capital investment licence, which could be closed at the end of the relevant contract if no longer required by the foreign contractor. This change in practice is likely to cause some inconvenience to foreign contractors, as it is generally considered more difficult to obtain a foreign capital investment licence than a temporary licence and commercial registration.

---

[13] The directive originates from the conclusions of a committee formed at the level of undersecretaries at the Ministry of Commerce, the Ministry of Finance and National Economy, the Ministry of Industry and Electricity and the Public Auditor's Office, as minuted on 16/2/1419AH (10 June 1998).

8 AGENCY AND DISTRIBUTION AGREEMENTS: REQUIREMENTS FOR REGISTRATION

Saudi Arabian law prohibits foreigners from engaging in trading activities in Saudi Arabia (with the exception of GCC nationals).[14] Consequently, if a foreign company wishes to sell goods within Saudi Arabia (as opposed to making direct sales into Saudi Arabia) it must appoint a local agent or distributor.

The appointment of an agent or distributor is governed by the commercial agency regulations of 1981 (the "Regulations"). The Regulations provide that a commercial agent or distributor must be either a Saudi national or a wholly Saudi-owned company, the board of directors and managers of a Saudi company acting as an agent or distributor must be Saudi and that the person signing on behalf of the agent must also be Saudi.

The Regulations provide that an agency or distribution agreement must be registered by the agent or distributor with the Ministry of Commerce within three months of its commencement. An application form must be filed stating the name, commercial registration number, address and manager of the agent or distributor, the type of goods covered, the name, nationality and address of the principal, the territory covered and the duration of the agreement. The application must be accompanied by an original copy of the agency agreement and (if it is not in Arabic) an Arabic translation thereof.

The Regulations provide that the following particulars must be contained in the agency or distribution agreement:

(a)   the capacity and nationality of each of the parties;
(b)   the subject matter and territory of the agency;
(c)   the duration of the appointment and methods of renewal; and
(d)   the mode of termination or lapse of the appointment.

Beyond this, the Regulations require only that the agreement be written and contain a sufficient description of the rights and obligations of the parties and their obligations towards customers regarding maintenance and spare parts. While the above requirements appear to be straightforward, the actual registration of an agency or distribution agreement has always been more problematic. In particular, the Ministry of Commerce has always, as a matter of practice, included additional provisions that must be included in agency or distribution agreements before permitting such agreements to be registered. The Ministry of Commerce has recently "reminded" agents and distributors that it will not register any agency or distribution agreements (or approve their renewal) unless such agreements contain explicit terms confirming:

(a)   that all products will conform to specifications (if any) laid down by the Saudi Arabian Standards Organization;
(b)   that all products should be accompanied by a certificate of origin;

---

[14] Although GCC nationals are, subject to certain conditions, entitled to participate in trading companies in Saudi Arabia (see Council of Ministers Resolution No. 104 dated 12/7/1416AH (4 December 1995)), GCC nationals cannot participate in trading activities as "agents" or "distributors", as these activities are restricted to Saudi nationals.

(c)   a commitment on the part of the agent or distributor to provide after sales service to consumers throughout Saudi Arabia;

(d)   an undertaking to immediately announce any defects or technical faults in the relevant products and to withdraw defective products from the market for repair or replacement at the expense of the principal;

(e)   a commitment to employ and train Saudi technical and management staff on the part of the agent or distributor; and

(f)   that all disputes between the agent and the principal will be looked into by the judicial authorities in Saudi Arabia.

The above requirements are more onerous than those set forth in the Regulations. The legal basis for the Ministry of Commerce requiring certain matters not included in the Regulations to be included in an agency or distribution agreement is unclear.

The obligation to register an agency or distribution agreement is imposed upon the agent or distributor (as opposed to the principal) and financial penalties of between SR5,000 and SR50,000 can be imposed for non-registration in accordance with the Regulations.

9   LITIGATION

9.1   Recovery of legal and other expenses by a successful litigant

The practice of the Board of Grievances[15] has generally been not to award costs to a successful litigant. This practice appears to be based on the assumption that a litigant should generally be able to present its own case and, consequently, costs incurred by the successful litigant in employing lawyers and other experts are unnecessarily incurred.

However, the practice of the Board of Grievances has not been consistent and the possibility of obtaining an order for costs cannot be entirely discounted.

Set out below is a translated extract from pleadings presented to the Board of Grievances,[16] in which a claim for costs by a successful litigant was allowed in part (accounting fees were awarded, legal fees were not):[17]

---

[15] The Board of Grievances (*Diwan Al-Mazalin*) has exclusive jurisdiction in relation to disputes between a private contractor and a Saudi government entity and all commercial disputes between private litigants other than in relation to commercial disputes heard by specialist quasi-judicial bodies (for example, disputes relating to banking matters are heard by the Committee for the Settlement of Banking Disputes); we believe that, contrary to the practice of the Board of Grievances, the *shari'a* courts would generally award costs to a successful litigant if appropriately requested; certain judicial and quasi-judicial bodies in Saudi Arabia are expressly granted the power to award costs (for example, the Primary and Supreme Labour Commissions and the Negotiable Instruments Committee), although sometimes these powers are not exercised.

[16] Case Ref. No. 1749/1/K/1411H before Administrative Chamber No. 2 the Board of Grievances; the pleadings were drafted by Prof. Dr. Abdul Fattah Khedr, Law Firm of Salah Al-Hejailan, Riyadh.

[17] The original judgement was appealed but upheld by the Review Committee of the Board of Grievances in 1419AH. Legal fees can, however, sometimes be recovered: for example, see the Second Judgment of the Review Committee of the Board of Grievances (Third Circuit) under No. 136/D, year 1417AH.

. . . claiming that the Board of Grievances has settled, in the past, on the practice of not allowing compensation for expenses, is a disputed issue. There is no reason that prevents the Board of Grievances from changing its opinion in accordance with the dictates of justice and equity . . .

It is true that there is no obligation – legal or religious – on a litigant to seek the help of a lawyer, but such an obligation is actual and imposed by the circumstances in which the owner of a lost right finds himself. We can confidently say that Islamic religion incites people to protect their legal rights and not to neglect them in any way, and to pursue their interests with all permitted means, including by applying to the relevant courts and obtaining legal, auditing or medical expertise etc. in order to provide the necessary evidence for a juridical case, under the Islamic rule that stipulates "the evidence is on the plaintiff", which rule puts the whole burden of proof on the plaintiff's shoulders.

How can an ordinary man take the stand of a lawyer? How can a plaintiff manage without drawing upon the experience of others to protect his rights, especially if such rights are related, for example, . . . to the execution of a large project, the value of which is hundreds of millions of riyals, with all that accompanies the execution of such a project, such as the drafting and signing of contracts, bookkeeping, collection of money and undertaking to execute administrative or contractual obligations and where the Saudi government obliges contractors to be subject to all related regulations? Who can understand the context of legal texts and be knowledgeable about which of them is cancelled and which is still applied? Such texts necessitate legal expertise to be understood in the light of the legal system of a given state.

If it is permitted for the courts to seek the help and assistance of legal and auditing experts and others – as happened in this present case when the honourable court nominated an accounting expert – then such right should be permitted, in the first place, to the litigants according to their estimation as to whether their cases require such expertise . . .

We should add that Islamic religion does not refuse or disallow this issue, and here our Master Moses (peace be upon him) requested God to strengthen him in his confrontation [with Pharaoh] by joining to him his brother Haron, because Haron had the ability to express himself better than Moses. This was mentioned in the Holy Qur'an in Taha Chapter: "And appoint for me a helper from my family, Haron, my brother. Increase my strength with him, and let him share my task (of conveying Allah's message and prophethood)", (vers. 29–32).

As well as in Al-Qassas Chapter: "and my brother Haron – he is more eloquent in speech than me: so send him with me as a helper to confirm me. Verily I fear that they will belie me", (vers. 34).

By this our client hopes that it has given to Your Honourable Court sufficient justification for the legal and accounting fees, because there was real harm caused by the defendant's error as we have proved and as was proved by the [appointed] expert.

Needless to say, the reluctance of the Board of Grievances to award costs to successful litigants provides an incentive for litigants to reach some form of negotiated settlement, rather than pursuing their remedies to the fullest extent through the Saudi courts.

9.2 Representation before the Saudi courts

The Council of Ministers recently resolved[18] to generally prohibit non-GCC nationals from appearing on behalf of third parties before the Saudi courts.

The resolution, however, permits non-GCC nationals to represent third parties before the Saudi "judicial authorities" in certain circumstances, namely where the non-GCC national is representing:

(a)   his wife, kin, relatives by marriage or relatives to the fourth degree;
(b)   any company or establishment owned by the non-GCC national; or
(c)   any person of whom the non-GCC national is a guardian or trustee.

The resolution formalizes the circumstances that non-GCC nationals can appear before the Saudi courts, whereas previously non-GCC nationals were, at least in theory, not permitted to appear.[19]

10 *ZAKAT* AND TAX ADVISORY SERVICES: NEW REGULATIONS

The Ministry of Commerce has issued regulations[20] in connection with the provision of *zakat* and income tax advisory services in Saudi Arabia (the "*Zakat* and Tax Advisory Services Regulations").

The *Zakat* and Tax Advisory Services Regulations prohibit the provision of *zakat* and income tax services by persons other than accountants licensed to practise the profession of accounting and auditing in Saudi Arabia and persons holding licences issued by the Ministry of Commerce pursuant to the *Zakat* and Tax Advisory Services Regulations.

The *Zakat* and Tax Advisory Services Regulations provide that only Saudi nationals and wholly Saudi-owned entities may hold a licence. In addition to general provisions dealing with the granting and revocation of licences, the *Zakat* and Tax Advisory Services Regulations also include a number of consumer protection provisions, such as:

(a)   Article 8 provides that the licensee must strictly adhere to the rules of conduct of the profession as well as the accounting standards and other professional standards issued by the Saudi Commission for Legal Accountants.
(b)   Article 9 provides that the licensee must participate in continuing educational programmes provided by the Saudi Commission for Legal Accountants.
(c)   Article 11 provides that the licensee is responsible for all losses suffered by clients or third parties that result from the licensee's [negligent] work.

The *Zakat* and Tax Advisory Services Regulations also include provisions relating to the maintenance of records for a period of not less than ten years and compliance by licensees with the general Saudi national employment requirements. It ap-

---

[18] Published in the Official Gazette, Issue No. 3747 dated 13/2/1420AH (28 May 1999).
[19] Ministry of Commerce Decision No. 1190 dated 16/2/1402AH (12 December 1981).
[20] Ministerial Decree No. 946 of 26/7/1419AH (15 November 1998).

pears that lawyers and law firms are not formally exempted from the scope of the *Zakat* and Tax Advisory Services Regulations, but it is thought that it was not the intent to prevent licensed lawyers from providing *zakat* or tax advisory services.

11 ESTABLISHMENT OF BRANCHES OF GCC-INCORPORATED BANKS

The Saudi banking market has recently been subject to a wave of consolidations. United Saudi Commercial Bank and Saudi Cairo Bank merged to form United Saudi Bank and United Saudi Bank is now in the process of merging with Saudi American Bank.[21] For a number of years, no branches of foreign banks have been permitted to be established in Saudi Arabia, although a number of offshore banks lend significant amounts into Saudi Arabia.[22] Limited foreign participation in locally incorporated banks is permitted under the foreign capital investment regime.[23]

We understand that it is the intention of the authorities to progressively liberalize the existing regime in line with understandings reached between the member states of the GCC, so as to enable GCC-incorporated banks to establish branches in Saudi Arabia. However, it is likely that any liberalization will be gradual and only one banking licence has been issued to date under the liberalized regime (to the Bahrain-incorporated Gulf International Bank, which is expected to commence limited operations in Saudi Arabia from the year 2000).

---

[21] Resulting in the number of locally incorporated commercial banks reducing to seven.

[22] The establishment of a branch of a foreign bank in Saudi Arabia is not prohibited as such, but the issuance of a banking licence for such a branch is subject to the approval of the Council of Ministers pursuant to Art. 3 of the Banking Control Law.

[23] Currently under Art. 5 of Ministerial Resolution No. 11/M/R dated 17/7/1410AH (corresponding to 12 February 1990).

United Arab Emirates

*Richard Price**

1 SOURCES OF LAW: JUDICIAL AND LEGAL SYSTEM

1.1 Extension of working hours of court for non-contentious transactions

As of 1 November 1998, the Dubai Court of First Instance announced that it would remain open between the hours of 5 pm and 8 pm every day (except Thursdays and Fridays) for non-contentious matters such as the signing of marriage contracts, the issuing of marriage certificates and issues relating to inheritance and endowment.

2 CONSTITUTIONAL AND ADMINISTRATIVE LAW

There have been no significant developments in the relevant period.

3 CIVIL LAW

There have been no significant developments in the relevant period.

4 COMMERCIAL LAW

4.1 A court may order specific performance of an agency agreement

The Federal Court of Cassation[1] has held that where a local agent is a valid registered agent with the Ministry of Economy and Commerce (the "MEC") such reg-

---

* Former Gulf Resident Partner, Clifford Chance, Dubai, UAE.
[1] Petition No. 99/18 Civil Cassation.

istration must be ordered to continue. This is unusual as it is an order for the contract to be specifically performed rather than the more familiar order for compensation for unjustified termination.

The French car manufacturer, Peugeot, was dissatisfied with the service provided by its appointed agent. They therefore applied to the MEC to cancel the agency agreement and the power of attorney given to the agent, which the MEC purported to do. The agent filed a complaint when it discovered that Peugeot had obtained a licence to import cars and spare parts to Abu Dhabi itself. The appeal to the Court of Cassation was based on the ground that the MEC's decision to cancel the agency contract was halted by an urgent judgment issued on 13 December 1994 in Case No. 456/1994 in Abu Dhabi. In that case, the MEC declared that the registration of the agent was still valid. The Court of Cassation accepted these arguments and therefore held that the granting of a licence to Peugeot contradicted Articles 3, 8 and 23 of the Commercial Agencies Law which restrict the practising of commercial agency business to local companies and prohibit the re-registration of an agency at the Commercial Agencies Register in the name of another agent, unless that first agency was terminated amicably or the termination was based on substantial reasons that convince the Commercial Agencies Committee. The Commercial Agencies Law also prevents the importation of any goods related to a registered commercial agency without the approval of the commercial agent or the MEC.

4.2 Draft Law on the formation of the Emirates Securities and Commodities Market and Committee

The Ministerial Legislatures Committee will be reviewing a draft law on the establishment of the UAE Securities and Commodities Market and Committee before it is presented to the Cabinet. The intention is to create a market where securities and commodities are traded within the Emirates. In its current form the draft law deals with a number of issues.

The types of instrument which will be traded include shares, securities and bonds, all agricultural products and all natural resources extracted from under the ground or sea after preparing them for commercial use. Market activity will be carried out through two electronically connected halls, one in Abu Dhabi and the other in Dubai. More halls may be set up in other cities in the UAE if this proves beneficial to the market. The market will take the form of a federal government institution which will be solely owned by the federal government and headquartered in Dubai.

A securities and commodities authority will be established to set up the market and to regulate it. The authority will be made up of a board of directors and an administrative body. The board will be answerable to the Cabinet and will have to report every six months on the market's activities. The administrative body will be in charge of carrying the board's decisions into effect and will be accountable to it.

The federal government will cover all expenses incurred by the authority in the first year, and half the expenses incurred during the second and third years. The Authority will receive its funding from a percentage of the registration fees, the annual fee imposed on companies and brokers in the market, fees imposed on trading and fees for services rendered by the market. The market will retain the balance of any fees extracted from members.

Dealing in securities listed on the market will be limited to authorized brokers. The board will issue codes dealing with the conditions for accepting brokerage companies, registration procedures and permits.

The draft law also deals with the issue of insider dealing. Article 37 provides that no one may deal in securities based on undeclared information that has come to his knowledge by virtue of his position and no one may spread rumours about the selling or buying of shares. Strict penalties for violation of this provision include a jail sentence of no less than three months and a minimum fine of AED100,000.

Although a significant amount of work is still required in order to put the draft law into effect, this is an important first step in the formation of a stock exchange for the UAE.

4.3 A creditor may not claim payment of instalments which are not yet due, even if the debtor is in default with some of the payments

The Dubai Court of Cassation[2] has held that where the parties have agreed that a debt will be paid by instalments, the creditor can only claim for instalments which have fallen due but have not been paid. The creditor cannot claim for the full amount of the loan and in particular, he cannot claim for payment of instalments which have not yet become due.

Etisalat sued one of its employees in relation to a loan granted by them. However, the defendant had resigned before repaying the loan and had defaulted in the payment of certain instalments. The plaintiff claimed the full loan amount.

The Court of Cassation held that where a creditor has extended to the debtor the facility of paying a debt by instalments, it was not prepared to read into the contract an implied term that should the borrower default in certain instalments, the whole loan becomes due. The court confirmed that it had no right to interfere in the contract by calling in the rest of the instalments before they became due.

4.4 A shipowner will avoid liability under a bill of lading where the damage to the goods occurred as a result of the negligence of a third party

The Dubai Court of Cassation[3] has held that the owners of a vessel cannot be held liable for damage caused to goods by a third party, even if the damage occurs before delivery of the goods to the consignee.

An insurance company was subrogated to the claim of the consignee. The claim was for damage to a cargo of air conditioner units shipped from the USA to Dubai. As the carrier under the Bill of Lading, pursuant to Article 275 of the UAE Maritime Code, the defendant carrier was responsible for loss or damage sustained by the goods during the period from the time he took delivery of the goods at the

---

[2] Case No. 276/97.
[3] Case No. 274/97.

port of loading to the time he delivered the same to the persons having the right to them at the port of discharge.

Before the Court of Cassation the plaintiffs argued that pursuant to Article 275 of the Code, the defendants were liable for any damage caused to the goods while they were in their possession, even if such damage occurred at the hands of a third party. The Court of Cassation rejected this argument and held that the carrier will escape liability if he discharges the burden of proving that the damage was the fault of a third party. In these circumstances, a third party means anyone other than the carrier or his representative. On the facts of this case, the Jebel Ali Ports Authority, which handled the goods after their discharge up until the time of delivery to the consignee, was neither a representative nor the agent of the carrier. The Court based its decision on the grounds that the carrier had no control or power of supervision over the Port Authority and the Authority charged customs and handling charges for its own account.

4.5 UAE Central Bank Circular on requirements for personal loans and the provision of credit facilities

In February 1998 it was reported that, on instructions from the President of the UAE, the Minister of Interior has issued a letter which was circulated to all banks and financial institutions in the country by the UAE Central Bank. The purpose of the letter was to highlight certain matters which should be taken into account when considering applications for personal loans and other credit facilities. Banks/financial institutions should not provide personal loans or credit facilities to the unemployed, individuals with a low income, individuals who cannot provide security for the repayment of a loan or guarantees that the loan will be repaid, or any other person which the bank/financial institution has reasonable grounds to believe will be unable to repay his/her debt. The letter goes on to state that in such circumstances neither the police nor the courts will consider the case and that any bank/financial institution which ignores these provisions will be responsible for the consequences of failing to comply. The exact legal status of the Ministry of Interior letter and Central Bank circular is unclear. In any event, it is understood that its application is likely to be limited to Abu Dhabi.

4.6 Reservation clauses on bills of lading

A recent Court of Cassation[4] judgment is indicative of a more reasonable judicial approach to reservation clauses on bills of lading.

A claim was brought by the consignee of the bill of lading against the carrier and the cargo insurers. The container of goods which was the subject of the claim was opened on arrival in Dubai and found to be empty. The bill of lading was claused with the words "said to contain" and "shippers load stow and count".

---

[4] Case No. 379/98.

The Court of Cassation-appointed expert stated that the container was delivered to the plaintiff with the seal intact. The court emphasized that the bill of lading constitutes absolute evidence of the condition of the goods at the time of shipment. In addition, the court went on to say that the reservations on the face of the bill are part of the contract of carriage entered into between the carrier and the shipper and are valid against a consignee. It is not, therefore, open to a consignee to argue that the terms of the bill of lading do not apply to him as he was not a party to the original contract. The court held that such cases turn on their facts and it is for the lower courts, based on the evidence and any expert witnesses, to assess whether the reservation clause on the face of a bill of lading is effective to exclude the carrier and/or the insurer's liability. The issue which the courts have to decide is whether the carrier has had the opportunity to examine the goods prior to shipment.

This case should be contrasted to many earlier judgments of the Court of Cassation, including a recent one,[5] in which the court held that a carrier is liable for goods shipped in a sealed container. One must assume, therefore, that where there is no reservation clause on the face of the bill of lading, the carrier will be held responsible for shortage or damage, even if the container is delivered sealed to the carrier at the port of shipment.

In this particular case the consignee brought a claim for both shortage and damage to goods. The carrier argued that the container delivered to the vessel was sealed and was marked CY-CY which meant that the carrier had not checked the container and had marked his reservation on the same by stating, in shorthand form, that he had taken delivery of the container from the container yard and bore no responsibility for its contents. The Court of Cassation placed the burden of proof firmly on the carrier to rebuff the assumption that the damage or loss had been caused during the voyage by showing that the damage was caused by force majeure or a third party. The carrier is under an obligation to maintain the goods in complete and good condition and this duty is not discharged until he delivers them in the same good condition, to the consignee or his representative. In circumstances where there is no reservation clause on a bill of lading and where the carrier has not discharged this burden of proof, the carrier will be liable for shortage and/or damage to cargo even if he receives a sealed container which he delivers at the port of discharge with the seal intact. The Maritime Code does not make specific provision for shipment of goods by container and, therefore, the rules as to liability are the same as for other shipments.

4.7 Banks may not charge compound interest exceeding 12 per cent in the Emirate of Abu Dhabi

The Federal Supreme Court of Abu Dhabi[6] has restated that it is permissible for banks to charge interest. However, it has held that they may not charge interest

---

5 Case No. 212/97.
6 Case No. 176/207.

beyond 12 per cent. and furthermore the bank may not charge compound interest even if the parties agree to this in writing in advance.

The plaintiff in this case sued the bank and asked the court to order that a settlement agreement made between himself and the defendant bank was null and void on the grounds that it charged compound interest. The bank had extended an overdraft facility to the plaintiff which was to be repaid by way of instalments and the borrower had issued post-dated cheques by way of repayment. The cheques bounced and, in order to avoid criminal proceeding instigated by the bank, the plaintiff agreed to sign the settlement agreement. The settlement agreement provided, without the knowledge of the plaintiff, for the charging of compound interest. The courts appointed an auditor to check the calculations and to ascertain how the instalments and the repayments were calculated.

The court reiterated that, even though Islamic principles of *shari'a* (which is the principal source of UAE law) state that interest is illegal, it is necessary in the interests of the UAE economy and has therefore been legalized pursuant to Articles 61 and 62 of the Abu Dhabi Law of Procedure No. 3 of 1970 as amended by Law Nos. 3 and 4 of 1987. However, pursuant to Article 62 the maximum interest which can be charged on any commercial transaction is 12 per cent and for any non-commercial transaction it is 9 per cent. The court held that the parties to a commercial contract do not have the right to contract out of these provisions as the purpose of the legislation was the protection of debtors. The courts therefore must enforce the maximum rates imposed by Article 63. In addition, any attempt by a bank to charge compound interest will be held to be null and void.

The court also held that, since banking transactions are commercial transactions, the Civil Code does not apply to them. In particular, Article 714 which states that any provision in a contract which provides for a "benefit in excess of the contract" will be void, does not apply to commercial transactions and consequently banks may charge interest.

5 EMPLOYMENT AND LABOUR LAW

5.1 Draft law on Pensions and Social Security for UAE nationals

The UAE draft law on Pensions and Social Security was recently approved by the UAE Cabinet and is awaiting final ratification by the President of the UAE. Provided the law progresses through to enactment in its current form, it will be applicable to UAE nationals employed both in the public and the private sectors. The Pension Scheme will be operated by way of a contribution from salary which may amount to 5 per cent of an employee's monthly salary. In order to be eligible for a pension, an employee must complete twenty years' service.

The draft law also deals with the issue of severance pay and sets out the level of compensation which a company must pay to its employees if they are made redundant. The level of compensation is calculated by reference to the length of service.

Finally, the draft law provides for the establishment of the General Authority for Pensions and Social Security (GAPSS) which will act as an independent body to help finance the scheme and to help reduce the need for government subsidies.

5.2 End of service benefits rules developed by the Court of Cassation

The Court of Cassation recently ruled than an employee is not entitled to end of service benefits if (a) his employment contract is for an unlimited period, or (b) he has not completed five years of continued service under a fixed term contract and his employment is terminated in the following circumstances:

(i)   the employee is absent, without a legal reason, for more than twenty days intermittently during the period of one year or more than seven days successively; or

(ii) the employee terminates his employment voluntarily without notice provided, however, that the employer was not in breach of his legal or contractual obligations towards the employee or the employer did not commit an act of aggression against the employee.

The Court of Cassation was asked to interpret Federal Law No. 8 of 1980 (the Labour Law). The plaintiff/employee sued his employer for end of service benefits and severance pay. In the Court of Cassation the defendant employer argued that the plaintiff had resigned in order to avoid dismissal for being absent for more than one month without excuse. In addition, the plaintiff had left his employment without notice. The Court of Cassation relied on Article 120 of the Labour Law and held that, on the facts of this case, the employee was found to have resigned in order to avoid being dismissed and this was sufficient grounds for disentitling him of his end of service benefits.

6 SOCIAL SECURITY LAW

6.1 Draft law on Medical Liability and Insurance

According to reports, the Ministry of Health has drafted a new law on Medical Liability and Insurance which is being considered by the relevant bodies.

One of the provisions which has been suggested is for hospitals and medical staff to be held jointly liable for any injury sustained by their patients as a result of the treatment provided. In addition, the draft law states that a doctor must obtain the prior consent of a patient to the proposed treatment, except in cases of emergency where consent cannot be obtained in advance.

The draft law also provides that both public and private practitioners must obtain medical insurance covering them, *inter alia*, against negligence. The government will subsidize a minimum of 80 per cent of the annual premium of such insurance for the public sector and the balance will be paid by the medical staff.

7 PROPERTY LAW

7.1 Draft law on property ownership

The UAE cabinet is considering a draft law entitled Non-national Ownership of Real Estate. Article 1 of this law states that "The ownership of all kinds of real estate in the UAE shall be restricted to UAE nationals. This shall include perfect and imperfect ownership and the right of usufruct." According to Article 2, any transfer of ownership of freehold property to foreigners will be null and void.

In accordance with Article 7 of the draft law, foreigners who currently own freehold property in the UAE must, in order to maintain their ownership, apply for registration of their property in the Emirate concerned within six months from the date that the draft law is implemented.

There appear to be two exceptions to this rule. First, by virtue of Article 6 of the draft law a foreign owner may transfer his ownership to a non-national by inheritance. It is not clear whether this also applies in circumstances where a UAE national is purporting to leave property to a non-national by way of inheritance.

In addition, by Article 4 of the draft law the headquarters of international organizations, diplomatic and consular missions and the residence granted to the head of the mission, are exempt from the provisions of the draft law and these entities are allowed to own real estate in the UAE.

The draft law is in line with rules in place in Abu Dhabi. However, it is in sharp contrast to the position in Sharjah where 24 per cent of the real estate market is said to be attributed to foreign investors or owners. The other Emirates allow for the ownership of real estate in some shape or form, albeit with certain restrictions.

8 INTELLECTUAL PROPERTY (TRADEMARKS)

There have been no significant statutory developments in the relevant period. There have, however, been other matters of interest.

8.1 Opening of the Patent Office and revised requirements for submission of applications

On 18 November 1998, the Gulf Corporation Council's Patent Office was officially opened under the direction of the Secretary-General Jamil Al Hejailan. The Patent Office is supported by the World Trade Organization. The intention is that individuals should be encouraged to invest in the development of new ideas within the industrial or trade markets in order to facilitate the introduction of new kinds of products.

The headquarters of the Patent Office are in Riyadh, Saudi Arabia.

Pursuant to the GCC's patent regulations, there are four requirements for the registration of a valid patent. These are:

(a) the invention must be new;
(b) it must involve an inventive step;
(c) it must be industrially applicable; and
(d) it must not contradict Islamic *shari'a*, public order, or the GCC's ethics.

The GCC's regulations enumerate a number of things which are not considered inventions and therefore cannot be patented. Amongst these are computer programmes, methods of surgical or therapeutical treatment of the human or animal body, methods of diagnosis applied to the human or animal body and rules and methods for doing business.

The regulations also set out the information and documents which must accompany a patent application. The application must be submitted in both Arabic and English and delivered to the Patent Office's headquarters.

Once the patent is registered with the GCC Patent Office, its owner is automatically afforded protection throughout all GCC member states. The patent is valid for fifteen years and can be renewed for a further five years. The patent cannot be extended beyond this twenty-year period. In order to obtain the extension, the applicant must justify the request.

If the patent is infringed, the inventor can file a complaint against the violating party. Acts of infringement include importing, selling, offering to sell, storing with the intent to sell and using the product protected under the patent.

8.2 The registered owner of a trademark will be granted protection irrespective of any arguments or challenges submitted, unless the registration is cancelled

The Court of Cassation[7] overruled both the Court of First Instance and the Court of Appeal in relation to the infringement of a trademark. A claim was brought before the Dubai courts for the protection of a trademark against a counterfeit product bearing the same trademark which was being imported and sold by a local trader.

The Court of First Instance and the Court of Appeal looked beyond the fact that the trademark was registered and considered whether it met the requirements for registration. The plaintiff-owner of the trademark appealed on the grounds that the previous courts should not have considered whether the trademark met the criteria for a registerable trademark (the Courts had held that the trademark did not have an independent status, was not new and creative and that, despite its valid registration, the plaintiff would not be granted protection).

The Court of Cassation held, based on the UAE Trademarks Law No. 37 of 1992, that Articles 5–26 state the procedure to be used when challenging the registration of a trademark. Any party wishing to challenge the decision of the Trademarks Committee of the Ministry of Economy and Commerce can do so by appeal to the Courts in accordance with those Articles and such Court may order the cancellation of the trademark. However, the registration of a trademark cannot be challenged if more than ten years have elapsed since its registration.

Therefore, if a trademark is registered in the Trademarks Register the proprietor will be entitled to use it from the date when the application was filed and will be entitled to protection against interference with such trademark. The trademark will be effective throughout its term unless it is cancelled and deregistered according to the rules and procedures stipulated under the law. No action had been filed for the cancellation of the trademark in this case and the plaintiff was therefore the proprietor of the trademark and entitled to protection. The hearing of a claim for infringement was not the appropriate forum to decide whether the trademark met the requirements of registration.

---

[7] Case No. 152/97.

9 FAMILY LAW AND SUCCESSION

There have been no significant developments in the relevant period.

10 CIVIL PROCEDURE AND EVIDENCE (ENFORCEMENT OF FOREIGN JUDGMENTS)

There have been no significant statutory developments in the relevant period. There have, however, been a number of Abu Dhabi and Dubai Court of Cassation cases of interest.

10.1 A fax message produces the effect of a "common instrument" and can serve as evidence

The Court of Cassation[8] has held that a fax message can serve as evidence pursuant to paragraph 1 of Article 11 of the UAE Law of Evidence.

This was an action in debt. On appeal to the Court of Cassation, the defendant argued that the lower courts had erred in law on the ground that, in reaching their decision, they had relied on a fax sent by the defendant to the plaintiff admitting the debt. By Article 11 (1) a common instrument is deemed to be issued by a person who puts his signature thereto, unless he expressly denies any handwriting, signature, stamp or thumb print attributed to him. A further argument raised by the defendant was that the contents of the fax admitting liability were inconsistent with the defendant's accounts which showed that a lesser amount of money was due to the plaintiff.

The court held that, as the fax amounted to a common instrument and was therefore admissible as evidence, it was not sufficient to contest it on the grounds that its contents did not correspond with the defendant's accounts. The court stated that a fax message can only be disputed on the grounds that it was not issued or signed by the party purporting to have issued or signed it, or by proving that it is inconsistent with the original copy.

10.2 Requirements to enforce a foreign arbitration award in the UAE

The Dubai Court of First Instance[9] has laid down the requirements for enforcing a foreign arbitration award in the UAE.

The owners and managers of a vessel had brought proceedings before a London arbitrator against the time charterer of their vessel for failure to pay hire, bunkers and port fees. The arbitrator held in favour of the owners and managers of the vessel and ordered the defendants to pay the sum of US$460,810.91 plus interest.

---

[8] Case No. 328/97.
[9] Case No. 190/98.

The owners and managers filed a claim before the Dubai Court of First Instance to enforce the award. The defendant argued, despite the agreement to submit to arbitration contained in the charter party, that the arbitrator did not have jurisdiction to hear the dispute. The defendant based his claim on Articles 20 and 24 of the Civil Procedure Law of 1992 alleging that the claim was personal and therefore UAE courts had jurisdiction to hear such a claim. The defendant also argued that he was not appropriately represented before the arbitrators.

The court held that Articles 20 and 24 of the Civil Procedure Law relate to the establishment of jurisdiction within the UAE and do not restrict the freedom of the parties to agree by contract that any disputes should be resolved by arbitration abroad. In view of this, and the fact that the parties had agreed to arbitration in the charter party, the UAE courts did not have jurisdiction in this matter. Furthermore, the defendant could not argue that he was not adequately represented before the arbitrator as he had been properly notified of the proceedings but failed to appear before the arbitrator.

Having reached this conclusion, the court further held that the following requirements must be met in order to enforce a foreign arbitration award:

(a)   the claimant must submit documents to the court confirming that the foreign arbitration award is final and cannot subsequently be challenged;
(b)   the claimant must confirm that the arbitration award can be enforced in the country in which it was issued; and
(c)   there must exist a reciprocity treaty between the UAE and the foreign country where the award was issued which provides that any judgments issued in the UAE will be enforceable in that country.

10.3 The Abu Dhabi Supreme Court of Cassation ratified a judgment of a French court against a trading company in Sharjah

The Abu Dhabi Supreme Court of Cassation[10] rejected the arguments of a trading company in Sharjah challenging the enforceability of a judgment given under French law by the French courts.

The French trading company filed the claim in the Sharjah Court of First Instance requesting that a judgment given by a French court should be enforced against the defendant.

The defendant appealed to the UAE Supreme Court of Cassation on the grounds that the French Court summons had not been properly served on the defendant in France and therefore the judgment should be declared to be null and void. The lower courts had held that this was a matter to be decided in accordance with the French law of procedure. On appeal the defendant argued that this was a breach of the agreement between the UAE and France in relation to the enforcement of judgments and that, therefore, the Sharjah courts should have decided the issue regarding the service of the summons by reference to that agreement.

---

[10] Case No. 41/17.

The Supreme Court held that the UAE courts cannot review the merits of the case where it has been decided in a foreign jurisdiction and under a foreign law. According to Articles 21 and 22 of the UAE Civil Procedure Law, the law of the country where the action is being heard will be applied to matters of procedure. Accordingly, the method of service of the summons falls to be determined according to French procedural law, unless such procedure is contrary to public policy in the country where the judgment is to be executed. In addition, the treaty between France and the UAE in relation to the mutual enforcement of judgments provides that the applicable law in relation to matters of procedure is the law of the country where the original action is filed.

A number of factors influenced the Supreme Court in reaching its decision to enforce the judgment. It had heard in evidence from the French Consul in Abu Dhabi that UAE judgments are enforceable in France under Article 509 of the French Law of Procedure. Further, Article 19 of the UAE Civil Procedure Law states that the law of the country where the contract is executed will apply. In this case the contract was entered into in France and therefore French law applied. The appropriate courts within the French judicial system had heard the case, the summons was effectively served by diplomatic channels and the plaintiff in this case had also filed a counterclaim before the French court (i.e. submitting to the jurisdiction of that court).

10.4 The courts can rely on English language documents in delivering their judgments and have a discretion in the appointment of experts

The Dubai Court of Cassation[11] recently clarified the law in relation to documents presented to courts in the English language.

The courts were faced with a straightforward debt claim and both the Court of First Instance and the Court of Appeal found in favour of the plaintiff and ordered the defendant to pay the sum owed plus interest and costs.

The defendant appealed to the Court of Cassation on a number of grounds.

One of the issues on which the judgment of the Court of First Instance was challenged was on the ground that the court had rejected the defendant's request that an expert should examine the plaintiff's books in order to ascertain precisely what sums were due to the plaintiff. On this point, the Dubai Court of Cassation ruled that the lower courts had discretion to pass judgment on a case by reference to some (rather than all) of the documents presented to them and, if they consider it necessary, they may refer certain matters to experts in the relevant field. However, a court does not have to appoint an expert because one of the parties has submitted a request to that effect, it merely has a discretion to do so.

The alternative ground on which the defendants challenged the judgments of the lower courts was that the courts had been wrong to rely on invoices and receipts provided by the plaintiffs which were in the English language. In this respect, the Court of Cassation held that the courts can rely on documents which are in the English language and which have not been translated, especially in cases where the de-

---

[11] Case No. 29/97.

fendant does not challenge the meaning of the English document. The court rejected the defendant's submission that they did not understand English holding that this was not a good defence.

10.5 An agreement between the parties to give jurisdiction to a foreign court is null and void where the defendant has a UAE domicile

The Dubai Court of Cassation[12] has held that an agreement giving jurisdiction to the courts of Saudi Arabia is null and void where the defendant has a UAE domicile or place of residence as it contravenes Articles 20 and 24 of the UAE Civil Procedure Law.

The contract between the plaintiff and the defendant was executed in Saudi Arabia and the plaintiff's claim was for sums due under that contract. The defendant had contracted to build the extension of the military hospital in Riyadh, Saudi Arabia and had employed the plaintiff as a sub-contractor.

The defendant's appeal was based on the exclusive jurisdiction clause contained in the contract between the parties which stated that any dispute would be settled by competent authorities in Saudi Arabia.

However, the Court of Cassation relied on Article 20 of the UAE Civil Procedure Law which states that: "with the exception of real actions (action in rem) concerning real estate located abroad, Courts shall have jurisdiction to hear actions lodged against a national and a foreigner having a domicile or place of residence in the state".

Therefore, with the exception of real estate cases, a defendant may be sued in his place of domicile and any contractual agreement to the contrary is, by virtue of Article 24, null and void.

10.6 A Dubai court does not have jurisdiction to hear a dispute where the defendant is domiciled in Ajman, even if the vessel's arrest is ordered in Dubai and the vessel is mortgaged to the applicant

Where a plaintiff sued a local trader based in Ajman before the courts of Dubai, the Court of Cassation[13] held that the Dubai court did not have jurisdiction to hear the matter. The claim had to be brought in Ajman which was the domicile of the defendant.

The defendant had a number of businesses both in Dubai and Ajman, including vessels registered in his name in Dubai. The plaintiff had taken a mortgage over one of these vessels as security for a loan granted to the defendant. The plaintiff obtained an attachment order from the Dubai court against the defendant's assets in Dubai and Ajman (including an order for the arrest of the vessel).

Two sets of proceedings, one in relation to the merits of the case and the other in relation to the arrest, were progressing through the courts at the same time. In both

---

[12] Case No. 155/97.
[13] Case No. 11/97.

sets of proceedings the defendant argued that the court did not have jurisdiction. However, the decisions of the lower courts were inconsistent on this issue. The Court of Cassation joined the two sets of proceedings and the judgment related to both.

The Court of Cassation held that in commercial actions filed against companies, the action should be filed at the court in which the company had its principal place of business or where it has its branch office, or the place where the contract was executed in full or in part, or, where damages are involved, in the place where the damage took place. On these facts, it was evident that the defendant's main place of business was Ajman and that the contract between the parties was not executed in Dubai. Additionally, the companies whose domicile was Dubai were not involved in the transaction which was in dispute and therefore were not relevant.

The Court of Cassation also held that the mere fact that a Dubai court has ordered the arrest of a vessel does not give it jurisdiction to hear the main action. As the mortgage was registered in Ajman, only the courts of Ajman could hear the case. The location of the arrest is, therefore, irrelevant.

The Court of Cassation therefore dismissed the attachment order and held that the Dubai court did not have jurisdiction to hear the main action.

10.7 The Dubai court has jurisdiction to hear a claim where part of the contract is executed in Dubai, despite the fact that the goods are shipped to Sharjah

The Dubai Court of Cassation[14] held that the consignee under a bill of lading can sue the carrier for compensation for shortage and damage to goods.

The contract provided for the carriage of goods from a port in Taiwan to Khalid port in Sharjah on a vessel owned by the defendants. In alleged breach of their obligations under the bill of lading, when the goods arrived at their destination there was a shortage and they were found to have deteriorated.

The Court of Cassation held that the Dubai courts do have jurisdiction to hear the matter even if the consignment was shipped to Sharjah, on the ground that the bill of lading was endorsed in Dubai. This conferred jurisdiction on the Dubai courts over the case, as part of the contract was executed in Dubai. The court stated that, in commercial matters, it has jurisdiction to hear a case if the person is domiciled or has his business in Dubai or if the contract was executed or implemented in part or in full in Dubai. The plaintiff in these circumstances can choose to file the case in any of the relevant jurisdictions.

10.8 An arbitrator must be and remain independent and impartial from the parties to an agreement

The Dubai Court of Cassation[15] has held that if an arbitrator appointed under an arbitration clause is not found to be impartial, the courts will strike down the arbitration clause and hear the case themselves instead.

---

[14] Case No. 212.
[15] Case No. 355/97.

The plaintiff brought a claim against the defendant for monies due under a construction contract. The defendant called on the Court of First Instance to dismiss the action on the ground that the parties had agreed to arbitrate any dispute that may arise between them.

The Court of Cassation reiterated the position that where the parties to a contract have agreed in writing that any dispute between them will be resolved by arbitration, the court would uphold their choice and would not have jurisdiction to hear the case. However, the arbitrator chosen by the parties cannot be involved in the dispute in question in any way. In order to maintain the impartiality and independence of the arbitrator he may not be a representative of either of the parties to the dispute. On the facts of this case the arbitrator was the engineer who had supervised the plaintiff's work during the construction period. In view of this relationship with the plaintiff, the court found that the arbitrator was likely to represent the defendant's interest and was therefore not impartial. This was a clear violation of the principle that the judiciary must be impartial.

It is not clear from the judgement why the court dismissed the arbitration clause in its entirety. The court could have simply appointed an alternative arbitrator. However, it chose to take jurisdiction over the case.

11 CRIMINAL LAW AND PROCEDURE

There have been no significant developments in the relevant period.

12 PUBLIC INTERNATIONAL LAW

There have been no significant developments in the relevant period.

13 PRIVATE INTERNATIONAL LAW

There have been no significant developments in the relevant period.

14 ENVIRONMENTAL LAW

14.1 Draft Federal Environment Law

The Draft Federal Environmental Law which is currently being referred to the UAE Cabinet contains harsh sanctions on those who pollute the sea, air and land. For example, the dumping of oil, oily mixtures, noxious substances or other substances polluting the environment will give rise to a minimum fine of Dhs150,000 and a maximum fine of Dhs500,000. Repeat offenders will be jailed for one to three years in addition to being fined the sums specified above. Foreign ships without pollution reducing equipment in UAE ports or UAE waters will face fines of between Dhs70,000 and Dhs300,000. Finally, the direct or indirect pollution of drinking water will be met with a fine of between Dhs500 and Dhs20,000.

Bahrain

Husain M. Al Baharna*

1 COMMERCIAL AGENCY

1.1 Law by Decree No. 8 for 1998 Amending Certain Provisions of Law by Decree No. 10 for 1992, Concerning the Commercial Agency

This new amending law replaces Articles 1, 3(h), 7, 9, 12, 15 and 25 of the 1992 Law on the Commercial Agency with new articles. The new Article 1 widens the definition of the Commercial Agency by stating:

A commercial agency is defined, under the provisions of this Law, as representing the principal in the distribution of goods and products or their display for sale and circulation, in return for a profit or a commission, or in providing facilities of any kind. These activities comprise agencies for land, sea and air communication or agencies for tourism offices or for travel and services or for insurance or for publication and distribution or for the press, promotion or advertising and any other commercial activities for which an edict from the Minister of Commerce is issued.

The new Article 7 of the Law provides:

1. The agent is entitled to a commission not exceeding 5 per cent of the price of the goods or products imported by a third party for the purpose of trade if such goods or products (that are covered in the agency agreement) were not directly imported from the principal himself, provided that such arrangements have been made in accordance with the procedures and conditions of the edicts issued by the Minister of Commerce.

---

* PhD in International Law (Cambridge); Barrister-at-Law of Lincoln's Inn; Council Member of ICCA; Member of the UN International Law Commission (ILC); Attorney, Legal Consultant and Arbitrator Bahrain; Former Minister for Legal Affairs, Bahrain.

2. The agent shall receive his commission from the principal in accordance with their agreement if the goods or products imported by third parties for the purpose of trade have been sent to them directly through the principal.
3. The agent is not entitled to any commission from the customer for the goods imported by him for his personal use only. Nor is the agent entitled to any commission for goods imported by third parties for the purpose of re-exporting the same goods (transit trade). Similarly, no commission is to be paid to the agent for goods and products imported for industry and, thus, exempted from customs tariff.
4. The Minister of Commerce may, in accordance with the procedures and conditions of the edict issued by him, exempt certain goods and products from the payments of commission on them to the agent if such exemption is in the public interest.

The new Article 9 of the law provides:

(a) The committee concerned which shall be formed by an edict to be issued by the Minister of Commerce, may terminate the registration of the agency of an unlimited period either by an agreement of both parties, or if either party makes such a request, notwithstanding the objection of the other party. But the injured party is entitled to claim compensation for the harm caused to him as a result of such an action.
(b) The agent, notwithstanding an agreement to the contrary, has the right to claim compensation for the damage suffered if his activities resulted in a clear success of his promotion of the principal's products in increasing the number of his customers, and accordingly, the principal's termination of the agency contract has deprived him from obtaining the profit or the commission resulting from such success.

The new Articles 3(h), 12, 15 and 25 of the Law are procedural. Article 2 of the new Amending Law of 1998 abrogates Articles 5 and 31(4) of the Law by Decree No. 10 for 1992, concerning the Commercial Agency, as well as any provision contrary to the 1998 Amending Law.

Article 4 of the new Amending Law authorizes the Minister of Commerce to issue the necessary edicts for the implementation of the law.[1]

2 COMPANY LAW

2.1 Law by Decree No. 10 for 1999 Amending Some Provisions of the Law of Commercial Companies No. 28 for 1975

Article 1 of this law provides for substitution of the provisions of Articles 60, 60(bis) and 110 of the Law of Commercial Companies by the following provisions:

Article 60
Taking into consideration Articles 60(bis) and 278 of this Law, all shareholders of joint stock companies shall be Bahraini nationals, without prejudice to the formation and ownership by nationals of the Gulf Cooperation Councils of joint stock companies.

---

[1] Official Gazette No. 2314, 1 April 1998.

Article 60(bis)
Taking into consideration the provisions of Articles 60 and 278 of this Law, the Minister
of Commerce may grant a license for the establishment of joint stock companies with the
participation of foreign capital or foreign expertise, provided that the participation of
Bahrainis in its capital should not be less than 51 per cent. However, the Minister of
Commerce may issue edicts providing that the percentage of the participation of the foreign capital could exceed 49 per cent of the capital.

The shares that represent the foreign capital shall not be transferred or disposed of by any
form of disposition during the period of three years from the date of the registration of the
company in the Register of Commerce, unless such disposition of shares has taken place
between persons of the foreign party alone.

Article 110
Shares and provisional certificates of the company may be transferable. Also, the company
may buy its shares for the purpose of investments and the Minister of Commerce shall
issue an edict providing for cases where the company is allowed to buy its shares for the
purpose of investment. The edict shall also provide for the maximum of shares that are
allowed to be bought by the company.

The disposition of shares shall not be enforced vis-à-vis the company of a third party
unless it is registered in the Register allocated for that purpose.[2]

2.2 Edict of Minister of Commerce No. 1 for 1999, Amending Certain Provisions of Minister of Commerce's Edict No. 11 for 1994

This new Edict by the Minister of Commerce provides for amendments of certain
provisions of the 1994 Edict concerning granting licences to non-Bahrainis to own
and deal with shares of joint stock companies. Article 1 of the Edict substitutes the
provisions of Article 1 of the former 1994 Edict by the following provision:

Article 1
Taking into consideration the provisions of Article 60(bis) of the Law by Decree No. 10
for 1999, concerning the amendment of certain provisions of the Law of Commercial
Companies, issued by Law by Decree No. 28 for 1975, non-Bahrainis may own and deal
with shares of Bahraini joint stock companies, in accordance with the provisions of the
Law of Commercial Companies with the exception of the shares of the Bahrain Flour Mill
Company and the Delmon Chicken Company. Dealings with and transfer of shares shall
be in accordance with the provisions of the Law of the Bahrain Stock Exchange Market
and regulations and Edicts thereof.

Article 2
Article 2 of the Minister of Commerce's Edict No. 11 for 1994, concerning the licence for
non-Bahrainis to own and deal with joint stock company shares is hereby abrogated.[3]

---

[2] Official Gazette No. 2362, 3 March 1999.
[3] Official Gazette No. 2365, 24 March 1999.

3 LABOUR LAW

Edict No. 2 for 1999, issued on 14 February 1999 by the Minister of Labour and Social Affairs concerning the equalization of the application of cases and procedures of Labour Law in the private sector to both Bahrainis and nationals of the Gulf Cooperation Council (GCC) on the same footing.[4]

4 TRANSFER AND IMPLANTATION OF HUMAN BODY PARTS

4.1 Law by Decree No. 16 for 1998 concerning the Transfer and Implantation of Human Body Parts

This Law comprises twelve articles. According to Article 1 of this law, specialized doctors of medicine may perform medical operations for extracting parts of the body of a human person, alive or dead, and thereafter, implanting those parts in the human body of another alive person, with the purpose of treatment and preservation of the latter's life. Such operations may be performed in accordance with the conditions and procedures provided in this law.

Article 2 of the law provides that a person may donate or bequeath a part of his body provided that he has full legal capacity to do so, and provided that the donation or the bequest takes the form of a written authorization signed and certified by two witnesses possessing full capacity to do so.

Article 3 prohibits the transfer of a part of the body of a living person, even with his own consent, if the extraction of this part will culminate in his death or will result in incapacitating him.

According to Article 4, the donor must be properly informed about all known and probable health consequences arising from the extraction of the donated part. These consequences must be brought to the attention of the donor by means of a written report provided by a specialized medical committee, having formerly performed a thorough medical examination over the donor. The donor may retract his donation unconditionally before the performance of the extraction operation over him. But the donor could not get back the part extracted from him after donating it in accordance with the law.

Article 5 of the law deals with the conditions and procedures required for the donation and the transfer of human parts from the body of a dead person. It is provided in the article that in such a case the consent of the nearest relative to the dead person, until the fourth degree of the kinship, is required. Such consent of the dead person's relatives should take the form of a written authorization. Moreover, among other procedural conditions required, the article provides that the dead person should not have made a will before his death, professing full capacity to do so, to the effect that no part of his body should be extracted. The will must be signed by two witnesses.

According to Article 7, the sale and buying of parts of a human body by any means is prohibited. Nor is it allowed to receive any financial return for such parts. More-

---

[4] Official Gazette No. 2360, 17 February 1999.

over, the specialized doctor who has knowledge of the same is prohibited from performing such an operation. This law was issued by the Amir on 13 June 1998.[5]

5 EDUCATION: UNIVERSITY OF BAHRAIN

5.1 Law by Decree No. 18 for 1999, Amending Certain provisions of the Law by Decree No. 12 for 1986 Establishing and Regulating the University of Bahrain

The Articles of the 1986 law affected by the amendments are Articles 2, 5, 8, 9, 10, 12, 15, 16, 17, 18(d), 20, 21, 30, 34(c) and 35 of that law. According to amended Article 2, the university is empowered to establish colleges or institutions or any other divisions thereof that are attached to the University. According to amended Article 3, the university aims to perform all the functions related to the university teaching and service research in its faculties and institutions, to its research centres and all its divisions in accordance with the law and with what its Council of Trustees and the University Council decide, with the aim of providing services to the Bahraini community.[6]

6 INTERNATIONAL CONVENTIONS

6.1 Space Convention

6.1.1 Law by Decree No. 1 for 1999 Concerning the Approval of the Amended Agreement of the Arab Organization for Space Communication

This law approves the amendments made on 14 May 1990, in respect of the Agreement of Arab Organization for Space Communication which was signed on 14 April 1976, by the Arab League Countries who are parties to the said Agreement as amended. Bahrain had already approved the said 1976 Agreement by virtue of Law by Decree No. 25 for 1976. The 1990 version of the amended Agreement of 1976 concerning the Arab Space Agreement was intended to bring some of the provisions of the 1976 Agreement up to date in accordance with current economic and commercial rules, with the aim of facilitating the administration and development of the Arabic Space Net.

Article 2 of the amended 1990 Agreement describes the Arab Organization for Space Communication as a specialized agency in the field of space communication, its science and its technology.

Article 3 deals with the goals and activities of the Organization. It states that the Organization aims, generally, to secure specialized services for all members and other users in the field of space communication, in accordance with suitable artistic and economic standards and means.[7]

---

[5] Official Gazette No. 2325, 17 June 1998.
[6] Official Gazette No. 2369, 21 April 1999.
[7] Law by Decree No. 1 for 1999, Official Gazette No. 2354, 6 January 1999.

6.2 Commercial, economic and technical cooperation

6.2.1 Law by Decree No. 19 for 1999, Ratifying the Agreement Between Bahrain and the Republic of Russia Concerning Commercial, Economic and Technical Cooperation

The ratification of this agreement which was signed by the parties on 12 April 1999, took place by virtue of this law on 2 May 1999.

According to Article 1 of this agreement, the two contracting parties are required to take all necessary steps to guarantee the progress and development of commercial, economic and technical cooperation in accordance with the applicable laws in their respective countries.

Article 2 of the agreement provides that the two parties shall grant each other the treatment of most favoured nation in all fields related to trade and economic cooperation between their respective countries.[8]

6.3 Civil aviation

6.3.1 Law by Decree No. 5 for 1998, Ratifying the Agreement for Civil Aviation Services between Bahrain and Japan

This law ratifies the Agreement for Civil Aviation Services, signed on 4 March 1998 between Bahrain and Japan. The ratifying law was issued by the Amir of Bahrain on 21 March 1998.[9]

6.3.2 Law by Decree No. 6 for 1998, ratifying the Agreement for Civil Aviation Services between Bahrain and Hong Kong

This law ratifies the Agreement for Civil Aviation Services between Bahrain and Hong Kong (China), signed on 3 March 1998. The ratifying law was issued by the Amir of Bahrain on 21 March 1998.[10]

6.3.3 Law by Decree No. 7 for 1998, Ratifying the Agreement for Civil Aviation Services between Bahrain and the People's Republic of China

This law ratifies the Agreement for Civil Aviation Services between Bahrain and China, signed on 24 February 1998. The ratifying law was issued by the Amir of Bahrain on 21 March 1998.[11]

---

[8] Official Gazette No. 2371, 5 May 1999.
[9] Official Gazette No. 2313, 25 March 1999.
[10] *Ibid.*
[11] *Ibid.*

6.3.4 Law by Decree No. 13 for 1998 Ratifying the Agreement for Civil Aviation Services between the Government of Bahrain and the Government of the United Kingdom

This agreement was signed between the two parties on 29 April 1998. It was ratified by the Amir of Bahrain on 24 May 1998.[12]

6.3.5 Law by Decree No. 14 for 1998, Ratifying the Addition of a New Article to the Agreement for Civil Aviation Services between the Government of Bahrain and the Government of the Netherlands, signed on 22 March 1989

This law ratifies the addition of a new Article 13(bis) to the Agreement for civil aviation services between the Government of Bahrain and the Government of the Netherlands, signed on 22 March 1989 and ratified by law by Decree No. 4 for 1993. This ratifying Law No. 14 for 1998 was issued on 23 May 1998.[13]

6.3.6 Law by Decree No. 18 for 1998, Ratifying the Agreement for Civil Aviation Services between the Government of Bahrain and the Government of Belgium

This law ratifies the Agreement for Civil Aviation Services between Bahrain and Belgium, signed on 30 June 1998. The ratifying law by the Amir of Bahrain was issued on 13 June 1998.[14]

6.3.7 Law by Decree No. 20 for 1998, Ratifying the Agreement for Civil Aviation Services Between Bahrain and Poland

This law ratifies the Agreement for Civil Aviation Services between Bahrain and Poland, signed on 20 October 1998. The ratifying law was issued by the Amir of Bahrain on 1 November 1998.[15]

6.3.8 Law by Decree No. 21 for 1998, Ratifying the Agreement for Civil Aviation Services between Bahrain and Turkey

This law ratifies Agreement for Civil Aviation Services between Bahrain and Turkey, signed on 26 October 1998. The ratifying law was issued by the Amir of Bahrain on 8 November 1998.[16]

---

[12] Official Gazette, No. 2321, 24 May 1998.
[13] Official Gazette, No. 2322, 27 May 1998.
[14] Official Gazette, No. 2329, 15 June 1998.
[15] Official Gazette, No. 2345, 4 November 1998.
[16] Official Gazette, No. 2346, 11 November 1998.

Qatar

*Najeeb Al-Nauimi**

1 JUDICIAL AND LEGAL SYSTEM

1.1 Law No. 6 of the year 1999 Concerning the Judiciary

This law was first issued on 9 May 1999 to abrogate Law No. 13 of the year 1971 of the Court of Justice system. The law has unified the *shari'a* and justice courts into one judicial unit and laid down the principles of jurisdiction for each court separately. It will come into force after one year from publication in the Official Gazette.

The most important innovation of this new law is that it creates the Court of Cassation to be the supreme court in Qatar to adjudicate upon objections and appeals raised against courts of appeal decisions of both divisions of *shari'a* and *Adlia*.

The second important feature of this law is the introduction of the High Judicial Council to preside over judiciary affairs and to secure the principle of judiciary independence.

The law then provides for the hierarchy of the courts and their jurisdictions, the courts general committees and a new system of judicial inspection.

Chapter 2, Article 3 of this new law makes the structure of the courts as follows:

(a) Court of Cassation;
(b) *shari'a* Court of Appeal;
(c) Appeal Court of Justice;
(d) *shari'a* Court of First Instance; and
(e) Court of Justice (First Instance).

* LLB; PhD; Former Minister of Justice, State of Qatar, Professor of Public International Law, University of Qatar; National President of World Jurists Association in Qatar; Ex-President Asian African Legal Consultative Committee 1995–96.

Article 5 provides that the Court of Cassation will be formed of the president and one or two deputies and enough member judges to form two panels or more – one for *shariʿa* and one for the other courts of justice and appeals:

(a)   the objection by way of Cassation to this court should be based on the con-travention of law or mistake as to its application or interpretation;
(b)   conflict of jurisdiction as between lower courts.

The new law provides for the jurisdictions of both *shariʿa* courts and courts of jus-tice when sitting in first instance and appeal.

Chapter 5, Article 23 of this law has stated the rules governing the High Judi-ciary Council, which will be formed as follows:

(a)   the head of the Court of Cassation;
(b)   the head of the *shariʿa* Court of Appeal;
(c)   the head of the Court of Appeal;
(d)   two elder judges of the Court of Cassation;
(e)   two elder judges of both Courts of Appeal; and
(f)   the head of the *shariʿa* Court of First Instance.

Article 24 states the powers and jurisdiction of this council as follows:

(a)   to give opinion on judicial matters and to study and suggest appropriate leg-islation to develop the judicial system;
(b)   to give opinion on the recruitment of judges, their promotion, and other af-fairs concerning their career; and
(c)   to decide upon appeals made concerning the judge's affairs.

Chapter 10, Article 47 lays down the rule governing judicial inspection, which has been newly introduced by this law. It provides for the formation of a judicial in-spection administration to be supplemented to the High Judicial Council to be headed by one of the courts of cassations' members, assisted by enough judges. The main objective of the administration is to inspect the judicial works of the judge of the lower courts.

2 CRIMINAL LAW AND PROCEDURE

2.1 Criminal Procedure Act of 1971, Law No. 21 of the Year 1993 Amending some of the Provisions of the Criminal Procedure Code of 1971

This is the first amendment made to the law since 1971 when the law of criminal procedure was enacted. This new law has touched upon very crucial issues relating to police investigations, public prosecution, trials and the rights of the accused during these stages.

Article 5 of this amendment gave the public prosecutor the power to check and see criminal information and complaints made to the police with reference to of-fences provided for in the Penal Code or any other incriminating law. Article 33 stated that the maximum period of custody of the accused during the investigation to be forty-eight hours and only to be sanctioned and renewed by the judge. Arti-cle 35 gave the public prosecutor (after the completion of the investigation) the power to pass the criminal procedure to the judge when the charge is formed, to appoint a date of the commencement of the criminal trial. Articles 181–183 make important improvements with regard to the lapse of a criminal suit which would happen in the following circumstances:

(a) if the accused died;
(b) in cases of crimes other than misdemeanour after a lapse of ten years from the date of committing the crime;
(c) in misdemeanour, after the lapse of three years after the date of the commitment of the crime;
(d) in cases of contravention after the lapse of one year; or
(e) if the above periods are interrupted by the investigation procedures or accusation, or the trial.

Another important amendment was imported into this law by drafting twenty-two Articles (191–205) when regulating rehabilitation cases in the following instances:

(a) upon application by the convicted person (only crimes and misdemeanour) a rehabilitation order will be granted by the criminal court, if two conditions are satisfied:
    (i) The punishment was totally executed or pardon is given or the punishment has been elapsed by time; or
    (ii) a six-year period has passed since the section of the punishment has been pardoned or expired in cases of crimes or a three-year period has passed in cases of misdemeanour.
(b) A convicted person is legally entitled to rehabilitation if the following conditions are satisfied:
    (i) if no punishment is passed against the convicted person during ten years (in crimes) and five years (in misdemeanours);
    (ii) the punishment was totally executed or pardoned or has been lapsed by time; or
    (iii) between five to ten years have passed since the conditions in paragraph (ii) above were met.

Providing that the consequences of the rehabilitation order have relinquished the conviction for the future, the person granted rehabilitation will gain his competency from lost rights due to that and all other criminal effects.

3 INTELLECTUAL PROPERTY AND COPYRIGHT

3.1 Law No. 25 of the Year 1995 Concerning the Protection of Intellectual Property and Copyrights

Before this law was enacted, Qatar had regulated copyrights and inteleectual property by Decree Law No. 16 of the year 1993, and Decree No. 50 of the year 1986 consenting to join the Arabian Agreement for Copyright Protection. Now, under this new legislature, all intellectual property and copyrights are covered and protected under Chapter 2, Article 2.

Article 3 is a defining article which reads:

Intellectual rights and copyrights which expressed by writing, sound, drawing, photography or [film] shall be generally protected . . . particularly the following:
1. books, pamphlets and other written material;
2. verbal patents that is debates, lectures, etc.
3. theatre and musical products;
4. musical products;
5. moving designs;
6. photography works;
7. cinema, television and broadcasting works;
8. practical arts works;
9. drawing, colouring, painting, architecture, stones digging works, embodiments and
    plans;
10. computer programmes and practices;
11. encyclopaedia works;
12. collecting and classifying of heritage materials.

The protection under this law for the above-mentioned "intellectual property and
copyrights" prevails over:

(a) Qatari intellectual property and copyrights both in and out of the state of
     Qatar;
(b) non-Qatari intellectual property and copyrights published or distributed in
     Qatar; and
(c) intellectual property and copyrights of any foreigners whose country has reci-
     procal treatment with Qatar.

Chapter 3, Article 9 provides for items of copyright, which are attributable to and
owned by the writer. The most important machinery for implementing this law and
giving the rights the appropriate protection was laid down in Chapter 7. Where
the

intellectual property and copyright protection Bureau was formed to [perform the] task of
executing the provisions of this law by exercising the following powers:[1]
1. informing the writers of the ideal means to practice their materialistic and moral
    rights;
2. laying down the basis of evaluation of writer in monetary terms;
3. adjudicating upon disputes between writers and others in accordance with this law;
4. the studying and following up of the problems concerning copyright within the local,
    Arabic and international level;
5. studying the lodging of applications for intellectual rights or copyright;
6. proposing the appropriate decisions to implement this law, especially in relation to the
    necessary systems of lodging the intellectual property or copyrights to the Bureau, the
    way of advertising for that system and the forms of registers of lodging.

Article 36 states the requirements for lodging the intellectual property or copyright to the Bureau and the information to be annexed with the lodging application.

---

[1] Art. 35, Law No. 25 of 1995.

Chapter 9, sections 42–46 provides for the crimes and punishments available under this law. The main offence defined by this law is the publication of intellectual property or writings, books, products or work without the written consent of the writer or patent's owner. The punishment under this law varies between imprisonment or a fine, and the law in this area is applicable to individuals as well as to shops, offices and companies that deal with copyright and intellectual property.

4 ECONOMIC AND INVESTMENT LAW

4.1 Law No. 9 of the year 1995 Concerning the Regulation of Investment of non-Qatari Capital in Economic Activity

This amendment was introduced to encourage foreign investors to enter the economic field of investment in Qatar by striking all fetters upon the foreign capital as stated by section 3(6) of Decree Law No. 25 of the year 1990, which is now the subject of the amendment. The main amendment was enacted in section 3 of the Law as follows:

Notwithstanding the provisions of s. 1(2) of this Law, the Minister of Finance, Economy and Trade may make a decision that non-Qatari persons (natural and fictions) to invest their money for the purposes of economic development or to give a public service or effect public utility – in industrial, agriculture, mineral, tourism or general contracts. Also, they may thereby by the same instrument import all necessary materials for these projects, which are not available in local markets.

The amendment in section 5 reads:

It is not allowed for a non-Qatari to apply for the above exemptive decision if all the investment capital is wholly owned by him unless a Qatari services agent is appointed.

Oman

Nicholas Edmondes*

1 SOURCES OF LAW, JUDICIAL AND LEGAL SYSTEM

Legal changes in Oman during 1998 and early 1999 were considerably affected by the economic climate which prevailed. In 1998, there was a prolonged period of very low oil prices, which in turn resulted in government revenue being significantly reduced. As a consequence, a number of legislative provisions were passed, aimed at generating additional income and restricting government expenditure.

At the same time, the Muscat Securities Market (which had enjoyed a remarkable rise in fortune during 1997 and early 1998) continued to decline, with the result that shares were generally trading at over 50 per cent below the levels which they had reached at the top of a long bull run. As consequence of this and the low oil price, monetary liquidity was very tight and economic growth within the public and private sectors was much restricted.

From a legal standpoint, these events also prompted a wholesale redrafting of the Financial Law (imposing much tighter and more centralized control on public expenditure) and the reorganization of the capital market in an attempt to try and encourage confidence in the management and regulation of the market.

2 CONSTITUTIONAL AND ADMINISTRATIVE LAW

2.1 The Financial Law

The issuance of the Financial Law (Royal Decree 47/98) reinforced the authority of the Minister of National Economy, as Supervisor of the Ministry of Finance, to

---

* Partner, Trowers & Hamlins, Sultanate of Oman.

control the government revenue streams and expenditure strictly in accordance with approved budgets. In the past, individual ministries had generally failed to keep within their budgetary limits. While much legislation is a consolidation of previously promulgated financial restrictions on units of the administrative apparatus of the state, there is no doubt that the timing of the Financial Law enabled the Ministry of Finance to exercise a greater level of control over budgeting and to restrict and control any excess expenditure. Individual ministries are prevented from being able to alter taxes, duties or other fees without the approval of the minister responsible for the Ministry of Finance (currently the Ministry of National Economy). Additionally, no laws or decisions exempting or waiving such taxes, duties or fees are permitted unless specifically approved in the first instance by the Financial Affairs and Energy Resources Council, and upon its decision, approved by the Council of Ministers. In essence, the procedural requirements for any changes to the fiscal system are such that it makes it difficult for ministries to work outside of the stated fiscal regime.

2.2 Capital Markets Law

A major development at the end of 1998 was the promulgation of a new Capital Markets Law which completely reorganized the structure of the Muscat Securities Market ("MSM"). The law came into force on 15 January 1999, two months after its publication. Up until this time, a single body (the MSM) had carried out the marketing and promotion and operation of the market itself, as well as the regulatory and supervisory role. Following the long bull run, which many attributed to the MSM's promotional policies, much criticism was levelled at the MSM for promoting the market without concentrating sufficiently on regulation and supervision. The evident conflict between these two roles was dealt with by the new law.

The regulatory functions have been separated out and are now the responsibility of a new government appointed entity, the Capital Markets Authority ("CMA"). This leaves the MSM to concentrate on the day to day running of the market. A separate Royal Decree (Royal Decree 82/98) established a third entity, the Muscat Depository and Securities Registration Company SAOC, with responsibility to handle registration of transactions and the deposit of securities. The company has taken over all registers, records, systems and staff previously managed by the Deposits and Transfer Department of the MSM, and is supervised by the CMA. Securities held by an investment fund are to be deposited with the new depository or an Omani bank.

The CMA is responsible for the organizing, licensing and monitoring the issue and trading of securities and for supervising the operations of the MSM. The CMA has power to control share price fluctuations by imposing or waiving upper and lower caps expressed as a percentage of the opening prices of securities. These powers have already been exercised to stimulate the market.

New enhanced disclosure rules were enacted by the law. Listed companies are now required to submit annual audited and semi-annual and quarterly unaudited reports on their activities. The lower limit of shareholding, owned by a person alone or with minor children, requiring disclosure, has been increased from 10 per cent to 15 per cent. However, any individual shareholding which is increased above this limit must be disclosed whether this increase is caused by way of purchase of shares, grant, inheritance or by will. Previously, disclosure was only required if the increase in shareholding occurred through trading of shares.

One of the main changes introduced by the new Capital Markets Law is that securities companies must now confine themselves to the practice of one or more of the following activities:

(a) promotion and underwriting of securities or financing the investment in securities;
(b) participation in the establishment of or in the increase of capital of companies which issue securities;
(c) depositing, setting-off and settlement of securities transactions;
(d) the establishment and management of securities portfolios and investment funds; or
(e) securities brokerage.

All companies wishing to perform these activities must now obtain a licence from the CMA. This change is likely to affect the ability of companies such as banks carrying out these activities alongside their general activities. Brokers are also required to form an association (which will act as an internal regulator of the brokerage business) and to establish a fund to protect investors who use brokers.

One of the more important provisions of the new Capital Markets Law is that new investment funds must now be established as joint stock companies. Up to one third of the fund's board of directors may be persons other than shareholders. This is an exception to the Commercial Companies Law which only allows up to two members of the board of a joint stock company to be non-shareholders. Share certificates and units issued in funds set up in this way will be listed and traded on the market.

The securities held by an investment fund are to be deposited with the new depository company or with an Omani bank, provided that such a bank is not either an owner or shareholder in the company which owns the fund nor the investment manager.

Investment funds are obliged to appoint an investment manager to manage all investment activities of the fund and to submit to the CMA the investment management contract for approval.

Commercial banks and certain investment companies are still allowed to establish investment funds with the approval of the CMA (and, in the case of a bank, in coordination with the Central Bank of Oman). In a departure from the previous system, investment units issued by funds established in this way, by banks or investment companies, may not be listed or traded in the market.

The new law introduces a degree of protection for minority shareholders who hold at least 5 per cent of a company's shares. Such shareholders may request the CMA's board of directors to suspend any resolutions of the general meeting of the company which favour a certain category of shareholders, or are against a certain category of shareholders, or are in the interests of the members of the board of directors. Within fifteen days of such a suspension a request may be made to the grievance committee of the CMA to invalidate the resolutions of the general meeting. However, if fifteen days elapse without action from the grievance committee then the suspension is voided.

In general, financial penalties for breach of the law have been increased ten-fold from levels in the old law.

Several new penalties have been introduced including a penalty of imprisonment of not more than three years and/or a fine of not less than RO5,000 on any person who carries out any of the activities regulated by the law or who offers securities for subscription or receives monies in respect of securities subscriptions in contravention of the provisions of the law, without being licensed.

Market manipulation in a manner contrary to applicable laws, regulations and guidelines is subject to imprisonment of not less than three months and a penalty of not less than RO3,000 and not exceeding RO10,000. The new law also imposes a general liability on a person who infringes the law, its regulations or guidelines and thereby causes damage to another party.

The new law reflects a big step in the right direction towards alignment with international practices. The establishment of an independent regulator is particularly welcome as is the establishment of a custodial body to be fully responsible for the transfer of ownership of traded securities and the maintenance of shareholder registers.

Implementation of the new law will be difficult. New and detailed supporting regulations are expected and are required to put flesh on the bones of the new structure. In the meantime, the market keeps working, necessitating a seamless shift of power from the old to the new.

One feature which reflects caution and the lessons learned from the 1998 crash and fluctuations in markets worldwide are the provisions to allow for control of share price movements by the independent regulatory body. Also, the emphasis on ensuring the effectiveness of dispute resolution and the accountability of senior officials involved in both the MSM and the CMA, through a referral to the grievance committee, are positive changes which should encourage investors.

2.3 Educational establishments

New laws were issued allowing private higher education facilities to be set up.

Royal Decree 41/99, which came into force on 1 June 1999, issues the regulations for private universities. The regulations provide that a private university can only be set up by a decision of the Minister of Higher Education, and with the approval of the Higher Education Council. The regulations also set requirements for a board of trustees to be set up, and provides that the founders cannot withdraw from the university until five years have passed from the date studies begin. Furthermore, the courses run at the university must be for a minimum of four years, and may only issue grades and certificates which are equivalent to other grades and certificates which are recognized in the Sultanate.

Royal Decree 42/99, which came into force on 1 June 1999, permits the establishment of private colleges and institutes. These may be established by a decision of the Minister of Higher Education, and also with the approval of the Higher Education Council, and may teach both academic and technical disciplines.

2.4 National Investment Funds

An important development during the year was the establishment (Royal Decree 81/98) of a new closed joint stock company under the name of "National Investment Funds Company SAOC". The company was promoted by the State General Reserve Fund of Oman and its shareholders are the leading civil service and military pension funds as well as the Public Authority for Social Insurance. The company's objective is to pool investment resources from its members and other privately invited institutional investors with a view to generating and developing a portfolio of shares. Although the establishment of this company was widely regarded at the time as being an attempt to improve liquidity in the Muscat Securities Market, which had suffered a dramatic downturn during the course of 1998, it is clear that the establishment of the company has had a limited impact on the market by the end of June 1999.

The company established its first fund, "the National Equity Fund", with an initial reported value of RO40 million which was raised through private subscription. An internationally recognized investment manager was appointed as investment manager of the Fund.

3 CIVIL LAW (CONTRACT AND OBLIGATIONS)

There have been no developments under this title.

4 CIVIL PROCEDURE AND EVIDENCE

Oman has taken steps to become a full member of the 1958 United Nations Convention on the Recognition and Enforcement of Foreign Arbitral Awards. Royal Decree 36/98 gave formal authority for Oman to accede to the Treaty. The Decree requires "the competent authorities" to take necessary steps to join the agreement. In order for the Convention to enter into law in Oman it is necessary for a further Royal Decree to be issued ratifying Oman's accession to the Decree.

Once ratification has taken place, arbitration awards issued overseas should be enforceable automatically notwithstanding the provisions of Articles 119—123 of Royal Decree 13/97[1] (which reconstituted the Commercial Court) which, among other things, required verification of certain matters before the Commercial Court will issue an enforcement order. Indeed, once the treaty is ratified, arbitration proceedings in Oman are likely to become more attractive particularly given the recently promulgated Arbitration Law (Royal Decree 47/97) which governs private arbitration in Oman and provides a framework for such arbitrations based on the Egyptian version of the UNCITRAL model law.[2]

---

[1] Reported in "Oman", *Yearbook of Islamic and Middle Eastern Law*, vol. 4 (1997–1998), pp. 375–385.
[2] *Ibid.*

5 COMMERCIAL LAW

5.1 Shipping

Ministerial Decision 197/98, which came into effect on 1 December 1998, implements unified regulations to ensure the safety of ships which are not covered by International Treaties with GCC countries. There are five main areas, which issue regulations on life-saving equipment, fire-fighting equipment, navigational equipment, construction of cargo and passenger ships, and the inspection and certification of ships. These regulations apply to "ships", which are defined as "any floating marine facility or unit", and the applicability of the regulations depends upon their length.

The Sultanate of Oman formally joined the Agreement for the Establishment of the Arab Organiation for the Classification of Ships by Royal Decree 57/98, which came into force on 15 September 1998.

5.2 Banking and finance

Ministerial Decision 48/98, which came into force on 1 August 1998, amends the regulations concerning financial support in the private sector for some economic and service fields, which were issued by Ministerial Decision 135/97. The amendments essentially extend the application of soft loans to agricultural and fisheries projects, and apply similar application provisions for agricultural and fisheries projects as already existed for industrial projects.

In 1994, the Central Bank of Oman deregulated interest rates in relation to commercial lending by Omani banks but retained an interest rate cap in relation to consumer loans, which were defined as loans for RO9,000 (roughly US$23,400) or less. The Central Bank has issued a new circular (BM 863 dated 16 January 1999) which represents a change in policy by removing all interest rate caps.

The reason for continuing to regulate interest rates in relation to personal consumer lending was essentially a simple form of consumer protection. The Central Bank has now decided not to attempt any kind of consumer protection role and is now approaching the issue of consumer loans purely from a banking regulatory point of view. Accordingly, there is no longer any interest rate cap on consumer loans, which are now defined by reference to the use to which the loan is to be put rather than by reference to amount – basically, consumer loans are loans granted to individuals or households for household purchases. Monitoring of personal loans is now by calculation of the proportion which they form of a particular bank's lending portfolio.

Non-bank lending continues to be subject to the rate cap set by the Ministry of Commerce and Industry under Article 80 of the Commercial Code (see below). There is still a possible interpretation that the MCI cap on interest rates might apply to foreign banks lending into Oman on the basis that they are not regulated by CBO but the better view is that bank lending, whether domestic or international, is not subject to the Article 80 interest rate cap.

The capital of the Central Bank of Oman has been increased from RO200 million to RO250 million by Royal Decree 10/99, which came into force on 1 March 1999.

The Central Bank has also issued amendments to the guidelines concerning Negotiable Certificates of Deposits (Central Bank Circular 854 dated 19 October 1998), and in reaction to the fall of the MSM share prices during 1997 and 1998 the CBO amended the guidelines on the provision for losses and writing off irrecoverable assets (Central Bank Circular 869 dated 26 May 1999). This is understood to have affected the basis upon which pledged security is valued for the purpose of each bank's financial statements.

Ministerial Decision 97/98, which came into force on 15 August 1998, specifies an interest rate of 10 per cent for loans and commercial debts in respect of non-banking transactions, although parties are free to agree a lesser rate. This Ministerial decision sets the rate of interest applicable under Article 80 of the Commercial Law, Royal Decree 55/90.

5.3 Medical regulations

The medical profession was generally reorganized through new decisions.

Ministerial Decision 52/98, entitled The Regulations on Paramedical Occupations, came into force on 15 June 1998, as did Ministerial Decisions 53/98 ("Regulations Related to Private Clinics and Hospitals") and 54/98 ("Conditions and Procedures Related to Issue of Licences to Practise Human Medicine and Dentistry").

Ministerial Decision 52/98 sets out the licensing procedures and qualifying conditions relating to individuals who wish to practise medicine in the following areas: radiography, physiotherapy, ophthalmic matters, circumcision, midwifery, nursing, laboratory technician work and as a dental technician. This Ministerial Decision also stipulates that current licensees should renew their licences within three months from the date of the Decision, or before the two-year expiry of the current licence, whichever is the later occurrence.

Ministerial Decision 53/98 sets out in detail the licensing procedures for private clinics and private hospitals, and the conditions which must be satisfied to obtain the relevant licence. The general provisions of this Decision also state that physicians authorized by the Minister of Health can inspect these establishments at any time without notice and can submit reports thereon. Penalties for breaches of the required standards include the revocation of the licence of the clinic or hospital.

Ministerial Decision 54/98 sets out the licensing procedures and qualifying conditions for doctors and dentists.

5.4 Taxation and customs duties

New amendments to business income tax have been introduced by Royal Decrees 26/99 and 27/99. The main effects of the new changes are to increase the rate of income tax payable by wholly Omani owned businesses and to equalize the tax rates applicable as between most listed and other companies. The new rates apply to the 1999 tax year and subsequently.

As a result of the changes, the tax rates applicable to different companies are now as follows.

5.4.1 100 per cent Omani owned companies

As before, the first RO30,000 of taxable income is exempt from tax. For taxable income over RO30,000, the previous rates of 5 per cent and 7.5 per cent have been increased to a single rate of 12 per cent.

5.4.2 Public companies listed on the MSM

Public (open joint stock) companies listed on the MSM irrespective of their foreign shareholding percentage are to be taxed at the rate applicable to 100 per cent Omani owned companies on income over RO30,000; this means they are now taxed at a rate of 12 per cent. This is a change from the old system which required a minimum Omani ownership.

5.4.3 Private companies 51 per cent or more Omani owned

All private companies (i.e. other than open (listed) joint stock companies) 51 per cent or more Omani owned will also now be taxed at the same 12 per cent rate as wholly Oman owned companies.

5.4.4 Private companies more than 49 per cent foreign owned

Private companies that are more than 49 per cent foreign owned (but are not wholly foreign owned) are to be taxed at the following rates:

Taxable income (RO)	Applicable rate
0–30,000	Exempt
30,001–130,000	15%
130,001–280,000	20%
280,001 and above	25%

5.4.5 Wholly foreign owned companies

The tax rates applicable to wholly foreign owned companies are unaffected and remain those set out in the Second Schedule to the 1981 Law of Income Tax on Companies:

Taxable income (RO)	Applicable rate
0–5,000	Nil
5,001–18,000	5%
18,001–35,000	10%
35,001–55,000	15%
55,001–75,000	20%
75,001–100,000	25%
100,001–200,000	30%
200,001–300,000	35%
300,001–400,000	40%
400,001–500,000	45%
500,001 and above	50%

5.4.6 MSM investment funds

The decree confirms that investment funds established under the new Capital Markets Law are to be treated for tax purposes as if they were wholly Omani owned companies. Investment funds will, therefore, enjoy the same privileged tax treatment as listed companies.

Existing investment funds established as joint investment accounts under the old Muscat Securities Market Law are also given the same tax treatment as listed companies (i.e. taxed on the same basis as wholly Omani owned companies, provided that foreign participation did not exceed 49 per cent). Such funds are not specifically dealt with under the new tax decree but it is expected that they will continue to enjoy the same tax treatment as before.

5.4.7 Customs Duties

The State Budget for 1999, issued by Royal Decree 1/99 indicated a significant reduction in government expenditure and an attempt to balance an austere budget in the light of an oil price which at that time had been languishing around $10 per barrel. The Ministry of Finance issued a number of decisions aimed at generating additional fiscal revenue including increased airport taxes (Ministerial Decision 45/98), a 100 per cent increase in duty for the import of pork products and alcohol (this had the effect of increasing the duty to 200 per cent). An increase in duty on the import of cars (with a higher rate of duty applying to vehicles with engine capacities of over 2500 cc (all comprised within Ministerial Decision 126/98)).

Ministerial Decision 7/99 increased customs duty from 5 per cent to 15 per cent for a list of "luxury goods". However, on closer analysis the specified "luxury" goods included most household items and packaged food products other than the most basic and staple foods. During the course of 1999 some of the lists have been amended to avoid confusion. The increased import duty rates did not, however, affect the existing customs duty exemptions available to newly established projects with foreign capital investment and the existing exemptions and reliefs available for the import of raw materials and import–export businesses.

5.4.8 *Tourism tax*

A tax for tourist services fees charged by hotels and other leisure facilities has been imposed at a rate of 4 per cent on the value of each transaction or service provided. The Decree imposes various obligations on tourist and leisure establishments to keep records of guests and clients and imposes penalties for not doing so.

5.4.9 *Double taxation treaties*

Oman has ratified double taxation treaties with Tunisia, the United Kingdom of Great Britain and Northern Ireland and Mauritius[3] and with the Republic of Italy (Royal Decree 36/99).

6 EMPLOYMENT AND LABOUR LAW

6.1 Amendments to the Labour Law

Royal Decree 13/98, which came into force on 15 March 1998, replaces Article 22 of Omani Labour Law 34/73, so that it is no longer the case that an employer's financial contribution to vocational training projects is calculated on the basis of the basic salary of the non-Omani worker working with that employer. Instead, RD 13/98 provides that each employer will pay an annual financial contribution to vocational training projects in accordance with decisions made by the Minister of Social Affairs, Labour and Vocational Training.

Royal Decree 11/99, which came into force on 1 March 1999, augments Article 19 of Oman Labour Law (RD 34/73) by stating that non-Omanis must comply with the Expatriate Residence Law (16/95) and it also states that the Minister shall issue decisions specifying the professions and work which cannot be practised by non-Omanis. RD 11/99 also amends Article 21(a) of RD 34/73 by stating that the Minister can now issue a decision specifying the ratio of Omani to non-Omani workers for individual sectors of the economy, rather than, as had previously been the position, merely in relation to the workforce employed by one employer. In addition, RD 11/99 cancels Articles 22 and 39 of RD 34/73.

6.2 Wages and benefits for Omani labourers

Ministerial Decision 222/98 (in force from 15 July 1998) specifies the minimum wage for Omani labourers working in the private sector (RO100 per month). The decision also states that employers shall provide labourers with accommodation and transport means where the circumstances of the work so require; otherwise, each employee shall be paid a monthly travel allowance in the sum of RO20. Article 5 states that wages and benefits for Omani labourers may not be less than those paid

---

[3] *Ibid.*

to their expatriate counterparts (based on the premise that those counterparts are at the same level of experience and undertaking work of the same nature as the Omani labourers).

6.3 Omanization and youth initiatives

Omanization continues to be a major political objective of the Omani government. During the course of 1998, a Diwan committee was set up with the purpose of following up Omanization policy and objectives.[4] It is understood that this committee's role is to advise the Sultan directly on the success of Omanization policies in general and the appropriate objectives of Omanization. The committee comprises a number of key government officials as well as members of the private sector drawn from various fields of industry and commerce.

In the meantime, a number of Ministerial Decisions were issued (many of them unpromulgated) relating to specific areas of activity which were required to be Omanized or partly Omanized. This included Ministerial Decision 41/98 which required that filling station workers should be at least 50 per cent Omani by the end of 1998. Unpromulgated decisions required all school bus drivers and domestic bottled gas distributors to become 100 per cent Omani by a specified time.

Royal Decree 76/98 established the Youth Projects Development Fund SAOC with the objective of raising funds for youth projects and for the encouragement of youth businesses and entrepreneurship. A number of private sector individuals and companies are understood to have contributed to the fund which is chaired by H.E. Mohammad bin Zubair bin Ali, His Majesty's Special Advisor on Economic Planning Affairs.

7 PROPERTY AND LAND LAW

There have been no developments under this title.

8 INTELLECTUAL PROPERTY

The implementing regulations of the Copyright Law came into force on 2 May 1998. Since that date there has been increasing application of the prohibition on the trade in non-original works. Article 9(a) of the implementing regulations, set down by Ministerial Decision 43/98, stated a prohibition on the import, circulation and possession of non-original works (excluding computer programmes) for the purposes of trade. This prohibition has had a noticeable impact on the sale of some non-original products. It is understood that import permits for certain products, such as video recordings, are now only issued by the Ministry of National Heritage and Culture for original recordings.

---

[4] *Ibid.*

The implementing regulations have recently been amended by Ministerial Decision 170/98, which came into force on 1 February 1999. The amendments remove the exception given to non-original computer programmes. As a result the prohibition on the import, circulation and possession of non-original works for the purposes of trade, now extends to non-original computer software.

While Ministerial Decision 43/98 states that it will come into force with effect from the date of publication, it also states that anyone who possesses a non-original work (not including computer software) which enjoys protection abroad should dispose of such items by 31 December 1998. The recent amendment to this Ministerial Decision applied a similar provision to non-original computer software, stating that such non-original software should be disposed of before 30 June 1999.

Since that date has passed, enforcement against traders of non-original computer software has been reported in the Oman press. Additionally, businesses which utilize non-original computer software in their operations should take immediate action to replace their existing software with original versions.

By Royal Decree 63/98, Oman approved the joining of the Paris Treaty for the Protection of Industrial Property and the Berne Treaty for the Protection of Literary and Artistic Works.

9 FAMILY LAW AND SUCCESSION

There have been no developments under this title.

10 CRIMINAL LAW AND PROCEDURES

Royal Decree 17/99, the Law for the Control of Narcotics and Psychotropic Substances, came into effect on 15 March 1999. Under this law, controls are placed on the manufacture, cultivation, production, possession and movement of specified substances. Certain exceptions are provided for licensed physicians and their patients, and also licensed pharmaceutical establishments. Unauthorized manufacture, cultivation, production, possession and movement of certain substances is punishable by a fine and/or imprisonment.

Articles 38 to 42 establishes a number of money laundering offences connected with the proceeds of drug trafficking. Article 38 details the criminal offences of money laundering. First, a person commits an offence where he or she remits or transfers funds when he or she is aware, or should be aware that those funds have been obtained from an offence of illegal trading in drugs. The onus of proof is upon the owner, possessor or user of the funds to prove that funds come from a legitimate source. Secondly, a person commits an offence by obtaining, possessing or using the funds when he or she knows, or should know, that those funds have been obtained through an offence of illegal trading in drugs.

Article 39 makes these provisions relevant to banks to the extent that they are obliged to comply with regulations issued by the Central Bank of Oman (CBO). These regulations provide that the banks must identify the source of funds, the background of their customers, and record other details. Article 40 imposes an obligation to register cash transactions, again, in accordance with CBO regulations.

Where banks are suspicious about the source of funds, they are permitted to breach their general obligation of confidentiality by notifying the CBO and the Royal Oman Police (ROP) of their concerns. Article 42 allows the ROP to exchange information with other governmental authorities (including those of foreign countries). There is an attempt to continue the general obligation of confidentiality which arises from the bank and customer relationship, by requiring the ROP and the CBO only to use the information made available in connection with investigations related to combatting money laundering.

11 PUBLIC INTERNATIONAL LAW

Developments in clarifying the border between UAE and Oman occurred with the issuance of Royal Decree 32/99. The Decree further demarcated border points between both countries

The Riyadh Arab Agreement of Judicial Co-operation was ratified by Royal Decree 34/99.

12 PRIVATE INTERNATIONAL LAW (CONFLICTS)

There have been no developments under this title.

Yemen

*Nageeb Shamiri**

1 CONSTITUTIONAL LAW

1.1 Boundaries of administrative duties

Republican Resolution No. 23/1998[1] in connection with certain changes in the boundaries of the administrative division in the Republic introduced the following:

(a) two new provinces (*muhafazat*) have been established: Al-Dhala' and 'Imran;
(b) certain districts have changed jurisdiction from some provinces to others, with a view to put an end to the former boundaries between ex-north Yemen and ex-south Yemen.

Al-Dhala' province includes the following districts:

(a) Al-Dhala' (the centre of the province);
(b) Al-Shu'aib;
(c) Al-Hussain;
(d) Jihaf;
(e) Al-Azarek;
(f) Al-Hasha;
(g) Damt;
(h) Qa'tabah; and
(i) Juban.

Provinces (a) to (e) are in ex-south Yemen and (f) to (i) are in ex-north Yemen. 'Imran province consists of nineteen districts, all of them in ex-north Yemen and a few from other provinces, e.g. Hajjah. Other changes in this respect include:

---

* LLD and member of the Supreme Judicial Council of Yemen.
[1] Dated 28 July 1998. Published in the Official Gazette, Issue 14, 31 July 1998.

(a)   three districts in Sana'a province (ex-north) have been attached to Al-Jowf
       province: 'Anan, Kharab Al-Marashy and Rajoosah;
(b)   Mukiaras district in Abyan province (ex-south) has been attached to Al-Bay-
       dha province (ex-north);
(c)   Al-Makaterah district in Ta'iz province (ex-north) has been attached to Lahej
       province (ex-south); and
(d)   Karish district in Lahej province (ex-south) has been attached to Ta'iz province
       (ex-north).

1.2 Elections law

Law No. 27/1999 in connection with the amendments to Elections Law No.
27/1996 was promulgated on 18 April 1999, the main changes being related to
seven sections (12, 13, 14, 15, 16, 17 and 76) which are as follows.

1.2.1 New Section 12

An official copy of the voters' lists for every constituency, certified by the chairman
of the main committee in the constituency, shall be exhibited in the main squares
of public places within the constituency, as well as the centres of the districts and
other places specified by the Supreme Elections Commission, for five days with effect from the third day of the period for revision and registry of the voters' lists. It
is within the rights of the branches of the political parties and organisations in the
constituencies, within the fixed period for declaration of the lists, to photocopy
the declared list, if the branches have so requested.

1.2.2 New Section 13

Every citizen resident in the constituency has the right to ask the main committee
to add his name to the voters' list if his name's insertion has been ignored without
due cause or to delete a name which has been enlisted without due right. Applications should be submitted to the headquarters of the committee within five days
with effect from the next day of declaration of the lists and should be registered according to the days of the submission thereof in a special register. Receipts should
be given to the applicants and every voter has the right to look at the register.

1.2.3 New Section 14

The committee concerned with the preparation of the application for insertion or
deletion should deal with such applications within a maximum period of eight
days with effect from the next day of submission of the applications. The committee may hear the applicant and anyone for whom the application has been submitted and may make whatever investigation it deems necessary.

1.2.4 New Section 15

The resolutions of the committee should be exhibited in public places (as provided for in section 12) for three days with effect from the resolutions.

1.2.5 New Section 16

Every vote in the constituency has the right to appeal against the resolution before the district court within five days with effect from the first day of exhibition of the resolutions. The court may take whatever investigation it deems necessary in order to give its ruling by admitting or rejecting the appeal, according to the facts of each case, by deletion or addition or maintaining the status quo, within eight days with effect from the expiry of the period allowed for appeals. The court should give the party concerned, as well as the main committee in the constituency, a copy of the ruling once it has been given. The main committee should exhibit the ruling in the places specified in section 12 for two days with effect from the next day of the expiry of the period allowed for appeals.

Every voter and the public prosecutor in the constituency has the right to appeal against the ruling(s) of the district court within a period of five days with effect from the expiry of the period allowed for appeals, by an application lodged with a judge seconded by the President of the Court of Appeal for the purpose and – if necessary – more than one judge may be seconded in order to distribute the work among themselves according to the constituencies. The decisions should be passed, and finally, within a maximum period of seven days with effect from the next day of the expiry of the period allowed for appeals, the court should furnish the party concerned and the supervisory committee in the governorate with a copy of the decision(s) once they have been passed. This committee should furnish the resolution(s) to the main committee concerned within twenty-four hours with effect from receiving them from the Court of Appeal.

1.2.6 New Section 17

The voters' lists should be amended according to the final resolutions within the next twelve days of the expiry of the period allowed for appeals before the Court of Appeal.

1.2.7 New Section 76

The candidate who achieves an absolute majority of the votes cast in the presidential elections shall be considered to be President of the Republic. If none of the candidates obtains that majority, there shall be a re-election as regards the two candidates who won the highest number of votes, within forty days with effect from the date of announcing the results of the last ballot.

1.2.8 Further additions

At the same time, five sections have been added after section 73, as follows.

1.2.8.1 New addition No. 73/2

Applications for the office of the President shall be submitted to the Speaker of the House of Representatives during the ten days following the announcement for submission of candidacy. The candidate himself shall submit the application in writing during working hours. If the candidate is the candidate of a political party, he should submit evidence to this effect.

Every applicant for candidacy shall be given a receipt regarding the documents filed in his application. The Presidency of Parliament shall scrutinize the applications to make sure that they fulfil the constitutional requirements by the applicants.

The names of the successful applicants shall be submitted to Parliament for secondment within one week with effect from the end of the period for scrutiny.

Parliament is under an obligation to second, for the office of President of the Republic, at least two persons, as preparation to have them as candidates for presidential elections by the people.

1.2.8.2 New addition No. 73/3

The applicant for candidacy of the office of President of the Republic has the right to withdraw his application by submitting a written application to the Speaker of Parliament before the names of the applicants are referred to Parliament for secondment.

1.2.8.3 New addition No. 73/4

The provisions of section 55 of Law No. 27/1996 are not applicable as regards the candidates for the presidential elections.

1.2.8.4 New addition No. 73/5

The President shall issue a resolution inviting the voters to elect the President of the Republic, after completion by the Parliament of the proceedings provided for on the preceding sections.

1.2.9 New additions after section 75

1.2.9.1 New addition No. 75/1

The news and publication thereof by the official media of the performance by the President of the Republic of his responsibilities and daily duties shall not be considered as election propaganda, if the President is among the candidates for the Presidential Elections.

1.2.9.2 New addition No. 75/2

Taking into consideration section 75/1 above, the Supreme Electoral Commission (SEC) shall regulate the use of the official media in the election propaganda by the candidates for the presidential elections in such manner as to realize equality as well as equal opportunities as regards space and time for all the candidates.

1.2.9.3 New addition No. 75/3

As an exception to the provisions of section 27 of Law No. 27/1996, every candidate for the office of the President of the Republic shall be granted a sum of money paid out of the State Treasury, acting on a proposal to this effect from the Presidium of Parliament and approval of Parliament, provided the sums shall be equal as regards all the candidates, in order to meet the expenses of the elections campaign for each of them.

1.2.9.4 New addition No. 75/4

Every candidate for the presidential elections shall convene at least one election campaign meeting in the centres of the governorates and the capital.

1.2.9.5 New addition No. 75/5

The candidates for the presidential elections may, in the last week of the time allowed for elections propaganda, hold debates broadcast by the official media. The SEC shall arrange such debates among the candidates.

1.2.9.6 New addition No. 75/6

Every candidate has the right to hold press seminars and conferences to explain his elections' manifesto or programme.

1.2.9.7 New addition No. 75/7

Every candidate may receive donations from Yemeni individuals or corporate bodies, provided that such donations go into a bank account to be opened in a bank, and provided too, that statements to this effect are submitted to the SEC; it is strictly forbidden to obtain any amounts from any foreign body.

1.2.10 New additions after section 77

1.2.10.1 New addition No. 77/1

The SEC shall give the successful candidate for the office of President of the Republic a "success certificate" in the presidential elections.

1.2.10.2 New addition No. 77/2
Every interested person shall have the right to appeal against the voting procedure or the results thereof, by an ordinary appeal petition, lodged at the Supreme Court, in accordance with the following conditions:

(a) lodging the petition should take place within forty-eight hours from the declaration of the final results of the presidential elections by the SEC;
(b) the appeal shall give grounds, and shall be limited to (i) the ballot procedure and (ii) the results thereof;
(c) the appeal should be accompanied by payment of an amount of YR250,000 to the treasury of the Supreme Court, as surety in the event that the appeal turns out to be untrue, and should be repaid in the event that the ruling is in his favour;
(d) the Supreme Court shall give its rulings as regards the appeals within a maximum period of fifteen days from lodging thereof.

1.2.10.3 New addition No. 77/3
The lodging of appeals shall not stop giving the successful candidate of the office of President of the Republic with the "success certificate", or to be sworn in before Parliament and commencing performing his responsibilities.[2]

1.3 Democracy: Sana'a Declaration

1.3.1 An International Forum of the Emerging Democracies

The Forum, which was opened officially by the President of the Republic of Yemen, President 'Ali 'Abdalla Saleh, was held in Sana'a during the period 28–30 June 1999, under the title "Managing the Twin Transitions: the Politics of Democratic and Economic Reform in Emerging Democracies". Seventeen States participated as follows: (a) Yemen; (b)Morocco; (c)Jordan; (d)Benin; (e)Bolivia; (f)El Salvador; (g)Georgia; (h)Ghana; (i) Guatemala; (j) Guyana; (k) Macedonia; (l) Malawi; (m) Mali; (n) Mongolia; (o) Mozambique; (p) Namibia and (q) Nepal.

In addition, delegates and observers from the donor countries attended, including, (a) the United States; (b) the United Kingdom; (c) Germany; (d) Japan; (e) the Netherlands; (f) Canada; and (g) the United Nations and the World Bank.

Political, civil and economic leaders, as well as senior officials and human rights activists, leading businessmen and other prominent public figures of the above countries participated. They discussed shared experiences and challenges and formulated common approaches, regarding the following subjects, which were the goals of the forum:

(a) politics of hard choice: political transition and economic reconstruction;
(b) building public trust: elections and legislatures;

---

[2] Author's note: it is expected that there will be certain important amendments in this respect, to provide for the right of Yemeni immigrants to take part in the presidential elections.

(c) participation: democratic decision-making; the vital voice of women; civil society; pluralism; and

(d) achieving good governance: controlling corruption; improving administration and strengthening the rule of law.

The Forum ended its session with a Statement Declaration.[3] Furthermore, the Republic of Yemen offered, in the final speech by the President of the Republic, to host an international conference on human rights.

2 JUDICIAL SYSTEM, COURTS AND CRIMINAL LAW

2.1 Supreme Court

The Supreme Court, the highest court in the land, has been re-shaped as follows:

(a) a new President and two deputies;

(b) a new attorney-general;

(c) nineteen presidents of the courts of appeal in the provinces, some of whom have been re-appointed; and

(d) a new director of judicial control.

New commercial courts and courts of first instance, as well as new commercial appeals divisions, have been established. Many changes in the public prosecution have taken place throughout the country, in addition to three refresher courses and two guideline books.

2.2 Military crimes and penalties

Law No. 21/1998, in connection with military crimes and penalties, replaces Laws Nos. 16/1994 and 6/1996 on the same subject. The sentences should be within the law's provisions and, under all circumstances, should not contravene the Constitution. According to the new law, the provisions apply to (a) the personnel of the armed forces; (b) those serving compulsory military service; (c) those serving during public emergency; (d) institutes, schools and centres for military training, and their students; (e) civilians working in the armed forces; (g) prisoners of war; and (h) allied military personnel of any country who are in the Republic, unless there are treaties or agreements (whether bilateral or international) which provide otherwise.

The provisions also apply to any crime committed in the bases, camps, institutions, factories, vessels, aeroplanes, vehicles or places used by military personnel for the benefit of the armed forces. Crimes committed against equipment, arms, documents or secrets of the armed forces and crimes committed by personnel are subject to the law's provisions when committed during the performance of their duties due to superior orders.

---

[3] See Part III of this volume at p. 502.

Every person subject to the law's provisions who commits an unlawful act abroad making him a perpetrator of a crime under the law, is an accused even if that act is not a crime in the country where he is resident. If that act is an offence there, he should be tried again before a military court in Yemen.

The punishments available under the law are as follows:

(a)   capital punishment;
(b)   lapidation (stoning until death);
(c)   retribution (less than capital punishment);
(d)   crucifixion;
(e)   amputation;
(f)   lashes;
(g)   imprisonment;
(h)   compensation (blood money), called *diyya* or *arsh*;
(i)   fine;
(j)   community service;
(k)   dismissal from military service; or
(l)   demotion of rank.

In addition, the provisions of the law mention non-entitlement to medals of honour and non-entitlement to promotion.

The military crimes/offences are as follows:

(a)   crimes regarding the enemy;
(b)   crimes regarding prisoners of war, e.g. maltreatment of them;
(c)   crimes during war;
(d)   insurrection crimes;
(e)   crimes regarding military duties and guards;
(f)   crimes of robbery and destruction, forgery, etc.
(g)   crimes of attacks on superior officers/commanders and disobedience of orders;
(h)   misuse of responsibilities;
(i)   crimes regarding military service – which include avoiding military service, absenteeism, sickness;
(j)   crimes regarding prisoners;
(k)   crimes regarding military courts;
(l)   crimes regarding military obedience requirements; and
(m)   crimes regarding public law and other laws in force.

2.3 Kidnapping

According to Law No. 24/1998 in connection with the struggle against kidnapping crimes, anyone who leads a gang for the purposes of kidnapping or stealing of a person or private property by force is punishable by death. It is punishable by imprisonment for:

(a)   twelve to fifteen years for kidnapping a person, and if the victim is female the period is twenty years, and if kidnapping is accompanied by malice, injury or attack, the period is twenty-five years, and that is without prejudice to capital punishment or *diyya* or damages if kidnapping is followed by murder, adultery etc.

(b)   ten to fifteen years if the accused has contacted a foreign country or gang in order to commit the same.

2.4 Civil service offences and discipline

The Prime Minister's Resolution No. 234/1998 in connection with the main regulations regarding administrative and financial offences and penalties was passed. The regulations deal with offences by "civil servants while performing their duties". The main parts of the regulations are as follows.

The said regulations apply to everyone governed by the Civil Service Legislation. They do not apply to judges, military forces, security forces or the police, public prosecutors, or diplomatic and consular cadres. The aims of the Regulations are:

(a)   to strengthen discipline and good behaviour at work;
(b)   to enable ministers to exercise its jurisdiction regarding investigation and discipline with a view to normal, efficient and smooth work and respect for the system and regulations of public duty; and
(c)   to direct the behaviour of civil servants towards a positive stance to work.

The Resolution mentions obligations, duties, rights, prohibitions, responsibilities and offences, including financial and administrative responsibilities and offences, investigations, trials and suspension.

2.5 Court fees

2.5.1 Court Fees Law No. 28/1998, promulgated on 16 May 1999

A fixed sum of YR300 (US$27) shall be paid as regards any civil, commercial or administrative case.

To explain further, there was a court fees law in ex-south Yemen, but none in ex-north Yemen, except for commercial cases. After reunification, in 1990, a court fees law was issued by the President by way of a Republican Resolution (Court Fees Law No. 43/1991), based on gradual percentage increases in court fees. Parliament recently made certain drastic changes and provided for a fixed sum in this respect, as stated above.

2.6 Advocates

The Advocacy Law No. 31/1999 was promulgated on 28 June 1999, the first law on this important subject to be promulgated in the Republic of Yemen since reunification. The law consists of nineteen sections, dealing with the following subjects:

(a)   definitions;
(b)   the lawyers' union (or Bar Council);
(c)   conditions to be fulfilled by anyone applying for registration to be licensed
      to practise as a private lawyer;
(d)   rights and obligations;
(e)   disciplinary council;
(f)   appeals against the decisions/resolutions of the union's executive body;
(g)   finances of the lawyers' union;
(h)   penalties for violations of the provisions of the law; and
(i)   general provisions.

There was a Law (No. 81/1997) in ex-north Yemen, and another (No. 12/1981) in ex-south Yemen. After reunification, Law No. 30/1992 was issued by the President, under the power conferred upon him by the Constitution, by way of a Republican Resolution (decree); thereby repealing the two previous laws on the subject.

However, the House of Representatives (Parliament) rejected Law No. 30/1992 and the result has been that there has not been any law regulating and governing the legal profession. Another sensitive issue in this respect has been the question of Islamic *shari'a* attorneys, many of whom are without any legal training or university background, who wanted to be treated like any other lawyer graduating from a law faculty. The issue has been resolved by a provision, in the Final Provisions, to the effect that the affairs of those who have been practising by a Resolution, equivalent to subsidiary legislation, by the Ministry of Justice.

3 COMMERCIAL LAW

3.1 Miscellaneous amendments to the Commercial Code

Law No. 6/1998 makes certain amendments to the Commercial Code as follows:

(a)   banking transactions and withdrawals: the account-holder has the right to dispose of his account balance at any time he so wishes;
(b)   the bank shall be entitled to cancel any facilities at any time it so wishes, by a notification to this effect to the customer, provided sufficient time is given to the customer to repay the debt;
(c)   the facilities will be cancelled:
      (i)   as a result of the death of the applicant for facilities, or
      (ii)   due to the fact that the applicant is subject to insolvency proceedings, or
      (iii) if the applicant is deemed incapacitated, or
      (iv)   the applicant's status as body corporate comes to an end, or
      (v)   if the applicant has violated the obligation of trust and honesty or has committed a serious mistake as to render the use of the facilities illegal and all the guarantees, if any, shall be returned;
(d)   the guarantees as regards satisfaction to a security bond;
(e)   making a cheque and use thereof; and
(f)   insolvency and conciliation.

Sections 608 and 789 of the Commercial Code regarding commercial and service agency shall be repealed as follows:

(a)   Section 608: the court shall deduct, from the deferred debt which has no terms or conditions attached to it regarding interest, an amount equivalent to the legal interest for the period from the date of judgment declaring insolvency until the date when the repayment of the debt becomes due.

(b)   Section 789: a conciliation contract may be reached, provided:
    (i)   there is a condition regarding fulfilment; and
    (ii)   that the debtor becomes solvent within a period specified in the conciliation contract; and
    (iii)   that the period shall not exceed five years with effect from the date of approval of the conciliation contract.

The following three sections shall be added and regarded as part of the Commercial Code:

(a)   there may be more than one commercial agent in the Republic according to the number of the items produced by the principal;

(b)   it is not permissible to have many service agents for a non-local principal in the service agency (air, freight), and in case the public sector waives his concession, the agency goes to the first agent in order in the Republic;

(c)   if there are presumptions to the effect that there are certain irregularities (deceit, etc.) as regards property *in rem* or *in personam* which is the property of the wife or children of the insolvent, which has been conveyed to them within the three years preceding the insolvency. The court shall make an inventory of the property and shall order that the property shall not be disposed of for a period not exceeding six months, and if afterwards it is proved that there have been irregularities, the court shall add the property to that of the insolvent.

3.2 Banks Law No. 38/1998

This law was promulgated and replaces the Banks Law No. 8/1972 enacted in ex-North Yemen, the Banking System Law No. 36/1972 enacted in ex-South Yemen and the Banks Law No. 36/1991 issued after reunification by Presidential Resolution. The law consists of the following provisions:

(1)   The provisions of this law shall not – unless it is otherwise expressly stated – restrict the application of the Commercial Companies Law, or the Islamic Banks Law, or any other law in force in the Republic. Furthermore, the provisions of the law do not apply as regards the Post Office Deposit Funds, or any other financial authorities which are specified by the Central Bank as such and a Resolution of the Council of Ministers is issued to this effect.

(2)   The Central Bank alone is conferred with the authority to grant licences for engagement in the banking business: the only exceptions being those banks established in accordance with special legislation. Furthermore, it is permissible for Yemeni nationals to establish banks, and, too, for foreign banks to open branches in the Republic of Yemen.

(3) No person may engage in the business of banking in the Republic unless he has been granted a licence to do so from the Central Bank. The branches of any bank in the Republic shall be considered to be one bank, unless there is an express provision to the contrary.

(4) The provisions of the law lay down the conditions according to which licences are granted to engage in banking business: such as the fees; written application, in addition to the memorandum and articles of association; a copy of the last financial statement or budget (in cases where the applicant is a foreign bank desiring to open a branch in the Republic). However, the following conditions should be fulfilled, otherwise no licence will be granted by the Central Bank:

   (a) each of the board of directors should be over the age of 25, and there should not be more than two members who are related;

   (b) the administrative experience of the senior staff should not be less than five years, in the field of banking, law, accountancy, financing or financial companies;

   (c) the three most senior staff in the bank should have banking experience of at least eight years;

   (d) at least three members of the board of directors should not be executives.

(5) The Central Bank should give its decisions as regards any application within sixty days of the application's submission.

(6) The Central Bank may withdraw the licence granted as regards the establishment of any bank, and may publish its decision in one of the following events:

   (a) if the licensee has not commenced business within six months following the granting of the licence;

   (b) if the licensee has ceased to perform any banking business, or if he wound up his business;

   (c) if the Central Bank has discovered that the licensee is performing the business in a manner prejudicial to the interests of depositors, or that the licensee has not enough money to satisfy his obligations towards the public, or that he contravenes any of the provisions of the law;

   (d) if the licence has been granted on the basis of documents or information submitted by the licensee, which had turned out to be incorrect;

   (e) if the bank which has been granted a licence has not complied with the provisions of the law within the period allowed by the Central Bank.

(7) The provisions of the law also mention:

   (a) the capital of banks, the minimum for each bank being YR1 million;

   (b) transactions which are forbidden and the restrictions;

   (c) financial statements, auditing of the accounts and inspection by the Central Bank as regards banks operating in the Republic;

   (d) responsibilities of the members of the board of directors, as well as the other senior staff, of a bank;

   (e) voluntary or compulsory winding-up and re-organization;

   (f) penalties.

3.3 Stamp duty

Law No. 44/1991, regarding stamp duty, was repealed by Law No. 5/1998. The repealed law consisted of forty-nine sections, in addition to an annexe of 11 pages.

There was a Stamp Duty law, No. 14/1969 in ex-north Yemen and similar laws, Nos. 6/1979 and 5/1983 in ex-south Yemen. After reunification, Law No. 44/1991 was promulgated in this respect, due to the fact that "it cost more time, effort and wages to collect such a duty", the law was abolished within the Government Administrative and Financial Reform Programme, which commenced in 1995.

3.4 Income tax

Law No. 12/1999 amended the Income Tax Law No. 31/1991. According to the amendments, the following bodies shall be exempted from paying income tax:

(a) humanitarian charitable societies, the activities of which are not for profit and the financial and material sources of which are from donations, grants and assistance only, and if they provide services of consideration, *yjat* should be nominal. However, the Income Tax Department has the right to impose tax if it ascertains that the society engages in commercial activities;
(b) fishing and agricultural co-operative societies, as well as other societies which are subject to the provision of the Societies Law, provided that:
(i) they are registered;
(ii) they do not engage in commercial activities, or engage in imports and exports for their benefit or the benefit of others; or
(iii) their activities are for the benefit of the members thereof.
(c) the income from lands invested for agriculture or horticulture or for the rearing of sheep, poultry, fish or honey;
(d) the technical institutes specializing in technological and vocational training;
(e) the profits from exporting Yemeni agricultural, industrial, fishing and handicraft products, according to the procedures regulating exports;
(f) the income of individuals from the interest on their deposits in banks and post office accounts and from income of their shares in public or shareholding companies;
(g) the profits of shares gained by public and shareholding companies, from their contributions in other shareholding companies, to the extent of their contributions after deducting 10 per cent of their value to cover expenses, etc.

3.5 Commercial companies

Commercial Companies Law No. 15/1999 amended section 245, paragraphs (b) and (c) of Law No. 22/1997.

According to the amendment, shareholders forming a commercial company should submit their application for registration accompanied by a copy of both the memorandum of association and the articles of association. In addition, the shareholders should authenticate their signatures before the Registrar (or attorney thereof), the Director of the Office of the Ministry of Supply and Trade in the province, or the district court.

3.6 Agency of foreign companies

Foreign Companies Agencies Law No. 16/1999 repealed two sections of Law No. 23/1997 as follows:

Every agent in the Republic, be that a natural person or body corporate, should have a stamp/seal mentioning his/its full name, name of the foreign firm, number of the registration of the firm and the firm's activities in the Agencies' Register, in printed form, in both Arabic and English, so as to be stamped in the applications for opening letters of credit for importing products or commodities which are the subject of the Agency, whether the agent is importing directly from the principal or is a broker only for import.

It is possible, as an exception to the above-mentioned, and without prejudice to the interests of the agent, to permit the direct importation through a person other than the registered agent if it is categorically proved to the Ministry that the registered agent has refused to stamp the application for letters of credit without justification.

Section 19 provided that if a dispute arose between the local agent and the foreign firm principal because of the agency contract, it shall not be possible for the Department concerned to register another local agent on the application of the principal, except after the dispute had been settled, whether amicably or through a final court judgment.

4 PERSONAL STATUS LAW

Personal Status Laws Nos. 27/1998 and 24/1999 were promulgated, amending Law No. 20/1992, according to which 115 of 351 sections have been amended, and some sections repealed completely, as follows.

4.1 Marriage and divorce

4.1.1 Polygamy

There were five conditions, the following of which were amended:

(a)   permission for up to four wives, provided justice to all;
(b)   ability of husband to support more than one wife; and
(c)   the would-be wife should be told that the husband is already married.

The following conditions have been repealed:

(a)   there should be legitimate interest (e.g. children); and
(b)   the present wife(ves) should be informed of the husband's intention to marry.

4.1.2 Registration of marriage contract

Previously, this should be done within a week with effect from the marriage contract, now, the condition has been changed to one month.

4.1.3 Accommodation

It is now possible to keep all wives in one home, provided all wives agree and it is possible for any one to change her mind at any time.

4.1.4 Dissolution due to inability to support

If the husband is married to more than one wife, with no ability to support or provide accommodation, each wife may apply for dissolution.

Previously, the judge would give the husband an option to keep one and divorce the rest; if the husband refused, the judge could order a dissolution to the wives who had applied. Now, if the husband is able to support some wives, the judge can give the husband an option to keep those he can support and divorce the rest. If the husband refuses, the judge can order a dissolution to the wives who have applied.

4.1.5 Zihar *(a form of separation)*

Previously, the husband had to fast for two consecutive months. If he could not do so, then he would have to feed sixty poor persons. Under the new amendment, the husband is now obliged to free a slave. If he cannot do so, to fast etc, (plus sections 120, 129, 132, 137, 143, 150 and 159).

Section 71 was repealed. It had provided for support of the ex-wife for a maximum of a year if the ex-husband has been unjustified in divorcing his wife.

4.2 Succession

Section 259 was amended as follows.

If the grandfather or grandmother dies, leaving sons and daughters who were alive and children of sons of or daughters who died before the deceased, and were poor and have not inherited anything from their dead fathers during the lifetime of their grandparents, and the latter had left a lot of property and had not left anything in a will, then:

(a) for the granddaughters, a share equal to one-sixth;
(b) for the grandsons, a share not exceeding one-fifth;
(c) if there is more than one son who died before the grandparents, then the grandsons or granddaughters would receive what the father would have received if

he had been alive, subject to an overall share not exceeding a third of the estate. This statutory will is given precedence over any voluntary will.

4.3 Marriageable age

Section 15 is a very important section regarding the age limit for marriage for both males and females. It used to be 15 until after reunification two years ago. Since 10 April 1999, there is no age limit, or minimum age for marriage, as regards females or males. The new provision, in this connection, is as follows:

The guardian of the (would be) wife may enter into a marriage contract as regards her, but shall not allow consummation (of the marriage) until after the wife shall have reached the age of puberty, even after the age of fifteen. At the same time, a guardian of a male may enter into a marriage contract, on behalf of his ward, below the age of puberty, if there is an interest in the said (marriage).

4.4 Children's rights

Many regional conferences were held in various provinces in the Republic, in preparation for the Yemeni Law on Child Rights, the last series of which conferences was held in Sana'a from 27–28 April 1999. The Ministry of Social Affairs and the Yemeni Council for Motherhood and Childhood Care had started regional workshops in various governorates in October 1998. The purpose was to obtain feedback and input on the law that had been prepared earlier.

The UNICEF representative in Yemen said that talks with the Yemeni authorities in this regard had started in April 1998. UNICEF financed the participation of experts from Lebanon and Tunisia to help draft the law, and expressed a hope that the law will be enacted before the end of the year 2000.

5 SOCIAL, COMMUNITY CARE AND EDUCATIONAL LAW

5.1 Eradication of illiteracy and Adult Education Law No. 28/1998

This is the first law promulgated since reunification on the subject, according to which there is stipulated training (which is non-conventional), aiming at both males and females between the ages of 10 and 60, to acquire certain professions and skills through short training courses, not exceeding one academic year.

The law states that eradication of illiteracy is a continuous religious, national, humane, development and political task and is a principle prerequisite for the religious, educational and cultural process in society, which works through creating and the continuation of opportunities, education and training for all Yemeni citizens who have been deprived of these previously, in full-time or part-time, with a view to raising their contribution in the progress of their country.

The main principles of the eradication of illiteracy programmes are as follows:

(a) the Islamic religion;
(b) the Constitution of the Republic of Yemen, in addition to the state's educational and cultural policies;
(c) history and national heritage of the Yemeni people and the Arab and Islamic peoples;
(d) social justice and equality and the right to knowledge for all;
(e) cooperation on the basis of Arab and Islamic solidarity and brotherhood, based on fraternity, liberty and justice;
(f) link between the educational programmes and work, in order to fulfil the requirements of society's progress;
(g) taking into consideration the characteristics and requirements or needs of the motives of adults, both male and female;
(h) taking into considerations that the eradication of illiteracy and adult education programmes are supplementary to regular education; and
(i) eradication of illiteracy and adult education programmes are to be linked to the economic and social development plans.

A Supreme Council for eradication of illiteracy and adult education is established as follows:

(a) the President of the Republic as chairman;
(b) the Prime Minister as vice-chairman;
(c) the Minister of Education as secretary-general;
(d) the Head of the Organization of Eradication of Illiteracy and Adult Education as recorder;
(e) the Ministers of Finance, Civil Service and Development and Planning and Information;
(f) deputy ministers in other ministeries; and
(g) any expert(s) or specialist(s) the Council deems proper to invite.

5.2 Technical, Educational and Cultural Organization (*jihaz mahuw al-'ummiyah wa ta'leem al-kibar*)

This has has been established as part of the Ministry of Education, but with body corporate status, with the following responsibilities:

(a) laying down a comprehensive strategy to put an end to illiteracy within a maximum period of twenty-five years;
(b) to plan, regulate and direct the programmes of eradication of illiteracy and adult education; prepare plans and curriculum for education together with the necessary technical requirements as well as following up the implementation of the activities thereof and assessing and developing the various aspects in this respect;
(c) to propose the practical steps and procedure to implement the stages, activities and spheres of adult education, according to the available resources;
(d) to develop and modernize the administration of the training as well as the female training centres and activities, together with the other training centres and activities;

(e)   to study and analyse the successful experiments and experiences of mankind in this field and to make use of the same to develop the cadres here;

(f)   to prepare an annual budget for the activities and programmes of eradicating illiteracy and adult education; and

(g)   to strengthen the relations with counterparts in other countries, as well as the regional, Arab and international organizations and to represent the Republic at conferences, meetings and symposia specializing in eradicating illiteracy and adult education.

5.3 Law No. 34/1998 in Connection with Amendments to Certain Provisions of Law No. 22/1990, in Connection with the Compulsory National Defence Service

This law was promulgated as follows. According to the said law, it is now possible for those persons who are subject to compulsory national defence service to pay a certain amount of money in lieu, provided that those amounts do not exceed 15 per cent of his total annual salary. The provisions of this law apply to all Yemeni nationals, whether resident in the country or abroad. Furthermore, the provisions of the law are inoperative should the circumstances of the country change.

5.4 Teachers and Educational Professions Law No. 38/1998

This law was promulgated and it is the first legislation on the subject since reunification. Its main principles are as follows:

(a)   The provisions of the law aim at creating a highly qualified and trained educational cadres, having confidence in their ability to deliver a better quality of education to the students; the realization of a better social place for teachers and all those working in the educational field, which enhances the mission of the educational cadres; the attraction of national qualified cadres to the educational field; the realization of psychological, professional, living stability for those working in the educational field.

(b)   The provisions of the law apply to all categories of teachers whose main responsibility is teaching; those categories of cadres assisting in the educational process, which include persons working in laboratories, librarians, headmasters and their deputies, academic, educational, social, health and administrative supervisors; those persons involved in the preparation and development of the curriculum, books and other educational methods; those persons involved in training (including those involved in the training of teachers – male and female); teachers working in the Qur'anic schools and nurseries; persons working in the Ministry of Education and its offices in the provinces and districts throughout the Republic.

(c)   The provisions of the law mention educational and technical jobs, appointments and promotions, in both these fields; the obligations and duties of those working in the educational field in addition to their rights and incentives, including salaries and allowances for bonuses (60 per cent), training courses, graduation, transfer, cost of living, rural (30–60 per cent), housing, risk (10 per cent) and medical allowances (including treatment abroad).

(d) Retirement from the teaching profession is either at the end of 35 years' service or at reaching the age of 60. It is possible to take early retirement.

(e) The provisions of the law also mention those practices in which the persons in the teaching profession are forbidden, such as anything contrary to the teachings of Islam, any partisan activities at or during work or the patronizing of certain students. The provisions of the law also provide for investigations and administrative discipline.

5.5 Private Educational Institutions Law No. 11/1999

This law was issue by the President of the Republic with the aim of regulating licences granted for opening private schools and institutions. The main principles of the law are as follows:

(a) The objectives and aims of the private schools and institutions are:
   (i)   addition of new educational capabilities to the ones available at present by the state, which will help to achieve the religious and national educational objectives;
   (ii)   direction of the national and foreign efforts and capabilities towards participation in qualifying and training of cadres essential for the economical and social development projects;
   (iii) rendering the present state basic education system more flexible, through the study of the curriculum and new methods of instruction, within the framework of the legislation, with a view to fulfilling the needs of renewing the system;
   (iv)   widening the study of useful foreign languages, in addition to other subjects, with a view to cadres having knowledge of foreign languages;
   (v)   providing the opportunity for competition in the field of education, through recruitment of experts in the education systems and programmes;
   (vi)   encouragement of popular efforts, as wells as the efforts of the national, Arab and foreign capital in the educational development efforts through investment in the field of education;
   (vii) providing the opportunity to foreign communities to go to educational institutions which render to them the educational services they need and which are consistent with the curriculum and system of education in their respective countries.

(b) The conditions to be fulfilled in order to grant a licence for the establishment of private schools and institutions under the provision of this law are:
   (i)   if the applications are submitted by corporate bodies, such as corporations and authorities of the public, mixed or private sectors, or individuals who have practised in the profession of education and have the expertise qualifying them to give effect to renewals in the means and

methods of instruction, or individuals who desire to invest in the sphere
of education who enjoy Yemeni nationality;

(ii) if the applications are submitted by non-Yemenis, including coun-
      tries which have valid bilateral agreements with the Republic of Yemen
      in the field of cultural and technical cooperation, provided such agree-
      ments have provisions to this effect, or on the basis of reciprocity;
      the friendly countries which have common original culture; the non-
      governmental foreign organizations which have educational coopera-
      tion with the Ministry of Education in the Republic of Yemen, or
      foreign investment institutions with permission to operate in the Re-
      public under official agreements, and provided that there is no con-
      tradiction with the main legislation on education in force; the educa-
      tion organization recognized by the Arab, Islamic and International
      organizations (e.g. UNESCO) or if non-Yemeni nationals are will-
      ing to invest in the field of education.

      The following points should be noted:

      –   a private education institution will be granted a licence in any
          one of the following events: (a) for a community where the in-
          habitants do not speak Arabic; (b) where a community's system
          of education in its country of origin is different from that in force
          in the Republic of Yemen; or (c) if the curriculum in the com-
          munity's country of origin are different from those in force in
          the Republic. However, under all of these circumstances, there
          should be a sufficient number of students in each community to
          justify the establishment of an educational institution, and that the
          services of that institution are only for the benefit of the commu-
          nities' students in the Republic of Yemen;

      –   furthermore, it is absolutely forbidden to grant licences to estab-
          lish private educational institutions or to allow any kind of edu-
          cation if it is proved that the body submitting the application is
          connected to, or has relations with, missionaries or Masonic or-
          ganizations;

      –   it is also forbidden to grant licences to political parties and orga-
          nizations, as well as charitable organizations to establish private
          educational institutions. Furthermore it is not permissible to es-
          tablish private educational institutions for political, partisan or sec-
          tarian objectives or motives.

(c) the licensing authority is the Ministry of Education;
(d) the supervisory authority is the Ministry of Education;
(e) the curriculum and procedure for admitting students, in addition to the sys-
     tem of examinations and awarding of certificates;
(f) the admininistrative and financial systems;
(g) the existing schools and institutions are given a maximum of one year to reg-
     ulate their administrative, financial and technical affairs in accordance with the
     provisions of this law.

5.6 Republican Resolution No. 128/1998 Regarding Awards of the President of the Republic for the Youth

According to these Republican Resolutions, three awards have been established for the youth (citizens of the Republic under 30 years of age) in the following subjects:

(a) reciting the Qur'an;
(b) technology and sciences; and
(c) arts and music, etc.

Every award is made as a sum of money, in addition to a certificate.

The subject to be presented by the youth must not have been published or taken from someone else's work and must be consistent with the Yemeni society's culture and national heritage, public morals and the national laws in force.

A committee shall be set up for the awards, consisting of:

(a) the Minister of Youth and Sports: Chairman;
(b) representatives of the Presidential Office, Yemen's universities, Ministries of Education and Culture and Labour, Deputy under-secretary of the Ministry of Youth and Sports: Members.

A sub-committee shall choose the subjects for the awards.

On 1 October every years, the Committee shall announce the invitation for papers for the awards, and shall recommend the financial awards in this respect. Those interested should submit their papers within three months from the date of publication and the Ministry shall refer the names of the participants as well as the subjects to the Committee.

Within six months, the Committee shall convene and shall nominate a national day for presentation of the awards, with effect from the year 1999.

5.7 Republican Resolution Nos. 193/1998 and 194/1998 Regarding the Establishment of Community Colleges in Sana'a and Aden

These Resolutions were issued under the Community Colleges Law No. 5/1996 as bodies corporate, with financial and administrative independence, subject to the laws and regulations in force. The objectives and aims to be realized are as follows:

(a) preparation of middle cadres to ensure provision of personnel with technical and professional skills necessary for development requirements;
(b) fulfilment and implementation of the principal objective of community participation in spreading education;
(c) establishment of a system of education that is characterized by flexibility and adaptation of modern technology and labour requirements; and
(d) participation in activization of training with a view to raising efficiency and professional standards.

5.8 Republican Resolution No. 14/1999 Regarding the Formation of a Commission from the Religious Clergy (or "ULAMA") Society, with Responsibility to Review and Approve the Curricula of the Principal Education Stage (years 1–9)

According to this Resolution:

(a) thirty religious clergy, from all schools of Islamic jurisprudence, representing all political parties as well as the various provinces of the Republic, have been chosen to form this Commission;

(b) the responsibilities assigned to the Commission, and the powers conferred upon that Commission are as follows:

  (i) to approve the philosophy, policies and objectives of the principal education stage curriculum, submitted to the Commission by the Ministry of Education; and

  (ii) to approve uniform and unified curricula for all students at the principal education stage (years 1–9) which is equivalent to the primary years and an intermediate three-year stage in other Arab states.

This step has been made necessary to unify the curriculum of the state schools and the Islamic religious schools. The latter have grown in number as well as importance during the last few years. The main aim is to put an end, if possible, to any chance of fundamentalism increasing, thereby creating chaos in the country in future.

6 HUMAN RIGHTS

The Republic of Yemen has ratified most of the major international conventions on human rights. Article 6 of the Constitution is a specific reference to Yemen's adherence to the Universal Declaration on Human Rights. Important human rights are enshrined separately in the Constitution.

In 1998, the government showed an increasing readiness to give high-level attention to human rights matters, most notably with the setting up of the Supreme National Human Rights Committee on 31 December 1998, chaired by the Foreign Minister. It continues to work to improve the provision for human rights.

The British Embassy, with the agreement of the Ministry of the Interior, is undertaking a series of events in 1998 and 1999 to support penal and judicial reform in Yemen.

6.1 Penal reform

During 28–29 September 1998, the British Embassy, in conjunction with the British Council, Penal Reform International (PRI) and the Yemeni Human Rights Information and Training Centre (HRITC), supported the first seminar in Yemen on Prison Reform and Human Rights. The aim of the seminar was to raise awareness of human rights among decision-makers, officials and senior prison staff.

During 25–29 October 1998, the British Embassy supported a five-day workshop for prison governors from five prisons, carried out by PRI and HRITC. This encouraged governors to focus on the rights of prisoners. As part of the workshop, the governors drew up action plans for the five prisons concerned. These contain practical steps which they can undertake to achieve real improvements in conditions for prisoners.

In November 1998, the British Embassy in Yemen funded a visit by two British Members of Parliament and one former Member of Parliament, a parliamentary clerk and a parliamentary librarian, as part of a project to help build the capacity of the Yemeni Parliament. This included a three-day training workshop aimed at helping four key parliamentary committees to strengthen their ability to play a full and effective role in Parliament. One of the four committees selected was the Parliamentary Committee on Human Rights.

During November and December of 1998, the embassy also funded a visit by three consultants from the Electoral Reform International Services (ERIS), organized in conjunction with the British Council, to help develop a long-term strategy for building the capacity of the SEC. The aim is to help the SEC enhance their role in the organization of future elections in Yemen, so that all citizens can exercise the political rights granted to them in the Constitution in the context of free and fair elections.

Two two-week training sessions for judges and others involved in the judicial process on national and international human rights law and its application in the courtroom are scheduled for early 1999. The aim is to increase awareness of human rights and of the different roles of those involved in the judicial process. The programme is being formulated in consultation with the Ministry of Justice, the Higher Judicial Institute, the Judicial Inspection Board and the Supreme National Human Rights Committee.

6.2 Children's rights

During the autumn of 1998, the British Embassy supported the project "Children Painting their Rights", aimed at raising awareness in Yemen of the rights of children. It focused particularly on the right to education and on the existing inequality between boys and girls in this respect.

7 LEGAL MAGAZINES, NEWSPAPERS AND BULLETINS

Al-Qistas is the first legal magazine since reunification and was started in mid-1998. It is a monthly magazine in Arabic, edited by a lawyer, with financial assistance from the Dutch and Danish Embassies in Sana'a and Riyadh respectively. It is an independent magazine, albeit it is subsidized by certain foreign bodies.

Al-Qahda Tyyah was started in October 1998 and is published fortnightly. It is, for the time being, financed by the Ministry of Justice and edited by Judge Nageeb Shamiri. It is addressed mainly to the public at large, to contribute to spreading legal and judicial awareness. It publishes information about the appeals decided by the Supreme Court of the Republic, as well as any resolutions, circulars or directions issued by the Ministry of Justice, Supreme Court or the Attorney-General. It provides a valuable service to the public.

Al-Tahkeem is a monthly bulletin, which was started in September 1998 by the Yemeni Centre for Conciliation and Arbitration, in the hope that in future it could become a monthly magazine dealing with international commerce.

Algeria

*Yamina Kebir**

The legislative activity during the year 1997 has not been very important in comparison with previous years, due to the fact that the legislative elections for the new assembly took place in June and in the interim period, no law was passed. Once it was elected and installed, the new assembly focused primarily on the enactment of rules for its internal organization and functioning.

The main fields for legislative activity were administrative, constitutional and economic with the pursuance of economic reforms.

1 ADMINISTRATIVE AND CONSTITUTIONAL LAW

Further to the legislative elections which were held on 5 June 1997, the Constitutional Council officially proclaimed the results of the elections. As a result of this, the various political parties were represented in the new assembly with the following number of seats:

National Democratic Gathering	155
MSP (Islamist)	69
National Liberation Front	64
Ennahda (Islamist)	34
Socialist Forces Front	19
Culture and Democratic Gathering	19
Independents	11
Workers' Party (Trotskyist)	4
Other small parties	5

Prior to the elections, Ordinance No. 97-07 of 1997 relating to the organization and process of the elections was passed, setting out the rules for the election of the

---

* Attorney-at-law, Algiers Bar, admitted to appear before the Supreme Court of Algiers. See also the article on the status of children and their protection in Algerian law in the country survey of Algeria covering the year 1997 in this *Yearbook* at p. 162.

National People's Assembly and the Council of the Nation in accordance with Articles 123 and 179 of the Constitution.

As far as the election of the National People's Assembly is concerned, Ordinance No. 97-07 reasserts the right of any Algerian citizen aged 18 to vote. It is to be noted that there is no discrimination with regard to gender; in fact all the Constitutions of Algeria since independence have guaranteed women's right to vote.

The citizens are invited to register with their constituencies and the electoral lists are established under the supervision of a committee composed of various personalities and chaired by a magistrate. The vote is personal and secret.

Proxy votes have been restricted to specific situations. It is to be recalled in this respect that abuses in the use of proxies during the elections of 1991 led to massive fraud. Proxy votes are now limited to persons in hospital, invalid or handicapped persons or those travelling aboard. Proxies are established by a deed sworn before the Chairman of the local elections committee and for persons in hospital, before the manager of the hospital.

The counting of the votes is public and takes place in the polling booth immediately after the poll. The results are gathered by the regional election committees and then transmitted to the Constitutional Council which must declare the poll within seventy-two hours of the receipt of regional results.

Any candidate or political party has the right to file complaints about the alleged irregularities of the voting by making a recourse before the Constitutional Council within two days of the announcement of the results. The candidate of the political party may produce a written memorandum within four days of registration of the recourse at the Constitutional Council. The Constitutional Council has three days to make its decision. If the Council considers that the recourse is justified, it may either cancel the contested election or amend the minutes of the results and decide that the candidate is elected. The Constitutional Council must, in making its decision, give the reasons.

The National People's Assembly is elected for a term of five years by proportional voting for several members on a list. Candidates to the election of the assembly are either presented by a political party or on an independent list. In the latter case, the candidate must be supported by at least 400 signatures.

The elected members of the Council of the Nation are elected for a term of six years and renewed every three years by half. They are elected by absolute majority for several members on a list by the members of the National People's Assembly and of the regional assemblies.

The President of the Republic is elected by uninominal voting on a second ballot at the absolute majority of votes cast. If there is no clear winner the first time, the candidates at the head of the list who obtained the highest number of votes go forward to the second ballot.

The election campaign starts twenty-one days before the ballot and all candidates must provide a political programme.

All candidates have an equal access to the media for electoral propaganda. The length of a television appearance is equal for all candidates to the presidential election – for legislatives, it varies according to the respective importance of the number of candidates presented by each political party.

The use of the equipment or resources of a legal entity or public organization is prohibited, as is the use of places of worship, schools or universities.

Electoral campaigns may be financed by funds originating from:

(a) contributions of political parties;
(b) subsidies by the state; or
(c) income of the candidate.

Candidates are strictly prohibited from receiving either directly or indirectly donations in cash or in kind from a foreign individual, legal entity or organization.

In the wake of the reforms of institutions, a new law organizing political parties was passed with the aim of clarifying the conditions and rules presiding over the funding of political parties and correcting the grave deviations which prevailed before the election of 1991 (Ordinance No. 97-09 of 6 March 1997).

The main provision of this Ordinance sets out the principle that no political party is entitled to use the constituent values of the national identity for its propaganda, which are Islamic, Arabic and Amazigh or to make use of practices contrary to the values of the Revolution of 1 November 1954.

A political party cannot be founded on a religious, linguistic, racial, gender or regional basis. Any link, whatever its nature, between a political party and a trade union or association is strictly forbidden.

In order to comply with the law, existing political parties were invited to amend their founding charters and names accordingly. As a consequence, the party Hamas (Islamist) changed its name to Mujtama' Harakat Essilm (MSP). Judges, members of the military and security forces, members of the Constitutional Council and high ranking civil servants cannot belong to a party.

Ordinance No. 97-04 of 11 January 1997 relating to the declaration of patrimony, required all members of Parliament, local assemblies and government, as well as civil servants and managers of publicly owned enterprises to make a formal declaration of their patrimony. This declaration, which is sworn in the month following their election or appointment before a special committee, is confidential; the principle of confidentiality does not apply to the declaration made by the President of the Republic, the President of the Constitutional Council, the Prime Minister and the members of Parliament, of the Government, the President of the Supreme Court and of the bank of Algeria are published in the Official Gazette within two months following their election or appointment.

2 COMMERCIAL LAW

The economic reforms that were launched in 1990 have been completed with the enactment of new laws and amendment of the existing ones, notably in the field of privatization.

The authorities had to recognize that the law on privatization, Ordinance No. 95-22 of 26 August 1995 had a very limited impact and that the process launched then was not a success. According to official records, only nineteen local companies had been privatized, out of a programme of 139.

The government was then prompted to propose a bill for the amendment of Ordinance No. 95-22 with the aim of making the conditions and process of privatization more flexible.

Ordinance No. 97-12 amending and supplementing Ordinance No. 95-22 of 26 August 1995 was passed on 19 March 1997. The main objective of the amendments was to facilitate the process of privatization and to enable employees of privatized enterprises to purchase the assets of the companies they work in.

As compared to Ordinance No. 95-22, the changes are the following. Article 1 defining the scope of the law has been enlarged in order to include the "assets which constitute an autonomous plant of a publicly owned company". Under this provision, even the smallest local companies are susceptible of being privatized. The other main amendment is relating to the public shareholding which has now become an additional method of acquiring shares for the privatization of publicly owned companies. In this context, employees of companies eligible for privatization are entitled to purchase the totality of the assets and for so doing to exercise their pre-emptive rights within three months of the date of notice of the offer for the transfer of assets. In such a case, employees are granted the benefit of payment by instalments.

The National Privatization Council has issued a list of publicly owned enterprises to be either partially or totally privatized and which covers all activities.

3 EMPLOYMENT AND LABOUR LAW

The significant development in this field during 1997 was the reduction of the legal weekly duration of work. This was reduced from forty-four to forty hours per week on five business days from Saturday to Wednesday. This is provided by Ordinance No. 97-03 of 11 January 1997.

4 INTELLECTUAL PROPERTY

Ordinance No. 10 of 6 March 1997 relating to copyrights and related rights superseded Ordinance No. 73-14 of 3 April 1973 which was abrogated. The new law introduces a considerable modernization of Algerian copyright law and provides extensive revisions on literary and artistic property.

The interesting point is that the range of works covered by protection has been considerably enlarged to include all works of intellectual creation.

The law expressly protects all books and other literary, artistic and scientific writings (including lectures), choreographic and musical works (including cinematographic works composed of animated sequences with or without sound), photographic works, drawings and printings, architectural, sculptural and graphic works (including plans), as well as software programmes, garment designs, translations, adaptations, music arrangements and other original transformations of literary or artistic works.

The right of author (individual or legal entity) remains in force and protected during his lifetime and accrues to benefit of his heirs for fifty years after his death.

The law also provides for fifty-year periods of protection for collective works, broadcasts and photographs from the date of their presentation to the public.

Infringement of law is a criminal offence which may be punished by imprisonment and fine through request for prosecution. Civil damages may be obtained before civil courts.

It is also to be noted that Algeria ratified the Berne Convention for the protection of literary and artistic works.

5 PUBLIC INTERNATIONAL LAW

In 1997, Algeria approved of and/or ratified a number of international treaties. These treaties are related to Maghrebine cooperation and inter-Maghrebine relations, double taxation and the promotion of investments. In addition, the Unified Treaty on Investment of Arab Capital in the Arab Countries has been ratified.

In line with the implementation of reforms towards a market economy, the following treaties were also ratified:

- the Convention Establishing the Multilateral Investment Guarantee Authority (MIGA); and
- the Convention on Settlement of Investment Disputes between States and Nationals of other States.

Decrees passed include:

- Presidential Decree No. 97-102, dated 28 Dhu'l-Kaada 1417, corresponding to 5 April 1997, giving notice of the amendment to paragraph 2 of clause 43 of the Convention on Children's Rights, adopted at the meeting of participating States in December 1995;
- Presidential Decree No. 97-103, dated 28 Dhu'l-Kaada 1417, corresponding to 5 April 1997, ratifying out the agreement made between the DPRA (Democratic and Popular Republic of Algeria) and the Hashemite Kingdom of Jordan concerning reciprocal encouragement and protection of investments, signed at Amman in August 1996;
- Presidential Decree No. 97-125, dated 19 Dhu'l-Kaada 1417, corresponding to 26 April 1997, setting up and defining the organization and working of the inter-Ministerial Committee charged with the implementation of the agreement banning the perfecting, manufacturing, storing or use of chemical weapons and also dealing with their destruction;
- Appendix to Presidential Decree No. 86-67, dated 16 May 1989, setting out accession to the international pact relating to economic, social and cultural rights, to the international pact concerning civil and political rights and also to the protocol referring to civil and political rights adopted by the United Nations General Assembly on 16 December 1996. This was published in the Official Gazette No. 20 of the DPRA on 17 May 1997;
- Presidential Decree No. 97-229, dated 23 June 1997, ratifying the agreement made between the State of Qatar and the DPRA concerning reciprocal encouragement and protection of investments, signed at Doha and dated 11 Jumada II 1417, corresponding to 24 October 1996;
- Presidential Decree No. 97-33, dated 13 September 1997, setting out the agreement for cooperation in the field of vocational training made between the DPRA and the Islamic Republic of Mauritania, signed at Nouakshott and dated 8 February 1997 (OG No. 61, dated 14 September 1997);
- Presidential Decree No. 97-339, dated 13 September 1997, ratifying the agreement for cooperation in the field of health, made between the DPRA and the Islamic Republic of Mauritania, signed at Nouakshott and dated 23 April 1997 (OG No. 61, dated 14 September 1997);
- Presidential Decree No. 97-341, dated 13 September 1997, setting out conditional accession on behalf of the DPRA to the Berne Convention for the pro-

tection of literary and artistic works, dated 9 September 1886, supplemented at Paris on 4 May 1896, revised at Berlin on 13 November 1908, supplemented at Berne on 20 March 1914 and revised at Rome on 2 June 1928, at Brussels on 26 June 1948, at Stockholm on 14 July 1967 and at Paris on 24 July 1971 and amended on 28 September 1979 (OG No. 61, dated 14 September 1997);

–   Presidential Decree No. 97-342, dated 13 September 1997, setting out the agreement made between the DPRA and the Government of the Republic of Indonesia, aimed at avoiding double taxation and laying down rules for reciprocal aid in the fields of income tax and wealth, signed at Jakarta on 28 April 1995 (OG No. 61, dated 14 September 1997);

–   Presidential Decree No. 97-357, dated 27 September 1997, ratifying the agreement made between the DPRA and the Government of the Arab Republic of Egypt, for mutual administrative assistance with a view to informing and inquiring into customs offences, signed at Algiers on 31 July 1996;

–   Presidential Decree No. 97-361, dated 27 September 1997, ratifying the agreement made between the DPRA and the State of Qatar for cooperation in the fields of education and science, signed at Doha and dated 24 October 1996 (OG No. 63, dated 28 September 1997);

–   Presidential Decree No. 97-373, dated 30 September 1997, setting out conditional accession on behalf of the DPRA to the convention concerning illegal repression against the security of maritime navigation, signed at Rome and dated 10 March 1998;

–   Presidential Decree No. 97-374, dated 30 September 1997, ratifying the agreement made between the DPRA and the Government of the Kingdom of Belgium concerning international road haulage and the passage of travellers and goods as also of the protocol appended thereto, signed at Brussels on 29 March 1994.

Morocco

*Michèle Zirari-Devif**

1 DROIT CONSTITUTIONNEL

Du 1er janvier 1998 au 30 juin 1999 un seul texte concernant le droit constitutionnel a été publié au Bulletin officiel. Il s'agit de la loi organique n° 8-98 modifiant et complétant la loi organique n° 29-93 relative au Conseil constitutionnel.[1]

Le Conseil constitutionnel a été créé par la Constitution de 1992. Jusque là le contrôle de la constitutionnalité, exercé par la chambre constitutionnelle de la Cour suprême, était très limité. Il intervenait dans des cas très peu nombreux et ce contrôle ne pouvait être mis en oeuvre que par le Premier ministre ou le président de la Chambre des Représentants.

La création du Conseil constitutionnel par la Constitution de 1992 a élargi le contrôle de la constitutionnalité des lois. Le conseil est chargé, comme l'était auparavant la chambre constitutionnelle, de l'approbation des lois organiques et du règlement de la chambre des représentants. Mais, selon la Constitution de 1992, ce Conseil peut se prononcer sur la constitutionnalité de toutes les lois dès lors qu'il est saisi par le Roi, le Premier ministre, le Président de la Chambre des représentants ou le quart de cette chambre.

A la suite de la révision constitutionnelle de 1996,[2] modifiant la composition du Parlement qui comporte désormais deux chambres, la Chambre des Représentants et la Chambre des Conseillers, une modification de la composition du Conseil constitutionnel s'imposait. C'est l'objet de la loi organique n° 8-98.

---

* Professeur à la faculté des sciences juridiques, économiques et sociales de Rabat-Agdal
[1] Promulguée par dahir n° 1-98-126 du 28 septembre 1998, Bulletin officiel du 5 octobre 1998, p. 531.
[2] Voir *Yearbook of Ialsmic and Middle Eastern Law*, vol. 3 (1996), p. 354 et vol. 4 (1997–1998), p. 429.

Le Conseil constitutionnel était jusque là composé d'un président nommé par le Roi, quatre membres nommées par le Roi et quatre membres nommés par le Président de la Chambre des représentants après consultation des groupes parlementaires.[3]

Après la modification apportée par la loi n° 8-98 le Conseil comprend:

(a) six membres désignés par le Roi;
(b) trois membres désignées par le Président de la Chambre des représentants après consultation des groupes;
(c) trois membres désignés par le Président de la Chambre des conseillers après consultation des groupes.

Le président du Conseil est désigné par le Roi parmi les membres qu'il nomme.

Le mandat des membres du Conseil qui était de six ans renouvelable une fois passe à neuf ans non renouvelable. Le renouvellement se fait par tiers tous les trois ans.

2 DROIT ADMINISTRATIF

En janvier 1999 est publié au Bulletin officiel un décret fixant les conditions et les formes de passation des marchés de l'Etat ainsi que certaines dispositions relatives à leur contrôle et à leur gestion.[4]

Ce texte qui se substitue à un décret du 14 octobre 1976[5] opère une refonte de la législation relative aux marchés publics. Il comporte quatre-vingt-sept articles répartis en sept chapitres. Selon son texte de présentation, il se propose d'adapter la réglementation des marchés aux exigences du contexte économique et financier actuel et vise notamment à asseoir de nouvelles règles en vue de garantir une meilleure gestion des marchés publics.

Les principales améliorations apportées par ce nouveau décret concernent l'amélioration de la transparence dans la passation et la gestion des marchés publics, en imposant notamment la communication par les administrations de leur programme d'action en début d'exercice budgétaire, l'institution d'un règlement de consultation précisant les critères utilisés par la commission de jugement des offres, l'information systématique des concurrents, la généralisation de l'ouverture des plis en séance publique ainsi que la motivation des décisions d'éviction aux soumissionnaires non retenus.

Le nouveau texte se propose également d'améliorer le libre jeu de la concurrence en assurant aux soumissionnaires l'égalité d'accès aux marchés publics. Ainsi, la procédure de l'appel d'offre est retenue comme règle générale pour l'octroi des marchés publics. Le recours aux marchés négociés et aux appels d'offre restreint devient exceptionnel.

Le nouveau décret vise également, la moralisation des marchés publics, la simplification des procédures et des règles régissant la gestion des marchés publics ainsi que la garantie du droit des entreprises.

---

[3] Loi organique n° 29-93 du 25 février 1994 relative au Conseil constitutionnel, promulguée par dahir n° 1-94-124 du 25 février 1994, Bulletin officiel du 2 mars 1994, p. 158.
[4] Décret n° 2-98-482 du 30 décembre 1998, Bulletin officiel du 7 janvier 1999, p. 3.
[5] Décret n° 2-76-479 du 14 octobre 1976 relatif aux marchés de travaux, fournitures ou services passés au compte de l'Etat, Bulletin officiel du 27 octobre 1976 p. 1140.

3 ORGANISATION JUDICIAIRE

Le 22 septembre 1998 est promulguée une loi n° 6-98 modifiant et complétant le dahir portant loi n° 1-74-338 du 15 juillet 1974 fixant l'organisation judiciaire du Royaume.[6]

Cette loi n'apporte pas d'innovation mais actualise heureusement le dahir du 15 juillet 1974 fixant l'organisation judiciaire du Royaume.[7] En effet, depuis la promulgation de ce dahir en 1974, l'organisation judiciaire a connu des modifications importantes, en particulier par la création, en 1993, des tribunaux administratifs[8] et en 1997 des tribunaux de commerce.[9] Le texte de 1974 est donc modifié en conséquence et son article premier prévoit que l'organisation judiciaire comprend les juridictions suivantes:

(a)   les juridictions communales et d'arrondissement dont l'organisation, la composition et les attributions sont fixées par un dahir portant loi;
(b)   les tribunaux administratifs;
(c)   les tribunaux de commerce;
(d)   les tribunaux de première instance;
(e)   les cours d'appel;
(f)   les cours d'appel de commerce;
(g)   la Cour suprême.

Les articles suivants apportent à la composition des juridictions, les modifications imposées par la création des nouveaux tribunaux

4 DROIT PÉNAL

Le 5 février 1999, une loi n° 11-99 modifie et complète l'article 446 du code pénal.[10]

Cette modification d'un seul article du code pénal pourrait passer inaperçue. Elle revêt cependant une importance certaine. L'article 446 du code pénal concerne le respect du secret professionnel par les médecins et toutes personnes dépositaires des secrets qu'on leur confie. Les deux premiers alinéas de l'article 446 n'ont pas été modifiés depuis la promulgation du code pénal en 1962; le premier alinéa sanctionne la violation du secret professionnel de un à six mois d'emprisonnement et d'une amende, le second autorise la dénonciation des avortements dont les personnes tenus au secret professionnel ont connaissance à l'occasion de leur fonction.

---

[6]   Promulguée par dahir n° 1-98-118 du 22 septembre 1998, Bulletin officiel du 1er octobre 1998, p. 516.
[7]   Bulletin Officiel du 17 juillet 1974, p. 1081.
[8]   Loi n° 41-90 instituant des tribunaux administratifs, promulguée par dahir n° 1-91-225 du 10 septembre 1994, Bulletin officiel du 3 novembre 1993, p. 595.
[9]   Loi n° 53-95 promulguée par dahir n° 1-97-65 du 12 février 1997, Bulletin officiel du 15 mai 1997, p. 520; Voir *Yearbook of Islamic and Middle Eastern Law*, vol. 4 (1997–1998), pp. 427–428.
[10]   Promulguée par dahir n° 1-99-18 du 5 février 1999, Bulletin officiel du 15 avril 1999, p. 201.

La loi n° 11-99 ajoute à l'article 446 un troisième alinéa qui autorise la dénonciation aux autorités judiciaires et administratives compétentes, des faits délictueux et des actes de mauvais traitements et privations perpétrés contre des mineurs de 18 ans lorsque les personnes tenues au secret ont eu connaissance de ces faits à l'occasion de l'exercice de leur profession ou de leur fonction. Citées en justice pour des affaires relatives à de telles infractions, elles demeurent libres de fournir ou non leur témoignage.

Cette modification du code pénal semble indiquer que le respect de la personne de l'enfant devient un préoccupation réelle du législateur marocain. Déjà en 1994, une circulaire du ministre de la Santé prescrivait en termes clairs et énergiques la dénonciation aux procureurs du Roi de tout cas de sévices exercés sur enfant, constaté par un médecin. Cette modification législative va dans le même sens permettant à toute personne d'agir sans crainte de violer le secret que sa profession lui impose.

5 DROIT DES AFFAIRES

On peut noter dans ce domaine la promulgation de deux lois. Il s'agit tout d'abord de la loi n° 13-97 relative aux groupements d'intérêt économique.[11]

La loi n° 13-97 définit dans son article premier le groupement d'intérêt économique (GIE) en prévoyant que deux ou plusieurs personnes morales peuvent constituer entre elles pour une durée déterminée ou indéterminée un GIE en vue de mettre en oeuvre tous les moyens propres à faciliter ou à développer l'activité économique de ses membres et à améliorer ou accroître les résultats de cette activité.

Le GIE est, par conséquent, essentiellement un groupement de moyens qui a pour but de permettre à ses membres la réalisation d'économies par la mise en commun d'un certain nombre de frais fixes (par exemple création d'un service informatique ou d'une bibliothèque commune).

L'activité du groupement doit se rattacher à l'activité économique de ses membres et ne peut avoir un caractère subsidiaire par rapport à celle-ci. Le but du groupement n'est pas de réaliser des bénéfices pour lui-même (art. 1er).

Le GIE, qui peut être constitué sans capital (art. 3), jouit de la personnalité morale à partir de son immatriculation au registre du commerce, sans toutefois que cette immatriculation emporte présomption de commercialité du groupement. En effet, le caractère commercial ou civil d'un GIE est déterminé par son objet, que ses membres soient ou non commerçants (art. 4 et 5).

Le chapitre II de la loi est consacré au contrat du groupement d'intérêt économique. Ce contrat est soumis aux règles générales de formation des contrats à l'exception de quelques règles de formes imposées par les articles 9 à 12: écrit obligatoire dont les membres peuvent se faire remettre copie, mentions obligatoires devant figurer dans le contrat (dénomination, objet, durée adresse, raison sociale du groupement).

Le chapitre III (art. 13 et 14) traite des concours financiers: Outre les apports pouvant être effectués en cas de constitution avec capital, la perception d'un droit

---

[11] Promulguée par dahir n° 1-99-12 du 5 février 1999, Bulletin officiel du 1er avril 1999, p. 165.

d'entrée peut être prévue ainsi que des cotisations destinées à couvrir les frais de fonctionnement. Les membres peuvent également consentir des prêts ou avances et décider que tout ou partie des bénéfices, s'il en existe, seront laissés à la disposition du GIE sous forme d'avance.

Les droits et obligations des membres sont prévus par le chapitre IV (articles 15 à 20). Ils sont déterminés par le contrat. A défaut ils sont présumés identiques. Les membres du groupement sont tenus sur leur patrimoine propre. Le GIE peut accepter de nouveaux membres dans les conditions prévues par le contrat. Tout membre, dans les conditions prévues par le contrat, peut se retirer à condition d'avoir rempli ses obligations ou peut céder sa participation.

Le groupement est administré par un ou plusieurs administrateurs choisis parmi ses membres ou en dehors d'eux. Les administrateurs sont responsables individuellement ou solidairement, selon le cas, envers le groupement ou envers les tiers, soit des infractions aux dispositions légales applicables au GIE, soit de la violation du contrat de groupement, soit des fautes commises dans leur gestion (chapitre V, articles 21 à 29). L'assemblée des membres est habilitée à prendre toute décision dans les conditions déterminées par le contrat (chapitre VI, articles 30 à 33). Les membres ont toute liberté pour déterminer les bases de répartition des bénéfices et des pertes (chapitre VII, articles 34 à 38).

Le contrôle des comptes du groupement peut être assuré par un ou plusieurs commissaires aux comptes, nommés par décision collective des membres, dans les conditions prévues par le contrat (chapitre VIII, articles 39 et 40).

Toute société ou association dont l'objet correspond à la définition du groupement d'intérêt économique peut être transformée en un tel groupement sans donner lieu à dissolution ni création d'un personne morale nouvelle. De même un GIE peut être transformé en société en nom collectif, sur décision unanime de ses membres sans donner lieu à dissolution ni création d'un personne morale nouvelle (chapitre IX, article 41).

La dissolution du GIE se fait, sous réserve d'autres causes de dissolution prévues par le contrat, par l'arrivée du terme, la réalisation ou l'extinction de son objet, une décision de l'assemblée de ses membres ou une décision judiciaire pour de justes motifs (chapitre X). La liquidation de fait conformément aux dispositions du contrat (chapitre XI).

Quel que soit l'objet du groupement le contrat doit être déposé au greffe du tribunal du lieu du siège et un extrait de ce contrat doit être publié au Bulletin officiel et dans un journal d'annonces légales. La même publicité doit accompagner les modifications du contrat, la dissolution ou la liquidation du groupement (chapitre XII).

Le chapitre suivant (XIII) prévoit les nullités des GIE et de leurs actes ou délibérations qui ne peuvent résulter que d'une violation d'une disposition expresse de la présente loi ou de l'une des causes de nullité des contrats en général.

Enfin les deux derniers chapitres sont consacrés aux dispositions pénales et aux dispositions diverses.

Le deuxième texte à signaler en droit des affaires est la loi n° 18-97 relative au micro-crédit.[12]

---

[12] Promulguée par dahir n° 1-99-16 du 5 février 1999, Bulletin officiel du 1er avril 1999, p. 172.

Depuis quelques années plusieurs associations de micro-crédit ont été créées au Maroc sans qu'aucun texte spécifique ne leur soit consacré. Ces associations étaient donc soumises au dahir du 15 novembre 1958[13] réglementant le droit d'association qui définit l'association comme "la convention par laquelle deux ou plusieurs personnes mettent en commun de façon permanente leur connaissance ou leur activité dans un but autre que de partager des bénéfices".

La loi n° 18-97 est consacrée aux associations de micro-crédit. D'après cette nouvelle loi, les associations de micro-crédit restent soumise au Dahir de 1958, mais également à des règles qui leur sont spécifiques.

La loi définit le micro-crédit comme "tout crédit dont l'objet est de permettre à des personnes économiquement faibles de créer ou développer leur propre activité de production ou de service en vue d'assurer leur insertion économique". Le montant du micro-crédit, qui ne peut dépasser 50,000 dirhams, est fixé par décret. Ce décret peut prévoir plusieurs niveaux de ce montant en fonction des objectifs de chaque association de micro-crédit et de ses moyens financiers.

Le chapitre II de la loi traite des conditions d'exercice de l'activité de micro-crédit. En ce qui concerne leur constitution, les associations de micro-crédit, comme toutes les associations, sont soumises à la procédure de la déclaration préalable au siège de l'autorité administrative locale, déclaration dont il est délivré récépissé.

Elles doivent, en outre, être autorisées par arrêté du ministre des finances, pris après avis du conseil consultatif du micro-crédit. Pour obtenir cette autorisation l'association doit remplir un certain nombre de conditions concernant ses statuts, ses moyens humains et financiers, son plan de développement et ses projections financières.

De plus, les fondateurs et les membres des organes d'administration ou de direction d'une association de micro-crédit doivent "être de bonne moralité" et n'avoir pas été condamnés pour contrefaçon ou falsification des monnaies ou effets de crédits publics, vols et extorsions, infractions à la législation des changes; ils ne doivent pas non plus avoir fait l'objet d'une liquidation judiciaire (article 7).

Toujours au chapitre II, l'article 8 prévoit que le taux d'intérêt maximum applicable aux opérations de micro-crédit est fixé par arrêté du ministre des finances après avis du conseil consultatif du micro-crédit. Ce taux d'intérêt ainsi que les conditions appliquées aux opérations doivent être affichés dans les locaux des associations.

Les ressources des associations de micro-crédit (chapitre III) sont plus importantes que celles des associations simplement déclarées prévues par le dahir de 1958. Elles comprennent en effet, outre les cotisations et contributions de leurs membres, les dons ou subventions publiques ou privés; les emprunts, les intérêts et commissions perçus sur les micro-crédit qu'elles octroient; les fonds mis à leur disposition dans le cadre de conventions de partenariat, de contrats-programmes conclus avec des administrations, des organismes publics et des collectivités locales; les ressources concessionnelles que l'Etat peut mobiliser à leur profit dans le cadre de la coopération bilatérale ou multilatérale; les revenus gérés par le placement de leurs fonds; le remboursement de principal des prêts.

Contrairement aux autres associations, elles peuvent également faire appel à la générosité publique sans autorisation préalable.

---

[13] Dahir n° 1-58-376 du 15 novembre 1958 réglementant le droit d'association, Bulletin officiel du 27 novembre 1958, p. 1909.

Le chapitre IV prévoit le contrôle des opérations de micro-crédit. Il impose la tenue d'une comptabilité régulière qui doit être conservée pendant dix ans.

Un comité de suivi des activités de micro-crédit est institué, qui est composé de représentants de l'administration; ce comité est chargé de veiller au respect des dispositions législatives et réglementaires.

Les associations sont tenus de procéder annuellement à un audit externe de leur gestion.

Les opérations de crédit opérées par les associations de micro-crédit sont exonérées de la taxe sur la valeur ajoutée. Les dons en argent ou en nature qu'elles reçoivent constituent des charges déductibles de l'impôt sur les sociétés et de l'impôt général sur le revenu (chapitre V).

Les associations de micro-crédit sont tenues d'adhérer à la Fédération des associations de micro-crédit dont les statuts ainsi que leurs modifications doivent être approuvés par le ministre des finances après avis du conseil consultatif du micro-crédit (chapitre VII).

Le chapitre VI crée un conseil consultatif du micro-crédit composé de représentants de l'administration, des associations des chambre professionnelles, de la fédération des associations de micro-crédit, d'un représentant de la banque du Maroc, un représentant du groupement professionnel des banques du Maroc et un représentant de l'association professionnelle des sociétés de financement. Ce conseil est consulté sur toutes les questions relatives à l'octroi et au développement du micro-crédit.

Le chapitre VIII prévoit des sanctions pour les associations qui ne se conformeront pas aux dispositions de la loi, mise en garde, avertissement, retrait d'autorisation par le ministre des finances, sanctions pénales pour l'exercice du micro-crédit sans autorisation ou par des personnes ayant subi les condamnations pénales énumérées à l'article 7.

Enfin le dernier chapitre, consacré aux dispositions diverses et transitoires, donne un an aux associations existantes pour se conformer aux dispositions de la loi.

6 DROIT DE L'EAU

Plusieurs textes d'application de la loi sur l'eau n° 10-95 promulguée le 16 août 1995,[14] ont été publiés au Bulletin officiel du 5 février 1998.

6.1 Décret du 4 février 1998 relatif aux modalités de fixation et de recouvrement de la redevance pour utilisation de l'eau du domaine public hydraulique[15]

Ce texte abroge les dispositions de l'arrêté viziriel du 30 janvier 1926 relatif aux redevances à verser au Trésor par les attributaires de prises d'eau que la loi sur l'eau avait maintenu en vigueur dans l'attente des textes d'application.

---

[14] Voir *Yearbook of Islamic and Middle Eastern Law*, vol. 2 (1995), pp. 97–111; *Yearbook*, vol. 4 (1997–1998), pp. 435–437.
[15] Décret n° 2-97-414 du 4 février 1998, B.O. 5 février 1998, p. 50.

Le décret précise les bases de calcul de la redevance due pour utilisation du domaine public hydraulique. Le calcul se fait en fonction du volume d'eau prélevé ou de l'énergie hydroélectrique produite. Ce décret est complété par deux arrêtés interministériels d'application: un arrêté relatif aux redevances d'utilisation de l'eau du domaine public hydraulique pour l'irrigation[16] et un arrêté relatif aux redevances d'utilisation de l'eau du domaine public hydraulique pour la production de l'énergie hydroélectrique.[17]

6.2 Décret du 4 février 1998 fixant la procédure d'octroi des autorisations et concessions relatives au domaine public hydraulique[18]

Ce décret. abroge les dispositions de l'arrêté viziriel du 1er août 1925 en ce qui concerne les autorisations et concessions de prélèvement d'eau (art. 25).

Les demandes d'autorisation ou de concession du domaine public hydraulique doivent être présentées au directeur de l'agence de bassin accompagnées de toutes les pièces justificatives nécessaires. Ces demandes donnent lieu à une enquête publique effectuée par une commission spéciale chargée de recueillir les réclamations des personnes intéressées.

Après l'enquête et l'avis de la commission, le directeur de l'agence de bassin décide de la suite à réserver. Le refus doit être motivé et notifié. L'autorisation est soumise à l'avis du président du conseil municipal concerné.

L'autorisation doit préciser, outre l'identité de l'attributaire, sa durée, l'usage de l'eau, le débit à prélever, toutes les caractéristiques du prélèvement ainsi que le montant de la redevance.

Le décret prévoit les dispositions spécifiques aux creusements de puits et réalisations de forages.

6.3 Décret du 4 février 1998 relatif à la délimitation du domaine public hydraulique, à la correction des cours d'eau et à l'extraction des matériaux[19]

Ce texte abroge les dispositions de l'arrêté viziriel du 1er août 1925 en ce qui concerne la délimitation du domaine public hydraulique et l'arrêté du directeur général

---

[16] Arrêté conjoint du ministre de l'économie et des finances, du ministre de l'équipement et du ministre de l'agriculture, du développement rural et des pêches maritimes n° 548-98 du 21 août 1998 relatif aux redevances d'utilisation de l'eau du domaine public hydraulique pour l'irrigation, Bulletin officiel du 7 septembre 1998, p. 510.

[17] Arrêté conjoint du ministre des finances, du commerce, de l'industrie et de l'artisanat, du ministre de l'agriculture, de l'équipement et de l'environnement et du ministre du transport et de la marine marchande, du tourisme, de l'énergie et des mines n° 520-98 du 12 mars 1998 relatif aux redevances d'utilisation de l'eau du domaine public hydraulique pour la production de l'énergie hydroélectrique, Bulletin officiel du 13 mars 1998, p. 216.

[18] Décret n° 2-97-487 du 4 février 1998 fixant la procédure d'octroi des autorisations et concessions relatives au domaine public hydraulique, Bulletin officiel du 5 février 1998, p. 51.

[19] Décret n° 2-97-489 du 4 février 1998 relatif à la délimitation du domaine public hydraulique, à la correction des cours d'eau et à l'extraction des matériaux, Bulletin officiel du 5 février 1998, p. 55.

des Travaux publics du 6 décembre 1924 réglementant les extractions de sable dans le lit des cours d'eau (art. 27).

L'article 2(g) de la loi sur l'eau prévoit que font partie du domaine public hydraulique les berges des cours d'eau jusqu'au niveau atteint par les eaux de crue dont la fréquence est déterminée par voie réglementaire pour chaque cours d'eau ou section de cours d'eau. Ce décret précise que la détermination de la fréquence des crues sera fixée par arrêté du ministre de l'équipement sur proposition du directeur de l'agence de bassin.

Le même texte fixe dans son chapitre II la procédure de délimitation du domaine public hydraulique. Lorsqu'il y a lieu, la délimitation du domaine public hydraulique est fixée par décret après enquête publique.

Le décret prévoit ensuite les procédures d'autorisation concernant les opérations de curage, approfondissement, élargissement, redressement ou régularisation des cours d'eau, les opérations d'excavation notamment pour enlever des matériaux de construction dans les lits de cours d'eau, ainsi que les autorisation d'effectuer ou d'enlever tout dépôt, plantation ou culture sur le domaine public hydraulique.

6.4 Décret du 4 février 1998 relatif à la composition et au fonctionnement des commissions préfectorales et provinciales de l'eau[20]

La loi sur l'eau prévoit dans son article 101, la création au niveau de chaque préfecture ou province d'une commission préfectorale ou provinciale de l'eau, chargée d'apporter son concours à l'établissement des plans directeurs d'aménagement intégré des eaux du bassin hydraulique, d'encourager l'action des communes en matières d'économie d'eau et de protection des ressources en eau contre la pollution et d'entreprendre toute action susceptible de favoriser la sensibilisation du public à la protection et à la préservation des ressources en eau.

Ce décret fixe la composition de ces commissions. Y siègent, d'une part des représentants de l'Etat et des établissements publics chargés de la production de l'eau potable, de l'énergie électrique et de l'irrigation (six représentants), d'autre part des représentants des collectivités régionales et locales, des chambres d'agricultures et de commerce et un représentant des collectivités ethniques (sept représentants).

6.5 Décret du 4 février 1998 relatif aux normes de qualité des eaux et à l'inventaire du degré de leur pollution[21]

La loi sur l'eau, dans son chapitre VI relatif à la pollution des eaux prévoit que l'administration fixe les normes de qualité auxquelles une eau doit satisfaire selon l'utilisation qui en sera faite. C'est l'objet de ce décret qui prévoit dans son article pre-

---

[20] Décret n° 2-97-488 du 4 février 1998 relatif à la composition et au fonctionnement des commissions préfectorales et provinciales de l'eau, Bulletin officiel du 5 février 1998, p. 58.

[21] Décret n° 2-97-787 du 4 février 1998 relatif aux normes de qualité des eaux et à l'inventaire du degré de leur pollution, Bulletin officiel du 5 février 1998, p. 58.

mier selon quels critères seront fixées les normes de la qualité de l'eau. La fixation des normes relève d'arrêtés conjoints des ministres de l'équipement et de l'environnement, après avis du ministre de la santé et du ministre dont relève le secteur concerné par lesdites normes.

Le chapitre II du décret prévoit la procédure de l'inventaire du degré de pollution des eaux prévus par l'article 56 de la loi sur l'eau. Cet inventaire est effectué au moins une fois tous les cinq ans par l'agence de bassin avec la collaboration des autorités et services concernés. Les résultats de cet inventaire sont centralisés et exploités au niveau de chaque agence de bassin. Des cartes de vulnérabilité à la pollution des nappes souterraines sont établies par l'agence.

6.6 Décret du 4 février 1998 relatif à l'utilisation des eaux usées[22]

L'article 57 de la loi sur l'eau prévoit que l'administration détermine les conditions d'utilisation des eaux usées et que tout utilisation des eaux usées est soumise à l'autorisation de l'agence de bassin.

Ce décret d'application interdit la réutilisation des eaux usées si elles n'ont pas été épurées. Les eaux usées, même épurées ne peuvent être utilisées à la boisson, à la préparation, au conditionnement ou à la conservation des produits ou denrées alimentaires, ni pour le lavage des récipients destinés à contenir des denrées alimentaires.

Toute utilisation d'eaux usées est soumise à autorisation de l'agence de bassin. La demande d'autorisation doit comporter tous les renseignements nécessaires notamment l'origine des eaux et l'usage qui en est prévu.

Les utilisateurs d'eaux usées à la date du décret disposent d'un délai de cinq ans pour se conformer aux dispositions du nouveau texte.

6.7 Décret du 4 février 1998 relatif à la délimitation des zones de protection et des périmètres de sauvegarde et d'interdiction[23]

Ce texte abroge les dispositions de l'arrêté viziriel du 1er août 1925 en ce qui concerne l'établissement des zones de protection. Il fixe les périmètres de protection autour des puits artésiens, puits et abreuvoirs publics réalisés par l'Etat ou pour son compte, prévus par l'article 2(c) de la loi sur l'eau. Ces zones sont constituées d'une zone immédiate intégrée au domaine public hydraulique et, éventuellement, d'une zone rapprochée et d'une zone éloignée qui ne sont soumises qu'à des servitudes. Ce dernier décret d'application de la loi sur l'eau fixe les règles et procédures relatives aux délimitations des périmètre de protection.

Il prévoit également la délimitation des périmètres de sauvegarde et d'interdiction prévus par les articles 49 et 50 de la loi sur l'eau. Les périmètres de sauvegarde

---

[22] Décret n° 2-97-875 du 4 février 1998 relatif à l'utilisation des eaux usées, Bulletin officiel du 5 février 1998, p. 59.

[23] Décret n° 2-97-657 du 4 février 1998 relatif à la délimitation des zones de protection et des périmètres de sauvegarde et d'interdiction, Bulletin officiel 5 février 1998, p. 61.

sont délimités dans les zones où le degré d'exploitation des eaux risque de mettre en danger les ressources existantes. Ils sont fixés par décret pris sur la base d'un dossier technique élaboré par le ministère de l'équipement, comportant tous les éléments nécessaires à la détermination de l'étendue du périmètre et des restrictions qui y seront applicables. Ce décret est soumis à l'avis du ministre de l'environnement et à l'avis du ministre des pêches lorsque des zones d'estuaire sont concernées.

Les périmètres d'interdiction sont délimités en cas de nécessité, dans les zones où le niveau des nappes ou la qualité des eaux sont déclarés en danger de surexploitation ou de dégradation. À l'intérieur de ces périmètres aucune autorisation ou concession de prélèvement d'eau n'est délivrée sinon pour la consommation humaine ou animale. Les périmètres d'interdiction sont déterminés par décret dans les mêmes conditions que les périmètres de sauvegarde.

7 DROIT DE L'ENVIRONNEMENT

On relève un seul texte dans ce domaine, le décret n° 2-97-377 du 28 janvier 1998 complétant l'arrêté du 24 janvier 1953 sur la police de la circulation et du roulage.[24]

A voir l'intitulé de ce texte on pourrait penser qu'il s'agit d'une modification du code de la route. C'est en réalité une disposition importante en matière d'environnement puisque, pour la première fois au Maroc, un texte intervient dans le domaine de la prévention de la pollution due aux gaz d'échappement.

Le décret prévoit que les véhicules automobiles fonctionnant à l'essence ou au gasoil doivent être conçus, construits, réglés, entretenus, alimentés, utilisés et conduits de façon à ne pas provoquer d'émission de fumée ou de gaz dépassant les valeurs de 4,5 pour cent de monoxyde de carbone et de 70 pour cent d'opacité.

Le contrôle des émissions s'effectue à l'occasion de chaque visite technique des véhicules automobiles (tous les ans à compter de la cinquième année à partir de la mise en circulation), la réception par type d'automobile à l'état neuf ou la mise à la consommation des véhicules importés. Le contrôle peut également être effectué à tous moments sur route par les agents verbalisateurs.

Ce décret prévoit également l'interdiction, sauf cas de nécessité dûment justifiée, de laisser en état de marche le moteur d'un véhicule en stationnement.

Les infractions à ce texte sont des contraventions punissables d'une peine d'amende et en cas de récidive d'une peine de prison de dix jours maximum.

Ce texte est entré en vigueur six mois après sa publication, soit le 5 août 1998. Cependant il n'est pas encore appliqué dans la réalité, faute semble-t-il des appareils nécessaires au contrôle des émissions. Son application n'ira pas sans de sérieuses difficultés. En effet, si le problème de la pollution atmosphérique se pose très sérieusement dans les grandes villes, il ne semble pas que les usagers en soient conscients ni même préoccupés. La vétusté d'un partie du parc automobile permet de douter d'une amélioration prochaine . . . malgré les prescriptions réglementaires.

Dans le domaine de l'environnement, on rappellera également les textes présentés sous la rubrique "Droit de l'eau".

---

[24] Bulletin officiel du 5 février 1998, p. 50.

Tunisia

*Afif Gaigi**

La législation tunisienne durant l'année 1998 n'a pas été marquée par de nombreuses lois nouvelles. On peut toutefois remarquer avec intérêt les lois nouvelles introduites en matière de régime de communauté de certains biens entre époux, en matière de droit international privé et en matière d'exercice de la profession d'avocat. On développera dans ce qui suit les textes les plus marquants et on se contentera de citer le reste des autres textes.

1 DROIT CONSTITUTIONNEL ET DROITS POLITIQUES ET FONDAMENTAUX

1.1 La loi constitutionnelle n° 98-76 du 2 novembre 1998

Cette loi modifie la constitution dans son article 75 (JORT n° 89 de l'année 1998). La loi rend désormais obligatoire la motivation de l'avis du conseil constitutionnel que doit être communiqué au président de la république. Cet avis s'impose à tous les pouvoirs publics sauf en ce qui concerne les questions prévues au paragraphe dernier de l'article 72 de la constitution.

1.2 La loi organique n° 98-77 du 2 novembre 1998

Modifiant la loi du 14 mai 1975 cette loi a octroyé à la seule autorité judicaire le pouvoir de retrait d'un passeport en cours de validité. La décision de retrait peut être rendue soit à la requête du représentant légal de l'enfant mineur, soit à la requête du juge d'instruction, du ministère public ou de l'administration selon les cas.

---

* Avocat à la Cour de Cassation – enseignant universitaire.

1.3 La loi 98-93 du 6 novembre 1998 (JORT n° 90 du 6 november 1998)

Cette loi a modifié et complété certaines dispositions du code électoral (JORT n° 90 du 10 novembre 1998) et ce en redéfinissant les conditions devant être remplies par tout candidat à la députation ainsi que l'attribution des sièges à toutes les listes selon la représentation proportionnelle sur la base du plus fort reste. Cette même loi a redéfini l'objet du recours au référendum qui peut désormais être organisé en application des dispositions des articles 2, 47 et 76 de la constitution.

Le decret n° 479/98 du 19 février 1998 a régi les modalités d'octroi des subventions autorisées aux partis politiques (JORT n° 19 du 6 mars 1998).

2 DROIT PÉNAL

La loi n° 98-33 du 23 mai 1998 (JORT n° 43 de l'année 1998) a redéfini les crimes commis par un fonctionnaire public ou assimilé lors de l'exercice de sa fonction et constituant un acte de corruption ainsi que les peines applicables. La loi a concerné également la personne qui aura abusé de son influence ou de ses liens auprès d'un fonctionnaire public ou assimilé et qui aura accepté des dons ou des avantages au profit d'autrui même justes. Les modifications ont visé la personne qui aura corrompu ou tenté de corrompre le fonctionnaire public pour accomplir un acte lié à sa fonction. La présente loi a visé aussi la délivrance des certificats médicaux de complaisance et faisant état de faits inexacts.

La loi a également ajouté de nouvelles dispositions punissant les actes de corruption en matière de marchés publics. De nouvelles dispositions de la loi ont concerné la sanction du fonctionnaire qui exerce une activité rémunérée ayant une relation avec ses fonctions sans autorisation préalable.

3 DROIT COMMERCIAL

3.1 La loi n° 98-39 de 2 juin 1998 (JORT n° 44 de l'année 1998)

Cette loi relative aux ventes avec facilités de paiement a fixé les règles régissant les ventes et prestations de services au consommateur donnant lieu à un paiement échelonné. La loi a déterminé les modalités à respecter dans le cas des ventes avec facilités en spécifiant notamment l'obligation de rédiger un écrit et les mentions obligatoires à insérer dans le contrat. Le consommateur dispose d'un délai de rétractation de dix jours. La loi à déterminé les obligations et les droits de parties, les infractions et les sanctions pénales applicables.

3.2 La loi n° 98-40 du 2 juin 1998

Cette loi a concerné les techniques de vente et la publicité commerciale. Son objet est de fixer les règles régissant les ventes avec réduction de prix, les ventes hors magasins et la publicité commerciale en vue d'assurer la transparence dans les transactions commerciale et de protéger le consommateur.

3.3 Les décrets 98-2327 et 2328 du 23 novembre 1998 (JORT n° 96 de l'année 1998)

Ces deux décrets ont été adoptés en application de la loi de 28 juli 1997 relative à l'organisation de l'activité du transport routier. Le premier fixe les clauses du contrat type de location de véhicules de transport routier de marchandises et le deuxième fixe les clauses du contrat type de transport de marchandises pour le compte d'autrui.

3.4 La loi n° 4/98 du 2 février 1998

Cette loi relative aux sociétés de factoring (JORT n° 11 de l'année 1998) a réglementé le domaine d'activité de ces sociétés et les conditions d'exercice de l'activité de cession de créances et la poursuite de leur recouvrement pour le compte d'autrui.

3.5 La loi n° 21/98 du 11 mars 1998 (JORT n° 21 de l'année 1998)

Cette loi concerne le transport international de marchandises. La loi a régi le fondement juridique du contrat, la responsabilité du transporteur, celle d'expéditeur, les actions pouvant résulter de ce contrat, les délais pour agir, les conditions contractuelles et les avaries communes.

3.6 La loi n° 22/98 du 16 mars 1998

Cette loi a modifié certaines dispositions du code de commerce maritime (JORT n° 23 du 20 mars 1998). La loi a redéfini la responsabilité et les obligations du transporteur, de l'armateur et de l'acconnier.

4 DROIT DE LA FAMILLE

La loi n° 98-91 du 9 novembre 1998 (JORT n° 91 avec un rectificatif au n° 95 de l'année 1998) a introduit en Tunisie un régime spécifique réglementant les biens communs entre époux. Cette loi apporte une nouveauté unique en son genre dans un pays soumis fondamentalement en ce qui concerne le droit de la famille à une législation inspirée directement du droit musulman. Le principe dans ce droit est la séparation des biens entre époux. En cas de décès l'épouse n'hérite que du $1/8$ ou de $1/4$ des biens de son époux selon qu'il y a ou il n'y a pas d'enfants. Le mari hérite quant à lui de $1/4$ ou de la $1/2$ dans les mêmes conditions. Cette législation peut engendrer des situations iniques surtout pour l'épouse qui ne possède pas de biens propres et lorsque les biens acquis pendant le mariage l'ont été au nom de l'époux. Etant

donné qu'il est difficile d'apporter de grands changements à une législation mar-
qué par son caractère religieux, on ne pouvait apporter de modifications que de
manière exceptionnelle et sur la base d'un consentement des parties concernées. La
nouvelle loi a ainsi institué un régime qui est fondé sur son acceptation expresse
par les époux au moment de la conclusion de l'acte de mariage ou par un acte écrit
ultérieurement. Ces derniers doivent déclarer expressément s'ils acceptent ou non
le régime de la communauté des biens. Toutefois ce régime ne s'applique qu'aux immeubles acquis après le mariage et destinés à l'usage familial ou à l'intérêt propre
de la famille. Sont exclus les biens acquis par voie de succession, donation ou legs.
Les immeubles destinés à un usage professionnel sont également exclus de ce régime.
La loi a réglementé en outre les dettes grevant ces biens, la publicité légale, leur administration et la dissolution de la communauté. Les époux peuvent évidemment
étendre l'effet de la loi à d'autres biens s'ils le désirent en le spécifiant expressément.

5 STATUT DE LA PERSONNE

Loi n° 98-75 du 28 octobre 1998 relative à l'attribution d'un nom patronymique
aux enfants abandonnés ou de filiation inconnue. Cette loi permet notamment au
père, à la mère ou au ministère public de saisir la juridiction compétente pour l'attribution du nom patronymique à l'enfant dont il est prouvé par l'aveu, par témoignage ou par tests d'empreintes génétiques que cette personne est le père de
cet enfant. Dans ce cas l'attribution du nom patronymique ouvre droit à la pension
alimentaire et à un droit de regard telle que la tutelle et la garde.

Dans le cas d'enfants abandonnés ou de filiation inconnue c'est le tuteur public
que choisit un nom et un prénom à ces enfants.

6 DROIT INTERNATIONAL PRIVÉ

La loi n° 98-97 du 27 novembre 1998 a promulgué un code de droit international
privé (Journal officiel n° 96 de l'année 1998). La présente loi a pour objet de déterminer la compétence judiciaire des juridictions tunisiennes, les effets en Tunisie de
sdécisions et jugements étrangers, les immunités juridictionnelles et d'exécution et
le droit applicable lorsqu'un rapport de droit est rattaché par l'un de ses éléments
déterminants à un ou plusieurs ordres autre que l'ordre juridique tunisien.

La loi a utilisé d'une manière générale les critères habituels applicables en matière
de droit international privé pour déterminer la compétence de tribunaux tunisiens
de la manière la plus large possible.

La loi a accordé l'immunité de juridiction à l'état étranger ainsi qu'à la personne
morale de droit public agissant au nom de sa souveraineté ou pour son compte en
sa qualité d'autorité publique sous réserve de réciprocité. Concernant la détermination de la loi applicable le nouveau code spécifie le caractère d'ordre public de la
règle de conflit seulement pour les droits dont les parties n'ont pas la libre disposition. La loi a fixé plusieurs critères et des exceptions pour la détermination de la loi
applicable selon qu'il s'agit des droits de personnes, des droits de la famille, des
successions, des biens, des obligations volontaires ou légales.

7 QUESTIONS DIVERSES

7.1 La loi n° 98-65 du 20 juillet 1998 (JORT n° 60 P1640)

Relative aux sociétés professionnelles d'avocats. Cette loi a introduit la possibilité d'exercer l'activité d'avocat sous la forme de sociétés professionnelles ayant la forme civile ou commerciale.

7.2 La loi n° 14/98 du 18 février 1998 (JORT n° 15 du 20 février 1998)

Cette loi est relative à la vente des boissons alcoolisées à emporter.

7.3 La loi n° 17/98 du 23 février 1998 (JORT n° 17 de 27 février 1998)

Cette loi concerne la protection contre les effets nocifs de la consommation du tabac et l'interdiction de cette consommation dans les lieux publics. Le décret n° 98-2248 du 16 novembre 1998 (JORT n° 94 de l'année 1998) a fixé les lieux affectés à l'usage collectif dans lesquels il est interdit de fumer.

7.4 La loi du 2 juin 1998

Cette loi a institué le code de la poste.

7.5 La loi 98/73 du 4 août 1998

Cette loi a porté simplification des procédures fiscales et réduction des taux de l'impôt (JORT n° 64 de l'année 1998)

7.6 La loi 98/74 du 19 août 1998

Cette loi est relative aux chemins de fer (JORT n° 67 de l'année 1998)

7.7 La loi de finances de 1999 (JORT n° 104 de l'année 1998)

On peut relever dans cette loi surtout la création d'un fonds de péréquation des changes destiné à couvrir les pertes découlant de la variation du taux de change subies par les banques.

On peut relever également la déduction des revenus et bénéfices réinvestis dans des entreprises qui s'installent à l'étranger en vue de commercialiser exclusivement des marchandises et des services tunisiens.

Pakistan

*Martin Lau**

1 INTRODUCTION

In the past two years the annual survey of Pakistani law was marked by pessimism: economic and political problems had left a visible impact on the legal system. In 1997 domestic politics were allowed to seep into Pakistan's Supreme Court leading to the *de facto* removal of the Chief Justice by his own court. In 1998 nuclear tests were used by the government to declare a state of emergency and to suspend all fundamental rights.

However, there were signs that at least Pakistan's higher judiciary was prepared to fulfil its role as the guardian of the Constitution and of the rule of law in Pakistan. There can be no doubt that this task has become more difficult in a period of sustained economic depression and mounting external and internal political problems. Externally, the second half of 1999 was witness to a serious military confrontation with India. Armed militants had – with the *de facto* support of the Pakistani army – infiltrated Indian positions beyond the UN monitored line of control which divides the former princely state of Kashmir into Azad Kashmir (which is in reality controlled by Pakistan), and into the Indian state of Jammu and Kashmir. The attempts by the Indian army to regain these positions led to intense fighting along the line of control and there were moments when a war between the countries could not be ruled out. The fighting only returned to its normal level, which consists of an exchange of artillery fire on a daily basis, when Prime Minister Nawaz Sharif openly withdrew his government's support from the fighters.

Internally, two trends can be identified which have had a direct impact on Pakistan's legal system. First, the unabated rise of religious extremism and sectarianism has found visible support in the political system. The most notable expression of this phenomenon was the murder of Samia Imran, a young woman from the

---

* Barrister, Lecturer in Law.

North West Frontier Province, who had sought the legal assistance of Hina Jilani and Asma Jehangir in her attempts to obtain a divorce from her husband. A group of armed men stormed the office of the two lawyers, situated in a quiet residential area of Lahore, and shot Samia Imran. One of the assailants was shot by a guard but the others escaped. The murder has to be placed in the category of the growing number of "honour killings", i.e. women who are murdered by members of their own family because of alleged moral impropriety. The event, tragic as it was, appeared to be a fairly straightforward murder case but the conduct of the investigation by law enforcement agencies has thrown serious doubts on the independence of the police from social and political pressures. The main suspects, namely the parents of the murdered woman, have been granted bail before arrest whereas at the same time abduction charges have been filed against Asma Jahangir and Hina Jilani. The counter-FIR was filed by Ghulam Sarwar, the father of the murdered woman, who also happens to be a former president of the NWFP Chamber of Commerce. An attempt to condemn the honour killing in the Senate failed after senators of the ruling party voted against it. At the same time there is a strong suspicion that the Lahore police tried to tamper with the evidence against the suspects by forcing eye-witnesses to change their testimony.

The second trend which can be identified is the government's attempt to stifle any opposition to its rule. The most notable manifestation of this trend was the detention of the journalist Najam Sethi on treason charges. Najam had given a paper in India which contained a very critical and pessimistic assessment of Pakistan's political future. The Lahore High Court's reaction to a *habeas corpus* petition brought by the wife of Sethi was lukewarm: there was no order to produce Sethi in court and it was only mounting international pressure which lead to his release.

There has also been a sustained campaign to malign established NGOs such as, for instance, Shirkat Gahr, a women's rights organization, and AGHS, a prominent human rights' law firm, and a clamp-down on newspapers, most notably on newspapers owned by the Jangh group.

At the same time the Urdu press has become increasingly sectarian and intolerant. On the political front Nawaz Sharif's government finds itself in an uncomfortable position: the economic depression can only be tackled by large-scale reforms. These reforms have now become a condition precedent for any international assistance by, for instance, the IMF. A proposed general sales tax, similar to a value added tax, has triggered widespread protests throughout the country. In addition provincial opposition parties have become more vocal and active in pressing for their demands for more provincial autonomy. There have been violent demonstrations in Baluchistan and a governor's rule has been imposed in the province of Sindh. In response to the civic unrest in Sindh, Nawaz Sharif's government constituted military courts. The new courts were completely independent from the established courts and it was only after two men had been sentenced to death and executed that these courts were declared to be *ultra vires* and therefore unconstitutional by the Supreme Court.

The emerging scenario is a curious one: the democratically elected government is increasingly resorting to what is deemed by the Supreme Court to be unconstitutional measures to govern the country and to maintain law and order. This is a sad reflection on Pakistan's democracy but has afforded the Supreme Court numerous opportunities to demarcate its jurisdiction and to refine its interpretation of the constitution of Pakistan.

This brief outline of developments in Pakistan during the period under review provides the backcloth to Pakistan's legal developments which will be examined below. The focus will be on the substantial number of constitutional cases which dealt with legal fall-out of the removal of the Chief Justice and the events surrounding his fall from office, especially the contempt of court proceedings against the Prime Minister, Nawaz Sharif, and the constitutional challenge to the 14th Amendment to the Constitution, as well as the imposition of a state of emergency and the establishment of military courts. However, there have also been interesting developments in other areas of law, notably in the fields of Islamic criminal and family law.

2 CONSTITUTIONAL LAW

2.1 The declaration of the state of emergency

On 28 May 1998 the President issued a proclamation of emergency stating that "a grave emergency exists in which the security of Pakistan is threatened by external aggression and internal disturbance beyond the power of the Provincial Government to control".[1] On the same day a second proclamation was issued suspending the right to move any court, including a high court and the Supreme Court, for the enforcement of all fundamental rights conferred by chapter I of part II of the Constitution.[2] The proclamations were issued in response to the testing of nuclear devices in India which in turn were followed by the testing of nuclear bombs by Pakistan. In a carefully argued judgment the Supreme Court decided that it did have the power to examine both the constitutionality of the imposition of a state of emergency and the suspension of the fundamental rights.[3] The Supreme Court did not invalidate the declaration of the state of emergency itself but found that the suspension of fundamental rights was in itself unwarranted being unproportional to the level of external aggression faced by Pakistan. Significantly the Supreme Court held that even the suspension of fundamental rights did not affect the operation of Article 4 of the Constitution, which provides that "To enjoy the protection of law and to be treated in accordance with law is the inalienable right of every citizen, wherever he may be, and every other person for the time being within Pakistan". The Supreme Court referred to a wide range of legal materials including the International Covenant on Civil and Political Rights and the European Convention of Human Rights and did not shy away from stressing the importance of being seen

---

[1] See Gazette of Pakistan, Extraordinary, Part 1, 28 May 1998, and Art. 232(1) of the Constitution of Pakistan.

[2] This was the third time that fundamental rights had been suspended under the 1973 Constitution. The first suspension was imposed by Zulfiqar Bhutto in 1973 but was in fact a continuation of an existing suspension. It was lifted in August 1974. However, with the imposition of martial law in 1977 the fundamental rights were again suspended: s. 2(3) of the Laws (Continuance in Force) Order 1977 (CMLA 1 of 1977). Fundamental rights were restored in 1985: s. 1 of the Proclamation of Withdrawal of Martial Law, 30 December 1985.

[3] See *Farooq Ahmad Khan Leghari v. The Federation of Pakistan* PLD 1999 SC 57.

as progressive and dynamic, especially in respect of the enforcement of fundamental rights.

2.2 The Anti-Terrorism Act 1997

The willingness of the Supreme Court to guard the Constitution and fundamental rights was tested again when the government decided to introduce military courts to try terrorists. The Anti-Terrorism Act 1997, though superficially similar to the Suppression of Terrorist Activities Act 1975, introduced three new features. First, the judges were appointed by the President on an *ad hoc* basis and did not enjoy any security of service, and second the confessions made to police officers were made admissible as evidence against the accused. In addition, the final appeal was an appellate tribunal and not a high court or the Supreme Court. The 1997 Act was challenged first in the Lahore High Court. The petitioner raised a number of points the most important being the contentions that the Act violated principles of Islamic justice and the Constitution because, first, the independence of the judges was not guaranteed, secondly, the jurisdiction of the Supreme Courts and the high courts had been removed, and finally that persons accused under the Act could be tried *in absentia*.

In *Mehram Ali v. The Federation of Pakistan*,[4] the Lahore High Court rejected by a majority of four to one all but one of these constitutional challenges. It appears from the law report that the Attorney General had given an undertaking that no trials *in absentia* would take place and that the oath for non-Muslim judges would be changed; with this assurance in place, the four judges of the Lahore High Court were content to uphold the validity of the Act. Only Judge Karamat Nazir Bhandari voiced a strong but lone note of dissent, holding that the 1997 Act was unconstitutional. In particular he pointed out that the establishment of a tribunal and an appellate tribunal which excluded an appeal to the High Court as a matter of right was unconstitutional and a departure from established principles. The Supreme Court of Pakistan agreed with his dissent and declared the Anti-Terrorism Act 1997 unconstitutional. Chief Justice Ajmal Mian in a carefully and concisely argued judgment concentrated on the constitutionality of the exclusion of the jurisdiction of the high courts and the Supreme Court, holding that the Act vitiates against the concept of the independence of the judiciary and Articles 175 and 203 of the Constitution. The Supreme Court made extensive references to and comparisons with the UK Prevention of Terrorism Act 1976 and the Indian Terrorist and Disruptive Activities Act (TADA).

It should be noted that the Supreme Court also referred extensively to various Islamic provisions on the independence of the judiciary. The judgment caused considerable disquiet in Pakistan since it amounted to a direct challenge of the government. However, Prime Minister Sharif was quick to concede defeat and undertook to abide by the decision. The judgment can be regarded as a significant victory of the Supreme Court but it should be noted that three persons had been executed under the provisions of an Act held to be unconstitutional by the Supreme Court.

---

[4] PLD 1998 Lah 347.

It must be regarded as disconcerting, to put it mildly, that the Supreme Court of Pakistan did not stay their executions until it had decided the constitutionality of the Act itself.

2.3 Fundamental rights

The successful defence of judicial independence constitutes an important development which has found in the above-mentioned judgement its most visible expression. The newly found assertiveness of the Supreme Court is also reflected in other constitutional cases. A whole series of cases confirmed – unsurprisingly – the constitutionality of the toppling of the former Chief Justice Sajjad Ali Shah by his own court.

In *Asad Ali v. The State*[5] the Supreme Court confirmed the constitutionality of the appointment of Ajmal Mian as the new Chief Justice of Pakistan. The case disposed of the original constitutional petitions which had challenged the appointment of Sajjad Ali Shah as the Chief Justice of Pakistan in 1994 and declared the appointment of Sajjad Ali Shah as "wholly unconstutional, illegal and contrary to the decision of this Court in the Al-Jehad case and accordingly declare it invalid, unconstitutional and of no legal consequence".[6]

In *Muhammad Ikram Chaudhury v. Federation of Pakistan*[7] four constitutional petitions which had challenged the removal of Sajjad Ali Shah as the Chief Justice were dismissed by the Supreme Court. The petitions had been filed under Article 184(3) of the Constitution which provides that "Without prejudice to the provisions of Article 199, the Supreme Court shall, if it considers that a question of public importance with reference to the enforcement of any of the Fundamental Rights conferred by Chapter I of Part II is involved, have the power to make an order of the nature mentioned in the said Article." Article 199 establishes the writ jurisdiction of the high courts.

Article 184(3) has been the jurisdictional basis of public interest litigation and in the past the Supreme Court has shown an ever increasing willingness to admit writ petitions against the government under this article. However, the Supreme Court was not prepared to have the same article being used to scrutinize its own judgments holding that "no writ can be issued by a High Court or the Supreme Court against itself or against each other or its Judges".[8] Obiter Chief Justice Ajmal Mian observed with barely hidden glee that "the situation would not have arisen if my learned brother Sajjad Ali Shah, J, would have agreed with me to decide the question of the appointment of the Chief Justice in Judges' Case in line with the view taken in the above case for the appointments of the Chief Justices of the High Courts". However, the exact ambit of Article 184(3) still awaits clarification.

This became apparent in the case of *Pakistan Tobacco Company Ltd ["PTC"] v. The Federation of Pakistan*[9] where PTC, the largest producer of cigarettes and the largest

---

5 PLD 1998 SC 161 and PLD 1998 SC 33.
6 *Ibid.*, at p. 44.
7 PLD 1998 SC 103.
8 *Ibid.*, at p. 108.
9 PLD 1999 SC 383.

purchaser of domestic tobacco, contended that various laws which fixed the purchase price of tobacco were unconstitutional being violative of the fundamental right to equality guaranteed under Article 25 of the Constitution. The Federation of Pakistan argued that the petitions were not maintainable because PTC was a commercial enterprise which had an individual grievance not amounting to a question of public importance. The Supreme Court held that

We are inclined to hold that the question whether a particular Constitution petition filed under Article 184(3) of the Constitution directly in this Court is maintainable is to be examined not on the basis as to who has filed the same, but the above question is to be determined with reference to the controversy raised in the Constitution petition, and if the controversy involves a question of public importance with reference to the enforcement of any of the Fundamental Rights the same will be sustainable.[10]

In the event the petition was dismissed on merits, the Supreme Court holding that the discriminating provisions were based on a reasonable classification and therefore not in breach of Article 25. Further, the Supreme Court found that the "object of the law-makers seems to be to safeguard the interest of the tobacco growers who belong to a down trodden/economically depressed class".

However, the former Chief Justice Sajjad Ali Shah was not so easily defeated. He filed a constitutional review petition against the judgement of the Surpeme Court in the celebrated judges' case of *Al-Jehad Trust v. Federation of Pakistan*[11] which had established that as a matter of constitutional convention the most senior judge of a superior court was to become the Chief Justice of that court. In *Sajjad Ali Shah v. Asad Ali*[12] the former Chief Justice argued that the seniority principle was only a convention which could not override the written Constitution. Furthermore, Sajjad Ali Shah had been appointed before the Supreme Court established the seniority principle as a constitutional convention and it should only be allowed to act prospectively. Unsurprisingly, the Supreme Court rejected this argument holding that a constitutional convention once recognized expressly by the court becomes as much part of the constitutional law of the country as the written constitution itself. It seems that the seniority principle has now become part of Pakistan's constitutional order, though a word of caution seems appropriate: the Constitution allows the President to appoint a Chief Justice from outside the court. This would not attract the seniority principle which at the present only refers to the sitting judges of the Supreme Court. This point was raised but was left unanswered: therefore there is still some scope for constitutional turmoil in the future.

Corruption and governmental harassment of political opponents was the issue in the case of *Ahmad Nawaz v. State*,[13] a case decided by the High Court of Karachi. The petitioner had moved the High Court complaining that after having lost a local election he was being harassed by the District Commissioner. In particular the Commissioner had demanded the payment of revenues which it was alleged

---

[10] *Ibid.*, at p. 389.
[11] PLD 1996 SC 324 and PLD 1997 SC 84.
[12] 1999 SCMR 640.
[13] PLD 1998 Kar 180.

the petitioner had not paid since 1987. When the matter came to court the petitioner had become afraid of the potential repercussions of his boldness and tried to withdraw his petition. However, the High Court refused to allow him to do so observing that "the grievance of the petitioner is not peculiar to him but a growing menace of mal-administration and it was necessary to lay down guidelines for the exercise vested in the administrations by law". Referring to the Objectives Resolution and the Principles of Policy of the Constitution the High Court proceeded to state the duties of a Deputy Commissioner which deserve to be quoted in full:

A Deputy Commissioner in a district is a highest officer of administration and holds responsible position. He has to act in accordance with law at all time. Not only that but but with the powers which are given to him in law more responsibilities are saddled on his shoulders corresponding to the powers. It is his duty to treat the poor and rich alike (and also winning and defeated candidate alike) in accordance with the Injunctions of Islam and teachings of Qur'an and Sunnah. He must treat all children of Adam (which includes non-Muslim citizens as well) without any discrimination which is not only the essence of Islamic way of life but also in consonance with Article 25 of the Constitution. He is a public servant and not a private employee of any person holding authority either in the federation or the federating unit. It is expected of the Deputy Commissioner that like Caesar's wife he should be above suspicion in his words, actions and dealings.[14]

An appeal against two public interest litigation cases decided by the Karachi High Court came before the Supreme Court.[15] The original petitions, which had been faxed to the High Court, had complained about the illegal construction of high rise buildings in Karachi with the connivance of the authorities. The High Court had reacted swiftly and had ordered not only an immediate stay of the construction work but had also ordered all service providers to disconnect the premises from water, gas and electricity supply. The owners of the buildings appealed to the Supreme Court contending that the order had deprived a large number of people from access to essential services without them having been afforded a proper chance to be heard. In order to support their claim they submitted a report indicating that most flats in the disputed properties were by now occupied. However, at the time of the hearing of the public interest petition the High Court had asked a court official to visit the disputed properties and to submit a report directly to the court. The court-led inquiry had found that none of the properties was occupied! There was therefore before the Supreme Court irrefutable evidence that in breach of the order of the High Court the petitioners had actually allowed persons to occupy the premises no doubt hoping that this would improve their legal position. The Supreme Court was not impressed and refused to interfere with the order of the Karachi High Court. The Supreme Court observed obiter that

We may point out that unfortunately it has become common practice in Karachi that some builders obtain approval of plans for raising buildings Ground-plus-One, but actually they construct multi-storeyed high-rise buildings on the sites to the detriment of neighbours in the locality concerned as it disturbs the amenities besides creating environmental problems.

---

[14] *Ibid.*, at p. 185.
[15] *Zubaida A. Sattar v. Karachi Building Control Authority* 1999 SCMR 243.

Such practice is to be deprecated as was pointed out in the judgment of this court in Abdul Razak. It may further be observed that some builders raise unauthorized constructions after obtaining status quo orders from the courts.[16]

Nawaz Sharif's controversial amendment of the Constitution which had inserted a new Article 63A allowing for the disqualification of a member of parliament on the grounds of defection from his party – commonly known as "floor-crossing" – was judicially reviewed in the case of *Wukala Mahaz Barai Tahafaz Dastorr v. Federation of Pakistan*.[17] The Supreme Court held the amendment to be constitutional but in holding so was able to establish for the first time with any decisiveness[18] the limits of constitutional amendments: the Supreme Court held that Pakistan's Constitution had a basic structure which could not be altered by constitutional amendment. However, the exact definition of what was protected as part of this basic structure was kept vague. Nevertheless the case is significant in that the Supreme Court has reserved the right to strike down an amendment to the constitution in the future. This might become a very relevant issue in the near future if the government manages to get the proposed 15th amendment to the Constitution passed. As mentioned in last year's survey, the amendment would make Islamic law the supreme law of the land overriding even the written Constitution.

3 ISLAMIC LAW

The Federal Shariat Court and the Shariat Appellate Bench of the Supreme Court have continued to play a decisive role in the shaping of the economic and legal system. The Shariat Appellate Bench is currently hearing the appeal of the government against the FSC's decision declaring all laws providing for the payment of interest un-Islamic.[19] The case had been pending before the Supreme Court for almost a decade and the somewhat sudden decision to hear the appeal now underlines the determination of the courts to exercise their power to the fullest extent possible. The case could potentially have grave implications for the government and for the economic system since the original decision, handed down by Tanzil ur Rehman, the former Chief Justice of the Federal Shariat Court, had declared even the payment of interest on foreign loans to be repugnant to Islam. There is some uncertainty about the outcome of the current appeal but it seems unlikely that the Appellate Bench will follow the radical and uncompromising line taken by the Federal Shariat Court.

In the meantime the Shariat Appellate Bench has overturned a decision of the Federal Shariat Court which had examined the Islamic *vires* of the appointment procedure of village headmen, called Lambardars.[20] The post was introduced in British

---

[16] *Ibid.*, at p. 248.

[17] PLD 1998 SC 1263.

[18] On the basic structure see also the case of *Mahmood Khan Achakzai v. Federation of Pakistan* PLD 1997 SC 426. That case concerned the constitutionality of the 8th Amendment which had introduced Art. 58 2 (b) into the Constitution.

[19] *Dr Mahmood ur Rahman Faisal v. Secretary, Ministry of Law, Justice and Parliamentary Affairs, Government of Pakistan* PLD 1992 FSC 1.

[20] *Maqbool Ahmad Qureshi v. Islamic Republic of Pakistan* PLD 1999 SC 484.

colonial times and constituted a central part of the administration of land and the collection of land revenue. The latter was a major source of income for the colonial regime. In Punjab the system of revenue collection was organized along collective lines, i.e. a village was responsible for the payment of land revenue in respect of all lands owned by its inhabitants. There was a record of each owner's land holdings for the purpose of revenue collection but all proprietors were jointly responsible for the payment of the land revenue. The village headman was responsible for the collection of the land revenue and was given in return a certain percentage of the revenue so collected. He was therefore a link between the population and the tax payers. Almost inevitably village headmen would come from prosperous land owning families who exercised considerable control and influence over the affairs in their respective villages. The position became over time *de facto* a hereditary one.

This was expressly sanctioned in the appointment procedures of village headmen contained in the West Pakistan Land Revenue Rules, 1968 which contain detailed rules on how the heir of a deceased village headman was to be identified as a successor to the headmanship. The Shariat Appellate Bench held this system to be un-Islamic because in Islam the appointment to a public office was to be made on the basis of merit and was not a hereditary entitlement. The decision will cause some upheaval in rural areas where the headmanship is an important post carrying with it considerable power and prestige.

3.1 Offence of *Zina* (enforcement of *Hadd*) Ordinance 1979

The Offence of *Zina* (Enforcement of *Hadd*) Ordinance, 1979 is a controversial law which makes any sexual intercourse outside a valid marriage an offence. Adultery carries the *hadd* punishment of stoning to death if certain evidential requirements are satisfied, namely that the act had been witnessed by four male adults of good character. If this requirement is not met the court can nevertheless impose a *tazir* punishment which can consist of whipping[21] and imprisonment. In the past a considerable number of women have been accused of adultery by their husbands inevitably exposing them not only to the danger of harsh punishments but also – even in cases of acquittal – to social stigmatization. In *Maqbool Ahmad v. Mohammad Anwar*[22] the husband had moved the Shariat Appellate Bench of the Supreme Court in order to overturn an order of acquittal made by the Federal Shariat Court. The husband had accused his wife of having committed adultery and both the wife and her alleged paramour were sentenced to five years' rigorous imprisonment, whipping of 30 stripes and a fine under section 10 of the Offence of *Zina* (Enforcement of *Hadd*) Ordinance, 1979 by the Court of Sessions. The Federal Shariat Court overturned this decision for lack of evidence. Against that order the husband appealed.

Taqui Usmani, the *ulema* member of the Supreme Court, in a concise and tightly reasoned decision, has finally put an end to the deplorable tendency of disgruntled

---

[21] It should be noted that the Abolition of Whipping Act, 1996 has repealed the Whipping Act, 1909. The Act has abolished whipping for all offences with the exception of offences committed under the 1979 Hudood Ordinances.

[22] PLD 1999 SC 935.

husbands to accuse their wives of adultery and expose them to severe punishments. Judge Usmani held that the *Zina* Ordinance has to be applied in conjunction with section 14 of the Offence of *Qazf* (Enforcement of *Hadd*) Ordinance, 1979. The *Qazf* Ordinace incorporates the Islamic procedure of *li'an* which allows for a divorce if the husband suspects his wife of adultery. Under the *li'an* procedure the husband swears before a judge that his wife has committed adultery. If he cannot produce the four witnesses required by Islamic law to prove that *zina* had been committed the court asks the accused wife to respond to the allegation. If she denies the allegation by swearing an oath herself the court dissolves the marriage.

Judge Usmani held that in all cases where a husband accuses his wife of adultery without being able to produce the four witnesses the wife has to be offered the *li'an* procedure. Only if she admits to having committed the offence in express terms can she be convicted for having committed the offence of *zina*. In the matter at hand the Supreme Court summoned the estranged couple and the *li'an* procedure was carried out. The husband swore five times that he accused his wife of adultery and believed she had committed the offence. The wife in turn swore five times that she had not committed adultery and the marriage was dissolved. It is somewhat surprising that the *li'an* procedure has in the past been virtually ignored by both trial courts and the Federal Shariat Court – in the present cases the wife was originally acquitted because of lack of evidence, but the *li'an* procedure had never been mentioned at all! The decision of the Shariat Apellate Bench of the Supreme Court has gone some way to check the considerable abuse of the *Zina* Ordinance by husbands determined to send their wives to prison.

Unusually the Offence of *Zina* (Enforcement of *Hadd*) Ordinance, 1979 also came up for consideration before the High Court of Lahore.[23] All appeals against convictions under the Ordinance have to be heard by the Federal Shariat Court and not by the provincial high courts. However, the facts of the case were such that the High Court was able to take cognisance of the matter.

These facts can be stated briefly: on the information received by a police informer that a residential house was used as a brothel the police obtained a search warrant under section 98 of the Code of Criminal Procedure from a magistrate and raided the house. Allegedly they found in the house an unmarried couple engaged in sexual intercourse and subsequently an FIR was filed on the basis that the offence of *zina* had been committed. The accused couple moved the Lahore High Court asking for the FIR to be quashed and the search to be declared illegal arguing that section 98 did not authorize a search in these circumstances and that the search had amounted to a violation of the petitioner's fundamental right to privacy. The High Court allowed the petition and took the opportunity to restate the legal position with regard to searches in the context of allegations of *zina*.

The basis of the judgement was provided by Islamic law, more specifically the Islamic concept of privacy. The *Zina* Ordinance had to be interpreted in the light of that principle: since the Offence of *Zina* (Enforcenment of *Hadd*) Ordinance, 1979, did not contain any provisions relating to the search of a house there was presumption that the police had no right to interfere with the privacy of the home. The High Court held that "The irresistible inference is that the common practice

---

[23] *Riaz v. Station House Officer, Police Station Jhang City* PLD 1998 Lah 35.

of the police to register cases under *Zina Hudood* Ordinance on the report of the Mukhbar (an anonymous informer) is totally unwarranted and [against] the Injunctions of Islam".

4 ISLAMIC CRIMINAL LAW

Islamic criminal law was also at the heart of a case decided by the Peshawar High Court. The case involved the offence of intentional murder which is governed by laws of *qisas* and *diyat*, now a permanent part of Pakistan's criminal law since the enactment of the Criminal Law (Amendment) Act, 1997.[24] However, in the present case the murder had been committed in the Malakand Division, a northern area of Pakistan, to which the Act does not apply. Instead, judges apply Islamic law directly, i.e. without reference to any legislation. The case involved a revenge killing: the murderer had suspected his victim to have killed his father more than twenty years ago. At that time he was only seven years old, but honour demanded that the death of his father should be avenged. The suspected killer had been charged with murder in 1977 but was acquitted because of lack of evidence.

However, there was ample evidence against the accused since two witnesses had actually been present when he shot his victim with a sub-machine gun and he was sentenced to *qisas*, i.e. death in the case of murder. In the appeal the Peshawar High Court was not asked to overturn the conviction but to reduce the sentence of death to one of imprisonment. The Peshawar High Court took notice of the custom of revenge killings observing that "In this part of the country it is a matter of tradition to avenge the murder of the father"[25] before examining the Islamic law of *qisas*. The High Court found that *qisas* could only be awarded if all requirements imposed by the Islamic law of evidence were met. In the present case the character of the two eye witnesses had not been examined and they had not sworn a special oath required by Islamic law. The sentence was reduced to one of life imprisonment thereby continuing a judicial policy of not awarding death sentences in revenge and honour killings. This policy was best expressed in the case of *Ajun Shah v. The State*[26] where the Supreme Court of Pakistan held that

A man is after all a creature of his environment. His action therefore must be judged in the background of the society to which he belongs. Though he may not be entitled to rely on the doctrine of provocation, still the above circumstances may be taken into account for not imposing the extreme penalty. We would, however, like to make it clear that we are not suggesting for a moment that private revenge can be regarded as mitigating circumstance. What we are really pointing out is that the question of sentence must in each case depend on the facts of the case and that in this particular case the criminality is not of a kind which should be visited with extreme penalty.

---

[24] *Sambali Khan v. The State* PLD 1998 Pesh 101.
[25] *Ibid.*, at p. 106.
[26] PLD 1967 SC 185.

However, it should be noted that there is no such leeway in a case of *qisas*. The Peshawar High Court was only able to reduce the sentence because it had found that the evidential requirements which have to be met to attract *qisas* had not been met. If *qisas* had been properly awarded the death penalty would have had to be confirmed by the court.

5 ISLAMIC FAMILY LAW

Two cases, both from the Lahore High Court, deserve special mention. In *Dr Anees Ahmad v. Uzma*[27] a marriage had been dissolved under the *khula* procedure swith the wife alleging that the husband had been cruel towards her. The Lahore High Court held that in cases where the marriage was dissolved because of cruelty, the wife was under no obligation to pay back the dower as consideration for the dissolution of the marriage.

In *Muhammad Yousaf v. Anis Bibi*[28] the relationship between the Guardians and Wards Act, 1898 and the Islamic law on custody of children came up for consideration. The case concerned a divorced couple who had at the time of the proceedings both married again. The father applied for the custody of the child arguing that the wife had lost her right of *hizannat* over the child because she had married a person not related to the minor within the prohibited degree. The Lahore High Court agreed that the mother had lost her right to *hizannat* but held that the custody would nevertheless not automatically revert to the father. The court was entitled to determine the welfare of the minor and since there was no evidence that the new wife of the husband would look after her new stepchild it was more prudent to grant the mother the custody of the child. The High Court observed that "Our experience with stepmothers in our society is not very healthy". The case is significant in that the High Court refused to grant custody in accordance with section 25 of the Guardians and Wards Act, 1898 which contemplates that regard should be had to the personal law of the parties. The decision amounts to an admission that social reality, in this case the court's experience with the way stepmothers treat their stepchildren, can necessitate a deviation from established principles of Islamic law.

Finally a recent, though as yet unreported, decision handed down by the Lahore High Court deserves to be mentioned. In writ petition 420 of 1999 decided in February 1999 the Lahore High Court[29] had to determine whether a woman could enter into a valid marriage without the consent of her parents. Briefly summarized, the case concerned a young woman who had married against the will of her parents. Her parents alleged that she had already been married to somebody else and when the woman fled the parental home they filed abduction charges against her husband. It appears that the police connived with the parents and agreed to file false charges against the husband and members of his family. Eventually, heavily armed police stormed the women's refuge run by the Ehdi centre in Karachi and attempted to bring

---

[27] PLD 1998 Lah 52.
[28] PLD 1998 Lah 67.
[29] I am grateful to Interrights which provided me with a transcript of the judgment.

her back to Lahore. The High Court of Karachi intervened and the young woman was allowed to live at a place of her choice during the pendency of the proceedings. When the matter came up for hearing in Lahore the High Court in emphatic terms denounced the police misconduct, quashed all criminal proceedings, and upheld the validity of the woman's marriage to the partner of her choice. The Lahore High Court's observations on the case deserve to be reproduced *in extenso*:

At a socio-moral plane the case had certain disconcerting overtones. Humaira was to be given in marriage to Mozzam in exchange of the latter's sister who was married to Humaira's brother. On the one hand there was anguish and pain of a father whose daughter had rebelled and refused to marry a person of his choice and had left her hearth and job to join someone with whom she had contracted. The father called it a sinful act and was not prepared to accept her under any circumstances. On the other hand there was a girl in distress, who lost prime of her youth, waiting for parental permission to join a husband of her choice. She was in a critical dilemma i.e. of facing the social consequence of going back to a family fold where she stood eternally stigmatized or to go back with Mahmood whom she stood married to. The former course was full of tension, uncertainty and carried a death threat whereas in the latter course although there was a death threat yet it meant a fulfilment of her desire, where she dreamt of security and if she survived the death threat she hoped for an ultimate release from the high walls of a feudal bondage. She choose the latter course and wanted society to accept it. Perhaps she was not asking for too much at this age of her life but she was refused. On disclosure of her marriage she was beaten up. Taken to the surgical theatre of a government run hospital. Her entire body was bandaged and she was detained for a month but she persevered. As per her perception a mock drama of her marriage with Mozzam Ghayas was staged where she cried and sobbed but her parents could not persuade her to join him. No *rukhsati* was performed and when they tried to force her she left the house. She was chased, harassed, abused, beaten and disgraced. This treatment was meted out to the only daughter of a father and at the latter's behest and the real brother spear-headed it.

The Lahore High Court also felt compelled to comment on the religious arguments raised by the father stating that

Behind the evangelistic facade there was a certain culture at play. It is that culture which needs to be tamed by law and an objective understanding of the Islamic values. Let us do a little self accountability and little soul searching both individually and collectively. Let there be no contradiction in our thoughts and actions. Male chauvinism, feudal bias and compulsions of a conceited ego should not be confused with Islamic values. An enlightened approach is called for otherwise an obsecurantism in this field may break the social fabric.

6 MISCELLANEOUS

The prosecutions of Asif Ali Zardari and his wife Benazir Bhutto, the former Prime Minister, for corruption, and in the case of the former also for murder, at times continue to generate bizarre legal proceedings. Only one needs to be mentioned by way of example in *The State v. Asif Ali Zardari*[30] the government appealed against a de-

---

[30] PLD 1999 Kar 144.

cision of the trial judge in the Murtaza Bhutto murder case to allow Zardari the facility of an air conditioner in prison. The High Court of Karachi dismissed the appeal holding that a prisoner under trial could be provided with an air conditioner if such was required for medical reasons.

In the field of legislation the Environmental Protection Act 1997 and the Eradication of Corrupt Business Practices Ordinance 1998 should be mentioned. A detailed review of these laws will be made in next year's survey.

7 CONCLUSION

The cases reviewed in this year's survey testify to the importance of Pakistan's higher judiciary in the protection of the constitutional order of the country. There can be no doubt that courts are guarding their independence jealously and that they are prepared to challenge the government directly and decisively. However, there are clear limits to the ability of the courts to protect the Constitution and the citizens against governmental lawlessness and repression. Nevertheless it seems justified to conclude this year's survey on a somewhat more optimistic note: at least Pakistan's higher judiciary seems prepared to uphold civil liberties and the rule of law.

The most visible manifestations of judicial activism in 1998 were the willingness to recognize the existence of a basic structure and the striking down of legislation deemed to be unconstitutional. Furthermore there is a marked trend to interpret Islamic law in a more liberal manner which has benefited especially women. Most notable are the cases involving the enforcement of the *Hudood* Ordinances: courts are increasingly unwilling to condone the abuse of these laws by zealous members of the public and the police alike. The same holds true for Islamic family law: interpretations favourable to women dominate the field.

Turkey

Sibel Inceoglu *

There have been very few significant statutory developments during 1998 and the current year 1999, but several important constitutional, administrative and case developments took place in Turkey.

1 CONSTITUTIONAL LAW

1.1 Constitutional amendment

The European Court of Human Rights in the case of *Incal v. Turkey*[1] declared that the state security courts cannot be considered "independent and impartial" within the meaning of Article 6 of the European Convention on Human Rights. The state security courts are composed of three judges, one of whom is a regular officer and member of the Military Legal Service, therefore according to the European Court, the applicant had legitimate cause to doubt the independence and impartiality of the state security court which found him guilty. This case had been the cause of the restart of the discussions on the state security courts in Turkey and on 18 June 1999 the constitutional provision governing state security courts (Art. 143) was changed.[2]

The state security courts were created by Statute No. 1773 of 11 July 1973, but that statute was annulled by the Constitutional Court on 15 June 1976. Security courts were later reintroduced into the Turkish judicial system by Article 143 of the 1982 Constitution, and the control of the Constitutional Court ended. Before the 1999 amendment, Article 143 read as follows:

State Security Courts shall be established to deal with offences against the indivisible integrity of the State with its territory and nation, the free democratic order, or against

---

* LLM, PhD, Associate Professor at the Law Faculty of Marmara University, Istanbul.
[1] The case of *Incal v. Turkey*, 41/1997/825/1031, 9 June 1998, http:/www.dhcour.coe.fr.
[2] Statute no. 4388, 18 June 1999, OG No: 23729, dated 18 June 1999.

the Republic whose characteristics are defined in the Constitution, and offences directly involving the internal and external security of the State.

State Security Courts shall consist of a president, two regular and two substitute members, one public prosecutor and a sufficient number of deputy public prosecutors.

The president, one regular and one substitute member and a public prosecutor from among first category judges and public prosecutors; one regular and one substitute member from among first category military judges; and deputy public prosecutors from among public prosecutors of the Republic and military judges, shall be appointed in accordance with procedures prescribed by their special statute.

The president, members and substitute members, and public prosecutors and deputy prosecutors of the State Security Court shall be appointed for four years; those whose term of office expires may be reappointed.

The High Court of Appeal is the competent authority to examine appeals against the judgments of the State Security Court.

Other provisions relating to the functioning, the duties and the power and the trial procedure of the State Security Court shall be prescribed by the statute.

In the event of declaration of martial law within the regions under the jurisdiction of a State Security Court, the latter may be transformed, in accordance with the provisions prescribed by statute, into a Martial Law Military Court with jurisdiction restricted to those regions.

On 18 June 1999, the sentence "However the provisions relating to the martial law and state of war are excepted" was added to the first paragraph of Article 143 and the last paragraph of the article was repealed. In addition, the most important developments are the amendments of paragraphs 2, 3 and 4. Paragraph 2 was changed, paragraphs 3 and 4 were joined, which state that:

State security courts shall consist of a president, two regular and one substitute member, the Principal Public Prosecutor of the Republic and a sufficient number of public prosecutors of the Republic.

The president, two regular and one substitute member and the Principal Public Prosecutor of the Republic from among first category judges and public prosecutors of the Republic; and public prosecutors of the Republic from among other public prosecutors of the Republic shall be appointed for four years by the Supreme Council of Judges and Public Prosecutors in accordance with procedures prescribed by its special statute; those whose term of office expires may be reappointed.

As a result of the said amendment, today the state security courts consist of civil judges and public prosecutors and work as a specialized court, the non-conformity between the Constitution and the *Incal* case of the European Court of Human Rights was ended.

1.2 Constitutional Court decisions relating to political parties

In 1998, two political parties – the Welfare Party and the Labour Party – were dissolved by the Constitutional Court.

The reasons for dissolution of the two parties are both different. The Welfare Party was dissolved because of its anti-secular activities, whereas the Labour Party was dissolved because of its activities against territorial integrity of the state and the unity of the nation.

On 21 May 1997, the Principal Public Prosecutor at the Court of Cassation applied to the Constitutional Court for an order for dissolving the Welfare Party. In his indictment, the public prosecutor accused the party of having become a centre for the execution of activities against the principle of secularism.

Article 69 paragraph 6 (amended on 23 July 1995) of the Constitution states that: "The decision to dissolve a political party permanently owing to activities violating the provisions of the fourth paragraph of Article 68 may be rendered only when the Constitutional Court determines that the party in question has become a centre for the execution of such activities."

Article 68 paragraph 4 reads:

The constitutions and programmes, as well as the activities of political parties shall not be in conflict with the independence of the State, its indivisible integrity with its territory and nation, human rights, the principles of equality and rule of law, sovereignty of the nation, the principles of the democratic and secular republic; they shall not aim to protect or establish class or group dictatorship or dictatorship of any kind, nor shall they incite citizens to crime.

The Constitutional Court, having reached the decision of dissolution, examined the declarations of the Welfare Party's Chairman, members of the Assembly and Mayors. Some of the declarations of those people are as follows.

The declaration of Necmettin Erbakan, the Welfare Party's Chairman in its Assembly group meeting:

The Welfare Party will get the governing power, will be established the order of justice. What is the problem? Will be the transition period harsh or will it be calm and without blood? . . . The Welfare Party will bring the order of justice, this is absolutely necessary. How will the transition period be? Will it be calm or harsh, pleasant or bloody, sixty million person will decide on that".

The Declaration of Sevki Yilmaz, the party's member of the Assembly reads:

Erbakan and his friends under the image of party they want to bring the Islam to this country. The public prosecutor understood that . . . the person who incited the people to use the weapons before the Muslims have the power to govern is either ignorant or treacherous as charged by others. None of the prophets allowed the war before obtaining the power to govern.

The declaration of Hasan Hüseyin Ceylan, the party's member of the Assembly states:

This country is ours but the regime is not...Turkey will collapse gentlemen, they say that the Turkey can be the Algeria? In that country they (fundamentalists) are 81 per cent, not 20 per cent, we will also reach 81 per cent. You, who imitate the savage west, do not try in vain . . . you will die in the hands of Kirikkale's people.

The declaration of Sükrü Karatepe, the party's Kayseri Mayor commented:

In a period in which our belief is not respected . . . I came to this ceremony [the ceremony for the memory of Mustafa Kemal Atatürk the founder of the Republic] shedding bitter tears... Muslims, always keep the anger, the grudge and the hate in your heart.

The declaration of Halil Ibrahim Çelik, the party's member of Assembly stated:

I want bloodshed, democracy will come in this manner. The Army could not overcome the 3500 PKK militants. How can it overcome six million defenders of Islamic rules.

The Constitutional Court decided that the Welfare Party's Chairman, some of its members of Assembly and mayors used the democratic rights and freedoms with their declarations and activities against the secularity as a means to abolish democracy and to establish an Islamic-rules order instead. It is natural to dissolve any parties which threaten the democratic order and it is necessary to dissolve the Welfare Party according to Articles 68 and 69 of the Constitution and Article 103 of the Political Parties Statute No. 2820.[3]

On 22 May 1996, the Principal Public Prosecutor at the Court of Cassation applied to the Constitutional Court for an order dissolving the Labour Party. He accused the party of having formed a programme intended likely to undermine the territorial integrity of the state and the unity of the nation (Arts. 2, 3, 14 and 69 of the Constitution and Article 78(a) of the Political Parties Statute No. 2820), having pursued the aim to create minorities (Art. 81 of Statute No. 2820). Article 69 paragraph 5 of the constitution states that: "The permanent dissolution of a political party shall be decided when it is established that the constitution and programme of the political party violate the provisions of the fourth paragraph of Article 68."

The Constitutional Court having examined the programme of the Party, held that it contained statements which had aimed to undermine the territorial integrity of the state and to create minorities. The Court found violation of Articles 78 and 81 of Statute No. 2820 and relied on some statements from the Party's programme, indicating that:

reactionism of Kurds and Turks . . . stop activities to make Kurdish and Turkish workers, labourers as enemies to each other and to ill-treat Kurds . . . to repeal all the prohibitions on Kurds . . . perfect freedom and equal rights to ethnic nations and languages . . . to guarantee the union of Turks and Kurds freely and equally . . . to support and guarantee the free development of the other national cultures and languages in the country.

According to the Constitutional Court there is no prohibition on individuals, as all individuals who live in Turkey are equal and all have an equal chance to work in every field including legislative, judicial and executive functions, therefore to request "freedom and equal rights to ethnic nations" means to claim the existence of other nations in a nation and to request the separation of those nations. This sort of unrealistic argument leads to the motives and reasons of terrorist organizations and some people who are ignorant on this subject attempt to realize terrorist actions. By drawing a distinction in its programme between the Kurdish and Turkish nations, the Labour Party had revealed its intention of working to achieve the creation

---

[3] The decision of Constitutional Court, E. 1997/1, K. 1998/1, 16 January 1998, OG 23266, dated 22 February 1998.

of minorities which – with the exception of those referred to in the Treaty of Lausanne and the Treaty with Bulgaria – posed a threat to the state's territorial integrity.[4]

1.3 The provisions annulled by the Constitutional Court

The Constitutional Court decision dated 14 December 1998 concerns the security of tenure of judges and public prosecutors. According to Article 139, paragraph 1 of the constitution, judges and public prosecutors shall not be dismissed or retired before the age prescribed by the Constitution; nor shall they be deprived of their salaries, allowances or other rights relating to their status, even as a result of the abolition of court or post. According to Article 140 paragraph 4 of the Constitution, judges and public prosecutors shall exercise their duties until they reach the age of 65, promotion shall be made according to age and the retirement of military judges shall be prescribed by statute.

On one hand, the provisions mentioned above declare a precise retirement age, but on the other they give the possibility to prescribe a different rule governing the retirement of military judges. Therefore the age of retirement of the military judges (determined by Military Judges Statute (No. 357)) is lower than civil judges and changes depending their official rank. In addition to this, when a military judge acquires all the attributes necessary to be promoted he can wait a maximum of two years for an available superior post and according to Article 21, paragraph 2 of the Military Judges Statute, if there is no suitable post available he can be retired before the age prescribed by the statute. The posts available are determined by the administration.

The chambers of the Council of Military Administrative Superior Court has applied to the Constitutional Court for a decision invalidating Article 21 paragraph 2 of the Military Judges Statute. According to the Constitutional Court, the retirement of the military judges before the age prescribed by statute because of an absence of post means giving a wide margin of appreciation to the administrative authority; therefore the provision disputed is against the constitutional principles of independence of the courts and security of tenure of judges.[5]

On 23 September 1996, the Constitutional Court annulled Article 441 of the Criminal Code, taking into consideration the principle of equality between man and woman, as an adultery crime committed by a man (Art. 441) was different from the adultery crime committed by a woman (Art. 440).[6] However, the result of the Constitutional Court judgment created a situation which is more unequal than the situation which existed before the judgment, as the crime of adultery for a man was invalidated, but the crime of adultery for a woman remained the same. In 1998

---

[4] The decision of Constitutional Court, E. 1996/1, 1997/1, 14 February 1997, OG No. 23384, dated 26 June 1998.
[5] The decision of the Constitutional Court, E. 1998/39, K. 1998/78,14 December 1998, OG No. 2392, dated 11 May 1999.
[6] See Sibel Inceoglu, in *Yearbook of Islamic and Middle Eastern Law*, vol. 4 (1997–1998), p. 460.

the Constitutional Court, taking into consideration the unequality, also annulled Article 440;[7] now there is no crime of adultery in Turkey.

Another Constitutional Court decision concerns Article 208 paragraph 2 of the Criminal Judgment Procedure Statute. As a rule, the indictment of the public prosecutor is notified to the defendant with a letter of invitation to the court (Art. 208, para. 1), but in cases which are litigated before the Courts of First Instance the indictments are not notified to the defendants (Art. 208, para. 2). The Constitutional Court taking into consideration Article 36 of the Constitution which says "everyone has the right of litigation either as plaintiff or defendant before the courts through lawful means and procedure" and Article 6, paragraph 3 of the European Convention on Human Rights, annulled Article 208, paragraph 2 of the Criminal Judgment Procedure Statute.[8]

2 CRIMINAL LAW

On 1 October 1998 the By-law of Arrest, Detention and Interrogation came into force.[9] The aim of this by-law is to describe the rights of the people arrested or detained and the authority and the responsibility of the officers who have authority to detain, arrest or interrogate. Some of the rights of the person detained are as follows: (a) the right to be informed about the reasons of detention, (b) the right to remain silent, (c) the right to call his/her lawyer, and (d) the right to inform his/her relatives. Those rights had already been prescribed by related statutes, but the by-law describing them has introduced some provisions which are not in conformity with the statutes. Therefore, the Istanbul, Ankara and Izmir Bar Associations applied to the Council of State to annul some of its provisions.

For instance, Article 21 describes the lawyer's authority to investigate the documents and records of the case, but some of those documents and records can be investigated with the permission of the public prosecutor. Another provision (Article 19) describes the right to appoint a lawyer. According to this provision, if the detained person does not have a lawyer, he or she has the right to request a lawyer from the Bar Association. However, a person detained for a crime which is within the state security courts' jurisdiction does not have the same right. Article 20 mentions the right to meet with a lawyer. It says that the detained person can always meet with his or her lawyer, but the person detained because of a crime which is within the state security courts' jurisdiction can meet with his or her lawyer when the period of detention is extended by the judge. It means that he or she can meet a lawyer after four days beginning from the day of arrest. Article 10 describes health controls employed in order to prevent unlawful methods at the inquiry; however, it states that the person detained and the physician are left alone when there is no reason to doubt the safety of the investigation and the security of the detained per-

---

[7] The decision of the Constitutional Court, E. 1998/3, K. 1998/28, 23 June 1998, OG No. 23638, dated 13 March 1999.

[8] The decision of the Constitutional Court, E. 1997/41, K. 1998/47, 14 July 1998, OG No. 23649, dated 24 March 1999.

[9] OG N0. 23480, dated 1 October 1998.

son or the physician. This provision gives the possibility to prevent the right of being able to stay alone with the physician and to talk to him or her freely.

The Council of State has not yet annulled any provision, but it has decided to stay the execution of Article 21.

3 HEALTH LAW

On 1 August 1998, the By-law of Patients' Rights came into force.[10] The aim of the by-law is to describe specifically the rights of patients which were already prescribed by the Constitution and statutes. Every patient has the following minimum rights:

(a) to request information on the health institutions and the physicians;
(b) to choose and to change the health institution and the physician;
(c) to request information written or orally on his or her health, the treatment which he or she will receive, the benefits and the probable harms of the treatment, the other treatment methods, the course of progress of the disease and the probable results which will happen if the treatment is refused (the right to have an informed consent);
(d) to be informed in a language which he or she can understand, without using medical terminology as far as possible;
(e) to request not to give information to his or her self or to his or her relatives on his or her illness;
(f) to examine his or her medical records by his or her self or by his or her representative; those records can be seen only by the people who are directly related to the treatment, and cannot become publicly known except in cases where the law allows disclosure;
(g) to be respected for his or her private life; and
(h) not to be treated without informed consent and to refuse the treatment with the exemption of a case in which there is a threat to his or her life or vital organs.

The By-law of Patients' Rights, in addition to those rights described, also has some prohibitions, for instance euthanasia is not allowed. Active euthanasia is absolutely illegal. Passive euthanasia depends on the condition of the patient. The patient can always refrain from giving consent at the beginning, but after the treatment commences the patient cannot withdraw consent if there is a threat to his or her life or vital organs. Another problematic provision concerns the authority of the physician to decide not to inform the patient in cases in which to inform the patient can effect his or her psychology and the progress of the illness negatively. The provision which gives such an authority to the physician and the provision which prohibits the right to refuse the treatment are argued among both physicians and lawyers.

---

[10] OG No. 23420, dated 1 August 1998.

4 CIVIL LAW

On 17 January 1998, the Protection of the Family Statute came into force.[11] According to this statute if one member of the family is the subject of violence the judge can decide new measures against the other member who has exercised the violence. The measures are as following:

(a) to warn the family member to refrain from the violence and the acts which frighten other members;
(b) to reserve the residence to the members who are the subject of violence and to warn the other member not to approach the residence;
(c) to warn not to disturb the family members by telephone or other communication means;
(d) to deliver the weapon or other instruments similar to a police officer;
(e) not to approach the residence after using drugs or drinking alcoholic beverages; and
(f) to pay a regular allowance to the other family members taking into consideration their standard of living.

The application period of those measures cannot be more than six months. If the family member violates the measures mentioned above, he or she shall be sentenced to between three to six months' imprisonment. The penalties of the acts which are separate crimes shall be added to this penalty.

---

[11] Statute No. 4320, 14 January 1998, OG No. 23233, dated 17 January 1998.

Syria

*Jacques El-Hakim**

1 PROCEDURAL LAW

1.1 Jurisdiction over disputes between two administrative state entities

Public sector entities in Syria are divided into two different groups; "administrative" entities (State agencies or autonomous organizations) governed by administrative law and public accounting and falling under the jurisdiction of the State Council, or "economic" entities (carrying out a commercial, industrial, financial or agricultural activity) governed by private law (civil, commercial, etc.) and private accounting and falling under the jurisdiction of ordinary courts.

Article 47(c) of the law of the State Council (No. 55 of 21 February 1959) authorized the General Assembly of the Consultancy Sections of the State Council to give legal opinions settling disputes arising between Ministries, State agencies, local or municipal entities. The Syrian Insurance Company (a State-owned commercial entity) contended that ordinary courts did not have jurisdiction over claims filed against it by another public sector entity. The State Council contended that it has an exclusive jurisdiction over these disputes and rendered an opinion thereon according to Article 47(c) of Law No. 55 of 1959 but the ordinary courts rendered a different judgment confirming their jurisdiction over the disputes. Those conflicting decisions could only be settled by a ruling of the Court of Conflict of Jurisdictions, headed by the First President of the Court of Cassation with the membership of one counsellor from the ordinary courts and one from the State Council (Art. 27 and 28 of the law on the Judicial Authority (legislative decree No. 98 of 15 November 1961)).

In its judgment No. 1 of 1993, that court ruled that the dispute fell under the jurisdiction of the ordinary courts, the State Council having no jurisdiction over commercial State entities.

---

* Professor of Law, Damascus University; Attorney at Law.

2 CIVIL AND CRIMINAL LAW

2.1 Law on antiques

Syria is among the richest countries in the world in antique civilizations and due to the increased number of excavations in the last decades and the growing demand for antiques, a great number of specialized thieves and influential people have developed a fruitful trade in antiques, particularly through neighbouring Lebanon, depriving humanity of previous cultural remains (since the origin of most of the stolen objects is then permanently lost) and damaging cultural sites which cannot be restored to their previous conditions. The previous law on antiques was drastically amended by Law No. 1 of 28 February 1999 which forbade the trade and export of antiques and considerably increased the penalties applicable to its violation. Experience showed that a reasonable penalty enforced strictly is much more efficient than a disproportionate one which will not be enforced on influential people anyway and will encourage the courts to discharge the infringers rather than condemning them to an unacceptable penalty.

Under the law, an object may be regarded as antique if it is more than 100 years old and has a historical, artistic or national value.

Antiques must be registered with the Department of Antiques (supervised by the Ministry of Culture) which can force the holder to sell them to it at the price it has appraised. Any transfer of their property must be recorded with that Department which can purchase them itself as mentioned above (Art. 34). Trade and export of antiques is forbidden and punished with ten to fifteen years imprisonment and a fine of SP100,000–500,000 (US$1 is now worth about SP50), i.e. with the same penalty as applicable to theft of antiques, which is absolutely illogical (Art. 57). Trade of antiques is developed in the whole world and, under the previous law, the merchants had to be registered with the Antique Department which controlled their activity and could purchase the items sold or exported. Many such items are of a minor value and are sometimes available in great quantities which makes it worth allowing part of them to be acquired by museums and cultural institutions in the world and making that human legacy be known and appreciated in other countries. The high value of antiques makes it impossible to stop their trade and it is much preferable to control that trade and levy taxes on their dealers instead of having the antiques smuggled abroad without control.

Smuggling of antiques is also punished with imprisonment (fifteen to twenty years) and a fine (from SP500,0000 to SP1 million) and the attempt thereof also falls under the same penalty (Art. 56). Unfortunately, there is no legal definition of smuggling, which is not acceptable in a criminal penalty. Unauthorized excavation or search of antiques is punished with the same penalty as theft and trade and the maximum penalty applies in cases of serious damage to the antiques (Art. 57(b)). Destruction, damage or modification of antiques is punished with five to ten years imprisonment and a fine of SP25,0000 to SP50,000 and the same penalty applies to manufacturing a false antique or selling it as genuine – in which case it must be confiscated (Art. 58). Lower penalties apply to the violation of other provisions of the law including the possession of antiques without registering them with the Antique Department or their transport without previous authorization (Art. 62).

Civil servants who do not prosecute infringers when they know about their offence are subject to the same penalties (Art. 63).

3 PRIVATE INTERNATIONAL LAW AND COMMERCIAL LAW

3.1 Joint accounts

Syrian law does not contain any provision regarding joint accounts, contrary to Lebanese law which confirmed their validity and legal effects authorizing every party to those accounts to freely operate them and withdraw any amount deposited therein. In case of death, the account has to be wound up and its balance equally divided between the parties without considering the origin of the deposits and which party made them. However, Syrian banks always opened joint accounts under the above-mentioned rules existing, in various pieces of legislation and resulting from international banking practice. Those rules being stipulated in the respective agreement concluded to open the account are as valid under Syrian law as any contractual stipulation, as long as they do not violate public policy.

A recent judgment from the Appeal Court of Damascus (10th Chamber, No. 366 of 26 October 1998) unfortunately violated those elementary principles as well as other legal provisions. A Lebanese couple had opened a joint account in Switzerland where they deposited various amounts. Before her husband's death, his wife withdrew an amount therefrom and some of the other heirs (children from the husband's previous marriage) contended that the above-mentioned amount was part of their inheritance and that they should receive their share thereof. The wife and her children contended that under Article 18 of the Syrian Civil Code, the law governing inheritance is the law of the deceased, i.e. Lebanese law, which confirms the validity of the joint account and the right of each party thereof to withdraw whatever amounts therefrom without proving that he or she previously deposited similar amounts. Since she withdrew those amounts during her husband's life, the latter could not be regarded as part of his inheritance. They also pointed out that the joint account was opened in Switzerland under Swiss law, and its stipulations authorized each party to withdraw whatever amounts therefrom. The judgment nevertheless ruled that:

(a) Since the deceased resided in Syria where the inheritance was opened, it was governed by Syrian laws. This statement obviously violates the express terms of Article 18 of the Civil Code.

(b) Under Syrian law, the stipulations of a joint account only applied to the parties' relationship with the bank but did not affect the relationship of the parties. Each party had to prove that he or she owned the amount deposited to be allowed to withdraw it. The judgment did not discuss the provisions of Syrian and Swiss laws governing the dispute and initiated a dangerous ruling in that matter and an obvious violation of the basic legal principles. The new amendment of the Commerce Code now examined by the Council of Ministers contained comprehensive provisions on joint accounts but even if the amendment is issued, one cannot predict whether it will receive the same interpretation as the other legal provisions governing that dispute. We hope that the Court of Cassation, which will settle the appeal made against that judgment, will take a more accurate position in that issue.

3.2 Interest due on a current account

A foreign airline company had deposited amounts resulting from the sale of its tickets in Syria in two current accounts opened at the Commercial Bank of Syria (which has a monopoly in that field) as per an agreement entitling it to 4 per cent interest. The bank deposited that interest in the account for several years, but all of a sudden cancelled that deposit and pretended to recover the interests following subsequent instructions of its general management contending that the amounts deposited had to be transferred, sooner or later, to the company's headquarters abroad and did not deserve the interest.

The company then sued the bank, asking for the implementation of their common agreement and pointing out that any amount duly deposited in its accounts could not be unilaterally withdrawn therefrom by the depositor.

In its judgment No. 3043 of 23 November 1998, the Damascus Appeal Court (11th Chamber) required the bank to return the amounts unduly withdrawn and to pay interest on the following periods, rejecting the bank's contentions on the following grounds:

(a)   Although it was State owned, the bank was nevertheless a commercial company subject to civil and commercial law. It was a private corporate body represented by its director general as per its basic law (Legislative Decree No. 20 of 28 September 1994) and was therefore the only party to the dispute, without any need to call the bank's tutorship authority (i.e. the Central Bank and the Minister of Economy and Foreign Trade) to the hearing since they were not a party to the agreement under dispute.

(b)   Interest was due on the amounts deposited in the accounts not only in implementation of the agreement governing them but on the basis of the provisions governing current accounts (Articles 400 and 402 of the Syrian Commercial Code). The bank could not therefore withdraw this interest once the amounts have been duly deposited nor could it refuse to pay it in the future.

4   LABOUR LAW

The Syrian Labour Code did not determine a retirement age but nevertheless authorized the employer to terminate the labour agreement when the employee reached that age. The courts then referred to the Code of Social Insurance to determine when the retirement compensation was due from the Social Insurance Organization, i.e. when the employee reaches the age of sixty or even fifty-five if the insurance premium were paid for twenty years which entitles him to a retirement pension. An employee recently sued his employer for dismissing him at the age of sixty, although he duly filled in the retirement form required by the Social Insurance which granted the employee the pension he was entitled to. Nevertheless the employee challenged his dismissal, contending that he continued working for his employer after his retirement. In a judgment rendered on 17 July 1999 (case No. 112), the Commission of Dismissals at the Labour Ministry (a court having jurisdiction over dismissal of employees) rejected the employee's claim for reinstatement, on the basis of the above-mentioned rules and in the absence of any evidence of the re-employment of the plaintiff for a subsequent period.

5 PROPERTY LAW

A recent judgment of the Court of Cassation (no. 532 of 15 October 1998) seriously violated the basic principles of property of chattels and the rules of evidence. The plaintiff was travelling by aeroplane with his wife and contended that they lost a suitcase worth SP71,500 with its contents. The airline carrier pointed out that his claim was not acceptable without determining who was the owner of the lost items (the husband or the wife who, in Syrian law, do not legally represent each other) and whether the plaintiff was acting in his personal capacity or on behalf of his wife and without identifying and appraising the lost items.

The Court of Cassation ruled that:

(a) the Court of Appeal (whose judgment was appealed of) had a sovereign power to describe and appraise facts even if no evidence was brought by the plaintiff);
(b) all chattels are deemed to be the husband's property unless his wife proves the contrary (this is contrary to Article 917 of the Civil Code whereby the common possession of the domestic items makes both husband and wife deemed to be the owners thereof unless one of them establishes their exclusive property thereon).

6 ENVIRONMENTAL LAW

Environmental problems have increased considerably in Syria during the twentieth century due to various factors, including the continuous growth of the population (now 17 million with a growth rate of about 3.8 per cent per year and the absence of family planning), industrial, tourist and urban development in rural areas affecting the limited agricultural lands, illegal drilling of wells, lack of sewerage installations, irresponsible use of chemical fertilizers, pesticides and plastic food packaging etc. Despite harsh legislation on forests inherited from the French Mandate (1920–1945), forests were considerably reduced due to criminal fires, drought and urban development. Some partial measures have been taken since the beginning of the twentieth century to restrict the most alarming aspects of pollution and damage to public health and the environment e.g. at the occasion of granting a licence regarding buildings, industries, mines and quarries, well drilling, tourist projects, etc. However, it is only in the last decade of the twentieth century that a global legislation has been issued on the environment thanks to the suggestion and assistance of the United Nations (FAO, WHO, etc). A State Ministry of Environment (herewith referred to as "the Ministry") was created, linked with the President of the Council of Ministers as well as a Public Organization of the Environment ("the

Organization") by Legislative Decree No. 11 of 21 August 1991, enjoying legal status and financial and legislative autonomy (Art. 2) and aiming at the safeguard of the environment and its protection from pollution (Art. 3). To reach those aims, the organization should study and prevent the existing problems, draft adequate laws and regulations, inform the public of the importance of the environment, appraise the dangers threatening the environment and establish criteria to protect it, control the activities and enterprises which might damage it and study the appropriate international conventions (Art. 3).

The Organization is administered by a Higher Council for the Protection of the Environment headed by the President of the Council of Ministers and constituted of the various Ministers concerned (Art. 6). That Council sets the general policy and plans regarding the environment, the problem criteria, the regulations and conditions of industrial enterprises and other activities threatening them (Art. 7). The Minister submits to that Council the general policy and planning schemes, controls the enforcement of environmental laws and regulations and sets up with the competent authorities an advisory technical committee and more restricted committees on specific issues, e.g. purity of air and criteria, population, soil and natural resources, information, etc. In addition, fourteen local committees were established in the various administrative regions (*mouhafazats*) headed by the governor (*mouhafez*) or a local counsellor in charge of health. These committees draft adequate decrees to protect the environment. The Minister also organizes the technical, administrative and financial activity of the Council and issues the proper decrees and instructions (Art. 4).

On 4 August 1994, a decree of the President of the Republic created a Centre of Environmental Studies linked with the Ministry, enjoying legal capacity and all the privileges of an administrative or public organization (public organizations in Syria are either administrative, i.e. governed by administrative law, or economic i.e. representing commercial entities subject to civil and commercial law). It is managed by an administrative council composed of several vice-ministers (Art. 4) and a director general with two assistants and several administrative and technical bodies (Art. 8).

All the legislation has not, until now, resulted in concrete achievements and the structure of the Ministry, the Organizations and the various councils is not yet operative. A law on the protection and development of the environment has been drafted and is expected to be issued soon. Real progress in that field cannot be achieved without extensive public information and the formation of competent and efficient staff for prevention and control.

Part III

Selected Documents and Legislation

Resolutions and International Agreements

United Nations–Iraq
Resolutions

S/RES/1205 (1998)
5 November 1998

RESOLUTION 1205 (1989)
ADOPTED BY THE SECURITY COUNCIL AT ITS 3939TH MEETING, ON 5 NOVEMBER 1998

The Security Council,

Recalling all its previous relevant resolutions on the situation in Iraq, in particular its resolution 1154 (1998) of 2 March 1998 and 1194 (1998) of 9 September 1998,

Noting with alarm the decision of Iraq on 31 October 1998 to cease cooperation with the United Nations Special Commission, and its continued restrictions on the work of the International Atomic Energy Agency (IAEA)

Noting the letters from the Deputy Executive Chairman of the Special Commission of 31 October 1998 (S/1998/1023) and from the Executive Chairman of the Special Commission of 2 November 1998 (S/1998/1032) to the President of the Security Council, which reported to the Council the decision by Iraq and described the implications of that decision for the work of the Special Commission, and noting also the letter from the Director General of the IAEA of 3 November 1998 (S/1998/1033, annex) which described the implications of the decision for the work of the IAEA,

Determined to ensure immediate and full compliance by Iraq without conditions or restrictions with its obligations under resolution 687 (1991) of 3 April 1991 and the other relevant resolutions,

Recalling that the effective operation of the Special Commission and the IAEA is essential for the implementation of resolution 687 (1991)

Reaffirming its readiness to consider, in a comprehensive review, Iraq's compliance with its obligations under all relevant resolutions once Iraq has rescinded its above-mentioned decision and its decision of 5 August 1998 and demonstrated that it is prepared to fulfil all its obligations, including in particular on disarmament issues, by resuming full cooperation with the Special Commission and the IAEA consistent with the Memorandum of Understanding signed by the Deputy Prime Minister of Iraq and the Secretary-General on 23 February 1998 (S/1998/166), endorsed by the Council in resolution 1154 (1998)

Reiterating the commitment of all Member States to the sovereignty, territorial integrity and political independence of Kuwait and Iraq,

Acting under Chapter VII of the Charter of the United Nations,

1. Condemns the decision by Iraq of 31 October 1998 to cease cooperation with the Special Commission as a flagrant violation of resolution 687 (1991) and other relevant resolutions;

2. Demands that Iraq rescind immediately and unconditionally the decision of 31 October 1998, as well as the decision of 5 August 1998, to suspend cooperation with the Special Commission and to maintain restrictions on the work of the IAEA, and that Iraq provide immediate, complete and unconditional cooperation with the Special Commission and the IAEA;

3. Reaffirms its full support for the Special Commission and the IAEA in their efforts to ensure the implementation of their mandates under the relevant resolutions of the Council;

4. Expresses its full support for the Secretary-General in his efforts to seek full implementation of the Memorandum of Understanding of 23 February 1998;

5. Reaffirms its intention to act in accordance with the relevant provisions of resolution 687 (1991) on the duration of the prohibitions referred to in that resolution, and notes that by its failure so far to comply with its relevant obligations Iraq has delayed the moment when the Council can do so;

6. Decides, in accordance with its primary responsibility under the Charter for the maintenance of international peace and security, to remain actively seised of the matter.

S/RES/1210(1998)
24 November, 1998

RESOLUTION 1210 (1998)

ADOPTED BY THE SECURITY COUNCIL AT ITS 3946TH MEETING,
ON 24 NOVEMBER 1998

The Security Council,

Recalling its previous relevant resolutions and in particular its resolutions 986 (1995) of 14 April 1995, 1111 (1997) of 4 June 1997, 1129 (1997) of 12 September 1997, 1143 (1997) of 4 December 1997, 1153 (1998) of 20 February 1998 and 1175 (1998) of 19 June 1998,

Convinced of the need as a temporary measure to continue to provide for the humanitarian needs of the Iraqi people until the fulfilment by the Government of Iraq of the relevant resolutions, including notably resolution 687 (1991) of 3 April 1991, allows the Council to take further action with regard to the prohibitions referred to in resolution 661 (1990) of 6 August 1990, in accordance with the provisions of those resolutions,

Convinced also of the need for equitable distribution of humanitarian supplies to all segments of the Iraqi population throughout the country,

Welcoming the positive impact of the relevant resolutions on the humanitarian situation in Iraq as described in the report of the Secretary-General dated 19 November 1998 (S/1998/1100),

Determined to improve the humanitarian situation in Iraq,

Reaffirming the commitment of all Member States to the sovereignty and territorial integrity of Iraq,

Acting under Chapter VII of the Charter of the United Nations,

1. Decides that the provisions of resolution 986 (1995), except those contained in paragraphs 4, 11 and 12, shall remain in force for a new period of 180 days beginning at 00.01 hours, Eastern Standard Time, on 26 November 1998;

2. Further decides that paragraph 2 of resolution 1153 (1998) shall remain in force and shall apply to the 180-day period referred to in paragraph 1 above;

3. Directs the Committee established by resolution 661 (1990) to authorize, on the basis of specific requests, reasonable expenses related to the Hajj pilgrimage, to be met by funds in the escrow account;

4. Requests the Secretary-General to continue to take the actions necessary to ensure the effective and efficient implementation of this resolution, and to review, by 31 December 1998, the various options to resolve the difficulties encountered in the financial process, referred to in the Secretary-General's report of 19 November 1998

(S/1998/1100), and to continue to enhance as necessary the United Nations observation process in Iraq in such a way as to provide the required assurance to the Council that the goods produced in accordance with this resolution are distributed equitably and that all supplies authorized for procurement, including dual usage items and spare parts, are utilized for the purpose for which they have been authorized;

5. Further decides to conduct a thorough review of all aspects of the implementation of this resolution 90 days after the entry into force of paragraph 1 above and again prior to the end of the 180-day period, on receipt of the reports referred to in paragraphs 6 and 10 below, and expresses its intention, prior to the end of the 180-day period, to consider favourably renewal of the provisions of this resolution as appropriate, provided that the said reports indicate that those provisions are being satisfactorily implemented;

6. Requests the Secretary-General to report to the Council 90 days after the date of entry into force of paragraph 1 above, and again prior to the end of the 180 day period, on the basis of observations of United Nations personnel in Iraq, and of consultations with the Government of Iraq, on whether Iraq has ensured the equitable distribution of medicine, health supplies, foodstuffs, and materials and supplies for essential civilian needs, financed in accordance with paragraph 8 (a) of resolution 986 (1995), including in his reports any observations which he may have on the adequacy of the revenues to meet Iraq's humanitarian needs, and on Iraq's capacity to export sufficient quantities of petroleum and petroleum products to produce the sum referred to in paragraph 2 of resolution 1153 (1998),

7. Requests the Secretary-General to report to the Council if Iraq is unable to export petroleum and petroleum products sufficient to produce the total sum provided for in paragraph 2 above and, following consultations with relevant United Nations agencies and the Iraqi authorities, make recommendations for the expenditure of the sum expected to be available, consistent with the priorities established in paragraph 2 of resolution 1153 (1998) and with the distribution plan referred to in paragraph 5 of resolution 1175 (1998),

8. Decides that paragraphs 1, 2, 3 and 4 of resolution 1175 (1998) shall remain in force and shall apply to the new 180-day period referred to in paragraph 1 above,

9. Requests the Secretary-General, in consultation with the Government of Iraq, to submit to the Council, by 31 December 1998, a detailed list of parts and equipment necessary for the purpose described in paragraph 1 of resolution 1175 (1998),

10. Requests the Committee established by resolution 661 (1990), in close coordination with the Secretary-General, to report to the Council 90 days after the entry into force of paragraph 1 above and again prior to the end of the 180-day period on the implementation of the arrangements in paragraphs 1, 2, 6, 8, 9 and 10 of resolution 986 (1995),

11. Urges all States, and in particular the Government of Iraq, to provide their full cooperation in the effective implementation of this resolution;

12. Appeals to all States to continue to cooperate in the timely submission of applications and the expeditious issue of export licences, facilitating the transit of humanitarian supplies authorized by the Committee established by resolution 661 (1990), and to take

all other appropriate measures within their competence in order to ensure that urgently required humanitarian supplies reach the Iraqi people as rapidly as possible;

13. Stresses the need to continue to ensure respect for the security and safety of all persons directly involved in the implementation of this resolution in Iraq;

14. Decides to remain seised of the matter.

United States–Iraq
Resolution

HR 4655 EH
105th CONGRESS
2d Session
H. R. 4655

AN ACT
To establish a program to support a transition to democracy in Iraq.

Be it enacted by the Senate and House of Representatives of the United
States of America in Congress assembled,

SECTION 1. SHORT TITLE.
This Act may be cited as the `Iraq Liberation Act of 1998'.

SEC. 2. FINDINGS.
The Congress makes the following findings:

(1)   On September 22, 1980, Iraq invaded Iran, starting an eight year war in which Iraq
        employed chemical weapons against Iranian troops and ballistic missiles against
        Iranian cities.

(2)   In February 1988, Iraq forcibly relocated Kurdish civilians from their home villages
        in the Anfal campaign, killing an estimated 50,000 to 180,000 Kurds.

(3)   On March 16, 1988, Iraq used chemical weapons against Iraqi Kurdish civilian op-
        ponents in the town of Halabja, killing an estimated 5,000 Kurds and causing nu-
        merous birth defects that affect the town today.

(4)   On August 2, 1990, Iraq invaded and began a seven month occupation of Kuwait,
        killing and committing numerous abuses against Kuwaiti civilians, and setting
        Kuwait's oil wells ablaze upon retreat.

(5)   Hostilities in Operation Desert Storm ended on February 28, 1991, and Iraq subse-
        quently accepted the ceasefire conditions specified in United Nations Security Coun-

cil Resolution 687 (April 3, 1991) requiring Iraq, among other things, to disclose fully and permit the dismantlement of its weapons of mass destruction programs and submit to long-term monitoring and verification of such dismantlement.

(6)   In April 1993, Iraq orchestrated a failed plot to assassinate former President George Bush during his April 14–16, 1993, visit to Kuwait.

(7)   In October 1994, Iraq moved 80,000 troops to areas near the border with Kuwait, posing an imminent threat of a renewed invasion of or attack against Kuwait.

(8)   On August 31, 1996, Iraq suppressed many of its opponents by helping one Kurdish faction capture Irbil, the seat of the Kurdish regional government.

(9)   Since March 1996, Iraq has systematically sought to deny weapons inspectors from the United Nations Special Commission on Iraq (UNSCOM) access to key facilities and documents, has on several occasions endangered the safe operation of UNSCOM helicopters transporting UNSCOM personnel in Iraq, and has persisted in a pattern of deception and concealment regarding the history of its weapons of mass destruction programs.

(10)   On August 5, 1998, Iraq ceased all cooperation with UNSCOM, and subsequently threatened to end long-term monitoring activities by the International Atomic Energy Agency and UNSCOM.

(11)   On August 14, 1998, President Clinton signed Public Law 105-235, which declared that"the Government of Iraq is in material and unacceptable breach of its international obligations" and urged the President "to take appropriate action, in accordance with the Constitution and relevant laws of the United States, to bring Iraq into compliance with its international obligations."

(12)   On May 1, 1998, President Clinton signed Public Law 105-174, which made $5,000,000 available for assistance to the Iraqi democratic opposition for such activities as organization, training, communication and dissemination of information, developing and implementing agreements among opposition groups, compiling information to support the indictment of Iraqi officials for war crimes, and for related purposes.

SEC. 3. SENSE OF CONGRESS REGARDING UNITED STATES POLICY TOWARD IRAQ

It should be the policy of the United States to support efforts to remove the regime headed by Saddam Hussein from power in Iraq and to promote the emergence of a democratic government to replace that regime.

SEC. 4. ASSISTANCE TO SUPPORT A TRANSITION TO DEMOCRACY IN IRAQ

(a)   AUTHORITY TO PROVIDE ASSISTANCE The President may provide to the Iraqi democratic opposition organizations designated in accordance with section 5 the following assistance:

(1) BROADCASTING ASSISTANCE
(A) Grant assistance to such organizations for radio and television broadcasting by such
organizations to Iraq.
(B) There is authorized to be appropriated to the United States Information Agency
$2,000,000 for fiscal year 1999 to carry out this paragraph.

(2) MILITARY ASSISTANCE
(A) The President is authorized to direct the drawdown of defense articles from the
stocks of the Department of Defense, defense services of the Department of Defense,
and military education and training for such organizations.
(B) The aggregate value (as defined in section 644(m) of the Foreign Assistance Act of
1961) of assistance provided under this paragraph may not exceed $97,000,000.

(b) HUMANITARIAN ASSISTANCE The Congress urges the President to use existing authorities under the Foreign Assistance Act of 1961 to provide humanitarian
assistance to individuals living in areas of Iraq controlled by organizations designated in accordance with section 5, with emphasis on addressing the needs of individuals who have fled to such areas from areas under the control of the Saddam
Hussein regime.

(c) RESTRICTION ON ASSISTANCE No assistance under this section shall be provided to any group within an organization designated in accordance with section 5
which group is, at the time the assistance is to be provided, engaged in military cooperation with the Saddam Hussein regime.

(d) NOTIFICATION REQUIREMENT The President shall notify the congressional
committees specified in section 634A of the Foreign Assistance Act of 1961 at least
15 days in advance of each obligation of assistance under this section in accordance
with the procedures applicable to reprogramming notifications under such section
634A.

(e) REIMBURSEMENT RELATING TO MILITARY ASSISTANCE
(1) IN GENERAL Defense articles, defense services, and military education and training provided under subsection (a)(2) shall be made available without reimbursement to the Department of Defense except to the extent that funds are appropriated
pursuant to paragraph (2).

(2) AUTHORIZATION OF APPROPRIATIONS There are authorized to be appropriated to the President for each of the fiscal years 1998 and 1999 such sums as may
be necessary to reimburse the applicable appropriation, fund, or account for the
value (as defined in section 644(m) of the Foreign Assistance Act of 1961) of defense articles, defense services, or military education and training provided under
subsection (a)(2).

(f) AVAILABILITY OF FUNDS
(1) Amounts authorized to be appropriated under this section are authorized to remain
available until expended.

(2) Amounts authorized to be appropriated under this section are in addition to
amounts otherwise available for the purposes described in this section.

(g) AUTHORITY TO PROVIDE ASSISTANCE   Activities under this section (including activities of the nature described in subsection (b)) may be undertaken notwithstanding any other provision of law.

SEC. 5. DESIGNATION OF IRAQI DEMOCRATIC OPPOSITION ORGANIZATION

(a) INITIAL DESIGNATION   Not later than 90 days after the date of enactment of this Act, the President shall designate one or more Iraqi democratic opposition organizations that the President determines satisfy the criteria set forth in subsection (c) as eligible to receive assistance under section 4.

(b) DESIGNATION OF ADDITIONAL ORGANIZATIONS   At any time subsequent to the initial designation pursuant to subsection (a), the President may designate one or more additional Iraqi democratic opposition organizations that the President determines satisfy the criteria set forth in subsection (c) as eligible to receive assistance under section 4.

(c) CRITERIA FOR DESIGNATION   In designating an organization pursuant to this section, the President shall consider only organizations that—

(1) include a broad spectrum of Iraqi individuals, groups, or both, opposed to the Saddam Hussein regime; and

(2) are committed to democratic values, to respect for human rights, to peaceful relations with Iraq's neighbors, to maintaining Iraq's territorial integrity, and to fostering cooperation among democratic opponents of the Saddam Hussein regime.

(d) NOTIFICATION REQUIREMENT   At least 15 days in advance of designating an Iraqi democratic opposition organization pursuant to this section, the President shall notify the congressional committees specified in section 634A of the Foreign Assistance Act of 1961 of his proposed designation in accordance with the procedures applicable to reprogramming notifications under such section 634A.

SEC. 6. WAR CRIMES TRIBUNAL FOR IRAQ

Consistent with section 301 of the Foreign Relations Authorization Act, Fiscal Years 1992 and 1993 (Public Law 102-138), House Concurrent Resolution 137, 105th Congress (approved by the House of Representatives on November 13, 1997), and Senate Concurrent Resolution 78, 105th Congress (approved by the Senate on March 13, 1998), the Congress urges the President to call upon the United Nations to establish an international criminal tribunal for the purpose of indicting, prosecuting, and imprisoning Saddam Hussein and other Iraqi officials who are responsible for crimes against humanity, genocide, and other criminal violations of international law.

SEC. 7. ASSISTANCE FOR IRAQ UPON REPLACEMENT OF SADDAM HUSSEIN REGIME

It is the sense of Congress that once the Saddam Hussein regime is removed from power in Iraq, the United States should support Iraq's transition to democracy by providing immediate and substantial humanitarian assistance to the Iraqi people, by providing democracy transition assistance to Iraqi parties and movements with democratic goals, and by convening Iraq's foreign creditors to develop a multilateral response to Iraq's foreign debt incurred by Saddam Hussein's regime.

SEC. 8. RULE OF CONSTRUCTION

Nothing in this Act shall be construed to authorize or otherwise speak to the use of United States Armed Forces (except as provided in section 4(a)(2)) in carrying out this Act.

Passed the House of Representatives October 5, 1998.

Attest:

Clerk.

END

Palestine

Wye River Memorandum

The following are steps to facilitate implementation of the Interim Agreement on the West Bank and Gaza Strip of 28 September 1995 and other related agreements including the Note for the Record of 17 January 1997 (hereinafter referred to as "the prior agreements") so that the Israeli and Palestinian sides can carry out their reciprocal responsibilities more effectively, including those relating to further redeployments and security, respectively. These steps are to be carried out in a parallel phased approach in accordance with the Memorandum and the attached time line. They are subject to the relevant terms and conditions of the prior agreements and do not supersede their other requirements.[1]

I FURTHER REDEPLOYMENTS

A Phase One and Two Further Redeployments

1. Pursuant to the Interim Agreement and subsequent agreements, the Israeli side's implementation of the first and second FRD will consist of the transfer to the Palestinian side of 13 per cent from Area C as follows:

–   1 per cent to Area (A)
–   12 per cent to Area B

The Palestinian side has informed that it will allocate an area/areas amounting to 3 per cent from the above (B) to be designated as the Green Areas and/or Nature Reserves. The Palestinian side has further informed that they will act according to the established scientific standards, and that therefore there will be no changes in the status of these areas, without prejudice to the rights of the existing inhabitants in these areas, including Bedouins; while these standards do not allow new construction in these areas, existing roads and buildings may be maintained.

The Israeli side will retain in these Green Areas/Nature Reserves the overriding security responsibility for the purpose of protecting Israelis and confronting the threat of terrorism.

---

[1] See also the text of the Sharm el-Sheikh Memorandum at pp. 487–490 of this *Yearbook*.

Activities and movements of the Palestinian Police forces may be carried out after coordination and confirmation; the Israeli side will respond to such requests expeditiously.

2. As part of the foregoing implementation of the first and second FRD, 14.2 per cent from Area (B) will become Area (A).

B Third Phase of Further Redeployments

With regard to the terms of the Interim Agreement and of Secretary Warren Christopher's letters to the two sides of 17 January 1997, relating to the further redeployment process, there will be a commitment to address this question. The United States will be briefed regularly.

II SECURITY

In the provisions on security arrangements for the Interim Agreement, the Palestinian side agreed to take all measures necessary in order to prevent acts of terrorism, crime and hostilities directed against the Israeli side, against individuals falling under the Israeli side's authority and against their property, just as the Israeli side agreed to take all measures necessary in order to prevent acts of terrorism, crime and hostilities directed against the Palestinian side, against individuals falling under the Palestinian side's authority and against their property. The two sides also agreed to take legal measures against offenders within their jurisdiction and to prevent incitement against each other by any organizations, groups or individuals within their jurisdiction.

Both sides recognise that it is in their vital interests to combat terrorism and fight violence in accord with Annex I of the Interim Agreement and the Note for the Record. They also recognise that the struggle against terror and violence must be comprehensive in that it deals with terrorists, the terror support structure and the environment conducive to the support of terror. It must be continuous and constant over a long-term, in that there can be no pauses in the work against terrorists and their structure. It must be cooperative in that no effort can be fully effective without Israeli–Palestinian cooperation and the continuous exchange of information, concepts and actions.

Pursuant to the prior agreements, the Palestinian side's implementation of its responsibilities for security, security cooperation and other issues will be as detailed below during the time periods specified in the attached time line.

A Security Actions

1 Outlawing and Combating Terrorist Organizations

a   The Palestinian side will make known its policy for zero tolerance for terror and violence against both sides.

b   A work plan developed by the Palestinian side will be shared with the US and hereafter implementation will begin immediately to ensure the systematic and effective combat of terrorist organizations and their infrastructure.

c   In addition to the bilateral Israeli–Palestinian security cooperation, a US–Palestinian committee will meet biweekly to review the steps being taken to eliminate terrorist cells and the support structure that plans, finances, supplies and abets terror. In these meetings, the Palestinian side will inform the US fully of the actions it has taken to outlaw all organizations (or wings of organizations, as appropriate) of a military, terrorist or violent character and their support structure and to prevent them from operating in areas under its jurisdiction.

d   The Palestinian side will apprehend the specific individuals suspected of perpetrating acts of violence and terror for the purpose of further investigation, and prosecution and punishment of all persons involved in acts of violence and terror.

e   A US–Palestinian committee will meet to review and evaluate information pertinent to the decisions on prosecution, punishment or other legal measures which affect the status of individuals suspected of abetting or perpetrating acts of violence and terror.

2 Prohibiting Illegal Weapons

a   The Palestinian side will ensure an effective legal framework is in place to criminalize, in conformity with the prior agreements, any importation, manufacturing or unlicensed sale, acquisition or possession of firearms, ammunition or weapons in areas under Palestinian jurisdiction.

b   In addition, the Palestinian side will establish and vigorously and continuously implement a systematic program for the collection and appropriate handling of all such illegal items in accordance with the prior agreement. The US has agreed to assist in carrying out this programme.

c   A US–Palestinian–Israeli committee will be established to assist and enhance cooperation in preventing the smuggling or other unauthorized introduction of weapons or explosive materials into areas under Palestinian jurisdiction.

3 Preventing Incitement

a   Drawing on relevant international practice and pursuant to Article XXII (1) of the Interim Agreement and the Note for the Record, the Palestinian side will issue a decree prohibiting all forms of incitement to violence or terror, and establishing mechanisms for acting systematically against all expressions or threats of violence or terror. This decree will be comparable to the existing Israeli legislation which deals with the same subject.

b   A US–Palestinian–Israeli committee will meet on a regular basis to monitor cases of possible incitement to violence or terror, and to make recommendations and reports on how to prevent such incitement. The Israeli–Palestinian and US sides will each appoint a media specialist, a law enforcement representative, an educational specialist and a current or former elected official to the committee.

B Security Operation

The two sides agree that their security cooperation will be based on a spirit of partnership and will include, among other things, the following steps:

1 Bilateral Cooperation

There will be full bilateral security cooperation between the two sides which will be continuous, intensive and comprehensive.

2 Forensic Cooperation

There will be an exchange of forensic expertise, training and other assistance.

3 Trilateral Committee

In addition to the bilateral Israeli–Palestinian security cooperation, a high-ranking US–Palestinian–Israeli committee will meet as required and not less than biweekly to assess current threats, deal with any impediments to effective security cooperation and coordination and address the steps being taken to combat terror and terrorist organizations.

The committee will also serve as a forum to address the issue of external support for terror. In these meetings, the Palestinian side will fully inform the members of the committee of the results of its investigations concerning terrorist suspects already in custody and the participants will exchange relevant information. The committee will report regularly to the leaders of the two sides on the status of cooperation, the results of the meetings and its recommendations.

C Other Issues

1 Palestinian Police Force

a   The Palestinian side will provide a list of its policemen to the Israeli side in conformity with the prior agreements.
b   Should the Palestinian side request technical assistance, the US has indicated its willingness to help meet these needs in cooperation with other donors.
c   The Monitoring and Steering Committee will, as part of its functions, monitor the implementation of this provision and brief to the US.

2 PLO Charter

The Executive Committee of the Palestine Liberation Organization and the Palestinian Control Council will reaffirm the letter of 22 January 1998 from PLO Chairman Yasser Arafat to President Clinton concerning the nullification of the Palestinian National Charter provisions that are inconsistent with the letters exchanged between the PLO and the Government of Israel on 9–10 September 1993. PLO Chairman Arafat, the Speaker of the Palestine National Council, and the Speaker of the Palestinian Council will invite the members of the PNC, as well as the members of the Central Council, the Council, and the Palestinian Heads of Ministries to a meeting to be addressed by President Clinton to reaffirm their support for the peace process and the aforementioned decisions of the Executive Committee and the Central Council.

3 Legal Assistance in Criminal Matters

Among other forms of legal assistance in criminal matters, the requests for arrest and transfer of suspects and defendants pursuant to Article II (7) of Annex IV of the Interim Agreement will be submitted (or re-submitted) through the mechanism of the Joint Israeli–Palestinian Legal Committee and will be responded to in conformity with Article II (7) (f) of Annex IV of the Interim Agreement within the twelve week period. Requests submitted after the eighth week will be responded to with Article II (7) (f) within four weeks of their submission. The US has been requested by the sides to report on a regular basis on the steps being taken to respond to the above requests.

4 Human Rights and the Rule of Law

Pursuant of Article XI (1) of Annex I of the Interim Agreement, and without derogating from the above, the Palestinian Police will exercise powers and responsibilities to implement this Memorandum with due regard to internationally accepted norms of human rights and the rule of law, and will be guided by the need to protect the public, respect human dignity and avoid harassment.

III INTERIM COMMITTEES AND ECONOMIC ISSUES

1   The Israeli and Palestinian sides reaffirm their commitment to enhancing their relationship and agree on the need actively to promote economic development in the West Bank and Gaza. In this regard, the parties agree to continue or to reactivate all standing committees established by the Interim Agreement, including the Monitoring and Steering Committee, the Joint Economic Committee (JEC), the Civil Affair Committee (CAC), the Legal Committee and the Standing Cooperation Committee.

2   The Israeli and Palestinian sides have agreed on arrangements which will permit the timely opening of the Gaza Industrial Estate. They also have concluded a "Protocol Regarding the Establishment and Operation of the International Airport in the Gaza Strip during the Interim Period".

3   Both sides will renew negotiations on safe passage immediately. As regards the southern route, the sides will make best efforts to conclude the agreement within a week of the entry into force of this Memorandum. Operation of the southern route will start as soon as possible thereafter. As regards the northern route, negotiations will continue with the goal of reaching agreement as soon as possible. Implementation will take place expeditiously thereafter.

4   The Israeli and Palestinian sides acknowledge the great importance of the Port of Gaza for the development of the Palestinian economy, and the expansion of Palestinian trade. They commit themselves to proceeding without delay to conclude an agreement to allow the construction and operation of the port in accordance with the prior agreements. The Israeli–Palestinian Committee will reactivate its work immediately with a goal of concluding the protocol within sixty days, which will allow commencement of the construction of the port.

5   The two sides recognize that unresolved legal issues adversely affect the relationship between the two peoples. They therefore will accelerate efforts through the Legal Committee to address outstanding legal issues and to implement solutions to these issues in the shortest possible period. The Palestinian side will provide to the Israeli side copies of all of its laws in effect.

6   The Israeli and Palestinian sides also will launch a strategic economic dialogue to enhance their economic relationship. They will establish within the framework of the JEC an Ad Hoc Committee for this purpose. The committee will review the four following issues: (1) Israeli purchase taxes; (2) cooperation in combating vehicle theft; (3) dealing with unpaid Palestinian debts; (4) the impact of Israeli standards as barriers to trade and the expansion of A1 and A2 lists. The committee will submit an interim

report within three weeks of the entry into force of this Memorandum, and within six weeks will submit its conclusions and recommendations to be implemented.

7   The two sides agree on the importance of continued international donor assistance to facilitate implementation by both sides of agreements reached. They also recognize the need for enhanced donor support for economic development in the West Bank and Gaza. They agree to jointly approach the donor community to organize a Ministerial Conference before the end of 1998 to seek pledges for enhanced levels of assistance.

IV PERMANENT STATUS NEGOTIATIONS

The two sides will immediately resume permanent status negotiations on an accelerated basis and will make a determined effort to achieve the mutual goal of reaching an agreement by 4 May 1999. The negotiations will be continuous and without interruption. The US has expressed its willingness to facilitate these negotiations.

V UNILATERAL ACTIONS

Recognizing the necessity to create a positive environment for the negotiations, neither side shall initiate or take any step that will change the status of the West Bank and the Gaza Strip in accordance with the Interim Agreement.

ATTACHMENT: TIME LINE

This Memorandum will enter into force ten days form the date of signature.
Done at Washington, DC this 23rd day of October 1998.

_____   _____
For the Government   For the PLO
of the State of Israel

Witnessed by:

_____
The United States of America

TIME LINE

Note: Parenthetical references below are to references in the "Wye River Memorandum" to which this time line is an integral attachment. Topics not included in the time line follow the schedule provided for in the text of the Memorandum.

1 Upon Entry into Force of the Memorandum

- Third further redeployment committee starts (I(b))
- Palestinian security work plan shared with the US (II(A)(1)(b))
- Full bilateral security cooperation (II(B)(1))
- Trilateral security cooperation committee starts (II(B)(3))
- Interim committees resume and continue; Ad Hoc Economic Committee starts (III)
- Accelerated permanent status negotiations start (IV)

2 Entry into Force: Week 2

- Security work plan implementation begins (II(A)(1)(b)); (II(A)(1)(c)) committee starts
- Illegal weapons framework in place (II(A)(2)(a)); Palestinian implementation report (II(A)(2)(b))
- Anti-incitement committee starts (II(A)(3)(b)); decree issued (II(A)(3)(a))
- PLO Executive Committee reaffirms Charter letter (II(c)(2))
- Stage 1 of FRD implementation: 2 per cent C to B, 7.1 per cent B to A. Israeli officials acquaint their Palestinian counterparts as required with areas; FRD carried out; report on FRD implementation (I(A))

3 Weeks 2–6

- Palestinian Central Council reaffirms Charter letter (weeks 2–4) (II(C)(2))
- PNC and other PLO organizations reaffirm Charter letter (weeks 4–6) (II(C)(2))
- Establishment of Weapons collection program (II(A)(2)(b)) and collection stage (II(A)(2)(c)); committee starts and reports on activities
- Anti-incitement committee report (II(A)(3)(b))
- Ad Hoc Economic Committee; interim report at week three; final report at week six (III)
- Policemen list (II(C)(1)(a)); Monitoring and Steering Committee review starts (II(C)(1)(c))
- Stage 2 of FRD implementation: 5 per cent C to B. Israeli officials acquaint their Palestinian counterparts as required with areas; FRD carried out; report on FRD implementation (I(A))

4 Weeks 6–12

- Weapons collection stage (II(A)(2)(b)); (II(A)(2)(c)) committee report on its activities
- Anti-Incitement committee report (II(A)(3)(b))
- Monitoring and Steering Committee briefs US on policemen list (II(C)(1)(c))

–   Stage 3 of FRD implementation: 5 per cent C to B, 1 per cent C to A, 7.1 per cent B
        to A
–   Israeli officials acquaint Palestinian counterparts as required with areas; FRD carried
        out; report on FRD implementation (I(A))

5 After Week 12

Activities described in the Memorandum continue as appropriate and if necessary, including:

–   Trilateral security cooperation committee (II(B)(3))
–   (II(A)(1)(c)) committee
–   (II(A)(1)(e)) committee
–   Anti-incitement committee (II(A)(3)(b))
–   Third phase FRD Committee (I(b))
–   Interim Committees (III)
–   Accelerated permanent status negotiations (IV)

End of Attachment

Palestine

The Sharm el-Sheikh Memorandum

on Implementation Timeline of Outstanding Commitments of Agreements

Signed and the Resumption of Permanent Status Negotiations

The Government of the State of Israel ("GOI") and the Palestinian Liberation Organization ("PLO") commit themselves to full and mutual implementation of the Interim Agreement and all other agreements concluded between them since September 1993 (hereinafter "the prior agreements"), and all outstanding commitments emanating from the prior agreements. Without derogating from the other requirements of the prior agreements, the two Sides have agreed as follows:

1. Permanent Status negotiations

(a)   In the context of the implementation of the prior agreements, the two Sides will resume the Permanent Status negotiations in an accelerated manner and will make a determined effort to achieve their mutual goal of reaching a Permanent Status Agreement based on the agreed agenda ie. the specific issues reserved for Permanent Status negotiations and other issues of common interest;

(b)   The two Sides reaffirm their understanding that the negotiations on the Permanent Status will lead to the implementation of Security Council Resolutions 242 and 338;

(c)   The two Sides will make a determined effort to conclude a Framework Agreement on all Permanent Status issues in five months from the resumption of the Permanent Status negotiations;

(d)   The two Sides will conclude a comprehensive agreement on all Permanent Status issues within one year from the resumption of the Permanent Status negotiations;

(e)   Permanent Status negotiations will resume after the implementation of the first stage of release of prisoners and the second stage of the First and Second Further Redeployments and not later than September 13, 1999. In the Wye River Memorandum,[1] the United States has expressed its willingness to facilitate these negotiations.

---

[1] See the full text of the Wye River Memorandum on p. 479 of this volume.

2. Phase One and Phase Two of the Further Redeployments

The Israeli Side undertakes the following with regard to Phase One and Phase Two of the Further Redeployments:

(a)   On September 5, 1999, to transfer 7 per cent from Area C to Area B;
(b)   On November 15, 1999, to transfer 2 per cent from Area B to Area A and 3 per cent from Area C to Area B;
(c)   On January 20, 2000, to transfer 1 per cent from Area C to Area A, and 5.1 per cent from Area B to Area A.

3 Release of Prisoners

(a)   The two Sides shall establish a joint committee that shall follow up on matters related to release of Palestinian prisoners;
(b)   The Government of Israel shall release Palestinian and other prisoners who committed their offences prior to September 13, 1993, and were arrested prior to May 4, 1994. The Joint Committee shall agree on the names of those who will be released in the first two stages. Those lists shall be recommended to the relevant Authorities through the Monitoring and Steering Committee;
(c)   The first stage of release of prisoners shall be carried out on September 5, 1999 and shall consist of 200 prisoners. The second stage of release of prisoners shall be carried out on October 8, 1999 and shall consist of 150 prisoners;
(d)   The joint committee shall recommend further lists of names to be released to the relevant Authorities through the Monitoring and Steering Committee;
(e)   The Israeli side will aim to release Palestinian prisoners before next Ramadan.

4 Committees

(a)   The Third Further Redeployment Committee shall commence its activities not later than September 13, 1999;
(b)   The Monitoring and Steering Committee, all Interim Committees (i.e. CAC, JEC, JSC, legal committee, people to people), as well as Wye River Memorandum committees, shall resume and/or continue their activity, as the case may be, not later than September 13, 1999. The Monitoring and Steering Committee will have on its agenda, inter alia, the Year 2000, Donor/PA projects in Area C, and the issue of industrial estates;
(c)   The Continuing Committee on displaced persons shall resume its activity on October 1, 1999 (Article XXVII, Interim Agreement);
(d)   Not later than October 30, 1999, the two Sides will implement the recommendations of the Ad-hoc Economic Committee (Article III-6, WRM).

5 Safe Passage

(a)   The operation of the Southern Route of the Safe Passage for the movement of persons, vehicles, and goods will start on October 1, 1999 (Annex I, Article X, Interim Agreement) in accordance with the details of operation, which will be provided for in the Safe Passage Protocol that will be concluded by the two Sides not later than September 30, 1999;
(b)   The two Sides will agree on the specific location of the crossing point of the Northern Route of the Safe Passage as specified in Annex I, Article X, provision c-4, in the Interim Agreement not later than October 5, 1999;
(c)   The Safe Passage Protocol applied to the Southern Route of the Safe Passage shall apply to the Northern Route of the Safe Passage with relevant agreed modifications;

(d)   Upon the agreement on the location of the crossing point of the Northern Route of the Safe Passage, construction of the needed facilities and related procedures shall commence and shall be ongoing. At the same time, temporary facilities will be established for the operation of the Northern Route not later than four months from the agreement on the specific location of the crossing point;

(e)   In between the operation of the Southern crossing point of the Safe Passage and the Northern crossing point of the Safe Passage, Israel will facilitate arrangements for the movement between the West Bank and the Gaza Strip, using non-Safe Passage routes other than the Southern Route of the Safe Passage;

(f)   The location of the crossing points shall be without prejudice to the Permanent Status negotiations (Annex I, Article X, provision e, Interim Agreement).

6 Gaza Sea Port

The two Sides have agreed on the following principles to facilitate and enable the construction works of the Gaza Sea Port. The principles shall not prejudice or preempt the outcome of negotiations on the Permanent Status:

(a)   The Israeli Side agrees that the Palestinian Side shall commence construction works in and related to the Gaza Sea Port on October 1, 1999;

(b)   The two Sides agree that the Gaza Sea Port will not be operated in any way before reaching a joint Sea Port protocol on all aspects of operating the Port, including security;

(c)   The Gaza Sea Port is a special case, like the Gaza Airport, being situated in an area under the responsibility of the Palestinian Side and serving as an international passage. Therefore, until the conclusion of a joint Sea Port Protocol, all activities and arrangements relating to the construction of the Port shall be in accordance with the provisions of the Interim Agreement, especially those relating to international passages, as adapted in the Gaza Airport Protocol;

(d)   The construction shall ensure adequate provision for effective security and customs inspection of people and goods, as well as the establishment of a designated checking area in the Port;

(e)   In this context, the Israeli Side will facilitate on an on-going basis the works related to the construction of the Gaza Sea Port, including the movement in and out of the Port of vessels, equipment, resources, and material required for the construction of the Port;

(f)   The two Sides will coordinate such works, including the designs and movement, through a joint mechanism.

7 Hebron Issues

(a)   The Shuhada Road in Hebron shall be opened for the movement of Palestinian vehicles in two phases. The first phase has been carried out, and the second phase shall be carried out not later than October 30, 1999;

(b)   The wholesale market-Hasbahe will be opened not later than November 1, 1999, in accordance with arrangements which will be agreed upon by the two Sides;

(c)   A high level Joint Liaison Committee will convene not later than September 13, 1999 to review the situation in the Tomb of the Patriarchs/Al Haram Al Ibrahimi (Annex I, Article VII, Interim Agreement and as per the January 15, 1998 US Minute of Discussion).

8 Security

(a)   The two Sides will, in accordance with the prior agreements, act to ensure the immediate, efficient and effective handling of any incident involving a threat or act of terrorism, violence or incitement, whether committed by Palestinians or Israelis. To this end, they will cooperate in the exchange of information and coordinate policies and activities. Each side shall immediately and effectively respond to the occurrence or anticipated occurrence of an act of terrorism, violence or incitement and shall take all necessary measures to prevent such an occurrence;

(b) Pursuant to the prior agreements, the Palestinian side undertakes to implement its responsibilities for security, security cooperation, on-going obligations and other issues emanating from the prior agreements, including, in particular, the following obligations emanating from the Wye River Memorandum:

(1) continuation of the program for the collection of the illegal weapons including reports;
(2) apprehension of suspects including reports;
(3) forwarding the list of Palestinian policemen to the Israeli Side not later than September 13, 1999;
(4) beginning of the review of the list by the Monitoring and Steering Committee not later than October 15, 1999.

9 The two Sides call upon the international donor community to enhance its commitment and financial support to the Palestinian economic development and the Israeli–Palestinian peace process.

10 Recognizing the necessity to create a positive environment for the negotiations, neither side shall initiate or take any step that will change the status of the West Bank and the Gaza Strip in accordance with the Interim Agreement.

11 Obligations pertaining to dates, which occur on holidays or Saturdays, shall be carried out on the first subsequent working day.

This memorandum will enter into force one week from the date of its signature.[1]

Made and signed in Sharm el-Sheik, this fourth day of September, 1999

For the Government of the State of Israel   For the Palestinian Liberation Organization

Witnessed by

For the Arab Republic of Egypt   For the United States of America

For the Hashemite Kingdom of Jordan

[1] It is understood that, for technical reasons, implementation of Article 2-a and the first stage mentioned in Article 3-c will be carried out within a week from the signing of this Memorandum.

Documents

Palestine

Statement of the Palestinian Central Council
Emergency Session
Gaza, 27 April 1999*

The Central Council held a series of meetings within the context of its emergency session which commenced on 27 April. The Council heard a full report presented by President Yassir Arafat, in which he gave an overview of various aspects of the political situation, and outlined the main tasks outstanding on the Palestinian front, at the forefront of which is the completion of the creation of our independent Palestinian state, with holy Jerusalem as its capital.

The President spoke about the Peace Process on the Palestinian and other Arab tracks which had begun at the Madrid Conference on the basis of Land for Peace, and the implementation of Security Council resolutions 242, 338 and 425, stressing that the Israeli Government bears responsibility for the total halt in this process, due to its rescinding on obligations for which it has signed, and its following an aggressive policy targeted at the Palestinian people, their land, and their rights, in flagrant violation of all agreements, covenants and treaties, and in disregard for the global consensus on the rights of the Palestinian people as an essential part of the peace process and a principal ingredient of its advance and its success, as well as in the stability of the situation in the region.

After listening to the report presented by the political leadership regarding the political situation, members of the committee discussed, in a democratic and responsible manner, all possible options that may be endorsed in these crucial times. There was full consensus that the State of Palestine, and its capital, holy Jerusalem, is a reality established on the basis of the natural rights of the Palestinian people to establish their own state, and on the basis of General Assembly resolution number 181 of 1947 and the Declaration of Independence of 1988, and that the Palestinian people with their sacrifice, their steadfastness and their struggle, are the original creators of this state and the determiners of its destiny, and that the Palestinian Liberation Organisation with its national and democratic institutions is the highest source of this national decision, which is neither negotiable nor subject to repeal.

The Council also reached consensus that the current Israeli policy, based on settlement, expansion, and the negation of the Peace Process freezing it in its tracks, as well as on the violation of the national and human rights of the Palestinian people, will in no way break our nation's resolve to obtain its rights and to mobilise all political and popular capacities to protect Palestinian land, the Palestinian people, and Palestinian rights, on the firmly established basis of national unity and the just and legitimate struggle to obtain the one national objective: the objective of terminating the occupation and obtaining self-determination, the establishment of the state, and the resolution of the case of refugees, on the basis of resolution 194, and of international law.

In this context the members of the Central Council paid respect to the presence of colleagues in the Hamas and Jihad movements during the Council's meetings, and affirmed that this initiative is a clear message that our people are united in confronting difficult circumstances, and that to wager on our division is to make a losing wager.

The Council reached consensus that the Palestinian people will not turn their backs on peace, as a strategic choice supported by all nations of the world, and sponsored and emphasised by them as one of the bases of regional and international stability.

The Council prized highly the stances taken by fellow Arab, Islamic and African countries, non-aligned countries, Russia, China and other European and Latin American countries, which were at the forefront in their full recognition of the Palestinian state, with holy Jerusalem as its capital.

The Council also prized the stances taken by the European Union, Norway, Japan and Canada, who supported the Peace Process and declared their recognition of the right of the Palestinian people to self-determination, including the establishment of their state, as a legal, unconditional right and a right that cannot be repealed, and which also took a marked stance on the case of Jerusalem and its sovereignty.

The Council received with much attention the letter of President Bill Clinton in which he stressed the commitment of the United States of America to the realisation of the objectives of the Peace Process, embodied in the implementation of resolutions 242 and 338, and the principle of Land for Peace, and his support of the aspirations of the Palestinian people to live freely on their own land, and also in consideration of settlements as factors destructive to the Peace Process.

The Council lauded the wide-ranging movements and consistent and productive efforts exerted by President Yassir Arafat on the Arab and international fronts, and which bore the fruit of a qualitative development in the stances of the world's nations regarding the Palestinian State, further establishment of its international legitimacy, and the development of its current and future relations.

The Council gave great importance to the passing of the five years set in the interim agreement, without the fulfilment of the requirements of this stage, at the forefront of which is Israeli withdrawal from the land, before the fulfilment of the final agreement between both parties. There was consensus that the reason for this is basically due to the policies and stances of the Israeli side, which bears full responsibility for the freezing of the Peace Process.

Consequently, the Central Council calls upon the international community and the United Nations, and particularly the sponsor countries and the countries which are signatory to the agreements, to work to compel Israel to implement its obligations in accordance with the agreements ratified between the Israeli Government and the Palestinian Liberation Organisation, in a way which would lead to the implementation of Security Council resolutions 242 and 338, and other pertinent international resolutions.

At the end of the sessions which the Council held over three days, the Council made the following resolutions:

First: To consider the meetings of the current session of the Council open, on condition that it reconvenes in a general meeting during the coming month of June.

Second: To move forward in taking the necessary steps and procedures to complete the fabric of the state and its institutions, and the dedication to its sovereignty, through forming a number of working committees, including the special committee for drawing up the draft constitution of the state. In this context the Council welcomes the response of the Secretary General of the League of Arab States, Dr Esmat Abdul Meguid, to the Palestinian request to form a Higher Arab Committee headed by him, to help draw up the draft constitution.

Third: The Central Council entrusts the Executive Committee with studying the sponsor countries' correspondence and with dealing with the correspondence in a manner which realises the higher interests of the Palestinian people.

Fourth: The Council stresses the central importance of the city of Jerusalem, and that all measures and plans which Israel has undertaken and still undertakes as an occupying force in Jerusalem and elsewhere, are null and void, illegal, and to be desisted from, and whose result must be reversed. In this context the Council affirms pertinent UN resolutions, and highly appraises the latest stance of the European Union regarding Jerusalem. It also values highly the steadfast stances of Arab, Islamic and non-aligned countries, in connection with Jerusalem.

Fifth: the Council calls upon all active groups amongst our people to confront with all national capacities the policy of settlements and the dispossession of land and demolition of homes, of building circular roads and highways, and the racist actions of Judaization which are taking place in Jerusalem and in all Palestinian lands, and the Council affirms, on the basis of international law and the resolutions of the General Assembly and the Security Council of the United Nations, the illegality and invalidity of these aggressive policies and practices. The Council entrusts the Executive Committee with taking necessary measures to confront this danger, and in this context the Council welcomes the convening of a conference of the parties signatory to the Fourth Geneva Convention on 15 July 1999, and calls for the taking of measures established in the Convention to compel Israel to implement this (convention) in occupied Palestinian lands.

Sixth: The Council lauds the steadfastness of our heroic prisoners and detainees in the occupation's prisons, and stresses its insistence that they be set free, and that their suffering be terminated.

Seventh: The Council stresses the need to consolidate the process of building the nation and dedicating to the rule of law and to democratic practices and the institutions of civil society.

The Central Council lauds the steadfastness of our great people and its rallying round its national leadership, and calls for further vigilance and preparedness during these historical moments in the destiny of our every struggling people, and affirms in all confidence that the dawn is coming, and that victory is nigh.

In the Name of God, the Merciful, the Compassionate: "We will favour our prophets and those who have faith in this life and in the day of reckoning".

The Casablanca Declaration of the Arab Human Rights Movement*

Adopted by the First International Conference of the Arab Human Rights Movement
Casablanca, 23–25April 1999

THE CAIRO INSTITUTE FOR HUMAN RIGHTS STUDIES

CIHRS is a professional, non-governmental research centre specialized in the study of human rights in the Arab world. CIHRS was found in April 1993 and started its activities in April 1994. The Institute views itself as part of the international and Arab human rights movement.

CIHRS is an Arab regional centre concerned with studying the structural factors affecting the human rights situation in the Arab world and finding approaches to upgrade them, giving special attention to issues of cultural specificity, human rights education and the dissemination of human rights culture.

CIHRS' activities include conceptual and applied research, education programmes, seminars, courses, periodical and non-periodical publications, as well as providing research facilities and consultation to interested researchers.

CIHRS conducts several programmes, and publishes a number of series of publications, a bulletin, a quarterly studies journal, in addition to two journals that feature translated articles from *MERIP* (Middle East Report) and *Reproductive Health Matters* in consultation with their editorial boards.

The Institute does not associate with any kind of politicized activity, and cooperates with other institutions on an equal basis in all political matters, except when it come to the International Human Rights Law.

CIHRS enjoys special consultative status with the Economic and Social Council of the United Nations and an observer status with the African Commission on Human and Peoples' Rights.

---

* Taken from the original English text. © Cairo Institute for Human Rights Studies, Cairo, Egypt.

THE FIRST INTERNATIONAL CONFERENCE OF THE ARAB HUMAN RIGHTS MOVEMENT: PROSPECTS FOR THE FUTURE

The Conference was organized by the Cairo Institute for Human Rights Studies (CIHRS) and hosted by the Moroccan Organization for Human Rights on 23–25 April in Casablanca, Morocco. It was attended by 100 participants and observers representing 40 human rights organizations from 15 Arab countries, in addition to a number of international experts as observers. The assembly of the participants culminated two months of discussion via fax and e-mail, in deliberation of 16 working papers. Based on these discussions, a draft "Casablanca Declaration" was prepared and discussed by the Consultative Panel (23 members from 10 countries) before the conference. The second draft of the Declaration was ready on 22 April. During three days the conference participants discussed a number of important issued in 16 parallel working groups and four panel sessions. The First Arab Human Rights Book Fair was held on the fringes of the Conference.

The Conference adopted the Casablanca Declaration and a programmatic document entitled "The Tasks of the Arab Human Rights Movement". It also issued a special decision in solidarity with human rights defenders in Tunisia and Syria.

THE CASABLANCA DECLARATION

At the invitation of the Cairo Institute for Human Rights Studies, and hosted by the Moroccan Organization for Human Rights, the *First International Conference of the Arab Human Rights Movement: Prospects for the Future* was held in Casablanca from 23 to 25 April 1999, to examine the human rights conditions in the Arab world, and the responsibilities, tasks and prospects of the Arab human rights movement.

After extensive discussions, the Conference declared that the only source of reference in this respect is international human rights law and the United Nations instruments and declarations. The Conference also emphasized the universality of human rights.

The International Setting

The Conference examined the international setting and conditions affecting the status of human rights specifically in the Arab world and affirmed the following:

–   The call for substantial reforms in the Untied Nations so as to make it more representative of the regions and peoples of the world, and more effective in fulfilling its role and in expressing the common interests and responsibilities of humanity.
–   The importance of drawing the attention to the grave consequences of using the principles of human rights for the realization of specific foreign policy objectives of some countries. It affirms that the Arab world is still suffering from the opportunistic, political and propagandist use of human rights by some major powers as evidenced by the double-standards employed by such powers, most notably the United States of America.
–   Calling upon the UN Security Council to review the international sanctions system and its application methods. The Conference also urges the UN Security Council to decide to immediately and unconditionally end the economic sanctions on Iraq, consid-

ering that their devastating effects on the civilian population could be likened to genocide.

– Rejecting the manipulation by some Arab governments of patriotic sentiments and the principle of sovereignty so as to avoid complying with international human rights standards.

– Rejecting any attempt to use civilizational or religious specificity to contest the universality of human rights. Commendable specificity is that which entrenches the dignity and equality of citizens, enriches their culture and promotes their participation in the administration of public affairs.

Peace and the Rights of Peoples and Minorities in the Arab World

The Conference declares its support for the proposed UN Decade for the Culture of Peace and affirms that acceptable peace is that which is based on respect for fundamental rights, justice and peoples' inherent dignity. It should also be based upon the provisions of international law, the UN resolutions, and the due respect of human rights – most notably the right to self-determination.

The rights of the Palestinian people are the proper standard to measure the consistency of international positions towards a just peace and human rights. The Arab human rights movement will apply this standard in its relations with the different international organizations and actors.

The Conference declares its full support for the right of the Palestinian people to self-determination and to establish their independent state on their occupied national soil – with Jerusalem as its capital – and the right of return for the refugees and to compensation in accordance with UN resolutions. The Conference demands the dismantling of settlements, the elimination of all forms of racial discrimination and human rights violations against the Arabs of Israel, and the elimination of the racist Zionism and the expansionist nature of Israel.

The establishment of a just peace requires the immediate and unconditional withdrawal of Israel from the Golan Heights and South Lebanon in accordance with UN Security Council resolutions.

Meanwhile, the Conference calls upon the contracting parties of the Fourth Geneva Convention on the Protection of Civilian Persons in Times of War to fulfil their legal obligations and to work towards compelling the Israeli occupation forces to apply the provisions of the Convention, considering that these provisions constitute the minimum standards required for the protection and safety of Palestinian civilians. In this regard, the Conference affirms that it is necessary that the High Contracting Parties comply with the UN General Assembly resolution to hold a special conference of the High Contracting Parties on 15 July 1999 to examine the measures required for the enforcement of the provisions of the Convention in the occupied territories. The Conference also calls upon international and Arab NGOs to join the international campaign to urge the High Contracting Parties of the Fourth Geneva Convention to work towards enforcing its provisions in the occupied territories.

The Conference values the positions of NGOs and states in support of the rights of the Palestinian people and the position of the European Union among them – especially the EU's refusal to recognize the Israeli stance on Jerusalem. The Conference also hails the European Commission's recommendation to embargo the goods produced in the Israeli settlements and calls upon all states to adopt similar positions.

The Conference urges the Palestinian National Authority to respect human rights, to establish the separation of powers, to dissolve State Security Courts, and to release political prisoners.

In discussing the issue of minorities in the Arab world, the Conference affirms its commitment to the right to self-determination and its strong condemnation of all acts of oppression, despotism and war that have been and are still being committed against minorities in the Arab world, especially the genocide, displacement and enslavement. The Conference affirms that the Arab human rights movement will treat such actions as crimes against humanity.

In this context, the Conference declares its support for the Kurdish people's right to self-determination and calls upon the United Nations to convene a special international conference with the participation of all the concerned parties to reach an integrated and comprehensive solution to the continued suffering of the Kurdish people.

The Conference also calls for an end to the war in Sudan and urges the establishment of peace within the framework of a formula that ensures the establishment of a democratic system of political plurality, participation in public life, and respect for human rights without discrimination between citizens – including securing the right of the citizens of South Sudan to self-determination.

The General Conditions of Human Rights in the Arab World

Despite the relative relaxation in the human rights situation in a number of Arab countries, the general picture remains gloomy in comparison with the progress realized in other parts of the world. This is exacerbated by the failure of the League of Arab States to provide an effective regional conflict-resolution system and mechanisms for the protection of human rights in the Arab world.

The Conference expresses its alarm at the continued absence of a modern legal structure in a number of Arab countries. This includes the lack of a constitution, a parliament and a modern judicial system, in addition to their persistent rejection of international human rights standards. This applies to Saudi Arabia and a number of Gulf states.

The Conference discussed at length the continuation of acts that completely suppress fundamental rights and freedoms and the persistence of legal systems based upon the codification of cruelty and violence in Iraq, Libya, Syria, Sudan and Bahrain. This is despite their accession to some of the most fundamental international human rights conventions and agreements. The Conference also discussed the prevalence in these countries of grave and flagrant human rights violations that cannot be accurately monitored because of the absence of the minimum requirements for fact-finding.

The Conference draws attention to the fact that acts of external aggression and military or economic violence against Iraq and Libya further aggravate the human rights situation there.

The Conference affirms that the acts of violence and armed internal conflicts, as in Somalia and Sudan, constitute in themselves a grave violation of the rights to life, physical integrity, life in peace and all other rights.

While expressing its concern at the situation in Algeria since the cancellation of elections in 1992, the Conference strongly condemns the crimes and massacres committed by armed groups and military militias against tens of thousands of citizens. The Conference also condemns the grave human rights violations committed by the state, specifically the enforced disappearance of thousands of people.

The Conference examined the human rights situation in the other Arab countries, which are characterized by defects in the rule of law and in institutional, legislative and other safeguards for the enjoyment of human rights and fundamental freedoms, in addition to infringements of the principle of the independence of the judiciary. These conditions lead to grave and systematic violations of human rights, especially the crime of torture. The Conference regrets the reversal in some countries, which had realized some relative improvement in the condition of human rights, such as Tunisia, Egypt, Yemen and Jordan.

The Conference welcomes the relative progress in the general human rights situation in Morocco in the last decade, due to the efforts of the Moroccan and international human rights organizations.

In this respect the Conference affirms the following:

1.   Generating pressure to reform and upgrade the institutions of the League of Arab States and to achieve the legislative and practical reforms necessary for safeguarding human rights and for ensuring the participation in and monitoring of these institutions by Arab citizens.

2.   Calling upon the League of Arab States to review all its conventions relating to human rights – especially the Arab Agreement on Combating Terrorism – and also to review the Arab Charter of Human Rights of 1994, with a view to drafting a new Arab convention on human rights, in cooperation with Arab human rights NGOs, so as to make it compatible with international standards. The Conference decided to form a working group to prepare a draft proposal for such a convention.

3.   Generating pressure to reform the legislation of Arab countries, especially those that contravene the freedoms of opinion, expression, and dissemination of information and the right to knowledge. Working towards ending the state's control of all media, and demanding that Arab governments legalize, in the framework of democratic constitutions and laws, the rights of assembly and peaceful association for all intellectual and political groups and forces, including the unarmed political Islamic groups.

4.   Calling upon all political Islamic groups to renounce violence and to end its practice, and calling upon the intellectual and political community and forces to abstain from practising intellectual terrorism through calling others apostates or traitors or defaming their characters.

5.   The need to initiate substantial political reforms in Iraq leading to a democratic system and constitution that would bring about the equality of citizens, abolish political confessionalism, allow for diversity as a basis of national unity according to the principle of equality in citizenship, and enshrine fundamental human rights.

6.   Calling for an end to the exceptional situation in Sudan and for convening a comprehensive constitutional conference with the participation of all the political and civil forces so as to ensure the restoration of democracy and peace.

7.   Calling for the consolidation of the political reforms begun in 1989 in Algeria so as to prepare the ground for ending violence and laying down arms; releasing those detained without trial; retrying those who had been tried under exceptional laws; revealing the fate of the "disappeared"; and bringing those responsible for the crimes of disappearance, torture and killing to justice. The Conference stresses the need for governments to respond to just and legitimate initiatives for opening a serious dialogue to establish peace and broaden public freedoms.

Responsibilities of the Arab Human Rights Movement

1.   Promoting the *struggle for democracy* and basing the general strategy of the movement on such a task. The Conference reaffirms that the aims of preserving the non-partisan nature of the movement and ensuring its independence from political parties do not exclude working towards a constant dialogue between human rights organizations and all political parties. Such a dialogue should aim at cooperation to consolidate democratic transformation and respect for human rights, and to draft a code of minimum stan-

dards for the respect of human rights and democracy that takes into consideration the specific political and social context of every single country.

2. Determining the *common priorities* of the Arab human rights movement in the realms of advocacy and protection. These include the following:
    -   Putting a final end to the practice of torture, and pursuing its perpetrators and bringing them to justice.
    -   Annulling martial and emergency laws, and affirming the need to respect freedoms of expression, assembly and association.
    -   Ending administrative and preventive detention and releasing all prisoners of conscience and those detained without charge or trial.
    -   Opposing exceptional courts, campaigning for laws and safeguards which guarantee the independence of the judiciary from any administrative manipulation or intervention.
    -   Introducing necessary reforms to the basic laws, revoking exceptional laws, and putting an end to arbitrary and extra-judicial executions or those resulting from unfair trials.

3. Struggling for the realization of *economic and social rights*, considering that human rights are integrated, indivisible and are not exchangeable. In this respect the Conference affirms:
    -   Securing citizens' rights to participation, including guaranteeing public oversight of the public revenues of the state, is the backbone of the application of the *right to development*.

4. Struggling for entrenching the values of *human rights in the Arab and Islamic culture*. This includes the following:
    -   Urging those Arab governments that did not ratify international human rights instruments to do so immediately and without reservations, and urging those that ratified them to lift their reservations, and to comply with the provisions of such instruments regarding the mechanisms of protection
    -   Urging academics, researchers and religious scholars to shed light on the roots of human rights in the Arab culture, to exhibit the contribution of the Islamic civilization in establishing the value of human rights, and to dismantle the artificial contradictions between some human rights principles and some obsolete fundamentalist interpretations. Calling upon all Arab intellectuals and politicians to refrain from entangling Islam in a confrontation with human rights, and to consider those rights provided by international human rights law as a minimum to build upon and not seek to reduce or call for their violation in the name of specificity or any other pretext.

5. Struggling for the recognition of *women's rights* as an integral part of the human rights system. This includes the affirmation of the following:
    -   Women's enjoyment of human rights in an integrated and comprehensive process that should encompass all facets of life within and outside the family.
    -   Real equality between women and men goes beyond legal equality to encompass changing the conceptions and confronting the stereotypes about women. Thus, it requires not only a comprehensive review of laws, foremost of which are personal status codes, but also the review and upgrading of educational curricula as well as the critical monitoring of the media discourse.
    -   In this respect, the Conference stresses the necessity of engaging women's and human rights NGOs in the process of reviewing current legislation and in upgrading

civil and criminal laws, with a view to resolutely confronting all forms of violence and discrimination against women.
- The Conference also calls upon the Arab governments that did not ratify the Convention on the Elimination of All Forms of Discrimination Against Women to do so expeditiously, and those that ratified it to lift their reservations.
- It also calls upon women's and human rights NGOs to work to refute these reservations, to challenge the culture of discrimination, and to adopted courageous stances in exposing the practice of hiding behind religion to legitimize the subordination of women. These NGOs should also give special attention to the continued monitoring of the compliance by Arab governments to their international commitments concerning women's enjoyment of their rights.
- The necessity of considering the possibility of allocating a quota for women in parliaments, representative institutions and public bodies as a temporary measure. This should stand until appropriate frameworks for women's voluntary activity take shape and until the awareness of the necessity of equality and the elimination of all forms of discrimination increases.

6. Confronting the violations of the *rights of the child* in the Arab world, especially those emanating from economic sanctions, the aggravation of armed conflicts in some countries, and the increase in the phenomena of street children and child labour. In this respect the Conference calls for the following:
    - Crminalising the engagement of children in armed conflicts, and supporting efforts aimed at raising the minimum age of military conscription to 18 years.
    - Prohibiting the employment of children in occupations that may harm their health, security, or morals.
    - Prohibiting the implementation of capital punishment in crimes committed by children under 18 years of age; this is until the abolition of capital punishment entirely.
    - Prohibiting the confinement of children in the detention places of adults.

7. Disseminating *human rights education* and culture on the basis that the first line of defence of human rights is citizens' awareness of their rights and their readiness to defend them. In this respect, the Conference has decided on the following:
    - The need to overcome all obstacles preventing access to the fora provided by the media and the educational institutions to disseminate the message of human rights. It is necessary to try by all means to convince governments to facilitate the work of human rights education institutions, to add the subject of human rights to the educational curricula, and to uproot all that contravenes the values of human rights from the current curricula.
    - Consolidating cooperation with the fora of artistic creativity and other non-governmental organizations in the realm of disseminating the culture of human rights, and focusing on some intermediary strata that could be able to play a vital role in this sphere, such as teachers, media personnel, judges and lawyers. In addition, it is necessary to design suitable plans to activate the role of preachers in mosques and churches in this respect.

8. With respect to upgrading and advancing the capabilities of the Arab human rights movement, the Conference draws attention to the signs of substantial developments in *international criminal justice* manifested by the opening for ratification of the Convention on the International Criminal Court, and also the possibility of bringing to justice the torturer Pinochet. The Conference affirms that such developments open the door to the possibility of trying war criminals and perpetrators of crimes against humanity.

This necessitates that human rights defenders develop new methodologies and tools to collect and document information that could be used as evidence before such trials.

9.　Protecting *human rights defenders* and their rights to receive information, hold meetings, contact all the concerned sides, and make use of local and international law to defend human rights.

In this respect, the Conference

- Absolutely condemns all the reservations made by 13 Arab states to the Declaration on the Right and Responsibility of Individuals, Groups and Organs of Society to Promote and Protect Universally Recognized Human Rights and Fundamental Freedoms;
- Affirms that the conduct of any Arab government toward human rights defenders will be the determinant by which, negatively or positively, the Arab human rights movement will deal with it;
- Stresses that it is necessary for human rights defenders to commit themselves to the professional standards and political neutrality, which require defending the victims of human rights violations regardless of their political or ideological affiliations. It is also necessary that human rights defenders apply the rules of democratic review established in the structures of civil associations and exercise complete transparency regarding their financing sources and expenditures. The Conference considers that the commitment to these principles is consistent with the very essence of the task of defending human rights. This calls for the founding of a body to represent civil society in overseeing the performance of human rights NGOs and their commitment to these standards.

10.　*Coordination between the Arab human rights NGOs*:

The Conference affirms that the minimum standard required for the fulfilment of these responsibilities and recommendations necessitates the elevation of bilateral and collective cooperation between Arab human rights NGOs to the highest level. Given the lack of national and regional coordination mechanisms and structures on the local and regional levels, the Conference considers these tasks of utmost importance. There is an urgent need for reviewing the present structure of relations between its components on the local, regional and international levels, taking into consideration the quantitative and qualitative developments of the human rights movement in the South. The movement should strive to found a new international mechanism based on continuous and dynamic consultation to promote the relationships of partnership and parity among its components. This is to help further the effectiveness of the movement on the international, regional and local levels.

Sana'a Declaration of the Emerging Democracies Forum

Sana'a (Saba) – We who attended the Emerging Democracies Forum in Sana'a, Yemen from 27 to 30 June 1999 from 16 countries, assembled to acknowledge our democratic achievements, to address common challenges we face in the transition to full democracy and to reaffirm our commitment to democratic rights and principles. The forum was a unique gathering, bringing together a diverse group of participants and countries whose democratic advances are less known.

We recognize that the transition process is not complete and that much needs to be done to consolidate our democratic systems and to implement further political and economic reforms.

While we are proud to have joined the growing community of democracies, the international community has tended to focus on countries that are considered strategically more important or are in crisis. However, democratic progress in our states contributes to peace, stability and prosperity both within and beyond our borders.

Reflecting the importance of all sectors of society in this endeavour, the participants at the forum included government officials, members of governing and opposition parties and representatives of labour, business and civic groups from Benin, Bolivia, El Salvador, Georgia, Ghana, Guatemala, Guyana, Macedonia, Malawi, Mali, Mongolia, Morocco, Mozambique, Namibia, Nepal and Yemen. We represent a diversity of democratic experience, but our attendance at this forum demonstrates the universality of the democratic idea. This group of nations with different traditions, cultures and historical experiences was brought together by a shared commitment to democracy and a belief that the promise of economic prosperity enjoyed by all citizens is more likely realized in a democratic political environment based on respect for human rights, popular participation and the rule of law. Further we share a commitment to:

- pursue economic reforms and secure fundamental workers' rights, while making every effort to educate and build widespread consensus for these goals;
- improve protection for human rights for all our people;
- hold regular free and fair elections, with special attention to the need to build public confidence in the process;
- develop our legislatures as an essential instrument for broad public participation as well as for policy debate and oversight of government;
- improve democratic governance at local levels;

- deepen our commitment to, and implement measures to ensure, the full participation of women in political life;
- ensure that the rights of minorities are represented and that every effort is made to engage marginalized groups in the political process;
- support the strengthening of civil society;
- uphold the freedom of the press;
- address the urgent challenge of corruption by instituting meaningful reforms, including those that increase governmental transparency; and
- foster judicial independence, enhance public access to legal redress and ensure that the laws are fairly applied to all.

These are the principles that brought us to Yemen, which we discussed in the context of our specific experiences. Following are some examples of measures recommended by forum participants that give concrete expression to our shared democratic principles.

The successful implementation of economic reforms is enhanced by:

- transparent and inclusive decision-making; the involvement of civil servants, the public, labour, business groups and political parties in the design and implementation of reforms;
- a social safety net to meet human needs and/or a complementary poverty alleviation programme; and
- a recognition of the role of the civic sector in the implementation of economic reforms, including the use of such groups to help deliver government-founded social services.

Public confidence in elections is enhanced by:

- working towards the establishment of independent election commissions that are non-partisan or politically balanced;
- regulating by legislation, government financing of elections to ensure that they are fair and equitable for all parties; and
- inviting election observers, whether domestic or international, to mount more comprehensive efforts, including the monitoring of registration.

The legitimacy of parties and legislatures is advanced by:

- the adoption of political parties of internal democratic procedures, ongoing training of political leaders and elected officials, and public accountability, and transparency;
- the implementation of legislative procedures that ensure public access to plenary and committee meetings, the holding of public hearings; and
- regulating by legislation, government financing of elections to ensure that they are fair and equitable for all parties.

Public participation democratic decision making is enhanced by:

- providing for private ownership of media and ensuring the impartiality of state-owned media through independent boards or other means;
- ensuring that governments and political parties take measures to increase the number of women in parliament and appoint women to key government posts;
- conducting civic education in schools, non-governmental organizations, parties and the media to address cultural attitudinal and legal barriers to the political and economic participation of women;

– encouraging governments and legislatures to enhance the viability of non-governmental organizations, including removing legal barriers and providing tax exempt status; and engaging non-governmental organizations in policy debates.

The achievement of good governance, the improvement of administration, controlling corruption and strengthening the rule of law can be advanced by:

– instituting public information mechanisms, such as budget transparency, freedom of information laws and the publication of regulations;
– depoliticising and professionalising the civil service;
– implementing a comprehensive programme to fight corruption, including institutions such as politically independent anti-corruption;
– commissions, ombudsmen and auditors general, codes of conduct and financial disclosure rules, and open procurement processes.

As a result of this conference, we hope to establish mechanisms between our countries to continue the sharing of ideas and experiences through consultations, exchange programmes, an interactive web and other means.

We also look forward to working together in a variety of international fora to promote democratic principles and practices. We intend to support the efforts of other countries that are beginning the process of democratic transition.

The participants express our appreciation to the President, the government and the people of Yemen and to the governments, organizations and corporations that helped organize and make possible this first emerging democracies forum.

Beirut Declaration
Recommendations of the First Arab Conference on Justice
Beirut, 14–16 June 1999*

Convened by the Arab Center for the Independence of the Judiciary and the Legal Profession (ACIJLP) in collaboration with the Geneva-based Center for the Independence of Judges and Lawyers (CIJL), hosted by the Bar Association in Beirut, and under the auspices of the Lebanese Minister of Justice, 110 Arab jurists from 13 Arab states participated in a conference on "The Judiciary in the Arab Region and the Challenges of the 21st Century". The conference, held on 14-16 June 1999, focused on four main topics:

1. The main challengers faced by judiciary institutions in the Arab region in the 21st century.
2. The main impediments and problems related to the independence of the judiciary in the Arab region.
3. The judiciary in the Arab region and international standards on human rights and the independence of the judiciary.
4. The basic safeguards for the independence of the judiciary in the Arab region.

The participants discussed the ability of the judiciary in the region to confront the various challenges resulting form international political and economic transformations and the new technological challenges. The ability to confront such challenges depends on the existence of real support for the independence of the judiciary in the Arab region.

Moreover, the judiciary's capacity to be a substantial power in Arab countries and to be an active party in entrenching democratic principles and the rule of law is pending on the progress of democratic development and respect for the law, including the subjection of the main powers to it. The discussions stressed that democracy is progressing with difficulty, which in turn affects the development of the judiciary in many Arab countries.

In the conference, participants discussed several papers and other issues in detail. They stressed the importance of articulating and implementing a set of recommendations which would be put into effect by individuals, jurist institutions and Arab governments. This action would serve as real support for the judiciary in enabling it to confront the challenges of

---

* Text provided by the Arab Center for the Independence of the Judiciary and the Legal Profession (ACIJLP), Cairo, Egypt.

the coming century, and would also contribute towards entrenching the rule of law and democracy in the Arab region.

The participants proposed the following recommendations.

First: Safeguards for the Judiciary

1. To include the UN Basic Principles on the Independence of the Judiciary into Arab constitutions and laws, and in particular, to penalize any interference in the work of the judiciary.
2. The state shall guarantee an independent budget for the judiciary, including all its branches and institutions. This budget shall be included as one item into the state budget, and shall be determined upon the advice of the higher judicial councils within the judicial bodies.
3. The executive power shall not intervene in the activities of judicial inspection in any form, nor shall it breach the independence of the judiciary through orders or circulars.
4. The public prosecution shall be considered a branch of the judiciary. The authority undertaking this prosecution shall be separate from those of investigation and referral.
5. Judges shall have immunity associated with their jobs. Except in cases of illegal acts, no judicial measures shall be taken unless upon a permission issued by the highest council.
6. Law suits shall not be transferred from the judges reviewing them unless for reasons related to incompetence.
7. It is important to reform the administrative structure and other work mechanisms pertaining to the work of judges, and to facilitate the means for an efficient administration of justice.
8. To link the work of the judiciary with a democratic environment on the basis that democracy is the approach for a more effective management of justice.
9. Lawsuits shall be distributed among judges of various courts through their general assemblies or according to their internal regulations in case such assemblies do not exist. Such distribution shall be made in a manner that guarantees the non-intervention of the executive.
10. Judges shall freely practice freedom of assembly in order to represent their different interests. In this regard, they shall have the right to establish an organization to protect their interests and guarantee their constant promotion.

Second: Electing and Appointing Judges

11. The election of judges shall be free of discrimination on basic of race, color, sex, faith, language, national origin, social status, birth, property, political belonging, or any other consideration. Particularly when electing judges, the principle of equal opportunity must be followed to guarantee that all applicants for a judicial position are objectively assessed.
12. Assuming the position of judge shall be possible, without discrimination, for all those who meet its requirements. The appointment of judges shall be made through the higher councils of the concerned judicial bodies.
13. No judges shall be appointed by virtue of temporary contracts. They cannot be disciplined unless by boards made from their bodies, provided that the decisions made by such boards shall not have immunity against being challenged, unless the decision is made by the highest council of the concerned judicial body.
14. The law shall stipulate the rules for appointing, delegating, transferring, promoting, and disciplining judges, as well as for all other matters related to their affairs, particu-

larly those concerning their livelihood while in office and in retirement. The aim of this is to guarantee in all cases their independence from the executive.

15.   A percentage of no less than 25 per cent of vacant judicial posts shall be allocated to lawyers and those working in legal issues, provided that the appointment is made by the highest judicial boards in the concerned judicial bodies.

Three: Qualification and Training of Judges

16.   The state shall endeavor, through specialized centers and institutes, to provide judges with an effective legal training in order to prepare them adequately to assume judicial posts. All aspects of the study and training programs shall be subject to the supervision of the judiciary.
      In the professional preparation of judges, the following principles shall be observed:
      (a)   To activate the Arab convention issued in Amman pertaining to the cooperation in the professional qualification of judges, and to reinforce the role of non-governmental organizations to secure their support for qualification programs and to serve as intellectual entities for judges, particularly in the field of human rights.
      (b)   These qualification programs shall focus on legal and professional training, as well as personal growth. The qualification programs shall particularly focus on managing and facilitating the role of the defense.
      (c)   To develop national institutions specializing in qualifying judges, whether by developing courses or financial and information resources supported by modern technological systems, in such a way that would guarantee the modernization of the judiciary, change educational courses in the faculties of law and develop infrastructure for the legal profession.

17.   To support continuous judicial education in developing an in-depth understanding of constitutional provisions in a way that would guarantee constitutional legitimacy, the structure of which is connected with the intelligent understanding of human rights.

18.   To urge the judicial authorities to constantly refer to international human rights treaties ratified by states, as being part of the states' legal structure and a framework of the values which societies should adopt and try to implement.

19.   To make the exchange of legal expertise between judges and lawyers, supporting human rights and freedoms, a firm methodology of Arab states, and a planned attitude of their legal systems in order to guarantee the objectiveness of their application and their consistence with modern concepts of advanced countries.

20.   To develop educational law courses in Arab countries that will give special consideration to human rights and freedoms and constitutional legitimacy, and affirm solidarity with efforts made by the United Nations in this regard.

Fourth: Judicial Review on Constitutionality of Laws

21.   States with no system for judicial review on the constitutionality of laws shall adopt such a system whether through establishing a supreme constitutional court for this purpose, or establishing constitutional councils to assume this task, provided that they are made of members of judicial bodies, lawyers, and law professors, and in a way that would guarantee the independence of such a court or council and secure the soundness of practicing its constitutional responsibility. All members of such a court or council shall be appointed without the intervention of the executive. The right of individuals to bring a constitutional lawsuit by means of original claim shall be guaranteed.

Fifth: Safeguards for the Rights of the Defense and a Fair Trial

22. To call on Arab states to ratify the optional protocol to the International Covenant on Civil and Political Rights (ICCPR), which enables individuals to bring their case before the Human Rights Committee after having exhausted national means of challenging through national judiciary without being able to obtain their rights.
23. Every defendant shall be guaranteed an attorney of his/her choice. In case the defendant is unable to afford lawyer's fees, the judicial authority shall appoint a lawyer to the defendant.
24. Laws applied in Arab states shall set short periods for suspension whether in the stage of gathering information or during interrogations. During these two stages, the minimum human rights and freedoms must be observed including the right to a defense, as well as the constraints necessary to protect human rights and freedoms and secure everyone's right to refrain from making statements that would condemn him.
25. No suspension shall be made against misdemeanours of which the sentence is no more than one year in prison. Also, those in preventive detention shall not be denied their right to obtain, from the state, a suitable compensation for his imprisonment in case there is legal ground.
26. Decisions on judicial litigation must be made according to previously set legal rules which respect human rights and freedoms, provided that parties have equal chances to a defense, whether with respect to the actual dispute or its legal factors.
27. Judicial disputes shall only be decided on by judges who are the most objective given the nature of the case and the circumstances surrounding it.
28. Only natural judges shall decide on disputes of a judicial nature.
29. There must be a guarantee that any trial, be it civil or criminal, is heard within a reasonable time that would secure a fair trial. Trials shall be conducted with modern technical means as much as can be provided.
30. Refraining from implementing judicial rulings by law enforcement officials is a crime the penalty of which shall be stiffened. Impeding the implementation of rulings shall be considered as refraining from the implementation.

Sixth: Women and the Position of Judge

31. No discrimination is permitted between men and women with respect to assuming the judicial responsibility. Women shall not be subject to any discrimination for assuming this position.
32. The rights achieved by Arab women in the field of the judiciary shall be supported and extended. Existing laws shall be cleared from impediments which prevent or restrict the practice of these rights.
33. Links shall be made between the issue of women's rights in the society and cultural and social development in concerned Arab countries. Studies which stress women's rights in conscious work and in society shall be conducted.
34. To exchange experiences among Arab countries to support equal rights for men and women while practicing judicial work.

Seventh: The International Criminal Court

35. To assert the role of the International Criminal Court and call upon Arab states to sign its Statute to support the Court and guarantee the effective practicing of its jurisdiction.

36. To call upon Arab states to increase participation in preparatory meetings assigned to set the procedural rules of the Court in order to form a general trend with respect to the Court's safeguards, and particularly its independence from the Security Council.

Part IV

Selected Cases

Arbitral Award

In the Matter of the Arbitration between Eritrea and Yemen*

IN THE MATTER OF AN ARBITRATION
PURSUANT TO AN AGREEMENT TO ARBITRATE
DATED 3 OCTOBER 1996

BETWEEN:
THE GOVERNMENT OF THE STATE OF ERITREA

and

THE GOVERNMENT OF THE REPUBLIC OF YEMEN

AWARD OF THE ARBITRAL TRIBUNAL
IN THE FIRST STAGE OF THE PROCEEDINGS
(TERRITORIAL SOVEREIGNTY AND SCOPE OF THE DISPUTE)

CHAPTER 1: The Setting up of the Arbitration and the Arguments of the Parties

Introduction

1. This Award is rendered pursuant to an Arbitration Agreement dated 3 October 1996 (the "Arbitration Agreement") between the Government of the State of Eritrea ("Eritrea") and the Government of the Republic of Yemen ("Yemen") (hereinafter "the Parties").
2. The Arbitration Agreement was preceded by an "Agreement on Principles" done at Paris on 21 May 1996, which was signed by Eritrea and Yemen and witnessed by the Governments of the French Republic, the Federal Democratic Republic of Ethiopia, and the Arab Republic of Egypt. The Parties renounced recourse to force against each other, and undertook to "settle their dispute on questions of territorial sovereignty and de-

---

* Extracts from the original text. Due to a lack of space, we have only reproduced Chapters I and X of the Agreement.

limitation of maritime boundaries peacefully". They agreed, to that end, to establish an agreement instituting an arbitral tribunal. The Agreement on Principles further provided that

> . . . concerning questions of territorial sovereignty, the Tribunal shall decide in accordance with the principles, rules and practices of international law applicable to the matter, and on the basis, in particular, of historic titles.

3. Concurrently with the Agreement on Principles, the Parties issued a brief Joint Statement, emphasizing their desire to settle the dispute, and "to allow the re-establishment and development of a trustful and lasting cooperation between the two countries", contributing to the stability and peace of the region.

4. In conformity with Article 1.1 of the Arbitration Agreement, Eritrea appointed as arbitrators Judge Stephen M. Schwebel and Judge Rosalyn Higgins, and Yemen appointed Dr. Ahmed Sadek El-Kosheri and Mr. Keith Highet. By an exchange of letters dated 30 and 31 December 1996, the Parties agreed to recommend the appointment of Professor Sir Robert Y. Jennings as President of the Arbitral Tribunal (hereinafter the "Tribunal"). The four arbitrators met in London on 14 January 1997, and appointed Sir Robert Y. Jennings President of the Tribunal.

5. Having been duly constituted, the Tribunal held its first meeting on 14 January 1997, at Essex Court Chambers, 24 Lincoln's Inn Fields, London WC1, UK. The Tribunal took note of the meeting of the four arbitrators, and ratified and approved the actions authorized and undertaken thereat. Pursuant to Article 7.2 of the Arbitration Agreement, the Tribunal appointed as Registrar Mr. P. J. H. Jonkman, Secretary-General of the Permanent Court of Arbitration (the "PCA") at The Hague and, as Secretary of the Tribunal, Ms. Bette. E. Shifman, First Secretary of the PCA, and fixed the location of the Tribunal's registry at the International Bureau of the PCA.

6. The Tribunal then held a meeting with Mr. Gary Born, Co-Agent of Eritrea, and Mr. Rodman Bundy, Co-Agent of Yemen, at which it notified them of the formation of the Tribunal and discussed with them certain practical matters relating to the arbitration proceedings.

7. Article 2 of the Arbitration Agreement provides that:

1. The Tribunal is requested to provide rulings in accordance with international law, in two stages.
2. The first stage shall result in an award on territorial sovereignty and on the definition of the scope of the dispute between Eritrea and Yemen. the Tribunal shall decide territorial sovereignty in accordance with the principles, rules and practices of international law applicable to the matter, and on the basis, in particular, of historic titles. The Tribunal shall decide on the definition of the scope of the dispute on the basis of the respective positions of the two Parties.
3. The second stage shall result in an award delimiting maritime boundaries. The Tribunal shall decide taking into account the opinion that it will have formed on questions of territorial sovereignty, the United Nations Convention on the Law of the Sea, and any other pertinent factor.

8. Pursuant to the time table set forth in the Arbitration Agreement for the various stages of the arbitration, the Parties submitted their written Memorials concerning territorial sovereignty and the scope of the dispute simultaneously on 1 September 1997 and their Counter-Memorials on 1 December 1997. In accordance with the requirement of Article 7.1 of the Arbitration Agreement that "the Tribunal shall sit in London", the oral proceedings in the first stage of the arbitration were held in London, in the Durbar Conference Room of the Foreign and Commonwealth Office, from 26 January through 6 February 1998, within the time limits for oral proceedings set forth in the Arbitration

Agreement. The order of the Parties' presentations was determined by drawing lots, with Eritrea beginning the oral proceedings.

9.   At the end of its session of 6 February 1998, the Tribunal, in accordance with Article 8.3 of the Arbitration Agreement, closed the oral phase of the first stage of the arbitration proceedings between Eritrea and Yemen. The closing of the oral proceedings was subject to the undertaking of both Parties to answer in writing, by 23 February 1998, certain questions put to them by the Tribunal at the end of the hearings, including a question concerning the existence of agreements for petroleum exploration and exploitation. It was also subject to the proviso in Article 8.3 of the Arbitration Agreement authorizing the Tribunal to request the Parties' written views on the elucidation of any aspect of the matters before the Tribunal.

10.   In its Communication and Order No. 3 of 10 May 1998, the Tribunal invoked this provision, requesting the Parties to provide, by 8 June 1998, written observations on the legal considerations raised by their responses to the Tribunal's earlier questions concerning concessions for petroleum exploration and exploitation and, in particular, on how the petroleum agreements and activities authorized by them might be relevant to the award on territorial sovereignty. The Tribunal further invited the Parties to agree to hold a short oral hearing for the elucidation of these issues.

11.   Following the exchange of the Parties' written observations, the Tribunal held oral hearings on this matter at the Foreign and Commonwealth Office in London on 6, 7 and 8 July 1998. By agreement of the Parties, Yemen presented its arguments first. In the course of these hearings, the Tribunal posed a series of questions concerning the interpretation of concession evidence, and the Parties were requested to respond thereto in writing within seven days of the oral hearings. On 17 July 1998, both Parties submitted their written responses to the Tribunal's questions. Eritrea indicated at that time that it anticipated a brief delay in submission of the documentary appendix accompanying its submission; this documentary appendix was received by the International Bureau of the PCA on 22 July 1998. On 30 July 1998, the International Bureau received from Yemen a submission entitled "Yemen's Comments on the Documents Introduced by Eritrea after the Final Oral Argument". Eritrea objected to this late filing by Yemen.

12.   In the course of the supplementary hearings in July 1998, the Tribunal informed the Parties of the intention to contact the Secretary-General of the Arab League, in order to ascertain the existence, and obtain copies, of any official Arab League reports of visits to any of the islands in dispute, particularly in the 1970s. A letter on behalf of the Tribunal was sent by fax to the Secretary-General of the Arab League on 20 July. His response, dated 28 July, was transmitted by the registry to the Co-Agents and the Members of the Tribunal.

* * *

Arguments of the Parties on Territorial Sovereignty

13.   Eritrea bases its claim to territorial sovereignty over these "Red Sea Islands" (hereinafter the "Islands")[1] on a chain of title extending over more than 100 years, and on international law principles of "effective occupation". Eritrea asserts that it inherited title to

---

[1]   The identification of the specific islands or island groups in dispute between the Parties has been entrusted to the Tribunal by Article 2 of the Arbitration Agreement (see para. 7, above), and is dealt with in the part of this Award dealing with the scope of the dispute. References to "the Islands" in this Award are to those Islands that the Tribunal finds are subject to conflicting claims by the Parties. The geographic area in which these islands are found is indicated on the map opposite page 1. [Editors note: maps are not included in this extract.]

the Islands in 1993, when the State of Eritrea became legally independent from the State of Ethiopia. Ethiopia had in turn inherited its title from Italy, despite a period of British military occupation of Eritrea as a whole during the Second World War. The Italian title is claimed then to have vested in the State of Eritrea in 1952–53, as a consequence of Eritrea's federation with, and subsequent annexation by, Ethiopia.

14.   Eritrea traces this chain of title through the relevant historical periods, beginning with the Italian colonization of the Eritrean mainland in the latter part of the 19th Century. The parties do not dispute that, prior to Italian colonization, the Ottoman empire was the unchallenged sovereign over both coasts of the Red Sea and over the Islands. By-passing the Ottomans and dealing directly with local rulers, Italy established outposts in furtherance of its maritime, colonial and commercial interests. Despite Ottoman objections, it proclaimed the Italian colony of Eritrea in 1890. Eritrea contends that in 1892 Great Britain recognized Italian title to the Mohabbakah islands, a group of islands proximate to the Eritrean coast.

15.   Eritrea asserts that, without challenging Ottoman sovereignty, Italy also maintained an active presence in other southern Red Sea islands at that time. Italian naval vessels patrolled the surrounding waters in search of pirates, slave traders and arms smugglers, and the colonial administration allegedly issued concessions for commercial exploitation on the Islands. According to Eritrea, there was no Yemeni claim to or presence on or around the Islands during this time. The Imam Yahya, who ultimately founded modern Yemen, occupied a highland region known as the *Gebel*, and, according to Eritrea, openly acknowledged his lack of sovereignty over the coastal lowlands known as the *Tihama*. This territorial arrangement was confirmed by the 1911 "Treaty of Da'an", an understanding between the Imam and the Ottoman Empire.

16.   Eritrea asserts that the weakening of the Ottoman Empire in the years immediately preceding the First World War fuelled Italian plans to occupy an island group known as the "Zuqar-Hanish Islands". These plans were preempted by a brief period of British military occupation in 1915, which was short-lived and, according to Eritrea, without legal consequences. At the end of the War, Italy purportedly renewed and expanded its commercial and regulatory activities with respect to what Eritrea refers to as the "Zuqar-Hanish and lighthouse islands". These activities are cited by Eritrea as evidence of Italy's intent to acquire sovereignty over the Islands.

17.   The question of sovereignty over the Islands formed part of the post-First World War peace process that culminated in the signature of the Treaty of Lausanne in 1923. While certain former territory of the defeated Ottoman empire was divided among local rulers who had supported the victorious Allies, Eritrea contends that none of the Arabian Peninsula leaders who had supported the Allies was in sufficient geographical proximity to the Islands to be considered a plausible recipient. The Imam of Sanaa was not a plausible recipient of the Islands, both because of his alliance with the Ottoman Turks, and because his sovereignty did not extend to the Red Sea coast. Eritrea cites Great Britain's rejection of claims made by the Imam in 1917–1918 to parts of the Tihama, and relies on the Imam's characterization of these territories as having been "under the sway of his predecessors" as acknowledging that the Imam indeed lacked possession and control at that time.

18.   Eritrea traces Great Britain's failure to persuade the remaining Allies to transfer the Islands to Arab rulers selected by Great Britain, or to Great Britain itself, through the unratified 1920 Treaty of Sèvres and the negotiations leading up to the conclusion of the Treaty of Lausanne in 1923. Eritrea relies on Articles 6 and 16 of the Treaty of Lausanne as having left the islands open for Italian occupation. Article 6 established the general rule that, in terms of the Treaty, "islands and islets lying within three miles of the coast are included within the frontier of the coastal State". Eritrea interprets this provision, and subsequent state practice under the Treaty of Lausanne, as withholding

the islands in question from any Arabian peninsula leader, because none of the Islands are within three miles of the Arabian coast. Eritrea further argues that the Imam could not have been given the disputed islands pursuant to Article 6, because his realm was neither a "state" nor "coastal" at the time the Treaty of Lausanne was signed.

19. Article 16 of the Treaty of Lausanne contained an express Turkish renunciation of all rights and title to former Ottoman territories and islands, and provided that their future was to be "settled by the parties concerned". Eritrea argues that because Article 16 did not transfer the Islands to any particular state, and did not specify any particular procedure for conveying ownership of the Islands, their ultimate disposition was left to general international law standards for territorial acquisition/conquest, effective occupation, and location within the territorial sea. Eritrea claims to find further support for this in subsequent state practice interpreting Article 16.

20. Eritrea asserts that by the end of the 1920s, Italy had acquired sovereignty over the disputed islands by effective occupation, and that neither the 1927 conversations between Great Britain and Italy, which came to be known as the "Rome Conversations", nor the aborted 1929 Lighthouse Convention were contra-indications. This effective occupation consisted, inter alia, of the construction in 1929 of a lighthouse on South Wets Haycock Island, which Eritrea claims led Great Britain to repeat acknowledgements of Italian sovereignty over the Mohabbakahs, previously made in 1892 and 1917. Eritrea finds further support for Italian occupation during this period in the dispatch of an expedition to the Zuqar-Hanish islands and their subsequent occupation by Italian troops. Eritrea asserts that in the period 1930–1940 Italy exercised sovereign rights over the Islands through the colonial government in Eritrea. Eritrea cites, inter alia, the granting of fishing licenses with respect to the surrounding waters, the grating of a license for the construction of a fish processing plant on Great Hanish, and the reconstruction and maintenance of an abandoned British lighthouse on Centre Peak Island. These satisfy, in Eritrea's view, the *corpus occupandi* requirement of effective occupation and, accompanied as they were by the requisite sovereign intent (*animus occupandi*), constitute the acquisition of sovereignty by effective occupation.

21. Eritrea further asserts that Yemen did not protest or question Italy's activities on the Islands during this time. Great Britain, however, sought assurances that Italian activities did not constitute a claim of sovereignty. Eritrea characterizes Italy's responses that the question of sovereignty was "in abeyance" or "in reserve" as a refusal to give such assurances. According to Eritrea, this formula was understood by both Italy and Great Britain as preserving Italy's legal rights while allowing Great Britain to withhold diplomatic recognition of those rights. Tensions between the two states on this and other matters led to conclusion of the 1938 Anglo-Italian Agreement, which Eritrea claims is probative of Italian and British views at that time. It is said to reflect, among other things, the parties' understanding that the Islands were not appurtenant to the Arabian Peninsula, and that Italy and Great Britain were the only two powers with a cognizable interest in them.

22. The 1938 Anglo-Italian Agreement also contained an express undertaking on the part of both Italy and Great Britain with respect to the former Ottoman Red Sea islands, that neither would "establish its sovereignty" or "erect fortifications or defences". This constituted, in Eritrea's view, not a relinquishment of existing rights, but simply a covenant regarding future conduct. Eritrea argues that, at the time of the Anglo-Italian Agreement, Italy's sovereignty over the Islands had already been established as a matter of law, and it remained unaffected by the agreement. Eritrea further asserts that in December of 1938, Italy formally confirmed its existing territorial sovereignty over the Islands by promulgating decree number 1446 of 1938, specifically confirming that the Islands had been, and continued to be, part of the territory of the Eritrean *Commissariato* of Dankalia.

23.   Eritrea characterizes the eleven-year British occupation of Eritrea that commenced in
       1941 in the wake of the Second World War as congruent with the law of belligerent
       occupation. Eritrea's territorial boundaries remained unchanged, and the territory of
       "all Italian colonies and dependencies" surrendered to the allies in the 1943 Armistice
       "indisputably included", in Eritrea's view, the Islands. The 1947 Treaty of Peace pro-
       vided for disposition of Italy's African territories by the Allied Powers, which was ac-
       complished in 1952 by the transfer to Ethiopia, with which Eritrea was then feder-
       ated, of "all former Italian territorial possessions in Eritrea". This marked, in Eritrea's
       view, the passing to Ethiopia of sovereign title to the Islands.
24.   Eritrea claims that the drafting history of the 1952 Eritrean Constitution confirms the
       inclusion of the disputed islands within the definition of Eritrean territory. This is, ac-
       cording to Eritrea, the only plausible interpretation of the phrase "Eritrea, including the
       islands" in the definition of the territory of Eritrea, and it is said to be supported by
       advice given to Ethiopia at the time by its legal adviser, John Spencer. Eritrea claims that
       this was further reinforced by similar language in subsequent constitutional and leg-
       islative provisions, in particular, the 1952 Imperial Decree federating Eritrea into the
       Ethiopian Empire, and the 1955 Ethiopian Constitution.
25.   Another basis for Ethiopian sovereignty put forward by Eritrea is the inclusion of the
       Islands within Ethiopia's territorial sea. Eritrea relies on the rule of international cus-
       tomary and conventional law that every island is entitled to its own territorial sea, mea-
       sured in accordance with the same principles as those applicable to the mainland. In
       Eritrea's view, a chain of islands linked to the mainland with gaps no wider than twelve
       miles falls entirely within the coastal state's territorial sea and therefore under its terri-
       torial sovereignty. Thus, measuring from the Mohabbakah islands, which Eritrea asserts
       were indisputably Ethiopian, Ethiopia's 1953 declaration of a 12-mile territorial sea en-
       compassed the Zuqar-Hanish islands.
26.   The 35-year period between 1953 and Eritrean independence in 1991 is characterized
       by Eritrea as one of extensive exercise of Ethiopian sovereignty over the Islands. This al-
       legedly included continuous, unchallenged naval patrols, which became increasingly
       systematic as the Eritrean Liberation Movement gathered strength. In addition, fol-
       lowing transfer of the administration of the lighthouses to Asmara by the British Board
       of Trade in 1967, Ethiopia is said to have further consolidated its sovereignty by re-
       quiring foreign workers on the lighthouse islands to carry passports and similar docu-
       ments, overseeing and regulating the dispatch of all provisions to the lighthouse islands,
       being involved in all employment decisions affecting lighthouse workers, approving
       all inspection and repair visits to the lighthouse islands, and tightly controlling radio
       transmissions to and from the lighthouse islands. Other alleged acts of Ethiopian sov-
       ereignty put forward by Eritrea include the exercise of criminal jurisdiction over acts
       committed on the Islands, regulation of oil exploration activities on and around the
       Islands, and an inspection by then President Mengistu and a group of high-ranking
       Ethiopian military and naval personnel during the late 1980s, for which Eritrea has sub-
       mitted videotape evidence.
27.   Eritrea claims that throughout the 1970s the two Yemeni states and their regional al-
       lies acknowledged Ethiopian control over the Islands by their statements and actions.
       It alleges that, until the early 1970s, neither North Yemen nor South Yemen had dis-
       played any interest in the Islands. Regional interest in the Islands is said to have been
       sparked by false reports of an Israeli presence there in 1973. According to Eritrea, the
       presumption on the part of Yemen, its neighbouring states and the Arab media that
       Ethiopia had leased the Islands to Israel constituted an acknowledgement of Ethiopian
       sovereignty. In support, Eritrea claims that the Arab states not only condemned Ethiopia
       for having made Ethiopian islands available to Israel, but also looked ultimately to
       Ethiopia for permission to visit the Islands in order to investigate the allegations of Is-
       raeli military activity.

28. Eritrea contends that the final years before Eritrean independence were marked by aerial surveillance and continuous naval patrols by Ethiopian forces.

29. Eritrea claims that, after winning its independence in 1991, it acquired sovereign title to the Islands and exercised sovereign authority over them. Eritrea asserts that, as they have been throughout recent history, Eritrean fishermen are dependent upon the Islands for their livelihood. Eritrean administrative regulations are said strictly to control fishing around the Islands, prescribing licensing and other requirements for fishing in the surrounding waters. Eritrea further contends that its vessels police foreign fishing vessels in order to enforce fishing regulations, seizing vessels that fail to comply. It asserts that Yemen did not maintain any official presence in the Islands, and that it was only in 1995 that Eritrean naval patrols discovered a small Yemeni military and civilian contingent purportedly engaged in work on a tourist resort on Greater Hanish Island. This led, in December 1995, to hostilities that ended with Eritrean forces occupying Greater Hanish Island, and Yemeni forces occupying Zuqar.

30. With respect to territorial sovereignty, Eritrea seeks from the Tribunal an award declaring that Eritrea possesses territorial sovereignty over each of the "slands, rocks and low-tide elevations" specified by Eritrea in its written pleadings, "as to which Yemen claims sovereignty".

* * *

31. Yemen, in turn, bases its claim to the Islands on "original, historic, or traditional Yemeni title". Yemen puts particular emphasis on the stipulation in Article 2.2 of the Arbitration Agreement, that "[t]he Tribunal shall decide territorial sovereignty in accordance with the principles, rules and practices of international law applicable to the matter, and on the basis, in particular, of historic titles". This title can, according to Yemen, be traced to the *Bilad el-Yemen*, or realm of Yemen, which is said to have existed as early as the 6th Century AD. Yemen advances, in support of this claim, map evidence,[2] declarations by the Imam of Yemen, and what it refers to as "the attitude of third States over a long period".

32. Yemen contends that its incorporation into the Ottoman Empire, from 1538 to *circa* 1635, and again from 1872 to the Ottoman defeat in 1918, did not deprive it of historic title to its territory. Yemen asserts that the creation of the Ottoman *vilayet* of Yemen as a separate territorial and administrative unit constituted Ottoman recognition of Yemen's separate identity. It relies on the work of 17th, 18th and 19th Century cartographers who allegedly depicted Yemen as a separate, identifiable territorial entity. Further map evidence is adduced in support of Yemen's contention that the Islands form part of that territory.

33. In further support of its assertions that Yemen maintained historic title to the Islands, Yemen retraces the drafting history of its 1934 Treaty with Great Britain, citing several exchanges of correspondence in which the Imam insisted, in one form or another, on his rights to the "Islands of the Yemen". Yemen cites Great Britain's rejection of the Imam's proposal to attach to the treaty a secret appendix concerning the Islands, on the grounds that the Islands, as former Ottoman possessions, were to be dealt with pursuant to Article 16 of the Treaty of Lausanne.

---

[2] Although Eritrea has also submitted cartographic evidence showing the Islands to be Ethiopian, Eritrean or, in any event, not Yemeni, it places relatively little weight on this type of evidence. Eritrea takes the position that maps do not constitute direct evidence of sovereignty or of a chain of title, thereby relegating them to a limited role in resolving these types of disputes.

34. Yemen argues that this did not constitute a denial of traditional Yemeni title, and puts forward documents that it claims support the characterization of British official opinion in the period 1933 to 1937 as being reluctant to challenge Yemeni title. Yemen further contends that the Treaty of Lausanne had no effect on Yemeni title, because Yemen was not a party to the Treaty, and because Turkey's renunciation of rights could not prejudice the interests of third parties. Yemen takes the view that the effect of Article 16 was not to make the Islands *terra nullius*, but rather, territory "the title to which was undetermined". Yemen argues in addition that Article 16 has, in any event, ceased to have effect between "the parties concerned", because of their own conduct, and that of third states, in recognizing, or failing to make reservations concerning, Yemen's sovereignty in respect of the Islands.

35. Another ground put forward in support of Yemen's claim that its original title extends to the Islands is "the principle of natural or geographical unity". Yemen argues that this doctrine is a corollary of the concept of traditional title, and that it operates in conjunction with evidence of the exercise of acts of jurisdiction or manifestations of state sovereignty. Yemen cites case law of the International Court of Justice and arbitral decisions in support of the premise that once the sovereignty of an entity or natural unity as a whole has been shown to exist, it may be deemed, in the absence of any evidence to the contrary, to extend to all parts of that entity or unity. According to Yemen, there is a "concordance of expert opinion evidence on the caricature of the islands as an entity or natural unity", including British admiralty charts, the *Red Sea and Gulf of Aden Pilot*, produced by the United Kingdom Hydrographic Office, and the *Encyclopaedia Brittanica*.

36. Yemen relies on various categories of evidence of sovereignty, which it asserts may serve to confirm and supplement the evidence of traditional or historic title, as well as constituting independent sources of title. These include economic and social links between the Islands and the Yemeni mainland, the exercise of sovereignty in the form of acts of jurisdiction, recognition of Yemen's title by third states, and confirmation of Yemeni title by expert opinion evidence.

37. Yemen cites case law and commentary in support of its contention that, within the appropriate geographical context, the private activities of individual persons constitute relevant evidence of historic title to territory. Yemen's analysis of these facts and activities begins with the names "Hanish" and "Zuqar", which, it asserts, have Arabic roots. Yemen also notes the presence on the Yemeni coast of inhabitants with names derived from the word "Hanish", and a family history, as fishermen, intertwined with that of the Islands. Yemen points out that, during the disturbances of 1995, two members of such a family were taken prisoner by Eritrean forces while fishing near Greater Hanish Island. Yemen also alleges the existence of anchorages and settlements on the Islands bearing distinctly Yemeni Arabic names. Yemen claims that, for generations, Yemeni fishermen have enjoyed virtually exclusive use of the Islands, even establishing, in contrast to Eritrean fishermen, permanent and semi-permanent residence there.

38. Yemen further asserts that the Islands are home to a number of Yemeni holy sites and shrines, including the tombs of several venerated holy men. It points to a shrine used primarily by fishermen, who have developed a tradition of leaving unused provisions in the tomb to sustain their fellow fishermen.

39. In addition, Yemen points out that the Islands fall within the jurisdiction of a traditional system of resolving disputes between fishermen, in which a kind of arbitrator may "ride the circuit" along the coast and among the Islands, in order to insure access to justice for those fishermen who are unable to travel.

40. Yemen emphasizes the economic links between the Islands and the Yemeni fishermen who rely for their livelihood on them and their surrounding waters, and who sell their catch almost exclusively on the Yemeni mainland. Yemen contrasts this with the situa-

tion of the Eritrean fishermen, pointing out that, because of the difficulty of hygienic transport of fish to the interior of Eritrea (including the capital of Asmara), Eritrea lacks a fish-eating tradition. According to Yemen, most Eritrean fishermen find a better market for their wares on the Yemeni coast. Yemen asserts that for centuries, the long-standing, intensive and virtually exclusive use of the Islands by Yemeni fishermen did not meet with interference from other states.

41. Yemen provides an historical review of alleged Yemeni acts of administration and control, which are said to supplement and confirm Yemen's historic title to the Islands, as wells as forming independent, mutually reinforcing sources of that title. The earliest of these acts, a mission sent to Jabal Zuqar by the King of Yemen in 1429 to investigate smuggling, predates Ottoman rule. In the Ottoman period, Yemen asserts that the Islands were considered part of the *vilayet* of Yemen, and that the Ottoman administration handled, inter alia, tax, security and maritime matters relating to the Islands. Yemen cites an 1881 lighthouse concession by the Ottoman authorities to a private French company, for the construction of lighthouses throughout the empire, which included some of the islands in the *vilayet* of Yemen. Yemen also cites 19th Century Ottoman maps and annual reports, which place the Islands within the *vilayet* of Yemen.

42. Yemen emphasizes that the post-Ottoman British presence on the islands was intermittent, and that Great Britain never claimed sovereignty over them. Following establishment of the Yemen Arab Republic in 1962, its Government allegedly asserted legislative jurisdiction over the Islands on at least two occasions. Yemen claims that its navy conducted exercises on and around the Islands, and that its armed forces played a key role in confirming the absence of Israeli troops on the Islands in 1973. In Yemen's rendition of the events surrounding the 1973 incident, the Islands are consistently characterized as Yemeni, rather than Ethiopian.

43. Yemen cites a number of examples of the issuance of licences to foreign entities wishing to engage in scientific, tourist and commercial activities in and around the Islands, and of the granting of permits for anchorage. Yemen presents evidence concerning the authorization given to a German company by the Yemeni Ministry of Culture and Tourism and the Yemen General Investment Authority in 1995 for the construction of a luxury hotel and diving centre on Greater Hanish Island. Yemen further asserts that it exercised jurisdiction over the Islands in respect of fishing, environmental protection, the installation and maintenance of geodetic stations, and the construction and administration of lighthouses, including the publication of relevant Notices to Mariners. Yemen has placed in evidence elaborate chronological surveys, covering a variety of time periods, of alleged Yemeni activities "in and around the Hanish Group".

44. Yemen contends that from 1887 to 1989, at least six states confirmed, by their conduct or otherwise, Yemen's title to the Islands. Yemen points out that upon conclusion of the Anglo-Italian Agreement of 1938, which Eritrea characterizes as being limited to future conduct, the Italian Government informed the Imam of Yemen that, pursuant to the agreement, Italy had undertaken not to extend its sovereignty on or to fortify the "Hanish Island group", and that it had, in the negotiations, "kept in mind . . . above all Yemen's interests". Yemen claims to find further acknowledgement of Yemeni rights in British practice and "internal thinking", as reflected in Foreign Office and Colonial Office documents of the 1930s and 1940s. French recognition of Yemeni title is said to include a request for permission to conduct military manoeuvres in the Southern Red Sea in 1975, and for a French oceanographic vessel to conduct activities near the Islands in 1976.

45. Yemen attributes similar evidentiary value to German conduct and publications, and to official maps published by the United States Army and Central Intelligence Agency, as recently as 1993. Yemen offers evidence of what it terms "revealing changes in Ethiopian cartography" in support of its contention that Ethiopia did not claim title

to the Islands. It relies particularly on Ethiopian maps from 1978, 1982, 1984 and 1985, on which all or some of the Islands appear, by their colouring, to be allocated to Yemen.

46. Yemen also puts forward cartographic evidence on which it relies as official and unofficial expert evidence of Yemeni title to the Islands. Such evidence serves, according to Yemen, as proof of geographical facts and the state of geographical knowledge at a particular period. Yemen supplements this cartographic evidence with the published works of historians and other professionals.

47. Yemen gives an historical review of this evidence, beginning with 17th and 18th Century maps depicting the independent *Bilad el-Yemen*. Yemen asserts that while some 18th Century maps fail to depict the Islands accurately, the more accurate of these attribute them to Yemen. Yemen places great emphasis on writings and maps reflecting the first-hand impressions of Carsten Niebuhr, a Danish scientist and explorer who visited the Red Sea coast from 1761–1764. Niebuhr's works suggest political affiliation and other links between the Islands and the Yemeni mainland.

48. Yemen further submits in evidence a large number of 19th and 20th Century maps, of varied origin, the colouring of which appears to attribute all or some of the Islands to Yemen. At the same time, it did not deny that certain Yemeni maps attribute the Islands to Ethiopia or Eritrea; or at least not to Yemen.

49. In addition to proffering cartographic and other evidence in support of its assertions of historic title to the Islands, Yemen argues that, until the events of December 1995, Ethiopian and Eritrean conduct was consistent with Yemeni sovereignty. Yemen alleges that as recently as November 1995, Eritrea acknowledged in an official communique to the President of Yemen that the Islands had ". . . been ignored and abandoned for many years since colonial times, including the eras of Haile Selassie and Mengistu, and during the long war of liberation".

50. Yemen insists that, during the Ottoman period, the Islands were consistently administered as part of the *vilayet* of Yemen, and that title never passed to Italy during the period of Italian colonization of the Eritrean mainland. Yemen cites several occasions on which, in its view, Italy had declined to claim sovereignty. These include exchanges between the British and Italian Governments in the late 1920s and 1930s and culminated in the 1938 Anglo-Italian Agreement which amounts, in Yemen's view, to a definitive agreement by both parties not to establish sovereignty over islands with respect to which Turkey had renounced sovereignty by Article 16 of the Treaty of Lausanne. Yemen interprets Italian decree number 1446 of December 20, 1938 not as a confirmation of existing territorial sovereignty but rather as a mere "internal decree providing for the administration of the islands to be undertaken from the Assab department of Eritrea".

51. Yemen argues further that the phrase "the territory of Eritrea including the islands" in the 1952 UN-drafted Eritrean Constitution does not refer to the disputed islands, because the official Report of the United Nations Commission for Eritrea, prepared in 1950, indicates Yemeni title to the Islands, by depicting them in the same colour as the Yemeni mainland on UN maps accompanying the Report. Yemen contests all Eritrean allegations of Ethiopian acts of sovereignty or administration, and asserts that Ethiopian conduct, particularly its publication of official maps on which the Islands were the same colour as the Yemeni mainland, constituted recognition of Yemeni sovereignty over the Islands.

52. According to Yemen, while Yemeni fishermen historically fished around the Islands and used them for temporary residence, Yemen exercised a wide array of state activities on and around them. These activities are alleged to have included, during the 1970s, the consideration of requests by foreign nationals to carry out marine and scientific research on the islands, periodic visits of Yemeni military officials to Greater Hanish and Jabal Zuqar, and related patrols on and around these islands. Yemen also claims to have protested the conduct of low-level military flights by France over the Hanish islands,

as well as Ethiopia's arrest of Yemeni fishermen in the vicinity of the Islands, and further asserts that it investigated a number of lost or damaged foreign vessels around Greater Hanish and Jabal Zuqar.

53. With respect to the 1980s and 1990s, Yemen alleges that various Yemeni air force and naval reconnaissance missions were conducted over and around the Islands. Yemen also asserts that it granted licenses allowing nationals of third states to visit the certain islands for scientific purposes and tourism, and that some of these visitors were accompanied by Yemeni officials. In 1988, Yemen is said to have embarked on a project to upgrade and build a series of lighthouses, accompanied by Notices to Mariners, on Centre Peak Island, Jabal al-Tayr, Lesser Hanish Island, Abu Ali, Jabal Zuqar and Greater Hanish Island. Yemen also claims to have erected geodetic stations on Greater Hanish and Jabal Zuqar and authorized construction of a landing strip on Greater Hanish, which was used frequently in the early 1990s. Yemen also contends that, during this period, it continued its patrols of the islands, arresting foreign fishermen and confiscating vessels found operating in waters around the islands without a Yemeni license.

54. With respect to territorial sovereignty, Yemen seeks from the Tribunal an award declaring "that the Republic of Yemen possesses territorial sovereignty over all of the islands comprising the Hanish Group of islands . . . as defined in chapters 2 and 5 of Yemen's Memorial".

* * *

Arguments of the Parties on the Relevance of Petroleum Agreements and Activities

55. In response to specific questions from the Tribunal, which were dealt with in supplemental written pleadings, at resumed oral hearings in July 1998, and in post-hearing written submissions, both Parties have presented evidence of offshore concession activity in the Red Sea. Yemen contends that its record of granting offshore concessions over the last fifty years reinforces and complements a consistent pattern of evidence indicating Yemeni title to the islands. As the granting of oil concessions serves to confirm and maintain an existing Yemeni title, rather than furnishing evidence of effective occupation, it need not, in Yemen's view, be supported by evidence of express claims. This is said to be congruent with Yemen's assertions of historic title.

56. In evidence of what it terms "longstanding and peaceful administration of its petroleum resources" on and around the Islands, Yemen has submitted agreements and maps concerning concession blocks granted or offered since 1974. One of these concession blocks (Tomen) encompasses some of the Islands, in this case, the "Hanish Group", while another (Adair) is bounded by a line that cuts through Greater Hanish. Yemen further relies on a 1991 hydrocarbon study of the Red Sea and Gulf of Aden regions carried out by the United Nations Development Programme (UNDP) and the World Bank. As this study enjoyed the participation of the governments concerned, particularly Ethiopia and successive Yemeni governments, Yemen relies on it as a useful overview of petroleum activities undertaken by the two states from the early 1950s.

57. Yemen relies on both case law (in particular the *Eastern Greenland* case)[3] and scholarly writing in support of its assertion that the granting of exploration permits and concessions constitutes evidence of title, addressing such evidentiary categories as: the attitude of the grantor state, its grant and regulation of the operation of the concession, ancillary government-approved operations, and the attitude of the concessionaire and of inter-

---

[3] Legal Status of Eastern Greenland (*Denmark v. Norway*), 1933 PCIJ (Ser. A/B) No. 53.

national agencies. In addition, Yemen derives from the absence of protests evidence of Ethiopian and Eritrean acquiescence.

58. Yemen invokes the presumption that a state granting an oil concession does so in respect of areas over which it has title or sovereign rights. The activity of offering and granting concessions with respect to blocks that encompass or approach the Islands constitutes, in Yemen's view, a clear manifestation of Yemeni sovereignty over the Islands. Yemen cites, in addition, express reservations, in the relevant agreements, of Yemeni title to the concession areas. In addition to demonstrating Yemen's attitude regarding title, the granting of these economic concessions to private companies is said to constitute evidence of the exercise of sovereignty in respect of the territory concerned. Yemen finds additional evidence of the exercise of sovereignty in Yemen's monitoring and regulation of the operations undertaken by the various concessionaires and the granting of permits for ancillary operations such as seismic reconnaissance.

59. Yemen further argues that a company will not enter into a concession with a state for the development of petroleum resources unless it is persuaded that the area covered by the concession, and the underlying resources, in fact belong to that state. Furthermore, the reservations of Yemeni title in the concession agreements submitted by Yemen are said to constitute express recognition by the concessionaires of Yemeni title to the blocks concerned. The UNDP/World Bank study constitutes, in Yemen's view, recognition of Yemeni title by these international agencies, as well as expert evidence to the same effect.

60. Yemen also proffers the UNDP/World Bank study as evidence of Ethiopian acquiescence. Because the study was prepared in collaboration with, and ultimately distributed to, all concerned governments, Ethiopia can, in Yemen's view, be held to have had notice of the existence and scope of Yemeni concessions implicating the Islands, without issuing the protests. Yemen relies further on other maps and reports published in the professional petroleum literature, of which it asserts Ethiopia and Eritrea should have been aware.

61. Finally, Yemen asserts that Ethiopian and Eritrean petroleum activities did not encompass or touch upon the Islands, and therefore provide no support for a claim of sovereignty. Despite this, Yemen alleges that it consistently made timely protests with respect to those Ethiopian concessions that, in Yemen's view, encroached in any manner upon its territorial sea, continental shelf and exclusive economic zone.

62. Eritrea, in turn, proffers evidence of offshore petroleum activities, conducted primarily by Ethiopia, at a time at which, it alleges "Ethiopia's title was already established". Eritrea cites oil-exploration related activities "on the islands" as confirming Ethiopia's pre-existing claim to sovereignty, which could not, in its view, be divested by Yemen's unilateral grants of offshore mineral concessions. Eritrea also argues that, in the absence of any physical manifestation of control either on islands or in their territorial waters, the mere granting of concessions by Yemen would not suffice to establish title through effective occupation, "even if the islands had been previously unowned".

63. According to Eritrea, the concession evidence put forward by Yemen is irrelevant, because it represents unilateral attempts by Yemen to establish permanent rights to the seabed, in violation of customary international law and the Untied Nations Convention on the Law of the Sea (the "Law of the Sea Convention"). Yemen's concession agreements are further said to be irrelevant because they were entered into only after the present dispute arose, were not accompanied by Yemeni government activities, and did not pertain to the territory in dispute. Eritrea also questions the factual accuracy of Yemen's allegations concerning concession agreements, pointing to Yemen's failure to submit in evidence copies of certain of these agreements.

64. Eritrea argues that, under both the Law of the Sea Convention and customary international law, mineral rights to the seabed can neither be acquired nor lost through the

unilateral appropriation of one competing claimant. Pending agreement with the opposite coastal state, Yemen was, in Eritrea's view, entitled only to issue concessions on a provisional basis. If the alleged concessions could not effectively confer the very mineral rights with which they purported to deal, they could not indirectly settle the question of sovereignty over the Islands. According to Eritrea, petroleum concessions are relevant only where they demonstrate the existence of a mutually recognized de facto boundary line. There had, in this case, been no attempt by Yemen to reach mutual agreement with Ethiopia or Eritrea.

65. Eritrea contends that the provisional character of any concessions issued by Yemen is derived not only from Article 87(3) of the Law of the Sea Convention, which permits the provisional granting of concessions, provided this does not prejudice a final delimitation, but also from Yemen's own continental shelf legislation, adopted in 1977, which provides that "pending agreement on the demarcation of the marine boundaries, the limits of territorial sea, the contiguous zone, the exclusive economic zone . . . shall not be extended to more than the median or equidistance line".

66. Eritrea further asserts that Yemen's offshore concessions were issued after 1973, with full knowledge of Ethiopia's sovereignty claims to the Islands. This is claimed not only to have implications for the delimitation of the surrounding seabed, but to limit as well the evidentiary value of Yemen's concession evidence in resolving the question of sovereignty.

67. Thus Eritrea argues that the post-1973 grant of concessions by Yemen reflects attempts to manufacture contracts with the disputed islands. This is further supported, in Eritrea's view, by the lack of any related Yemeni state activity pertaining specifically to the territory in dispute. According to Eritrea, concessions can be brought to bear on the question of territorial acquisition in two ways. The first is exemplified by the deep sea fishing concession granted by Italy to the *Cannata* company in the 1930s, which led inter alia to construction of a commercial fishing station on Greater Hanish Island. According to Eritrea, the *Cannata* concession was accompanied by the direct involvement of state officials, including Italian troops stationed on the island.

68. Another way in which concessions may be relevant to territorial acquisition is that reflected in the *Eastern Greenland* case. *Eastern Greenland* does not, in Eritrea's reading, necessarily require the physical presence of a particular state official, but rather activities by individuals who, while not themselves employees of the state, act under colour of state law. Eritrea cites doctrine in support of its position that the concession activity of private individuals is relevant only when it involves some kind of real assertion of authority, since "the exercise or display must be genuine and not a mere paper claim dressed up as an act of sovereignty". Eritrea argues that the scope of Yemeni and private activity with respect to petroleum concessions "does not approach the quality and significance of Ethiopia's long-standing pattern of governmental activities on and around the disputed islands". Eritrea further asserts that the few concession agreements actually placed in evidence by Yemen ultimately bear little or no relationship to the islands in dispute.

69. In addition, Eritrea characterizes much of Yemen's petroleum activity as pertaining to "marine scientific research", rather than economic exploitation. Article 241 of the Law of the Sea Convention expressly precludes marine scientific research activities from constituting the legal basis for any claim to any part of the marine environment or its resources.

70. Eritrea argues that its failure to protest Yemeni concessions does not amount to acquiescence, particularly in light of military and political upheaval in Ethiopia during the relevant period. Eritrea has submitted evidence aimed at demonstrating that the 1991 UNDP/World Bank report relied upon by Yemen as evidence of notice to Ethiopia may never have been received by Ethiopia, embroiled as it then was in the fall of the Mengistu

regime and the end of the civil war. And even if it had been ultimately received, Eritrea posits that in 1991, knowing it would soon lose its entire coastline to the soon-to-be independent Eritrea, Ethiopia would have had no reason to protest Yemeni concessions.

71. Even if it had had actual notice of some or all of Yemen's concessions, Eritrea contends that it was entitled to rely on their being provisional under Article 87(3) of the Law of the Sea Convention and under Yemen's own 1977 continental shelf legislation.

72. Finally, at the oral hearings in London in July 1998, Eritrea produced evidence of a 1989 Ethiopian concession agreement which, in its view, included at least some of the Islands, notably Greater Hanish, on which Eritrea relies as evidence of related activities which are said to have taken place on Great Hanish Island, including the placement of beacons. Moreover, it has introduced evidence of publication in 1985 of a series of maps, one of which is entitled "Petroleum Potential of Ethiopia" and purports to encompass a block of the Red Sea that includes the Hanish islands.

* * *

CHAPTER X: Conclusions

440. Having examined and analysed in great detail the extensive materials and evidence presented by the Parties,[25] the Tribunal may now draw the appropriate conclusions.

Ancient Title

441. First there is the question of an "ancient title" to which Yemen attaches great importance; moreover the Agreement for Arbitration requires the Tribunal to decide the question of sovereignty "on the basis in particular of historic titles". Yemen contends that it enjoys an ancient title to "the islands", which title existed before the hegemony of the Ottoman Empire and indeed emanates from medieval Yemen. It contends, moreover, that this title still subsisted in international law at the time when the Turks were defeated at the end of the First World War, and that therefore, when the Ottoman Empire renounced their generally acknowledged sway over the islands by the Treaty of Lausanne in 1923, the right to enjoy that title in possession "reverted" to Yemen.

442. This is an interesting argument and one that raises a number of questions concerning the international law governing territorial sovereignty. No one doubts that during the period of the Ottoman Empire – certainly in the second Ottoman period 1872–1918 – the Ottomans enjoyed possession of, and full sovereignty over, all the islands now in dispute, and thus not only factual possession but also a sovereign title to possession. When this regime ceased in 1923, was there a "reversion" to an even older title to fill a resulting vacuum?

443. It is doubted by Eritrea whether there is such a doctrine of reversion in international law. This doubt seems justified in view of the fact that very little support for such a doctrine was cited by Yemen, nor is the Tribunal aware of any basis for maintaining that reversion is an accepted principle or rule of general international law. Moreover, even if the doctrine were valid, it could not apply in this case. That is because there is a lack of con-

---

[25] The Tribunal wishes to note the sheer volume of written pleadings and evidence received from the Parties in this first phase of the arbitral proceedings. Each Party submitted over twenty volumes of documentary annexes, as well as extensive map atlases. In addition, the Tribunal has carefully reviewed the verbatim transcripts of the oral hearings, which together far exceed 1,000 pages. The Tribunal further notes that the majority of documents were submitted in their original language, and the Tribunal has relied on translations provided by the Parties.

tinuity. It has been argued by Yemen that in the case of historic title no continuity need be shown, but the Tribunal finds no support for this argument.

444. Yemen's argument is difficult to reconcile with centuries of Ottoman rule over the entire area, ending only with the Treaty of Lausanne (see Chapter V, above). This is the more so because, under the principle of intertemporal law, the Ottoman sovereignty was lawful and carried with it the entitlement to dispose of the territory. Accepting Yemen's argument that an ancient title could have remained in effect over an extended period of another sovereignty would be tantamount to a rejection of the legality of Ottoman title to full sovereignty.

445. The Treaty of Lausanne did not expressly provide, as the Treaty of Sèvres would have done, that Turkey renounced her territorial titles in favour of the Allied Powers; which provisions would certainly have excluded any possibility of the operation of a doctrine of reversion. Yemen was not a party to the Treaty of Lausanne, which was therefore *res inter alios acta*. Nevertheless, none of the authorities doubts that the formerly Turkish islands were in 1923 at the disposal of the parties to the Lausanne Treaty, just as they had formerly been wholly at the disposal of the Ottoman Empire, which was indeed party to the treaty and in it renounced its sovereignty over them. Article 16 of the Treaty created for the islands an objective legal status of indeterminacy pending a further decision of the interested parties; and this legal position was generally recognized, as the considerable documentation presented by the Parties to the Tribunal amply demonstrates. So, it is difficult to see what could have been left of such a title after the interventions of the Ottoman sovereignty which was generally regarded as unqualified; and its replacement by the Article 16 regime which put the islands completely at the disposal of the "interested parties".

446. There is a further difficulty. Yemen certainly existed before the region came to be under the domination of the Ottomans. But there must be some question whether the Imam, who at that period dwelt in and governed a mountain fortress, had had sway over "the islands". Further, there is the problem of the sheer anachronism of attempting to attribute to such a tribal, mountain and Muslim medieval society the modern Western concept of a sovereignty title, particularly with respect to uninhabited and barren islands used only occasionally by local, traditional fishermen.

447. In keeping with the dictates of the Arbitration Agreement, both Parties, and Yemen especially, have placed "particular" emphasis on historic titles as a source of territorial sovereignty. They have, however, failed to persuade the Tribunal of the actual existence of such titles, particularly in regard to these islands.

448. Eritrea's claims too, insofar as they are said to be derived by succession from Italy through Ethiopia, if hardly based upon an "ancient" title, are clearly based upon the assertion of an historic title. There is no doubt, as has been shown in chapters V, VI and VII above, that Italy in the inter-war period did entertain serious territorial ambitions in respect of the Red Sea islands; and did seek to further these ambitions by actual possession of some of them at various periods. Major difficulties for the Eritrean claims through succession are, as has been shown above in some detail, first the effect of Article 16 of the Treaty of Lausanne of 1923, and later the effects of the provisions of the Italian Peace Treaty of 1947. But there is also the fact that the Italian Government, in the inter-war period, constantly and consistently gave specific assurances to the British Government that Italy fully accepted and recognized the indeterminate legal position of these islands as established by treaty in 1923. No doubt Italy was hoping that the effect of her active expansionist policies might eventually be that "the parties concerned" would be persuaded to acquiesce in a *fait accompli*. But that never happened.

449. So there are considerable problems for both Parties with these versions of historic title. But the Tribunal has made great efforts to investigate both claims to historic titles. The difficulties, however, arise largely form the facts revealed in that history. In the end neither Party has been able to persuade the Tribunal that the history of the mat-

ter reveals the juridical existence of an historic title, or of historic titles, of such long-established, continuous and definitive lineage to these particular islands, islets and rocks as would be a sufficient basis for the Tribunal's decision. And it must be said that, given the waterless and uninhabitable nature of these islands and islets and rocks, and the intermittent and kaleidoscopically changing political situations and interests, this conclusion is hardly surprising.

450. Both Parties, however, also rely upon what is a form of historic claim but of a rather different kind; namely, upon the demonstration of use, presence, display of governmental authority, and other ways of showing a possession which may gradually consolidate into a title; a process will illustrated in the *Eastern Greenland* case, the *Palmas* case, and very many other well-known cases. Besides historic titles strictly so-called the Tribunal is required by the Agreement for Arbitration to apply the "principles, rules and practices of international law"; which rubric clearly covers this kind of argument very familiar in territorial disputes. The Parties clearly anticipated the possible need to resort to this kind of basis of decision – though it should be said that Yemen expressly introduces this kind of claim in confirmation of its ancient title, and Eritrea introduces this kind of claim in confirmation of an existing title acquired by succession – and the great quantity of materials and evidences of use and of possession provided by both Parties have been set out and analysed in Chapter VII above, together with chapter VIII on maps and Chapter IX on the history of the petroleum agreements. It may be said at once that one result of the analysis of the constantly changing situation of all these different aspects of governmental activities is that, as indeed was so in the *Minquiers and Ecrehos*[26] case where there had also been much argument about claims to very ancient titles, it is the relatively recent history of use and possession that ultimately proved to be a main basis of the Tribunal decisions. And to the consideration of these materials and arguments this Award now turns.

Evidences of the Display of Functions of State and Governmental Authority

451. These materials have been put before the Tribunal by the Parties with the intention of showing the establishment of territorial sovereignty over the islands, in Judge Huber's words in the *Palmas* case,[27] "by the continuous and peaceful display of the functions of state within a given region". But the kind of actions that may be deployed for this purpose has inevitably expanded in the endeavour to show what Charles de Visscher named a gradual "consolidation" of title. Accordingly, the Tribunal is faced in this case with an assortment of factors and events from many different periods, intended to show not only physical activity and conduct, but also repute, and the opinions and attitudes of other governments (the different classes of materials are set out above in Chapter VII).

452. It is well known that the standard of the requirements of such activity may have to be modified when one is dealing, as in the present case, with difficult or inhospitable territory. As the Permanent Court of International Justice said in the *Legal Status of Eastern Greenland* case, "[I]t is impossible to read the records of the decisions in cases as to territorial sovereignty without observing that in many cases the tribunal has been satisfied with very little in the way of the actual exercise of sovereign rights, provided that the other state could not make a superior claims".[28]

453. This raises, however, a further important question of principle. The problem involved is the establishment of territorial sovereignty, and this is no light matter. One might

---

[26] Minquiers and Ecrehos (*UK v. France*), 1953 ICJ 47.
[27] Island of Palmas (*US v. Netherlands*), 2 RIAA 829 (1929).
[28] Legal Status of Eastern Greenland (*Denmark v. Norway*), 1933 PCIJ (Ser. A/B) No. 53.

suppose that for so important a question there must be some absolute minimum requirement for the acquisition of such a right, and that in principle it ought not normally to be merely a relative question.

454. It may be recalled that this question of principle did arise in the *Palmas* case, but there Huber was able to meet it by appealing to the particular terms of the *compromise*, which, said Huber, "presupposes for the present case that the Island of Palmas (or Miangas) can belong only to the United States or to the Netherlands and must form in its entirety part of the territory either of the one or of the other of these two Powers, parties to the dispute", and "[t]he possibility for the arbitrator to found his decision on the relative strength of the titles invoked on either side must have been envisaged by the parties to the Special Agreement".

455. The Arbitration Agreement in the present case, however, is in different and even unusual terms. The Tribunal is required only to make "an award on territorial sovereignty" and "to decide the sovereignty". The compromissory provision which led Huber to the possibility of deciding only on the basis of a marginal difference in weight of evidence cannot be said to apply in the present case.

456. There is certainly no lack of materials, evidence, or of arguments in the present case. The materials, on the contrary, are voluminous and the result of skilled research by the teams of both Parties, and of the excellent presentations by their counsel. But what these materials have in fact revealed is a chequered and frequently changing situation in which the fortunes and interests of the Parties constantly ebb and flow with the passage of the years. Moreover, it has to be remembered that neither Ethiopia nor Yemen had much opportunity of actively and openly demonstrating ambitions to sovereignty over the islands, or of displaying governmental activities upon them, until after 1967, when the British left the region. For, as shown above, the British were constantly vigilant to maintain the position effected by the Treaty of Lausanne that the legal position of "the islands" was indeterminate.

457. In these circumstances where for all the reasons just described the activities relied upon by the parties, though many, sometimes speak with an uncertain voice, it is surely right for the Tribunal to consider whether there are in the instant case other factors which might help to resolve some of these uncertainties. There is no virtue in relying upon "very little" when looking at other possible factors might strengthen the basis of decision.

458. An obvious such factor in the present case is the geographical situation that the majority of the islands and islets and rocks in issue form an archipelago extending across a relatively narrow sea between the two opposite coasts of the sea. So there is some presumption that any islands off one of the coasts may be thought to belong by appurtenance to that coast unless the state on the opposite coast has been able to demonstrate a clearly better title. This possible further factor looks even more attractive when it is realized that its influence can be seen very much at work in the legal history of these islands; beginning indeed with the days of Ottoman rule when even under the common sovereignty of the whole region it was found convenient to divide the jurisdiction between the two coastal local authorities (see paras 132–136, above). Moreover, in the present case, the examination of the activities material itself shows very clearly that there was no common legal history for the whole of this Zuqar–Hanish archipelago; some of the evidence not surprisingly refers to particular islands or to sub-groups of islands.

459. Thus the Tribunal has found it necessary, in order to decide the question of sovereignty, to consider the several subgroups of the islands separately, if only for the reason that the different subgroups have, at least to an important extent, separate legal histories; which is only to be expected in islands that span the area between two opposite coasts. This may seem only a natural or even manifest truth, but Yemen in particular has emphasized the importance it attaches to what it calls a principle of natural unity of the islands, and some comment on this theory is therefore required.

Natural and Physical Unity

460. Yemen's pleadings insist strongly on what it calls "the principle of natural or geophysical unity" in relation to the Hanish group of islands; Yemen uses the name of the "Hanish Group" both in its texts and in its illustrative maps to encompass the entire island chain, including the Haycocks and the Mohabbakahs (the present comments do not refer of course to the northern islands of Jabal al-Tayr and the Zubayr group, which will be considered separately later on).

461. This "principle" is described in Chapter 5 of the Yemen Memorial, where impressive authority is cited in support of it, including Fitzmaurice, Waldock and Charles de Visscher. That there is indeed some such concept cannot be doubted. But it is not an absolute principle. All these authorities speak of it in terms of raising a presumption. And Fitzmaurice is, in the passage cited, clearly dealing with the presumption that may be raised by proximity where a state is exercising or displaying sovereignty over a parcel of territory and there is some question whether this is presumed to extend also to outlying territory over which there is little or no factual impact of its authority. The Tribunal has no difficulty in accepting these statements of high authority; but what they are saying is in fact rather more than a simple principle of unity. It will be useful to cite Fitzmaurice again:

> The question of "entity" or "natural unity"
> This question can have far-reaching consequences. Not only may it powerfully affect the play of probabilities and presumptions, but also, if it can be shown that the disputed areas (whether by reasons of actual contiguity or of proximity) are part of an entity or unity over which as a whole the claimant State has sovereignty, this may (under certain conditions and within certain limits) render it unnecessary– or modify the extent to which it will be necessary – to adduce specific evidence of State activity in relation to the disputed areas as such – provided that such activity, amounting to effective occupation and possession, can be shown in the principle established by the Island of Palmas case that "sovereignty cannot be exercised in fact at every moment on every point of a territory".[29]

462. Thus, the authorities speak of "entity" or "natural unity" in terms of a presumption or of probability and moreover couple it with proximity, contiguity, continuity, and such notions, well known in international law as not in themselves creative of title, but rather of a possibility or presumption for extending to the area in question an existing title already established in another, but proximate or contiguous, part of the same "unity".

463. These ideas, however, have a twofold possible application in the present case. They may indeed, as Yemen would have it, be applied to cause governmental display on one island of a group to extend in its juridical effect to another islands or islands in the same group. But by the same rationale a complementary question also arises of how far the sway established on one of the mainland coasts should be considered to continue to some islands or islets off that coasts which are naturally "proximate" to the coast or "appurtenant" to it. This idea was so well established during the last century that it was given the name of the "portico doctrine" and recognized "as a means of attributing sovereignty over offshore features which fell within the attraction of the mainland".[30] The relevance of these notions of international law to the legal history of the present case is not far to seek.

464. Thus the principle of natural and physical unity is a two-edged sword, for if it is indeed to be applied then the question arises whether the unity is to be seen as originating from the one coast or the other. Moreover, as the cases and authorities cited by Yemen clearly show, these notions of unity and the like are never in themselves roots

---

[29] 32 BYIL (1955–56) 73–74.
[30] D. O'Connell, *The International Law of the Sea* 185 (1982).

of title, but rather may in certain circumstances raise a presumption about the extent and scope of a title otherwise established.

465. In spite of unity theories, the fact is that both Parties have tacitly conceded that, for the purposes at any rate of the exposition of their pleadings, it may be accepted that there can be sub-groups within the main group. The nomenclature within common use indicates at least three of the sub-groups: the Mohabbakahs; the Haycocks; and what it will be convenient at least for the moment to call the Zuqar-Hanish group and its many satellite islands, islets and rocks. These names will all be found in the *British Pilot and Sailing Directions for the Southern Red Sea* (Yemen has cited this publication as authority for regarding all these islands as one group, but of course if one is concerned with them as sailing hazards or landmarks when traversing the Red Sea there is really no other way to do it). There are also the two northern islands: Jabal al-Tayr, and the group of which the biggest island is Jabal Zubayr. The Tribunal will now consider its conclusions in respect of each of the three subgroups and then, finally, the northern islands.

466. Thus, in order to make decisions on territorial sovereignty, the Tribunal has hardly surprisingly found on alternative but to depart from the terms in which both Parties have pleaded their cases, namely by each of them presenting a claim to every one of the islands involved in the case. The legal history simply does not support either such claim.[31] For, as has been explained above, much of the material is found on examination to apply either to a particular island or to a sub-group of islands. The Tribunal has accordingly had to reach a conclusion which neither Party was willing to contemplate, namely that the islands might have to be divided; not indeed by the Tribunal but by the weight of the evidence and argument presented by the Parties, which does not fall evenly over the whole of the islands but leads to different results for certain sub-groups, and for certain islands.

The Mohabbakahs

467. The Mohabbakah Islands are four rocky islets which amount to little more than navigational hazards. They are Sayal Islet, which is not more than 6 nautical miles from the nearest point of the Eritrean mainland coast, Harbi Islet and Flat Islet; all three of these are within twelve nautical miles of the mainland coast. Finally, there is High Islet, which is less than one nautical mile outside the twelve-mile limit from the mainland coast, and about five nautical miles from the nearest Haycock island, namely South West Haycock.

468. Eritrea has sought to show that Italy obtained title to the Mohabbakahs along with the various local agreements Italy made with local rulers (see para. 159, above), which led to its securing title over the Danakil coast; this was not protested by Turkey and

---

[31] In this connection it is interesting to see the statements made in the 1977 "Top Secret" memorandum of the Ministry of Foreign Affairs of the Provisional Military Government of Socialist Ethiopia, discussed above in para. 245. This memorandum refers to islands in the southern part of the Red Sea that "have had no recognized owner", with respect to which Ethiopia "claims jurisdiction" and "both North and South Yemen have started to make claims". South Yemen's position is that the islands were illegally handed over to Ethiopia by the British when Britain was giving up its rights in the protectorate of Aden. It adds "the North Yemen government has now raised the question of jurisdiction over the islands". It goes on to recommend bilateral negotiations which seem in fact to have been entered into before the time of this memorandum for it goes on to say that "[b]oth states . . . have informally mentioned the possibility of dividing the islands between the two of them. The proposal is to use the median line, which divides the Red Sea equally from both countries' coastal borders, as the dividing line . . . Ethiopia rejected this proposal as disadvantageous".

came to be recognized by Great Britain. The diplomatic history has some interest for this case, especially in highlighting the question of whether South West Haycock is a Mohabbakah island, or part of a separate group of Haycocks, or part of a larger "Zuqar-Hanish group" (see para. 215, above, for the 1930 Italian claim to sovereignty over South West Haycock).

469. Eritrea thus contends that the Mohabbakahs were comprised within what was passed to Ethiopia and so to Eritrea after the Second World War and that this is affirmed by the reference in Article 2 of the 1947 Peace Treaty to the islands "off the coast" and by the constitutional arrangements.

470. Yemen claims that the only islands Eritrea secured jurisdiction over through local rulers were the islands in Assab Bay; and that, because formerly both coasts of the Red Sea fell under Ottoman rule; and because after the end of the First World War Yemen reverted to its "historical title"; and also because the Mohabbakahs are properly to be perceived as a unity with the Haycocks and the Zuqar-Hanish group, title to all these islands lies with Yemen. The Tribunal rejects this argument.

471. The Tribunal has already noted that there is no evidence that the Mohabbakah islands were part of an original historic title held by Yemen, even were such a title to have existed and to have reverted to Yemen after the First World War. And, even if it were the case that only the Assab Bay islands passed to Eritrea by Italy in 1947, no serious claims to the Mohabbakahs have been advanced by Yemen since that time, until the events leading up to the present arbitration.

472. The Tribunal need not, however, decide whether Italian title to the Mohabbakahs survived the Treaty of Lausanne, and passed thereafter to Ethiopia and then to Eritrea. It is sufficient for the Tribunal to note that all the Mohabbakahs, other than High Islet, lie within twelve miles of the Eritrean coast. Whatever the history, in the absence of any clear title to them being shown by Yemen, the Mohabbakahs must for that reason today be regarded as Eritrean.[32] No such convincing alternative title has been shown by Yemen.

It will be remembered indeed that Article 6 of the 1923 Treaty of Lausanne already enshrined this principle of the territorial sea by providing expressly that islands within the territorial sea of a state were to belong to that state. In those days the territorial sea was generally limited by international law and custom to three nautical miles, but it has now long been twelve, and the Ethiopian territorial sea was extended to twelve miles in a 1953 decree.

473. At this point it will be convenient to look at the ingenious theory enunciated by Eritrea, based on the undoubted rule that the territorial sea extends to twelve miles not just from the coast but may also extend from a baseline drawn to include any territorial islands within a twelve-mile belt of territorial sea. Thus the baseline can lawfully be extended to include an entire chain, or group of islands, where there is no gap between the islands of more than twelve miles; the so-called leapfrogging method of determining the baseline of the territorial sea. As already mentioned, the entire chain or group of these islands consists of islands, islets, or rocks proud of the sea and therefore technically islands, with no gap between them of more than twelve miles. The only such gap is the one between the easternmost island (the Abu Ali islands) and the Yemen mainland coast.

---

[32] See D. Bowett, *The Legal Regime of Islands in International Law* 48 (1979), where he says of islands lying within the territorial sea of a state, "Here the presumption is that the island is under the same sovereignty as the mainland nearby"; and he also interestingly quotes Lindley, *The Acquisition and Government of Backward Territory in International Law* 7 (1926), writing, it may be noted, in the mid-1920s that "An uninhabited island within territorial waters is under the dominion of the Sovereign of the adjoining mainland".

474. The difficulty with leapfrogging in the instant case is that it begs the very question at issue before this Tribunal: to which coastal state do these islands belong? There is a strong presumption that islands within the twelve-mile coastal belt will belong to the coastal state, unless there is a fully-established case to the contrary (as, for example, in the case of the Channel Islands). But there is no like presumption outside the coastal belt, where the ownership of the islands is plainly at issue. The ownership over adjacent islands undoubtedly generates a right to a corresponding territorial sea, but merely extending the territorial sea beyond the permitted coastal belt, cannot of itself generate sovereignty over islands so encompassed. And even if there were a presumption of coastal-state sovereignty over islands falling within the twelve-mile territorial sea of a coastal-belt island, it would be no more than a presumption, capable of being rebutted by evidence of a superior title.

* * *

475. Therefore, after examination of all relevant historical, factual and legal considerations, the Tribunal unanimously finds in the present case that the islands, islet, rocks, and low-tide elevations forming the Mohabbakah islands, including but not limited to Sayal Islet, Harbi Islet, Flat Islet and High Islet are subject to the territorial sovereignty of Eritrea. It is true that High Islet is a small but prominent rocky islet barely more than twelve miles (12.72 n.m.) from the territorial sea baseline. But here the unity theory might find a modest and suitable place, for the Mohabbakahs have always been considered as one group, sharing the same legal destiny. High Islet is certainly also appurtenant to the African coast.

The Haycocks

476. The Haycocks are three small islands situated along a roughly southwest-to-northeast line. They are, from south to north, South West Haycock, Middle Haycock and Northeast Haycock. South West Haycock is some 6 nautical miles form the nearest point of Suyul Hanish, though there is the very small Three Foot Rock about midway between them.
477. As already mentioned above, the Haycocks do have a peculiar legal history and it is for this reason mainly that they need to discussed separately here. That legal history is very much bound up with the story of the Red Sea lighthouses. But one might begin the salient points of this legal history by recalling the 1841, 1866 and 1873 *firmans* of the Ottoman Sultan (see para. 97, above), by which the African coasts of the Red Sea and the islands off it were placed under the jurisdiction and administration of Egypt, though of course the whole of this part of the world was then under the sovereignty of the Ottoman Empire. There seems little doubt that this African-coast administration would have extended to the Mohabbakahs and the Haycocks. At this time the territorial sea was limited to three miles, and there were still grave doubts about the nature and extent of the territorial waters regime. Nevertheless there was a feeling, based upon considerations of security as well as of convenience, that islands off a particular coast would, failing a clearly established title to contrary, be under the jurisdiction of the nearest coastal authority. As mentioned above, this was sometimes called the "portico doctrine".
478. Another stage in this legal history is at the end of the nineteenth century, when the British Government was interested in the possibility of establishing an alternative western shipping channel through the Red Sea, which needed lighting if it was to be used at night. Various islands were considered as sites for a light (see paras. 203, 204, above), including South West Haycock, which in the end proved to be the successful candidate.

This involved inquiries about the "jurisdiction" under which the island would come, and the British Board of Trade satisfied itself that South West Haycock was subject to Italian jurisdiction and at any rate probably not Ottoman.

479. In 1930, when the Italians were constructing a lighthouse on South West Haycock, there was an instructive correspondence between the Italian and British Governments. An internal Foreign Office memorandum reveals the opinion that "the establishment of the Italian colony of Eritrea makes it difficult, therefore, to resist the claim that the islands off the coast of Eritrea are to be considered as an appendage of that colony".[33] This was the official reaction to a letter from the Royal Italian Government of 11 April, claiming South West Haycock, *inter alia* for reasons of its "immediate vicinity" to the Eritrean Red Sea coast.

480. Eritrea employs these arguments to support its claim to the Haycocks, but puts it in the form of a succession derived from the Italian colony of Eritrea, and by way of the subsequent federation of Ethiopia and Eritrea, through to Eritrean independence in 1993. There are difficult juridical problems with this theory of succession, not least the terms of the Italian armistice in 1943 and the peace treaty of 1947, whereby Italy surrendered her colonial territories for disposition by the Allies and in default of agreement amongst them, to disposition by the United Nations, which of course is what actually happened to Eritrea. However this may be, the geographical arguments of proximity to the Eritrean coast remain persuasive and accord with the general opinion that islands off a coast will belong to the coastal state, unless another, superior title can be established. Yemen has failed, in this case, to establish any such superior claim.

481. The Eritrean claim to the Haycocks also finds some support in the material provided by both Parties for the supplementary hearing on the implications of petroleum agreements. None of the Yemen agreements extends as far to the southwest as the Haycocks; the 1974 Tomen–Santa Fe agreement appears to encompass the Hanish group, but stops short of the Haycocks. On the other hand, the fully documented agreements of the Eritrean Government and Shell, Amoco and BP do cover the areas of the Haycocks, and of course the Mohabbakahs. There was no protest from Yemen, though Yemen did protest when an agreement with Shell appeared to it to trespass upon its claim to the northern islands.

482. Therefore, after examination of all relevant historical, factual and legal considerations, the Tribunal unanimously finds in the present case that the islands, islet, rocks and low-tide elevations forming the Haycock Islands, including, but not limited to, North East Haycock, Middle Haycock, and South West Haycock, are subject to the territorial sovereignty of Eritrea. It follows that the like decision will, apart from other good reasons noted above, apply to High Islet, the one island of the Mohabbakah subgroup that is outside the Eritrean territorial sea.

483. There remains a question whether the South West Rocks should for these purposes be regarded as going along with the Haycocks. No doubt South West Rocks are so called because they lie southwest of Greater Hanish and there is no other feature between them and that island. There is some evidence that South West Rocks were, at various times, considered to form the easternmost limit of African-coast jurisdiction. While the British Foreign Office documentation relied on by both Parties reflects divergent views (referring in at least one case to Italian jurisdiction over South West Rocks as "doubtful"), the Parties agree that in the early 1890s, Italy responded to direct British inquiries concerning potential lighthouse site with assertions of jurisdiction over all of the proposed sites, including South West Rocks. Furthermore, Italy did not object to

---

[33] Foreign Office Memorandum dated 10 June 1930, prepared by Mr Orchard.

the subsequent British suggestion that the Sublime Porte be informed of the Italian position. This thinking surfaced again in 1914, in Great Britain's initial proposal for a post-war distribution of relinquished Ottoman territory, which would have placed everything east of South West Rocks under the sovereignty of "the independent chiefs of the Arabian mainland".

484. In light of this, it seems reasonable that South West Rocks should be treated in the same manner as the other islands administered from the African coast: the Mohabbakahs and the Haycocks. South West Rocks are therefore unanimously determined by the Tribunal to be subject to the territorial sovereignty of Eritrea.

The Zuqar–Hanish Group

485. There remains to be determined the sovereignty over Zuqar and over the Hanish islands, and their respective satellite islets and rocks, including the island of Abu Ali, to the east of the northern end of Zuqar, which was for long a principal site for a lighthouse.

486. This has not been an easy group of islands to decide on, one reason for this being that, positioned as they are in the central part of the Red Sea, the appurtenance factor is bound to be relatively less helpful. A coastal median line would in fact divide the island of Great Hanish, the slightly greater part of the island being on the Eritrean side of the line. Zuqar would be well on the Yemen side of a coastal median line.

487. The Parties have put before the Tribunal many aspects of the local legal history which are said to point the decision one way or the other. These have all been examined in detail in the chapters above. It is however already apparent from that examination that any expectation of a clear and definite answer from that earlier legal history is bound to be disappointed. The Yemeni idea of a reversionary ancient title has been discussed earlier in this chapter and found unhelpful in regard to these islands. More helpful perhaps is the material which suggests that, when the Ottomans decided in the later nineteenth century to grant to Egypt the jurisdiction over the African coast, this possibly included islands appurtenant to that coast, and according to some respectable authorities this did not include this central group of islands, both Zuqar and Hanish being regarded as still within the jurisdiction of the *vilayet* of Yemen. If this was so, though that position can hardly have been carried over to the present time in spite of Article 16 of the Treaty of Lausanne, it would constitute an impressive historical precedent. Hertslet's opinion about the proper distribution of jurisdiction over the islands of the Red Sea clearly impressed the British Foreign Office, but it seems to be Hertslet's view of what should be done about all the islands in the Red Sea rather than evidence of existing titles.

488. There are some echoes of the idea of Yemeni title to be found in the earlier part of the present century in for example the record of the negotiations between the Imam and a British envoy, Colonel Reilly, in which talk the Imam is said to have referred to the need to return to him certain Yemeni islands. But there is no doubt that the main grievance the Imam had in mind was the island of Kamaran and its surrounding islets, which was then occupied by the British. There was also a claim which an internal Foreign Office memorandum referred to as the Imam's claim to "unspecified islands". The British civil servants were quite prepared themselves to speculate that these islands might have included Zuqar and Hanish, which had been temporarily occupied by the British in 1915. But it is in the end difficult to attach decisive importance to a claim which could not be specified with any certainty.

489. Eritrea seeks to derive an historical title by succession, through Ethiopia, from Italy. There is no doubt that Italy had serious ambitions in respect of these central islands in the 1930s and did establish a presence there. But as has been seen above that position was constantly neutralized by assurances to the British Government that Italy fully accepted that the legal status of the islands was still governed by Article 16 of the Treaty of Lausanne. And then there is also the difficulty of deriving a title from Italy in view of the provisions of the Italian Peace Treaty of 1947.

490. Then of course there are the maps. These islands are large enough to find a place quite often – though by no means always – on even relatively small-scale maps of the region. It is fair to assert that, thanks to the efforts of counsel and especially those of Yemen, the Tribunal will have seen more maps of every conceivable period and provenance than probably have ever been seen before, and certainly a very much larger collection than will have been seen at any time by any of the principal actors in the Red Sea scene. In fact, the difficulty is not so much the interpretation of a plethora of maps of every kind and provenance, as it is the absence of any kind of evidence that these actors took very much notice of, or attached very much importance to, any of them. The Tribunal is of the opinion that in quite general terms Yemen has a marginally better case in terms of favourable maps discovered, and looked at in their totality the maps do suggest a certain widespread repute that these islands appertain to Yemen.

491. As to the other aspects of the legal history of this central group, it does inevitably reflect the ebb and flow of the interest, or the neglect, as the case may be, of both sides, varying from time to time, and qualified always by the unattractive nature of these islands, relieved from time to time by occasional usefulness, as for siting navigational lights, or by their sometimes perceived or imagined strategic importance; for they have never been considered "remote" in the sense of Greenland or the Island of Palmas. Accordingly, in the Tribunal's opinion, although some of this older historical material is important and generally helpful and indeed essential to an understanding of the claims of both Parties, neither of them has been able on the basis of the historical materials alone to make out a case that actually compels a decision one ways or the other. Accordingly the Tribunal has looked at events in the last decade or so before the Agreement of Arbitration for additional materials and factors which might complete the picture of both Parties' cases and enable the Tribunal to make a firm decision about these two islands and their satellite rocks and islets. The Tribunal is confirmed in this approach by the fact that both Parties have anticipated the need for such material by providing supplementary data in connection with the hearings held in July 1998. It should be added, however, that the more recent legal history of these islands shows in some respects differences between Zuqar and Hanish. Because this is so, the islands should be, and will be, considered separately . It would be wrong to assume that they must together go to one Party or the other. In this extent the Tribunal rejects the Yemen theory that all the islands in the group must in principle share a common destiny of sovereignty.

492. Of the recent events perhaps the first heading to look at is that of the Red Sea lighthouses which have featured in the arguments of both Parties. It is evident from the lighthouse history, again dealt with in detail in chapter VI above, that the undertaking by a government of the maintenance of one of these lights has generally been regarded as neutral for the purpose of the acquisition of territorial sovereignty, although it should also be remembered that, when Great Britain wished in 1892 to secure the building of a light for the proposed western shipping channel, the British Government was anxious to know which government had "jurisdiction" over the chosen site on South West Haycock, and Italy not only made a claim but had its claim to jurisdiction recognized by the British Government. Four lights have been constructed by and appear to be maintained by Yemen in the area now being dealt with (though it

should be added that such lights are of course no longer manned). These are sited as follows: on the island of Abu Ali, which is some 3 nautical miles west of the northern tip of Zuqar, on the south-eastern tip of Zuqar; on Low Islands which is off the north-eastern tip of Lesser Hanish; and on the north-eastern tip of Greater Hanish. The latter was constructed in July 1991 by Yemen and there is in evidence a picture of it with an inscription giving the name of the Republic of Yemen. It can hardly be denied that these lights, clearly intended to be permanent installations, are cogent evidence of some form of Yemen presence in all these islands.

493. Of relatively recent events, Eritrea attaches much importance to the history of Ethiopian naval patrols and the log books which evidence their occurrence, and which involved in particular the islands of Zuqar and Hanish; and this is indeed a possible factor where the islands must be taken as a group; for these were patrols in these waters generally rather than voyages to particular islands. There is no doubt that these patrols occurred on a large scale, and they are fully examined in Chapter VII and it is well known that these islands were used by the rebels, probably mainly as staging posts and relatively safe anchorages for vessels attempting to convey supplies to the rebel armies fighting on the mainland of Ethiopia, some of them possibly from Yemen, which is known to have sympathized with the rebel cause.

494. A strange aspect of these naval patrols possibly over a matter of several years – though the actual evidence Eritrea has been able to provide leaves a number of blank periods – is the lack of protest from Yemen. If Ethiopia had been patrolling the islands on the assumption that it was merely patrolling its own territory, then the lack of Yemen protest is all the more remarkable and calls for some explanation which Yemen has not altogether provided. Yemen was of course preoccupied with its own civil war between 1962 and 1970; and a good deal of this naval patrolling must have been in the high seas rather than in the territorial sea of the islands. Eritrea claims that the Ethiopian naval patrols were also enforcing fishing regulations. This seems credible for it would have provided cover for inspecting the papers of vessels even on the high seas and the rebels would hardly have confined their supply operations to ships flying the Ethiopian flag.

495. And yet these logbooks of naval patrols give relatively little evidence of activity on or even near to the islands. It is interesting to consider in this context the press statement issued by the Yemen Embassy in Mogadishu on 3 July 1973 stating "the Y.A.R. always maintains its sovereignty over its islands in the Red Sea, with the exception of the islands of Gabal Abu Ali and Gabal Attair which were given to Ethiopia by Britain when the latter left Aden and surrendered power in our Southern Yemen". This surmise was of course mistaken. But is does amount to a statement that Yemen at the time had no presence in either of these two mentioned islands and had little idea what was happening there. This, however, was the time of the Arab press rumours of Ethiopia having allowed Israel the use of certain Red Sea islands. This same press release stated that Yemen had, accompanied by journalists and press correspondents, investigated the position on "Lesser Hanish, Greater Hanish, Zuqar, Alzubair' Alswabe', and several other islands at the Yemeni coast". These were found to be "free from any foreign infiltration whatsoever".

Presumably this was also the inspection by the military committee of the Arab League (see para. 321, above). This statement has the ring of truth. It most probably was the position that these islands, including Zuqar and both Hanish islands, were then normally empty of people or activity other than that of small coastal fishermen plying their traditional way of life and calling at the islands when their work took them there. But it is significant that Yemen could apparently take the above inspection party without any repercussions from Ethiopia.

496. There is much that is ambiguous and unexplained on both sides in this evidence of naval patrols. On balance the episode appears to the Tribunal to lend some weight to the Eritrean case. But again it is a matter of relative weight. There is no compelling case here

for either Party. And again it is very difficult on the basis of this material to give it great weight in claims to land territory.

497. The petroleum agreements made by Yemen and by Ethiopia (and then by Eritrea) from 1972 onwards do surprisingly little to resolve the problem, for these agreements, in so far as they extended to offshore areas, were not really concerned with the islands at all, but with either the outer boundary formed by the extent of the then exploitable depths of seabed, or by the coastal median line, which was the temporary boundary actually contemplated for such agreements by the 1977 Yemeni continental shelf legislation. As was reflected by the questions put to the Parties in the closing moments of the July 1998 hearings, the agreements seemed almost to ignore the islands; not surprisingly, considering that the volcanic geological nature of the islands meant that they were totally uninteresting to the oil companies.

498. As already stated above, the Tribunal attaches little importance to the agreements by both Parties with Shell for geological investigations. The area covered by the contract activities likely traversed these islands. But the Tribunal has little doubt that Shell was operating with the permission of both Parties, and was getting information primarily for its own use, in order to decide about which areas of the continental shelf it might be worth making production agreements.

499. When it comes to actual agreements for exploration, whether in the form of full petroleum production-sharing agreements or less than that, two of the agreements made by Yemen encompassed the Zuqar–Hanish Islands totally (one with Adair, which was very short-lived and never went into effect, and one with Tomen-Santa Fe), while the agreements made by Ethiopia (Ethiopia/Shell) avoided extending to these islands or, in the instance of the Ethiopia-IPC/Amoco agreement of 1989, cuts across Greater Hanish, the division apparently depending on precisely how one plots the coastal median line.

500. After the careful examination of the contract areas of the oil agreements of both Parties, the conclusions to be drawn from this material seem to be reasonably clear. Eritrea can and does point to the IPC/Amoco agreement with Ethiopia which cuts the Island of Hanish. There are various versions. In some versions of the attempts to draw the contract area on a map, only the tip of Hanish is within the Eritrean side of the line; in others the line appears to portray most of the island as Eritrean, leaving only a relatively small portion of it to Yemen. It is surely apparent that the contract area was defined simply in terms appropriate for the essentially maritime interests of the contracting party, and that this, in conformity with normal practice where there is no agreed and settled maritime boundary, was made the coastal median line, ignoring the possible effect of islands. It seems in effect to have been agreed and drawn on the illustrative map of the contract simply ignoring the islands. If Ethiopia had had it in mind to use the agreement for the purpose of illustrating a claim to the island of Hanish, Ethiopia would surely not have given itself only two-thirds of the island; it would have had the line make an excursion round and embrace the whole island. As it is, it seems to the Tribunal that the Ethiopian and Eritrean agreements are in effect neutral as far as the present task of the Tribunal is concerned; as indeed Eritrea argued. This does not mean that the Eritrean claim to these islands is unfounded; but it does mean that the oil agreements do little to assist that claim, except in so far as the IPC/Amoco Agreement tends to neutralize the Yemeni argument that petroleum agreements as such provide confirmation of sovereignty.

501. Yemen, besides the unconvincing suggestion that the Shell Company's seismic investigation of a large area right across the southern Red Sea somehow confirms the Yemeni claims to the Zuqar and Hanish islands, has in the Tomen-Santa Fe seismic agreement of 1974–75 referred to an agreement in which the contract does apparently embrace both Zuqar–Hanish, or most of Greater Hanish Island. This also resulted in certain activities by the company, including a collection of samples from Zuqar (see

para. 409, above). This again does not establish that Yemen has validated its claim to both these islands. But as concluded above, the agreements produced by both parties fail to establish evidence of sovereignty. Perhaps it helps to see these petroleum agreements of the 1970s in perspective to remember that in 1973 there was a Yemeni inspection of the islands, with journalists and representatives of the Arab League military committee, that found all these islands empty.

502. It was later that there was more activity; notably the construction in 1993 by the Total Oil company of an air landing strip on Hanish, for the recreational visits of their employees, and as a by-product of their concession agreement with Yemen. That agreement did not encompass either Zuqar or Hanish. Nevertheless, the fact that there were regular excursion flights constitutes evidence of governmental authority and the exercise of it. Nor did it apparently attract any kind of protest from Eritrea; though of course by this time the civil war was over and Eritrea was established as an independent state.

503. As neither Party has in the opinion of the Tribunal made a convincing case to these islands on the basis of an ancient title in the case of Yemen, or, of a succession title in the case of Eritrea, the Tribunal's decision on sovereignty must be based to an important extent upon what seems to have been the position in Zuqar and Hanish and their adjoining islets and rocks in the last decade or so leading up to the present arbitration. Anything approaching what might be called a settlement, or the continuous display of governmental authority and presence, of the kind found in some of the classical cases even for inhospitable territory, is hardly to be expected. For very few people would wish to visit these waterless, volcanic islands except for a special reason and probably a temporary one. Nevertheless, it is clear from the documents mentioned earlier in this Award that both Yemen and Ethiopia had formulated claims to both islands at least by the late 1980s and had indeed it would seem held secret negotiations on the claims; which negotiations, at least according to the Eritrean "Top Secret" internal report, had at first promised a compromise solution on the basis of a median line which would presumably have given Zuqar and Little Hanish to Yemen and Greater Hanish to Ethiopia. But this came to nothing. So now one must look at the *effectivités* for the solution.

504. Yemen has been able to present the Tribunal with a list of some forty-eight alleged Yemeni happenings or incidents in respect of "the islands", which occurred in the period between early 1989 and mid-1991. This list is not confined to the central group, for there is included for example the decisions of the 1989 London Conference on the lighthouses, and the building of a lighthouse on al Tayr in July 1989. It is evident though that Zuqar features very prominently in the list. It is also evident that Eritrea has relatively very little to show in respect of Zuqar. The Tribunal has no doubt that the island of Zuqar is under the sovereignty of Yemen.

505. In respect of Hanish the matter is not so clear cut. The Eritrean claim is well established as a claim and is clearly of great importance to that very newly-independent country. The refusal to agree to a Yemeni aerial survey of the Islands and Ethiopia's responsive claim of title to some of them is significant. So also is its arrest of Yemeni fishermen on Greater Hanish and its assertion, in response to Yemen's protest to the Security Council, that the area was within Ethiopian jurisdiction.

506. There was some emphasis by Eritrea on a scheme to put beacons on Hanish to assist Amoco's seismic testing; there is no clear evidence that they were actually installed. Any such installation of beacons covered several locations, of which Great Hanish Island was only one, and would have been short-lived; the evidence provided by Eritrea mentions two weeks, and provides for removal of the beacons on completion of the seismic work. Moreover, the beacons were placed by the oil company, Amoco, with only a limited role for the Ethiopian government in protecting the oil company personnel and the temporary beacons from the attentions of "random individuals". Finally, there is evidence of the issuance, in 1980, of an Ethiopian radio transmitting license to Delft

Geophysical Company, which provided for a station to be located at "Greater Hanish Island, Port of Assab vicinity".

507. Yemen has more to show by way of presence and display of authority. Putting aside the lighthouse in the north of the island, there was the Ardoukoba expedition and camp-site which was made under the aegis of the Yemeni Government. There is the air landing site, as well as the production of what appears to be evidence of frequent scheduled flights, no doubt mainly for the off-days of Total employees; and there is the May 1995 license to a Yemeni company (seemingly with certain German nationals associated in a joint venture scheme) to develop a tourist project (recreational diving is apparently the possible attraction to tourism) on Greater Hanish.

* * *

508. Therefore, after examination of all relevant historical, factual and legal considerations, the Tribunal finds in the present case that, on balance, and with the greatest respect for the sincerity and foundations and claims of both Parties, the weight of the evidence supports Yemen's assertions of the exercise of the functions of state authority with respect to the Zuqar–Hanish group. The Tribunal is further fortified in finding in favour of Yemen by the evidence that these islands fell under the jurisdiction of the Arabian coast during the Ottoman Empire; and that there was later a persistent expectation reflected in the British Foreign Office papers submitted in evidence by the Parties that these islands would ultimately return to Arab rule. The Tribunal therefore unanimously finds that the islands, islet, rocks, and low-tide elevations of the Zuqar-Hanish group, including, but not limited to, Three Foot Rock, Parkin Rock, Rocky Islets, Pin Rock, Suyual Hanish, Mid Islet, Double Peak Island, Round Island, North Round Island, Quoin Island (13°43'N, 42°48'E), Chor Rock, Greater Hanish, Peaky Islet, Mushajirah, Addar Ail Islets, Haycock Island (13°47'N, 42°47'E; not to be confused with the Haycock Islands to the southwest of Greater Hanish), Low Island (13°52'N, 42°49'E) including the unnamed islets and rocks close north, east and south, Lesser Hanish including the unnamed islets and rocks close north east, Tongue Island and the unnamed islet close south, Near Island and the unnamed islet close south east, Shark Island, Jabal Zuqar Island, High Island, and the Abu Ali Islands (including Quoin Island (14°05'N, 42°49'E) and Pile Island) are subject to the territorial sovereignty of Yemen.

Jabal al-Tayr and the Zubayr Group of Islands

509. Both the lone island of Jabal al-Tayr, and the Zubayr group of islands and islets, call for separate treatment, as they are a considerable distance from the other islands as well as from each other. They are not only relatively isolated, but also are both well out to sea, and so not proximate to either coast, though they are slightly nearer to the Yemeni coastal islands than they are to the coast and coastal islands of Eritrea. Both are well eastward of a coastal median line. Here again, the Tribunal has had to weigh the relative merits of the Parties' evidence, which has been sparse on both sides, of the exercise of functions of state and governmental authority.

510. The traditional importance of both groups has been that they have been lighthouse islands (the Zubayr light was on Centre Peak, the southernmost islet of the group). It will be clear from the history of the Red Sea lighthouses (see Chapter VI, above) that, although, or perhaps even because, lighthouses were so important for 19th and early 20th century navigation, a government could be asked to take responsibility or even volunteer to be responsible for them, without necessarily either seeming to claim sovereignty over the site or acquiring it. The practical question was not one of owner-

ship, but rather of which government was willing, or might be persuaded, to take on the responsibility, and sometimes the cost, if not permanently then at least for a season.

511. It will be recollected that Centre Peak in the Zubayr group was an island in which Italy, in its 1930s period of colonial expansion, had taken a great interest; the Centre Peak light was abandoned by the British in 1932, but reactivated by Italy the following year. The British sought and obtained the usual assurances about the Treaty of Lausanne status of the island (see paras. 216–218 above). So for a time at least this group fell under the jurisdiction of the authority on the African coast.

512. Yet during the Second World War and the subsequent British occupation of Eritrea, it was decided that Great Britain was under no obligation to maintain the Centre Peak light or indeed the Haycock light.

513. An important turning point in the history of the northern islands of Jabal al-Tayr and the Zubayr group was the 1989 London conference about lighthouses. This was rather different from previous conferences. This conference was to be the last of its kind, because its main purpose was to liquidate the former international arrangements for administration of the lights and the sharing of costs. The final arrangements made for the lights (which were then still of the greatest importance for navigation) were therefore intended to be permanent. No further conference was envisaged.

514. It will be remembered that Yemen was invited to the conference as an observer on the plea to the British Government that the two lighthouse islands of Abu Ali and Jabal al-Tayr, "lie within the exclusive economic zone of the Yemen Arab Republic", and that because of this Yemen was willing to take on the responsibility of managing and operating the lights. It was also the fact that Yemen had already installed new lights on both of these sites. The offer from Yemen was gratefully accepted by the conference. There had been hopes that Egypt might take on the work but Egypt was not willing to do so.

515. The matter of sovereignty was not on the agenda of the conference, nor was it discussed. Yemen's own request to be invited to the conference had wisely avoided raising the matter. Moreover, there were at the conference the usual references to the Treaty of Lausanne formula concerning indeterminate sovereignty.

516. Nevertheless, the decision of the conference to accept the Yemeni offer over the lights does reflect a confidence and expectation of the member governments of the conference of a continued Yemeni presence on these lighthouse islands for, at any rate, the foreseeable future. Repute is also an important ingredient for the consolidation of title.

517. There is also another matter where Yemen is able to show what amounts to important support for its case over these northern islands, and that is the substantially new information on petroleum agreements that was made available to the Tribunal at the supplementary hearings held for this purpose in July 1998. There are two such agreements which appear to be relevant for the islands presently under determination.

518. First, there is the agreement made by the Yemeni Government with the Shell company on 20 November 1973. The western boundary of the contract area in this agreement is drawn so as to include within it the Zubayr group. It does not include Jabal al-Tayr, but passes at a distance which might encompass the territorial sea of that island, depending on the breadth of the territorial sea allowed to it for the purposes of a maritime delimitation.

519. The second is the Hunt Oil production sharing agreement ratified on 10 March 1985. The western contract area boundary of this agreement again includes the Zubayr group, but also appears from the illustrative map to brush the island of Jabal al-Tayr, and of course plainly includes a part of its territorial sea.

520. These agreements were not protested by Ethiopia (though it should be remembered that the Hunt agreement was made at a time when the Ethiopian civil war was still raging).

521. Neither Ethiopia nor Eritrea has made any petroleum agreements encompassing these islands. Eritrea did, however, make agreements in 1995 and 1997 with the Anadarko Oil Company, which extended in the direction of these islands and towards what appears to be an approximate median line between coasts. Yemen protested this line on 4 January 1997 as a "blatant" violation of the territorial waters of both groups and of her economic rights "in the region". This was, of course, some time after the signature of the Agreement on Principles and indeed the Arbitration Agreement initiating these proceedings.

522. The legal history of these northern and isolated islands has been mixed and varied. It has been seen that even as late as 1989 it was assumed that their sovereign status was still indeterminate in accordance with the status impressed upon them, until it should be changed in a lawful way, by the Treaty of Lausanne. Nevertheless, by 1995 it was doubtful whether any dispute over Yemen's claim to them would be agreed to be submitted to this Tribunal. Even Eritrea at one point made a proposal for the agreement in which these islands were not mentioned.

523. The Tribunal has not found this particular question an easy one. There is little evidence on either side of actual or persistent activities on and around these islands. But in view of their isolated location and inhospitable character, probably little evidence will suffice.

524. Therefore, after examination of all relevant historical, factual and legal considerations, the Tribunal unanimously finds in the present case that, on the basis of the foregoing, the weight of the evidence supports the conclusion that the island of Jabal al-Tayr, and the islands, islets, rocks and low-tide elevations forming the Zubayr group, including, but not limited to, Quoin Island (15°12'N, 42°03'E), Haycock Island (15°10'N, 42°07'E; not to be confused with the Haycock Islands to the southwest of Greater Hanish), Rugged Island, Table Peak Island, Saddle Island and the unnamed islet close north west, Low Island (15°06'N, 42°06'E) and the unnamed rock close east, Middle Reef, Saba Island, Connected Island, East Rocks, Shoe Rock, Jabal Zubayr Island, and Centre Peak Island are subject to the territorial sovereignty of Yemen.

The Traditional Fishing Regime

525. In making this award on sovereignty, the Tribunal has been aware that Western ideas of territorial sovereignty are strange to people brought up in the Islamic tradition and familiar with notions of territory very different from those recognized in contemporary international law. Moreover, appreciation of regional legal traditions is necessary to render an Award which, in the words of the Joint Statement signed by the Parties on 21 May 1996, will "allow the re-establishment and the development of a trustful and lasting cooperation between the two countries".

526. In finding that the Parties each have sovereignty over various of the Islands the Tribunal stresses to them that such sovereignty is not inimical to, but rather entails, the perpetuation of the traditional fishing regime in the region. This existing regime has operated, as the evidence presented to the Tribunal amply testifies, around the Hanish and Zuqar islands and the islands of Jabal al-Tayr and the Zubayr group. In the exercise of its sovereignty over these islands, Yemen shall ensure that the traditional fishing regime of free access and enjoyment for the fishermen of both Eritrea and Yemen shall be preserved for the benefit of the lives and livelihoods of this poor and industrious order of men.

Osman v. Elasha

IN THE SUPREME COURT OF JUDICATURE
IN THE COURT OF APPEAL (CIVIL DIVISION)
ON APPEAL FROM THE HIGH COURT OF JUSTICE
FAMILY DIVISION
(MR JUSTICE CONNELL)

FAFMI 1999/9632/2

Royal Courts of Justice
Strand, London, W2A 2LL

Thursday 24 June 1999

Before
LORD JUSTICE STUART-SMITH
LORD JUSTICE PILL
LORD JUSTICE THORPE

————

HALA BIN OSMAN   Appellant

v.

ELASHA MAJDI ELASH   Respondent

————

(Computer Aided Transcript of the Stenograph Notes of
Smith Bernal Reporting Limited, 180 Fleet Street
London EC4A 2HD   Tel: 0171 421 4040
Official Shorthand Writers to the Court)

————

MISS GERALDINE MORE O'FERRALL (instructed by Messrs Miles & Partners, London E1 7EZ) appeared on behalf of the Appellant Mother.

MR NICHOLAS CARDEN (instructed by Sally Morris, Middlesex) appeared on behalf of the Respondent Father.

———————————

*   Taken from the original text from Smith Bernal Reporting Limited.

543

JUDGMENT
(As approved by the court)

Crown Copyright

LORD JUSTICE STUART-SMITH: I will ask Lord Justice Thorpe to give the first judgment

LORD JUSTICE THORPE: Last week Mr Justice Connell ordered the peremptory return of three boys abducted by their mother from the Sudan. On Tuesday we granted her application for permission to appeal. Today we decide the appeal.

For the facts I take the words of Connell J. from a note of the judgment below agreed by counsel and approved by him.

The father was born in 1956 and is now 43. The mother was born in June 1970 and is 29. On 19 December 1986 they married in the Sudan. The father lived in this jurisdiction previously and earlier had bought a property which he still owns. Having married in the Sudan, in February 1987 the mother and father came to the United Kingdom. In England on 1 April 1989 F was born. Also in England on 3 April 1991 M was born. In 1991 the mother, father and the two boys returned to the Sudan.

There is an issue between the parents that the mother at some time after August 1991 commenced a relationship with a Mr M. On 23 April 1993 a third boy was born in the Sudan. In May 1993 the father came to the United Kingdom. In December 1993 the mother followed and brought the three boys. In April 1994 she returned to the Sudan with the children. She has not lived in this jurisdiction since that time.

In 1995 the mother and father divorced in the Sudan. For a period the children ceased to live with the mother. On 15 June 1995 the mother married Mr M in the Sudan. On 17 September 1995 the mother went to the equivalent of the Magistrates' Court in Sudan. She applied for the children to be returned to her and that the father should not interfere with the custody of the children with her. On 20 November 1995 an order was made by the court which appears in terms to be a consent order. The mother said she did not in truth consent. It was not possible to decide the issue.

An order was made for the children to remain living with the father's family. The mother, as local law indicates, was disqualified from obtaining custody by reason of her re-marriage. The children were looked after by the mother's family and in particular the maternal grandmother. However the maternal grandmother had other difficulties which prevented this. The order therefore provided that the children live with the father's mother. The order also contained provision for contact Thursday and Friday alternating. It incorporated provision for the mother to visit at any time.

On 2 April 1996 the mother gave birth to K. In July 1997 the father remarried in the Sudan. His wife and daughter are in the Sudan.

In April 1999 the mother was enjoying contact to the three children. On 9 May the mother together with the four children and her second husband came to the United Kingdom. Upon arrival at Heathrow she sough asylum in this jurisdiction. She did not tell the father or his family of her intention to come to the United Kingdom. The mother's reason for taking this dramatic step was that she was deprived of seeing the children as and when she wanted. She was dissatisfied with the provision of the order of 20 November 1995 and, accordingly, decided to come here and claim asylum. In those circumstances she was accommodated in temporary accommodation. Her claim for asylum will be considered on 4 October 1999.

On 21 May the mother filed a statement in support of her application for residence and to prevent the removal of the children from England and Wales. On the same day she obtained an *ex parte* order from Mrs Justice Hale. On 28 May Mr Justice Bodey continued that order. On 4 June Her Honour Judge Pearlman ordered that the children remain in the interim care and control of the mother and ordered the injunctions to continue.

In relation to those facts the judge made the following additional findings. He said:

> In relation to the parents, the mother's future is uncertain. Her background is in the Sudan – only in this jurisdiction very recently, it is not known what is the basis of her asylum or the prospects of success. All that is known is that the application will not be considered until 4 October 1999. The father on the other hand has spent half his time in England and half his time in the Sudan. In his oral evidence he said in recent times he had given up his work, had bought a property in the Sudan – his intention is or was until the issue of these proceedings – to return to the Sudan and live there and live in the property – intended to put this into practice later this year or sometime next year. I heard his evidence and accept this was his plan, only interrupted as a result of these proceedings. In my view it is clear that the children had habitually resided in the Sudan until 9 May 1999. They are Sudanese children removed by the mother from familiar surroundings to the United Kingdom. They speak a very limited amount of English. The children are now living in temporary accommodation. There is much doubt as to their future and that of the mother.

Mr Justice Connell recorded the submissions of the parents thus:

> The mother says, adjourn the residential application and grant her interim residence in the meantime for future consideration of her application at a later stage when the outcome of her application for asylum is either decided upon or when more is known about it . . .
>
> The father says, these are Sudanese children, their whole background is Sudanese and the court should make a peremptory order for their return.

He directed himself as to the law by adopting a recent judgment of Mr Justice Charles in the case of *Re Z (Abduction: non-Convention Country)* [1999] 1 FLR 1270. In that judgment Mr Justice Charles conducted a full and scholarly view of the modern case law and distilled a number of propositions which Mr Justice Connell rightly found to be of great assistance. He said:

> In the light of that case, which is a helpful guide, it is clear that in this case and it is common ground, that the welfare of the children is the paramount consideration. Equally, as stated by Charles J., there is a presumption that the prima facie position is in favour of returning the children to the country from which they were wrongfully removed. Thirdly, the presumption can be displaced in certain circumstances. Fourthly, the application by the father was promptly made – the children have been in the country for six weeks. The question is – is the presumption displaced?

Mr Justice Connell turned then to the expert evidence which was not in dispute. A Miss Ragab told the judge that

> The most important fact in Sudanese personal law, mainly Muslim *shari'a* law, [was that] once a divorced mother has remarried . . . the care of the children moves to the maternal grandmother. If the maternal grandmother is unable . . . to care for them, care moves to the paternal grandmother in all cases.

That expert had filed a written report before giving oral evidence. In her written report she had said:

. . . there is no Welfare Officer in Sudan. However, the court would have testimony of witnesses close to the families, because socially the Sudanese community is very close. The court normally takes full account of the social background of the children and their families, and the economic capacity of the custodian, the health of the carer and above all what would be the best interest of the children, according to the Sudanese culture. Despite the same principles, the concept is different from the British concept.

Mr Justice Connell then recorded the submission of the mother's counsel in these terms:

Accordingly it is submitted by Miss More O'Ferrall that it is contrary to the best interests of the children to order return to Sudan as in the present circumstances the mother has no chance of any order or opportunity of changing the contact arrangements . . .

Miss More O'Ferrall lays considerable stress upon *Re JA (A Minor) (Abduction: non-Convention Country)* [1998] 1 FLR 231 which contains a consideration of United Arab Emirates and Muslim *shari'a* law.

The judge then cited at length from the judgment of Lord Justice Ward in *Re JA* before concluding as follows:

It can be seen from the consideration of that passage that in different case the Court of Appeal has emphasised different aspects of matters re abduction from a non-Convention country — different emphasis on different circumstances in the cases. Hence the apparent contradiction between *Re JA* and *Re M*.

Here the evidence of the expert is that the courts in the Sudan do take account of the best interests of the children but they do so in accordance with Sudanese law and culture, which involved different concepts from British concepts. With a Sudanese Muslim family habitually resident in the Sudan this is scarcely surprising.

I cannot conclude that Ward LJ's view was that the courts in this jurisdiction would never make an order for return when *shari'a* law applied, particularly if the children's best interests required that solution. Each case must be decided on its own circumstances. The approach of the courts of the competing jurisdiction is an important feature but is not conclusive. In my view the courts in Sudan will apply Muslim law which is appropriate and acceptable to this Muslim family.

Before us Miss More O'Ferrall renews her reliance on the case of *Re JA* and her submission that the absence of justice for her client in Sudan adversely affects the welfare of the children. She says that the judge has made an order that separates the children from both parents and returns them to a jurisdiction where there can be no discretionary review of all relevant facts and circumstances to determine child welfare but only the rigid application of *shari'a* rules that deprive the children of a natural upbringing. As in *Re JA* she says this court should overturn the peremptory order on the grounds that the Sudanese system is inimical to child welfare

The ease of international and intercontinental air travel has created the evil of international child abduction. The response of the international community has been the negotiation of the Convention on the civil aspects of international child abduction signed at the Hague on 25 October 1980. Its ratification by the United Kingdom was followed by its introduction into domestic law by the Child Abduction and Custody Act 1985. The Convention has been extremely successful. Since 1980 no less than 57 states have joined the club. For the purposes of this judgment I shall refer to states that have acceded as members and those that have not as non-members.

However, there has been an obvious limitation to this success. The members states by and large all derive their sense of law and justice from the Judaeo-Chritsian route. No state that settles civil and family disputes according to Islamic law has joined the club. The nearest approach is the making of bi-lateral treaties between France and Spain on the one hand and North African states on the other. There is also the prospect of accession by states with predominantly Muslim populations. For instance Turkey has signed the Convention but not yet ratified it and Turkmenistan is a full member. When a state accedes to the Convention existing members have the option to recognise the accession, thus creating binding treaty rights between the states, or to withhold recognition. The Treaty is only effective between the acceding states and those existing members who have recognised accession.

It must be emphasised that the Convention is limited to the provision of regulation to ensure the swift return of abducted children. One of the underlying principles is that it is for the country of origin to determine the conflict between the parents that has culminated in flight. The Convention does not provide any regulation for the determination of that underlying dispute. That is for the *lex fori*.

Of course the successful operation of the Convention depends upon mutual confidence that the family dispute will be determined in the country of origin according to standards and principles of justice broadly comparable to those available in the returning state. However, as the number of club members has increased it may be increasingly difficult to maintain that confidence. For instance the break-up of the USSR and the former Yugoslav Republic has seen the accession of a number of individual jurisdictions. Besides Turkmenistan, Uzbekistan has acceded, as have Moldavia and Belarus. The United Kingdom has recognised the accession of Turkmenistan and recognition of the other states is pending.

Before recognising accession the Foreign and Commonwealth Office makes enquires locally to satisfy itself that there is in place a central authority and a justice system capable of providing the reciprocal service that the Convention requires. However, I do not understand there to be any requirement of minimum standards of the family justice system in the acceding state. Whilst consideration was given to setting such a requirement, it was decided that there was too obvious a risk of invidious comparisons and inflammatory exclusions. To this extent arrangements have developed since June 1997 when the official solicitor, as central authority, was directly involved with vetting, as noted by Lord Justice Ward in *Re JA* at 240A. Of course the maintenance of mutual confidence within the member states is crucial to the practical operation of the Convention. But the promotion of that confidence is probably most effectively achieved by the development of channels for judicial communication such as the Seminar for Judges convened in 1998 in Holland by the Hague Conference on Private International Law.

The welfare principle as paramount has been the cornerstone of the family justice system in this jurisdiction for many years. We regards it as a touch stone in measuring the quality of other family justice systems. Article 3 of the United Nations Convention on the Rights of the Child 1989 requires no less. But what constitutes the welfare of the child must be subject to the cultural background and expectations of the jurisdiction striving to achieve it. It does not seem to me possible to regard it as an absolute standard. It would be quite unrealistic to suppose that the concept of child welfare is equally understood and applied throughout the 57 member states. The further development of international collaboration to combat child abduction may well depend upon the capacity of states to respect a variety of concepts of child welfare derived from differing cultures and traditions. A recognition of this reality must inform judicial policy with regard to the return of the children abducted from non-member states.

The principles determining outcome of applications for the return of children abducted from non-member states have been considered in a line of cases in this court, culminating in the case of *Re JA*. In that case the leading judgment was given by Lord Justice Ward, as it was in its immediate predecessor *Re P (A Minor) (Child Abduction: Non-Convention Country)* [1997] 2 WLR 223. In the earlier case this court allowed an appeal from the decision of Mr Justice Stuart-White who had felt himself constrained by authority to determine the application as though notionally made under the Convention when his instincts suggested that the opposite outcome would be better for the child. After a full review of the authorities Lord Justice Ward emphasised that the welfare consideration is always paramount. In the later case of *Re JA* he had occasion to consider a point raised by a respondent's notice that had not been considered by Mr Justice Singer. The point was defined thus:

> . . . because the best interests of the child is the court's paramount consideration, it is necessary that the court have regard to the way in which the issue is likely to be resolved in the competing jurisdiction so as to satisfy itself that the question will be decided along broadly similar welfare lines to the way we have to judge the issues which arise.

The expert evidence established that in the State of Sharjah the mother had care of the child, subject to the father's guardianship, until the age of 12, when care passed automatically to the father. The mother's care had to be exercised within about 100 miles of the father's home and the court had no discretion to entertain her application to relocate to the United Kingdom. Lord Justice Ward, having reviewed the authorities, said:

> These authorities seem to me clearly to establish that it is an abdication of the responsibility and an abnegation of the duty of this court to the ward under its protection to surrender the determination of its ward's future to a foreign court whose regime may be inimical to the child's welfare. If driven to it, I would reluctantly say that the decision of this court in *Re M (Abduction: Peremptory Return Order)* [1996] 1 FLR 478 was decided *per incuriam*.

Whilst I am in agreement with the first sentence of the citation I do not share his view that the decision in *Re M* was reached *per incuriam*. I believe that it holds a legitimate place in the stream of authority, bearing in mind that statements of judicial principle are always susceptible to the requirements of family cases.

In *Re M* Lord Justice Waite had said at 480:

> Underlying the whole purpose of the peremptory return order is a principle of international comity under which judges in England will assume that facilities for a fair hearing will be provided in the court of the other jurisdiction, and that due account will be taken by overseas judges of what has been said, ordered and undertaken to be done within the English jurisdiction. That is of course reciprocal. It has to be presumed that judges in other countries will make similar assumptions about the workings of our own judicial system.

As a general principle of private international law that seems to me to be properly stated. In support of the approach adopted by Lord Justice Waite in *Re M*, I would also cite the decision of this court in *Re S (Minors) (Abduction)* [1994] FLR 297, seemingly not cited in *Re JA*. There the appellant mother submitted that the question was:

> whether or not the court should order a peremptory return to a jurisdiction which does not apply a similar system of law to that governing decisions over the welfare of children adopted in the courts of England.

The country in question was Pakistan, which meant that "Muslim law principles will be applied to the case unless there are overriding reasons to the contrary". In deciding the issue Balcombe LJ adopted the approach of the Master of the Rolls in *Re F* [1991] Fam 25 and held that it would not be appropriate to deny the Pakistan courts jurisdiction merely because they would try to give effect to what was the child's welfare from the Muslim point of view. In a concurring judgment Lord Justice Nolan said:

> But it is implicit in s 1(1)(a) [of the Children Act 1989] that the paramountcy of the child's welfare is to be observed consistently with the law to which the child is subject.

I am also attracted by a passage from the judgment of Mr Justice Brennan in an Australian case, cited with approval by Lord Justice Ward in the case of *Re P*. The sentence which I extract from the citation is this:

In any event, when the Family Court is determining an application for the return of a child to the place of the child's ordinary residence, the capacity, sensitivity or procedures of the courts of that country are likely to be of minor importance unless the evidence shows that those courts are unlikely to make and to enforce orders deemed to be appropriate in that society to protect the child and to serve his or her best interests.

That citation emphasises the importance of according to each state liberty to determine the family justice system and principles that it deems appropriate to protect the child and to serve his best interests. There is an obvious threat to comity if a state whose system derives from Judaeo-Christian foundations condemns a system derived from an Islamic foundation when that system is conceived by its originators and operators to promote and protect the interests of children within that society and according to its traditions and values.

What weighed with Lord Justice Ward in *Re JA* was not so much that child welfare would not be considered as that the mother would have right to apply in Sharjah to relocate to this jurisdiction. The inter-relationship between the wrongful international abduction of children and the rights of a parent to relocate on separation have always seem to me to be intricately interconnected. In this jurisdiction we do not refuse the application of the parent with the residence order the right to exercise that responsibility in another jurisdiction, unless the decision is clearly shown to be incompatible with the paramount welfare consideration; see *Chamberlain v. De La Mare* [1983] 4 FLR 434. Such an approach reinforces the obligation on the parent with the responsibility of providing the primary home to apply for permission to relocate and not to abduct. But the approach that we adopt is by no means universal or even common place even amongst the member states. Obviously the adoption of a more restrictive approach to relocation applications increases the pressure and temptation to abduct.

The Council of Europe has worked hard, and continues to work hard, for the harmonisation of family law amongst its membership. However, the number and diversity of the member states makes this a difficult if not impossible goal. Even the European Union has as yet made no endeavour to map out a common approach to family law. I have no doubt that the number and the diversity of the states that have joined the Hague club have made it impossible to formulate minimum standard requirements of other family justice systems before recognising accession. As a matter of logic if we make no investigation and in litigation permit no criticism of the family justice systems operating in the member states, I am extremely doubtful of the wisdom of permitting the abducting parent to criticise the standards of the family justice system in the non-member state of habitual residence, save in exceptional circumstances, such as those therein defined by the Master of the Rolls in *Re F* at page 31 when he referred to persecution, or ethnic, sex, or any other discrimination. I am equally doubtful of the principle enabling a judge in this jurisdiction to criticise the standards or paramount principles applied by the family justice systems of a non-member state save in such exceptional circumstances.

In summary there are three relatively recent decisions of this court on defences to peremptory return applications asserting that the system of justice in the foreign state threatened the paramount welfare principle. They are of course *Re S*, *Re M* and *Re JA*. Only in the last case did the defence succeed. But in my opinion that was not because this court was signalling a change of course but because expert evidence established that risk of harm to the child if return were ordered.

Of these three cases perhaps that which is nearest on the facts to this is the case of *Re S*. In neither case was there any specific evidence of harm or risk of harm. In each there was a generalised attack on the application of Muslim perceptions of child welfare. Both states had received system of law during the brief flowering of the British Empire. Pakistan applied section 17 of the Guardians and Wards Act 1890 in these terms:

In the vent of a dispute involving the physical care of a child, the court shall be guided by what, consistently with the law to which the minor is subject, appears in the circumstances to be for the welfare of the minor.

Post independence both states have chosen to move to an orthodox Islamification of family law. In such circumstances it would seem to me to be particularly insensitive of a court in London to hold that that move offended a concept of child welfare that we retain.

I agree with Mr Justice Connell that outcome in particular cases is particularly dependent on the factual matrix. His findings of fact cannot be challenged. Nor can his directions as to the law be faulted. In may opinion he was plainly right in his conclusions.

I would dismiss this appeal.

LORD JUSTICE PILL: I agree. The judge found the following facts at page 161:

In my view it is clear that the children had habitually resided in the Sudan until 9 May 1999. They are Sudanese children removed by the mother from familiar surroundings to the UK. They speak a very limited amount of English. The children are now living in temporary accommodation, there is much doubt as to their future and that of the mother.

At page 168:

In relation to the welfare of the children: in May 1999 they were settled in the Sudan. They appear to be doing pretty well. The eldest boy won a prize for "ideal pupil". They saw the mother and had extended contact. The abduction took place when they were on extended contact. In this country they are strangers. Their future is uncertain. The father says, and I accept, that he intends to return this year or next year to Khartoum when he has bought a house. The mother's broader family is in the Sudan — has lived there for the last five years.

As to the law which would be applied in the Sudan, the judge received evidence from an expert who set out the principles of law which apply in circumstances such as the present.

The judge concluded at page 167:

Here the evidence of the expert is that the courts in the Sudan do take account of the best interests of the children but they do so in accordance with Sudanese law and culture, which involves different concepts from British concepts. With a Sudanese Muslim family habitually resident in the Sudan this is scarcely surprising. In my view the courts in Sudan will apply Muslim law which is appropriate and acceptable to this Muslim family.

It is not disputed that in the Sudan there is a judicial system which operates under the rule of law. What is submitted is that the operation of the Sudanese rule that in present circumstances the mother cannot obtain a residence order, is unacceptable and inconsistent with English law notions of child welfare even though substantial access by the mother to the children is provided.

I have no difficulty in accepting the judge's conclusion that the application of Muslim law to this Muslim family is appropriate and acceptable. It is submitted on behalf of the mother that the welfare of children, paramount in English law, must take priority over notions of international comity and respect for foreign courts in non-Convention states. In my judgment the two are not inevitably in conflict. These are Sudanese children. Their welfare may well be served by a decision in accordance with Sudanese law which may be taken to reflect the norms and values of the Sudanese society in which they live. That is a principle which the judge was entitled to take into account upon the facts of the case, thereby giving paramounty to the welfare of the children. A solution in accordance with local law is capable of being in the best interests of the children.

In *Re F* [1991] 1 FLR 1 Lord Donaldson MR stated at page 5:

Which court should decide depends, as I have said, on whether the other court will apply principles which are acceptable to the English courts as being appropriate, subject always to any contra-indication such as those mentioned in Art 13 of the Hague Convention, or a risk of persecution or discrimination, but prima facie the court to decide is that of the State where the child was habitually resident immediately before its removal.

Lord Donaldson also approved a statement made by Lord Justice Balcombe in *G v. G (Minors: Abduction)* [1991] 2 FLR 506. Lord Justice Balcombe stated:

. . . in enacting the 1985 Act, Parliament was not departing form the fundamental principle that the welfare of the child is paramount. Rather it was giving effect to a belief that in normal circumstances it is in the interests of children that parents or others should not abduct them from one jurisdiction to another, but that any decision relating to the custody of children is best decided in the jurisdiction in which they have hitherto normally been resident . . .

Those statements of principle were repeated in this court in *Re S (Minors) (Abduction)* [1994] 1 FLR 297. Lord Justice Nolan stated:

It is settled law that although Pakistan is not a signatory to the Hague Convention, we must apply the philosophy of the Convention to the case before use; see *G v. G* . . . and *Re F* . . . This philosophy is that in normal circumstances it is in the interests of the children that parents or others should not abduct them from one jurisdiction to another but that any decision relating to the custody of children is best decided in the jurisdiction in which they have hitherto been normally resident . . .

Lord Justice Nolan went on to consider the facts of that case which involved Pakistan. He added:

In the present case the argument before us is that Sir Gervase Sheldon wrongly failed to appreciate or take sufficient account of the fact that the attitude of the Pakistani courts towards the welfare of the children would differ significantly from that of an English court.

Having considered the facts, Lord Justice Nolan said:

In my judgment, Sir Gervase Sheldon was fully entitled to take the view that, for Muslim children of Muslim parents whose home hitherto has been in Pakistan, the principles of Pakistani law are appropriate *by English standards* — my emphasis

The principle I have identified will not of course be decisive in every case. There will be cases in which the links between the children and the foreign state are less strong than they are in the present case. There may also be cases, as Lord Donaldson MR contemplated, in which the notions of children's upbringing in the foreign state are wholly repugnant to English notions of provision for the welfare of children. On the present facts, however, the conclusion of the judge was in my view unimpeachable. Like Lord Justice Thorpe, I also do not agree with the suggestion that *Re M* [1996] 1 FLR 478 was decided *per incuriam*.

I agree that the appeal should be dismissed.

LORD JUSTICE STUART-SMITH: I also agree, for the reasons given by my Lords.

Order: Appeal dismissed; detailed assessment of parties' costs; children's wardship to terminate on departure.

Case Comment: Cross-border Abduction of Children

David Pearl*

In recent years, English courts have been experiencing problems associated with international child abduction. Of particular concern is whether or not to order the peremptory return of children abducted by one of the parents from a country which is not a party to the Hague Convention on Child Abduction (1980). Since 1980, 57 states have become parties to the Convention, but no state that settles family disputes according to Islamic law has acceded, although countries with a predominant Muslim population from the former USSR, such as Uzbekistan, are likely in due course to sign and accede. Turkey has signed the Convention, but not yet acceded.

The Convention applies to children who are aged under 16 years who have been wrongfully removed or wrongfully detained outside their countries of habitual residence. The Convention has two underlying principles. First, it is accepted by those countries who have acceded that it is normally is the best interests of an abducted child to be returned as speedily as possible. Second, the courts in the state in which return is requested acknowledge that it can trust the authorities, including the courts, of the country of habitual residence to uphold the welfare of the abducted child.

The issue which has exercised the English judges recently is the principle which should determine the outcome of applications for the return of children abducted from non-member states. It arose in a stark form in relation to Pakistan,[1] the UAE[2] and most recently in *Osman*.[3]

The facts of *Osman* were as follows. There were three boys, born in 1989, 1991 and 1993. The parents are Sudanese Muslims and they married in Sudan. They lived in the UK from 1987 to 1991 when the parents and the two children born at that time returned to Sudan. In May 1993 the father returned to the UK and in December the mother followed with the (by now) three boys. She did not remain here for long and she returned to the Sudan with the children in April 1994.

The marriage ended by divorce in Sudan in 1995. The mother remarried a Mr M and a Sudanese court ordered that the children live with the father's family. This decision was taken in compliance with the *shari'a* law as applied in Sudan that the mother was no longer qualified to have the care of the children (*Hadana*) because of her remarriage. It would seem

---

* Judge
[1] In Re S [1994] 1 FLR 297.
[2] In Re JA [1998] 1FLR 231.
[3] Reported in *The Times* Law Report of 7 July 1999. The full text of this case is on p. 543.

that the mother's mother was unable to care for the children in any event. The mother was given contact with the children.

The mother came to the UK in May 1999 with her second husband, a fourth child who was the child of her and the second husband, and the three children. She claimed asylum in the UK, and applied for residence orders and orders preventing the removal of the children from England and Wales. The matter was the subject of court hearings in the High Court and the Court of Appeal.

There was expert evidence before the High Court Judge on the Sudanese law. The expert (Miss Ragab) told the court "the most important fact in Sudanese personal law was that once a divorced mother has remarried . . . the care of the children moves to the maternal grandmother. If the maternal grandmother is unable . . . to care for them, care moves to the paternal grandmother in all cases." She said that the Sudanese court would take account of what would be in the best interest of the children according to Sudanese culture. The exclusion rule is based on a *hadith* of the Prophet and finds a place in schools of Sunni Islam, and today in many of the Codes of Personal Status. In Sudan, the *shari'a* law would be applied by courts there by reason of the Law on Custody of Children 1932 and section 5 of the Civil Procedure Act 1985.

When the matter was before Connell J at first instance, he made an order for the return of all the children to Sudan. The mother's counsel on appeal to the Court of Appeal criticized this approach. She said that the judge had made an order that separated the children from both parents and returned them to a jurisdiction where there can be no discretionary review of all the relevant facts and circumstances to determine child welfare, but only the rigid application of *shari'a* rules that deprive the children of a natural upbringing.

The decision of Connell J was upheld by the Court of Appeal. In a wide-ranging judgment Thorpe LJ, in particular, considered the cultural dimension of cases such as these. He referred to the importance of "according to each state liberty to determine the family justice system and principles that it deems appropriate to protect the child and to serve his best interests". He went on to remark that there is an obvious threat to comity if a state whose system derives from Judaeo-Christian foundations condemns a system from an Islamic foundation "when that system is conceived by its originators and operators to promote and protect the interests of children within that society and according to its traditions and values". In adopting this approach, Thorpe LJ was following the principles set out by the earlier Court of Appeal case of *Re S*,[4] which involved children removed from Pakistan. He also seemed to be influenced by the lack of minimum standards required even among those countries signed up to the Hague Convention. He said

As a matter of logic, if we make no investigation and in litigation permit no criticism of the family justice systems operating in the member states, I am extremely doubtful of the wisdom of permitting the abducting parent to criticise the standards of the family justice system in the non-member state of habitual residence, save in exceptional circumstances.

He places a different emphasis to the more interventionist approach adopted by Ward LH in *Re JA*,[5] a case relied upon by the mother in this appeal.

This case illustrates the difficulties which English courts face in circumstances of this kind. There would appear to be two ways forward. First, there may be some scope for the making of b-lateral treaties between the UK and Muslim countries. Both France and Spain have successfully negotiated such treaties with North African countries. It would then be possible to extend the initiatives introduced by the organization Relate enabling mothers from

---

[4] [1994] 1 FLR 297.
[5] [1998] 1 FLR 231.

the UK to visit their children on a more regular basis in the Muslim countries concerned. A second way forward is to develop initiatives with the courts in Muslim countries for creating "mirror" orders from the courts in those countries which "mirror" the orders of the English courts. This is already being considered in the UAE.

It is hoped that English courts will continue to adopt a sensitive approach to these issues, for it is only by such means that we can lessen the hurt caused to the lives of children caught up by the webs of discord created by their parents.

Part V

Book Reviews, Notes and News

Book Reviews

Islamic Institutions in Jerusalem, by Yitzhak Reiter, Kluwer Law International, 1997, 120pp £39.00

This title is the 15th volume in the Arab and Islamic Laws Series published by Kluwer Law International. The book itself is published in cooperation with the Jerusalem Institute for Israel Studies. The institutions focused on are the *shari'a* courts, pious endowments (*waqf*) and holy places. The burden of the book, however, is a discussion of *waqf* property and its administration.

In the first chapter dealing with the structure of Muslim institutions under Muslim and non-Muslim rules, the author gives a very general view of the subject, particularly concerning the structure of these institutions under Muslim rule, which, of course, is the longest period of their existence. The *shari'a* courts and *waqf* have been in existence since the 7th century and have played a great role in the lives of the Muslim community prior to the British mandate over Palestine at the beginning of the 20th century. Indeed, the *shari'a* courts played a decisive role with respect to the lives of the Christian community in Palestine. Since the liberation of Jerusalem by Saladin from crusaders' occupation in the 12th century, it was to the *shari'a* courts that the various Christian sects in Jerusalem applied for the determination of their respective rights in the Christian holy places and in particular the Church of the Holy Sepulchre.

Under the British mandate, the Supreme Muslim council was created. Quoting, with apparent approval from another author, the creation of this body is deemed by both as "an act of appeasement towards the Palestinian Muslim" by "Britain's first Jewish High Commissioner in Palestine" (p. 5). The creation of this body was in fulfilment of Britain's obligations under the League of Nations mandate and the British undertaking under the Balfour Declaration. As mandatory, Britain was under a further obligation to arrange, as successor to the Ottoman government, the management of Islamic institutions.

Under Israel, "[m]ost *waqf* property has been declared absentee property, according to the Law of Absentee Property of 1950, and handed over to a government custodian" (p. 7). The justification for this is given as the absence of the administrators of the *waqf* property. Under the *shari'a* all that is required is the appointment of new administrators, as indeed was done in pursuance to an amendment to the law and the release of some of the property (pp. 7–8). *Waqf* is not the property of the administrators and it is perhaps the only ju-ridical person, with its independent personality, that has been recognized by the *shari'a*. The seizure of the property and its continued possession by the custodian are unlawful. The author, however, seems to accept the action of Israel without discussion, although he ac-knowledges the specific characteristics of *waqf* property.[1] In a later section, the author dis-cusses the administration of *waqf* property in Jerusalem by Palestinian Administrators. How-ever, no discussion is to be found of administration by the custodian of absentee property in general and Jerusalem in particular, and whether the income is being applied by the cus-todian for the charitable or family purposes in favour of which the *waqf* has been created.

In dealing with the *shari'a* courts in the second chapter, the author concentrates, in the main, on the Jordanian and Israeli periods. During Jordanian rule, the West Bank (includ-ing East Jerusalem) formed part of the Hashemite Kingdom of Jordan, and it was natural to treat the *shari'a* courts as part of the *shari'a* judicial system of the Kingdom. However, "Israeli law does not recognize the East Jerusalem *shari'a* court and as such, the court's judg-ments cannot be implemented nor enforced by the Israeli Execution Offices" (p. 15). The author does not reflect on the extraordinary situation of having a functioning court whose judgments lack the means of enforcement. This extraordinary situation has arisen from the fact that, contrary to international law, Israel does not consider itself an occupying power, but, at the same time, does not fulfil its obligations to the persons who have come under its jurisdiction as an occupier or of the court which it has allowed to continue to function as a court. Israel has created its own *shari'a* court (the Jaffa court) which, after Israel's occupa-tion of West Jerusalem in 1967, acts in jurisdictional competition with the Jerusalem court. However, the author points out that the Jaffa court, on application by the party concerned, normally follows or relies upon a prior decision, if any, of the Jerusalem court. The author does not deem it pertinent to refer to the raid by Israeli security officers of the Jerusalem court and the seizure of all its documents.

In chapters 3, 4 and 5, the author deals mainly with *waqf* or pious endowments. He rightly points out the intrinsic internal conflict in the traditional concept: the conflict between per-petuation of the founder's purpose and perpetuation of the assets endowed for that pur-pose. Adherence to these two aspects has, in the past and to some extent in the present, pre-vented full development of *waqf* property. However, the author gives examples of novel ways accepted by the Jerusalem *shari'a* court for overcoming this problem. One would add that the *waqf* concept was a creature of Muslim jurists. There is nothing to prevent its development by modern Muslim jurists to meet changing economic circumstances.

The author gives, as one of the examples of proper development, the transformation of the inactive Muslim *waqf* cemetery of Bab al-Zahra to a commercial centre to the great be-nefit of the *waqf*. The same result could have been obtained had the Muslim Mamila Ceme-tery, which is in the centre of West Jerusalem, been allowed by Israel to continue under its Muslim control. The author points out that, during the British mandate, the *waqf* department permitted the construction of a number of shops and apartments and the Palace Hotel on the grounds of the cemetery. However, after Israel's occupation of West Jerusalem in 1948, the remainder of the cemetery was turned into a public garden with no benefit to the *waqf*. The asset is valuable and could help the *waqf* more than the Bab al-Zahra cemetery. Unfor-

---

[1] For the evidence acceptable to the custodian for the declaration of a property as absentee, see the Klugman Report of 10 September 1992 prepared by an Israeli inter-ministerial team published in *The Palestinian Yearbook of International Law*, vol. IX, 1996/1997, pp. 417–435. The report states that the custodian acted on a mere affidavit of any Israeli stating that the owner of a Palestinian property was absent. No investigation or even a meeting with the deponent is conducted. Thousands of Palestinians have been dispossessed of their property in Jerusalem and elsewhere on the basis of such evidence.

tunately, while the author is obviously concerned about development of *waqf* property he has failed to discuss this important asset (p. 81). Similarly, he makes no reference to another important *waqf* asset, the inactive Jewish Cemetery in al-Tur (Mount of Olives) area where the Intercontinental Hotel has been built on *waqf* property. His only reference to this cemetery, which fails to mention its Muslim *waqf* status, is that it has been desecrated under Jordanian rule. This cemetery has been inactive for decades, and although it is *waqf* Muslim property, its character as a cemetery was respected during Jordanian rule. Other *waqf* property in the Jerusalem areas, which has been denied even to the beneficiaries, is half of the village of Lifta, which is *waqf* property (p. 26). Israel has turned the inhabitants of the village into internal refugees and the village stands empty of its rightful residents. To expand the West Wall Plaza, Israel demolished an entire quarter, the Maghribi neighbourhood, all of which was *waqf* property. The inhabitants were made homeless. According to the author "a cluster of old buildings known as the *Abu Midyan al-Ghawth Waqf* in the *al-Maghribi* Quarter was vacated and demolished" (pp. 26 and 91).

The last chapter deals with holy places and concentrates in the main on the Dome of the Rock and the al-Aqsa Mosque.

In conclusion, this book represents an Israeli view of its subject. Its shortcomings seem to stem from unquestioning acceptance of Israeli policies as if they represent an objective assessment of the situation. It could have greatly benefited from some critical analysis.

Anis Al-Qasem

The Distinguished Jurist's Primer, by Ibn Rushd, 2 volumes, Garnet Publishing, vol. 1 (1994) 660pp, Vol. 2 (1996) 675pp, £60.00 each

The Centre for Muslim Contribution to Civilization has been involved now for a number of years in one of its main projects, namely the translation of a series of books which have been chosen for their outstanding importance during the classical period of Islamic thought and civilization. Ibn Rushd's *Bidayat al-Mujtahid* is one such book. The full title of the book is *Bidayat al-mujtahid wa-nihayat al-muqtasid*, i.e. "The beginning for the one who exercises independent reasoning and the end for the one who exercises moderation". This impressive work on *ikhtilaf* within the Sunni schools of law has been translated into English in two volumes by Imran Ahsan Khan Nyazee from Michigan, and reviewed by Dr Muhammad Abdul Rauf from Cairo under the title of *The Distinguished Jurist's Primer*. Both volumes include the same introduction and short preface, the preface being a translation of the section in the *Bidaya* just before the beginning of the *Kitab al-Tahara*. The extensive introduction contains a short biography of Ibn Rushd, a few pages on the "Significance and Method of *Bidayat al-Mujtahid*", and lastly some comments on the translation itself. There is also a very useful glossary at the end of each volume.

Volume One contains 17 books ending with "The Book of Foods and Beverages" – an error in the contents listing however has numbered this incorrectly as 18. Volume Two begins with "The Book of *Nikah*" and contains 39 books ending with "The Book of *Aqdiya*". The edition used for the translation was published in Beirut by Dar al-fikr (no date).

In the very useful introduction to the translation, we are told something on the life of Ibn Rushd (520/1126–595/1198). Famous in the Medieval West under the name of Averroes, he was known as the "grandson" (*al-hafid*), his grandfather being a famous Maliki jurist, *qadi* and the *imam* of the Great Mosque of Cordoba. Brought up and practising for the most part within the Maliki *madhhab*, Ibn Rushd himself eventually become the chief *qadi* of Cordoba. He wrote extensively on medicine and philosophy and a number of his significant works are now available in English. In the second section, it is explained that the *Bidaya* is a book of law that not only records the main points of difference between the Sunni *madhahib* (including the Zahiris), but also gives the reasons for their disagreement. The translator gives us some explanation of the definition of *fiqh*, the role of the *mujtahid*, the nature of *taqlid* and discusses at length the fact that in the *Bidaya*, Ibn Rushd "did not propose a new theory of interpretation", but that his aim was to "try and find a common ground between the different principles of interpretation that are preferred by the leading schools" (p. xxxvi).

Comment is also made on the arrangement of chapters and the sub-chapters which are divided into detailed issues, and the criteria for selecting the particular issues. Nyazee quotes Ibn Rushd himself who claims "our intention in this book is to establish the issues expressly stated by the texts, agreed upon or disputed, and to mention issues about which the texts are silent, but in which disagreement of the jurists of the regions has become well-known" (p. xxxvii). Perhaps most importantly, Ibn Rushd's purpose in writing the book was to produce a work whereby one could become a *mujtahid*. He claims this in the last paragraph of the Book of *Kitaba* (p. 468), "It is however, a strength of this book that through it a person can attain, as we have said, the status of *ijtihad* as he proceeds along with the knowledge of the Arabic language and of *usul al-fiqh* that is sufficient for this purpose. It is for this reason that we thought that the most suitable title for this book would be if we name it: *Bidayat al-Mujtahid wa Kifayat al-Muqtasid*".

Finally, there is a note on the translation itself, that in effect this is the first time that an entire manual of Islamic law has been translated into English from the original Arabic. The translator reminds us of the difficulties of rendering into another language the conciseness of *fiqh* texts, the lack of exact equivalents concerning much of the legal terminology and the prior knowledge of the law assumed by the authors of such texts (pp. xl–xli). In view of this, the translator has helped the reader by providing additional notes in some places, though this is by no means exhaustive.

It is in fact the short preface to the work which gives us an insight not only to Ibn Rushd's own attitude to *usul al-fiqh* but his attempt at imposing some sort of rational structure to the whole body of detail which essentially lies a the basis of *fiqh* and specifically, *ikhtilaf* literature. Using frequent citations from the Qur'an, he discusses the whole problem of *qiyas* as a principle of law, the necessity of resorting to various types of *qiyas*, the complexity of language where it becomes necessary to distinguish the particular ruling from the general and vice versa, the relationship between prohibition and punishment, finally ending with the six causes that lead to conflict of opinion.

Regarding the main corpus of the translated text, it must be said that overall the translator, Imran Nyazee has achieved a very competent translation of a large, interesting and sometimes complex text. The English for the most part reads fluently and the reader is alerted both in the introduction and throughout the translation to many of the stylistic and contextual difficulties that arise and how Nyazee has attempted to deal with them. However, there are also certain shortcomings within the *Bidaya* itself with which the translation has not always been able to deal, simply as it lies outside the scope of the work. Overall, the issues fall into the following categories: (a) incorrect sources when using legal opinions, (b) ambiguities in the Arabic which remain ambiguities in the English as well, (c) Nyazee's own understanding of certain sections wherein he has inserted the occasional "they say", "he says", etc, when it is not actually clear who is saying what, (d) his statements in parentheses aimed at clarifying the text and (e) the use of Pickthall's translation of the Qur'an which for the purpose of establishing greater clarity of meaning and necessary distinctions within the context, is changed quite often.

Some of these issues have quite simply been pointed out as an extra footnote. One such example is at the end of the Book of (Ritual) Purification (p. 95) which, being the first book, contains throughout many of Nyazee's own comments about the translation of the *Bidaya* and frequent explanations of the legal terminology. Nyazee informs the reader in a footnote that in translating Ibn Rushd's use of legal opinions, he "found on certain occasions that opinions have incorrectly been attributed to the Hanafites and Shafi'ites or to the founders of these schools. This could be the case for other jurists too. Ascertaining whether each and every opinion has been correctly attributed to its author is beyond the scope of this translation" (p. 95). This particular difficulty extends also to verifying the eighteen hundred traditions (including reference to the *Sahih* compilations) which have been used in support of the arguments of the jurists, but which again could be not be documented because of the limits of the project (p. xli).

Difficulties and variables in the translation appear quite early on in the text. One such example appears on p. xliv where Ibn Rushd is discussing the three channels through which the *ahkam* were received from the Prophet: word, act and approval. He continues that regarding those points about which the Lawgiver (*al-shari'*) is silent, most people (*al-jumhur*) say that the method of attaining them is analogy (*qiyas*).

Though Nyazee has used Pickthall's translation of the Qur'an, he has changed the odd word here and there for clarity of meaning. Concerning the verse on menstruation (Q. 2:222), Pickthall translates *adan* as an "illness", whereas Nyazee uses "suffering" (p. 47). However, the reader is not given any explanation as to why the change was deemed necessary. Likewise, the Qur'anic verse *"in kuntum junuban, fa'attaharu"* (Q5:6), has been translated by Pickthall as "and if you are unclean, purify yourself". Nyazee has changed this to "and if you are involved in a major *hadath*, purify yourself" (p. 43). Yet these exact words from the Qur'an have been translated further on as "and if you are involved in *janaba*, purify yourself" (p.

47). The fact is that *hadath* refers to ritual impurity, both minor and major including sexual impurity, whereas the state of *janaba* refers more specifically to major ritual impurity or to be precise, sexual impurity. Nyazee uses the term "major *hadath*" when discussing the obligation and manner of *ghusl* after such impurities in general. Further on, however, he is comparing and contrasting the *ahkam* governing explicitly the two states which nullify a woman's purity and require major ablution, i.e. both the menstruant and the woman who is in the state of *janaba*, which he qualifies in parenthesis as "sexual defilement" (p. 49). The Qur'an demands a major ablution for these two types of impurities. The word "unclean" therefore falls short of conveying the different nuances and legal and social consequences of a term such as *junub* in the purity laws. Nyazee's use of certain terminology in some places and not in others, further reflects the difficulty of unravelling the density of arguments in the *fiqh* texts.

In elaborate *fiqh* texts such as the *Bidaya*, it becomes imperative that there is a level of consistency in how the Arabic terms are translated. Different meanings for one word, albeit similar meanings, often result in confusion in the translating process. Thus in the discussion on cohabitation with menstruating women and the acts that are permitted (pp. 59–60), Nyazee translates "no part of the body of the menstruating woman is polluted, except for the outlet of blood" (p. 60). *Najis* has been translated here as polluted, whereas in fact, it could also have been translated as simply "impure", especially since the glossary translates the term *najasa* as "legal or actual impurity". The word "polluted" means nothing and everything in contemporary purity discussions. In the same section, Nyazee translates the famous *hadith* "*innal mu'min la yanjus*" as "the believer is never unclean". This time the word "unclean" is used to translate *yanjusu*.

Interestingly, this section also provides an insight into Ibn Rushd's acceptance and respect for individual *ijtihad* within the schools and despite his Maliki allegiances, no particular attempt is made to argue the validity of the Maliki opinion over the others. In the section on "Intercourse in the period of purity before bathing" (pp. 60–61), Ibn Rushd points to a dilemma stemming from the Qur'anic verse "and when they have purified themselves, then go in unto them as Allah has enjoined upon you" (Q.2:222). His discussion points to the problem of actually defining what is meant by *tahara* in this context, i.e. does "*fa'idha tatahhrana*" refer simply to the end of menstruation, i.e. the cessation of blood, or is it achieved only after purification with water? If water is necessary for purification, is it obligatory to wash the whole body or just the private parts? The discussion points out that Abu Hanifa's interpretation of the concept of *tahara* here is that intercourse could take place as the woman is pure by virtue of no longer bleeding. Malik, however, disagrees, arguing that only a full wash with water would signify purity. Nyazee manages to keep the rather complex discussion comprehensible. Ibn Rushd concedes that in the final analysis, it is up to the individual *mujtahid* to decide for himself how he reads these verses and that "one is inclined to say, 'each *mujtahid* is right'" (p. 62).

An example of Ibn Rushd's skill at legal discourse, and Nyazee's own competent style in translating the issues and the legal terms can be found in Volume Two in the Book of *Nikah*. Regarding *fasid* dowers, Nyazee translates:

If dower consists of *khamr, khinzir*, fruit that has not yet begun to ripen, or a stray camel, Abu Hanifa is of the opinion that the contract is valid if it contains a provisions for *mahr al-mithl*. From Malik there are two narrations about it. First, the invalidity of the contract and its rescission before seclusion and after it, which is also Abu 'Ubayd's opinion. Second, that if the marriage is consummated, the contract is effective and she has [the right to] *mahr al-mithl*. The reason for their disagreement is whether the *hukm* of marriage is the same as the *hukm* of sale. Those who held that it is the same said that marriage becomes void with the *fasad* of dower, just as sale becomes void with the *fasad* of the price. Those who maintained that the validity of dower is not a condition for the validity of marriage, upon the evidence that fixation of dower is not a condition for the validity of the contract, said that marriage is effective and becomes valid with the *mahr al-mithl* (p. 32).

The section is interesting for various reasons. It puts forward the juristic debate over the categorization of a marriage contract, that despite so many similarities between the contracts of sale and marriage, the *fuqaha* remained undecided or perhaps even reluctant to equate marriage contracts with contracts of sale. Furthermore, it reflects on the distinct nature of marriage contracts in which a *mahr* is always implied and obligatory, even though it may neither be mentioned or fixed. Thus there is always a tension in the Maliki school between stating that the *mahr* must not be *fasid* or defective as this would nullify the marriage contract and still recognising that mention of a *fasid mahr* would not nullify the contact if the couple were to subsequently consummate the marriage contract – for then a *mahr al-mithl* would be due!

As a final comment, I welcome this translation enormously. Islamic classical texts lie at the basis of so much scholarly research and are invaluable sources for both the Islamist and anyone else who wishes to understand the development of Muslim thought and civilization. Translations into English of such great works that allow us insight into the minds of the Muslim world's most outstanding scholars unfortunately remain very limited; thus, there is still a wealth of literature on *tafsir*, *fiqh*, etc which remains inaccessible to an audience unable to read this level of Arabic. Furthermore, as the interest in *fiqh* grows in contemporary Islamic studies, this translation will be of particular interest to both the academic, the lawyer, as well as the teacher and student of comparative legal/cultural studies. My own view is that the Centre for Muslim Contribution to Civilization made an excellent choice in undertaking this translation; I look forward to their future publications.

Mona Siddiqui
University of Glasgow

The Origins of the Islamic Law: the Qur'an, the Muwatta' and Madinan 'Amal, by Yasin Dutton, Curzon Press, 1999, 264pp, £40.00

Scholars and researchers of Islam more than often blur the fine distinction between *shari'a* and Islamic law (*fiqh*), assuming they are synonymous. Nothing could be further from the truth – *shari'a* subsumes *fiqh*, but not the reverse.

Linguistically, *shari'a* means the big flowing river to which people flock; the road leading to it is called *shara*. Technically, *shari'a* is viewed by Muslim scholars as the road that God chooses for his people. It means the following:

First: Al-Tawheed (ones of God) as defined in the Qur'an 42:13, "The same religion has He established for you as that which He enjoined on Noah".

Second: *Fiqh* (jurisprudence) as defined in the Qur'an 5:48, "To each among you have We prescribed a law".

This remark is more befitting this scholarly book, written by Yasin Dutton, which deals exclusively with both Islamic law and *shari'a*. The author makes it clear that his main concern is the method used by Imam Malik bin Anas to reach a legal binding decision on religious matters. He acknowledges the existence of two schools, the classical and modern Western views on *shari'a*, but he sets himself the task of proving the existence of a middle course called the third view. This middle course, which hitherto has not yet been researched or analysed thoroughly, is to be found in *Al Muwatta*, a book written by Imam Malik bin Anas, a renowned scholar.

In many respects the third view is traditional, but it diverges from both the classical and modern views, and shares certain similarities with the modern view. The classical view is based on the Qur'an and the Sunna, whereas the modern view is sceptical of the Sunna as a normative model.

Throughout the book, the author never fails to prove this middle course pioneered by Imam Malik through his reliance on the people of Madina's *amals* (living traditions of the prophet). He eloquently managed, though in a classical manner, to give a lucid and detailed account of Imam Malik's life, his environment, authenticity of the text of *Al Muwatta*, its arrangements and reasons for compilation, and finally how *amal* is understood by Malik. Of importance here is his recount of the encounter between Malik and the Khalifa Al Mansur who asked Imam Malik to gather his knowledge in a book and told him that he will order everyone to follow it, even by force. Imam Malik's refusal and his justification is clear testimony to the tolerance and openness held by the Imam and those alike at that time. Also, the refusal emanates from the deep belief of Imam Malik that he was not the sole holder of true knowledge of the religion and that acknowledging and accepting other jurists' contributions and their opposed views on *hadith* or the Qur'an is a prerequisite for a true understanding of Islam. To say, therefore, as suggested in the book, that Malik's refusal carries a political element represented by his fear that the book might be misused by political authority, lacks historical evidence, to say the least.

Since Western scholars, such as Schacht and Goldziher, dispute the normative value of the Sunna, and cast serious doubt on its authenticity, Dutton explains in the second part the techniques used in *Muwatta* by providing cases which clearly demonstrate the practicality of the third view. In Malik's view, *amals* explain how the Qur'anic message was lived out in the lives of men from the time of the Prophet right up until Malik's time. Therefore, whenever there is an ambiguity in the Qur'anic text, Malik contrasts the relevant *hadith* with the *amal* in Madina and makes the latter prevail. Many examples are given to illustrate the case, such as *Zihar* (an oath made by a man on his wife by saying you are to me like my mother's back), inheritance due to children. However, the author in such examples has tended to focus more on jurists' differences than showing how *amal* is used to explain or rule out the ambiguity of the text.

Many techniques of Qur'anic interpretation, such as the assumption of inclusion (*Umum*) and literal meaning (*Zahir*), exception to *Umum* and paired of chapters (*Takhsis al-Umum*), and many others are discussed in the second part to show how Muslim jurists held different views on certain matters, and how Malik made up his own mind. However, the author sometimes tends to simplify or overlook some facts, as in the example of "exception to Qur'an by Qur'an", a case arises when two Qur'anic verses would give seemingly different judgments on the same topic. For example, when Utham (the third Muslim Khalifa) was asked if it is permitted for a Muslim who owns two slave sisters to have sexual relations with both, his answer was one verse of the Qur'an allows it and another forbids it. However, Utham, as reported, while recognizing the possibility of permissibility, he, like the majority of companion, disapproved of the practice.

The verse (Q4:23) which forbids such practice reads as follows "Prohibited to you (for marriage) are your mother, daughters, sisters; father's sister . . . and two sisters in wedlock at one and the same time, except for what is past". The other verse which, as alleged, permits it is Q4:24: "Also [prohibited] women already married, except those whom your right hand possess". The word except relates back to already married women and not sisters. Jamal aldin Al-Qasimi, in his book "Mahasin al Taweel" (p. 94) says the exception here is applicable for those women who are already married and still have a husband in Dar al harab (land of war) and who become as a result of captivity owned by Muslims. Therefore, the exception denoted in the verse by the word *illa* is restricted to married women not sisters. Regrettably, the author did not tell us of Malik's view and how he made his opinion.

The detailed description of cases, though appearing sometime, but by no means easy, unwarranted, is mainly motivated by the author's desire to be faithful to his project of underlining the third view and questioning the Western thesis. He proved that the interplay between the Qur'an and Sunna is in the sense that the latter complements the former, and that the supposed contradiction (like the testimony of one witness) that sometime appears, must be understood in the context that the Prophet is clearly a source of extra Qur'anic judgment but this extra Qur'anic element is considered to be within the general principle outlined by the Qur'an rather than separate sources. Moreover, his distinction between Sunna and *hadith*, and his refutation of Western scholars, like Schacht, deserves credit and congratulation.

As a final word, this book is not destined for the general reader, but rather for the specialist in *shari'a*. The book is thoroughly researched, with valuable footnotes and bibliography – more evidence of the vitality and self-confidence of the author. No doubt it will endure as an important study for anyone interested in *Al-Muwatta* and what could be called the "third view".

Ahmad Mahmmoud Ajaj

A History of Islamic Legal Theories: An Introduction to Sunni: usul al-fiqh, by Wael B. Hallaq,
Cambridge University Press, 1997, 294pp, £35.00

For all Muslims of whatever persuasion, the *shari'a* is the body of commandments, religious, legal and social, given by Allah through the Prophet Mohammed. Qur'an and Sunna
(the Prophet's deeds, utterances and unspoken approval) are the two foremost and unchallenged sources of the divine laws, although each of the Sunnis have recorded their own accounts of the Prophet's traditions. Because not all worldly problems have their solution in the
Second Book and the Sunna, matters which lay altogether outside the purview of these two
impeccable sources had to be regulated. This is when Sunnis and Shiis draw apart.

Consensus of opinion (*ijma'*) in the community was believed by the Sunnis to be the
safest way of ascertaining the law. This was justified by an interpretation of certain verses of the
Qur'an, and by sayings of the Prophet to the effect that "there can be no consensus of error
or misguided behaviour among people". In the process of interpretation and reaching consensus, resort was also made by the Sunnis to reasoning by analogy (*qiyas*): that is to say that
in order not to step beyond the limits of the sacred law, a rule of law found in the Qur'an or
derived from the Sunna was applied by analogy to cases not directly covered by it, on the ground
of a common *'illa* (the underlying principles or objectives of a *shari'a* injunction).

For the Shiis, consensus is acceptable only when it is the consensus of *ahl al-bait* (the
family of the House of the Prophet) on when it is endorsed by the infallible Iman. Analogy
(*qiyas*) is rejected by the Shiis on the ground that God's dictates cannot be derived from
subjective assumptions. Instead of analogy the Shii jurist is exhorted to follow the path of
individual reasoning based on sound reason (*'aql*).

Other Islamic sects, such as the Zeidis, Ibidis and Ismailis, have their own secondary
sources from which they derive rules of law unavailable in the Qur'an or the Sunna.

Hence, when a work is presented under a salient title as a *History of Islamic Legal Theories*, the reader expects to find therein a historical study of the legal theories taught by the
major Islamic sects. What would also induce the reader in that belief is as the use of "theories" in the plural. It would have served the book better, had the comparatively inconspicu-
ous subtitle, "An introduction to Sunni *usul al-fiqh*" been the only title of the book.

Another discomforting matter is the bold statement found in the preface that "unfortunately until now there had been no text that presents students interested in Islamic law as well
as Islamists at large with an intelligible, manageable account of Islamic legal theories. This
introduction is designed to fill the existing gap" (p. viii).

I do not believe that such a statement is fair on the plethora of past authors who have tackled the same subject, in a great number of languages. That having been said, the scholarly
value of the book is not to be denied. The author has presented the reader with a well-
connected historical account of the developments of the Sunni sources of the law and the
methods for finding that law. He did not merely report the various phases of the development but had selected a number of scholars and thinkers who had been instrumental in ad-
vocating new ideas which may or may not have had a practical bearing during the lifetime
of their authors, but nevertheless had helped shape later stages.

Sometimes the opposition to some of these thinkers was itself a developing impetus.
The development relayed to us is a succession of novel detached ideas, but of context and lives
which have generated new thinking. Not only are we told that but also why and how.

From the time of the Prophet and his companions to contemporary scholars, Professor
Hallaq reviewed what sources of law had been used during a given time and what methods
had been relied on to determine less obvious sources. For doing that he had relied on his own

example, he had placed Mohammed Ibn Idris al-Shafi'i (d. 820), known by his capacity and later part of his name as Imam al-Shafi'i in the historical context giving value to his contribution, for having registered a middle position between two extremes; the rationalists on one hand and on the other those who thought that all human conduct must be firmly regulated by authoritative texts, and that human reasoning has no place in religious matters.

The teachings of the scholars chosen by Hallaq for being outstanding in the field of *usul al-fiqh* have been examined in the light of the teachings of their contemporaries or predecessors. In short, the teachings of each scholar under the author's scrutiny was not assessed independently and abstractly but in an overall context which must have influenced and brought him to develop what was available to him, modify it or even rebut it.

The author is to be thanked for the painstaking labour which was needed to research his work. These subjects would have, in my view, benefited his book: namely the Mu'tazilas – which he quotes in passing – legal stratagems (*hiyal*) and the role of authoritative rules on developing the law.

I believe the Mu'tazilas would have deserved an in-depth treatment, not least for their subsequent failure and the triumph of their adversaries. After all, the Mu'tazilas were able, during the first centuries of Islam, to teach their ideas more or less freely and at one time as *confessio fidei* under the Caliph al-Ma'mun (p. 827).

The legal stratagems (*hiyal*) have contributed to shape Sunni law, people and, most particularly merchants, who had recourse to legal stratagems in order to avoid *shari'a* inconvenient mandatory dictates without technically breaking them. Such stratagems came into use during the Abbeside Caliphates, chiefly among Hanafis and Shafiis. As for autocratic rules, their influence in the Islamic world for developing the law cannot be ignored. Turkey is a one major case in point, for Kemal Ataturk embarked Turkey in 1926 on a policy of secularism maintained by the state until today. In Syria the first military dictator Husni al-Za'm repealed the *Majalla* and imposed on the country a civil code, while the French, who had ruled Syria for the preceding two decades, did not dare touch on the matter. President Bourguiba who ruled Tunisia as a de facto dictator, brought in 1956 a law of personal status which was remarkably radical when compared with the traditional teaching of the *shari'a*.

Closer in time, the Sultan of Oman imposed in 1974 a secular Penal Code despite religious objections.

None the less, *A History of Islamic Legal Theories* remains a very useful book for students of religious studies who want to know not only how but also why the principles of Sunni jurisprudence had taken a direction at a given time.

It is clear from the author's firm authority that he knows his subject inside out and that this book is the brain-child of many years of researches and thinking.

We are thankful to Professor Hallaq for having shared his knowledge with the readers. A more carefully drafted title of his work and a few additional materials would have spared much of the criticism reported in this review, leaving, plain to see, the praise that he deserves.

Nabil Saleh

Legal Pluralism in the Arab World, by Baudouin Dupret, Maurits Berger and Laila al-Zwaini (eds.), The Hague, Kluwer Law International, 1999, 280pp including bibliography and index

This volume is a result of a meeting in Cairo in 1996 and opens with a short preface by the scholar whose "founding article" (Dupret at p. 29) is the subject of considerable attention in the first of the book's three sections. John Griffiths' "What is Legal Pluralism?"[1] is considered by the editors – and evidently many others – to have "most completely and radically formulated the sociological theory of legal pluralism".[2] Brian Tamanaha, whose 1993 article attacking "The Folly of the 'Social Scientific' Concept of Legal Pluralism"[3] is another frequent reference in the first part of the book, states that legal pluralism is "one of the dominant concepts in the field of legal anthropology, and has been claimed as the key concept in a postmodern view of law".[4] He also observes that there is no absolute consensus on the definition of legal pluralism, and it may be seen in affirmation of this that the first two essays in this section of theory, as well as Griffiths' preface, are devoted to further explorations of definition, serving as a fairly intensive introduction for the uninitiated to the debate on the theory.

According to Tamanaha, admittedly its most vocal critic, the "core credo of legal pluralism" is that "there are all sorts of normative orders not attached to the state which nevertheless are *law*."[5] This issue of what is "law" – or rather, the assertion that beyond "state law", all sorts of other normative orders are law and entitled to be named as law, is, or perhaps more fairly has been perceived to be, a major preoccupation in the debates on legal pluralism.[6] Griffiths' category of "weak legal pluralism" (corresponding to Woodman's of "state law pluralism")[7] is not at issue here, indicating as it does the situation in which the state itself recognizes a plurality of norms or sources of legislation which it will enforce – the recognition of customary law or religious law by colonial states in addition to their state-issued legislation and norms being the original model for the development of the theory.[8] In the Arab world, separate and sectarian laws for recognized religious communities in matters of personal status are a classic illustration of this kind of state law pluralism.[9]

It is rather the idea of "strong legal pluralism" (deep legal pluralism according to Woodman) that provoked the ire of Tamanaha and, it seems, the definitional problems that beset the theory. According to Woodman: " This second category is formulated on the assumption that there exist bodies of law with no necessary relationship to the state. This view arises from a sociological, rather than a technical legal notion of law."[10]

---

[1] J. Griffiths, "What is legal pluralism?", *Journal of Legal Pluralism*, no. 24 (1986), 1–55.

[2] Paraphrasing the editors at p. xi.

[3] B. Z. Tamanaha, "The folly of the 'social-scientific' concept of legal pluralism", *Journal of Law and Society*, vol. 20, no. 2 (1993), pp. 192–236.

[4] *Ibid.*, p.192.

[5] *Ibid.*, p.193. Emphasis in the original.

[6] See Baudouin Dupret in this volume suggesting that "many of the theoretical problems associated with legal pluralism are actually terminological in origin or, to be more precise, stem from the desire to give legal and/or political concepts (such as law, tradition, the state etc.) a socio-anthropologicial dimension". B. Dupret, "Legal pluralism, normative plurality, and the Arab world", pp. 29–40 at p. 29.

[7] G. R. Woodman, "The idea of legal pluralism", pp. 3–19 in this volume, at p. 5.

[8] See M.B. Hooker, *Legal Pluralism: An Introduction to Colonial and Neo-Colonial Laws*, Oxford, 1975.

[9] This is not incompatible with Woodman's brief consideration of "religious law" and "whether it can be an element in situations of legal pluralism".

[10] Woodman, "The idea of legal pluralism", p. 6.

Once the qualification of a "technical legal notion of law" is put in, it is already clear that there is some kind of definitional difference between "technical legal law" and other "bodies of law". And Griffiths distances himself from the insistence on law as terminology in the preface to the current volume:

[W]hile the intellectual struggle for recognition of the idea of legal pluralism was frequently waged in terms of the definitions of terms, in particular the term "law", that is not, in my opinion, what the struggle was really about. What was at stake was how social order, and in particular the place in social order of more or less law-like forms of social control should be conceived.[11]

It seems from this that the heat has more or less gone out of the argument over whether or not other forms of social control could or should be called "law". The idea of "more or less law-like forms of social control" will be immediately familiar to any scholar or student of law and society in the Arab world, as is amply demonstrated in the lucid and informative case studies contained in the remainder of this volume. Certainly such forms of social control are instantly recognizable from existing empirical work and a no more than average attentive consideration of any given 'legal' context. This is indeed so much the case that it would surely take a legal scholar quite formidably and single-mindedly bent upon a perspective of "legal monism"[12] to manage during the course of his or her work not to recognize both the "limits of law" (Allott) and the controlling (and frequently over-riding) strength of other normative systems or repertoires, to borrow from Dupret.[13]

Nevertheless, it is undoubtedly the case that legal pluralism theorists do not appear to have turned their attention to the "Arab-Muslim" world. More broadly, according to Dupret, the "theoretical, sociological and anthropological approach to legal and religious norms" have been neglected in existing studies.[14] Barry Hooker, whose *Legal Pluralism: An Introduction to Colonial and Neo-Colonial Laws*[15] examines situations of "state law pluralism" arising from legal transplants or receptions[16] and is one of the earlier standard references on legal pluralism, explicitly misses out the Arab world (with the exception of Algeria under French colonial rule).[17] Nor is this essentializing tendency special to law, or to analyses of religion: Fred Halliday proposes avoiding both "rampant relativism" and "bland universalism" by "matching an analytic universalism with a historical particularism," an approach that legal anthropologists, legal sociologists and lawyers might do well to consider.[18] In this volume, Dupret insists that scholars across the disciplines refuse the idea of "Arab-Islamic exceptionality": "We should mark our distance from the studies of Arab countries of Islamic tradition which have made the mistake of essentializing Islam and societies of Muslim tradition."[19]

It is here that one of the major strengths of the current volume lies: in its insistence on integrating the consideration of law and normative plurality in the Arab world into frame-

---

[11] Griffiths, "What is legal pluralism?", p. vii.
[12] Legal monism being, according to Griffiths, "not merely a preference for a particular terminological practice (in which 'law' is reserved for social control by the state)" but "[f]ar more importantly, it is a particular, and untenable sociological view, one associated historically with Austinian legal postivism and nineteenth century bourgeois liberalism" (pp. vii–vii).
[13] Dupret himself advocates in this volume the "analytical advantage of a sociology of normative plurality" over a theory of legal pluralism, in "Legal pluralism", n.4, p. 29.
[14] *Ibid.*, p. 37.
[15] Hooker, *Legal Pluralism*.
[16] Woodman, "The Idea of Legal Pluralism", p. 5.
[17] See K. Balz, "*Shari'a* and *Qanun* in Egyptian law: a systems theory approach to legal pluralism", in *Yearbook of Islamic and Middle Eastern Law*, vol. 2 (1995), pp. 37–53, p. 38, n. 9.
[18] F. Halliday, *Islam and the Myth of Confrontation: Religion and Politics in the Middle East*, London 1996, p. 15.
[19] Dupret, "Legal pluralism", p. 37.

works and mechanisms of comparison used to orient and articulate observation of law and normative plurality elsewhere in the world. Kilian Balz in the second volume of this Yearbook attributes to the same motivation his article on using systems theory to analyse the *shari'a/qanun* paradigm more commonly asserted and discussed purely in its own terms and referential framework.[20] This should serve both to test the theory (see Dupret p. 37) and to render the topics under discussion more recognizable to those whose regional interests do not necessarily include the Arab world.[21]

This effort is made primarily through the case studies, divided between the second and third sections of the book. The second includes articles on aspects of legal pluralism (or normative plurality) in Palestine (Botiveau),[22] Syria (Berger), and Morocco (Rosen), along with an interesting consideration of the implications of legal pluralism for implementation of the International Convention on the Rights of the Child including a consideration of reservations submitted by various Arab and non-Arab Muslim states,[23] and two other contributions dealing with the treatment of unfair terms and with a comparison of the treatment of "Islamic norms" in Belgian and Egyptian courts. The final section of the book collects eight contributions specific to Egypt, ranging from financial regulation through a fascinating account of the *haqq al-'arab* method of conflict resolution, using a 1996 case from Upper Egypt as an illustration.[24] In most cases the authors set their information in an analytical framework that facilitates comparison and draws out the ambiguities, the distinctions and the overlaps between the "jurisdictions" and norms they are examining. This takes us already considerably further than the "accumulation of ethnographic knowledge" referred to by Griffiths in his preface (p. ix) as an important start for the study of legal pluralism in the Arab world.

Some of the case studies on Egypt also raise more clearly the challenges to human rights norms (and/or law) that may be presented by the recognition, accommodation and enforcement, within "state law pluralism", of norms that fall short of those standards or are at odds with them. Ahmed Hamad prefaces his discussion in this volume of State Council rulings on the rights of apostates as follows:

Our aim is [...] to give concrete evidence of how plurality of legal systems may lead to legalizing human rights abuses. However, that is not to say that plurality in legal systems always implies human rights abuses, nor that the existence of a unified system automatically leads to the respect of these same right ...[T]he conjecture implicit here is that the probability of the occurrence of such abuses increases in pluralistic systems, as long as one of the components of this pluralism is a relatively archaic system that was developed before the present awareness of human rights.[25]

---

[20] Balz, "*Shari'a* and *Qanun*", n. 17, pp. 38–39.

[21] This indeed was among the points raised in conclusion of a workshop discussion on legal pluralism convened at the Summer Academy of the *Working Group on Islam and Modernity* in Casablanca, September 1999. The group included Balz, Dupret, Laila al-Zwaini and Rudolph Peters (another contributor to this volume). Some of the points made in this review arose in the course of discussions with these and other participants at the summer academy and I duly record my gratitude and state of indebtedness to them and to that forum!

[22] It is unfortunate that a significant error in Botiveau's article slipped through the editing stage in the form of a note stating that East Jerusalem "remains for the moment under Israeli sovereignty", which of course is not and never has been the case (p. 78 note 1).

[23] M. Paradelle, "Legal pluralism and public international law: an analysis based on the International Convention on the Rights of the Child", pp. 97–112.

[24] Ben Nefissa, S., "*He Haqq al-'Arab*: conflict resolution and distinctive features of legal pluralism in contemporary Egypt", 145–157.

[25] A.S. Hamad, "Legal plurality and legitimation of human rights abuses: a case study of State Council rulings concerning the rights of apostates", pp. 219–228, at p. 219.

The challenge to freedom of religion has been discussed elsewhere,[26] as have the implications of systems of legal pluralism for the rights of women. In this volume, Nagla Nassar points to some of the distinctions between Egyptian family law "on the books" and "non-legislated norms"[27] with a view to reflecting on the status of women, but it is surprising to find that the index contains no entry for "gender". The perspective of feminist jurisprudence, or of the "women's law" scholars, is a disappointing omission from this volume in view of the particular impact of legal pluralism (or normative plurality) on women as subjects of those laws and norms. Looking at the public/private split in the law under colonial regimes in Africa, Ann Stewart notes that it takes a "particular legally structured form":

> It is also gendered: women's activities are regulated through customary law because of their position within the family and clan but also through work in the subsistence and informal economies. It equally divides those who live urban, middle-class, market economy lives from those who live in rural areas.[28]

An attention to the race, class and living of the subject of the law as well as to gender is a feature of feminist jurisprudence and women's law. Studies of situations of normative plurality (or, as defined by Stewart, "analyses of the interaction of regulatory regimes")[29] from these perspectives have been developed with particular strength in work by African and South Asian women legal scholars and activists.[30] In the meantime, in many states in the "North", the reach of state law is extending into the traditionally "private" sphere, while traditionally "public" functions are being privatized.[31] The "liberal" thesis of the public/private divide is also blurring in the intended reach of international legal instruments - inevitably, those relating to women's and children's rights and other aspects of the "private" sphere, not co-terminous with the family but certainly including it. The frequent reservations by Arab states to the Convention on the Elimination of All Forms of Discrimination against Women on pretexts arising directly from state law pluralism (incompatibility of the norm of gender "equality" in family life with what the particular state considers the requirements of the *shari'a*) to some extent support Woodman's observation in this volume that "The ideals of the rule of law and equality before the law as propounded in the context of legal positivism do indeed seem to be opposed to state law pluralism."[32]

Recent media attention to the phenomenon of "crimes of honour" in Jordan and the efforts being made by women's groups and others to challenge them include references to "codes of honour" and the strength of non-legal rules governing women's lives which may be ac-

---

[26] For example in Arjomand, S.A., "Religious human rights and the principle of legal pluralism", in J. Witte and J. D. van der Vyer (eds.), *Religious Human Rights in Global Perspective*, The Hague, 1996.

[27] N. Nassar, "Legal plurality: reflections on the status of women in Egypt", pp. 191–204, at p. 191.

[28] A. Stewart, "Should women give up on the State? The African experience", pp. 23–44 in S. M. Rai and G. Lievesley, *Women and the State: International Perspectives*, Taylor and Francis, 1996, at p. 28.

[29] A. Stewart, "Debating gender justice in India", 4 *Social and Legal Studies* (1995) 253–274 at p. 270.

[30] Particular reference might be made to research by the sister projects Women and Law in Southern Africa and Women and Law in Eastern Africa; and to the work of various affiliates of Women Living under Muslim Laws; for an example of this research activity in Pakistan see F. Shaheed, "Engagements of culture, customs and law: women's lives and activism", in F. Shaheed, S.A. Warraich, C. Balchin and A. Gazdar (eds.), *Shaping Women's Lives: Laws, Practices and Strategies in Pakistan*, Shirkat Gah, 1998, pp. 61–79.

[31] See H. Barnett, *Introduction to Feminist Jurisprudence*, London, 1998, pp. 64–79.

[32] Woodman, "Idea of legal pluralism", p. 12, note 5.

commodated by the state law system, if not formally recognized.[33] In the Arab world as in South Asia and Africa, women legal scholars and activists grapple with the complexities of normative plurality as it affects the lives of its subjects, including the "primary hold of custom over the realm of gender relations [which] negates access to any potential benefits provided by law."[34] How is the state law, when it is there, to be used in strategies of response and challenge to norms abusive of women, in situations where "there is a view from within the societies that women who attempt to enforce their rights are an urban Westernized elite. [...] championing this type of lifestyle and denying custom"?[35]

In short, there is a considerable amount of work in progress in the Arab world that could fit into a framework of studies on normative plurality, broadly defined, and which stands to considerably extend and enrich the discussions of the scope, patterns and impact of interacting regulatory regimes in the region. In the meantime, the studies collected here are an excellent contribution both to learning and to teaching, and merit attention from a broad range of disciplines and regional specialization.

Lynn Welchman

---

[33] Compare: N. Shah, "Faislo: the informal settlement system and crimes against women in Sindh", in Shaheed, *et al.* (eds.), *Shaping Women's Lives*, n. 30; and "Pakistan: violence against women in the name of honour", Amnesty International, September 1999, pp. 227–252.

[34] Shaheed, *Shaping Women's Lives*, p. 71.

[35] Stewart, "Should women give up?", p. 28.

Marriage on Trial: A Study of Islamic Family Law, by Ziba Mir-Hosseini, IB Tauris, 1997, 245pp, £14.95

All to often, lawyers seeking information on the law of marriage and divorce in the Middle East are forced to rely on the bare text of the Statute of Personal Status, which seeks to amend and reform, in some instances, the traditional Islamic law. Ziba Mir-Hosseini's book *Marriage on Trial* seeks to show how the law is, in practice, interpreted and applied by the courts of two jurisdictions, Morocco and Iran.

The study of Iran is perhaps of the greater interest, because of the fluctuation which has occurred in the legal system of that country within the comparatively recent past. The enactment of the Family Protection Act in 1967 put Iran firmly in the forefront of Islamic law reform, abolishing as it did what the preamble of the act referred to as "the nightmare provision of the Civil Code", the provision which reiterated the rights of a Muslim husband to repudiate his wife at will, without showing cause and without recourse to a court of law. With the establishment of the Islamic Republic, traditional Islamic law again prevailed, although as Mir-Hosseini shows, with some significant changes. One of the most important of these changes is perhaps Article 1130 of the Civil Code, as amended in 1982, which provides that the court may order a husband to divorce his wife or to effect a divorce on his behalf if it is satisfied that the continuance of the marriage is causing hardship for the wife. The author describes the proceedings in several cases where the wife has pleaded hardship and which illustrates how hardship is construed by the courts, as in Iran.

There is also an examination of cases which illustrate the anomaly which exists in the law of Iran, whereby a husband may not be prevented by the court from exercising his right under the *shari'a* to repudiate his wife but which can, however, refuse to register such a divorce, thus retaining for the wife all her marital rights, including the right of maintenance.

Unlike the law of Personal Status in Iran, the law in Morocco has not been subject to violent change. Despite the enactment of a Code of Personal Status, the law has always remained, in essence, traditional Maliki. Mir-Hosseini again, through a discussion of cases, shows how the courts in Morocco are, in practice, applying the law and again, as in a case in Iran, demonstrates the concept of harm as it is interpreted by the courts.

Inevitably, the book does not provide answers to all the questions which lawyers would put – for example to what extent, if at all, do the courts implement traditional Maliki doctrine and award a judicial *Khul'* to a wife who has failed in a plea for divorce on the grounds of harm? However, the book is not intended to be entirely within the legal framework. It is extremely well-produced and well written, and it is constantly fascinating. It will be of great interest to anyone, whether a lawyer or not, who is interested in the contemporary Muslim world.

Doreen Hinchcliffe

Muslim Family Law, by David Pearl and Werner Menskie, Sweet & Maxwell, 3rd edn., 1998, 600pp, pb £55.00

David Pearl's textbook of *Muslim Personal Law* has long been a standard work of reference for both student of law and legal practitioners seeking information on the law of the Muslim world, and the publication of the third edition will be greatly welcomed.

The third edition has been given the new title of *Muslim Family Law* and is the result of collaboration between David Pearl and Werner Menskie. As in the two earlier editions, the emphasis is on the Islamic law of personal status as it is applied in the Indian sub-continent. The case law of the three republics of India, Pakistan and Bangladesh is examined in detail and the authors ably illustrate the extent to which the law of the three republics now differs, not only as a result of the enactment of legislation such as the Muslim Family Law Ordinance of Pakistan and Bangladesh, but also as a result of judicial interpretation of the law. Of particular interest in this context is the different approach of the courts to the controversial question of post-divorce maintenance.

A significant portion of this third edition is devoted to the problems of Islamic law which arise in the United Kingdom and shows how Muslims, in particular South Asians who are resident in the United Kingdom seek to conduct their affairs as far as possible within an Islamic context. They also claim that a new form of *shari'a* has now come into existence, which they term English Muslim or *Angrezi Shariat*. They acknowledge that this new *shari'a* is not officially recognized by the State but argue that nevertheless, it is a dominant legal force. This section of the book will attract the interest, not only of lawyers, but also of anyone having an interest in the field, perhaps in particular those interested in the area of social studies.

Muslin Family Law is a welcome addition to the literature in English on a subject which is becoming of ever-increasing importance, both to academics and to legal practitioners. The views expressed by the authors are often controversial and will, of course, not meet with universal acceptance, but whether readers agree with the authors' opinions or not, they will find the book consistently thought provoking and of great interest.

It is a pity that a work of such distinction is marred by an inadequate index but no doubt this defect will be remedied when it goes, as it undoubtedly will, into a further edition.

Doreen Hinchcliffe

The Palestine Yearbook of International Law, by Anis Kassim (ed.), Vol. IX, 1996/1997, Kluwer Law International, 476pp, £135.00

This valuable reference work is published by Kluwer Law International in cooperation with Al-shaybani Society of International Law. Dr Anis F. Kassim continues his excellent work as editor in chief of the book.

The volume opens with an In Memoriam of Elmer Berger written by a longtime friend of Dr Berger, Dr W. T. Mallison. The reviewer, who also had the privilege of knowing and working with Dr Berger, shares the sentiments of Dr Mallison and feeling of great loss for a man who was both distinguished and dignified in person and intellectual honesty.

As customary, this volume is divided into Articles, Law Reports, For the Record, Special Report, Book Reviews and Bibliography. Three of the articles deal with matters related to Jerusalem, the fourth deals with Israeli continued control of Palestinian water while the fifth is a study of judicial review in Palestine.

Professor John Quigley's article on Jerusalem, "The illegality of Israel's encroachment", is a timely contribution to the debate on rights to the Holy City. The author reviews Israel's housing construction in East Jerusalem, pointing out that after the Oslo Declaration of Principles in 1993, Israel's policy of confiscating Palestinian property in the city aimed at the creation of a demographic and geographic reality that would preempt every future effort to question Israeli sovereignty in East Jerusalem. These Israeli activities, the author concludes, are in violation of the Declaration of Principles and of the law of belligerent occupation. He then considers Palestinian and Israeli claims to Jerusalem. "What is remarkable about Israel's claim of sovereignty," he writes, "with respect to both sectors [of Jerusalem] is that it has never spelled out a legal basis". Publicly, the only basis that is mentioned is "historic connection" and "sentimental attachment to the city on the part of the Jews in later history". On the other hand, "Palestine's claim to Jerusalem is founded on the longtime status of the Palestinian Arabs as the majority population of Palestine". "Ironically," the author rightly concludes on the question of claims, "it is likely to be the PLO that will provide Israel for the first time with a legal basis for its claim to Jerusalem".

Leah Tsemel, the Israeli lawyer renowned for her defence of Palestinian prisoners and detainees, contributes an article on "The Continuing Exodus: the Ongoing Expulsion of Palestinians from Jerusalem". She discusses the machinery adopted by Israel since 1967 to annex the city, enlarge the municipality area by the inclusion of more Palestinian land and through treating Palestinian Jerusalemites as permanent residents. In the opinion of Israel's High Court, permanent residency "has a declarative aspect, which expresses the reality of the permanent residency. When this reality disappears, there is no longer anything to which the permit can adhere, and it is automatically revoked, without any necessity for formal revocation". Because of this ruling and Israel's administrative policy, the author concludes "the best strategy for Jerusalem Palestinians seeking to preserve their permanent residence status is to live continuously within Jerusalem's post-1967 municipal boundaries". The author continues: "But even those Palestinians willing to do so are not safe. Israel has adopted a policy of restricting the growth of Jerusalem's Palestinian population and housing, issuing hundreds of house demolition orders and deploying a mixture of bureaucratic obstacles and measures meant to make Palestinian life in Jerusalem difficult". The author considers the impact of these policies on Palestinian Jerusalemites, and rightly treats the exclusion of East Jerusalem from the interim arrangements as a major achievement for Israel, for they were left without legal or political protection pending the conclusion of negotiations on the status of Jerusalem.

John V. Whitbeck, an international lawyer in London and Paris, has been a longtime advocate of a solution for sovereignty over Jerusalem based on "joint undivided sovereignty". He contributes an article called "The Road to Peace Starts in Jerusalem: the Condominium Solution". "As a joint capital", he says, "Jerusalem could have Israeli government offices primarily in its western sector, Palestinian government offices principally in its eastern sector and municipal offices in both".

The question of water control is the subject of an article by Gamal Abouali, an associate in a New York law firm, called "Continued Control: Israel, Palestinian Water and the Interim Agreement". In his opinion, "the water-related provisions of the agreements concluded thus far between the Palestinians and Israelis have been extremely detrimental to the Palestinian side, and seemingly oblivious to the presence of applicable international law". He provides in this well researched study a legal and factual background a basis for his recommendations to negotiators in the final round of negotiations. Six core principals should, in his view, guide the negotiations: (1) sole Palestinian control of endogenous water resources; (2) true joint management of shared resources; (3) equitable allocation of waters from shared resources; (4) Palestine's rights to the Jordan river; (5) the illegality of water consumption by settlements; and (6) Palestine's right to compensation for past illegal consumption.

Looking to the future of Palestine, Professor Adrien K. Wing, Sonya Brauschwig and Qais Abdel-Fattah provide an insight into various options available for the practice of "Judicial Review in Palestine". They review Palestinian constitutional developments in connection with this topic and four foreign systems of judicial review: the British, the American, the Israeli and South African, and conclude with a recommendation of "an enumerated form of review" as adopted by the South African model under which the constitution would set forth a bill of rights and expressly allows for judicial review of both the procedural and substantive elements of legislative and executive decisions. With respect, this is exactly what the 1996 draft of the Basic Law for the Palestinian Authority, discussed by the authors, had intended to achieve. The constitutional court would rule on the constitutionality of legislation and executive decisions and the administrative tribunal would rule on the legality of administrative decisions and acts.

In the Law Reports section, this volume of the *Palestinian Yearbook* reproduces the judgment of the Israeli Supreme Court sitting as High Court of Justice in *Bilbeisi v. General Security Service*. The underlying question before the court was whether the use of torture (called "pressure" by the court) by members of the Defendant against Palestinian detainees during interrogation was lawful. The Israeli Landau Commission (headed by no less a judicial figure than a former President of the Supreme Court) had already in 1987 approved the use of "moderate measure of physical pressure". To the shame of the Israeli High Court of Justice, the ruling in this case gave further endorsement of the legality of such action in order to obtain confessions or information from a Palestinian detainee.

In the Special Reports section, this volume has done a valuable service through the publication of two reports: the first is the report of an *ad hoc* commission created in 1930 by the Council of the League of Nations entrusted with the settlement of the rights and claims of the Jews and Muslims with regard to the Wailing Wall (the Western Wall), and the second is the Klugman Report of 1992, a report prepared by an Israeli interministerial committee created "to collect and examine all the data relevant to houses leased, rented or purchased on behalf of private bodies, non-profit associations or individuals out of state budget or with any other assistance form the state and its agencies in East Jerusalem".

The League of Nations Commission concluded in its report "[to] the Moslems belongs the sole ownership of, and the sole proprietary right to, the Western Wall" and "[to] the Muslims there also belongs the ownership of the Pavement in front of the Wall and of the adjacent so-called Moghrabi (Moroccan) Quarter opposite the Wall". As to Jewish rights, the Commission concluded "[t]he Jews shall have free access to the Western Wall for the purpose of devotions at all times" subject to various explicit stipulations mentioned in the report.

The Klugman Report is instructive in particular as to the way in which the custodian of so-called absentee property decides the question. The report reveals that decisions are taken by the custodian on the basis of an affidavit submitted by any Israeli to the effect that the property was absentee property. No inspection or examination or meeting with the deponent takes place, and the occupants of the property are evicted to allow Israeli occupation. This report challenges the legality, even under Israeli law, of much of the acquisition of the property in East Jerusalem (and indeed the whole of Palestine) by the custodian.

Anis Al-Qasem

United Arab Emirates Court of Cassation Judgments 1989–1997, by Richard Price and Essam Al Tamimi, Kluwer Law International, 1998, 384pp, £70.00

This book, as its title indicates, is a collection of summarized decisions rendered by the highest courts of the United Arab Emirates – the Courts of Cassation – over the last few years.

For lawyers engaged in legal practice in the West, the publication of a set of judgments rendered by Western courts would be another work to be added to the innumerable complications of court judgments. For lawyers practising in the Gulf it is, I believe, a first in the English language and most certainly a welcomed achievement which deserves recognition.

It is a matter of fact that court judgments in most Gulf countries are either buried in dusty drawers at the clerk's office, as soon as the parties concerned have had their interest exhausted, or are not published on account of a misplaced confidentiality. A small number of judgments are indeed translated from Arabic to another language and published, but that is when the non-Arab party to a dispute either wishes to vent anger about the treatment he has received in a foreign jurisdiction or, on the contrary, to boast about a judgment obtained against adverse odds.

It is to be hoped that lawyers practising in the Gulf countries will follow in the example of Messrs Price and Al Tamimi and will undertake the same task in their respective jurisdictions. As for the confidentiality issue, all that they would have to do is to refrain from publishing the names of the parties, as these two authors have done. Omitting the names of the parties has not diminished the usefulness of the published case summaries. These names neither add to, nor reduce the benefit one could gain from the courts' findings.

Although there is no system of binding precedent in the UAE, the Courts of Cassation decisions are very persuasive before the lower courts, as the two authors explain in their introduction. Knowing the law, as interpreted by the courts, is invaluable, for statutory provisions are often written in abstract or digest form and need to be expounded. The most authoritative construction we could expect is from the courts. The more so because law books are scarce and law gazettes practically non-existent, if we exclude the two excellent newsletters distributed by Al Tamimi & Company and Afridid & Angell to their respective clients.

Besides the introduction, the book is divided into 10 parts, namely "Commercial Transactions Cases", "Civil Procedure Cases", "Maritime/Transport Cases", "Banking Cases, "Insurance Cases", "Arbitration Cases", "Jurisdiction Cases", "Tradename Cases", "Family Cases" and "Miscellaneous Cases". Each part is endowed with a table of contents which allows easy reference.

I chose to follow through the summarized cases in the book, two matters of which are of particular import to the international business community: the matter of "interest" and that of "foreign currency trading". The result is as follows:

Concerning interest; a credit card company may charge interests as high as 24 per cent if the cardholder agrees (Dubai Court of Cassation Judgment No. 201/91 of 28 December 1991) – parties to a commercial contract are free to stipulate any interest rate for the late payment of a debt (Dubai Court of Cassation Judgment No. 261/96 of 22 February 1997) – interest on a debt will be payable from the date on which the debt becomes due and not from the subsequent judgment date (Dubai Court of Cassation Judgment No. 52/97 of 6 April 1997) – compound interest charged by a bank is illegal and contrary to Islamic *shari'a* principles (Abu Dhabi Court of Cassation Judgment No. 26/18 of 31 December 1996).

The different leanings of the Courts of Cassation are clearly perceivable. Dubai's Court is responsive to business requirements, while the Federal Court of Cassation of Abu Dhabi might take into consideration strict *shari'a* principles which have not been cast aside by clear-cut statutory provisions.

The divergence of the two approaches is particularly plain when we look at the other legal matters, namely "foreign currency trading". In its judgment of 29 October 1996 (p. 23 of the book), the Abu Dhabi Court of Cassation held that currency transactions which are, in essence, speculative in the rise and fall of a currency's value, are contrary to the principles of Islamic law and therefore illegal. The judgment was based on the premise that the buying and selling of foreign currency is done via speculation to generate profit and, therefore, no actual goods or currency were transacted by the sale or purchase.

That was not the view of the Dubai Court of Cassation. In its judgment No. 17/89, delivered on 12 March 1990, the Court held that dealing in foreign currency through a brokerage firm or stock market is legal and that the essence of such a contract was neither in the nature of gambling or betting. Unfortunately, the Dubai judgment is not published in the book, but was mentioned in Essam Al Tamimi's article published in *Al Tamimi's Law Update* of April 1997.

United Emirates Court of Cassation Judgments reports a number of other legal principles of significance, such as the validity and effect of a non-competition clause; liquidated damages; payment to sub-contractors, arbitration clauses in commercial agency agreements and many others.

This collection of UAE judgments is priceless for lawyers who are interested in the development of the legal system of the Emirates and for those looking for an answer to a specific problem, and although it should be obvious that not all problems find a solution in the collection, a great deal of them do.

Businessmen, contractors, bankers and other persons who have business with, or who wish to pursue business interests in the Emirates, are advised to keep a copy of the book in their libraries.

Richard Price and Essam Al Tamimi deserve our thanks for the pioneering work they have done. Hopefully their example will be followed in other Gulf jurisdictions, so that neither the law nor its practice remains uncommunicated, a current shortcoming which is against the essence of justice.

Nabil Saleh

The Law of Business Contracts in the Arab Middle East, by Nayla Comair-Obeid, Kluwer Law International, 1996. xiii + 235 pp, £77.00

Muslim countries are faced with a difficult divergence between the demands of the international economy, based on Western ideas of contract law, "aimed first and foremost at making profit", and those of Islamic law "distinguished by the pre-eminence of the moral order". This book addresses the problems raised by this divergence, qualified by Dr Comair-Obeid as "thorny and urgent".

After an introduction dealing with the reasons for writing the book and the general background of the Islamic law of contract, the work is divided into two parts: Part One examines relevant aspects of the classical *shari'a* law of contract against the background of the demands of the modern world; Part Two discusses the extent to which the *shari'a* has been adopted in the contemporary legislation of the Arab world. Part One is divided into two chapters, Chapter 1 dealing with aspects of Islamic contract law viewed as part of the "Moral order, obstacle to contractual liberty" (the object of the obligation, ancillary conditions, the prohibition of *riba* and *gharar*), Chapter 2 with those aspects of the Islamic "Moral order as an instrument for the protection of the autonomy of the will" (optional clauses and defects of consent). Part Two is also divided into two. Chapter 3 deals with the adoption of Western-style ideas of contract by Arab countries (categorized as those which have accepted a limitation on Islamic ideas and those in which Islamic ideas have more significance). Chapter 4 looks at a specific topic, that of *riba* in those jurisdictions, dealing with Islamic banking techniques and the distinction between civil and commercial approaches towards interest.

There is a glossary of Arabic terms, a bibliography and an index. Some problems should be mentioned, although they need to be viewed in the context of the very positive general assessment below.

The parts of the work which deal with comparison with Western law have not received as much attention as they ought. For example, French law is taken as representative of "Western" law without explanation or justification. The choice of French law as a point of comparison is itself unexceptional, as it is the ultimate source of the modernist legislation in the Arab jurisdictions under scrutiny, but the absence of a preliminary caveat to the effect that it is only one of many types of Western law is unsatisfactory, and is made worse by a partial caveat to this effect on p 101. Indeed, passages providing comparative discussions with "Western" law seem to be inserted on a haphazard basis: if there is a logical reason for their presence, this is not apparent nor specifically stated. For example, the introduction contains an interesting comparison of French *cause* with its equivalents (or lack of them) in Islamic law. The comparatist's appetite is whetted, but disappointment follows, as this is the only comparative discussion of this type for some 90 pages.

Although Dr Comair-Obeid's command of English is remarkable, some infelicities have crept in. At times there is a lack of clarity, which can be compounded by gallicisms (such as "moral violence") and mistranslations, a particularly serious example of which is the translation of *conventionnel* as "conventional" rather than "contractual", which is seriously misleading for those who do not speak French. Another example of a linguistic problem is the consistent use of the term "ancillary conditions *shurut*" (emphasis added). This seems to be a minor point, but in fact it is an essential one. In the expression as drafted, it seems that *shurut* qualifies "ancillary conditions", rather than *shurut* being qualified by these words. This makes no sense, so one concludes that the words "ancillary conditions" are intended to qualify *shurut*, i.e. they are intended to distinguish this kind of *shurut* from another kind. If this is the case, the word "conditions", being used adjectivally, must be singular, giving "ancillary condition *shurut*". Generally, the quality of writing is lower in the beginning of the book and improves thereafter.

There are various minor problems, such as the lack of a note on the transliteration system used, some inconsistencies in the formatting of the footnotes, some problems with the index (for example, the word "pledge" is not mentioned in the index, despite there being an interesting passage on the acceptability of the requirement of a pledge as an ancillary condition), some typographical errors and, particularly, some problems with paragraphing (e.g. on p. 48 the first sentence of the second paragraph should form the last sentence of the previous paragraph).

On the positive side, Dr Comair-Obeid's assessment of the need for such a work as this is certainly correct, and it fills that need very creditably indeed.

Dr Comair-Obeid has used the Cartesian structural method, which is unfamiliar to most common lawyers. This method, standard in French academic writing, demands that any work be structured by division and successive sub-division into two. In some circumstances it can lead to an artificial and inappropriate organization, with a confusing amount of categories, but in the right hands it can, as here, result in a very logical and coherent overall structure (despite the relatively minor exceptions referred to above), the strength of which is compounded by the way in which Dr Comair-Obeid has made morality and its relation to contractual liberty in Islamic and Western law the central, linking theme of her thinking. These qualities give a cohesion to the whole book which is difficult to achieve in this type of work. This is no mean achievement, as many of the areas were previously uncharted, and others have been most skilfully reorganized and adapted for the needs of the book.

The author displays an admirable depth and breadth of knowledge and research in Islamic law, French law and the laws of the numerous Arab countries chosen, both in detail and in general overview or "feel". She mostly deals very well with the difficult problem of compressing the large amount of information and concepts necessary for understanding the issues without caricature or excessive inaccuracy, and is particularly strong on the philosophy underlying the Islamic rules. She is very thorough, dealing with all the schools, never loses sight of her central theme, and reaches clear conclusions on the approach which she feels Arab countries should take, but without manipulation of the viewpoints of others. This book is a very valuable contribution to the literature and can be thoroughly recommended.

As a postscript to the assessment above, it has become almost traditional for books dealing with the Arab world to examine a range of jurisdictions at the sort of level of analysis shown here. Such studies are very valuable, but detailed works, focusing on one jurisdiction, are in very short supply, and it would be extremely useful if the author could put her knowledge and talent to work on detailed studies of individual jurisdictions, by building on and expanding what has already been achieved.

There remains the thorny question of price. Obviously such a work is highly specialized and the market is thin, and no doubt the publishers see the potential market for such books as being practitioners, especially law firms, for whom the price is no doubt affordable. However, such an amount does pose significant problems: it puts the book out of the reach of students, if not lecturers, and in these days of increasing budgetary restraints, is a figure at which even university libraries balk. Such pricing does not assist the spread of the study of Islamic and Middle Eastern law. Some moderation of prices, or some scheme such as a reduction for students, would be very helpful.

Nicholas Foster

Arab Islamic Banking and the Renewal of Islamic Law, by Nicholas D.Ray, Graham & Trotman, 1995, xi + 195 pp, £60.00

In his introduction, Dr Ray identifies a gap in writings and information sources on Islamic banking in European languages. He laments the "virtual absence of competent discussion and correct information in Western financial journals". On the level of more specialized banking literature, he points to the lack of any in-depth study of an Islamic bank over a period of years. The more academic works are seen as either too limited in their ambit, failing to examine the way in which the medieval principles are being applied to contemporary circumstances, or making the opposite mistake, of not studying the Islamic legal principles enough.

Dr Ray's aim is to fill this gap. He attempts to do so by providing two things: an exposition of the medieval Islamic law on the subject as used in modern Islamic banking, and a case study of Faisal Islamic Bank of Egypt.

The first section, constituted by Chapters I and II, deals with Islamic banking and the legal principles applicable thereto. Chapter I starts with a general introduction to the book and a justification of the approach it takes. It then provides an introduction to Islamic banking, consisting of a historical section, an account of the main Islamic Financial Institutions, the aims of Islamic banking, the structure of Islamic banks and their successes and difficulties. The rest of the chapter is devoted to a summary of general principles of Islamic law. Chapter II looks in more detail at the Islamic law banking techniques of *murabaha*, *musharaka* and *mudaraba* (*ijara* is not dealt with) as well as at the way in which some Western financial transactions, such as share dealing, options and futures, are viewed in Islamic law.

The second section, constituted by Chapter III, studies the Faisal Islamic Bank of Egypt. Chapter IV assesses the growth rate of all Arab Islamic banks and Chapter V is a short conclusion. There is an appendix containing translations of selected fatwas on Islamic banking, a bibliography and an index.

To deal first with the problems.

The most significant difficulty is in the structure of the book. Attempting to fill both the perceived gaps in the literature in one work is understandable, laudable, and fairly common, but in this work at least the author falls between two stools by taking this approach. The first (legal) section is quite a detailed account in many ways, but is not really detailed enough for a specialist lawyer, and is probably too detailed for a banker or economist interested primarily in the case study. The second (case study) section is very interesting, but suffers from the mirror-image of the problems of the first section. Most lawyers would not need the amount of detail provided by the case study and, if they bought the book, would probably only glance at the second section. This section, combined with an extended version of the passage on the history of Islamic banking, a section providing some more factual information about Islamic banks and banking in general and their relative significance in the world banking landscape, prefaced by a short introduction to Islamic banking and techniques, could have been a book in itself. This would have allowed Chapter I to be expanded into a separate book dealing with the legal aspects of Islamic banking.

In addition, the degree of detail in the first section is rather uneven: it deals with some areas, such as the treatment of Western financial transactions, the interaction of Islamic banks with regulatory requirements and secondary markets, in less detail than might have been expected. The omission of *ijara*, justified by its similarity to Western concepts of leasing, leaves an unfortunate gap.

On another structural level, Chapter IV, although providing useful general information about the development of Arab Islamic banks, sits oddly with the very detailed analysis of the Faisal Islamic Bank of Egypt.

Concerning non-structural aspects, the work is presumably a revised edition of Dr Ray's thesis (or work done during this period) and it bears some evidence of this.

There are some rather unguarded statements: for example, *'ina* is referred to as a "stupid ruse" – it could be described as "transparent" perhaps, but hardly stupid if it achieves the desired result. Along similar lines, but more seriously, Dr Ray takes a more positive view of the prospects for Islamic banking than some (including this reviewer) would consider justifiable after a relatively short period of activity, and, although he does discuss some of the significant problems, could have developed the discussion of this area more.

Chapter I has substantial discussion of the Islamic banking techniques before they are examined in detail, and a brief preliminary description of their main aspects, or the placing of the discussion as a conclusion, would have made the text easier to follow.

The latest figures available are from 1990 in a work published in 1995, which reduces the value of the analysis.

Some niggling aspects should also be mentioned. There is an occasional lack of polish in areas such as the relationship between text and footnotes and in the technical aspects of the footnotes themselves. The sole appendix is confusingly called "Appendix I". A glossary of Arabic technical terms, often seen in other such works, would have been a useful addition.

A likely explanation of many of these difficulties is that they derive from the sheer magnitude of the task which the author set himself and the originality of the work. It is therefore unfair to lay too much emphasis upon them. Indeed, undue stress on the criticisms would give quite a wrong impression. Dr Ray succeeds in his main aims and various other aspects of the book deserve much praise.

On the level of the discussions concerning the general success of Islamic banking, Dr Ray delineates some of the main lines of the debate in an area where those lines were previously quite nebulous. This is a very positive and significant contribution, providing a useful starting point for further debate and study. As regards the factual background to these discussions, the account of the history of Islamic banking and the major players is very helpful, as well as being of general interest.

On the purely legal side, the introduction to Islamic law is a model of concision, and the exposition of the use of the medieval Islamic law in the contemporary context and the theoretical problems associated with such use is a most welcome advance in the field. One particularly effective technique is the use of two examples to illustrate a point, one from the Middle Ages and one from modern times. The complexities of technical areas are clearly set out and even the differences between the different schools, so often a source of confusion to the student of Islamic law, are easily understandable.

The amount of research undertaken is formidable (especially helpful are the numerous references to fatwas given by Islamic Supervisory Boards and the translations of selected fatwas which appear in the appendix) and the bibliography is a useful tool for future research.

The case-study of the Faisal Islamic Bank of Egypt is thorough and comprehensive, providing not only a case-study of the bank itself, but also a detailed comparison with the non-Islamic Egyptian banks.

Despite some shortcomings, this book has much to recommend it and is a very useful contribution to the burgeoning literature on Islamic banking.

Nicholas Foster

Notes and News

OBITUARY OF TAN SRI DATUK PROFESSOR
AHMAD MOHAMED IBRAHIM (1916–1999)

Many readers of the *Yearbook* will have noted with sadness the passing of Ahmad Ibrahim on 17 April 1999. His reputation as a Muslim scholar, not just in Malaysia and Singapore, where he spent his working life, but also in the Middle East and the West, was immense. His legacy in innumerable capacities is so great that we will be well into the next millennium before we can truly assess its significance. Not only was he a scholar of total dedication and almost incredible productivity, he was also a jurist and public servant who served the governments of either Malaysia or Singapore throughout his life. He founded two law schools (the Law Faculty, University of Malaya, and the Kulliyyah of Laws, International Islamic University, Malaysia), and was a teacher and academic administrator of lasting influence and achievement. In terms of his subject, Islamic law, he did not simply have no peer; he *was* Islamic law in the minds of everyone who was involved in the subject in his part of the world. He was a household name. He led research and teaching in the subject for several decades, and wrote or inspired practically the entire literary output on the subject to date in Malaysia and Singapore.

Ahmad Ibrahim was born in Singapore on 15 May 1916. He was educated at Raffles college, where he obtained the London Bachelor of Arts degree at 19. He obtained a place at St John's College, Cambridge with a Queen's Scholar award (1935), graduated with first class honours (1939) and was admitted to the Middle Temple, taking a Certificate of Honour in the Bar Finals (1941). He was appointed a Magistrate in Singapore (1946), and practised as an Advocate and Solicitor, appearing in some well-known cases such as the *Maria Hertogh* case.[1] He became Crown Counsel (1957) and was appointed Singapore's first State Advocate-General (1959–1963) and then Attorney-General (1963–1967). He then served as Singapore's Ambassador to the United Arab Republic (1967–1968). During this period he was responsible for drafting the Women's Charter 1961 and the Administration of Muslim Law Enactment 1966.

In 1972 he joined the University of Malaya and became the first Dean of the Law Faculty. On the establishment of the International Islamic University, Malaysia in 1983, he was appointed the first Dean of the Law Faculty, later Sheikh of the Kulliyyah of Laws. Only those with knowledge of the great problems of legal education in Malaysia, with its pluralistic so-

---

[1] *In re Maria Hertogh* [1975] MLJ 12, [1951] MLJ 164.

ciety and laws, can appreciate the depth of his achievements. Throughout his academic life Ahmad had an abiding interest and concern for legal education generally.

As a scholar, Ahmad Ibrahim was an expert in the common law as well as Islamic law, specializing in family law of all kinds in Malaysia's legal system, and constitutional law. His bibliography fills many pages. No task of legal writing was too high or too low or too broad for his expert touch. He even took enormous pleasure in reporting cases for local journals far into his old age. He was never happier than when working in the library or writing an article. In terms of Islamic law scholarship, Ahmad will be remembered by Muslim jurists principally for his ground-breaking book, *Islamic Law in Malaya* (1965), and for *Family Law in Malaysia and Singapore* (1978);[2] they will also know of his book *The Distribution of Estates According to Shafi Law*(1976).[3] However, a constant stream of articles on Islamic law topics brought his original work right up to date and dealt with a wide variety of practical and theoretical legal issues; and his scholarship covered many different areas of law, even such subjects as civil procedure, the legal system and labour law. His Inaugural Braddell Memorial Lecture, "Towards a History of Law in Malaysia and Singapore" (1970) is a classic of its kind. His work is never purely technical, but shows constantly his concern for law and the society and people it serves, as well as his deep religious convictions.

He founded journals, notably the *Jernal Hukum* (IIUM) and the *Journal of Malaysian and Comparative Law* and the *Annual Survey of Malaysian Law* (UM). He established the Diploma for the Administration of the Islamic Judiciary for Qadis, *Shari'a* Court Judges and Religious Department officials, and the Diploma in *Shari'a* Law and Practice, for the practising profession at IIUM. He chaired the *Shari'a* and Civil Law Technical Committee of the Prime Minister's Department, a committee whose objective is to codify and standardize Islamic Laws for all the 13 states of the Malaysian Federation, Islamic law begin a state subject under the Constitution.

Even this astonishing *cursus honorum* conveys little of Ahmad Ibrahim's influence. He held so many academic, professional and administrative positions, that he was constantly in touch with hundreds of people and all aspects of legal and academic life.

His productivity put younger colleagues to shame. He could have excused himself with a vast number of his pressing and very time-consuming practical commitments for faculty, government and profession, and latterly with old age, yet he always made time for his writing, and did not know how to say "no" to a request. He was a man of tireless energy who nonetheless never appeared hard-pressed or tense. Unlike others whose achievements are at the cost of attention to the needs of others, Ahmad was always ready to spend time advising and talking with young colleagues and friends in his office or informally in the staff room. He was never longwinded, but never gave less than whole attention to what was needed. He was wise, helpful and encouraging. He never appeared to think that criticism of another was ever appropriate, except perhaps for unpunctuality or laziness.

His colleague and successor as Dean, Tan Sri Professor Harun Hashim, tells movingly in a memorial for the *Malayan Law Journal* of his friend's last few hours:

---

[2] Now in a third edition under the title *Family Law in Malaysia* (1997).

[3] A bibliography up to 1986, with extensive academic comment and further details of Ahmad Ibrahim's career, can be found in "Islamic and Malaysian law: the contribution of Professor Ahmad Ibrahim", by M. B. Hooker, in M. B. Hooker (ed.), *Malaysian Legal Essays: A Collection of Essays in Honour of Professor Emeritus Datuk Ahmad Ibrahim* (1986). A piece in the same volume, "Ahmad Ibrahim in the Service of Islam", by Al-Mansoor Adabi, deals with his practical achievements as a Muslim. The bibliography (by no means complete) lists 18 books and 187 articles, almost all written between 1965 and 1985.

On Friday 16 April 1999 he was still at work in the Faculty, at 5.00pm, when he wrote "At last I have completed writing my book", and handed the manuscript he had been working on for some time to his secretary. In the early hours of 17 April he breathed his last. He worked tirelessly all his life. He had never been hospitalised . . . His example of scholarly leadership and research will always be a beacon for those who come after him. In spite of the public's admiration and respect for his brilliance and leadership he was a shy and humble person. Truly, he was Allah's chosen servant.

It was always said of Ahmad Ibrahim that he would never know how to retire. He was a scholar right to the end and leaves too large a gap for any single person to fill.

Andrew Harding

Index

587